MUTINY DOES NOT HAPPEN LIGHTLY

The Literature of the American Resistance to the Vietnam War

edited by

G. LOUIS HEATH

The Scarecrow Press, Inc.

Metuchen, N.J.   1976

Other Scarecrow books by G. Louis Heath:

The Hot Campus: The Politics That Impede Change in the
Technoversity (1973)

The Black Panther Leaders Speak (1976)

Off the Pigs! The History and Literature of the Black Panther Party (1976)

Vandals in the Bomb Factory: The History and Literature
of the Students for a Democratic Society (1976)

Library of Congress Cataloging in Publication Data
Main entry under title:

Mutiny does not happen lightly.

Bibliography: p.
Includes index.
1. Vietnamese Conflict 1961-1975--Protest
movements--Sources. 2. Vietnamese Conflict,
1961-1975--United States--Sources. 3. United
States--Politics and government--1945-   --Sources.
I. Heath, G. Louis.
DS559.62.U6M87   959.704'31   76-4825
ISBN 0-8108-0922-2

For my relative Mikal Kristiansen
who died in the Norwegian Resistance during World War II
and for the many who served their country
in the American Resistance during the Vietnam War

CONTENTS

This widened war has narrowed domestic welfare
programs, making the poor, white and Negro bear
the burdens both at the front and at home....

Martin Luther King, Jr.

If it's a blanket question, yes, I would give my
blood to North Vietnam. I think that would be in
the oldest tradition of this country.

Robert F. Kennedy

I served in Vietnam. But I know now that they
(draft evaders) were right. And they were the
only real heroes to emerge from that mess.

Patrick J. Walsh
Oak Park, Illinois

I. PREFACE*

This compilation of literature from groups that opposed the Vietnam War is a significant historical work that will enable subsequent generations to interpret and learn from the Vietnam tragedy. It is important that this volume be disseminated and read. I was proud as a Senator from Alaska to be a part of The Resistance to the Vietnam War from the very outset, meaning the period the Gulf of Tonkin Resolution was introduced and passed. Only Wayne Morse of Oregon and I publicly opposed in the Senate the American involvement in Vietnam as early as 1964. We were the small part of the Senate Establishment that resisted the war.

G. Louis Heath, distinguished professor and author, and runner-up in the Second and Third Annual Robert F. Kennedy Journalism Award competitions, has skillfully edited the literature of "The American Resistance to the Vietnam War" into a highly reliable and readable book. The documents in this excellent book offer a cross-section of Resistance writing from 1964 through 1974. In addition, of particular value are Dr. Heath's excellent chronology and bibliography on Vietnam.

> Ernest Gruening
> 1707 Willow Drive
> Juneau, Alaska
> May 6, 1974

---

*Ernest Gruening died at age 87 on June 26, 1974. His life was an exemplary one of courage and the crusade for social justice. During the Vietnam War he became one of the few reasons for young people to believe in the American system. As editor of The Nation, diplomat, senator, and governor, he served his country well.

II. ON THE EDITING

Mutiny Does Not Happen Lightly: The Literature of
the American Resistance to the Vietnam War   consists of
flyers, leaflets, letters, reports, manuals and documents
produced by or relating to the antiwar movement in the
United States from 1964 to 1974.   The first material included
comes from the May 2nd Committee in 1964 and the last material originates with Amnesty International of the U.S.A. in
1974.   The ephemera were collected in the decade beginning
in 1964 from over one hundred groups, many of them organized on university campuses.   The date and location of
collection and the source of each item in this volume are indicated.   The groups collected from are included in the section, "Resistance Groups Referred to in this Book."   Almost
2,400 items were collected in ten years and the items here
included were selected so as to present an accurate cross-
section of the American Resistance to the Vietnam War during 1964-1974.   Most of the items do, however, reflect the
years 1964-1971, and especially 1967-1971, since an organized resistance was much more urgent and therefore more
active in those years.

The bibliography was begun at the University of California at Berkeley in 1964 and completed in 1974 at Illinois
State University.   It focuses on The Resistance, the problems
and prospects of the war, and background materials, especially of a scholarly sort, in order to provide a wide-ranging
compilation of works that illuminate the tragedy of the Vietnam War and the struggle of the American people to end it.

The title, Mutiny Does Not Happen Lightly, refers to
the high level of political deception, military misadventure,
and popular exasperation necessary to produce revolt and resistance in the American electorate.   The title is taken from
the caption of the document numbered 93 herein, concerning
the San Francisco Presidio stockade mutiny of 1969, proof
that The Resistance was not limited to civilians.

I have referred to the documents I have collected as "literature" in the title. The term "ephemera" does not capture their eloquence, integrity, bitterness, and desperation. The American Resistance produced on dilapidated mimeographed machines a great underground literature that expresses one of the great moral, political, and military agonies of our time. This literature certainly rivals the much acclaimed Soviet dissidents' underground writings known as "samizdat."

G. L. H.

III. ON THE RESISTANCE

I spent the academic year 1964-65 at the University of Uppsala in Sweden. From fall 1964 when I arrived to fall 1965 when I departed, the Vietnam War grew rapidly. I could see that the world was in for something more than a painfully passing crisis like the Cuban Missile Crisis or the invasion of the Dominican Republic. Although I was busy teaching and studying sociology at the University of Uppsala, I devoted much time to reading the world press, especially French, British, Swedish, and American. I read about the special forces in Vietnam, President Diem, and the bombing that was becoming an important part of the American military effort. We were becoming involved in a real war. One afternoon, sitting in the reading room at the University of Uppsala library, I reflected: "This thing is escalating and a large-scale resistance is beginning. It must be massive because millions will be affected." I recall being very uneasy with the thought. Even the geographical isolation of Sweden from the States could not thereafter give me even temporary peace of mind concerning the war in Southeast Asia. Return to the United States could only mean dealing in some way with a barbarous war.

I had a good friend in Uppsala, Nils-Åke Ericsson, with whom I talked politics for many hours. Nils was an activist in Laboremus, the youth arm of the ruling Social Democratic Party. He regarded Lyndon Johnson as "our good friend" in September of 1964, but by spring referred to him as a "damned imperialist." I underwent a similar change of attitude. I was "All the Way with LBJ" in the 1964 November elections but as the Vietnam conflict widened I developed a great personal dislike for Lyndon. I did not believe in the Vietnam War or any war and I was eligible for the draft.

One year after returning to the University of California at Berkeley, I was ordered to report for a pre-induction physical examination at the Oakland Induction Center on August 17,

1966. I failed my exam for overweight: 280 pounds. Thereafter, I was ordered to report for another physical every
three months. I failed each time, seven times in all. However, despite my continuing rejections, I felt morally compelled to claim C. O. or conscientious objector status to express my opposition to war in general and the Vietnam War
in particular. When I became a C. O. on the basis of religious belief, my Orcville, California draft board sought to
reduce its own requirements for service by exempting me
from the physical standards. My draft board seemed intent
on punishing me for being the only C. O. in Butte County.
They sent me to the Oakland Induction Center to be passed
through the physical exam as a C. O. That is, a routine pass
was ordered as no combat would be involved in any service
I would undertake. But even the military examiners would
not pass me to accommodate my draft board. My beliefs
protected due to the size of my body, and my body happily
still in one piece because it was too big, I became gratefully
free to join The Resistance to the Vietnam War.

I was typical of thousands who joined The Resistance.
I was a frequent participant but not a full-time or professional activist. I was never any kind of leader or hero of The
Resistance. I participated in every protest march that was
organized in the San Francisco Bay Area and when I became
an assistant professor at Illinois State University in 1969 I
traveled to marches in Washington, D. C., Chicago, and St.
Louis. I wrote a lot of letters to congressmen and I counseled numerous draft-eligible men for the Central Committee
of Conscientious Objectors (CCCO). We at CCCO advised
many young men of their right to C. O. status under the law.
Of course, no government agency was providing this critical
information.

When the war was effectively over in 1971, I worked
for amnesty for those who had refused military service in
Vietnam. As a visiting summer professor at McGill University in 1972, the University of British Columbia in 1973, and
Dalhousie University in 1974, all Canadian universities, I
encountered a sizable number of Americans who had sought
refuge from conscription into an immoral and illegal war.
They had fled not out of cowardice but because of conscience.
Certainly, by the end of our involvement in Vietnam, we
knew we had made a mistake and that we should welcome the
war resisters home. They were right when most Americans
had been wrong. We should not punish them for our mistake,
even through the device of "conditional" amnesty. The national fear is, of course, that once the super-patriots stop

pointing a finger at those who "shirked their responsibility, "
they might lower their hands and see the blood of 50, 000
killed and many more wounded young men who had been
largely sent to Southeast Asia against their will in a futile
endeavor.

Something else I did from 1964 to 1974 was to compile this book. Everywhere I went I collected the literature
of The Resistance. In 1966, I recall reading every book I
could find in the Bancroft Library at Berkeley on the Norwegian Resistance during World War II. Every book moved
me greatly and told me much about the difficulty and suffering of resisting war. But every book--about twenty of them
--was written as a narrative, usually by someone personally
involved. No book collected the literature of the great Norwegian Resistance. I felt at the time that this was a great
loss. I hope this volume remedies this deficiency of the
book world in the case of Vietnam by recording some of the
more telling literature of The American Resistance.

G. L. H.

IV. CHRONOLOGY

<u>1964</u>---May 2nd Committee, a group of young people who op-
pose the use of American troops in Vietnam, is organized on
March 14 in New Haven, Connecticut as an ad hoc committee
to plan and execute a demonstration in New York City on
May 2 to demand withdrawal from Vietnam. Escalation of
the Vietnam War after the August 2-4 Gulf of Tonkin incident
in which two U.S. destroyers are attacked by North Vietnamese torpedo boats and U.S. forces engage in retaliatory
attacks. Wayne Morse and Ernest Gruening are the only U.S.
Senators to oppose American involvement from the very outset. The only American soldiers engaged in fighting are
those acting as advisers to the South Vietnamese army. Nguyen Van Troi is executed on October 15 for attempted assassination of Secretary of Defense Robert McNamara.

<u>1965</u>---Vietnam War escalates dramatically. Nationwide
demonstrations. In June, U.S. field commanders are authorized to commit U.S. troop units for direct combat. The
draft becomes the target of anti-war protests. Students for
a Democratic Society sponsors draft resistance activities:
speaking to high school students who are about to register
and proposing alternatives; organizing community meetings
to talk about the war, the draft, and democracy; organizing
inductees and their families to creatively disrupt the draft
centers; and, urging soldiers not to fight. SANE-sponsored
"March on Washington for Peace and a Negotiated Settlement
in Vietnam" on March 22. "March on Washington to End the
War in Vietnam" on April 17. The Vietnam Day Committee
in Berkeley sponsors protest meetings known as "Vietnam
Days" on May 21 and 22 and demonstrates against President
Johnson on June 25 and 26 in San Francisco. Mass demonstrations on August 6-9 called the "Assembly of Unrepresented
People." More than forty groups demonstrate against the war
in several cities on August 6, the day the atom bomb was
dropped on Hiroshima 21 years earlier. The Vietnam Day
Committee organizes an attempt to stop a troop train at Santa
Fe Station in Berkeley on August 12. It holds a huge com-

munity protest meeting against American military intervention on October 15 and follows this on October 16 with massive civil disobedience. Medical Aid Committee, headquar-
tered in Berkeley, sends medical supplies to both North and
South Vietnam to help victims of the war. SDS leader Tom
Hayden, the U.S. Communist Party's Herbert Aptheker, and
Yale Professor Staughton Lynd travel on a "fact-finding mission" to Hanoi in December.

1966---Numerous sit-ins, teach-ins, fasts, vigils, meetings,
leaflettings, and picketing in opposition to the Vietnam War
throughout the country. Bill exempting non-volunteering
draftees from service in Vietnam is defeated in Congress.
All-woman's march on the Oakland Induction Center in California on February 23 sponsored by the Women's March Committee, Vietnam Day Committee. PFC James Johnson, Pvt.
Dennis Mora, and Pvt. David Samas refuse to fight in Vietnam on the grounds that it is illegal, immoral, and unjust.
On their way to speak at an anti-war demonstration in New
York City on July 7, they are jailed and held incommunicado
by military police. The privates, who took basic training
at Ft. Hood, Texas, become known as the "Fort Hood Three."
They become a rallying point for The Resistance. The House
Committee on Un-American Activities subpoenas anti-war ac-
tivists to appear in Washington, D.C. on August 16. The
Student Mobilization Committee is organized in December.
SMC becomes the largest student antiwar group with many
thousands of members and chapters at hundreds of colleges
and high schools. SMC focuses on large, mass actions.
Considerable number of draft eligible youth begin fleeing to
Canada.

1967---The first viable national antiwar coalition, the National Mobilization Committee, organizes successful national
demonstrations in April and October. Massive draft resistance. Anti-war leaders visit North Vietnam. Demonstrations
against Defense Secretary Robert McNamara at Harvard University. Large march against CIA recruiters at Columbia
University. Thousands participate in Vietnam Week, April
8-15. SDS national president Nicholas M. Egleson visits
North Vietnam during the summer at the invitation of the
Peace Committee of North Vietnam. American anti-war
activists attend a conference in Bratislava, Czechoslovakia,
sponsored by Czechoslovakian Peace Committee, September
6-13. Rennie Davis, former member of the SDS National
Council, travels to North Vietnam in October. Ché Guevara
killed in Bolivia on October 8. Stop the Draft Week, October

16-21. Disruptive and frequently violent demonstrations at
induction centers and college campuses during the week.
Demonstrators arrested at a Chicago induction center. Demonstrations by thousands at the Oakland, California Army induction center on October 16 lead to clashes with police, the
use of tear gas, and arrests. On October 18, hundreds of
students sit-in against Dow Chemical recruiters at the University of Wisconsin; rock-throwing, injuries to 65 demonstrators and policemen, and arrests. On October 20, eight
thousand students boycott classes at Brooklyn College to protest police intervention and arrests on campus the previous
day, in disturbances connected with a protest against U.S.
Navy recruiters. Blockade of a Princeton University military
research building in a protest against university relations with
the Institute for Defense Analysis; sit-in at Harvard University interferes with campus recruitment by Dow Chemical;
and, obstruction of interviews by CIA representatives at the
University of Colorado, all during October. Mass anti-war
march on Washington, D.C. on October 21. Sit-in against
the CIA at Stanford University; sit-in against Marine Corps
recruiters at the University of Iowa leading to arrests and
occasional violence; and an anti-Dow sit-in at the University
of Rochester, followed by a student strike protesting disciplinary suspensions imposed as a result of the sit-in, all
during November. SDS national organizers Jeff Jones, Cathy
Wilkerson, and Steve Halliwell are invited to visit Hanoi by
the North Vietnam Student Union. Upon arrival in Cambodia
in December, they are unable to complete the trip as the
Hanoi government cancels all foreign visits due to the intensity of American bombing.

1968---Rallies, marches, leafletting activity, and petitions
proliferate. Liberal churches, Protestant, Catholic, and
Jewish, begin to play a crucial role in The Resistance. Anti-
war activists work with the American Deserters Committee
in Sweden. Americans in West Berlin publish anti-war paper,
Where It's At, open a GI coffee house, and encourage GI's
to desert. National Mobilization Committee (Mobe) establishes
first GI coffee houses in U.S. Vietnamese communists launch
ferocious Tet offensive against thirty South Vietnamese provincial capitals on January 30. President Johnson declares
in early February that the offensive ends in complete military
failure, but the episode is credited with giving the communists a temporary psychological advantage and having an ad-
verse impact on the minority of the Americans who had been
optimistic about the war. The National Security Council decides to abolish draft deferments of youths enrolled in gradu-

ate school on February 15. Sit-in at Columbia University to
"smash the military" at the university on February 27.
President Johnson announces that the U.S. is unilaterally halt-
ing the bombing of 90 per cent of the North Vietnamese territory on March 31. He announces he will not seek a second
term of office. "Weeks of Resistance" during the spring.
Civil rights leader Martin Luther King, Jr. assassinated on
April 4. Rioting is set off in the ghettos of more than 80
cities. Rally at Columbia University on April 23 to protest
the university's relation to the Institute for Defense Analysis
leads to a shutdown of the university after six days of disorders. Preliminary peace talks begin on May 10. Presidential primary candidate Robert F. Kennedy assassinated on
June 6. Vernon Grizzard, Ann Scheer, and Stewart Meacham
travel to Hanoi in July to receive three American pilots who
had been prisoners of war in North Vietnam. Mass anti-war
demonstrations staged by the National Mobilization Committee
to End the War in Vietnam to coincide with the Democratic
National Convention in Chicago, August 26-30. Considerable
violence and numerous arrests result. Twenty American
anti-war activists travel to Budapest, Hungary in September
to confer with representatives of North Vietnam and the National Liberation Front of South Vietnam. All bombing raids
in North Vietnam end October 31. City College of New York
activists are involved in a week-long non-disruptive anti-war
sit-in during early November that is finally broken up by the
police. GI Week staged by several anti-war groups during
the week prior to the November national elections. The
Peace and Freedom Party collects enough voter signatures in
California to qualify as a party on the November election ballot. The party fields candidates opposed to the war in Vietnam. Richard Nixon is elected President largely on the basis
of his promises to end the war. Hemispheric Conference to
End the Vietnam War in Montreal, Canada, November 28-
December 1. Spokesmen for the Vietcong attend. Harvard
students sit-in against ROTC in December, forcing cancella-
tion of a faculty meeting on the issue. Attempted fire-bomb-
ing of an ROTC installation at Washington University in St.
Louis on December 3. SDSer Tom Hayden confers with the
North Vietnamese delegation at the Paris peace talks, especially with Colonel Ha Van Lau.

1969---Opposition to ROTC and defense research on campus.
SDS National Council pledges support to the Vietnamese communists and Ho Chi Minh. Anti-war activists break up a
board of trustees meeting at Stanford University in January
in a protest against counter-insurgency and war-related re-

search. Demonstrators greet President Nixon's limousine, January 20, along the Pennsylvania Avenue Inaugural parade route with shouted obscenities and a shower of sticks, stones, and empty beer cans. They burn small American flags and shout support for the Vietnamese communists. One hundred arrested. Picketing drives away a CIA recruiter from the University of Houston in February. Regional SDS conference at Princeton University on February 3 endorses "Smash the Military Machine in the Schools" spring offensive program. Trial of "Conspiracy 8" (later 7) begins for conspiracy charges as a result of rioting at the time of the 1968 Democratic National Convention. The eighth man, Black Panther Bobby Seale, is arrested on March 25 and goes on trial in Chicago on September 24 with the other seven, but is severed from the trial on November 5 when Judge Julius Hoffman sentences him to four years in prison for contempt as a result of disruptive trial behavior. He is eventually acquitted of all charges as are the other seven defendants.

Anti-Draft Week, March 16-22, sponsored by the National Mobilization Committee. Activities as follows: Washington, D.C.--Major demonstration at the National Headquarters of the Selective Service System; a coffin containing turned-in draft cards is used to block the door. Demonstrators, including the Rev. Malcolm Boyd, sit down to block the entrances to the building. Local students engage draft board members in debate at their homes and places of business, stage guerrilla theatre demonstrations around the city, and rally on college campuses in the evenings to discuss the war and draft. Area high school students conduct activities around The High School "We Won't Go" Statement, including assemblies in several schools on the draft and petitions for draft counseling. Dayton, Ohio--March in the predominantly black West End of Dayton, beginning at a National Guard armory, passing a veteran's home, and ending with a rally at a second armory. High school programs in the West End. Massive demonstration at the city's central draft board. Attempted comply-in designed to impede Selective Service operations with floods of legal information submitted by local registrants. Hackensack, New Jersey--Picketing of local draft boards on all days of Anti-Draft Week and sit-ins on two days. Pray-in involving area clergy. Heavy leafletting at shopping centers and bus terminals. Local PTA sponsors a debate between residents and the head of the New Jersey Selective Service System. Circulation of "We Won't Go" statements in high schools. Philadelphia--The "Spectre of Death," a figure robed in black, appears in silence at draft boards and seats himself in the presence of board members and

clerks. Non-violent sit-ins during the week. San Antonio,
Texas--The "Spectre of Death" appears here too. "Death"
comes to one of a list of local residents selected by lottery
during the week. He is reported as "drafted" and becomes
a "victim" of the war machine in a guerrilla theatre demonstration. Sit-ins at local boards. Buffalo--On March 19,
students at the State University of New York circulate hundreds of powers of attorney to other citizens. These citizens then inspect the students' Selective Service files in order to impede the draft. Parents and clergymen appear at
the local boards to talk and sit-in. Los Angeles--Blockade
of induction centers on March 18 and draft boards on the
19th. An especially large demonstration at Local Board 82
in Hollywood. "We Won't Go" statements circulated on LA
college and high school campuses. Demonstrations at the
homes of Selective Service Board members. Ames, Iowa--
Large groups of local residents visit the city's draft boards
at the beginning of the week. Iowa State University students
disrupt ROTC exercises on campus. The week ends with one
of the first "End the War in Laos" demonstrations in the
country. The following are some of the other locations in
which the National Mobilization Committee organizes demonstrations and related activities March 16-22: Boston, Stam-
ford, Conn., New York City, Rockland County, N.Y., Harrisburg, Lewisburg, Pa., Rochester, N.Y., Minneapolis,
Syracuse, Potsdam, N.Y., Pittsburgh, Akron, Cleveland,
Detroit, Mt. Pleasant, Mich., Grand Rapids, South Bend,
Milwaukee, Chicago.

    Anti-war conferences sponsored by Cleveland Area
Peace Action Council on March 29 and September 13 at Case-
Western Reserve University. Vietnam Moratorium organized
during the spring. Demonstration against war-related research at American University; occupation of building at
George Washington University to protest university complicity
in military recruitment and war research; non-violent sit-ins
against ROTC and military recruiters at Boston University
and Fordham University; and mass protests in opposition to
ROTC and defense research at Kent State University, all during April. Sit-in at Johns Hopkins University against ROTC
and military recruiting; occupation of an administration building at Dartmouth College in protest against ROTC and military recruiting; and, takeover of a meeting room at Northeastern University in Boston in opposition to ROTC, all during May. SDS splits into three small groups at its summer
convention and begins to decline rapidly. A small group
dominated by the Progressive Labor Party becomes the main
core. The formation of the New Mobilization Committee

Against the War in Vietnam (New Mobe) replaces the National Mobilization Committee (Mobe) in July. The Student Mobilization Committee (SMC) is instrumental in helping to organize New Mobe and winning the call for a mass action in Washington, D.C. as the immediate focus for the new coalition. The New Mobe is composed of scores of organizations, including radical, New Left, and pacifist groups.

National Anti-War Conference, July 4-5, at Cleveland State University. Rennie Davis leaves U.S. on July 15 for Hanoi to take custody of two American fliers and a U.S. Navy seaman held prisoner of war by the North Vietnamese. SDS delegation visits Cuba in July to meet with Viet Cong and North Vietnamese representatives. Consultations with Van Ba, head of the delegation representing the Provisional Revolutionary Government of South Vietnam (Vietcong). Plans for a mass "National Action" made at a meeting in Cleveland, August 29-31. Protest against September 14-18 International Industrialists Conference at the Stanford Research Institute, a leading brain center for counter-insurgency research. New York Fifth Avenue Vietnam Peace Parade Committee meets September 15 to plan strategy for November 15 march on Washington. Regional Student Anti-War Conference at Wayne State University in Detroit in October. Anti-ROTC Rally, front lawn of student union at Wayne State on October 1. Revolutionary Youth Movement (RYM) mass "National Action" against the war on October 8-11 in Chicago. Substantial number of SDS Weathermen arrested on October 8 for their participation in violent activity in downtown Chicago. March demanding that the "U.S. Get out of Vietnam Now" on October 11. Rally at People's Park the same day is dedicated to Albizo Campos, leader of the Puerto Rican liberation struggle. Massive nationwide mobilization against the Vietnam War on October 15. Student Strike nationwide on November 14. "March on Washington to Bring All the GI's Home Now" on November 15 proves one of the largest demonstrations against the war.

1970---Multi-issue reformist organization, the National Coalition against War, Racism and Repression, is formed. The Coalition holds Strategy Action Conferences June 27-28 and September 11-13 in Milwaukee and carries out the following activities: rally against genocide at the United Nations in New York City on October 5; protest against President Nixon's "phony peace plan" during his motorcade to Key Biscayne, Florida on October 11; rally to indict Nixon and Agnew when Vice President Agnew visits Chicago on October 19; demonstration against chemical and biological warfare in

Newport, Indiana on October 24; mass meeting and rally on
political repression in Los Angeles on October 25; demonstrations nationwide on October 30 at induction centers, welfare offices, and factories to dramatize the related issues of
war, the draft, poverty, and unemployment; mass vigils and
marches in cities and towns across the country to express
opposition to the war on October 31; protests at trial of anti-
draft demonstrators in Rochester, New York, during November; varied actions on the issue of genocide in San Francisco,
New Orleans, Los Angeles, Atlanta, Seattle, Chicago, and
Detroit from December 15 to 30; and, mass meeting, march,
and rally on inflation, poverty, unemployment, and the war
in South Bend, Indiana on December 22. The ongoing activities of the Coalition are: 1) leafletting factories and talking
with workers, especially the war as it relates to inflation and
unemployment; 2) speaking engagements at churches, schools,
unions, women's groups, etc.; 3) distribution of leaflets and
guerrilla theatre in front of churches and other institutions;
4) opening of coffee houses, especially near military installations and universities where anti-war activists can gather to
plan action; 5) draft counseling; 6) leafletting military installations and USO offices; 7) leafletting at unemployment offices
and welfare offices; 8) house-to-house leafletting, especially
in black and brown areas; 9) teams that design their own activities centered upon the problems of their own communities;
10) vigils; and 11) a media committee that solicits radio and
TV appearances and newspaper coverage.
    Nationwide protests on April 15 sponsored by the Viet-
nam Moratorium Committee. National boycott of Standard
Oil, one of the largest war contractors. American troops invade Cambodia on April 30. Massive non-violent civil disobedience and other forms of non-violent mass actions in
Washington, D.C. and other cities in early May, 1971. Four
Kent State University students shot dead on May 4. Over
100,000 march in Washington, D.C. on May 9 to register
their opposition to the Cambodian invasion and the murder of
students at Kent State University and Jackson State College.
National antiwar conference held in Cleveland during June.
Demonstrations are called for October 31 and the National
Peace Action Coalition (NPAC) is organized. The New Mobilization Committee and the National Peace Action Coalition
feud. New Mobe prefers civil disobedience and "direct action" while NPAC is inclined to mass, peaceful demonstrations. City-wide meeting of the Student Mobilization Committee at the Peace Center in Cleveland on June 14. Emergency
National Conference against the Cambodia-Laos-Vietnam War,
June 19-21 at Cuyahoga Community College, Cleveland, Ohio.

Students from 240 universities join with representatives from
33 labor unions, representatives from Third World organizations, women's leaders, high school students, and others.
The conference, attended by 1,500 people, plans massive
demonstrations in the fall to support the demand for immediate withdrawal of all U.S. troops from Southeast Asia. Virtually everyone from the conference, along with over 1,000
people from Cleveland, demonstrate against the war in front
of the Cleveland-Sheraton Hotel while Vice President Agnew
is speaking on Saturday evening, June 20.

National Peace Action Coalition sponsors local anti-
war demonstrations on August 6-9, the period from Hiroshima
Day to Nagasaki Day. On August 29, the Brown community
of Los Angeles carries out a massive anti-war demonstration
stressing that the Vietnam War is intimately linked to the
fight against racism. Violence and arrests result. Chicanos
in Denver and Los Angeles participate in Mexican Independence Day marches and rallies. Bail fund money is collected
for Chicanos arrested in the August 29 Chicano Moratorium
"police riot." NPAC sponsors massive anti-war demonstrations on October 31 in major urban centers, especially San
Francisco, Seattle, Chicago, Detroit, Cleveland, Columbus,
Boston, New York City, Philadelphia, Washington, D.C.,
Denver, Atlanta, Austin, and Houston. The demonstrations
relate the war to the issues of racism, inflation, unemployment, political repression, GI rights, and women's liberation.
Citizens of San Francisco and Massachusetts vote in November on a referendum calling for immediate withdrawal from
Vietnam. Secretary of Defense Melvin Laird warns of the
total resumption of the bombing of North Vietnam following
heavy attacks on November 20-21. On December 4-6, at the
Packinghouse Labor Center in Chicago, over 1,500 people,
representing 29 states, 34 labor unions, 150 colleges, 40
high schools, and hundreds of community peace groups meet
in a National Convention of the U.S. Antiwar Movement to
plan massive antiwar activities for the spring.

1971---People's Coalition for Peace and Justice (PCPJ)
founded at a Chicago conference attended by over 500 delegates, January 8-10. Gallup Poll in January shows that 73
per cent of the American people want the U.S. out of Vietnam
by the end of 1971; 59 per cent believe it was a mistake for
the U.S. to go into Vietnam in the first place; and six out of
ten who do not believe it was a mistake at first still want all
Americans out by the end of 1971. President Nixon orders
massive bombing in Vietnam, Cambodia, and Laos. Following the initiatives of the National Student Association, many

groups organize around the idea of the "People's Peace
Treaty." All anti-war elements become more unified, especially the National Peace Action Coalition and People's Coalition for Peace and Justice. Emergency national student anti-
war conference at Catholic University in Washington, D.C.,
February 19-21. "Speak Out Against the War" on April 1 at
Hunter College, New York City. "Tribute in Action to Martin Luther King, Jr.," April 1-4. Theme: "Freedom from
Hunger, War, and Oppression." Nationwide local activities
on April 1, including marches to dramatize the people's hunger for housing, jobs, and peace. April 2: fasts; teach-ins;
and, special programs in schools. April 3: tax protests
and resistance activities on a community level. April 4:
local demonstrations to mark the assassination of Dr. King,
who among his many contributions to the cause of social justice, opposed the Vietnam War.
    Third World Task Force against the War in Southeast
Asia activities: Washington, D.C.--April 2, teach-in at Howard University's Crampton Auditorium; April 3, mass rally
and march. Detroit--April 3, mass march and rally. Chi-
cago--April 3, mass march down State Street to the Chicago
Coliseum. Cleveland--April 3, antiwar action in memory of
Martin Luther King, Jr. New York City--April 2, high
school student strike; teach-in at Manhattan Community College.
    National Peace Action Coalition and other groups work-
ing on spring antiwar actions buy an ad in the New York
Times for Wednesday, April 7, to answer President Nixon's
April 7 speech before he speaks. Women's March on the
Pentagon, April 10. Operation Dewey Canyon III, organized
by the Vietnam Veterans against the War, takes place in
Washington, D.C., April 18-23. Vietnam vets, their families, and the families of POW's and GI's killed in Vietnam
engage in intensive lobbying, vigils and guerrilla theatre depicting search and destroy missions, torture, and other activities of U.S. forces in Indochina. "Women Speak Out
against the War," April 21, Washington, D.C. The People's
Coalition for Peace and Justice and the National Peace Action
Coalition sponsor the highly successful "Spring Action Campaign," including the April 24 mass march, the week-long
People's Lobby, and the May Day actions, all in Washington,
D.C. Many Federal agencies sponsor individual activities
during the week before the April 24 demonstrations. Prominent among these is a mass "Gathering for Peace" held at
the National Institute of Health on April 23 where Pete Seeger
introduces his newest song, "The Last Train to Nuremburg."
National Peace Action Week, April 19-24, culminates in the

largest antiwar demonstrations in American history on April
24 in Washington, D.C. and San Francisco. A half million
march in D.C. "Algonquin Peace City" opens in Rock Creek
Park in Washington, D.C. on April 24.

Mayday International, May 1-7: Major demonstrations
in large cities around the world protest U.S. foreign policy.
On May 1, SCLC Mule Train and hundreds who marched
from Wall Street to Washington arrive in Algonquin Peace
City. They set up camp and join in the Celebration of the
People's Peace. "Massive Assembly" in Washington, D.C.
on May 2 demanding: 1) Immediate withdrawal of all U.S.
military air, land, and sea forces from Vietnam, and that
the U.S. set the date now for completion of withdrawal; 2)
$5,500 Guaranteed Annual Income for a family of four; and,
3) Free all political prisoners. "People's Lobby" on May 3
and 4 at Congress and government agencies in order to carry
on dialogue with Congressmen, government employees, and
officers of government departments in support of the People's
Peace Treaty and the three demands issued during the Massive Assembly on May 2. Early morning leafletting and nonviolent picketing at government buildings and other locations
on May 5, day of "Nationwide Moratorium on Business as
Usual." At noon, march to the Capitol for sustained nonviolent action at the Capitol and other locations.

Antiwar demonstrations on May 5 on campuses and in
communities around the country to commemorate the massacre
of students at Kent State University and Jackson State College
and the nationwide outcry against the invasion of Cambodia.
Civilian antiwar activists convert Armed Forces Day, May 10,
into a Solidarity Day with antiwar GI's by joining them in
peace activities at military bases. President Nixon and other
heads of state greeted with demonstrations at NATO International Conference on Cities in Indianapolis, May 25-28.
People's Coalition for Peace and Justice Conference, Milwaukee, Wisconsin, June 25-27. The possible unification of
NPAC and PCPJ is the major convention issue. It is concluded that the fallacy of the NPAC approach is that it is trying to work through Congress for an immediate end to the
war and that a failing of both NPAC and PCPJ is that they
are not winning working class support. Three thousand people attend the Anti-War Convention of the National Peace Action Coalition at Hunter College in New York City on July 2-
4. NPAC sponsors Hiroshima-Nagasaki Days, August 6-9;
a nationwide moratorium with local civil disobedience, October 13; Day of Solidarity with Vietnam Veterans, October
28; National Peace Action Weeks, October 25-November 5;
National Peace Action Day, a day of massive regional anti-

war demonstrations, November 6; a mass rally and "March
for Life" in Washington, D.C., November 6; and, mass nonviolent civil disobedience in D.C., November 8.

1972---Under the pressure of national elections, President
Nixon partially fulfills his 1968 campaign promise to end the
war quickly. He reduces the large American army in Vietnam to a token force, although intermittently enlarging the
bombing throughout Southeast Asia. Agents of the Nixon re-
election committee break into Democratic Party national headquarters in June and are apprehended. On November 7, Nixon is re-elected to a second term. POWs are returned to
the U.S. in prisoner exchanges. The U.S. is now largely
out of the external crisis of Vietnam and moves immediately
into the internal governmental crisis known as "Watergate."

V. RESISTANCE GROUPS
REFERRED TO IN THIS BOOK

American Deserters Committee
American Friends Service Committee (AFSC)
American Guild of Variety Artists
American Labor Alliance
American Servicemen's Union
Americans for Democratic Action
Americans for Peace in Vietnam
Amnesty International of the U.S.A.
Amnesty Rescue Committee
Ann Arbor Committee to End the War in Vietnam
Ann Arbor Peace Action Coalition
Ann Arbor Youth Conference on a People's Peace
Another Mother for Peace (Palo Alto, California)
Asian Americans for Action (New York City)
Association of Student Governments
Atlanta Federation of Teachers
Atlanta Mobilization Committee
Atlanta Peace Coalition
August 6-9th Committee
Austin Peace Action Coalition (Austin, Texas)

Bay Area Peace Action Coalition (San Francisco)
Beacon Hill Support Group (Boston)
Berkeley Faculty-Student Ad Hoc Peace Committee
Berkeley Friends of SNCC
Berkeley Strike Coordinating Committee
Black and Brown Task Force (Chicago)
Black Caucus, Newark Teachers Union, Local 481
Black Christian Nationalists
Black Economic Development Conference
Black Moratorium Committee against the War
Black Panther Party
Black Student Union (Los Angeles)
Black Unitarians for Radical Reform
Black United Front (Cairo, Illinois, and numerous other towns
    and cities)

Boston Coalition for Peace and Justice
Boston Female Liberation
Boston Resistance
Buffalo Peace Council
Businessmen and Executives Move against the War in Vietnam

Cambridge Veterans for Peace
Capitol Area Peace Action Coalition (Albany, New York)
Case-Western Reserve University Women's Liberation
Catholic Peace Fellowship
Cedar Falls Peace Action Coalition (Cedar Falls, Iowa)
Central Committee of Conscientious Objectors (CCCO)
Chicago Medical Committee for Human Rights
Chicago National Association for the Advancement of Colored
    People (NAACP)
Chicago October 31 Peace Action Coalition
Chicago Peace Action Committee
Chicago Peace Council
Chicago Strike Council
Chicago Vietnam Moratorium Committee
Chicago Welfare Rights Organization
Chicago Women's Liberation Union
Chicano Moratorium Committee (Los Angeles)
Cincinnati Peace Coalition
Clergy and Laymen Concerned about Vietnam
Cleveland Area Peace Action Coalition (CAPAC)
Cleveland Coalition for Peace and Justice
Cleveland Lawyers against the War
Columbia University Women's Liberation
Columbus Peace Action Coalition (Columbus, Ohio)
Committee for Independent Political Action
Committee of Kent State Massacre Witnesses
Committee of Liaison with Families of Servicemen Detained
    in North Vietnam
Committee of Returned Volunteers
Committee of Student Concern (Drake University)
Community for New Politics (Berkeley, California)
Computer People for Peace (New York City)
Concerned Black Citizens of Tacoma (Tacoma, Washington)
Concerned Citizens of Palo Alto (Palo Alto, California)
Concerned Democrat Council (Los Angeles)
Concerned Officers Movement
Congress of Racial Equality (CORE)
Connecticut Peace Action Coalition
Connecticut Valley Peace Action Coalition (Northampton,
    Connecticut)
Contra Costa Citizens against the War in Viet Nam (Contra

Costa County, Calif.)
Crusade for Justice

D.C. Area Movement Committee
D.C. Committee to Free Angela Davis
Denver Stop the War Committee
Des Moines Area Moratorium Committee
Detroit Area Laymen
Detroit Coalition to End the War Now
Detroit Committee to End the War Now
Detroit Metropolitan Rights Organization
DuBois Clubs

Emergency Committee against Genocide
Episcopal Peace Fellowship
Eureka-Noe Valley Concerned Citizens (California)

Families of Resisters for Amnesty
Federally Employed Women (Washington, D.C.)
Fellowship of Reconciliation (FOR)
Florida Peace Action Coalition (Tampa, Florida)
Fort Hamilton GIs United
Fort Hood Three Defense Committee (Ford Hood, Texas)
Fort Worth-Dallas Peace Action Coalition
Free University of New York (FUNY)
Friends of the Vietnam Day Committee

Gay Liberation Front
Gay Liberation Front, Women's Caucus (New York City)
GI-Airman Coalition (Fort Lewis and McCord Air Force
     Base)
GI-Civilian Alliance for Peace (San Francisco)
G.I. Projects
GIs United against the War in Vietnam (Patterson AFB, Ohio
     and Ft. Bragg, N.C.)
Godzilla Committee to End the War in Vietnam Before It
     Ends Everything Else (Berkeley, California)
Grand Rapids Peace Action Coalition (Michigan)
Greater Boston Peace Action Coalition

Haight Ashbury Viet Nam Committee (San Francisco)
Health Professionals for Peace (New York City)
High School Students against the War in Viet Nam (San Fran-
     cisco)
High School Student Mobilization Committee (Chicago)
Honeywell Project
Houston Committee to End the War in Vietnam Now

Houston Peace Action Coalition

Independent Campus Women, San Francisco State College
Independent Socialist Club (Berkeley)
Independent Socialist Clubs of America
Individuals against the Crime of Silence (Los Angeles)
Interfaith Conference for Peace
International Longshoremen Workers' Union
Iowans for Peace in Vietnam

Japanese American Citizens League
Jeanette Rankin Rank and File (New York City)
Jewish Peace Fellowship
Jews for Urban Justice

Kalamazoo Women's Liberation (Michigan)

La Raza Unida Party (Colorado)
Labor Leadership Assembly for Peace
Latin American Student Union (Chicago)
Law Students against the War
Lawrence Peace Action Coalition (Lawrence, Kansas)
Lawyers Committee on American Policy towards Vietnam
League of Southern Co-operatives
Long Island Women's Liberation Front
Los Angeles October 31 Out Now Committee
Los Angeles Peace Council

Madison Area Peace Action Coalition (Wisconsin)
Making a Nation (MAN)
Manhattan Church Women United
Manhattan Community College Third World Coalition
Martin Luther King, Jr. Commemorative Committee
Maryland Council to Repeal the Draft
Massachusetts Referendum '70
May 2nd Committee
Mayday Collective
Medical Committee for Human Rights
Methodist Peace Fellowship
Mexican-American Youth Organization
Michigan Council to Repeal the Draft (Ann Arbor)
Michigan Strike Support Coalition
Mid-Peninsula Free University (MFU)
Militant Action Caucus of the National Peace Action Coalition
Military Wives for Peace
Milwaukee Coalition for Peace and Justice
Milwaukee Organizing Committee

Minnesota Mobilization Committee
Minnesota Peace Action Coalition (Minneapolis)
Minnetonka Peace Action Coalition (Minnesota)
Mohawk Valley Peace Action Coalition (Utica, New York)
Motor City Coalition (Detroit)
Movement for a Democratic Military
Movement for Puerto Rican Independence
Movimiento Pro Independicia (New York City)

Nashville Peace Action Coalition (Nashville, Tennessee)
National Action Group
National Association for the Advancement of Colored People
    (NAACP)
National Black Anti-war Anti-draft Union
National Black Task Force
National Caucus of Labor Committees (Philadelphia)
National Coalition against War, Racism, and Repression
National Conference of Black Draft Counselors
National Conference of Black Lawyers
National Council of Black Women
National Council of Churches
National Council of Rabbis
National Council to Repeal the Draft
National Federation of Temple Sisterhood
National Lawyers Guild
National Mobilization Committee to End the War in Vietnam
    (Mobe)
National Organization of Women (NOW)
National Peace Action Coalition (NPAC)
National Resist
National Student Association (NSA)
National Student Committee, National Student YMCA
National Welfare Rights Organization (NWRO)
Neighbors for Peace (New York City)
New Democratic Coalition (Cleveland)
New England Resistance
New England Women's Coalition
New Haven Liberation School (New Haven, Connecticut)
New Haven Peace Action Coalition
New Jersey Libertarian Alliance
New Mobilization Committee to End the War in Vietnam
    (New Mobe)
New Orleans Peace Action Coalition (New Orleans, Louisi-
    ana)
New Party
New University Conference (NUC)
New York Coalition for Peace and Justice

New York Ethical Culture Society
New York Fifth Avenue Vietnam Peace Parade Committee
New York Moratorium Committee
New York New Democratic Coalition
New York Peace Action Coalition
New York Radical Feminists
New York Resistance
New York Third World Task Force
New York University Christian Movement
New York University Law Students against the War
Niagara Peace Action Coalition (Niagara Falls, New York)
Non-Violent Training and Action Center
North Beach Viet Nam Committee (San Francisco)
Northern California Committee for Trade Union Action and
    Democracy
Northern California Strategy Action Conference Organizing
    Committee

October 31 Peace Action Committee (Chicago)
Ohio New Party
Ohio Peace Action Council
Operation Black Unity (Cleveland)
Orlando Peace Center (Orlando, Florida)

Pacific Northwest New Mobe
Palm Beach Peace Action Coalition (West Palm Beach, Flor-
    ida)
Parents Plea for Peace (Modesto, California)
Park Action Committee (St. Louis Park, Missouri)
Peace and Freedom Party (PFP)
Peace, Power and People
Penn State Coalition for Peace
People against Racism
Peoples Coalition for Peace and Justice (PCPJ)[1]
Peoples Committee of Inquiry
Philadelphia National Peace Action Day Committee
Philadelphia Resistance
Philadelphia YWCA
Pittsburgh Peace and Freedom Center
Portland Peace Action Coalition (Portland, Oregon)
Potrero Hill Peace Committee (Potrero Hill, California)
Progressive Labor Party
Publishers for Peace
Puerto Rican Student Union (New York City)

Quaker Peace Action Group (Baltimore, Maryland)

Radical Libertarian Alliance
Radical Student Union (Berkeley and UCLA)
Radical Women
Resist!
Rhode Island Peace Action Coalition (Providence, Rhode Is-
    land)
Richmond College Women's Liberation (Richmond College,
    New York City)
Rocky Mountain Peace Action Coalition (Denver, Colorado)

Safe Return Amnesty Committee
St. Louis Peace Action Coalition
St. Louis Peace Council
San Diego Peace Action Coalition
San Diego Women United against the War
San Diego Women's Center
San Francisco GI-Civilian Alliance for Peace
San Francisco October 31 Committee
San Francisco Peace Center
San Francisco State College Vietnam Day Committee
San Jose State College Vietnam Day Committee
Seattle GI-Civilian Alliance for Peace
Seattle Liberation Front
Seattle October 31 Committee
Seattle Peace Action Coalition
Servicemen's LINK to Peace
Socialist Workers Party (SWP)
Society for Individual Liberty (Philadelphia)
Soldiers Defense Fund
South Florida Peace Action Coalition (Miami)
Southern Christian Leadership Conference (SCLC)
Southern Conference Educational Fund
Southern Regional Council
Southern Student Organizing Committee (SSOC)
Spartacist League
Springfield Collective
Springfield Peace Action Coalition (Springfield, Illinois)
Standard Oil Boycott Committee
Stanford Anti-War Movement (Stanford University)
Stanford Committee for Peace in Vietnam
Strike Coordination Committee (Berkeley, Calif.)
Student and Youth Coordinating Committee
Student Committee for a SANE Nuclear Policy (SANE)
Student Health Organization (SHO)
Student Nonviolent Coordinating Committee (SNCC)
Student Peace Union (SPU)
Students for a Democratic Society (SDS)

Tallahassee Peace Action Coalition (Tallahassee, Florida)
Tallahassee Women's Liberation
Tampa Area Peace Action Coalition
Teachers Committee for Peace in Vietnam
Temple University Women's Liberation
Texas Coalition against the War
Texas October 31 Coalition (Austin, Texas)
Third World Task Force against the War in Southeast Asia
Trade Union Committee for Peace
Trade Unionists for Peace
Trumbull County Peace Action Coalition (Niles, Ohio)

Union of American Hebrew Congregations
United Black Trade Unionists, Inc.
United Farm Workers Organizing Committee (UFWOC)
United Methodist Board of Social Concerns
United Pastors Association (Cleveland)
United Poor People's Union (Los Angeles)
U.S. Committee to Aid the National Liberation Front of
    South Vietnam
United Women's Contingent
United World Federalists
United Youth for Peace (Berkeley, Calif.)
University Christian Movement
University of Chicago Students Against the War
The Urban Coalition

Veterans for Peace (Berkeley, Chicago, Cleveland, and num-
    erous other cities)
Vietnam Day Committee (VDC)
Vietnam Moratorium Committee (VMC)
Vietnam Veterans against the War
Villagers Opposed to the War in Viet Nam (Albany Village,
    University of California at Berkeley)

War Resisters League
War Tax Resistance
War Tax Resisters League
Wasatch Area Peace Action Coalition (Ogden, Utah)
Washington Area Peace Action Coalition (Washington, D.C.)
Washington, D.C. Church Women United
Washington, D.C. Coalition for Peace and Justice
Washington, D.C. Labor for Peace
Washington Mobilization Committee
Washington Peace Center
Welfare Rights Mothers (New York City)
West Side Peace Committee (New York City)

Women against the War (Florida State University)
Women for Peace
Women Mobilized for Change (Chicago)
Women Strike for Peace
Women's Coalition
Women's International League for Peace and Freedom
    (WILPF)
Women's Liberation (Hofstra University)
Women's Party
Women's Peace and Unity Club (Chicago)
Workers World

Young Socialist Alliance (YSA)
Young Women Committed to Action (Boston and Cleveland)
Youth against War and Fascism

NOTE

1. The People's Coalition for Peace and Justice was founded
    at a Chicago conference attended by more than 500
    delegates, January 8-10, 1971. It was a linear des-
    cendant of the New Mobilization Committee to End the
    War in Vietnam (New Mobe), which was formed in
    July, 1969 and which sponsored the November 15,
    1969 rally against the war in Washington, D.C. and
    the May 9, 1970 demonstration in response to the in-
    vasion of Cambodia and the murder of students at
    Kent State University and Jackson State College.   The
    New Mobe was a descendant of the National Mobiliza-
    tion Committee (Mobe), which sponsored anti-war
    demonstrations in New York and San Francisco on
    April 15, 1967; in Washington, D.C. on October 21,
    1967; and at the Chicago Democratic National Conven-
    tion, August 26-30, 1968.

VI

THE LITERATURE OF
THE AMERICAN RESISTANCE
TO THE VIETNAM WAR

1. WHAT IS THE MAY 2ND MOVEMENT?

We, as students in the richest but most brutally confused country in the world, cannot understand that world and
our part in it with the a-historical education we receive in
our universities. In order to make ourselves into effective
social beings and in order to discover, sharpen, and use the
power of our knowledge, we should organize ourselves in the
broadest possible way to combat that lack of education. For
it is a lack, a vacuum, that leads to political degeneration
and default. The May 2nd Movement was formed to fight
against a politics of default, specifically by organizing student protest and revolt against our government's savage war
on the people of Vietnam.

May 2, 1964, saw the first major student demonstrations against the war in Vietnam. In New York City, 1000
students marched through Times Square to the United Nations
to protest what was then called "U.S. intervention" on behalf of the legitimate government of South Vietnam. More
than 700 students and young people marched through San Francisco. In Boston, Madison, Wisconsin, Seattle, there were
simultaneous smaller demonstrations. A start, but nowhere
near enough. Nowhere near enough because very few students
even knew about the war, or if they did, knew what it means,
or what they could do about it. Now thousands know the nature of the war in Vietnam and its corollary deceit in the
press and in our universities, and its concomitant at home.
The May 2nd Movement calls that war and the resulting lies
about it at home the products of an imperialistic system.

The chief imperialistic power in the world today is
the United States, which has a business empire that perme-
ates the non-socialist world, extracting the superprofits made
possible by monopoly control. U.S. economic strangulation
of other countries causes horrible living conditions, including
mass starvation, to prevail. The people who live in these
countries have tried every "legal," non-violent recourse to
break out of their misery, only to be violently suppressed or
granted phony independence, without political freedom or economic improvement. They are driven to revolution as the
only means of liberation from imperialistic domination. To

3

keep them down the U.S. business empire requires the largest
military empire in world history.   Besides 3600 bases abroad,
the U.S. military empire includes the "native troops," the
U.S. trained, equipped and paid armies of the puppet military
dictators (Ky, Tshombe, Branco).   Ruling their countries for
the benefit of foreign business, getting personal wealth and
power as their out, these traitors serve to conceal the foreign nature of their country's oppression.

The May 2nd Movement opposes this 1965 version of
imperialism--the corporations that exact superprofits, the
military machine that enforces the system by violence, and
the cultural establishment that maintains the system, abroad
and at home, by racism, ignorance, lies and suppression of
the socially creative forces within man himself.

National liberation movements are emerging in country after country around the world.   Some have already been
victorious: Cuba, North Vietnam, Indonesia, China.   Others
are carrying on pitched armed struggle against imperialism
or are building toward it: Dominican Republic, Venezuela,
Panama, Puerto Rico, British Guiana, Colombia, Guatemala,
Brazil, Congo, South Africa, Rhodesia, Angola, Mozambique,
Iran, Vietnam, Laos, Thailand, Philippines.   This is the
many-fronted third world war.   The May 2nd Movement,
recognizing that there can be no peace without freedom, supports and joins the struggles for national liberation.   We de-
fect politically from the corruption of culture, mind and body
that is the price the privileged must pay in our country for
a share in the booty of exploitation.

The university offers no explanation of what's wrong,
of what's happening in a world principally marked by revolution.   Instead, it grooms us for places as technicians, managers and clerks within the giant corporations, or to be professional apologists for the status quo within the giant multi-
versities, or to fit some other cog-space that needs the special "sensitivity" that only the polish of factory education can
bring.   University courses on China put forward the same
formula as the war comic books--a communist conspiracy
resulting in a blue-ant hill.   Usually there is no course at
all on revolutionary Cuba, one of the major developments of
our lifetime, only 90 miles away.   Philosophy is not interested in how to understand (let alone change) the world, only
in how to evade it.   Literature is concerned with form alone.
Students jump from major to major in search of relevancy,
then, finding it nowhere, either quit or settle for banality.

The university is doing its job, supplying the system with loyal, well-trained, intelligent servants--who are moral, cultural and social morons. Lest this job prove too much of a burden for overstrained college administrations, it is shared with other institutions, from the movies to the Peace Corps.

Out of this understanding of imperialism as responsible for the poverty of our lives, and out of the void of inaction of the existing peace and left groups on the campuses, the May 2nd Movement was formed. M2M is campus based, attempting to organize students to fight the system and not docilely (or gripingly) accept it.

The major issue facing U.S. students at this time is the war against the people of Vietnam. This war is also against the interests of the students and almost the entire population of the United States. Nine billion dollars has already been cut from the ever-decreasing "peace" portion of the federal budget. The war has been used against steel workers, who were told that they were not permitted to strike because of the "national emergency." The administration will demand that black Americans stop protesting in an attempt to cover angry faces with a mask of "national unity."

Most people realize that the U.S. is not fighting for freedom and democracy in Vietnam, that the Vietnamese people want nothing more than the U.S. to get out. We say to those who are being forced to kill and die for the interests of imperialism--DON'T GO. The May 2nd Movement is launching an anti-induction campaign on the campuses. This campaign will organize existing resistance to the draft, based on the refusal to fight against the people of Vietnam. Each campus and each community should say, "No one from this college (or community) should be drafted." Declarations and literature will be circulated, forums and meetings held, demonstrations organized and acts of disobedience engaged in. The theme will be "WE WON'T GO."

We are beginning a program of approaching workers at the factory gate to talk to them about the war in Vietnam and why it is against the interests of workers. This project comes out of the understanding that while students make up an important section of the population, industrial workers make, load and transport the goods, and are therefore the key for stopping the war in Vietnam--for stopping the whole system. While workers' militancy has become more apparent in recent years, we realize that organizing a radical

workers' movement in this country is a long range goal, and
one that essentially must be done by workers. All the more
reason to begin projects now to involve workers in the peace
movement and as allies of the student.

Some chapters of May 2 plan campaigns to donate
blood and other medical aid to the National Liberation Front
of South Vietnam, to concretely show our support for national liberation struggles. Receiving blood from U.S. college
students will be a terrific morale boost to the Vietnamese
people. Collecting pledges for blood on campus can also
show where the administration stands, as collecting for civil
rights did at Berkeley.

Vietnam is not the slap in the face administered to
students by U.S. foreign policy. During the summers of
1963 and 1964, 150 U.S. students traveled to Cuba to see the
meaning of a Revolution. They went in spite of a state department "ban" on travel to Cuba. Even worse, they came
back and told students throughout the country, with their experience and with slides, that Cuba was building a just society. The organizers of the trips (including members of
M2M) face between five and twenty years in jail. We are
now organizing defense for them on the campuses. We must
fight for our right to travel anywhere and see for ourselves
what is happening--we don't find out in our classes and newspapers. The ban on travel to Cuba (and China, North Korea,
North Vietnam, liberated parts of South Vietnam, Albania) is
not an isolated Civil Liberties issue. It is part of the U.S.
government's policy of suppressing people around the world.
Fighting against the ban is part of our struggle for liberation.

This struggle is also being waged in the universities.
Whatever the immediate cause--libraries open 24 hours a day,
free tuition, real teaching and learning--it comes down to
this: In whose interest is the university run? Theirs or
Ours? May 2nd chapters put forward the idea that students
must fight for control of their schools, and that by working
together we can win fundamental changes in our day-to-day
life.

A creative response to university mis-education is the
Free University of New York. May 2nd supports the Free
University and May 2nd members in and around New York
City participate in it as students and teachers. We will work
toward spreading the idea of F.U.N.Y. and help in the initia-

tion of Free Universities in other areas.

These activities are the focus of our daily work of educating and organizing: Talking to each person on campus, going door to door, literature tables, street rallies, speaking up in class about pertinent issues.

Two special vehicles of education and agitation are the Free Student and M2M study groups. Four issues of FS have already been published so far and have sold over 70,000 copies. It has become an important voice of the student movement on many campuses, reaching not only activists, but thousands of students not in contact with the movement in any other way. FS has reported and analyzed the major student events: Berkeley, the March on Washington. It has included long features on Vietnam, Congo, Malaysia-Indonesia, Columbia University (including a complete rundown on who the trustees are) and the right of travel to Cuba. A regular feature has been the International Student column. The editorials have analyzed the student movement, the university, the war in Vietnam, the need for a long term outlook in building a movement, and have helped develop a consciousness within the student movement. Free Student is sold by all M2M chapters and members, in addition to many friends and other groups. It is used in organizing support and recruiting new members.

Study groups, such as on Vietnam, are meant for learning what is vital but not taught within the school. They are unlike most classes, where alleged experts provide descriptions of things for us to feed back in tests. The members of a study group come together to help each other increase their understanding of areas they feel necessary in order to be better able to fight for social change. The study group develops an analysis of events which is not right or wrong because a professor says so, but is judged by whether it aids in projecting the strategy and tactics of political struggle.

Our ideas have to correspond to reality if we are to organize large numbers of people to fight against a brutal system. We are in the process of developing an ideology based on anti-imperialism and support for the struggles of national liberation. To have an ideology means that we have beliefs based on studied understanding and analysis of the world situation. We put those beliefs forward for debate and for testing, and if they are proven, we base our actions up-

on them.   Our ideology enables us to see through events that
confuse and mislead.   Many people who are against the war
in Vietnam, but who are "non-ideological," are deceived by
Johnson's peace offensive.   They believe, because it would be
nice if it were true, that the administration's calls for negotiations represent a real desire to end the war.   This, in
spite of the two years of pretense at negotiations the U.S. engaged in during the hardest fighting of the Korean war, and
the hypocrisy of calling for a return to the Geneva agreements, which the U.S. has--literally--violated in every possible way.

        We reject non-ideological radicalism.   There is no
such thing as non-ideology.   Those who have "non-ideology"
cannot counter the prevailing ideology--decaying liberalism.
Only if the members of an organization share a conscious understanding of their task, can they work together over a long
period of time without suspicion, distraction and manipulation.
Of course, organizations with differing ideologies can work
together for common goals.

        When the student protest movement refers to "the es-
tablishment," we are not kidding.   That which we are out to
change--be it a university or a government--is built on a
tremendously powerful structure of material and organization.
The money and resources available to it are immense.   We
will change nothing unless we organize ourselves, forge ourselves into a united and disciplined force and match the
strength of the establishment in confrontations.   We can do so
because our strength is based on people, not cash.   M2M is
building an organization of students that recognizes, and
works to satisfy, our needs as students and as men and wom-
en.   These needs are inseparable from the worldwide struggle for liberation.   One can choose to oppose this struggle,
or to join it.   To oppose it is to be a murderer.   To join
together and fight to change this murderous society is the only way for any of us to live with decency and dignity.   We
will succeed when large numbers of students have the insight,
the dedication and the will to organize themselves, to join the
struggle with other sections of the population, and to see it
through.

                                            September 1965

May 2nd Movement
640 Broadway
New York City

(Collected October 12, 1965)

2. NATIONAL MOBILIZATION COMMITTEE
    TO END THE WAR IN VIETNAM

5 Beekman Street, New York, N.Y. 10038
(212) 964-6436

CHICAGO . AUGUST 1968

September, 1968

Dear Friend,

As we lick our wounds and analyze the political lessons of the battle of Chicago, we must not lose sight of the
urgency of a continuing, many-faceted program to challenge
the status quo of war and racism with decent, viable, human
relationships. Hundreds of Americans and thousands of Vietnamese are being killed every week that the war is allowed
to continue. The victims of repression and poverty continue
to suffer in the ghettos and in large sections of the white non-
community. Young people are still being brought up in a society which stresses the false values and assumes the ultimate righteousness of the American Empire.

Our presence in Chicago caused the guilt-ridden Johnson-Humphrey-Daley administration to bring out into the open
the forces of intimidation and political suppression which are
used far more brutally and regularly in the ghetto and in Vietnam. Despite the fact that Chicago ripped to shreds the
Democratic facade, the Democratic administration and its Republican and Wallace-ite alter-egos are pressing their fraudu-
lent election campaigns in a desperate attempt to pacify the
American people. First the stick, and now the meaningless
carrot. After the rigged conventions and the clubs, the polling booths.

Chicago was strong in the militance and courage of the
demonstrators and weak in over-all participation at the broad
range of forces that make up our total movement. It's not
surprising that millions decided, hope against hope, to play
the McCarthy game as long as it seemed to offer a viable

9

alternative (or supplement) to active resistance. In the end, hundreds of them joined us in the streets or learned that the police state could find them out even in their hotels. It is not surprising that many others stayed away from Chicago because of uncertainty as to the nature of the confrontation that would take place or out of reluctance to face police state tactics of Humphrey-Daley head on. But Chicago revealed that it is possible to stand up to such tactics and win politically.

Now we must reunite our forces and proceed to the tasks ahead. In this spirit the administrative committee adopted the following program at its meeting in Washington, D.C. on September 14. It provides a framework within which a wide variety of activities can take place and in which we can reintroduce some of its political content that was partially obscured in the fury of the Chicago street scenes. You will see that the stress for the coming weeks is on the local actions and local initiatives without which periodic national mobilization would have little meaning. But together these local initiatives will form a national pattern whose impact will be unmistakable.

Let us hear from you, your reactions, plans and reports.

Sincerely,

Dave Dellinger
Chairman of the National
Mobilization

CHAIRMAN: DAVE DELLINGER . NAT'L COORDINATOR: ROBERT GREENBLATT . PROJECT DIRECTORS: TOM HAYDEN: RENNIE DAVIS

PROGRAM

1. Confront the candidates: When the presidential candidates speak this fall, demonstrators should confront them with the issues of Vietnam and Black Liberation. Public gatherings for the candidates should be leafletted to remind people that the election is a contemptible mockery without any meaningful choice on Vietnam. Schedules of appearances of the candidates will be printed weekly in the Guardian, and are available through this office.

2. National GI Week: November 1-5 will underscore
American support for the right of soldiers to return to civilian life. Observing National Week is a way to vote for the
immediate withdrawal of troops from Vietnam, oppose U.S.
imperialism and militarism, and express kinship and concern
for the men who face orders to fight and die in an immoral
and illegal war. Delegations should visit army bases and
army towns throughout the country to talk with soldiers and
report their grievances. On November 2 and 3, Vietnam
Sabbath, churches and synagogues will hold special services
for American servicemen, calling for their withdrawal from
Vietnam and demanding amnesty for deserters, court-martialed prisoners, draft resisters, and other political opponents
of the war. Throughout the week, public hearings in many
communities should bring out the extent to which Vietnam
veterans reject the government's war. Airports, bus and
train stations, and USO centers should be blanketed with leaflets of support from the peace movement.

3. Anti-war Rallies: Country-wide public rallies on
the eve of the election, Monday evening, November 4 (in
some cases during the preceding weekend) will bring our
movement together to insure that this election will not be
seen at home or abroad, as a fair expression of American
public opinion. These rallies will give us an opportunity to
present a range of programs and policies that are frozen out
of the election.

4. Election Strike: On Election Day, we vote "no"
to Humphrey, Nixon, and Wallace, not with a "stay at home"
boycott, but with an active campaign to raise the relevant political issues in the streets. While boycotting the major
presidential candidates, we vote with picket signs, flaming
draft cards and discharge papers, and our feet and bodies.
While focusing on November 5, we talked with hundreds of
people about creating the machinery necessary to continue
and broaden the movement after the elections. While des-
cending by the thousands on the "home towns" of the major
candidates as they vote, we announce our determination to
place the next president in the same crush of public pressure
that became too much for LBJ last March. We propose a
student strike to close down American universities and high
schools on election day. Many people will vote for opposition candidates or for local peace candidates, but Tweedle-
de-de, Tweedle-de-dum, and Tweedle-de-dumber will not receive our votes. We make it clear that the war and racial
oppression must be ended no matter who is elected.

5. On to Washington: Finally we look to the new
year as a time to assert our determination to resist another
four years of war, political repressions, poverty and racism. National action could focus on the House of Reps. on
January 3, if the electoral college fails to give a majority
to any candidate, or on the inauguration of January 20, or
both.

SUMMARY OF ADMINISTRATIVE COMMITTEE MEETING
HELD IN WASHINGTON ON SEPTEMBER 14 CHAIRED BY
DAVID DELLINGER

Gerald Schwinn; Box 380, Cooper Station, NYC, Comm. of
    Returned Volunteers
Tim McCarthy; 1779 Lanier Place, NW, Washington, DC,
    Washington SDS
Richard Ochs; 3 Thomas Circle, Washington DC
Rod Robinson; 5 Beekman Street, NYC, Resistance
Ken Katz; 199 Church Street, New Haven, Conn., Conn.
    Peace Coalition
Irving Beinin; 170 E. 3rd Street, NYC, The Guardian
Emily Sack; 312 E. 84th Street, NYC
Lenny Brody; 5 Beekman Street, NYC, Resistance
Karl Baker; Box 6252, Univ. of Rochester, Rochester, NY
    SDS
Tom Hayden; 6468 Benvenue, Oakland, Ca., National Mobili-
    zation
Alan Gross; 336 E. 6th Street, NYC, ROC
Bob Kowollik; 5 Beekman Street, NYC, Resistance
Judith Simmons; 906 Maple Ave., Rockville, Md., SANE,
    Washington Mobilization
Dave Dellinger; 5 Beekman St., NYC, National Mobilization
Rennie Davis; 5 Beekman St., NYC, National Mobilization
Betty Hellman; 5 Beekman St., NYC, National Mobilization
Harry Ring; NYC, SWP
Lew Jones; 41 Union Square West, NYC, YSA
Susan La Mont; 305 E. 21st St., NYC, NYSMC
Mike Maggi; SMC National staff; 9 S. Clinton St., Chicago,
    Illinois
Larry Seigle; YSA
Pat Grogan; YSA
John Tillman; NYC, NBAWADU
Walter Reeves; NBAWADU
John Wilson; 100 Fifth Ave., NYC, SNCC
Willy Lousallen; 100 Fifth Ave., NYC, SNCC

Irwin Gladstone; 135 W. 4th Street, NYC, National ROC
Josh Brown; 135 W. 4th Street, NYC, NYROC
Marcia Kailen; Washington, D. C.
Abe Bloom; 3313 Hardell Street, Wheaton, MD. , Washington
    Mobilization
John Benson; 312 N. 37th Street, Philadelphia, Pa. , Phila-
    delphia Mobilization
Leland Sommers; 1717 19th Street, NW, Washington, DC,
    Washington Mobilization
Thomas L. Hayes; 300 Ninth Ave. , NYC, Episcopal Peace
    Fellowship
Gabrielle Edgcomb; 3515 Idaho Avenue, NW, Washington, DC
Walter Schneir; 42-34 Elbertson, Wilmhurst, NY
Arnold Johnson; 23 W. 26th Street, NYC, Communist Party,
    USA
Marc Bedner; 1101A Hellerman Street, Philadelphia, Pa. ,
    Univ. of Pa. Vietnam Week
Richie Lesnik; 312 N. 37th Street, Philadelphia, Pa. , Univ.
    of Pa. , Vietnam Week
Eric Weinberger; 17 E. 17th Street, NYC, Fifth Avenue Vi-
    etnam Peace Parade Committee
Bill Ayers; 616 Felch, Ann Arbor, Michigan, Ohio-Michigan
    SDS
Terry Robbins; 3118 Lorain #4, Cleveland, Ohio, Ohio-Michi-
    gan SDS
Joan Campbell; 3030 Eaton Road, Shaker Heights, Ohio,
    CAPAC
Barbara Beming; Wellfleet, Massachusetts, Liberation
Sidney Lens; 5436 Hyde Park, Chicago, Illinois
Bradford Lyttle; 217 Mott Street, Apt 2R. NYC, NECNVA
Louis Kampf; 763 Massachusetts Avenue, Cambridge, Mass. ,
    RESIST
Allan Brick; Box 271, Nyack, NY, Fellowship of Reconcilia-
    tion
Trudi Schutz; 2016 Walnut Street, Philadelphia, Pa.
Ron Young; Box 271, Nyack, NY, Fellowship of Reconcilia-
    tion
Marty Teitel; 4630 Newhall Street, Philadelphia, Pa.
Josie Teitel; 4630 Newhall Street, Philadelphia, Pa.
Sandy Lutz; 5 Beekman Street, NYC, National Mobilization
Arthur Waskow; 1808 Wyoming, Washington, DC
Gary L. Heath; 2299 Piedmont Ave. , Berkeley, California
Lee Webb; 1945 Calvert Street, NW, Washington, Ramparts
Jim Estes; 160 N 15th Street, Philadelphia, Pa. , AFSC
Bernice Smith; 112 Calvert Road, Rockville, Md.
Barbara Bick; 2231 Bancroft Place, NW, #1, Washington,
    DC

Tibi Texler; 20-25 Seagirl Blvd., Far Rockaway, NY, SCEF
Nona Stanton; 643 N 33rd Street, Philadelphia, Univ. of
    Temple Vietnam Committee
Greg Sandow; 27 Stanhope Street, Boston, Mass., New Eng-
    land Resistance
Terry Gross; 36-11 217th Street, NYC, Rhode Island Re-
    sistance
Ted Yarow; 531 W. 122nd Street, NYC, IWMRDC
Helen Gurewitz; 1112 Quebec Street, Silver Springs, Md.,
    Washington Mobilization
Richard M. Gold; 4939 Wayne Avenue, Philadelphia, Pa.
Edward Henderson; 5509 4th Street, NE, Washington, DC

Agenda: Brief reports.
          Concerns relating to press, Daley TV programs
          and possibility of response.
          Program suggestions and prospective for future.

Sidney Lens opened the meeting with an 8-point report.

    1.   Chicago still feels like a police state with hys-
teria running strong. There were 660 odd arrests during
the week of the convention and 51 other arrests since September 1. 100 stranded people need travel money. Bail
has been running high and is still needed, and there are
$8900 in loans to be repaid.
    2.   There is a move by Judge Campbell to indict five
leaders, Dellinger, Hayden, Davis, Jerry Rubin and Abbie
Hoffman.
    3.   A follow-up demonstration is planned for Septem-
ber 28 by the Chicago Peace Council and Women Mobilized
for Change.
    4.   A press conference was held announcing the Chi-
cago Rebuttal Paper with fair coverage.
    5.   The National Council of Churches has refused to
hold conferences in Chicago. Much mileage was obtained
from the report of Dr. Quentin Young of the Medical Committee on Human Rights.
    6.   One hundred newsmen have banded together to
follow through with reports to counter attacks by Chicago
authorities.
    7.   A "Don't Forget Chicago" ad has been placed in
the Nation and New Republic.
    8.   Donna Gripe of Legal Defense requests statements
from brutalized participants or witnesses be sent to 127
North Dearborn, 6th floor, Chicago, Illinois.

Dave Dellinger reported that when he and Keith Lampe had sent a telegram to Metromedia requesting equal time a response was received indicating it would be granted if the program appeared. News media people in cooperation with American Documentaries have worked out a possible format including interviews in rebuttal.

Rennie Davis was asked to make a proposal for a fall program, "election offensive." In introducing two dove-tailing projects, Rennie summarized proposals, stemming from meetings he had held after Chicago on both coasts. One proposal outlined plans related to the election period for decentralized actions focusing on the illegitimacy of the three major Presidential candidates and injecting the issue of Vietnam into the election. The other idea dealt with building a viable anti-war coalition representing active forces in motion, and encouraging broader participation in the National Mobilization. The specific decentralized actions revolving around the election period (the first idea) would corroborate the attempts to strengthen the organizational framework (the second idea). Specific proposals for action include:

1. The Mobilization staff would publicize the itineraries of Humphrey, Muskie, Nixon, Agnew and Wallace and help coordinate continual confrontations of mass demonstrations wherever they speak or travel.

2. The anti-war movement would focus on the plight of the soldier which is ignored by Presidential aspirants, and dramatize support of the right of the soldier to come home. Rennie outlined a "National GI Week" to be held during the election period (Nov. 1-5). Mobe would encourage sympathetic church services on Nov. 3, send delegations to forts, investigate stockade conditions, hold press conferences, leaflet, promote amnesty for deserters and organize public hearings featuring returning GIs.

3. Mobe would encourage the American peace vote to refuse to give legitimacy to the three major candidates and instead "strike the election" through a series of actions on Nov. 5. Proposed actions include:

   a. A national student strike on November 5
   b. Picketing and leafletting at polling places
   c. Sit-ins at polling booths until meaningful choices are presented
   d. National demonstrations and draft card turn-ins at the sites where the candidates themselves vote
   e. Actions at Humphrey & Nixon campaign headquarters, the evening of Nov. 5

       f.   Rallies in major cities the night of the elections
           where people can demonstrate their repudiation
           of the election farce.

Rennie concluded that if the elections were thrown into the
House of Representatives we should converge on Washington
for that event in a manner similar to Chicago.

      Dave interjected reports from two absent Mobe co-
ordinators, Donald Kalish and Sidney Peck. Kalish endorsed
GI week, and stressed continuing pressure be exerted against
draft boards and concerns like Dow Chemical in an effort to
apply the diversity of the movement and enunciate specific
political content. On structure, he emphasized the participation of new geographical areas and a larger role for women
in the Mobilization. Peck wrote that he was willing to focus
on the illegitimacy of the Presidential candidates, but didn't
want to rule out support of local candidates or other Presidential candidates like Halstead and Cleaver.

      A long discussion followed with sentiments expressed
that the emphasis in the fall should not be on the Presidential candidates, but on the issue of the war which has been
blurred by the resignation of Johnson and the Paris peace
talks. Others felt we should focus not only on the candidates
and the disintegration of the Democratic Party, but the rise
of the fascist dangers of a police state. Lee Webb and Arthur Waskow advised we lucidly present ourselves as the alternative to the electoral system, united as an extra-parlia-
mentary power in the streets to express the opposition denied by the ballot box. To dramatize the central issue of
the Vietnam war, Lee suggested the anti-war rallies be
planned for the Saturday prior to election day, to use a weekend date and avoid competition of work schedules and election returns. He advised no disruption to the voting be
planned in order not to conflict with the ordinary voter's
pride in his voting privilege. Several people argued that our
program must appeal not only to radicals but to a broader
constituency by soliciting the lower middle class, the working
class, and the dissident liberals. Tom Hayden warned not to
alienate voters by attempting to tamper with their belief in
the electoral system. Sidney Lens joined with Tom and Brad
Lyttle in exhorting the Mobilization to assume a non-violent
stance.

      Tom Hayden explained that the removal of Johnson to
silence the anti-war sentiment underscores the strategic relationship of the war to the election and the candidates. He

felt the outlined Davis proposal would successfully surface
anti-war, anti-racist sentiment, would allow moderates to
participate in the rallies and permit more militant action for
the youth. He explained that working classes wouldn't be
changed by "cooling it" or by educational statements, but that
the work with the armed forces during GI week would prepare new ground. He argued against the conservative tone
being injected into the meeting.

When discussion was channeled to the particular plan
to follow the candidates, Tim McCarthy said that no candidate should speak unencumbered by demonstrations and suggested the Guardian publish the schedules of the candidates
to facilitate organization. Irving Beinin called for militant
demonstrations to challenge the rigged elections by recreat-
ing Chicagos all over the country. Dave explained that a
post-Chicago demonstration in Flint, Michigan had used picketing and leafleting and had created an organized mass walk-
out during a candidate's speech. Dave said that while the
Mobe could disseminate information, it could not resolve on
exclusive patterns for the local demonstrations. In contrast,
Brad Lyttle felt Mobilization could make recommendations on
the tone and spirit of the demonstrations which should be nonviolent and finally, Sid Lens warned if we prevented speeches
from being heard, we would appear to represent the voice of
fascism and not of democracy.

In exploring the ideas for a GI Week, John Tillman reported he had been working on a Vietnam Sunday in which
ministers across the country would speak out against the war.
It was also suggested the plans emphasize the plight of the
black GIs, that we defend the right of the GIs to demonstrate,
and coordinate our efforts with a Japanese protest strike beginning October 21. When some speakers felt that GI Week
would deflect from other issues, Lee Webb suggested that it
should be placed after elections to facilitate lengthier planning
and to project our focus beyond the specific election period.
A vote recommended the choice of a date for GI Week be
sent to the Steering Committee. Concerning the date for the
proposed election rally it was voted that the Steering Committee set a date during the election week but not on Tuesday
itself. The suggestion to encourage people at polling places
to organize counter polling booths to vote on other candidates
or issues was defeated.

Discussion then focused on the idea to demonstrate at
the sites where the major candidates would vote. Speakers

felt it was better to stay and sink roots in local communities by picketing and distributing five million leaflets against
the war.   A vote recommended we supplement local actions
and leafletting with an attempt to dramatize the issues (particularly the draft) at areas where candidates cast votes.
(Minnesota, New York and Maryland would be emphasized.)
Another vote expressed opposition to civil disobedience or
disruption inside the polling places.

     Concerning structure revisions in the National Mobili-
zation, Rennie Davis proposed the present Steering Committee be abolished and that after regional discussions, regional
representatives be elected to the Committee.   He suggested
a more aggressive, organized staff, capable of developing
long range organizing projects in addition to single national
actions he supported.   He recommended regional staffs with
national staff.

     Dave explained that the steering committee, which has
been composed of officers and committee chairman, was intended to be small and capable of day to day decisions.   He
thought it must jump the generation gap and open itself to
young representation, not only on a regional but functional
basis.   Strong opposition was expressed by Harry Ring who
said that structural proposals were actually designed to build
an organization to supplant the present broad coalition, and
that people who would be eliminated would not necessarily be
inactive, but simply be left out.

     A committee was set up to discuss these proposals,
composed of Rennie Davis, Dave Dellinger, Irving Beinin,
Barbara Bick, John Wilson, Greg Sandow, Steve Halliwell,
and Harry Ring.

     The next meeting was set for October 12, and struc-
tural revision discussions were postponed to the meeting to
be held after the 12th.

LET US HEAR FROM YOU

Name_____

Address_____

_____Phone_____

Organization_____

What are you planning?_____

MOBILIZATION LITERATURE FOR ELECTION WEEK

(indicate quantity needed)

leaflet for GIs (single sheet)   _____

Vietnam GI (newspaper)   _____

"National GI Week" posters   _____

GI Week bumper stickers   _____

election buttons   _____

please enclose a donation to cover expenses

return to: National Mobilization Committee
                  5 Beekman Street
                  NYC   10038
                  phone: 964-6436

(Received from the National Mobilization Committee on September 23, 1968.)

3. WE WON'T GO

The war in Vietnam is not a war for freedom or democracy. It is a war against the people of Vietnam.

The government has no right to draft any citizen to participate in such a war.

We, the students of the United States, refuse to be drafted. We do not recognize the right of the government to draft our fellow students. We refuse to be turned into killers and corpses for a war that is not ours.

Name   Address   School

_____

_____

_____

We authorize the publication of our names with the above declaration.

- -

JOIN   The   M A Y   2nd   M O V E M E N T

National membership cards cost $2 per year. Members receive a monthly report of May 2nd activities and plans. (Let us know your mailing address changes.)

Members who are working together on a campus or elsewhere organize in a May 2nd chapter. Often the national office is able to provide new members with the names of other members in the same area, so that a chapter may be formed. Chapters elect representatives to the National Coordinating Committee, which also includes national staff workers. The NCC meets regularly to decide national policy.

MAY 2nd MOVEMENT, 640 Broadway, room 307, New York, N.Y. 10012. Tel: (212) 982-5550

(Collected August 10, 1964)

4. YOU DON'T HAVE TO GO!!!

NO DRAFT FOR VIETNAM!   OUR FIGHT IS HERE!

In Oakland, this week, a lot of people have "discovered" just what kind of "democracy" we really have. A lot of people have learned what some of us have known for a long time (especially around Mission HS)--what makes this country run: police clubs!

The reason more and more people are coming into conflict with the system is because they are coming to hate the rich man's war in Vietnam.

Young men are throwing away their lives in a war run by the rich and for the rich. Racism and poverty keep the establishment in power. The cops, army, big business and the school authorities work together to push us into a war that we had no part in making and no reason for continuing.

We must stand together and resist this war. Support liberation in Asia, Africa and Latin America. Our fight is for freedom and democracy right here at home.

Vietnam, Santo Domingo, the Congo, to name just a few, should be free of U.S. domination. Support this fight.

You don't have to join the rich man's army. And if you do join, you can fight for your rights inside, too.

Join this fight for freedom here. Learn more about what you can do to stay out of the army, or what you can do inside it.

Come to a rally Friday (tonight) at 7:30 -- 22nd & Mission to support the anti-draft demonstrators in Oakland, and to continue the fight against the U.S. war in Vietnam.

SPEAKERS WILL INCLUDE YOUNG MEN WHO ARE REFUSING TO GO TO VIETNAM!

21

"I ain't going to Vietnam. I got nothing against
those people. If I'm gonna die fighting, it's gonna
be fighting against the slumlords and loan sharks
and crooked politicians and cops right here in San
Francisco. "

---Come and talk with the young man who made
that statement.

TIME: Tonight at 7:30 p. m.   PLACE: 22nd & Mission

SPEAKERS FROM: Black Anti-Draft Union

Stop-the-Draft-Week

Progressive Labor Party
Mission Youth Organization

Come and get up and speak your piece!
Come and join the fight!

Sponsored by S. F. Draft Resistance Union--621-3995 and
824-2523

labor   donated

(Collected February 22, 1968 at the San Francisco Draft Resistance Union, 22nd & Mission, San Francisco, California.)

5. LET THE PEOPLE SPEAK

Demonstrate Your Opposition to the Vietnam War

Grant Park
Wednesday August 28th
1 p.m. to 4 p.m.

The majority of the American people want the United States to stop the bombing and get out of Vietnam. The politicians are in Chicago threatening to continue the war and to suppress opposition. This is the only demonstration for which the city has issued a permit despite repeated requests by many groups.

The political bosses at the Democratic Convention and the political boss of Chicago, Richard J. Daley, are obviously afraid to hear what the people want. They have turned Chicago into an armed camp and have tried to scuttle free speech so that they wouldn't have to listen to the innumerable Americans WHO WANT THE UNITED STATES TO GET OUT OF VIETNAM.

The people of this country have been grossly deceived and misrepresented by the Johnson-Humphrey-Daley team. These are the men who promised peace in 1964, then escalated the war to the point where 200,000 American boys (and countless Vietnamese) have been killed or wounded. These are the men who evidently believe that the American people have no rights, that only government bureaucrats can decide whether we live or die.

This totalitarian mentality, which goes hand in hand with the illegal war in Vietnam, must not go unchallenged. If we reassert our right to be free citizens, we must show our determination to stop the slaughter in Vietnam.

We urge all Chicagoans to join with the thousands coming from across the country in a massive antiwar demonstration at Grant Park, Wednesday from 1 p.m. to 4 p.m.

23

LET THE
PEOPLE BE HEARD

National Mobilization Committee
Room 315, 407 S. Dearborn 939-2666

(Collected from the Special Collections, Regenstein Library,
University of Chicago on February 4, 1974. Collected by
the library staff in Chicago on August 28, 1968.)

6. PEACE IS COMING ... BECAUSE THE PEOPLE
   ARE MAKING THE PEACE

On February 5, the National Student and Youth Conference on a People's Peace will convene in Ann Arbor. When it is concluded on the afternoon of February 7, a major drive for peace in Vietnam will have been initiated.

Last September, the Provisional Revolutionary Government (PRG) presented an eight-point peace plan to the Paris negotiations. It was ignored by U.S. and South Vietnamese negotiators, but in December a sixteen-member delegation of Americans went to Vietnam to work out the conditions of the treaty. The document they brought back is supported by the PRG, the Democratic Republic of Vietnam, and several womens', student, and neutralist groups. The basic theme of the treaty is the American and Vietnamese people are not enemies, yet the war is being waged without their consent.

At the conference, 2500 people from across the country will discuss ways to take the treaty to all the American people. National ratification will demonstrate to the Nixon-Ky administrations that the people reject the U.S. involvement in support of an illegitimate regime and instead call for self-determination and peace in Vietnam.

Now is the time to get involved. Everybody in the Ann Arbor area is urged to attend the conference and work for a people's peace. There is much to be done in terms of providing housing for incoming delegates and recruiting people to work at the conference. Those interested in helping or seeking more information can talk to members of Students for the Peace Treaty in the Fishbowl or call our offices.

NATIONAL STUDENT AND YOUTH
CONFERENCE ON A PEOPLE'S
PEACE
761-4648, 763-1107, 08, 09
UAC OFFICES, 2nd FLOOR UNION

25

PROPOSED AGENDA FOR
STUDENT-YOUTH CONFERENCE ON THE PEOPLES PEACE

TIME: ACTIVITY:

FRIDAY, FEBRUARY 5, 1971

12:00 on   REGISTRATION

ALL AFTERNOON   FLICKS & LITERATURE

3:00   WOMEN'S CAUCUS

5:00   ORGANIC FOOD FEAST

7:00   PLENARY: SPEECHES (10 MIN.
                          EACH)

    I.   GENERAL INTRODUCTION
        Allyne Rosenthal
   II.   NIXON STRATEGY
        Dr. Robal Ahmad
  III.   S. VIETNAM SITUATION
        Cynthia Frederick
  IV.   N. VIETNAM SITUATION
        Trudy Young
   V.   GI SITUATION
        Winter Soldier GI
  VI.   NSA PRESENTATION
        NSA delegate (Introduc-
             tion)

AGENDA RATIFICATION

CORRECTIVES

SATURDAY, FEBRUARY 6, 1971

9:00   LARGE WORKSHOPS:
                          NSA SUMMATION & IN DEPTH
                          STUDY OF PEACE TREATY
                          1. Organizing Skills

11:30   LUNCH

1:00   CAUCUSES AFTER LUNCH

2:30   CONSTITUENCY WORKSHOPS
                               (labor, student's, GI's, Women,
                               people of color, press):
                               I. Organizing skills
                               II. Treaty enforcement

8:00   CULTURAL EVENTS

SUNDAY, FEBRUARY 7, 1971

9:30   PLENARY: Nature of agenda to
                               be determined by committee
                               comprised of 3 members of
                               NSA, Mid-west Peace Treaty
                               Coordinating Committee, and
                               1 representative of each work-
                               shop

                               LUNCH

1:00   REGIONAL MEETINGS

(Received from the Special Collections/Archives Division, University of Michigan library, Ann Arbor, Michigan, February 4, 1974. Collected by the library staff on February 5, 1971.)

7. STUDENT MOBILIZATION COMMITTEE
TO END THE WAR IN VIETNAM:

WHO WE ARE

The Student Mobilization Committee to End the War in Vietnam is the mass national organization of American youth united in uncompromising struggle against the war in Vietnam.

Our program is simple. We fight for the immediate and unconditional withdrawal of all U.S. troops and material from Vietnam, for abolition of the draft, against all forms of campus complicity with the war in Vietnam, for self-determination for Vietnam, women, and Black and Third-World America, for constitutional rights for GIs and high school students.

We are an action organization, with a strategy of building mass actions of the kind that have already brought millions of Americans into the streets in opposition to the war. We intend to continue uniting even larger and broader sections of the student and academic community and GIs than ever before.

As part of this strategy, we have always participated as fully as possible in the broad adult antiwar coalitions that have initiated mass demonstrations and will continue to do so, urging these coalitions to extend organized antiwar sentiment through massive, independent actions like November 15.

BASIC PRINCIPLES

The SMC has become a mass organization of antiwar youth not haphazardly or by accident, but as the result of conscious adherence to certain basic principles. These principles have enabled the SMC to win even larger numbers of youth to its side while maintaining an uncompromising and uncooptable opposition to the policies of the American government.

28

Total Immediate Withdrawal

From the beginning of the antiwar movement, the student wing has taken the lead in making the demand for immediate withdrawal of all U.S. troops the central demand of the entire movement.

Anything less denies the right of self determination for the Vietnamese people. Anything less can be coopted and accommodated by the government while it continues the war unabated. Anything less is exactly what Nixon is already doing.

Non-Exclusion

The SMC welcomes and encourages the participation of everyone who opposes the war and is willing to work with the SMC on its projects. Our aim is to continue broadening the movement, not to narrow it by imposing irrelevant requirements upon those who would join us. Only through a united effort, with full rights for every participant, can we build a movement powerful enough to force the withdrawal of all U.S. forces from Vietnam.

Democracy in the Movement

The SMC has always stood for full democracy in decision making. The central expression of this policy is our open conferences, held at least twice a year, in which any individual or group can participate. All major campaigns of the SMC are decided upon at such conferences, which all SMCers are urged to attend after full discussion and a democratic vote.

Mass Actions Independent of All Parties and Institutions of the Government

Independent mass actions have been the most effective weapon of the antiwar movement. They provide a focal point for local, regional and national organization of the growing antiwar sentiment, and serve as a constant reminder to the government that there exists a powerful opposition which they don't control and can't ignore. And these mass actions encourage those millions just beginning to oppose the war to express their views by joining the antiwar movement.

This is what the government fears most. The fact

that we can't be bought and we won't shut up means that we
will continue to grow, organizing the majority we already
represent, until we include in our ranks the forces necessary
to compel the Administration to end the war.

PROGRAMS OF ACTION

During the week of April 13-18, the focus of the
Spring antiwar offensive, SMC's will initiate campaigns on every aspect of American society related to the war. The focus of the week will be an April 15 national student strike
and massive, united actions around the country to bring all
the GIs home from Vietnam now!

High School Antiwar Organizing

Antiwar militancy has swept through the high schools
in the past year. High school students turned out by the
hundreds of thousands all over the country for October 15
and November 14-15. In the past year hundreds of high
school SMC's have been organized.

The SMC is initiating a major national campaign
around the HIGH SCHOOL BILL OF RIGHTS to force school
boards and administrations to grant students political rights
they are entitled to in order to organize in their schools
against the war.

Campus Complicity

Many major universities have been turned into virtual
training schools for "counter insurgency" and secret research
centers for more sophisticated weapons of genocide. Nearly
all colleges and universities have ROTC, a direct arm of the
military, a Board of Trustees linked to war corporations
through boards of directors, university investments in war industries, etc. The SMC is pledged to drive these and all
other manifestations of the war machine off campus.

When 147,000 workers struck General Electric last
October the SMC supported the strike and initiated a "GE off
campus" campaign as a blow against the second largest war
producer in the country. In some areas SMCers forced GE
recruiters off campus and in many places they conducted
campaigns to get their schools to participate in the boycott
of GE products. This gave the anti-war movement a chance

to zero in on another war industry and to approach workers who are fighting for wage increases to keep pace with sky-rocketing, war-induced inflation.

The overwhelming majority of students oppose the war. SMCers have to explain to them the pervasiveness of the war machine's involvement in the campus and map out the ways of organizing the student body to drive the war machine off the university altogether.

Working With Antiwar GIs

The war in Vietnam affects most strongly the 3-1/2 million GIs. The vast majority of them oppose it but they face a special kind of intimidation by the military hierarchy. The SMC very early made it clear to GIs that when they moved against the war they would have the full support of the civilian movement. We did this realizing that they would re-spond.

What was clear to the SMC several years ago is now painfully evident to the brass. A Lieutenant Colonel in Viet-nam was quoted in the Feb. 2 Newsweek as saying: "the Movement is here at last--and it could become contagious." We agree.

SMCers have been active in building a number of GI demonstrations and in defense cases like the Ft. Jackson 8. In some areas they've helped with publication and distribution of GI newspapers.

Last summer the SMC started the GI Press Service which is now an informational service for more than sixty antiwar GI newspapers. The Press Service is available to civilians and should be used to keep up with this section of the movement and help gain support for GI antiwar efforts.

Third World Liberation and the Fight Against the War

The SMC sees an intimate relationship between the racist war in Vietnam and racist oppression in the United States, and supports self-determination for Vietnam and Black America. Third World people, oppressed to begin with, suffer added and exacerbated oppression from the war and its effects at home.

Third World GIs have been in the forefront of GI anti-
war activity. Third World committees of the SMC work to
build antiwar actions like April 15 in Third World communities, colleges, and high schools. The SMC is actively working on the March 22-29 national Black referendum on Vietnam as part of the effort to organize Third World antiwar
activity.

The Third World liberation movement has come under
severe attack by the same government that is attacking the
Vietnamese people. The SMC helps defend all victims of political repression, in particular the Black Panther Party.

Political and Legal Defense of the Movement

As the antiwar movement has grown considerably it
has come under repressive attack from the war-makers.
When any of us is attacked, we are all attacked, and we are
determined to wage the most effective political and legal defense. We speak for the majority, and we will mobilize that
majority behind any defense campaigns. In particular, we
see the trial of the "Conspiracy" defendants as a most serious attack on antiwar leaders, and the SMC defends them to
the utmost and calls on the entire movement to do likewise.

Women's Liberation

The SMC sees the Women's Liberation movement as
an important and growing part of the general movement of
various sections of humanity for the right to control their
own lives. This movement helps demonstrate to its participants what the Vietnamese struggle for self-determination is
all about.

As an under-employed, under-paid section of the working population women are among the hardest hit by the war-
induced inflation. In a militaristic society they are forced
to carry an increasing burden at home when men are sent off
to war.

The SMC welcomes the participation of all women and
Women's Liberation groups in the anti-war movement and encourages educational activity to show the link between the social, physical and economic oppression of women and the oppression of Vietnam through U.S. intervention.

Workers and the War

In some places local unions have participated in anti-war actions. The SMC recognized the powerful role organized labor can play in the fight against the war and will try to involve speakers and local unions in April 15 activities. It will watch for further opportunities to mobilize campuses linking up with strikes against major war producers like GE.

Local SMCs should explain to students the anti-war sentiment expressed in the refusal of workers to sacrifice wages "in the National (war) interest" and the importance of involving so powerful a sector of the population in the anti-war movement.

The Draft

Tens of thousands of young men every year are forced, either by being drafted or enlisting, to fight in a war which they do not support and which is not in their interests.

The Student Mobilization Committee demands the complete and immediate abolition of the draft. Forcing an end to the racist and oppressive draft would be a tremendous blow to the ability of the U.S. government to continue the war.

March 16-22 was National Antidraft Week. The SMC Conference supported and built the week of activities in local areas across the country. The struggle against the draft should continue. Actions around the draft should seek to unite the broadest layers of Americans against the draft. They should be massive and independent of the government's parties and institutions. Local areas should determine tactics of struggle. As with the mass struggle for the immediate withdrawal of U.S. troops from Vietnam our demand should be clear and simple: ABOLISH THE DRAFT.

JOIN THE SMC

For more information clip and mail to--------------------

Student Mobilization Committee
1029 Vermont Avenue, N.W. Suite 907
Washington, D.C. 20005   202-737-0072

____ I would like to organize an SMC at my school.

____ Please send more information on SMC's plans for building the Spring antiwar offensive.

____ Enclosed is a donation of $_____

____ Please send a literature order form.

Name_____

Address_____

City _____State_____

Zip _____Phone_____

School and/or Organization_____

_____

(Collected November 22, 1970 at Radcliffe College.)

8. WE ARE GOING TO STOP IT

We must be serious about implementing the Peace Treaty with the Vietnamese people. Already 73 per cent of the people of the United States favor immediately ending the war, but the government continues to defy these wishes and in fact intensifies the conflict. Thus the people have been forced to design their own treaty and now we must put it into effect. We must end and can end the war now.

WE CAN STOP IT

The movement has the power to bring the war to an end now if it can unify itself to exert maximum pressure. Last spring's response to the Cambodian invasion almost forced Nixon to give up the struggle, but since then the forces opposing the war have been unable to deal with Nixon's new strategy. Yet this strategy depends upon an increasingly shaky base of support--the mythical silent majority which feels threatened by the disastrous economic effects of our military policy. The rise in taxes, prices and the threat of unemployment have begun to break the complacency of this group. This strengthens the peace movement tremendously and means that the social cost of maintaining the Indochina war goes up tremendously.

THE PEACE TREATY AND UNITY

Bringing the diverse anti-war groups together requires that they see their common interest. The PEACE TREATY PROVIDES THAT MEANS. It appeals to all age groups and can attract people who have been inactive up until now. Campus and city-wide referendums should be set up and when possible run by the anti-war movement. Special efforts should be made to involve new groups in the implementation of the treaty--from welfare mothers to church groups. Door-to-door canvassing should have good results in many types of neighborhoods. But young people, especially students, will still have to play the role of catalyst that

35

they have done before. If the peace treaty is to be more
than another pointless petition people must see it as something real rather than just another gimmick to give some
people a way to work off frustration. More people than ever
are opposed to the war but they are unwilling to go down a
blind alley. They must be convinced that they have the power
to end the war.

MAY DAY BELONGS TO THE PEOPLE OF THE WORLD

Historically May 1 has been the day of the oppressed.
May 1 demonstrations have touched off major changes from
reform to revolution and this year should be no exception.
On May 1 people in Europe, Asia, Latin America and Africa
will be expressing their solidarity with the Vietnamese people. We should join in that struggle. On May 1 people
should mass in Washington and present the government with
the peace treaty, demanding that Nixon respond within two
days by calling an immediate end to the war. If the government refuses to heed the will of the majority for peace after
years and years of patience the people should begin to implement the treaty themselves. Beginning on May 3 and continuing for the rest of the week people who presented the treaty
and the thousands that will join them should close down the
functioning of the federal government through massive civil
disobedience. The demonstrations should be non-violent but
disruptive--blocking streets, marches, strikes at schools and
other places of work. To be effective--i. e. : to provide the
spark that can coalesce the people who oppose the war into
activity--we must be willing to do more than march. At the
same time our tactics should not be seen as provocative even
though those sorts of tactics may well be just. Civil disobedience is disruptive but it doesn't force the people involved
to make a choice between revolution and the system. Revolution is a necessity, but many people who oppose that war
don't yet believe this and they shouldn't be excluded from the
movement. Civil disobedience will allow groups as diverse
as church and youth groups to take part. It also means that
people will be taking some risks, opening themselves to arrest. But mass arrest penalties for white people are still
relatively light and the demonstration will not be Gandhi-like.
People can and should defend themselves from attack.

MAYDAY-MAYDAY-MAYDAY

The presentation of the peace treaty May 1 in Washington should be linked with simultaneous demonstrations in all major cities and on all campuses. Washington is the most important focus, but May 1 should be a nation-wide movement. On May 3 and 4 when disruption begins in Washington young people will have to make a choice as to whether to come to D.C. or stay in their areas. Hopefully, most cities can contribute to both efforts with an initial focus on Washington during the first week of May and gradually moving that emphasis through strikes and demonstrations back to regions. This means that young people will be called upon for several weeks of sustained activity, something which will require a great deal of hard work and sacrifice. Thus we must begin now to inform people from everywhere of our plans, explaining our views on Nixon's new strategy. Talking with people from dormitory to unemployment office will be helpful. Women's groups, which will hopefully play a leading role in May Day, are critical. The anti-war movement must realize that its past chauvinist practices have hurt women and weakened our chances for peace.

BEYOND MAY 1

The demonstration in Washington, although critical to the success of the peace treaty, cannot be an end in itself. People should not drop ongoing projects but should relate them to the war. One of the weaknesses of the peace movement has been its inability to relate imperialism to the lives of non-student non-hip communities. Actually, great numbers of people in factories, offices as well as unemployment and welfare lines have begun to become aware that Vietnam affects their lives and that until the war is ended the job of reconstruction of this country is impossible. But if this kind of awareness is to grow, if this kind of unity can develop, it will be necessary for the movement to change. Elitist attitudes will have to change. We will have to talk to and learn from people we normally ignore. In fact, the movement should no longer be an "it"--a thing separate from the people but part of them.

GETTING IT TOGETHER

Any serious attempt to implement the treaty will require some organization. Many people, because of the limitations of past organizations, are leary of any sort of coordination, but it would be a tragedy if the forces represented
at this conference had no way to really followup on May 1
and the treaty. Our skepticism must and should lead to constructive ideas, not negativism. Whatever is done, efforts
to avoid elitism, chauvinism and narrowness of view should
be made. Concerning May 1, coordination could be
achieved through a network of communication setups at this
conference. Switchboards and a national communications network, utilizing services like LNS and developing a liberation
broadcasting service for FM stations should be developed.
There should also be a May Day committee made up of several people elected from each region (members could rotate)
as well as several people elected from each constituency
group (women, GIs, etc.). The representatives from each
region should preferably include at least one woman. This
group could meet several times before May 1 and could make
sure that local, regional and national coordination around the
treaty can occur.

IMPLEMENTATION

1. Community and student organizing around the
Peace treaty, concentrating on involving new people and relating their concerns to the war.
2. Campus and city-wide referendums on the peace
treaty prior to May 1.
3. Presentation of peace treaty and demonstration in
support of the treaty in Washington on May 1. Demand that
the government withdraw immediately from Vietnam. Simultaneous May Day demonstrations in other cities and campuses.
4. If the government refuses to accept the peace
treaty, massive civil disobedience begins in Washington. Intense education at the local level, leading to strikes, etc.
5. Continuing organizing on the local level to implement the peace treaty.
6. Coordination of May Day and the peace treaty will
be achieved by a committee composed of two people elected
from each region and two people represented by the constituency groups.

                                        Seattle caucus

(Collected by the library staff, Special Collections, Suzzallo Library, University of Washington, Seattle on April 22, 1971.   Collected by the compiler on June 27, 1973.)

9. ANTI-WAR CONFERENCE--MARCH 29, 1969

Hatch Auditorium--Case-Western Reserve University

SCHEDULE OF EVENTS:

11:00 a.m. to 12 noon: REGISTRATION
12 noon to 1:45 p.m.: KEYNOTE SPEECHES

> SIDNEY LENS: "The Vietnam War--Is the End in
> Sight?"
> DON GUREWITZ: "The Youth Revolt--Campus, High
> School and Among GIs"

2:00 to 3:45 p.m.: WORKSHOPS

I. New Programs for the Peace Movement:
Panelists: Dr. Sidney Peck, Dr. Eugene Perrin,
Sheldon Schector, Esq., Syd Stapleton

II. Building the Peace Movement among Women:
Panelists: Louise Peck, Enid Stern, Marie Tuck

III. The Church as a Spokesman for Peace:
Panelists: Rev. James Hobart, Rev. Robert Bonthius

IV. High School Students in the Fight for Peace:
Panelists: Max Kirsch, Jerry Whiting, Molly Kirsch

V. Defense of Constitutional Rights:
Panelists: Joan Campbell, Al Stern, Benjamin Sheerer

Possibly other panels will be held on Labor and The Peace
Movement and Black Students, The Draft and the War.

REGISTRATION, OPEN TO THE PUBLIC, WILL BE FROM
11 A.M. TO NOON
Adults $2.00, College Students $1.00, High School Students 50¢

CLEVELAND AREA PEACE ACTION COUNCIL
13101 Euclid Avenue
Cleveland, Ohio 44112
PHONE: 761-5574

STEERING COMMITTEE PROPOSAL FOR
JOINT MINORITY-MAJORITY RESOLUTIONS

The Steering Committee Recommends an escalated autumn offensive against the war in Vietnam which shall include endorsement of the following three national actions being organized by associated groups:

1.   A Southern California campaign in August centered on
the summer White House and included a mass march on
August 17.

2.   An enlarged "reading of the war dead" type action in
Washington during the first days of September.

3.   An October 15 moratorium on "business as usual" in
order that students, faculty members and concerned citizens can organize in their own communities against the
war.

The Steering Committee also recommends two massive national actions for which administrative and organizing personnel
shall be provided by this conference and its appropriate committees:

1.   An October 11 action in Chicago related to the beginning of the conspiracy trial.   Planning on this action was
initiated by other groups.   It will therefore be necessary
to negotiate on tactics and means of collaboration with
these other groups to assure the development of plans and
tactics capable of mobilizing the largest number of people.

2.   A broad, mass, legal November 15 demonstration as
near the White House as possible in support of the demand for immediate withdrawal of all U.S. forces in Vietnam.   The demonstration is to include:

a. A mass march

b. A rally with speeches as near the White House as
possible which will include but not be limited to the
following program:

1.   Withdrawal of support from the Thieu-Ky government; self-determination for the people of
Vietnam

2.   Immediate and total withdrawal of all U.S.
     troops and supplies and dismantling of U.S.
     bases in Vietnam;
3.   Defeat of the ABM and related missile pro-
     grams and swift progress toward disarmament;
     an end to chemical-biological warfare research
     and development;
4.   Immediate implementation of a program to end
     racism, repression and poverty in the U.S.
5.   Free speech for GI's

The March and rally will last from 11:00 a.m. to
5:00 p.m.

c. Those who wish to stay in Washington will meet
that evening for planning of subsequent days' strategy
and tactics;

STEERING COMMITTEE PROPOSAL FOR
JOINT MAJORITY, MINORITY RESOLUTION

d.   It will be expected that an associated demonstration will be planned for the same time on the West
Coast.

(Nothing proposed in the foregoing should be taken to limit
the planning and implementation of other programs developing from this conference.)

G.I.-Veteran Workshop Proposals for Washington Action:

Voted 36-2

Since the participation of G.I.'s requires it, the mass demonstration in fall is proposed as a legal demonstration.

Overall proposal, unanimously adopted:

1.   That the Peace Movement launch the decisive phase of
anti-Vietnam War pressure with a massive convergence of
forces on Washington, D.C.

2.   That the central theme of this mass action be immediate cease-fire and immediate withdrawal of all U.S. forces
from Vietnam, supported by an ultimatum signed by masses
of Americans.

3.   That all participating groups be welcomed to add their own slogans and demands, representing the needs of their constituencies.   It is of utmost importance that G.I.'s be involved in the demonstration in Washington.   Therefore, we propose that one of the slogans for the march be "Free Speech for G.I.'s!"

4.   That this conference demand that President Nixon appear in person before the entire assembly to account for his actions in Vietnam and receive the ultimatum of the American people for an end to the killing.

5.   That the workshop recommends that the date of the national action be October 25th because (a) it will allow enough time for campuses to organize and (b) it will provide the best prospects for weather conditions suitable for travel to Washington and outdoor activities there.

6.   That build-up activities be initiated in all communities immediately following this Cleveland conference with door-to-door gathering of signatures on the ultimatum, thus bringing the issues to the people and building the grass-roots strength of the various participating organizations.

7.   That building actions throughout the country take place regularly, preceding the Washington action, focusing on military bases and nearby transportation centers.   By directive of the Department of the Army, civilians may demonstrate and distribute literature on open Army bases (see: AGAM-P (M) (27 May 69) DCS PER-SARD).

8.   That G.I.'s themselves be informed of and encouraged to participate and take a leading role in planning and carrying out the national build-up with simultaneous activities of their own choosing.   This is now possible with the cooperation of the network of G.I. base papers and national G.I.-oriented papers and the support groups of civilians near the bases that have papers.

(Collected by the Special Collections Division, 20700 North Park Blvd., John Carroll University, Cleveland, Ohio on March 29, 1969.   Collected by the compiler on March 24, 1972.)

10.   BRING THE WAR HOME

sds

The June National Convention of SDS has called for a National Action in Chicago on Sept. 26-28 with the following slogans: IMMEDIATE WITHDRAWAL OF ALL US OCCUPATIONAL TROOPS FROM VIETNAM AND ALL FOREIGN COUNTRIES, FROM BLACK AND BROWN COMMUNITIES AND FROM THE SCHOOLS; SUPPORT FOR BLACK AND BROWN LIBERATION; FREE HUEY NEWTON AND ALL POLITICAL PRISONERS; NO MORE SURTAX; INDEPENDENCE FOR PUERTO RICO; SOLIDARITY WITH THE CONSPIRACY 8; SUPPORT FOR GI'S RIGHTS AND REBELLIONS. The time and place were picked to coincide with the beginning of the trial of the 8 "conspirators" involved in last summer's demonstrations against the war and the Democratic convention.

We in SDS see this action as an important step in building the anti-imperialist movement in the U.S., one which allies with the international anti-imperialist movement. The enemy of the vast majority of the American people and of the people of the world is U.S. imperialism which tries to smash the struggles for national liberation of the Vietnamese and other black and brown peoples throughout the world, also oppresses the vast majority of white Americans.

But, imperialism gains white Americans' compliance by giving them a privileged position among the oppressed peoples of the world. Through the privilege of higher wages, a relatively higher standard of living and an ideology of white chauvinism, the imperialists try to make the struggles of national liberation of third world peoples seem to be against their interests. We must make it clear to white working people that the basis for their exploitation and oppression is imperialism and that only by allying with the struggles of the Vietnamese, blacks, and browns within the territorial boundaries of the U.S. and all other struggles for self-determination can their own oppression be ended. This alliance must

44

be a priority if Americans are to be part of the world wide
socialist revolution, rather than build a narrow isolated fight
for white privilege.

In the past, SDS has committed a serious error by
not taking an active enough role in transforming the anti-war
movement into an anti-imperialist movement. The majority
of American people are already opposed to the war. Beyond
that, it is clear that the majority of the American people are
also increasingly oppressed by U.S. imperialism: higher
taxes, urban crisis in housing, social services and schools,
the growing number of young men from black, brown and
white working class communities who are drafted and dying,
and profits being made by a small number of avaricious imperialists while poverty and illness continue to be a major
fact of life for millions of Americans. All of this is the
price that Americans must pay to maintain the privilege of
sharing the wealth of the richest nation in the world, of having the advantage of scraping the "crumbs off the imperialists' table."

Because of this, it is now possible and necessary to
build not simply an "anti-war movement," but an anti-imperialist movement; not simply calling for "end the war now
--bring the troops home," but organizing to "bring the war
home." And, rather than diminishing our base, raising anti-
imperialist issues in a militant way will expand the base of
the movement to include vast numbers of working people and
working class youth, by speaking directly to how the black
struggle and the Vietnamese struggle relate to them. This
is especially true because only a militant anti-imperialist
movement has a chance of winning.

Any radical or revolutionary organization that does
not recognize this, and does not take the issue of imperialism to the people, is, at this time, working against the interests of the MAJORITY of the American people, and the
interests of the oppressed and exploited people of the whole
world.

Furthermore, the development from an anti-war to an
anti-imperialist movement not only results in new tactics and
new slogans, but creates new leadership as well. The anti-
imperialist movement must be led by organizations such as
The Black Panther Party, the Young Lords Organization, the
Third World Liberation Front, La Raza and other revolutionary Third World groups, and by the Young Patriots, SDS,

and other white organizations that understand and support the
Third World struggles for national liberation, and are actively committed to the struggle against imperialism.

Broad-based organizations that have led the anti-war
movement until now must use their resources and skills to
build anti-imperialist actions, but must also be willing to follow the leadership of those within this country most oppressed
by, and most willing to lead the attack against U.S. imper-
ialism--in fact, those black and brown groups that daily lead
the attack.

This is the summer we have seriously begun to go into working class communities, high schools, shops and factories. The national action this fall will be a major focus
of that organizing, and the demonstrations must show that opposition to the Vietnam war--and this entire system--has
spread to new sectors of the population.

From the Chicago national action, we will build the
November 8th Movement. November 8th will be a time when
organizations and individuals carry out decentralized actions
across the country against U.S. imperialism. Such actions
will allow people in every part of the country to participate,
and will put every town and city power structure under attack.
The combination of the Chicago action and the regional actions in November can provide a new focus, and tremendously increase the possibilities of organizing against the war,
imperialism and racism.

There is a specific reason that the national action
should be held in Chicago:

For millions of Americans, the city of Chicago has
come to symbolize the repressiveness and brutality of the
state. At a time when the movement--and particularly black
and brown people--face severe repression, it is critical that
we affirm that the only way to fight repression is by bringing
the issues to the people, and winning them to fight even harder against the exploitative and oppressive system we live under. By retreating, or failing to continue to act aggressive-
ly in support of the Vietnamese and other oppressed peoples,
we only convince the ruling class of our weakness. There
are only two ways to meet repression: one is to give up;
the other is to fight and organize until the system that makes
repression inevitable is destroyed.

The action in Chicago, in and of itself, will be the movement's statement of our intention to continue the struggle.

Furthermore, it is critical that when Bobby Seale and others are under indictment by the courts, the movement responds by reaffirming its commitment to the issues that brought us to Chicago last year and demonstrates our determination to continue fighting against the war, imperialism and racism.   There is no better place to do this than in the city where the alleged "conspiracy" took place; no better time than when the "conspirators" are to be tried in the ruling class court.

The national action will be introduced at the United Front against Fascism Conference, called by the Black Panther Party in Oakland, starting July 15.   We hope that delegates and organizations at this conference in Cleveland will vote to support and participate in this national action.

ALL POWER TO THE PEOPLE!

FREE HUEY!

THE DUTY OF EVERY REVOLUTIONARY IS TO MAKE THE REVOLUTION!

BRING THE WAR HOME!

(Collected by the Dean of Faculties Office from The College of Wooster chapter of SDS, Wooster, Ohio on October 24, 1971.   Received from the College of Wooster on February 14, 1973.)

11. STUDENT MOBILIZATION COMMITTEE
TO END THE WAR IN VIETNAM

June 6, 1970

Dear Friend,

The past month saw the beginning of campus strikes of proportions unprecedented in American history. Originally a response to Nixon's announcement to spread the war into Cambodia, the strike obtained the peak of activity around the murder of students at Kent, Augusta, and Jackson.

The strikes on the campuses have been accompanied by a revulsion of incalculable intensity among people of the country as a whole at the escalation of the war and at the massacres. This revulsion offers us a chance to reach out to new forces and to build an antiwar movement more powerful and bigger than anything seen before.

On June 19-21, a National Emergency Conference against the Vietnam, Laos, Cambodia War has been called by over 110 individuals and organizations, including strike committees, labor leaders, and antiwar coalitions across the nation. The purpose of this conference is to evaluate the past month and plan the future of the antiwar movement. The conference, from all indications, looks like it will be the broadest national conference of its kind. The Cleveland Area Peace Action Council has agreed to host the conference and help is urgently needed in the office. If you can come down anytime, the number to call is 621-6516.

Registration starts at 12:00 noon on Friday, June 19, at Cuyahoga Community College. For advance registration, please fill out the enclosed form.

A significant part of the conference will be speaking here June 20, at a $250 a plate fund raising dinner for the Republican Party. More information will follow on that demonstration.

48

The SMC will hold a city-wide meeting on Sunday, June 14 at 3:00 pm at the Peace Center, 2102 Euclid Avenue, second floor. At this meeting we will discuss Mr. Agnew. Be sure to be there as it will be an important meeting.

Last but not least, is finances. The SMC is going more into debt every day. If every person on the mailing list could send just one dollar, it would cover a good portion of our bills. At a time when the antiwar movement is growing so rapidly, we cannot afford to let finances hold us back. Won't you please help?

SEE YOU AT THE MEETING.

SMC STAFF

2101 Euclid Ave., Cleveland, Ohio.   44115 (216) 621-6516

AN IMPORTANT PART OF THE NATIONAL EMER-GENCY CONFERENCE AGAINST THE CAMBODIA-LAOS-VIETNAM WAR TO BE HELD IN CLEVELAND JUNE 19-21 AT CUYAHOGA COMMUNITY COLLEGE.

Join us at East 30th and Cuyahoga Community College Avenue at 5:30 p. m.   The march begins at 6:00.   We will be picketing peacefully at the Sheraton Cleveland Hotel from 7:00-8:00 p. m. while Vice President Agnew addresses a $250-a-plate Republican party fund raising dinner.

JOIN US TO DEMAND THE IMMEDIATE WITHDRAW-AL OF TROOPS FROM SOUTHEAST ASIA AND PARTICI-PATE IN THE NATIONAL EMERGENCY ANTI-WAR CON-FERENCE.

Sat. June 20

assemble 5:30

Cuyahoga Community
College & E. 30

march begins 6:00

picket line 7:00

Sheraton Cleveland Hotel
Public Square

Called by The Cleveland Area Peace Action Council

Please clip and mail to: Peace Center, 2102 Euclid Ave.,
Cleveland, Ohio 44115: Phone: 621-6516

____ I would like more information on the Emergency Anti-
War Conference.
____ I would like more information on the Agnew demonstra-
tion.
____ I would like to work in the Peace Center to help build
the conference and the demonstration. Call me.
____ I would like to be a marshal at the conference and at
the demonstration. Call me.
____ Enclosed is my financial contribution to help pay for the
costs of the conference and demonstration.

           NAME:_____ Phone No.:_____

           ADDRESS:_____ Zip:_____

Labor donated

(Received from the Peace Center, 2102 Euclid Ave., Cleveland, Ohio on June 12, 1970. The demonstration occurred
at the Public Square, Sheraton Cleveland Hotel, Saturday,
June 20, 1970.)

12. A CALL TO AN EMERGENCY NATIONAL CONFERENCE
Against the Cambodia Laos Vietnam War

FRIDAY - SATURDAY - SUNDAY

JUNE 19-20-21

CUYAHOGA COMM COLLEGE

CLEVELAND OHIO

Fri: Registration & housing begin 12 noon

Campus Center Bldg./Keynote speakers

Sat: Session until 5 PM/Demonstration

against Agnew, early evening

Sun: Sessions until 8PM

The purpose of the emergency conference is simple
and to the point: to plan anti-war demonstrations and other
anti-war activities of the most massive kind centering on the
crucial issue of withdrawal from the war and conducted in a
peaceful and orderly fashion.   This is the way to involve immense masses of ordinary people, trade unionists, GIs and
their families, students, moderates, liberals and radicals,
young and old, and all those who oppose the war regardless
of their differences on various other matters.   Excerpted
from the Conference Call.

Sponsor list information (Organizations listed for identification
purposes only):

Rev. Charles Adams, pastor, Detroit
Lawrence Adler, UE District, Cleveland
Atlanta Mobilization Committee
Beacon Hill Support Group, Boston
Berkeley Faculty Student Ad Hoc Peace Committee
Berkeley Strike Coordinating Committee
Fred Brode, Chairman, Houston CEWV
Cambridge Veterans for Peace

51

Kay Camp, Natl Chairman, WILPF, Philadelphia
Chicago Strike Council
Chicago Veterans for Peace
Prof. Noam Chomsky, MIT
Joe Cole, Ft. Jackson 8
Committee of Kent State Massacre Witnesses
Stephanne Coontz, Seattle
Laura Deriz, H S SMC leader, San Francisco
Detroit Coalition to End the War Now
Malcolm C. Dobbs, President, Los Angeles chapter, Social
    Workers Union
Sid Feinhersh, U of Mass. Mobilization Committee
Harold Feldman, Veterans for Peace, Philadelphia
Leo Fenster, Sec'y, Cleveland District Auto Council UAW
    AFL CIO
Carl Finamore, Chicago Strike Council
Grady Glen, President, Frame Unit Local, 600 Dearborn,
    Mich.
Jerry Gordon, Chairman, CAPAC
Shirley Grant, United Poor People's Union, Los Angeles
Dick Gregory
Don Gurewitz, National Coordinator, SMC
Conn Hallinan, President, AFT Local 570, Berkeley
Fred Halstead
Robert Hare, pastor, Cleveland
Independent Campus Women, San Francisco State
Miche Judkins, Vice-president, Chicago Independent Union of
    Public Aid Employees
James Latterly, Co-chairman, Detroit Coalition
Ben Lesos, Treasurer, Concerned Democrat Council, Los
    Angeles
Jerry Lennon, rep. AFSCME Council 42, Los Angeles
Carol Lipman, National Executive Secretary, SMC
Herb Mogidson, Individuals Against the Crime of Silence
John McConn, Co-ordinator, Massachusetts Referendum '70
Pvt. Joe Miles, Ft. Richardson, Alaska
Joe Miller, Field Organizer, United Electrical, Radio &
    Machine Workers of America (WE) Minneapolis

--I plan to attend the conference center.   (The names of others in your area who plan to attend.)

--I need housing for Friday-Saturday for ____ people.

--Enclosed--Registration Fee ($5 adults/ $2 students)

--I cannot attend.   Enclosed is my donation of $____.
Please keep me informed.

Name	Address	City
State	Zip	Phone
Organization	Union	
School	SEND TO: Conference-CAPAC	
	2102 Euclid	
(216) 621-6516	Cleveland, Ohio 44105	

(Distributed June 15, 1970 at Cuyahoga Community College,
Cleveland, Ohio.   Collected in the Special Collections, Cleveland State University, June 11, 1972.)

13. WAR/GAME

Once more the fat-ass corporation executives and lying politicians are getting together for a ruling class festival --The World Davis Cup Tournament in Cleveland Heights. They'll sit back watching this game the same way they oversee the people of the world. Tricky Dick pig Nixon is even supposed to show up.

But those dudes just can't indulge in this bullshit game anymore. There's a war going on in the world--People's War! The people of Vietnam, Latin America and the Black and poor whites in the U.S. have all been enslaved by these U.S. corporation executives. That's what imperialism is about--colonizing whole nations, and raping and slaughtering the peoples of the world. But the game of the rich has caught up to Pig America! The Vietnamese have kicked ass out of U.S. occupational troops. More and more GI's will no longer listen to Pig Nixon's orders, and are turning their guns around on the REAL ENEMY. The Provisional Revolutionary Government in Vietnam has led the Vietnamese people to complete victory. This isn't a jive victory like we read about in the pig papers to cover up the truth that the rich businessmen are running scared and losing turf!

Pig cops occupy black communities in the same way U.S. troops occupy foreign nations to keep the people down and make profits. Last summer Ahmed Evans forced these racist pigs to deal with the people! He told the racist pigs to get out of Glenville. Ahmed must be free! He must be free to continue that struggle.

We're getting together and fighting the rich businessmen and their pigs in the streets, the schools and anywhere they appear. We see that struggle as the only way to revolution. SDS is calling a national action October 8-11 to bring the war home in support of the struggles for self-determination of the Blacks and Vietnamese. But there's no reason to wait for Chicago!

The sides are drawn.   High noon, Saturday
                                        September 20   SDS

54

Which side are you on?   Roxboro School
                                Cleveland Heights

                    (Take Roxboro rd. off Fairmount blvd.)

            A REVOLUTION IS NOT A SPECTACLE!

            THERE ARE NO SPECTATORS!

EVERYONE PARTICIPATES WHETHER THEY KNOW IT OR NOT

(Received from the Reference Librarian, Capital University,
2199 E. Main St., Columbus, Ohio on June 4, 1972.   Collected by the library on November 17, 1971.)

14. NEW MOBILIZATION COMMITTEE
     TO END THE WAR IN VIETNAM

STEERING COMMITTEE MEMBERS
OF THE NEW MOBILIZATION COMMITTEE

The following are the members of the Steering Committee of
the New Mobilization Committee to End the War in Vietnam.
Beside most individuals is the organization with which each
is primarily affiliated. These organizations can be considered "participating organizations" of the total coalition --
The New Mobilization Committee.

(The Steering Committee is the body responsible for all decisions regarding The New Mobilization Committee and the
activities and demonstrations it sponsors.)

Co-chairmen of the New Mobilization Committee are marked
with an *.

Mia Adjali -- United Methodist
Marc Beallor -- W.E.B. DuBois Club
Norma Becker -- The Fifth Avenue Vietnam Peace Parade
    Committee
Irving Beinin -- editor, The Guardian
Barbara Bick -- Women Strike for Peace
Abe Bloom -- The Washington (DC) Mobilization Committee
Irwin Bock -- Veterans for Peace (Chicago)
Allen Brick -- Fellowship of Reconciliation
Balfour Brickner -- Union of Hebrew Congregations
Katherine Camp -- Women's International League for Peace
    and Freedom
Joan Campbell -- churchwoman, Cleveland
Dan Collins
Marjorie Colvin -- GI Civilian Alliance for Peace (San Fran-
    cisco)
Tom Cornell -- Catholic Peace Fellowship
Bill Davidson -- Resist
Rennie Davis
*David Dellinger -- editor, Liberation Magazine
*Douglas Dowd -- Professor, Cornell University

Gerhard Elston -- National Council of Churches
Al Evanoff -- District 65, Retail, Wholesale, Department
    Store Workers Union, AFL-CIO
Mark Feinstein
Richard Fernandez -- Clergy and Laymen Concerned About
    Vietnam
John Froines -- Conspiracy
Gene Gladstone -- Michigan Mobilization Committee
Carleton Goodlett
Jerry Gordon -- Cleveland Area Peace Action Council
Sanford Gottlieb -- Sane
Bob Green -- Philadelphia Resistance
Robert Greenblatt -- Professor, Columbia University
Fred Halstead -- Socialist Workers Party
Alice Hamburg
Robert Haskell -- Episcopal Peace Fellowship
David Hawk -- Vietnam Moratorium Committee
David Herreshoff -- Detroit Coalition to End the War Now
Gus Horowitz -- Socialist Workers Party
Ralph Hudgins
Arnold Johnson -- Communist Party, USA
James A. Johnson
Frank Joyce -- People Against Racism
*Donald Kalish -- Southern California Peace Action Council
Sylvia Kushner -- Chicago Peace Council
James Lafferty -- Detroit Coalition to End the War Now
Paul Lauter -- Resist
*Sidney Lens -- Chicago Peace Council
Carol Lipman -- Student Mobilization Committee
Lincoln Lynch -- The Urban Coalition
Bradford Lyttle -- War Resisters League
John McAuliff -- Committee of Returned Volunteers
*Stewart Meacham -- American Friends Service Committee
Joe Miles -- Active duty GI
Joseph Miller -- Philadelphia Sane
Allan Myers -- editor, GI Press Service
Otto Nathan -- War Resisters League
Vern Newton -- New Democratic Coalition
*Sidney Peck -- Professor, Case-Western Reserve University
Ann Peery -- Ohio Peace Action Council
Max Primack
Msgr. Charles Owen Rice
Carl Rogers -- Servicemen's LINK to Peace
Richard Rothstein
Howard Samuels -- former Undersecretary of Commerce
Irving Sarnoff
Lawrence Scott -- A Quaker Action Group

Larry Siegle -- Young Socialist Alliance
Peer Vinther
Arthur Waskow -- Institute for Policy Studies (Washington,
    D.C.)
Charlotte Weeks -- Women's Liberation (Cleveland)
Abe Weisburg -- The Fifth Avenue Vietnam Peace Parade
    Committee
*Cora Weiss -- Women Strike for Peace
John Wilson
Mary Wylie -- United Methodist
Peter Yarrow
Ron Young -- Fellowship of Reconciliation

. . . .

Mia Adjali -- United Methodist Churchwoman, Detroit
Joan Campbell -- Churchwoman, Cleveland
Dan Collins -- State Chairman of New York New Democratic
    Coalition
Frank Joyce -- People Against Racism
Mary Wylie -- United Methodist
Moe Foner -- Local 1199, Drug and Hospital Workers Union,
    AFL-CIO
Larry Swingle -- St. Louis Peace Council
John Sullivan -- New Party
Rick Feigenberg -- RYM II
Ken Sherman -- New Mobilization, Buffalo
Roger McDonald -- Student Mobilization Committee
Robert Jones -- Unitarian Universalist

(Distributed during July and August, 1969.   Collected August
27, 1969.)

15. NEW MOBILIZATION COMMITTEE
TO END THE WAR IN VIETNAM

National Action Office, 1029 Vermont Avenue, N.W., Washington, D.C. 20005.   (202) 737-8600

September 17, 1969

Dear Friends,

What follows is the most complete list[*] of the Steering Committee that we were able to assemble as of September 17. There are undoubtedly omissions--we apologize. If you note any omissions, please let us know immediately so we can make the necessary addition(s). There will also undoubtedly be mistakes and inaccurate information--please let us know about them right away also. You will also note that there are some names for whom there is no information or incomplete information--if you can help us with that, please do. In the near future, we will also prepare a similar list of all those who have attended meetings of the Washington Action Committee.

For the Washington Action,

Don Gurewitz, New Mobe Staff

Steering Committee
New Mobilization

Norma Becker	Abe Bloom
Irving Beinin	Irwin Bock
Barbara Bick	Allan Brick

---

[*]Compiler's note: The complete list has been considerably edited for purposes of inclusion in this book. The names of Steering Committee members appear in other documents in this volume.

Katherine Camp
Marjorie Colvin
Bill Davidson
Myrtle Feigenberg
Gene Gladstone
Jerry Gordon
Bob Green
Robert Greenblatt
Dave Hawk
Dave Herreshoff
Fred Halstead
Barry Johns
Arnold Johnson
Donald Kalish
Gloria Karp
Sylvia Kushner
Sidney Lens
Carol Lipman

Brad Lyttle
John McAuliff
Stewart Meacham
Joe Miles
Joe Miller
Allan Myers
Otto Nathan
Sidney Peck
Ann Perry
Max Primack
Carl Rogers
Irving Sarnoff
Lawrence Scott
Larry Siegle
Arthur Waskow
Cora Weiss
John Wilson
Ron Young

Carol Andreas
1941 Orleans, Apt. 631
Detroit, Mich. 48207
961-5553
Carol is one of 3 rotating
representatives of the Detroit
Coalition along with Herreshoff and Lafferty.

Marc Beallor
222 17th St., Rm 1228
New York, N.Y.
924-8620
W.E.B. DuBois Clubs

Norma Becker
68 Charles St.
New York, N.Y. 10014
212-691-5748
Fifth Ave. Parade Comm.

Abe Bloom
3313 Harrell
Wheaton, Md.
Wh 2-5393-H
933-1144-0
Wash. Mob., Project Director

Irving Beinin
197 E. 4th St.
New York, N.Y.
170 E. 3rd St.
New York, N.Y.
212-673-1593
Parade Comm., Guardian

Barbara Bick
2231 Bancroft Pl., N.W. #1
Wash., D.C.   20008
202-483-5384 WSP

Irwin Bock
4140 N. Oakley
Chicago, Ill.
321-922-0065,   478-9337
Vets for Peace (431 S. Dear-
    born, Chicago)

Allan Brick
FOR
Box 271
Nyack, N.Y.
914-358-4601

Sue Susman
3 William St.
Great Neck, NY
United Methodists, Women's
   Division
Board of Missions
516-457-4674

Ethel Taylor
1505 Ashford Way
Philadelphia, Pa. 19151
WSP
(215) Mi2-9078

Bill Troy
17 E. 17th St.
New York, N.Y.
Parade Comm. 255-1075

Ottilie Van Allen
4838 Park Ave.
Washington, D.C.

George Vickers
232 W. 16th St.
New York, NY 10011
Methodist Women
(212) 675-5902-home
Mu2-3633-office

Peer Vinther
Box 471
Cooper Station
New York, NY 10003
YSA

Arthur Waskow
1520 New Hampshire
Washington, D.C.
Institute for Policy Studies

Marilyn Webb
2318 Ashmead Place, NW
Washington, D.C. 20009
Women's Liberation

Miss Cora Weiss
5022 Waldo
Bronx, NY 10471
(212) 549-4478

Steve Wilcox
1029 Vermont Ave., NW
Washington, D.C. 20005
737-8600

Mr. George Wiley
1419 H St. NW
Washington, D.C. 20005
347-7727

Rev. Herman Will
100 Maryland Ave., NE
Washington, D.C. 20002
Methodist CSC
(202) 543-6336

Grace Williams
148 Delancey St.
New York, NY 10002
CRV
(212) 228-4505

Ron Wolin
857 Broadway, Rm. 307
New York, NY 10003
(212) 675-8465

Leroy Wolins
1380 E. Hyde Park Apt. 302
Chicago, Ill. 60615
Vets for Peace

Richard and Mary Wylie
2120 16th St., NW
Washington, D.C.

Trudi and Ron Young
1029 Vermont Ave.
Washington, D.C. 20005
New Mobe, 737-8600

(Distributed nationally September 17, 1969. Collected September 20, 1969.)

16. NEW MOBILIZATION COMMITTEE
    TO END THE WAR IN VIETNAM

PRESS OFFICE   FOR FURTHER INFORMATION
1029 VERMONT AVE., N.W., THEODORE W. JOHNSON
  ROOM 1002   212-427-7422
202 737-5244 (if no answer
202 737-8600)

BIOGRAPHICAL DATA
ON NEW MOBILIZATION CO-CHAIRMEN

Mr. David Dellinger: 54 years old; Graduated magna cum
laude from Yale University in 1936; Elected to Phi Beta
Kappa; Received a Henry fellowship to study in England; Attended New College at Oxford University in England; Enrolled in Union Theological Seminary in New York City in
1939; Jailed for one year in 1940 and again for two years in
1943 for refusal to register for the draft during World War
II; Presently resides in Glen Gardner, New Jersey; Father
of five children; Founded Liberation Magazine in 1956 and
has served as its editor since then; Was co-chairman of the
National Mobilization Committee which organized the April 15,
1967 mass peace march in New York City and the Pentagon
Demonstration in October of that year; Serves as co-ordina-
tor of the Fifth Avenue Peace Parade Committee in New York
City; Served on the War Crimes Tribunal sponsored by Bert-
rand Russell in Stockholm in May 1967 and in Copenhagen in
November 1967; Has visited Cuba in 1960, 1964, January and
November 1968; During the summer of 1966 toured the Far
East, including Japan, Cambodia, South Vietnam and China;
Has been to North Vietnam in November 1966 and in May-
June 1967; Helped to organize a week long meeting between
Americans and Vietnamese from both the Democratic Repub-
lic of Vietnam (North Vietnam) and the National Liberation
Front in Bratislava, Czechoslovakia in September 1967;
During 1968 and 1969 made several trips to Paris to meet
with the delegations of the Vietnamese and Americans to the
Peace Talks; Has been responsible for the arranging of sev-
eral releases of prisoners of war from North Vietnam; Is

presently on trial in Chicago as part of the Conspiracy Eight
--those charged with alleged conspiracy as a result of activities at the Democratic Convention in Chicago in August
1968.

Dr. Douglas F. Dowd: 50 years old; 4 years in the U.S.
Army Air Force during World War II; Earned AB (1948) and
PhD (1951) from the University of California, Berkeley;
Lectured at the University of California from 1950 until 1953
when he joined the faculty at Cornell University; Now Pro-
fessor of Economics at Cornell University in Ithaca, New
York; Primary fields of teaching are economic history, econ-
omic development and the Economics of Race and Poverty;
Published various articles and books, including MODERN
ECONOMIC PROBLEMS IN HISTORICAL PERSPECTIVE,
THORSTEIN VEBLEN; and (with Mary Nichols) STEP BY
STEP; Was Guggenheim fellow in 1959-60 and a Fulbright
fellow in 1966-67; Active in political affairs having served
as campaign manager and candidate for elective offices; Active in Civil Rights movement in the early sixties; One of
the founders of the teach-in effort on college campuses over
the Vietnam war beginning in 1965; One of the founders of
the National Mobilization Committee to which the New Mobilization Committee is successor; Active with Resist, a support organization for anti-war, anti-draft, and anti-repres-
sion groups.

Mr. Sidney Lens: Currently a resident of Chicago; Author
of 11 books including, A WORLD IN REVOLUTION, THE
CRISIS OF AMERICAN LABOR and POVERTY, AMERICA'S
ENDURING PARADOX; In addition has written several hundred published articles and is a frequent contributor to radical and progressive publications; Has spent the major part
of his life as a labor organizer; In the 1930's he was instrumental in organizing of the sit-down strike of the Congress of Industrial Organizations; Has also participated in
the organization of the unemployed; Organized the taxi-driver
strike in Washington, DC; At one time was an official of the
Building Services Union in Chicago; He is a contributing editor to LIBERATION MAGAZINE; Has traveled through 90
foreign countries during his life-time; Played a part in the
indictment of the Capones in the 1930's. Has long been active in the anti-Vietnam war movement, having been instrumental in the sponsorship of various mass demonstrations;
Is active with the Chicago Peace Council; Is presently pre-
paring a new book on the Military-Industrial Complex.

Mr. Stewart Meacham: Presently the Peace Education Secretary of the American Friends Service Committee; A graduate of Davidson College; He earned the Bachelor of Divinity Degree from Union Theological Seminary in New York
City in 1934; Served as Presbyterian pastor in Birmingham,
Alabama; Later worked for eight years with the National
Labor Relations Board in Washington, DC; Served as Labor
advisor to the commander of the United States occupation
forces in Korea, following World War II; subsequently worked
for the Amalgamated Clothing Workers Union in New York
City; Was one of several responsible for the direction of the
Hillman Foundation; From 1951 to 1955 he was in India for
the Methodist Board of Missions; Later was associate secretary of the Committee on World Literary and Christian Literature; Joined the American Friends Service Committee more
than 10 years ago; In 1967 made a two month trip around
the world, spending considerable time in Japan, South Vietnam, Thailand and Cambodia; Traveled for three weeks in
South Vietnam, talking with people of widely varying backgrounds and opinions; During this time he had ample opportunity to observe Vietnamese life closely; Had extensive conversations with Thich Tri Quang, and other religious leaders,
students, newspaper editors, and people in public life; Went to
Hanoi in July 1968 and arranged with others for the release
of American prisoners in North Vietnam.

Dr. Sidney Peck: 42 years old; Presently Associate Profes-
sor at Case-Western Reserve University in Cleveland;
Earned BA degree in 1949 from the University of Minnesota;
Earned his MS (1951) and PhD (1959) from the University of
Wisconsin; Married and the father of two children; Major
fields of teaching are Industrial Sociology, social theory, and
social stratification; Has taught at the University of Wiscon-
sin (Milwaukee), Carleton College (Minnesota), the Milwaukee-
Downer College, Lawrence University of Michigan, and Case
Western Reserve University; Spent three years doing industrial research in Milwaukee; Is a member of several professional and honor societies; Has published many articles
and book reviews as well as a book, THE RANK AND FILE
LEADER; Has served as the co-chairman of the Ohio Peace
Action Council and as chairman of the Cleveland Area Peace
Council; Primary organizer of the July 4, 1969 conference
which planned the activities to take place in mid-November
in Washington and which organized the New Mobilization Committee; Indicted last January on two counts of aggravated assault and two counts of resisting arrest stemming from activities in Chicago at the time of the Democratic Convention

last August;   These charges carry a maximum sentence of
12 years and maximum fine of $22,000;   His trial is ex-
pected to begin sometime in November.

<u>Mrs. Cora Weiss</u>: Housewife from the Bronx, New York
City;   Serves as the representative of the New York City
Women Strike for Peace to the national body of that organization;   Former executive director of the Afro-American
Student Association in New York City;   Worked with the recently assassinated Tom M'Baya to arrange an airlift of 700
East African students to schools in the United States;
Serves on the board of the US Servicemen's fund;   Long active in national and New York City anti-war activities;   Has
visited Paris on several occasions recently to meet with the
representatives of all sides in the talks proceeding there to
end the war;   Was instrumental in the visit of Vietnamese
women to Canada this past summer and arranged meetings
in Canada between these women and representatives of US
peace groups.

(Distributed by the New Mobilization Committee to End the
War in Vietnam on September 17, 1969.   Collected September 20, 1969.)

17. JULY 4-5 NATIONAL ANTI-WAR CONFERENCE STEERING COMMITTEE

Norma Becker
168 Charles St.
New York, N.Y.
212-691-5748

Barbara Bick
2231 Bancroft Pl. NW, #1
Washington, D.C. 20008
202-483-5384

Douglas Dowd
Dept. of Economics
Cornell Univ.
Ithaca, N.Y.
307-272-6594 (home)
275-4892 (office)

Rennie Davis
The "Conspiracy"
109 N. Dearborn #606
Chicago, Ill.
312-641-5955

Dave Dellinger
Liberation Magazine
339 Lafayette St.
New York, N.Y. 10012
212-674-0050

Al Evanoff
Dist. 65
13 Astor Pl.
New York, N.Y. 10003
212-533-7200

Rev. Richard Fernandez
3500 Hamilton St.
Philadelphia, Pa.
EV 2-7920 (215)

Jerry Gordon
3194 Oak St.
Cleveland, Ohio
216-321-8714 (home)
781-2137 (work)

Fred Halstead
228 10th Ave.
New York, N.Y. 10001
212-565-5471

Arnold Johnson
23 W. 26th St.
New York, N.Y.
(212) 685-5755

Donald Kalish
Dept. of Philosophy
U. of California
Los Angeles, Cal. 90024
213-GR 2-0194 (home)
825-1476 (work)

Sidney Lens
5436 Hyde Park Blvd.
Chicago, Ill. 60615
312-NO 7-5437

Carol Lipman
Student Mobilization
857 Broadway #307
New York, N.Y. 10003
212-675-8465

John McAuliff
c/o CRV
Box 380 Cooper Sta.
New York, N.Y. 10003
212-228-4470

Stewart Meacham
c/o AFSC
160 N. 15th St.
Philadelphia, Pa. 10102
215-LO 3-9372

Carl Rogers
Comm. for 27
1029 Vermont Ave. NW
Room 200
Washington, D.C. 20005
202-638-4126

Sidney Peck
3420 Milverton
Cleveland, Ohio
216-991-6759 (home)
216-368-2624 (2620) (work)

Irving Sarnoff
555 N. Western Ave #3
Los Angeles, Ca. 90004
213-462-5188

Maxwell Primack
7436 S. Oglesby
Chicago, Ill.
312-374-0815

Cora Weiss
5022 Waldo
Riverdale, N.Y.
212-KI 9-4478

National List of Delegates

Name	Number of delegates

COUNCILS

Cleveland Area Peace Action Council	6
Chicago Peace Council	6
Fifth Ave. Vietnam Peace Parade Committee	6
Minnesota Mobilization Committee	3
San Francisco GI-Civilian Alliance for Peace	3
Seattle GI-Civilian Alliance for Peace	3
Southern California Peace Action Council	6
Texas Coalition Against the War	3
Washington Mobilization Committee	3

OTHER AREAS

Arizona
    Prof. Morris Starsky, Scottsdale   1
Atlanta
    Rev. Henry Bass   1
    Eleanor Bockman   1
    Nancy Collinson, AFSC   1
    Sharon Nalman, SMC   1
    Britt or Nan Prendergast   1
Bay Area
    Donald Duncan   1
    Edward Keating   1
    Robert Scheer, Ramparts   1

AREA	Number of delegates
Boston-Cambridge	
Russell Johnson, AFSC	1
Prof. Noam Chomsky	1
Jerry Grossman, PAX	1
Eric Mann, SDS Regional	1
Barbara Chis, GI-CAP	1
New England Resistance	1
Buffalo	
James Hansen, Buffalo Coordinating Comm.	1
Columbus-Dayton	
Ohio Peace Action Council	1
Julian Balley	1
Dayton Area Coordinating Comm., Yellow Springs	1
Denver	
Mary Walter, Denver Stop the War Committee	1
Des Moines	
AFSC, Des Moines	1
Comm. of Student Concern, Drake	1
Iowans for Peace in Vietnam	1
Detroit	
Olga Penn, Women for Peace	1
Prof. David Herreshoff, Wayne State	1
Atty. Michael Smith, coordinator, April 5 Action Comm.	1
Rev. Richard Venus, CALCV	1
Madison	
Francis Boardman, U. of Wisc.	1
Madison CEWV	1
Milwaukee	
Evelyn Knapp, WILPF	1
Prof. Arnold Kaufman	1
Milwaukee Organizing Committee	1
Michael Gelizan, Jewish Vocational Services	1
New Orleans	
Robert Zeiner, GROW	1
Oregon	
Steven Deutch, U. of Oregon, Eugene	1
AFSC, Portland	1
Philadelphia	
William Davidson, Resist	1
Robert Eaton, April Action	1
Phila. SMC	1
Naomi Marcus, WILPF	1
Dr. Robert Rutman, SANE	1
Ethyl Taylor, WSP	1

	Number of delegates
AREA	
Pittsburgh	
Ad Hoc Comm. for Peace, c/o Prof. Arthur Tuden	3
Rochester	
Niagara Reg. Coordinating Comm.	1

NATIONAL ORGANIZATIONS

Americans for Democratic Action	2
American Friends Service Committee	2
American Labor Alliance	2
Black Panther Party	2
Catholic Peace Fellowship	2
Communist Party	2
Clergy and Laymen Concerned	2
CORE	2
DuBois Clubs	2
Episcopal Peace Fellowship	2
Fellowship of Reconciliation	2
Independent Socialist Clubs of America	2
Jewish Peace Fellowship	2
Labor Leadership Assembly for Peace	2
Lawyers Comm. on American Policy Towards Vietnam	2
National Action Group	2
National Black Anti-war Anti-draft Union	2
National Council of Churches	2
National Council of Rabbis	2
National Lawyers Guild	2
National Mobilization Committee	2
National Student Association	2
National Welfare Rights Org.	2
Progressive Labor Party	2
The Resistance	2
SANE	2
Socialist Party	2
Socialist Workers Party	2
Southern Conference Educational Fund	2
Southern Christian Leadership Conference	2
SNCC	2
SSOC	2
Student Mobilization Committee	2
Teachers Committee for Peace in Vietnam	2
Vets for Peace	2

	Number of delegates
Nat'l Org. (cont.)	
War Resisters League	2
Women's Int. League for Peace and Freedom	2
Women Strike for Peace	2
Workers World	2
Youth Against War and Fascism	2
Young Socialist Alliance	2

ACTIVE DUTY GI GROUPS, PAPERS AND COFFEE HOUSES

About Face & Echo-Mike Coffee House, Los Angeles	1
The Ally, Berkeley	1
Bond-ASU, New York	1
Counterpoint, Seattle	1
Fatigue Press & Oleo Strut, Killeen, Texas	1
Flag in Action, Tennessee	1
FTA, Louisville	1
The GI Organizer, Killeen, Texas	1
Head On, Camp Lejeune, N.C.	1
Last Harass, Hill Station, Ga.	1
Open Sights, Washington, D.C.	1
Rough Draft, Norfolk, Va.	1
Short Times & UFO, Columbia, S.C.	1
S.O.S., San Francisco	1
Shelter Half, Tacoma	1
GI's United Against the War in Vietnam, Ft. Bragg, N.C.	1
Ultimate Weapon, Philadelphia, Pa., Ft. Dix	1
USAF, Wright-Patterson AFB, Ohio	1
Shakedown, Wrightstown, N.J., Ft. Dix	1
Top Secret, Boston	1

INITIATING ENDORSERS AND/OR STEERING COMMITTEE

Norma Becker	1
Barbara Bick	1

PROPOSED CONFERENCE AGENDA

I. WELCOME -- Jerry Gordon, Chairman, Cleveland Area Peace Action Council

II. GREETINGS AND MESSAGES

III. REPORT ON CONFERENCE PURPOSE AND ORGANI-
ZATION -- Sidney M. Peck, Co-Chairman, National
Mobilization Committee

IV. ADOPTION OF AGENDA

V. CONFERENCE RULES PROPOSAL FROM STEERING
COMMITTEE

VI. CREDENTIAL PROPOSALS FROM STEERING COM-
MITTEE -- Rev. Richard Fernandez, Clergy & Laymen Concerned

VII. ACTION PROGRAM: PANEL TO CONSIST OF:
Irving Sarnoff--Chairman, So. Calif. Peace Action
Council
Stewart Meacham--American Friends Service Com-
mittee
Students for a Democratic Society spokesman
October 15 Mobilization spokesman
Doug Dowd--New Universities Conference
Jerry Gordon--Chairman, Cleveland Area Peace Ac-
tion Coalition
Dave Dellinger--Chairman, National Mobilization Com-
mittee
Panel presentations to be followed by floor discussion
and decision.

VIII. WORKSHOPS ON PROPOSED ACTIONS

IX. REPORT BACK FROM WORKSHOPS

X. IMPLEMENTATION

XI. ANNOUNCEMENTS AND RESOLUTIONS

Note: Dave Dellinger was the steering committee majority
spokesman and Jerry Gordon was the steering committee minority spokesman.

(Distributed August 27, 1969 at Cleveland State University,
Cleveland, Ohio. Collected on the same date.)

18.   ON ORGANIZING FOR CIVIL DISOBEDIENCE

The enclosed booklet is being distributed to New Mobilization organizers across the country, to help them in planning for Anti-Draft Week, March 16-22. It is designed particularly to aid those planning demonstrations in which civil disobedience will play a part.

Non-violent civil disobedience has roots deep in the American tradition. Mohandas [Mahatma] Gandhi, the most famous proponent of nonviolence in this century, drew inspiration from the example of Henry David Thoreau, who protested the American invasion of Mexico in the 1940's, and recorded his experience in the essay On the Duty of Civil Disobedience. Nonviolence has continued to play a role in American political life through the nineteenth and twentieth centuries, from the opposition of Eugene V. Debs and others to American involvement in the first World War, to the great example of the Reverend Martin Luther King.

Following are two passages from Thoreau's essay on civil disobedience:

> There are thousands who are in opinion opposed to
> slavery and to the war, who yet in effect do nothing to put an end to them; who, esteeming themselves children of Washington and Franklin, sit down with their hands in their pockets, and say that they know not what to do, and do nothing; who even postpone the question of freedom to the question of free trade, and quietly read the prices--current along with the latest advices from Mexico, after dinner, and, it may be, fall asleep over them both. What is the price--current of an honest man and patriot today. They hesitate, and they regret, and sometimes they petition; but they do nothing in earnest and with effect. They will wait, well disposed, for others to remedy the evil, that they may no longer have it to regret. At most, they give only a cheap vote, and a feeble countenance and God-speed to the right, as it goes by them.

> If the alternative is to keep all just men in prison,
> or to give up war and slavery, the State will not
> hesitate which to choose. If a thousand men were
> not to pay their tax-bills this year, that would not
> be a violent and bloody measure, as it would be to
> pay them, and enable the State to commit violence
> and shed innocent blood. This is in fact the defi-
> nition of a peaceable revolution, if any such is pos-
> sible.

The demonstrations of Anti-Draft Week will include
acts of civil-disobedience in more than sixty cities in all
parts of America. This constitutes the largest coordinated
action of this sort ever seen in this country.

The actions for the New Mobilization Committee's
Anti-Draft Week (March 16-22) have multiplied in the last
week or two and the national organizers have been unable to
keep up with the developments in the hundreds of cities that
are planning activities for the week. It appears that virtually every city in the country will have some kind of action for
the week, and at least one hundred cities plan full-scale
marches on draft boards or induction centers on the 19th.
Over half of these demonstrations will include non-violent
civil disobedience.

In Washington, D.C. a major demonstration will occur
at the National Headquarters of the Selective Service System;
a coffin containing turned-in draft cards will either be carried into the building or be used to block the door. Demonstrators, including the Rev. Malcolm Boyd, will then sit
down to block the entrances to the building. On other days
of the week, local students will engage draft board members
in debate at their homes or places of business, will stage
guerilla theater demonstrations around the city, and will rally
on college campuses in the evenings to discuss the war and
the draft. Many of the District's high school students are
planning activities around the High School "We Won't Go"
Statement including assemblies in several schools on the
draft and petitions for draft counselling.

The Washington program is similar in many features
to scenarios developed in other locations. The details vary
from place to place and may change slightly as the week
progresses, but the following examples illustrate the range
of activities which have been undertaken around the country,
as citizens actively demand an end to the draft and the war:

Dayton: In the predominantly black West End of Dayton, a march has been planned which will begin at a National Guard armory, pass a Veterans' home, and end with a rally at a second armory. In addition, black organizers in Dayton have planned high school programs in the West End and have challenged local recruiting agents to a debate with a black Vietnam returnee and another Dayton anti-war organizer on WDAO, the local black radio station. Meanwhile, opponents of the war at the University of Dayton and elsewhere in the city are planning a large demonstration at the city's central draft board, with a comply-in designed to carry the SSS operations to their illogical conclusions with floods of legal information submitted by local registrants.

Hackensack, N.J.: New Jerseyans will picket Hackensack draft boards on all days of Anti-Draft Week and will sit in on two days, Wednesday and Thursday. One of these demonstrations will be a pray-in involving area clergy. Heavy leafletting will occur at shopping centers and at bus terminals. The local PTA is sponsoring a debate between residents and the head of the New Jersey Selective Service System and negotiations are underway for an anti-war spot on WJRB radio. In addition, organizing and circulating of "We Won't Go" Statements are underway in North Jersey high schools.

Philadelphia: The "Spectre of Death" has been seen in Philadelphia draft boards in the last few weeks. A figure robed in black has appeared in silence and has seated himself in the presence of the board members and clerks. The efficiency of the SSS workers has been noted to fall off considerably during these visitations. Other cities have picked up the idea, and the Spectre may shortly become a national figure. The highly active Philadelphia peace community is also planning demonstrations which will include nonviolent sit-ins during the week of March 16th.

San Antonio: The Spectre is here also, and "death" will come to one of a list of local residents selected by lottery during the week; he will report to be "drafted" and will become another "victim" of the war machine in a guerrilla theatre demonstration. Here also a sit-in at local boards is planned.

Buffalo: A group of students at the State University, Buffalo, will circulate thousands of powers of attorney to other citizens of this city on March 19th. The Selective

Service Law stipulates that registrants may enable others to inspect their files, and it is certain that some of the files at the Buffalo S.S. center will be amply inspected on that date. On Tuesday and Wednesday of Anti-Draft Week, Buffalo parents and clergymen plan to appear at the boards, to talk and to sit-in.

Los Angeles: Southern California will be the scene of many demonstrations during the week. Plans include the blocking of Induction centers on Wednesday the 18th, and draft boards on the 19th. One action in particular deserves notice: Local Board #82 in Hollywood is thought by L.A. organizers to be the largest in the nation, and there will be an all-day demonstration there on the 19th. During the week "We Won't Go" statements will be making the rounds of California college and high school campuses, and demonstrations at the homes of Selective Service Board members will continue through the 21st.

Ames, Iowa: Local residents in large groups plan to visit the city's draft boards at the beginning of the week. On Wednesday Iowa State University students plan to disrupt ROTC exercises on campus, and the week will end with one of the first "End the War in Laos" demonstrations to be organized in the country. Iowans are hoping thus to dramatize the continued opposition the government will face if it pursues its foreign policy.

These are only samples out of a broad range of activities planned by local organizers for the week.

The following is a partial listing of towns and cities in which demonstrations and related activities are planned for the New Mobilization Committee's Anti-Draft Week, March 16-22:

Boston	Lewisburg, Pa.	Akron
Stamford	Buffalo	Cleveland
New York City	Rochester	Detroit
Rockland Cty, N.Y.	Minneapolis	Mt. Pleasant, Mich.
Hackensack	Syracuse	Grand Rapids
Philadelphia	Potsdam, N.Y.	South Bend
Harrisburg	Pittsburgh	Milwaukee
		Chicago

(Distributed during January, February, and March, 1969. Collected August 27, 1969.)

19. ARE YOU GOING INTO THE MILITARY
SERVICE SOON?

Are you going into the military service soon? Do you
know someone who is? Do you know about these antiwar
newspapers? They are all put out by active-duty servicemen
or veterans. Most stress rights and legal aid at court martial. And all contain news not in the approved military press.

THE ALLY
Box 9276
Berkeley, California 94709

THE BOND
156 Fifth Ave. room 633
New York, N.Y. 10010

COUNTERPOINT (Ft. Lewis)
515 20th Street East
Seattle, Washington 98120

FATIGUE PRESS (Ft. Hood)
101 Avenue D
Killeen, Texas 76544

FLAG-IN-ACTION (Ft. Camp-
bell)
P.O. Box 2416
New Providence, Tenn. 37040

FUN, TRAVEL & ADVENTURE
532 N. 20th St. (Ft. Knox)
Louisville, Kentucky

LAST HARASS (Ft. Gordon)
P.O. Box 2994
Hill Station
Augusta, Georgia

SHORT TIMES (Ft. Jackson)
P.O. Box 543
Columbia, So. Carolina

TASK FORCE
P.O. Box 31268
San Francisco, Ca. 94131

THE ULTIMATE WEAPON
(Ft. Dix)
c/o Lesnick
312 North 37th Street
Philadelphia, Pa. 19104

VETERANS STARS AND
STRIPES FOR PEACE
P.O. Box 4598
Chicago, Illinois 60680

VIETNAM GI
P.O. Box 9273
Chicago, Illinois 60690

HEAD-ON (Camp Lejeune)
P.O. Box 879
Jacksonville, No. Carolina

GIG LINE (Ft. Bliss, Tex.)
(New: address unknown)

Servicemen everywhere are fighting for freedom of speech, press, and property ownership. Yet the brass, through illegal harassment and misuse of justice, take these basic freedoms away from servicemen.

FREE MEN FIGHT ONLY IN DEFENSE

Save this leaflet or give it to someone you think can use it. All of these papers have been started in the past two years, and the list is complete or soon will be

VETERANS FOR PEACE
874 Broadway   room 504
New York, New York   10003

(Distributed March 27, 1969 at the student union, Millikin University, Decatur, Illinois.   Collected March 27, 1969.)

20. STUDENT MOBILIZATION COMMITTEE
TO END THE WAR IN VIETNAM

Meeting, September 15

857 Broadway, New York, N.Y. 10003 Phone: 212-675-8466	MARCH ON WASHINGTON .. NOV. 15TH TO BRING ALL THE GI'S HOME NOW!

Help plan N.Y. participation
ATTEND NEXT PARADE COMMITTEE

MEETING

Monday, Sept. 15th
7:30 P.M.
Washington Square Methodist Church
137 West Fourth St.

Dear Friend,

As you can see from the enclosed copy of the Mobi-
lizer Wallposter, the Student Mobilization Committee has
greeted the opening of the fall 1969 American school semes-
ter with a concerted effort to build the Fall Antiwar Offensive
among a student population that is overwhelmingly opposed to
the war and ready to act against it. Even before school officially opened, students in over 50 New York schools had indicated they wished to organize participation on their campuses.

We approach this fall antiwar program with great opti-
mism--not only for the response it will receive from thousands
of high school and college students, but realizing that antiwar
actions now speak for the majority of the American people
and can draw in numbers of new activists into our ranks from
all layers of society. The Nov. 15th March on Washington
to Bring All the GI's Home Now can really expose the phony
maneuvers of the Nixon administration to lull the American
people and demonstrate the full power of the antiwar movement.

This optimism, coupled with a sense of urgency as the war continues, is reverberating throughout the entire anti-war movement, its oldest and newest constituencies. After 1,000 representatives of all sectors of the movement planned out the fall offensive in Cleveland over July 4th weekend, they went forward determined to unite the greatest number of people around this program of action. The New Mobilization Committee Steering Committee has already set up a broad working committee to carry out the building of the Nov. 15th March. The new Washington office is fielding speaking tours, getting out initial publicity, seeking permits, speakers, etc. In short, we're on our way. Contact the New Mobe at the following address: 1029 Vermont Ave., NW, Suite 900, Washington, DC 20005; phone (202) 737-8600.

Our primary need now is to get going, to plunge into building this historic action in a concerted, coordinated way. Only through such an all-out organizational effort on the part of every section of the antiwar movement can we realize the full potential of this fall program and bring hundreds of thousands to Washington. To this end, the SMC urges all organizations to be sure to send representation to the up-coming New York Fifth Ave. Vietnam Peace Parade Commit-tee meeting to begin this necessary planning and organiza-tion. <u>The meeting is scheduled for Monday, Sept. 15th, at 7:30 PM at Washington Square Methodist Church, 137 W. Fourth St</u>. As with past massive mobilizations of antiwar sentiment, through these coalition meetings we can coordi-nate our work in this key N.Y. region.

In line with the need for continued collaboration among all groups in the antiwar movement, as we move ahead, SMC will keep you informed of activities among antiwar students. We hope we can continue to work together with your organi-zation to build the Fall Antiwar Offensive. Please fill out the attached coupon and return it to us.

In peace,

Joanna Misnik,
National SMC Staff

----

clip & mail to: NY SMC, 857 Broadway, Rm. 307, NYC
                                    10003.

name of organization_____

address_____phone_____

___Our group will help publicize SMC activities.

___Please continue to keep our organization informed of your
   regular mailings.

___Enclosed is $____ to help carry out SMC's fall antiwar
   program.

(Distributed during the first two weeks of September, 1969.
Collected December 28, 1969.)

21. SAN FRANCISCO INVITES YOU!
HISTORIC CONGRESS ON SOUTH VIETNAM*

"In face of the imperative requirements of the new situation and tasks, responding to the deep aspirations of the broad social strata, the historic all South Vietnam Congress of people's representatives, meeting the 6th, 7th and 8th of June, 1969, <u>set up the Provisional Revolutionary Government of the Republic of South Vietnam.</u>" --From the declaration on program of action, signed by Huynh Tan Phat, President of the new Provisional Revolutionary Government.

By taking this firm step forward, the well organized and highly capable forces in South Vietnam, who are engaged in an heroic struggle to establish freedom and independence in their homeland, have made a positive move in the direction of truly representative government in South Vietnam. The Provisional Revolutionary Government, which has been recognized by 21 countries to date, becomes the political head of the "broad social strata" in South Vietnam which is determined to settle for nothing short of complete independence. The National Liberation Front becomes simply the military arm of that government.

Madame Nguyen Thi Binh now becomes the Foreign Minister of the Provisional government and under that title continues her brilliant diplomatic career at the Paris peace talks.

Briefly summarized, the 12-point program of action adopted by the new provisional government undertakes: to step up military and political struggle to compel the U.S. government to withdraw totally and without conditions; to abolish the "disguised colonial regime" in Saigon, overthrow its entire structure and organize general elections; prepare

---

*This document was distributed to delegates to the National Anti-War Conference held July 4-5, 1969, the founding conference of the New Mobilization Committee to End the War in Vietnam.

to form a coalition government of all political forces that
stand for peace, independence and neutrality; to provide for
improvement in the life of the people at every level--re-
ligious, social and political equality, human and civil rights,
land reform, industrial development; to move towards reunification of the country by mutual agreement; to carry out a
foreign policy of peace and neutrality.

Included in its foreign policy statement, the Provisional government aspires "to achieve active coordination
with the American people's struggle against the U.S. imperialist war of aggression in Vietnam."

In October, 1967, progressive people in both North
and South Vietnam organized a Vietnamese Committee for
Solidarity with the American People. To respond in kind
and to try to do our part to achieve active coordination with
the Vietnamese people's struggle, a San Francisco group
has organized the American Committee for Solidarity with
the Vietnamese People. Our one central purpose is to
spread information about our government's involvement in
this disgraceful war and to support the growing demand for
complete withdrawal. We urge concerned citizens in other
areas to set up local chapters.

AMERICAN COMMITTEE FOR SOLIDARITY
WITH THE VIETNAMESE PEOPLE

4945 California St. San Francisco 94118
Margaret Driggs, Secretary

The American Committee for Solidarity with the Vietnamese
People, San Francisco Chapter, INVITES delegates to the
National Anti-War Conference to establish chapters of this
SOLIDARITY Committee in their home areas. We believe
that it is more important than ever to get honest information
to the general public to help to escalate the peace movement
and consolidate the demand for an immediate end to hostili-
ties in Vietnam. We support the Provisional Revolutionary
Government of the Republic of South Vietnam and its 12-
point program for lasting peace and independence. To serve
as a source of information on Vietnam and our government's
involvement there is our sole reason for organizing this
committee. We invite support on the broadest possible base

and we are wide open for suggestions, ideas, and practical assistance. While in Cleveland, the undersigned invites national sponsorship of the Committee for Solidarity.

MARGARET DRIGGS,
Delegate from San Francisco

EXECUTIVE BOARD, SAN FRANCISCO CHAPTER:

Fred Chard, Chairman   Mahbi Gill, Vice Chairman
Margaret Driggs, Sec.   Florence Steinman, Treasurer
Marie Chapman, Publicity   Rita Robillard, Research
Nguyen Van Luy, Advisor

BAY AREA SPONSORS:

Rev. Edward L. Peet, Methodist Federation for Social Action
Dr. Holland Roberts, World Peace Council
Dr. Phillip Shapiro, Veterans for Peace
Elsa Peters Morse, writer
H. J. Phillips, Ph. D.
Vincent Hallinan, attorney
Terence Hallinan, attorney
L. W. Hedley, Ph. D.
Dr. J. L. Wertheimer, San Francisco State College
Enola D. Maxwell, Lay Preacher, Olivet Presbyterian Church
Grace R. Hazelrigg, Monterey Peace Action

(Distributed July 4, 1969 in San Francisco.   Collected on the same day.)

22. THE G.I. MOVEMENT:

ITS IMPORTANCE IN DEFEATING IMPERIALISM MUST BE UNDERSTOOD

by Sam Karp and Bob Tomashevsky*

We have been involved in GI organizing for close to a year now. This critical analysis shall attempt to set forth some basic propositions that we have developed through our work. They basically deal with the movement's relationship to GI organizing, a critique of different tendencies within the GI movement, and the beginnings of the development of a program to help strengthen the GI movement.

Every institution in this country is exhibiting the symptoms of youth's dissatisfaction with the status quo. Though some struggles are at higher levels of consciousness than others, their genesis and relationship to each other are becoming apparent. The armed forces, though a recent arrival, is no exception. The movement has been quite lax in its understanding and support of our brothers who are struggling in one of the most difficult areas. In spite of the heavy sentences, harassment and intimidation that GI's face, almost every military installation has felt the rising anger of dissatisfied GI's. The armed forces, particularly the army, are beginning to shake at their very foundations. Morale is low,

---

*Sam Karp was active in draft resistance work in the Boston area, spent 4 years in ROTC, refused his commission and entered the army for 4-1/2 months' active duty as a reservist. There his activities included the founding of Shakedown and the Fort Dix Coffee House Project. He worked there with the project until the end of July '69.

Bob Tomashevsky spent 2 years as an organizer with the taxi drivers union, AFL-CIO, worked with New York Regional SDS primarily doing draft work, and then moved to GI work which included aiding Fort Dix GI's with Shakedown and setting up the Fort Dix Coffee House Project. He worked with the project until the end of July '69.

no one gives a fuck, FTA (Fuck the Army) is the prevailing spirit. In other words, GI's are pissed off and have begun to move.

This rupture is sharply related to the war in Vietnam. Most GI's returning from Nam are disgusted with the experience they were forced to become a part of. This disgust is also increasing with each new cycle of guys coming into basic training. It should be pointed out that yesterday's rebelling working-class youth and high school students are today's angry GI's. Part of what it comes down to is that they know they're being pushed through fucking training programs, which in actuality, leave them ill-prepared for the hazardous life in Nam. This is not to imply that we are seeking to demand a better-trained army, but instead to understand the nature of the army in regard to the value of the individual soldier. It makes them nothing but cannon-fodder for generals to deploy, of which Hamburger Hill is but one sorry example. Most new recruits believe the war is wrong for different reasons. Primarily they believe that it is a mistake which was made by the politicians and the brass. The "V" sign and the fist (the latter especially among black GI's) have easily replaced the salute. They don't want to go to Nam, and almost everyone actively seeks individual ways of avoiding it; few, obviously ever succeed.

By now most movement people should be aware of the numerous insurrections, riots, and rebellions that have occurred recently.

The Movement's Response

Recently many articles have appeared in the movement press expounding the virtues of deserting and going AWOL. "Come to Canada and be a man!", "Soldiers are pigs!", and "To remain in the imperialist U.S. Army rather than leaving is comparable to being a Nazi" are some of the sentiments that those of us who work in GI organizing are troubled about, particularly the growth of the widespread support for these views. Obviously, one fights the imperialist army on any front available. The questions to be answered then are: Is one tactic more politically sound than another? Does one type of emphasis draw energy and resources away from the other? And, most importantly, which method, at this time, will really lead towards a movement which will defeat imperialism?

Last year there were, by Pentagon count, over
250,000 AWOL's and over 53,000 desertions. This individual approach, although done in massive numbers, has not
made much of a dent in the fighting strength of the U.S.
Army. That dent has clearly come from the heroic struggle
of the Vietnamese people under the leadership of the NLF
and the Provisional Revolutionary Government. Through the
draft the system has no problem replacing any GI's lost to
the "Green Machine." At best we can say that this significant development reflected a certain disenchantment in its
time and laid the ground-work for the more fruitful organizing tasks before us now.

The guys who split do so for many reasons, ranging
from personal considerations such as missing one's wife,
woman or family, flight from harassment or intimidation,
fear of battle in Nam, to political considerations. The cor-
relation between imperialism, albeit mostly in Vietnam, and
the high rates of AWOL and desertion cannot be denied.

Most guys who split come back on their own or are
caught. The problems they face upon their return are aggravated, for they now face jail (stockade), restrictions and
fines. In every stockade the majority of the "prisoners" are
there for AWOL. Thus the AWOL faces even worse screw-
ing than that which he was attempting to escape from.

The lot of the self-imposed exile is even worse. He
is transplanted into an unfamiliar environment and usually
finds it too difficult to cope with, so he ends up coming back
or getting strung out on drugs. Politically he feels impotent,
for in reality he is. He can do little to effect change in the
U.S. except to encourage further desertions. He is an out-
sider in a foreign land. The reports of the growing exile
movement are either exaggerated or outright falsehoods.
Groups like the various ADC's (American Deserter Committees) should not be encouraging desertion, but instead should
encourage guys to return and fight. In other words, as a
political movement their importance is dubious at best when
compared with the potential and actual developments occurring within the army. The desertion movement would make
sense only if there were a counter-force to desert to. In
Vietnam, when an ARVN soldier deserts, he has another
force, the NLF, that he can join. We have no such force
and it appears doubtful that one will evolve at this time. We
are not a peasant country, and for the time being guerrilla
bands in the countryside are no more than a romantic illu-

sion. The forms of urban warfare may lead to new conceptions in guerrilla fighting, but for the most part we are still
engaging in legal, above-ground organizing. We must build
as openly as we can while we are still able to. (This does
not mean that we should not be clandestinely developing methods of helping GI organizers to split when faced with heavy
charges.)

Political Priorities

One of the healthiest developments within this country
(and abroad) has been the emergence of the GI movement.
Not unlike the movement in general, there are many tendencies exhibited as to which type of organizing is best. The
range is from National Committees, paper committees, civilian-run groups, veterans' groups, coffee-house projects, to
on-base organizing projects. These tendencies have manifested themselves in the thirty-odd underground GI newspapers which now exist. We will go further into the differences between these groups later on. The point to be made
here, however, is that the movement must see that political
priorities now dictate that GI organizing is a far superior
method of defeating U.S. imperialism as it is manifested by
the army to the tactic of encouraging desertion. The time
has come for the movement to give its full support to the
GI's who are staying and fighting from within rather than to
those who drop out. Guys are going to split for any number
of reasons, regardless of movement propaganda. There is
just no longer any need for the "Be a man and go to Canada"
jive when relevant, important political work is taking place
daily inside all branches of the military.

Towards Increasing Contact

Another major criticism that we have heard from many
soldiers about both the movement and movement people is the
noted reluctance with which the movement aids, works with,
and supports GI's. The GI on a pass in a town or city that
is strange to him is lonely and is frowned upon by many so-
called "hip" people. Though it is changing slowly, the preva-
lent belief is that "soldiers are pigs." This kind of narrow-
mindedness and elitism must be fought if we are going to
build a united revolutionary movement of the people in this
country. Collectives, movement groups, and SDS chapters
should have at least minimal contacts with GI's on bases in

close proximity. Both can learn from and support each other. For example, the practices of imperialism will be
much more discernible to college students through working
with GI's. SDS chapters should see themselves as furthering this kind of understanding. Many bases have had stockade revolts. These should be well publicized, especially in
the areas close to where they occur. Legal support and defense committees are also needed as the army attempts to
isolate and play down what's really happening. For example,
if one read the New York Times article which quoted only
from "army sources" about the Fort Dix stockade revolt of
June 5th, one would have been led to believe that there was
only a "minor incident" rather than a revolt which involved
over 200 men and the near destruction of two cell blocks.
The army has brought charges against 38 of the GI's; some
of them face sentences of up to 40 years.

In the New York City, Newark, and Philadelphia areas
the Fort Dix GI newspaper, Shakedown, is distributed most
Sundays at bus, rail, and airline terminals. This is another
constructive way in which radical civilians can aid the GI
movement. An alliance between SDS chapters and GI's on
bases near them should become a reality. Joint concerts,
dances, film showings, rallies, etc. should also be worked
towards. We must break out of our pedantic intellectual
chauvinism and go to the people! Perhaps some of the blame
for this gap between GI's and the movement lies on the organizers who have been doing GI work (ourselves included)
who have, at times, become too isolated from the movement.
Newsreel is planning several films on what's going on in the
army, which should also help heighten awareness and lead to
real growth. At the very least, it is the responsibility of
all revolutionaries to rap with soldiers any time they can.

GI Coffee Houses

There are now six GI coffee houses and several others
being planned. They can serve important functions in aiding
on-base organizing; they cannot, however, replace or be a
substitute for it. They can best be seen as a useful transi-
tional form to reach GI's and make them aware of what's
happening in the movement and at other bases. At coffee
houses literature can be made available; aid can be given in
the printing and distribution of underground GI newspapers;
help can be extended in obtaining legal aid and publicity for
GI organizers and other GI's in trouble on the base; GI's

can rap with each other and other movement people; and relevant political films can be shown.

Coffee houses have had varying degrees of limited success for basically one reason: there are not yet enough
movement people in the army organizing and giving them direction (more on this later). This is probably the reason
why there is a strong tendency for coffee houses to remain
just that--a place for a bunch of guys to come, shoot the
bull, relax, and kill time as painlessly as possible until they
ETS (get out). Given that most military installations are
purposely isolated from populated areas, coffee houses can
be an excellent link in breaking down that conscious confinement which separates the movement from GI's and GI's from
the movement.

Coffee house staffs, in conjunction with GI's, should
communicate more with the movement. More literature
should be prepared aimed at high school, community college,
university, and working-class youth. A movement pamphlet
on what to expect in the army, as well as on what is happening in the GI movement, should be written for distribution at
induction centers. Active duty GI's should be encouraged to
speak to and acquaint themselves with the different radical
projects in their proximity. In ways like this, coffee houses
increase their value to the movement and can become a
more integral part of the struggle.

The GI Underground Press

The over 30 GI newspapers vary in many respects,
but they can be divided into two general tendencies: gripe-
sheet, hip culture, reformist type and those that seek to aid
in the on-base organizing of masses of GI's toward basic
change. The former are at this point the overwhelming majority of them. The most politically advanced are Vietnam
GI; Shakedown (Fort Dix); FTA (Fort Knox); The Last Harass
(Fort Gordon); and The Ally, which has a national perspective and should be read by those trying to develop an understanding of the problems facing the GI movement.

The papers which seek to involve GI's as organizers
are not only the best politically but are also the most relevant to today's GI struggle. Most civilian-run types (Trot,
Student Mobilization Committee, peace groups, etc.) are
written with the help of few contacts on the base and are

geared to "Peace in Vietnam" and other fucking legalisms.
They appear irregularly with heavy distributions whenever
there is a peace march.   They have very little to do with on-
base organizing and are basically paper front groups which
exhibit the manipulativeness and opportunism that will make
it difficult to accomplish any growth in the GI movement.
The few pacifist/liberal-type newspapers will never be able
to rally masses of GI's to their ideas as long as they remain isolated in their intellectual elitism.

A common problem encountered in most GI newspapers
is their over-emphasis on letters and articles which amount
to little more than petty bitching.   It is the job of the politically conscious organizer to relate these to their roots and
show how to change the conditions which created them rather
than just to attack the fucking food, the low rate of pay,
short haircuts, or fucking disciplinary procedures.   It is the
difference between a liberal pragmatist approach on the one
hand and an attempt to develop a Marxist-Leninist critique as
a guide to action on the other.

The American Servicemen's Union

The movement's understanding of the growth of the GI
movement has been quite incomplete.   As we said earlier,
some of the blame must be placed on those of us who have
been engaged in active GI work.   We criticize ourselves for
reinforcing the isolationism that has hampered many areas of
development within the movement.   However, much of this
misunderstanding and confusion about the GI struggle has been
the result of the sectarian propaganda put forth by the American Servicemen's Union (ASU).

As a result of experiences over a long period with the
ASU, both in discussions of theory and in practice, it has become necessary for us, in the interest of the future development of the GI movement, to undertake a radical criticism
of the Union.   We hope that from this criticism all can
"learn from past mistakes to avoid future ones" and to "cure
the sickness to save the patient."   We proceed in the Marxist-Leninist spirit of criticism/self-criticism, attempting to
point out errors and shortcomings as related to GI political
and organizational work, while at the same time hoping to
add somewhat to the movement's knowledge of what the army's
all about.   This critique should in no way be construed as an
attack on the rank and file membership of the ASU.

"Shit from Shingles"

The ASU was the first organization that correctly understood the importance of initiating struggle within the military in this country. The Union grew out of the struggle that Andy Stapp was engaged in while a GI at Fort Sill, Oklahoma. There, Stapp and several other GI's founded the ASU in the summer of 1967. Since that time Stapp has remained the self-appointed Chairman of the ASU without elections or any real participation of GI's in decision-making.

While the Union correctly saw the growing restlessness of the GI and his initial awakening to the power that lay with GI's when organized, neither its theory nor its practice in the last two years has ever fully demonstrated the dialectical relationship between the leading group and the masses in a struggle. This concept, correctly applied "from the masses, to the masses," should be seen as one of the guiding principles of Communist thought and practice. There is no need to dwell on the importance of trusting, serving, and learning from the people; however, Stapp had the audacity to claim at a recent meeting, "Soldiers don't know shit from shingles." This is no isolated statement, but is reflected clearly in the practice of the ASU.

Herein lies the principal contradiction within the ASU: its lack of trust for and failure to be responsible to the masses. Yet this contradiction cannot stand in isolation. There are many secondary and subordinate contradictions that flow from this primary aspect.

"Reforms Are a By-Product"

We certainly are not the first to accuse the Union of reformism and the demands themselves as being merely reforms. The question here is not to determine whether the demands in themselves are reformist, but in what political context they are used. As Comrade Lenin wisely points out, "Reforms are but a by-product of the revolutionary struggle." Reforms can be used as a tool for strengthening and furthering the development of the revolution if the main concern is the revolutionary advancement of the masses. If it is not seen in this light, the preparation of the masses will undoubtedly be set back.

In examining the demands (laid out over two years
ago and not modified since), from what our practice has
taught us we find that their application to the struggle not only impedes revolutionary growth and development, but also
tends to take the struggle away from the principal contradiction in the world today ("The contradiction between the revolutionary peoples of Asia, Africa and Latin America and the
imperialists headed by the United States..."--Lin Piao) and
from the ruling class in whose control the military establishment lies.   Instead, it lays primary emphasis on many contradictions that exist among the people in an antagonistic
manner.

Ignoring Racism

Let us concern ourselves for the moment with a brief
discussion of the third and eighth demands, which involve two
of the most pressing questions facing our movement.   The
third demand reads simply: "racial equality." Although the
Union and its Chairman Stapp, in public speeches, at rallies,
and in the movement press, talk a great deal about "fighting
racism," in practice its emphasis is on obtaining "racial
equality."   Discussing "racial equality" ignores the growth of
the black liberation struggle in this country.   It fails to understand the existence of the black colony inside the mother-
country, which leads to a neglect of the importance of understanding the role and organization of black leadership in
struggles in the military, the high schools, community colleges, universities, in the shops, and on the streets.

The Union deals with racism in practice by avoiding
struggling against it.   In an article that appeared in April's
Movement, Stapp said, "The only GI's that have ever quit
the union have quit on the grounds that they didn't want to be
in a union with a bunch of black people.   These are racist
GI's and we say good riddance to them" (our italics).   Is this
how to combat racism?

Ignoring Imperialism

The eighth demand, seen as the "most important demand" by the Union, states "the right to disobey illegal or-
ders--like orders to go and fight in an illegal war in Vietnam."   There are two serious criticisms in practical application of this demand.   First, it wrongly places emphasis on

legalism. Our experiences in and around the military have
taught us, from even our first contacts with GI's, that the
problems of fighting legalism that the movement has encountered in the universities are almost non-existent in the military. GI's, most of whom are from working-class backgrounds and off the streets, don't need to be told that law is
shit and serves only the rich. They know. They've lived
under it and in many cases were forced into the army because of it. The second criticism is much more serious.
By regarding the war as an "illegal" war, the Union completely ignores the United States as the imperialist aggressor
all over the world--a fact that more and more GI's seem
ready to understand at this time. In reducing the primary
contradiction in the world today to a fucking legalism, the Union plays a reformist role which may be inevitably transformed into an instrument for strengthening the role of the
state and, in turn, harming the development of the revolutionary masses.

In not confronting <u>racism</u> and U.S. <u>imperialism</u> head
on, but muddling over them, the Union attempts to organize
the masses around the lowest common denominator. This is
objectively right wing opportunism.

<u>MP's Are Not Pigs</u>

Aside from the "theory" laid out in the eight-point
"program," there are two specific political positions of the
Union which warrant criticism. First, the Union repeatedly
regards <u>all</u> MP's as pigs. Even though many have enlisted
for that position, many others have been conscripted into that
role, a role that they certainly don't enjoy performing. Others who enlisted quickly learn that the army isn't what they
thought it would be: fun, travel, and adventure. Our experiences have shown many MP's helping their brothers in the
stockade by smuggling letters and messages, underground
newspapers, and cigarettes to the men, plus many more useful aids that cannot be discussed publicly. Granted, a few
sadistic guards have made it rough on a number of prisoners,
but to categorically brand all MP's as mercenary pigs is an
incorrect handling of a contradiction that exists among the
people and is a mechanical application of civilian concepts
(such as the "union") to the military.

The Role of Officers and "Lifers"

    The second politically incorrect and harmful position
is the Union's denouncement of all officers and "lifers" as
class enemies. Again, in an article in the April Movement,
Stapp says, "Organizing against the war and organizing
against the officers is really the same thing. You have got
to take advantage of the class hatred that the men feel toward their oppressors ... the officers are all for the war."
The Union equates this position to the structure of a factory.
It contends that "lifers" are comparable to foremen and that
officers are comparable to managers. When workers strike
in a factory, the ASU says they are striking against the foremen and the managers. There are many points of contradiction in this position. Officers certainly cannot be considered
as all one class. They perform two main tasks in the military: (1) giving orders, and (2) decision making. All officers give orders, and most have the decision-making power
over individuals; very few, though, have the decision-making
power to continue to perpetuate the system. Generals and
other specific high-ranking officers should be criticized on
the basis of their class privilege.

    More than half of today's officers come from ROTC,
and nearly 90 per cent of these merely fill their two- to
three-year commitments. The majority of them have been
working-class guys who have accepted the fact of having to
go into the army, so why not "go as an officer," or who have
depended on the $50/month allowance and the easily available
ROTC scholarship which affords them an "education." These
officers are known throughout the military for being lax in
their eagerness to uphold military discipline and bearing.
The other major source of officers is Officer Candidate
School (OCS). These are basically guys who were drafted
or enlisted out of fear of induction and were sold a bill of
goods by the recruiter to become "leaders of men" and
"gentlemen." They too are exclusively non-ruling-class guys
who hope to get better jobs on the outside with a commission.
To call them class enemies is not to understand the importance of settling contradictions among the people.

    To also consider all "lifers" as class enemies is
again not to understand how they, as all of us, are oppressed
by a reaffirmation of their own alienation by a system that
drives them to assume that role. This accounts for the growing number of black and third world lifers--men who know

that the same disease-ridden, poverty-stricken, rat-infested, jobless community awaits their return after "serving to defend democracy."

For the Union to advocate taking advantage of this so-called "class hatred" is pure opportunism. Certainly GI's have a dislike for their officers and sergeants, but to avoid laying down an analysis of the class structure of the military or of society can cause many of our potential comrades to be mistaken for the enemy. Just as in a factory one struggles against the foremen and managers, GI's should struggle against officers and lifers. Yet in both cases an understanding of who actually runs and profits from the structure must be laid out so as to neutralize and divide the allies of the ruling class. To make no attempt to do so is harmful to the masses, for it permits mistaken and incomplete viewpoints to exist at the expense of the advancement of the revolutionary struggle. In all cases, it is a total denial of the process by which people move.

> The only way to settle questions of an ideological nature or controversial issues among the people is by the democratic method, the method of discussion, of criticism, of persuasion and education, and not by the method of coercion or repression.
>
> (Mao Tse-tung)

On Leadership

The organization of the Union itself is somewhat unclear. From our experiences with it, Andy Stapp must be considered 95 per cent of the Union himself. Nearly everywhere the Union is represented, Stapp is there. Nearly every article written about the Union is written by Chairman Andrew Stapp. To say the least, the Union is top down, elitist, and undemocratic. To our knowledge and to the better knowledge of former Union members, there has never been a Union meeting, either on a local or national level, in the two years of the Union's existence.

Stapp contends that there are "Union organizers" on nearly every base in the country, in Europe, and throughout Asia. Our experience with "Union organizers" is that they are in two basic categories: first, there are guys who once saw a copy of the BOND, the Union newspaper (written and edited primarily by Stapp), liked the anti-army/anti-authoritarianism line, sent in a dollar to join for a free subscrip-

tion, and have never had any further contact with the Union.
For those who have had additional contact with the Union, it
has been primarily in the form of legal assistance. Second-
ly, many so-called "Union organizers" have told us that they
joined the Union for "free legal advice." The Union has
played an important role in providing legal services to GI's
and in publicizing individual acts of rebellion, yet at the expense of suffering from Stapp's opportunism in playing up the
ASU. The foremost position in Stapp's practice has been to
promote the Union even at the expense of furthering the struggle of the GI movement. With few exceptions, almost every
Union member we have come into contact with has seen
through the facade of Stapp and "his" Union. For almost
everyone who has any political dealings with Stapp, the ASU
has come to stand for the Andrew Stapp Union. The movement must learn the harmful consequences of silently permitting individualism and opportunism in this form to exist.

Stapp has flooded the movement press with articles
claiming nearly every GI action and struggle as one organized and led by the ASU. Those who attended the UFAF Conference heard him run down these "Union" successes. Stapp
always seems to find time to attend every public rally in New
York and in many parts of the country. His availability
comes from his lack of involvement in any on-going work.

Opportunistic Tactics

Whenever a struggle intensifies at a base, Stapp can
certainly be expected to appear. The political theory that
best describes the Union is that of the "theory of spontaneity."
We must remember that spontaneity is opposed to taking a
line against the foundations of imperialism; it is a line which
favors the "least resistance"; in essence, it is a line of opportunism and of pure and simple trade unionism!

When 200 black GI's at Fort Hood refused orders to go
to Chicago last August, Stapp was on the first plane from
New York. He again must be credited with providing legal
assistance to the 43 GI's who were charged; on the other hand,
he claimed that the entire struggle was organized and directed
by "Union organizers." Most of the 43 GI's never heard of
Stapp or "his" Union before he appeared. Many of those GI's
have openly expressed their disgust for Stapp and his oppor-
tunistic tactics. (This can be further verified in the SDS-
published pamphlet of an interview B. Dohrn had with one of

the 200 black GI's who refused to go. It was also pointed out to us by staff members of the Oleo Strut--the coffee house at Fort Hood.)

Even in an attempt to get one of the authors of this article to join the Union a year ago, Stapp's line was "I'd like to let you come to the Union meeting with the Fort Dix GI's, but the guys would be uptight about a non-union member sitting in. Why don't you just pay a dollar...." When this person arrived at Fort Dix and met some of the "Union organizers" there, he found that they hadn't heard from Stapp in months.

At the recent SDS National Convention, the ASU prepared a four-page pamphlet entitled "What We Want, What We Believe," obviously meant to parallel the Black Panther Party's ten-point program. Interestingly enough, the third and eighth demands had been changed. "Racial equality" became "We demand an end to racism in the Armed Forces," and "... fight in an _illegal_ war in Vietnam" (our italics) became "... fight in Vietnam." Again Stapp portrayed the Union as one thing to the movement while his practice characteristically remained the same. When questioned by one of the authors of this article at the GI Workshop at the Chicago NC as to the change in the wording of the demands, Stapp's response was, "The wording was changed at a recent Union meeting, but the meaning is still the same."

Stapp at Fort Dix

Our most recent encounter with the ASU and its leadership prompted us to compile this political critique. This struggle centered around support for the 38 prisoners charged in the aftermath of the stockade rebellion at Fort Dix on June 5th.

GI's who have been active in the struggle at Fort Dix, in conjunction with SDS organizers at the coffee house there, developed three demands in an attempt to actively organize support for the brothers in the "pound." The demands are: (1) drop all charges against the 38; (2) abolish the stockade system within the military; and (3) free Huey P. Newton, the New York Panther 21, the Presidio 27 and all political prisoners. It was agreed by all that a requirement for groups joining in an ad hoc defense committee to support these guys in their action had to agree to support and organize around the three demands, each demand being of equal importance.

Since a few of the men charged with the heaviest offenses were ASU members, negotiations with the Union took
place to agree upon the three demands. After two unsuccessful meetings between Stapp and several different representatives of the Fort Dix coffee house (including the authors), with New York Regional SDS and YAWF members
present, Stapp still balked over the third demand, saying that
he couldn't say "Free Huey" every time he spoke about the
Fort Dix 38. One of his examples was that in speaking at a
union meeting of truck drivers he "couldn't very well mention 'Free Huey'." Again a specific example of combating
racism by not dealing with it. Note that at rallies, Stapp
mouths pro-Panther slogans freely and every week sends a
different article claiming the successes of the Union into the
BPP newspaper. Recently Stapp verbally agreed to support
the three demands, but he has yet to mention them in the latest issue of the Bond or in an article about the revolt in
the August issue of the Movement.

Stapp's analysis of the Dix rebellion is that it was a
deliberate attempt to bust the ASU--"an international 'union-
busting' tactic on the part of the army." This is not only
unfounded, but it attempts to divert attention from the significance of the revolt which was initiated by over 200 courageous GI's. Once again the Union's dishonest evaluation and
overt opportunism in placing the Union's interests over the
emerging GI movement have set back the on-going struggle,
and they will continue to impede this struggle unless the
movement becomes fully conscious of the dangers implicit in
the Union.

Conclusion

The time has come to begin considering entering the
army as organizers. From our experience at Fort Dix (verified by movement people in and around other bases), we
have realized the growing necessity and importance of having
movement organizers in the army. Collectives of movement
people on any one base in the country (and there are only a
dozen or so major bases) would be an invaluable aid in furthering the struggle.

This does not mean that individuals within the movement should allow themselves to be drafted. It is not an
easy or simple move, but with adequate preparation--learn-
ing about military law and procedure, pre-arranging civilian

and legal contacts near your base, speaking with GI's, with
vets, and with military organizers, getting into excellent
physical condition, and being able to rely on a developed program for action--the results would without a doubt be a
worthwhile sacrifice. A detailed program is now being developed and will be available for the movement's use very
soon.

The primary task of these cadre of organizers would
be to develop a mass approach to struggle among other GI's,
breaking down the myth that "you can't fight City Hall"; demonstrating and teaching (daily and from past experience) that
power is and should be "to the people." Cadre should discuss the nature of the war within the context of imperialism
and be prepared to discuss what a people's army is as opposed to an imperialist army. Giving historical examples,
cadre ought to be able to relate how the Armed Forces have
been used both at home and abroad to put down the people.
They should also conduct a simultaneous attack on racism if
we are to succeed where prior attempts have failed or fal-
tered. Cadre must see themselves as developing other cadre
and mass forms from their companies and units. The army
really is a paper tiger when compared with the power of organized, class-conscious people; however, as long as individual drop-out and cop-out approaches are continued in lieu
of building a mass counter-movement from within, the army
will be able to absorb, contain, withstand, and prevail in-
ternally.

Imperialist America will not fall only of its own ac-
cord--that would be an example of a vulgar, mechanistic interpretation of history. It will fall when it is weakened by
its own contradictions and by the masses of people who are
organized to protect themselves collectively and to seize what
is rightfully theirs.

As the Russian Revolution has taught us, soldiers who
are pressed into protecting someone else's interests which
are diametrically opposed to their own, have had no difficulty
in and are quite capable of understanding and acting in their
own interests.

Soldiers of the conscripted Kerensky Army who had
been fighting for years in an imperialist army eventually became the heart of the Red Army. For a revolution to come
about in this country, the army will have to be at least
neutralized. However, if enough people do their work well,

major sections of the army could very well take a positive
stance in the battle against imperialism.

Without a people's army the people have nothing.
--Mao

(Distributed at Boston University, February 22, 1969.   Collected June 11, 1969.)

23.   CONSTITUTION OF THE STUDENT PEACE UNION

The Student Peace Union aims to enlist the energy, talents and idealism of students in the cause of peace. For this purpose it invites students to organize so that through their study, mutual help and encouragement they may become instruments of achieving a peaceful world at home and abroad.

Especially in this age of possible nuclear destruction of the world the members of the Peace Union dedicate themselves to working for the survival of humanity.

The structure of the organization will be dependent on the desires of the local members in each school. The national organization will merely be a service that may help the local groups where they need and desire that help. For this reason no structure is outlined for local areas or schools. In this manner we believe that the process of peace may be more creatively and enthusiastically promoted.

BYLAWS OF THE STUDENT PEACE UNION OF GEORGETOWN UNIVERSITY

1- The Student Peace Union will accept no funds from the University.

2- The Student Peace Union of Georgetown University will have no hierarchical structure but will be aided by a steering committee made up of five members.

3- Meetings will be held at the call of the committee.

4- Members will be those who associate themselves with works of peace promoted by the organization.

(1967 Constitution of The Student Peace Union, Georgetown University. Collected by the compiler October 4, 1971.)

24. LETTER FROM HO CHI MINH TO CHARLOTTE POLIN

November 25, 1965

My dear niece,

I have received your letter. I sincerely thank you for your thoughtful words with regard to the Vietnamese people who are fighting for national freedom and independence. You and the American progressive people, specially the youth feel indignant at the barbarous crimes perpetrated in Viet Nam by the U.S. imperialists who have thus besmeared the honour of the American people and the noble traditions of the United States. These are sincere feelings of all honest Americans when they see the U.S. aggressors daily sowing ruins and death in a country some ten thousand miles away from the United States, and which has no other desire than to live in independence, freedom, peace, and friendship with the American people.

I am glad to learn that you and many other young Americans are actively endeavouring under varied forms to help push forward the movement against the war of aggression in Viet Nam and in support of the Vietnamese people. I highly appreciate these efforts of yours and of the American youth, students and other friends who are valiantly fighting for freedom, justice and for friendship between our two peoples.

The U.S. imperialist aggressors will certainly be defeated.

The Vietnamese people will be victorious.

Note: The above is Ho Chi Minh's letter to Charlotte Polin, radical activist in Youth against War and Fascism (YAWF) and the Free University of New York (FUNY). Note that Ho Chi Minh addresses Ms. Polin affectionately as "niece."

I wish you good health and good success.

With affectionate greetings

(Signed)

Uncle Ho

(Collected June 18, 1967 at the Free University of New York)

25. COMMITTEE OF LIAISON WITH FAMILIES OF
SERVICEMEN DETAINED IN NORTH VIETNAM

365 West 42nd Street, New York, N.Y. 10036

(212)-765-1490

January 27, 1970

Dear _____

We assume that by this time you have received the letter from North Vietnam which was forwarded to you by members of our Committee. We are enclosing an Information Sheet which explains the work of the Committee of Liaison.

The North Vietnamese have said that prisoners will be able to receive and send one letter a month. As noted in the Information Sheet, you may send letters directly to North Vietnam (note the mail address and route). If you would like us to forward them for you, please enclose but do not affix stamps as we will be sending them on in packets. We are also enclosing a letter form which you might wish to use, whether you send it directly or through us. Prisoners can also receive one package, not over six pounds in weight, every other month.

To insure the safe and rapid delivery of mail from prisoners, the North Vietnamese will send periodic packets of letters through our office. The letters will then be dispatched immediately to the families to whom they are addressed.

The only way to secure the eventual release of prisoners is through the decision by the United States to end the war. But in the meantime we are pleased to be able to assist in the communication between men and their families. We hope to forward letters on to you again soon.

Sincerely,

(signed) Maggie Geddes

(Rec'd. from the Committee of Liaison on Feb. 10, 1970.)

104

March 9, 1970

Dear <u>Mrs. Hess</u>:

We have just received word from Hanoi that a letter from <u>Dale Hess</u> to you has been mailed from North Vietnam and is expected to arrive here shortly, perhaps in the next week or two. As soon as it arrives, along with 86 others in the same package, we will send it to you immediately. Please forgive the mimeographed letter but we wanted you to know right away, particularly the large number of families for whom this will be the first letter.

As a result of arrangements made with the North Vietnamese, mail from captured pilots will be sent to this office in bundles for remailing to families. The Committee of Liaison, which includes members of various anti-war organizations, also forwards letters to captured pilots, although families are able to send letters, once per month, and a package, of six pounds or less every month, directly. Both letters and packages should be addressed to:

> Name of serviceman, serial number
> Camp of Detention of U.S. Pilots Captured in the
>   D.R.V.
> Hanoi, Democratic Republic of Vietnam
> <u>via</u> <u>Moscow</u>, <u>U.S.S.R.</u>

We understand that three more packages of mail are on their way and as has been announced by the postmaster general of Hanoi, in all, 318 letters are expected in this period. Since December, we have forwarded 266 letters; and as of this mailing we have official conformation of 219 servicemen held by the North Vietnamese.

We are very pleased to be able to perform this service and hope that you will feel free to be in touch with us if you have any questions. In the meantime we continue to work for the immediate and complete withdrawal of all U.S. troops from Vietnam; to bring an end to the fighting, killing and capturing and to hasten the day when all families will be reunited, American and Vietnamese.

Sincerely yours,

(signed)

Cora Weiss   Dave Dellinger

(Received from the Committee of Liaison on March 18, 1970.)

May 4, 1970

From: Rev. Richard Fernandez

To: The families of the 335 presently confirmed prisoners
     held in North Vietnam.

Re: Information on correspondence with prisoners.

On April 20th I returned from a three-week trip to
Laos and North Vietnam. In North Vietnam I spoke with officials responsible for communication between pilots held in
detention there and their families here. The following information was emphasized to me by the North Vietnamese authorities and we are anxious to make sure that you are aware
of it:

1) The Vietnamese recommend that families use the air-let-
    ter form (enclosed) for correspondence.

2) Communication to pilots should be limited to matters of
    family and health.

3) Pilots are allowed to receive one letter per month and
    one package every other month (not over six pounds
    in weight).

Detention Camp authorities have said that they do not
wish to receive several letters and/or packages per month for
a given pilot from different members of the same family.
Families should make arrangements for alternating letters
each month if different members want to write.

The North Vietnamese authorities indicated that, from
this point forward, they will not feel responsible for forwarding letters and packages that do not adhere to the above.

If the letter form is mailed directly it can go in another envelope but the mail route, "via Moscow, U.S.S.R.," should definitely be included in the address. If letters are sent to the Committee of Liaison for forwarding please enclose but do not affix stamps as we send letters on in packets. The Committee cannot forward packages for families.

While I was in Hanoi, Prof. Douglas Dowd of Cornell University and I met with three pilots; Cdr. Robert Schweitzer of Lemoore, California; Cdr. Walter Wilbur of Virginia Beach and Lt. Col. Edison Miller of Santa Ana, California. The three men were in good health, and said they had daily exercise and reading material. The three pilots advised us that they had been getting letters and packages from their families, and asked that packages include toilet articles and canned foods. In particular they mentioned soap, shaving cream (no razors or blades), toothpaste, powdered milk and cream, instant coffee, and non-melting candy. They said they do not need clothes.

Also, in my discussions with the Vietnam Committee of Solidarity with the American People, the Committee of Liaison's contact in North Vietnam, we confirmed that since December over 800 letters have been sent from Hanoi through the Committee of Liaison. Of those, 156 letters are still on their way from Hanoi to families here.

We hope that this information clarifies some aspects of correspondence for you. If you have any further questions please do not hesitate to contact us.

(Received from the Committee of Liaison on May 11, 1970.)

26. WHY NORTH VIET-NAM IS BEING BOMBED

(Youth Against War and Fascism)

IT IS ELEVEN YEARS SINCE THE GENEVA AGREE-
MENTS WERE SIGNED GUARANTEEING RE-UNIFICATION
ELECTIONS AND THE INDEPENDENCE, UNITY, SOVER-
EIGNTY AND TERRITORIAL INTEGRITY OF THE WHOLE OF
VIET-NAM. IT IS ELEVEN YEARS SINCE THE BLOODY
VIOLATION OF THESE AGREEMENTS BY THE U.S. GOV-
ERNMENT BEGAN. FOR THE PEOPLE OF VIET-NAM AND
FOR US, THIS IS THE ELEVENTH HOUR.

On February 7, 1965 the U.S. began its systematic
air massacre of the Democratic Republic of Viet-Nam (North
Viet-Nam). Now the U.S. government is planning shortly to
order the bombing of HAIPHONG, an industrial city of half
a million people, which is Hanoi's seaport, and of HANOI it-
self--a beautiful capital with a population of over a million,
with its precious industries, and cultural treasures dating
back centuries. The U.S. also plans to bomb the system of
dikes in the Democratic Republic of Viet-Nam (DRV) which
keeps the North Viet-Namese from drowning and starving.

IN THE NAME OF HUMANITY, LET US ACT BEFORE
IT IS TOO LATE!
SAVE HAIPHONG!
SAVE HANOI!
PREVENT THE BOMBING OF THE DIKES AND DAMS
WHICH WOULD KILL THREE MILLION NORTH VIET-
NAMESE THROUGH DROWNING AND STARVATION!

WHY IS THE U.S. BOMBING NORTH VIET-NAM?

Because, for a small and poor Asian country (population 18 million), the Democratic Republic of Viet-Nam has
achieved economic miracles! During over eighty years of
French colonialism, the Viet-Namese lived like serfs, working 12 to 17 hours a day, seven days a week, rummaging in

garbage heaps for food, never knowing what it was like to
have either national independence or industry. In 1945 as a
result of the anti-fascist victory and of the Viet-Namese people's August Revolution, led by the Viet-Minh, the Viet-Namese forced out the French and Japanese oppressors and established the Democratic Republic of Viet-Nam. On January
6, 1946, nation-wide elections were held, in both the North
and the South, which democratically elected the Ho Chi Minh
government. That the elections were entirely free and fair
was attested to by American observers, and many foreign experts on Viet-Nam such as the French historians Philippe
Devillers and Jean Chesneaux.

The government of the Democratic Republic of Viet-
Nam was recognized internationally even by the French, but
in March 1946 the latter decided to re-conquer their former
prize colony, and the Viet-Namese were forced to fight the
First Resistance War which ended only with the signing of
the Geneva Accords in July of 1954. They are now fighting
the Second Resistance War--against the U.S. aggressors who
come from eight thousand miles away to bomb, blast and
burn them.

North Viet-Nam is being bombed because it is the only industrialized economy in all of Southeast Asia. The economic miracles achieved by the Democratic Republic of Viet-
Nam, the first former colonial country to take the Socialist
path, were a most inspiring example to the peoples of South-
East Asia (including South Viet-Nam, where the U.S. had
never built any industry and where at least 80 per cent of
U.S. aid money at all times went for openly-avowed military
purposes) to all of Asia (particularly India) and to Africa and
Latin America as well.

Under Socialism, North Viet-Nam solved every problem that its giant neighbor, India, had been unable to solve
under Capitalism. In North Viet-Nam, famine and drought
were omnipresent, and in 1945 two million North Viet-Namese
starved to death. Though the Red River Delta of North Vietnam is the most densely-populated region in the world, and
though the DRV has a per capital land-holding of only a fifth
of an acre (one third that of an Indian peasant) the DRV not
only solved the famine problem but even began exporting rice!

Two other problems that plague India, housing and il-
literacy, long ago were solved by the DRV. Under the
French, tens of thousands of Viet-Namese slept in the

streets, as in Calcutta and Bombay now. Over 95 per cent
of the people of the DRV are literate. Whereas when Viet-
Nam was ruled by the French there were only 500 university
students for the whole of Indo-China (i.e. North & South Viet-Nam, Laos & Cambodia) today Hanoi graduates over
27,000 a year!

       Just as the U.S. is attempting to drown in blood the
Liberation struggle of the South Viet-Namese people because
it is the model for liberation struggles everywhere, so North
Viet-Nam is being bombed to bits because it shows all colonial and former colonial countries, it shows the so-called
Third World of Asia, Africa and Latin America by living example that Socialism can solve their problems. According
to the October 14, 1965 "Viet-Nam News Agency Bulletin"
(issued daily in Rangoon, Burma) between February and October 1965 the U.S. bombed no less than 124 educational establishments in the DRV, killing a large number of teachers
and students. This is done not only to terrorize the North
Viet-Namese people, but also because the U.S. did and does
not want Socialist North Viet-Nam's impressive educational
system to remain an example to the poor folk of the world.

       In the medical field, the Democratic Republic of Viet-
Nam is the only nation in Southeast Asia to have completely
wiped out cholera, plague, and small-pox. Between February 1965 and July 11, 1965 alone, the U.S. bombed no less
than fifteen hospitals and medical establishments, some of
them, like the Quynh Lap Leper Sanitarium (where U.S. pilots killed 180 patients in 14 bombing raids) and the Tuberculosis Hospital No. 71 (over 40 patients and five doctors
killed) the finest treatment centers of their kind in all of
Asia.

       The Democratic Republic of Viet-Nam is being bombed
because it built "an independent national economy" with economic and technical aid from the Socialist Camp, but largely
by its own labor--and hand labor at that! On the ruins of a
debilitating war, and with bare and bleeding hands, the North
Viet-Namese built an impressive infant industry that became
the Showplace for Socialism in Southeast Asia. North Viet-
Nam has been called "the Ruhr of Southeast Asia." Experts
on South-East Asia have highly praised the DRV's accomp-
lishments, such as Alex Josey, South-east Asian correspond-
ent for "Reynolds News" and a member of the British Labor
Party for over twenty-five years. Josey says that North
Viet-Nam is the most advanced country in South-East Asia

and has already solved many of the problems that remain unsolved in the rest of this area. "North Viet-Nam is making
material progress unequalled by any country in South-East
Asia," he also wrote. "While living standards in Malaya,
Thailand, Ceylon and elsewhere in the region remain static
or get worse, North Viet-Nam is marching forward."

By bombing the DRV, the U.S. seeks to dissuade all
countries from taking the Socialist path by showing that
through its preponderant military power it can negate every
benefit a Socialist State can bring to its people.   One of the
main appeals that Socialism has for the masses of the world
is its promise of Security, and the U.S. power structure
seeks to make a mockery of Socialism by subjecting the
North Viet-Namese to Insecurity--fear of the bombings, which
would cause insecurity on the job; insecurity over food, due
to the bombings hampering transportation and supply; fear of
illness, injury and death, and of their dwelling places being
destroyed.   Thus, by bombing the DRV, the U.S. seeks to
prove that even though a country may adopt Socialism, it will
not be able to give its people the benefits of Socialism: economic, political, social and psychological security.   For always, over it will hang the sword of Damocles--destruction
by the U.S.

This is the "message" the U.S. is transmitting to all
of Asia, Africa, and Latin America: Even though Socialism
brings about much more rapid industrialization than capitalism, better stick with Capitalism.   Because if you adopt Socialism, your economic development will still be set back
decades--by bombings!   This is the real reason for the clam-
or in Washington, led by General Curtis LeMay, to "bomb
North Viet-Nam back into the Stone Age"!

FOR THE SAKE OF THE MARTYRED AND SUFFER-
ING PEOPLE OF THE DRV, WHO TILL THE WINNING OF
INDEPENDENCE FROM THE FRENCH NEVER HAD A GOOD
DAY IN THEIR LIVES, AND FOR THE SAKE OF ALL OP-
PRESSED PEOPLES EVERYWHERE WHO HAVE STRUGGLED
AGAINST POVERTY, OR WHO WOULD LIKE TO, LET US
VOCIFEROUSLY CONDEMN GENERAL CURTIS LEMAY'S
SUBHUMAN SLOGAN "BOMB NORTH VIET-NAM BACK INTO
THE STONE AGE"!   DEMAND THAT THE U.S. GOVERN-
MENT CEASE TO IMPLEMENT THIS BARBARIC POLICY.
DEMAND AN END TO ALL BOMBINGS OF NORTH VIET-
NAM!

According to the "New York Times" of December 3, 1965, the bombing of North Viet-Nam is "so widespread that Hanoi and its port, Haiphong--the major population and industrial centers--are left as mere 'islands.' " The industrial center of Nam Dinh, third largest city in the DRV, has already been bombed, and its textile factories destroyed or badly damaged. According to "Newsweek" magazine of October 11, 1965 (p. 44) and Bernard Fall writing in the December issue of "Ramparts," the U.S. has almost completely leveled the new and important industrial city of Vinh, capital of the Province of Nghe An, surrounded by glorious tradition, where President Ho Chi Minh was born.

Senator Stennis, Chairman of the Armed Services Preparedness Sub-Committee, Richard Nixon, Mendel Rivers, Sen. Richard Russell and others making speeches calling for the bombing of Haiphong and Hanoi are ordered by the White House to put out these "trial balloons" to test American public opinion regarding the bombing of Haiphong and Hanoi. WE MUST PUNCTURE THESE TRIAL BALLOONS BY LETTING LYNDON JOHNSON AND THE STATE DEPARTMENT KNOW THAT WE ARE VEHEMENTLY OPPOSED TO THE BOMBINGS OF HAIPHONG! Before it is too late, we must do all we can to prevent further escalation in the air war of destruction against North Viet-Nam.

Haiphong is not only Hanoi's seaport, but the life-line of the whole DRV. The DRV cannot live without foreign trade! It buys its industrial base (i.e. purchase of heavy industrial equipment) through the exporting of its agricultural surplus! If Haiphong Harbor is dynamited and its port facilities destroyed, it will cause severe food and material shortages, and wreck the economy of the DRV. Now, the Republican Party has passed a Resolution calling for the blockading of North Viet-Nam. By imposing a complete "Cordon Sanitaire" and "Cordon Militaire," the U.S. hopes to completely strangle the DRV.

The precious industries and factories in the Hanoi-Haiphong area mean the world to the North Viet-Namese, who since the winning of national independence lovingly and laboriously built them up. The hypocritical Lyndon Johnson defended the bombing of North Viet-Nam at one of his press conferences by saying, "There is no blood in a steel bridge." We must let him know that we know very well that there is blood in every bridge, road, highway, dam, power plant, etc. that the U.S. is destroying--the blood, sweat and tears of the

North Viet-Namese who sacrificed everything to work day in,
day out, to build them. Haiphong is a city of strong working-class tradition, proud of the industries it has built. That
city has led the whole country in emulation drives! And attacks on Haiphong and Hanoi would massacre the civilians of
these densely-populated metropolitan cities!

Not only are the U.S. aggressors planning to bomb
Haiphong and Hanoi, and the whole economic-industrial complex of the DRV. Splashed all over the U.S. and world
press are their monstrous plans to bomb North Viet-Nam's system of dikes and dams! This genocidal act would drown and
starve three million North Viet-Namese--at least one million
of them would die outright, and the other several millions
from starvation and disease--including horrible plagues--over
a period of a year. "U.S. News & World Report" in its December 6, 1965 issue contains a horrifying admission: "U.S.
bombers have already crippled part of the irrigation system
in North Viet-Nam. In the months ahead, the U.S. may
strike at the high dikes protecting the Red River Delta--
would knock out agricultural production for at least a year."

The French press has demanded that the U.S. government openly renounce any intention to bomb the dikes. Of
course, the U.S. refused. BUT IT IS OUR DUTY AS CITI-
ZENS OF THE NATION WHICH IS CARRYING OUT AND
PLANNING THESE DIABOLICAL ACTS, TO DO ALL IN OUR
POWER TO MAKE LYNDON JOHNSON REVERSE HIS POLI-
CY, AND PUBLICLY DECLARE THAT HE WILL NOT BOMB
THE DIKES. We must make it clear that, negotiations or no
negotiations, we demand that the U.S. stop all bombings
against North Viet-Nam because it is a Hitlerian crime
against humanity to bomb and destroy the precious accomp-
lishments and economic livelihood of a poor, helpless little
country which has nothing to fight back with and is defenseless under U.S. air attacks.

Right now, the bombing of Haiphong has first priority
on the Pentagon's list. In addition, the Washington strate-
gists have other "projects" high on the priority list which
would strike at the life and welfare of millions of civilians
in North Viet-Nam. As "U.S. News & World Report" puts
it in its December 6, 1965 issue:

"There are other important targets in North Viet-Nam
that have not been touched by American bombs. Public utili-
ties are one. Also on the list are cement and fertilizer
factories, and two Chinese-built blast furnaces."

On December 15 and again on December 21, the U.S.
did indeed attack the DRV's public utilities--by destroying
the Uong Bi Thermal Power Plant! That power station was
one of the Viet-Namese people's brightest and most beloved
achievements. It supplied most of the electricity to the
Hanoi-Haiphong area, and by knocking it out, the U.S.
caused a massive power blackout, and brought industry to a
virtual standstill. 550 workers were employed at Uong Bi.
The U.S. dropped 3,000-pound bombs--the biggest used in
any war--to destroy them and their economic achievements.
Nearby coal mines, textile factories and other economic establishments were also heavily bombed, as well as heavily-
populated civilian areas in the suburbs of Haiphong!

LET US EXERT OUR ENERGIES TO PREVENT A
REPETITION OF SUCH HEARTLESS AND HORRENDOUS ACTS
OF AGGRESSION! LET US MOVE HEAVEN AND EARTH TO
PREVENT THE BOMBING OF HAIPHONG! LET US MAKE
A HERCULEAN EFFORT, WHILE THERE IS STILL TIME,
TO PREVENT THE BOMBING OF HANOI, AND THE DIKES,
AND THE WHOLE ECONOMIC-INDUSTRIAL COMPLEX OF
THE DRV!

LET US DEMAND AN END TO THE MASSACRE AND
MUTILATION OF A POOR DEFENSELESS LITTLE NATION!
A NATION WHOSE ONLY "CRIME" IS THAT IT CHERISHES
ITS NATIONAL INDEPENDENCE AND ITS OWN FORM OF
GOVERNMENT. LET US DEMAND AND ACT NOW FOR AN
END TO THE BOMBING OF THE DEMOCRATIC REPUBLIC
OF VIET-NAM!

This pamphlet has been endorsed by, among others:

Jacques Broucharde	Sandy Kaymen
Joe Ben-David	Kazu Okada
Joanna S. Eisenberg	John Phelps
Roland Hirsch	Paul Prensky
Robert Hirschfield	Alan Shapiro
Robert A. Hollis, Post #15	Austin Straus
American Legion Comdr.	Armand Storace
Jane Jaffe	Trudith Storace

(Mimeographed pamphlet collected at the Free University of
New York, August 27, 1966.)

27. U.S. COMMITTEE TO AID THE
    NATIONAL LIBERATION FRONT
    OF SOUTH VIETNAM

103 Macdougal St Room 5 NY 10012 Tel YU 2-7162

You, the American Citizen, have the obligation to try to repair the damage being done to the Vietnamese people by your government.

WE THEREFORE urge you to send medical equipment or money for medical aid, not to the military puppet regime in Saigon, but directly to the National Liberation Front of South Vietnam. This is the only government which truly represents the people and can see that your aid gets to those who really need it.

SEND medical supplies (list of suggested items supplied on request) to:

> The Liberation Red Cross, c/o Mr. Trom Xuan Pho, Commercial Attache, Room 608, 2A Des Voeux Road, Central, Hong Kong.

MAIL contributions by International Bank Draft via Registered Mail to:

> The National Liberation Front of South Vietnam Mission, 100-60972, Ceskoslovesnka Obchodni Banka, A.S., Prague, Czechoslovakia.

or to the National Liberation Front Mission in Paris, Algiers, or Moscow.

CABLE money to: "Vinacor," Hong Kong.

(Receipts for medical purchases will be forwarded on request.)

DO NOT send money for medical aid to our committee--we will gladly accept separate contributions to help us to further publicize the need for medical aid in Vietnam. In addition to our button (pictured above, in red and blue at 25¢ each), we

115

have for sale a large selection of Vietnamese literature.
Send $1.00 to cover costs for a bibliography and price list.
Speakers on the National Liberation Front available.

---------------------- tear here ----------------------

SUPPORT THE COMMITTEE
TO AID THE NATIONAL LIBERATION FRONT

1. I would like to: WORK WITH US-CANLF___ Be on mailing list____

2. Skills (typing, lettering, speaking, etc.):_____

3. Resources: Car____ Office equipment____ Space____
    Other_____

4. Languages: Viet____ Mandarin____ Cantonese____
    Other _____

Name_____Age____ Phone_____

Address(es)_____School_____

STATEMENT OF POLICY

20 November 1965

THE U.S. COMMITTEE TO AID THE NATIONAL LIBERA-
TION FRONT OF SOUTH VIETNAM (CANLF) supports the
aim of the National Liberation Front of South Vietnam (NLF)
for "Independence, Democracy, Peace, and Neutrality." We
support the right of the people of Vietnam for self-determina-
tion--without the presence of U.S. troops--and we agree with
the important NLF statement of March 22, 1965:

1. The U.S. is the aggressor and has violated the
    Geneva Agreements.
2. The NLF is determined to achieve an Independ-
    ent, Democratic, Peaceful and Neutral South Vi-
    etnam, with a view to national reunification.
3. The NLF will liberate South Vietnam and defend
    North Vietnam.
4. The NLF is ready to receive all assistance, in-
    cluding weapons.
5. The whole United People will defeat the U.S. ag-
    gressors and the Vietnamese traitors.

The CANLF supports the NLF position on negotiations as contained in Article 2 of their March 22 statement, and as further explained in their September 25, 1965 statement--that in order for negotiations to begin, the U.S. must agree to the following principles: 1) Withdrawal of all U.S. troops, 2) A return to the 1954 Geneva Agreements, 3) Respect for the rights of the NLF as "the only genuine representative of the 14 million South Vietnamese people," which must have its decisive voice in the formation of any new government in South Vietnam.

The CANLF calls for an immediate ceasefire and an end to the bombings of both North and South Vietnam, and the immediate withdrawal of all U.S. troops from Vietnam.

It is the purpose of the CANLF to bring to the U.S. public an awareness of the just and moral aims of the Vietnamese people in their resistance to efforts by the U.S. government to "pacify" their country. In doing this, we hope to arouse public indignation at the unjust nature of the U.S. position and actions, and thus bring about a call for peace--a peace which will allow the Vietnamese to determine their own affairs.

The resistance of the people of South Vietnam is an indigenous movement of politically and religiously diverse groups (and individuals) which was organized in response to years of oppression and illegal action by the U.S. government and its various "puppet" regimes in Saigon. In order to counteract the U.S. government's propaganda--which falsely teaches the public that the "enemy" is an outside, "communist" aggressor--we will continue to make use of various educational means. These are: To make available to the U.S. public literature from North and South Vietnam; to disseminate analyses and reprints of the structure and political nature of the NLF and the DRV (Democratic Republic of Vietnam-- North Vietnam); to provide expert speakers on the history of the NLF and DRV for formal discussions, street meetings, teaching, etc.; and to work with all groups for recognition of the legitimacy of the NLF in its struggle for victory and liberation. In addition, we urge all people to send medicines or money for medical supplies to the NLF through their foreign missions.

The U.S. government is trying to stifle, at tremendous cost and risk, a liberation struggle which is setting the example for all oppressed people. Those in this country who are for "Peace," but refuse to concern themselves with who the people

"on the other side" are, what is motivating them to fight, and
why the U.S. is <u>really</u> involved in Vietnam, are by default
supporting the policies and efforts of the U.S. government to
stop the liberation struggles of people everywhere.

THEREFORE it is not enough to be for peace--a "peace"
that would keep the Vietnamese from completing their struggle
for liberation.   Rather, if this war is to be stopped, if escalation is to be prevented, if the "brutalization" of our own
country is to be reversed, if the rights of the Vietnamese,
the Americans, and all peoples are to be protected, it is the
position of CANLF that THE PEOPLE OF THE UNITED
STATES MUST SUPPORT THE NATIONAL LIBERATION
FRONT OF SOUTH VIETNAM AND ITS VICTORY.

> The U.S. Committee to aid the National Liberation
> Front of South Vietnam is an ad hoc organization with
> its headquarters at 103 Macdougal Street, New York,
> N.Y. 10012, Room 5.   Telephone (212) YU 2-7162.

(Collected May 10, 1966, New York City)

28. WHERE IS THE PEACE MOVEMENT IN THE BAY AREA HEADED?

The goal is a nationwide peace movement which can coordinate nationwide protest demonstrations.

The goal is mobilization and organization of grassroots anxieties about the war into vigorous opposition, and to work toward participatory democracy.

The goal is to spread the truth about the war--by means of speakers, newspapers, pamphlets, research projects, classes and community meetings--to offset the control of the mass media and the universities by the liberal Establishment's cold war ideology.

In order to build such a three-phased movement of direct action, community organization and education-research we must begin. The Vietnam Day Committee, which organized the Teach-in on campus in May and the picket against Johnson, has undertaken this task. We need you to join us.

Come this Tuesday night to our kickoff summer meeting where we will organize some of the following projects:

Door-to-door canvassing of Oakland to discuss the war.

A mass drive throughout Berkeley and Oakland on Saturday, July 10 for signatures on a petition asking the President to withdraw the troops from Vietnam immediately.

A "peace vote" in Oakland at the end of the summer.

Setting up a speakers' bureau to send speakers to PTA's, labor unions, churches, fraternities and sororities.

Mass leafleting of the soldiers at Fort Ord, The Presidio, and other installations.

A second "Vietnam Day" to be followed by civil disobedience, on Oct. 15 and 16.

A Congress of Unrepresented Peoples on Sunday August 8 to pass resolutions demanding that the USA withdraw from Vietnam, and then a march to the office of Congressman Jeffrey Cohelan presenting the resolutions to him and asking him questions about his stand on the war.

A bi-weekly newspaper.

A research project on the involvement of the University of California in the war in Vietnam.

These ideas scratch only the surface of the possibilities of work to end the war in Vietnam. We will organize as many projects as there are people to work. Please come Tuesday night to help make the above projects successful, or to add new ones.

THE VIETNAM DAY COMMITTEE (Campus Chapter)

(Collected November 22, 1966 at the University of California at Berkeley.)

29. STOP THE TROOP TRAIN!

Another troop train is coming through Berkeley taking American boys to Vietnam to kill and be killed in a country where the U.S. does not belong.

We must demonstrate against the war machine; we must stop the train and give our anti-war literature to the soldiers. To oppose the immoral war in Vietnam and to block the war machine is moral; to take orders from an immoral state is immoral. The police will be on hand to try to help the war machine go through--without a second's stop. We will be there too.

We are not demonstrating against the soldiers. We consider the soldiers to be our brothers--brothers who have been conscripted against their will and forced to kill by a government which has forgotten how to tell the truth. We want to stop the war machine and tell the soldiers what is really going on in Vietnam.

thursday, august 12
SANTA FE STATION, BERKELEY 1300 University Avenue
TENTATIVE TIME: 8:45 a.m.

For the exact arrival time call the Vietnam Day Committee Wednesday night, or come over to the office for further information.

2407 Fulton St., Berkeley 549-0811 or 845-6637

Car pools will be leaving for the Santa Fe Station at approximately 8 a.m. from the corner of Bancroft and Dana.

(Collected August 13, 1965 at the University of California at Berkeley.)

30. FUTURE COMMUNITY PROTEST MEETING AND MASSIVE CIVIL DISOBEDIENCE PLANNED BY THE VIETNAM DAY COMMITTEE

The Vietnam Days of May 21 and 22 on the Berkeley campus were very successful in bringing vast numbers of people in the Bay Area into involvement with protest over Johnson's foreign policy. We estimate that peak crowds at the campus protest meeting reached 10,000 to 15,000, while the total number of people who came was at least 50,000. Besides this, we estimate that the peak radio audience of KPFA was one quarter of a million, with at least half a million listening to part of the program broadcast from the campus.

Inspired by this success, the Vietnam Day Committee has decided to hold on October 15 another community protest meeting against American military intervention and to follow this on October 16 with massive civil disobedience. Already speakers are being invited, and this program is being developed with the aid of the large number of workers who made Vietnam Day such a success.

Now the Vietnam Day Committee is beginning to coordinate its activities more and more with local and national groups. Thus, it is expected that October 15 and 16 will have a heavy impact on the American political scene. We hope that in the process of development of these events, the uniting of the activist peace and other political groups will lead to a new force in America, and that this force will effect the end of Johnson's interventionist policies.

> Jerry Rubin
> Steve Smale
> Co-chairmen of
> Vietnam Day Committee

If you want to help on this and other projects, call:
Jerry Rubin 848-3158

Enclosed is my contribution to help further the work of the
Vietnam Day Committee

Name_____$_____

Address_____

Make checks payable to: Vietnam Day Committee. Send to
Prof. Smale, Box 2201, Berkeley, California

(Collected June 23, 1965, University of California at Berkeley.)

31. AUG. 6TH PROTEST

JOIN MORE THAN 40 GROUPS TO PROTEST THE WAR IN VIETNAM

Every year on August 6th concerned people around the world commemorate and mourn the devastation of Hiroshima. Today, 21 years later, as the bombs continue to drop on Asia, the New York 5th Ave. Peace Parade Committee has called on Americans to join people throughout the world in protesting the Vietnam war. Deeply disturbed by our government's actions in Vietnam, hundreds of thousands have responded to this call. We are not in favor of this war, and we shall raise our voices and march through our streets to show President Johnson and the world how we feel. WHEN SILENCE MEANS CONSENT, NO ONE CAN AFFORD TO BE SILENT!

MASS MARCH ON MARKET ST.

11 a.m.

THE MARCH WILL BEGIN AT DRUMM AND MARKET STS., S.F.

BRING YOUR OWN SIGNS

RALLY AT CIVIC CENTER

1 p.m.

SET UP YOUR OWN TABLE

Speakers

Mrs. Ann Samas (Mother of a soldier who recently refused to fight in Viet Nam)
Robert Scheer
Vincent Hallinan
Pete Camejo
Sidney Roger

124

Special Events

Puppet play - Knives in the Drawers
Anti-war Pageant
The Committee
Public Discussion
Snake Dancing
Music - The Five Year Plan

NO MORE HIROSHIMAS!

GET OUT OF VIETNAM!

THE FOLLOWING IS A PARTIAL LIST OF GROUPS SUP-
PORTING THE AUGUST 6th MARCH:

Bay Area Peace Coordinat-
  ing Comm.
Berkeley Friends of SNCC
Berkeley VDC
Bring the Troops Home Now
  Newsletter
Bullets in the Bay Comm.
Citizens for Kennedy-Fulbright
  (Berkeley)
College of San Mateo Liber-
  al Caucus
Committee for Independent
  Political Action
Communist Party USA
Community for New Politics
  (Scheer Campaign)
Concerned Citizens of Palo
  Alto
Contra Costa Citizens Against
  the War in Viet Nam
Eureka-Noe Valley Concerned
  Citizens
Godzilla Comm. to End the
  War in Viet Nam Before it
  Ends Everything Else
Gondor Committee
Haight Ashbury Viet Nam
  Comm.
High School Students Against
  the War in Viet Nam (San
  Francisco)

Independent Socialist Club
Independent Truth Center
Iranian Students Association
Moslem Student Association
No. Beach Viet Nam Comm.
Northern California Guardian
  Committee
Potrero Hill Peace Comm.
Progressive Labor Party
San Francisco Peace Center
San Francisco State VDC
San Jose State College VDC
Socialist Workers Party
Spartacist
Stanford Committee for Peace
  in Viet Nam
Students for a Democratic So-
  ciety
United World Federalists (stu-
  dent division)
United Youth for Peace (Berk-
  eley)
Vets for Peace (Berkeley)
Villagers Opposed to the War
  in Viet Nam (Albany)
Women for Peace (Berkeley)
Women's International League
  for Peace and Freedom (San
  Francisco
Young Socialist Alliance

OTHER ACTIONS

Anti-Napalm Vigil, UTC, Redwood City (Bayshore East to
     Harbor Blvd. exit). Mondays-Fridays, 12 noon to
     1 p. m. and 7 p. m. to 8 p. m.

August 6-9th. Friends (Quakers). Continuing Vigil at Oak-
     land Army Terminal. For info: TH3-7557.

August 7-9th. Stanford Campus. White Plaza, 3 Day Vigil.
     For info: 325-3405.

August 5-13th. Peace Booth at San Mateo County Fair.
     10 a. m. to 10 p. m.

Port Chicago supplies over 90 per cent of all munitions &
     explosives for the War in Viet Nam.

RALLY--1 p. m. Sunday, Aug. 7, Concord City Plaza,
     Willow Pass & Grant Sts.

WALK-- 2 p. m. to dock gate at Port Chicago.

ACTION-- 5 p. m. Individuals will stop munitions trucks.
     For info: 934-3323 or 841-8919.

Dance on 2400 Telegraph Ave., Berk., Fri. Aug. 5th, 9 to
     11 p. m. Berkeley & San Francisco State VDC,
     (tentative).

(Collected in San Francisco, California on August 4, 1965.)

32. BRIEF NOTES ON THE WAYS AND MEANS OF "BEATING" AND DEFEATING THE DRAFT

1. <u>Be a C.O.</u> Write your local draft board requesting the special conscientious objector form sss 150. Now if you don't have religious or philosophical reasons that cause you to be against war "in any form," don't let it bother you. Mark yes on that question anyway, or mark out the "in any form" if you want to be more honest about it. It's fairly certain that your local board will turn you down. However, you can then appeal their decision, be investigated, appeal again and so on. The whole process takes about a year, and by that time we'll have stopped the war in Vietnam (we hope). For further information on the C.O. process, write: Central Committee for Conscientious Objectors, 2006 Walnut St., Philadelphia, Pa. 19103, or War Resisters League, 5 Beekman St., New York 38, N.Y. Have fun.

2. <u>Have a demonstration!</u> during your pre-induction physical. This is a way for political objectors to get a 4-F and cause the military a lot of trouble. Arrive at the examining center wearing signs: END THE DRAFT NOW! or GET OUT OF VIETNAM or the like. Wear buttons. Leaflet your fellow prospective inductees. Tell them what army life and the war in Vietnam are really all about. Be determined and the officers will be only too glad to be rid of you.

3. <u>Refuse to sign</u> the loyalty oath and don't mark the RED list. If you do, they will arrest you. They'll investigate you and if you've been fairly active in any of the 'subversive' campus movements, they won't want you.

4. <u>Be 'gay.'</u> Play the homosexual bit. Mark 'yes' or don't mark the "Homosexual Tendencies" line on forms. Psychiatrist may give you the run-around but stick with it. If you're really game, be obviously one of the 'gay' boys. Besides flicking your wrist, move your body like chicks do, hold cigarette delicately, talk melodically, act embarrassed in front of the other guys when you undress. Ask your girl-friend to give you lessons or watch the Frisco North Beach crowd any week-end night. 'Gay' bars are also found down in the Tenderloin--Turk Street area.

127

5. Note from doctor. If you have a 'friendly' family doctor
or can buy one, you'll find he's extremely handy. Get a
signed note from him attesting to an allergy, a trick knee or
elbow or shoulder or back trouble, or asthma. Don't forget
to mark appropriate places on induction forms and you've
got it made. Without a Dr.'s note, you'll have to do a
pretty good job of faking these things. Certain chemicals
will temporarily induce allergies--see your chemist.

6. Be an epileptic. Borrow the standard epileptic medal
from a friend and wear it. Mark the form properly, tell the
Dr. and you're in good shape. If you want to have some
fun, read about and fake a seizure. It's fun and you'll really
give them a head-ache.

7. Jail record. Most of us aren't lucky enough to have a
felony record, but if you've got one--use it. They insist on
it: you'll see signs all over the place telling you what a
crime you'll be committing if you don't tell them. Misde-
meanors--if you've got enough of them--are a good deal.
Suspicion of burglary or robbery or murder are also nice
bets.

8. Play psycho. If you've ever been to see a 'headshrinker'--even once--by all means mark so on forms. A
note from him and a little bit of acting with this will go a
long way. Chew your fingernails. Talk about the Viet Cong
being out to get you. Tell them you're a secret agent for
God Johnson. Or be sincere and tell the Dr. how much you
enjoy walking on the Golden Gate bridge. Use your imagination, have a ball, and you'll blow their minds without having
yours blown up.

9. Arrive drunk. Being late here really helps. They may
send you away to come back another day, but it'll look good
to have it on your record. If you do this bit enough times,
they'll probably run you back to the headshrinker to find out
why. Then play it cool (the booze will help) and you've got it
made.

10. Arrive high. They'll smell it, and you won't have to
admit it. If you want to go about the addiction scene in a
really big way, use a common pin on your arm for a few
weeks in advance. Check with your friends who 'shoot' to
see if the marks look good; then you'll have no trouble con-
vincing the Drs.

11. <u>Be an undesirable</u>. Go for a couple of weeks without a shower. Really look dirty. Stink. Long hair helps. Go in barefoot with your sandals tied around your neck. Give a wino a bottle for his clothes and wear them. For extra kicks, talk far-out (some pot will help here). One doctor is probably all you'll have to see, and he'll be only too happy to get you out of the place.

12. <u>Be a 'fucque-up'</u>! Don't do ANYTHING right. Forget instructions, don't follow orders, and generally do just about everything wrong. Apologize profusely for your mistakes, and they'll probably tell you how sorry they are for having to give you a 4-F.

13. <u>Be a trouble-maker</u>. Refuse to follow orders. (You don't have to, you're not in the army.) Let them know exactly what you think of them. Be antagonistic; smoke where the signs say NO SMOKING. Pick a fight with a fellow inductee, or better yet, one of the officers or doctors.

14. <u>Bed-wetting</u>. Tell them you wet the bed when you're away from home. If they don't defer you, prove it when you're inducted.

Extra Special Service for those who really care. Join the army or any of the other military branches and really screw up the works. Tell your buddies the truth about the scene in Vietnam. They'll listen to you; you're one of them. Use the base bulletin boards for posting official-looking leaflets about the whole military mess. Please be careful. If you want to be effective at this, you can't be caught. For the man with real guts. (Detailed pamphlet on this is currently in preparation.)

A deluxe booklet containing all the many ways and means and whys of 'beating' and defeating the draft is nearing completion and will soon be issued at nominal cost. If you have any suggestions or personal anecdotes on draft evasion and army infiltration, please forward them to: Dept. 2017-J, 2407 Fulton Street, Berkeley, California. Atten: Sidney. Also contact above at 549-0811 for draft counseling and additional information.

(Collected July 17, 1965 in Berkeley.)

33. ANTI-DRAFT COMMITTEE

An Anti-Draft Committee has been formed by members of the Vietnam Day Committee, Students for a Democratic Society, and other interested individuals. We are a broadly-based group with various points of view, and encourage everyone who opposes the draft for any reason to join us.

The Anti-Draft Committee has several major perspectives:
1. Applying for "conscientious objection" on political and moral grounds.
2. Total non-cooperation with Selective Service.
3. Publicizing the many methods of beating the draft.
4. Attempting to clog up the machinery of the draft system.
5. Undermining the war effort from within the army.

Activities we are planning include:
1. Campus--noon rallies, wide distribution of anti-draft literature, and informal discussions.
2. High schools--encouraging and assisting area high school students to organize anti-draft activities within their schools.
3. Induction Centers--leafletting and talking to draftees about the war in Vietnam.
4. Community petitions and community meetings in support of our activities.

The Anti-Draft Committee has planned two workshops during the VDC protest on the 15th and 16th. The first workshop will be held following Dave Dellinger's speech on Friday afternoon around 3:00 PM. The exact time and place will be announced from the podium. The workshop will discuss the various perspectives for anti-draft activity. On Saturday at the Oakland Army Terminal we will sponsor an action workshop, where we will form several committees to make specific plans for future activities.

A meeting to make final plans for the workshops will be held on Tuesday at 6:00 PM in 145 Dwinelle Hall. For

130

further information about the Anti-Draft Committee contact
Mark Stahl or Steve Cherkoss at Vietnam Day headquarters,
2407 Fulton, 549-0811.

(Collected October 28, 1965 at the University of California
at Berkeley.)

34. WOMEN: MARCH AGAINST THE WAR

March with us to the Oakland Induction Center where we will present our demands and voice our opposition to the war.

OUR PLANS

On WEDNESDAY, FEBRUARY 23, we will hold an all-woman's march on the Oakland Induction Center.

Women on the Berkeley campus are urged to attend a NOON RALLY on Wednesday. At 10:00 p.m. the march will leave the campus.

Other women who wish to join the march are urged to MEET IT AT 1:15 P.M. AT CONSTITUTION SQUARE IN BERKELEY (Center & Grove).

The march will proceed down Grove & should arrive at the Induction Center at about 1:15 p.m.

Those who will not be able to join the march are urged to MEET AT THE INDUCTION CENTER (14th & Clay) at 3:15 p.m. There will be a rally when the march arrives, and a delegation of women will present the demands of the march to the commander of the induction center, requesting they be conveyed to the President, Commander-in-Chief of the Armed Forces.

We ask that men do not participate in this demonstration. We urge women to dress conservatively, preferably in black.

OUR DEMANDS

As women who are deeply concerned about the illegal and immoral war in Vietnam, we demand:

that the United States Government bring our husbands, sons, and brothers home now.

that our government recognize and negotiate with the National Liberation Front for the withdrawal of U.S. troops.

132

self-determination for the Vietnamese people.

that there be open public discussion and debate on the war.
As a beginning we demand that Secretary of Defense MacNa-
mara and other government officials testify in public sessions
before the Senate Foreign Relations Committee.

that the disciplinary reclassification of the Ann Arbor, Michigan demonstrators be rescinded and that such policies be
never again used.

> Women's March Committee
> Vietnam Day Committee
> 2407 Fulton, Berkeley
> 549-0811

JOIN THE WOMEN'S MARCH: WED., FEB. 23

(Collected February 28, 1966 at the University of California
at Berkeley)

35. ADVICE TO DEMONSTRATORS

The Oakland Police are irrational and unpredictable. Any participant and, in fact, any observer of this or any demonstration in Oakland is subject to some risk. Present plans call for a lengthy sit-in which might well result in arrests and convictions. Because of the issue, sentences could be stiffer than any we have experienced. For those who are not prepared to risk arrest we will hold a supporting picket line outside the sit-in. Those who participate in the sit-in should be prepared for the possible consequences and should follow the instructions of the monitors. We urge the following procedures if you are arrested:

1) We will try to raise bail money as quickly as possible. Unless you have a specific hardship, we urge you to stay in jail until enough money is raised to bail out every one. If money comes in at the rate we expect, we hope to have everyone out within from 24 hours to over a week. There is a small possibility of eventual bail reduction and even release on OR (Own Recognizance). We urge cooperation in filling OR Forms, etc.

2) Insist on your right to a phone call, and either call 845-4123 or have the person you call phone that number, (write the number on your hand). We will need to get a list of the names of those arrested.

3) Anyone who wishes general information about the arrests or the people arrested should call Th8-4754.

4) Bail donation checks should be made out to CFJ Anti-war Bail Fund. Phone 549-0690 for bail information. If you know someone who wishes to put up your bail, urge them to put the money in the fund ear-marked for you.

5) The VDC has secured the Council for Justice (CFJ) to co-ordinate legal defense. Any lawyer who wishes to involve himself in this case should first call Peter Franck, legal co-ordinator for the CFJ at 845-4123.

6) Do not waive any of your constitutional rights.

7) A defendant's meeting will be called at the first convenience to discuss legal strategy.

8) We urge minors (under 18) and aliens to avoid arrest.

9) Good luck.

(Collected in Oakland, California, August 5, 1966.)

36. ATTENTION ALL MILITARY PERSONNEL

You may soon be sent to Vietnam. You have heard about the war in the news; your officers will give you pep talks about it. But you probably feel as confused and uncertain as most Americans do. Many people will tell you to just follow orders and leave the thinking to others. But you have the right to know as much about this war as anyone. After all, it's you--not your congressman--who might get killed.

Why Are We Fighting in Vietnam?

We are supposed to be fighting to protect democracy in Vietnam, and yet our own government admits that South Vietnam is run by a dictatorship. General Ky, the latest military dictator, is as bad as they come. In a recent interview he said: "People ask me who my heroes are. I have only one--Hitler. I admire Hitler because he pulled his country together when it was in a terrible state." (London Sunday Mirror, July 4, 1965).

General Ky doesn't mean much to us; we're not even sure how to pronounce his name, but the South Vietnamese have lived under men like him for years. As far as the Vietnamese are concerned, we are fighting on the side of Hitlerism; and they hope we lose.

Who Is the Enemy?

U.S. military spokesmen have often said that their greatest problem is finding the enemy. The enemy, they say, is everywhere. The old woman feeding her chickens may have a stock of hand grenades in her hut. The little boy who trails after the American soldiers during the day slips out to give information to the guerillas at night. The washerwoman at the American air base brings a bomb to work one day. It is impossible, say the military, to tell which are the Viet Cong and which are the civilians.

And so, because the whole Vietnamese people seem to be the enemy, the military is taking no chances. They use tear gas--a weapon designed for use against civilians. They order American troops to fire at women and children--because women and children, after all, are firing at American troops. American fighter planes destroy civilian villages with napalm; American B-52's are flattening whole regions. That is why the war in Vietnam is so often called a "dirty war."

When the South Vietnamese people see you in your foreign uniform, they will think of you as <u>their</u> enemy. You are the ones bombing their towns. They don't know whether you're a draftee or a volunteer, whether you're for the war or against it; but they're not taking any chances either.

Free Elections

The Vietnamese would like to vote the foreigners out of their country, but they have been denied the chance. According to the Geneva Agreement of 1954, there were supposed to be elections throughout Vietnam in 1956. But the U.S. government was certain that our man in Vietnam, Premier Diem, would lose. So we decided not to allow any election until we were sure we could win. Diem set up a political police force and put all political opposition--Communist and anti-Communist--in jail. By 1959, it was clear there weren't going to be any elections, and the guerillas known as the Viet Cong began to fight back. By 1963 our government was fed up with Diem, but still wasn't willing to risk elections. Our CIA helped a group of Vietnamese generals to overthrow Diem and kill him. Since then there have been a series of "better" military dictators. General Ky--the man who admires Hitler --is the latest one.

Fighting for Democracy

Your job as a soldier is supposed to be "to win the people of South Vietnam." Win them to what--democracy? No, we keep military dictators in power. What then? The American way of life? But why should they care any more about our way of life than we care about theirs? We can't speak their language or even pronounce their names. We don't know anything about their religion or even what it is. We never even heard of Vietnam until Washington decided to run it.

You are supposed to be fighting "to save the Vietnamese people from Communism." Certainly Communist influence is very strong in the National Liberation Front, the rebel government. Yet most of the people support the NLF.
Why? Many of the same people who now lead the NLF led
the Vietnamese independence movement against the Japanese
during World War II, and then went on to fight against
French colonial rule. Most Vietnamese think of the NLF
leaders as their country's outstanding patriots. In fact,
many anti-Communists have joined the guerrilla forces in the
belief that the most important thing is to get rid of foreign
domination and military dictators. On the other hand, very
few Vietnamese support the official government of General
Ky. His army has low morale and a high desertion rate.

The Guerrillas

The newspapers and television have told us again and
again what a tough fighter the Vietnamese guerrilla is. Short
of ammunition and without any air cover, he can beat forces
that outnumber him five or ten to one. Why do they have
such high morale? They are not draftees; no draftees ever
fight like that. They are not high-paid, professional soldiers.
Most of them are peasants who work their fields; they can't
even spare the ammunition for target practice.

Their secret is that they know why they are fighting.
They didn't hear about Vietnam in the newspapers; they've
lived there all their lives. While we were in high school,
they were living under the Diem regime and hating it. Now
American planes are bombing their towns and strafing their
fields; American troops have occupied their country; and if
they complain out loud, an American-supported dictator sentences them to jail or the firing squad. Is it any wonder
that they fight so fiercely?

Crushing the Resistance

The war in Vietnam is not being fought according to
the rules. Prisoners are tortured. Our planes drop incendiary bombs on civilian villages. Our soldiers shoot at wom-
en and children. Your officers will tell you that it is all
necessary, that we couldn't win the war any other way. And
they are right. Americans are no more cruel than any other
people; American soldiers don't enjoy this kind of war. But

if you are going to wage war against an entire people, you have to become cruel.

The ordinary German soldier in occupied Europe wasn't especially cruel, either. But as the resistance movements grew, he _became_ cruel. He shot at women and children because they were shooting at him; he never asked himself _why_ they were shooting at him. When a certain town became a center of resistance activity, he followed his orders and destroyed the whole town. He knew that SS men were torturing captured resistance fighters, but it wasn't his business to interfere.

Following Orders

As a soldier you have been trained to obey orders, but as a human being you must take responsibility for your own acts. International and American law recognize that an individual soldier, even if acting under orders, must bear final legal and moral responsibility for what he does. The principle became a part of law after World War II, when the Allied nations, meeting in London, decided that German war criminals must be punished even if they committed war crimes under orders. This principle was the basis of the Nuremberg trials. We believe that the entire war in Vietnam is criminal and immoral. We believe that the antrocities which are necessary to wage this war against the people of Vietnam are inexcusable.

Oppose the War

We hope that you too find yourself, as a human being, unable to tolerate this nightmare war, and we hope that you will oppose it. We don't know what kind of risks we are taking in giving you this leaflet; you won't know what risk you will be taking in opposing the war. A growing number of GIs have already refused to fight in Vietnam and have been court-martialed. They have shown great courage. We believe that they, together with other courageous men who will join them, will have influence far out of proportion to their numbers.

There may be many other things you can do; since you are in the service, you know better than civilians what sorts of opposition are possible. But whatever you do, keep your

eyes open. Draw your own conclusions from the things you
see, read and hear. At orientation sessions, don't be
afraid to ask questions, and if you're not satisfied with the
answers, keep asking. Take every chance you get to talk to
your fellow soldiers about the war.

You may feel the war is wrong, and still decide not
to face a court-martial. You may then find yourself in Vietnam under orders. You might be forced to do some fight-
ing--but don't do any more than you have to. Good luck.

Vietnam Day Committee
2407 Fulton Street
Berkeley, California
549-9611

(Collected in San Francisco, California on August 2, 1966.)

37. GRAND JURY, COUNTY OF ALAMEDA

COURT HOUSE, OAKLAND 7, CALIFORNIA

January 27, 1966

To the Honorable, The Superior Court
of the State of California
In and for the County of Alameda

Under the applicable sections of the California Penal Code and under the instructions given by the Presiding Judge of the Superior Court, it is the duty of the Grand Jury to inquire into and report on the needs and operations of County government, and to submit such recommendations as it may deem appropriate.

During the term of this Grand Jury, there have been a large number of criminal prosecutions, a series of arrests, and many demonstrations requiring police supervision, which have been directly related to activities on the Berkeley Campus of the University of California and which have had a profound impact upon Alameda County government. This impact has been reflected in added court costs and congestion, extensive costs to County and local police agencies, and numerous police operations which have resulted in the dilution of the services otherwise available for local community protection. Because of this burden upon local government, the 1965 Grand Jury feels an obligation, in fully carrying out its responsibility to the Superior Court and to the community, to objectively analyze this situation and to offer constructive conclusions and suggestions.

The Berkeley Campus has increasingly become the primary base for activities throughout the Bay Area which have involved law violations and disorder. This fact, coupled with the central University function of educating young people, points up the obligation of the University to share with the community its responsibility for keeping this burden within reason and within the rule of law.

141

The Grand Jury is concerned with the fact that facilities of the Berkeley Campus of the University of California have been made available to organizations such as the "Vietnam Day Committee," whose leaders and membership are composed largely of persons who are not students or otherwise associated with the University. The "Vietnam Day Committee" has its headquarters off the Campus and its objectives and activities are unrelated to the educational purposes of the University. Yet it has been able to use Campus facilities on numerous occasions during the past several months to organize and implement actions which have detrimentally affected the surrounding community (see Appendix A). Particularly serious is the use by this group of the Berkeley campus for a staging area for unlawful off-campus activities, such as the attempts to interfere with the passage of troop trains through Berkeley and Emeryville in August, 1965, and the open advocacy and planning of "civil disobedience," which in reality involves the deliberate violation of criminal laws.

These and other incidents, occurring on the Berkeley Campus or resulting from activities which took place there, have created an extraordinary burden on governmental services, which has been borne by the County of Alameda and the cities surrounding the Campus. When law and order broke down on the Campus, such as during the so-called "Free Speech Movement" demonstrations of October and December, 1964, the agencies of local government were required to step in and regain control of the situation. Likewise, where Campus activity was directed at creating incidents in the community-at-large, such as the marches and troop train demonstrations of the "Vietnam Day Committee," local authorities were required to enforce the law and preserve order. Hundreds of police officers, months of court time, and the services of numerous other public officials and agencies have been necessary to handle the problems emanating from the Berkeley Campus. The total cost of these services has amounted to thousands of dollars over the past two years (see Appendix B). In addition, the Berkeley situation has repeatedly required the diversion of manpower and resources, and has involved difficulties in operation, which has deprived the citizens of our community of essential governmental services which could otherwise be made available for their benefit.

It is naturally more costly when the full machinery of our law enforcement and legal system must be invoked to handle Campus situations, which could be better, more easily, and less expensively controlled by the disciplinary powers available to the Regents and Administration of the University. Nevertheless, when this disciplinary authority is not fully utilized, or when Campus officials are unwilling or unable to handle the situation, local government has a responsibility to preserve order. It is for this reason that the University must fully carry out its reponsibilities, so that the extraordinary burden on local government and the taxpayers, which has been experienced by this County during the past two years, can be eliminated.

Recommendations

1. The University Administration should consistently and firmly enforce all University regulations, should take appropriate disciplinary measures whenever rules are violated, and should fully carry out its responsibility for the maintenance of law and order on the Campus.

2. The University Administration should promulgate and enforce clear directives forbidding the use of University facilities for unlawful off-campus action.

3. The University Administration should diligently enforce its own regulations which limit the use of Campus facilities to students, faculty and staff for purposes which are related to the educational function of the University.

4. The University should extend full cooperation to local authorities in the investigation and/or prosecution of criminal cases which originate on the Campus.

5. The State Legislature and the Regents of the University should provide for the reimbursement of county and city government when conditions on or related to the University Campus require extraordinary law enforcement or other local governmental services.

6. The State Legislature, with the cooperation of the Regents, should enact new legislation to improve University control over outsiders coming on and/or using University property and facilities for purposes unrelated to the educational goals and functions of the University.

    In order that the taxpayers of Alameda County may be protected, that the facilities of the University may be preserved for the fulfillment of its educational objectives, and that these recommendations may be evaluated for implementation, copies of this document are being forwarded to the Governor of California; the President, the Chancellor at Berkeley, and the members of the Board of Regents of the University of California; the Board of Supervisors of Alameda County; and the members of the Alameda County delegation to the California State Legislature.

Respectfully submitted,

1965 GRAND JURY OF ALAMEDA COUNTY

Henry A. Bruno, Foreman

Appendix A

University Facilities Granted to Vietnam Day Committee

Permission was granted to the "Vietnam Day Committee" to use the following facilities of the Berkeley Campus of the University of California during the months of September, October, and November, 1965.

Date	Time	Facilities
Sept. 15	12-1 p.m.	Sproul Steps
Sept. 16	7:30 p.m. on	30 Wheeler
Sept. 18	7-10 p.m.	155 Dwinelle
Sept. 20	12-1 p.m.	Sproul Steps
Sept. 21	4-6 p.m.	2000 Life Science Bldg., (LSB)
Sept. 22	7:20-10:30 p.m.	4093 LSB
Sept. 23	7:30 p.m. on	30 Wheeler
Sept. 28	7:30-10 p.m.	204 Engineering
Sept. 29	12-1 p.m. 9:30-10 p.m. 7:30-10:30 p.m.	Sproul Steps 15 Dwinelle 4093 LSB
Sept. 30	7:30 p.m. on 4-12 p.m.	30 Wheeler Wheeler Auditorium
Oct. 2	No time listed	Wheeler Auditorium
Oct. 3	12-4 p.m. 7:30-10:30 p.m.	155 Dwinelle 145 Dwinelle

Date	Time	Facilities
Oct. 5	7 p.m. on	204 Engineering
Oct. 6	7:30-10:30 p.m.	4093 LSB
Oct. 7	7:30 p.m. on	30 Wheeler
Oct. 8	4-6 p.m.	155 Dwinelle
Oct. 9	12-3 p.m.	11 Wheeler
Oct. 11	4-6 p.m.	2000 LSB
Oct. 12	4-6 p.m. 7-11 p.m.	2000 LSB 204 Engineering
Oct. 13	12-1 p.m. 3-6 p.m. 3:15-5 p.m. 4-6 p.m. 7:30-10:30 p.m. 7:30-11:00 p.m.	Sproul Steps Wheeler Auditorium 2003 LSB 2000 LSB 4093 LSB 204 Engineering
Oct. 14	4-6 p.m. 7-10 p.m. 7:30 p.m. on	2000 LSB 11 Wheeler 30 Wheeler
Oct. 15	8 a.m. to 8 p.m. 2-8 p.m. 2-8 p.m. 5-7 p.m. 6-7 p.m.	Lower Student Union Plaza Wheeler Auditorium 145 Dwinelle Sproul Steps 126 Barrows 110 Wheeler 104 Cal Hall 106 Cal Hall 4093 LSB 4505 LSB 308 LeConte
Oct. 16	11-3 p.m.	Wheeler, Rooms 30, 100, 110, 120, 200, 210
Oct. 20	No time listed	Sproul Steps
Oct. 21	7:30 p.m. on	30 Wheeler
Oct. 19	7-10 p.m.	204 Engineering
Oct. 26	3-5:30 p.m.	106 Calif. Hall
Nov. 4	2:30-5 p.m. 7:30-10 p.m.	120 Wheeler 101 Wheeler
Nov. 11	2:30-5 p.m. 7:30-10 p.m.	120 Wheeler 101 Wheeler

Date	Time	Facilities
Nov. 16	12-1 p. m.	Sproul Steps
Nov. 18	2:30-5 p. m.	120 Wheeler
	7:30-10 p. m.	101 Wheeler
Nov. 19	6 p. m. -12	145 Dwinelle
Nov. 20	9-10 a. m.	Sproul Steps

NOTE: In addition to the above facilities, the Vietnam Day Committee was granted the use of the following facilities on November 21, all day from 9 a. m. to 5 p. m. for the "West Coast Regional Conference of the Committees Against the War in Vietnam": Wheeler Auditorium, Rooms 20, 24, 102, 103, 104, 121, 122, and 123 Wheeler Hall.

Appendix B

Cost to Local Government

The following reports from governmental agencies in Alameda County reflect a partial summary of the extraordinary expenses which have been required of city and county government as a result of activities related to the Berkeley Campus of the University of California.

Alameda County Sheriff's Department

The following are the man hours and cost for the Sheriff's Department in connection with the "Free Speech Movement" (FSM) and the Vietnam Day Committee (VDC) demonstrations:

October, 1964 (FSM)	914 hours	$ 3,628.60
December, 1964 (FSM)	3673	14,405.31
October 15-16, 1965 (VDC)	3875	16,235.17
November 20, 1965 (VDC)	2126	8,905.12
		$ 43,174.20

The above figures do not include two groups of fifty men each, which were dispatched during August 1965 to support and assist the police departments of Berkeley and Emeryville during VDC demonstrations against troop trains. In addition to the costs set forth above, numerous key personnel of the Sheriff's Department were forced to devote their

working time to matters related to the above events before
and after the actual incidents, and a great number of personnel were involved for over two months in the court trials of
the FSM defendants.   During the incidents enumerated herein,
the entire Sheriff's Department was placed on a twelve-hour
shift basis in order to handle the regular crime-suppression,
patrol and custodial functions, as well as to police the emergency incidents discussed above.

Berkeley Police Department

During the period October 1964-January 1965, expenses
involved in the handling of "Free Speech Movement" demonstrations on the Berkeley Campus amounted to $9,722.54.
This includes only direct costs and does not cover the expense of officers appearing in court as witnesses, trial preparation, or other miscellaneous or indirect costs incurred by
the City of Berkeley.

During the period from May to December 1965, protest activities of the VDC required the mobilization of off duty
police officers on thirteen separate occasions at considerable
overtime cost to the City, as the chart shown below indicates:

Date	Incident	Hrs. of Overtime	Cost	Misc. Cost
May 21, 22	Vietnam Protest Teach-in & March	202	$ 950.00	
August	Troop Train Dem- onstrations	596	2,755.00	
Oct. 15, 16	Vietnam Protest Marches (2)	1085	5,093.00	$ 452.00
Nov. 20	Vietnam Protest March	719	3,441.00	997.00
Total cost		2602	$12,239.00	$1449.00

Total cost of policing VDC activities: $13,668.00. This
does not include the loss incurred because of the injury and
5-month period of recuperation of a Sergeant injured during
the October 16 demonstration.

Oakland Police Department

The following salary costs are reported by the Oakland

Police Department. These figures do not include logistical or miscellaneous expenses.

Date	Location	Man Hours	Salary Cost
2 Oct 64	Univ. of Calif. (FSM)	1125	$ 4,927.50
3 Dec 64	Univ. of Calif. (FSM)	1999	8,755.26
12 Aug 65	34th & Wood (Troop Trains-VDC)	90	406.49
15 Oct 65	Oakland Army Base, etc. (VDC)	5104	23,325.00
20 Nov 65	Oakland Army Base, etc. (VDC)	4851	22,046.94
	DeFremery Park, etc. (VDC)	4779.5	21,248.50
			$80,711.87

NOTE: The City of Oakland was partially reimbursed by the University of California, in the amount of $4580.78, for expenses incurred on 2 Oct 64.

Municipal Court

        The Municipal Court for the Berkeley-Albany Judicial District reports that extraordinary costs directly chargeable to the trial of FSM defendants amounted to $28,096.75 for the twelve-month period ending December, 1965. This does not include the salaries of regular personnel of the Court, including the Judge, whose efforts were redirected to the handling of this case, nor does it include overtime for regular employees or the cost of utilizing an additional court room, additional cost for marshals, or other expenses which were provided out of the regular Court budget or the budgets of other County departments.

Other Expenses

        The expense summaries set forth above do not include a number of additional costs to County government. Personnel and miscellaneous costs incurred by the District Attorney's Office and the Alameda County Probation Department, as well as the costs of other Courts in the County, are not reflected above.

        Considerable expense was also incurred by the State of California and the Federal Government because of the mobilization of large numbers of California Highway Patrol-

men, National Guardsmen, and military personnel required
by various incidents described in this report.

(Collected in Oakland, California on March 18, 1966.)

38. WE DEMAND FREEDOM FOR G.I.s

The three soldiers who refused to fight in Vietnam were jailed and held incommunicado, on their way to speak at an anti-war demonstration. The three privates, Mora, Samas, and Johnson, refused to fight in Vietnam on the grounds that it is illegal, immoral, and unjust. They hope that their action, as well as the suit that they have instituted against McNamara, will free others who feel the same way about the war from being forced to commit murder in Vietnam.

Stokely Carmichael for SNCC, Floyd McKissick for CORE, A. J. Muste, Staughton Lynd and Dave Dellinger of the Fifth Avenue Committee have pledged their support. Pledge your support to these brave soldiers who may be the first of many to take a stand against the war.

DEMONSTRATE

OAKLAND INDUCTION CENTER

FRIDAY, JULY 15

Picket: 10 AM to 5 PM, 1515 Clay St. (5th & Clay), Oakland
Rally at 5 PM, Lafayette Sq. (12th & Jefferson), Oakland

WE NEED YOUR HELP

To continue our efforts against the war in Vietnam and to aid the three soldiers in their courageous struggle, we need your financial support. Please send contributions to Steve Meisenbach, c/o August 6-9 Committee, 2001 Milvia, Berkeley, California. Thank you.

AUGUST 6-9 COMMITTEE MEETING

A general meeting of the August 6-9th Committee for the International Days of Protest will take place at 8:00 PM on Thursday July 14 at LeConte School Auditorium, Ells-

150

worth and Russell. Committee meetings will start at 7:00
PM. All are welcome. Further info. at 845-9159.

AUGUST 6-9th COMMITTEE

(Collected July 15, 1966 at the University of California at
Berkeley.)

G.I.'s ARRESTED
FOR OPPOSING THE WAR

Three G.I.'s formerly stationed at Fort Hood, Texas,
and on leave in New York City were arrested July 7 just one
half hour before they were to speak to a public meeting to
explain legal proceedings which they have instituted against
the Vietnam war, which they consider "illegal, immoral and
unjust." They were taken, two of them in handcuffs, to Fort
Dix, New Jersey, where they are being held under tight restrictions.

The three are PFC James Johnson, 20, Pvt. Dennis
Mora, 25, and Pvt. David Samas, 20. They were drafted
into the Army last December, took basic training at Fort
Hood and signal training at Fort Gordon, Georgia. They became friends in training and found that they all felt the war
in Vietnam was wrong.

Ordered to Vietnam

They completed the signal school and were assigned to
the 142nd Signal Battalion, 2nd Armored Division, Fort Hood,
Texas. There they found they were under orders to go to
Vietnam.

"Now all we had discussed and thought about was real.
It was time for us to quit talking and decide. Go to Vietnam and ignore the truth or stand and fight for what we know
is right."

They were given 30-day leaves before reporting to Oakland Army Terminal in California for shipment to Vietnam. They decided not to go to Vietnam and to make a legal case of it. They went to New York and contacted an Attorney to seek an injunction in Federal Court based on the illegality of the war. They contacted the Fifth Avenue Vietnam Peace Parade Committee and asked for help.

On June 30 they held a news conference and announced that they were filing the injunction, that they would report for the Oakland Army Terminal as ordered when their leave was up July 13, but that they would not go to Vietnam.

They Said:

"We have been told that many times we may face a Vietnamese woman or child and that we will have to kill them. We will never go there--to do that--for Ky!... We have made our decision. We will not be a part of this unjust, immoral and illegal war. We want no part of a war of extermination. We oppose the criminal waste of American lives and resources. We refuse to go to Vietnam!"

Widespread Support

They have been supported in their stand by leaders of the civil rights groups and by the entire anti-war movement. Stokely Carmichael, Chairman of the Student Nonviolent Coordinating Committee (SNCC) and Lincoln Lynch, associate national director of Congress on Racial Equality (CORE) appeared with them at the press conference to give the support of their organizations.

Master Sergeant Don Duncan, who spent 18 months in the Special Forces in Vietnam, then refused a commission and quit the army because he had become convinced the war was wrong, sent a message of support saying: "Your actions, if properly motivated, take a strength greater than that required to go to Vietnam. To persevere will be an act of personal bravery far beyond the capabilities of most of us, certainly far beyond anything I have ever done."

A committee to aid the three soldiers in their case was formed called the Fort Hood Three Defense Committee, with prominent people across the country as sponsors.

After their announcement, though they were still on leave, attempts were made to intimidate them and even to bribe them to drop the case. Pvt. Samas's parents were contacted by police and told that if their son would drop the case, he would be given an Army discharge. Then, only 30 minutes before they were to speak on their case before a public meeting, they were arrested.

Floyd B. McKissick, national director of CORE, declared that the arrests "were made explicitly to prevent these young men from exercising their First Amendment right to freedom of speech and were reminiscent of 'police state tactics.' Recently in Baltimore at its National Convention, CORE went on record as being opposed to the Vietnam war and pledged to aid and support those who would not serve in Vietnam."

Telegram

The Fifth Avenue Vietnam Peace Parade Committee sent a telegram to the U.S. Attorney General and the Secretary of Defense saying: "The peace movement will continue to aid in every possible lawful way anyone, civilian, soldier, sailor or Marine, who opposes this illegal, immoral war. The young men in the armed services are entitled to know the truth about the war and to engage in discussions about it. Citizens are likewise entitled to communicate the truth about the war which they consider immoral and unjust.

The anti-war movement, with hundreds of thousands of active participants across the country is backing the three soldiers now being held at Fort Dix. We defend their right to free speech, their right to their day in court, and their right not to participate in a war which they consider immoral and unjust.

The Three Soldiers Involved Are:

PFC James Johnson, 20. Born in East Harlem. Graduated from Rice Parochial High school. Attended Bronx Community College for a year before being drafted. He is Negro.

Pvt. Dennis Mora, 25. Born in Spanish Harlem. Attended Bronx High School of Science. Graduated from CCNY with a B.A. in History. A case worker for the New York City Department of Welfare until being drafted. He is Puerto Rican.

Pvt. David Samas, 20. Born in Chicago. Was attending Modesto Junior College in California when drafted. Married this June. Of Italian, Lithuanian background.

For further information contact The August 6-9 Committee, 2001 Milvia, Berkeley

telephone 845-9159

Send contributions, with checks payable to A. J. Muste, to Soldiers Defense Fund, the above address.

(Collected August 1, 1966 at the University of California at Berkeley.)

39. PICKET PRESIDENT JOHNSON

President Johnson is coming to San Francisco on June 25 and 26 to speak at a commemoration of the 20th anniversary of the United Nations. Yet our government's actions in Vietnam and the Dominican Republic have served to undermine the United Nations.

The mandate for peace that President Johnson received from the American people has been betrayed. He is following Goldwater's policies of escalation, brinksmanship and gunboat diplomacy.

WE DEMAND:

END THE WAR IN VIETNAM NOW

The Vietnam Day Committee Is Organizing Demonstrations to Take Place on June 25 and 26:

Come at 7:00 p.m. Friday, June 25th to picket Johnson Directly in front of the Fairmont Hotel, San Francisco.

Come at 8:00 a.m. Saturday, June 26th to picket Johnson at the S. F. War Memorial Opera House on Van Ness between Grove and McAllister, S. F.

At 1:00 p.m. we will hold our own commemoration of the United Nations in the Civic Center across the street from City Hall. We are inviting representatives from various countries to address our meeting.

If you wish to help or want further information, phone Jerry Rubin at 845-6637.

Send contributions to: Vietnam Day Committee, c/o Prof. S. Smale, Box 2201, Berkeley, California.

(Collected August 21, 1965 in Berkeley, California.)

40.   PRESS RELEASE FROM THE
       VIETNAM DAY COMMITTEE

        The Vietnam Day Committee, which sponsored the re-
cent 36-hour protest teach-in on the University of California
campus, a meeting which drew upwards of 35,000 people, is
sponsoring protest demonstrations against the appearance of
Pres. Lyndon Johnson at the 20th commemoration of the UN
in San Francisco June 26.

        The Committee believes that it is sheer hypocrisy for
Johnson to commemorate the UN when his administration is
doing so much to destroy that organization in Vietnam and the
landing of U.S. troops in the Dominican Republic--acts of aggression in violation of the UN charter.   In Vietnam the
Johnson administration acts in violation of the Geneva treaty.
In addition to all this, it is the US which is largely responsible for keeping China out of the UN in spite of the fact
that many of the outstanding political problems of the world
require the participation of China in a settlement.   In view
of all these actions, how can Lyndon Baines Johnson commemorate the UN?

        We urge the people of the Bay Area to protest hypoc-
risy and aggression.   We urge Lyndon Johnson to refrain
from coming to San Francisco for the 20th commemoration
of the U.N.

        If Johnson comes, let the American people who pro-
test war and big-bullyism turn out to demonstrate that LBJ
does not represent us.   Let the world's press see how deeply we protest Johnson's war policies.   We know that the city
of San Francisco is investing a lot of money and effort in
this 20th commemoration and that city officials hope that the
meeting will be held without any disruption from dissenters.
But the Vietnam Day Committee believes that LBJ's appearance in the U.N. on the commemoration meeting is an insult
to those of us who believe in the U.N. as a force for peace.

        The Vietnam Day Committee has written to Chief of
Police Thomas Cahill informing him that we plan to picket

LBJ Friday night, June 25 at the Fairmont Hotel and Sat. morning, June 26, at the War Memorial Opera House. In view of the growing opposition to the war in Vietnam, we expect 3000 to 5000 people marching on our lines. We expect to be able to exercise our rights as citizens and to peacefully picket the President. We plan to picket directly in front of the Fairmont Hotel on Friday night and directly in front of the Opera House on Sat. morning. We will probably be meeting with Chief Cahill soon.

In addition, after LBJ speaks on Sat. we will hold our own commemoration of the UN in the Civic Center directly opposite City Hall. We have invited representatives from more than 45 countries, ranging from France to Tanzania ... in addition to other noted speakers. From Johnson we can expect homilies and pieties. Perhaps his advisers will caution him against repeating his schoolboy's orations about his country's flag in foreign soil. Our meeting will truly commemorate the U.N. We hope that representatives in the U.N. will take advantage of this opportunity to speak directly to the American people.

On the question of civil disobedience, the Vietnam Day Comm. announces that it has no plans at this time for civil disobedience but that it is considering all forms of nonviolent action.

The peace movement is growing in the U.S. as more and more people become disenchanted with the fact that while they may have voted for Johnson, the policy they receive is Goldwater's. The Vietnam Day Committee is receiving support from many groups for its June 25-26 demonstrations. We invite the citizens of the Bay Area to attend our commemoration of the U.N. at noon on June 26 in Civic Center. Lyndon Baines Johnson has forfeited any right to speak or act for us; nor can he represent us at the U.N. On June 25 and 26 we will demonstrate how we feel.

Morris Hirsch, Professor of Mathematics UC Steering Comm.
    VDC
Paul E. Ivory, Acting Asst. Prof. of Economics UC Acting
    Co-Chairman VDC
Jerry Rubin, Co-Chairman, VDC

REPLY TO PROFESSOR SCALAPINO

Professor Scalapino, in slandering the organizers and speakers of Vietnam Day, to be held Friday and Saturday on the Berkeley Campus, has confused the purpose of the meeting to such an extent that one must consider it deliberate.

The purpose of Vietnam Day is to present to the Bay Area Community alternatives to current U.S. policy. The information and ideas that will be related on these days cannot be found in the mass media, the State Department white paper, or even in university classrooms. We are contributing to democratic dialogue by expressing the views which, although widespread in Asia and Europe, are rarely presented to American people. Professor Scalapino calls such objectivity "propaganda."

Professor Scalapino has implied that the only people who are qualified to discuss Vietnam in public are academic or State Department experts on Vietnam. We do have such technical experts on the program: Professor Stanley Sheinbaum, who designed the strategic hamlet program for the Government, but now regrets it, is one example. But to restrict public discussion to "experts" leads to a dangerous elitism because in the end decisions on foreign policy are based on value judgments, not on just simple recording of facts. The issues in Vietnam are too important to be settled by cold war gamesmanship or academic hairsplitting. One of the purposes of Vietnam Day is to transfer the discussion from the Rand Corporation to the streets.

But more important than this, the problem of Vietnam is the problem of the soul of America. What the State Department is doing in our name in Vietnam is tied directly to Alabama, the Dominican Republic, the state of freedom of the press of America, and the scope of our literature. We think that people like Bob Parris of the Student Nonviolent Coordinating Committee, Norman Mailer and Dr. Benjamin Spock have much to say that is relevant to Vietnam.

Professor Scalapino makes much of the fact that we have included entertainers in the program. Had he bothered, he would have counted less than three hours of entertainment scattered throughout the main program. He conveniently juxtaposes speakers and entertainers and calls them all "performers." Which of our speakers does Professor Scala-

pino consider entertainers or performers?   Senator Gruening?
Isaac Deutscher, world-renowned writer on the Soviet Union?
Bertrand Russell?   Ruben Brache, the representative of the
Dominican rebels in the United States?   Professor Marvin,
Chairman of the International Relations Department, San
Francisco State College?   Bui Van Anh, Counselor of the
Vietnamese Embassy in Washington?

We offered Professor Scalapino and Professor Burdick,
who attacked us yesterday, as much time as they wanted at
any hour.   If they fear the public will be misinformed, they
do the public a great disservice by attacking the meeting instead of participating in it as others who support the State
Department are doing.

They refuse to take part because they fear four aspects of the meeting:

1.   Vietnam Day is giving a platform to intellectuals who
     are not favored by the State Department as Professor
     Scalapino is, but who, nevertheless, have much to say
     about Vietnam: people like Robert Scheer, Professor
     Staughton Lynd, Dave Dellinger, M. S. Arnoni, Edward
     Keating, and Felix Greene.
2.   The meeting goes beyond the narrow definition of aca-
     demic expert and challenges the authority of Professors
     Scalapino and Burdick.
3.   The meeting will spread some dangerous ideas to masses
     of people.
4.   The protest movement against the war is successful and
     is spreading.

One week the State Department, well aware of the nature of the program, promises to send speakers.   The next
week they back out, giving as an excuse, "lack of balance,"
Professors Scalapino and Burdick and the State Department
afraid to take the best time in our program and face an audience which has just heard fresh and unconventional ideas on
Vietnam?   Are they afraid that in this atmosphere their
cliches, apologies, and academic excuses for injustice will be
exposed?

                              Professor Morris Hirsch
                              Professor Stephen Smale
                              Jerry Rubin

(Collected June 4, 1965 at the University of California at
Berkeley.)

41. MEDICAL AID COMMITTEE

Everyday the people of Vietnam are being killed, wounded, their homes devastated by the weapons of modern war. Intensive attacks using steel fragmentation bombs, napalm and toxic chemicals sprayed from the air have been used, often indiscriminately on the civilian population. While this unjust, cruel war continues, it is the people of Vietnam who suffer most. Since 1957, well over 300,000 have been killed and 400,000 injured or tortured. It is these innocent people living in the villages who need your help.

On November 6, the San Francisco Chronicle reported that Pope Paul donated $50,000 to the victims of the war in both North and South Vietnam. He made an appeal for others to follow suit.

There is a desperate need to send medical supplies which will help to save lives. Medical equipment and drugs of all kinds are needed, especially antibiotics and antiseptics. Even the simplest equipment for first aid posts such as forceps, scissors, needles and sutures are desperately needed in addition to amputation saws and blood plasma. Money can buy these supplies. The people of Vietnam need your help!

The Medical Aid Committee will send all contributions to the International Red Cross in Geneva, Switzerland, which has already agreed to deliver the aid to victims of the war in North Vietnam and civilian controlled areas of South Vietnam. This guarantees the greatest possible efficiency.

In North Vietnam our help takes the form of medical supplies handed over to the North Vietnamese Red Cross in Hanoi.

The National Liberation Front of South Vietnam is supplied with medical and surgical supplies through its representatives.

160

Money handed over to us will be used for the purchase of relief goods and medical supplies according to the wishes of the donors.

(This is an excerpt from a letter received by the Medical Aid Committee from the International Red Cross in Geneva, dated October 15, 1965.)

By contributing to the Committee the American people will be able to render immediate relief to those who are innocently suffering as a consequence of the U.S. Government intervention and military actions.

Medical aid being collected and sent to the victims of our government's foreign policy is a dramatic protest that has a concrete effect ... they need the bandages and blood!

Need it be added that when men, women and children lie hurt and bleeding, the political views of the victims are as irrelevant as those of the Good Samaritan.

--Senator Robert F. Kennedy
S.F. Chronicle, Nov. 6

"If it's a blanket question, yes, I would give my blood to North Vietnam. I think that would be in the oldest tradition of this country."

I am enclosing _____ as a donation for the Medical Aid Committee for Vietnam.

NAME_____

ADDRESS_____

Medical Aid Committee
P.O. Box 1128
Berkeley, California

If you wish to be on our mailing list, please enclose this form.

(Collected January 3, 1965 in Berkeley, California.)

42. PEACE ON EARTH

"I have never talked or corresponded with a person knowl-edgeable in Indochinese affairs who did not agree that had elections been held at the time of the fighting (1954), pos-sibly 80% of the population would have voted for the Commu-nist Ho Chi Minh as their leader."

> -Dwight D. Eisenhower,
> in his book <u>Mandate for Change</u>,
> p. 372

The United States is fighting against the people of Vietnam. WHY?

"People ask me who my heroes are.   I have only one--Hitler."

> -Saigon Premier Nguyen Cao Ky

Wouldn't it be better to let the Vietnamese people decide for themselves what form of government they want--even if it's communist--and stop this needless killing of Vietnamese peasants and American G.I.s??

As Hell is war and war is Hell
Against your officers, unite!
I enjoin you, soldiers, to rebel
And proclaim, "We shall not fight!"

A vision to me there came one night
More horrendous than any dream.
Before my eyes the ghastly sight!
Grotesque bodies, the piercing scream
Of a woman with her baby dead
In her arms.   Decapitated men I saw,
And over the land a flood of red,
Mounds of bodies, the havoc of war.

"Who wrecks this curse upon the land?
What is the hideous sight?"

I looked to God to understand
And answer came by morning's light.

Who are the guilty? You and I.
For we drop bombs from the sky
On Viet Nam's soil far away.
"This is for their good," we say.

But most culpable of all
Are those who slaughter with their guns,
And those who cause the bombs to fall,
Our soldiers, they, the guilty ones.

So to you now, I make this plea:
"Refuse to kill, refuse to die,
Throw down your arms; unite with me,
Defy the draft and join the cry!
As Hell is war and war is Hell
Against your officers, unite!
I enjoin you, soldiers, to rebel
And proclaim, 'We shall not fight.' "

America! How can you be
Again what you were once to me?
Great foundations in history laid,
Ideals of freedom, just laws made.
Principles of a great nation:
Liberty and toleration.

A land of freedom, you expressed
The right of people to protest
Views which were not their own.
Freedom for people to dissent
From the views of the government,
To make their feelings known.

And now abroad a war you wage,
Felt by some to be an outrage.
But even while you force your hand
Overseas, on domestic land,
A greater danger lies.

Your people filled with fear and hate
For Communists, they now equate
Pacifism with treachery.
America! How can you be?
Again, what you were once to me?

My country, I grieve at your fate,
When you no longer tolerate
Thoughtful men who feel otherwise
Than you; they fear to criticize
Their Divine Nation's policy.

(Collected October 17, 1966 at Stanford University.)

43. AN OPEN LETTER TO ALL PERSONNEL IN VIET NAM

One year ago, I was stationed in Bien Hoa. When I was there I became very bitter at the hullabaloo going on in the States about the Viet Nam situation. I felt that I had something to say to the college students, but had no way to. Well, I am enrolled at the University of California now. A fellow journalist, John Maybury, and myself have formed a program by which you can say something to the students, to the citizens of America. We know you have many things to say and we want to hear them. Your comments will be published exactly as you write them. We are tired of repressed news, distorted views, and administrative hogwash; you are the ones there, and you can have an honest voice. Please write, send photographs, or see about our questionnaire. I personally want you to have a voice.

> James Grantham
> Student, University of Calif.
> Former airman at Bien Hoa
> 839 #D Embarcadero del Norte
> Goleta, California 93017

Working with:
  John Maybury
  EL GAUCHO, Student Newspaper
  University of California,
    Santa Barbara

TO ALL PERSONNEL IN VIET NAM:

Perhaps you are aware of the great controversy in the States about the situation in Viet Nam. We, here in the States, hear only journalistic editorial comments and are given inaccurate views. This has led (as you know) to big anti-war demonstrations here and especially in the University of California. Well, now is your chance--we want to hear from you! Please write anything you wish on your views and send them to James Grantham, 839 #D Embarcadero del Norte, Goleta, California 93017. Your views and comments will be published exactly as you write them.

165

Now you can have a voice!

1. Name _____

2. Age _____   3. Rank _____

4. Branch of Service _____

5. Where stationed _____

6. Hometown _____

(Answer Yes or No or explain if you wish)

7. Do you regret U.S. involvement in Viet Nam?

8. How do you think the South Vietnamese feel about U.S. involvement in the war?

9. How do you feel the war is going?

10. Do you think U.S. forces are being used effectively?

11. What is life like where you are? Explain your duties, schedules, conditions: Free time, clothes, food, travel-- anything like that.

12. Is there any problem with political investigators and VIP's from Stateside?

13. Do you favor escalation of the war?

14. Which seems more effective--infantry or bombers?

15. How do you feel about college students demonstrating against the war in Viet Nam? What can college students at home do to help you?

16. How is the news you get, your communication links? Do you have any comments or complaints about Stars and Stripes, for instance?

17. What do you think of the USO shows? Of entertainment in general where you are located?

18. Do you have any special gripes?

19. What general concluding comments would you like to
      make to college students and all others here at home?

By no means feel restricted to this page.   The more the bet-
ter--use the margins, the back, and other sheets if you desire.   Also include photos--anything publishable.

(Collected at the University of California at Los Angeles on
July 17, 1965)

44. "YOU DON'T BELIEVE IN WAR, BUT WHAT'S THAT GUN YOU'RE TOTIN'?"

What if you're <u>against war</u>? or the fighting in Vietnam? The <u>law</u> says you <u>may be eligible</u> to become a CONSCIENTIOUS OBJECTOR (Selective Service Classification 1-A-O or 1-O). A "Conscientious Objector" or "C.O." is a man who says "my conscience or my belief tells me it's wrong to kill, it's wrong to bomb or shoot and destroy people. I won't do it. Instead, I'll do 'alternative service' like the work done in poor communities on development, teaching or organization, that's good for the country, and other people."

WHO CAN FILE?

The law may not cover everybody who's against the war. It says a man can be a C.O. "who by reason of religious training and belief, is conscientiously opposed to war in any form." A lot more men fit this description than you may think right off, especially after recent court cases broadening the "religion" clause. You're certainly not limited to formal religion. You may think of yourself as agnostic or an atheist. Thinking about religion has changed; one famous theologian, Paul Tillich, says, in effect, that religion is "ultimate concern," a measure of intensity, and that you may be considered "religious" without knowing it. Court cases have broadened the definition of religion so that it may include agnostics and humanists.

No one knows who will get C.O. status from his draft board and who won't. Even though the law may not cover everybody, <u>any man can file</u> Form 150 (Special Form for C.O.'s) asking to be a C.O. If you are conscientiously against war--

    --you may want to file for C.O. because you think you qualify clearly under the law;

    --you may want to file for C.O. even if you're not sure you come under the law; but you want to ex-

press your beliefs honestly and let your draft board
decide;

--you may want to file for C.O. to tell your draft
board and everybody else that you're against the
war;

--you may want to file for C.O. to try to get the government to broaden the law to cover all men who
don't want to kill people; this would take an Act of
Congress or a Supreme Court decision.

TO FIND OUT IF YOU'RE LIKELY TO QUALIFY AS A C.O.,
TALK WITH SOMEONE WHO HAS HAD EXPERIENCE IN
COUNSELING MEN FOR CONSCIENTIOUS OBJECTION:
YOUR OWN MINISTER WILL PROBABLY BE ABLE TO AS-
SIST YOU.

(Collected at the University of Washington at Seattle on May
22, 1967.)

45. FOR INFORMATIONAL PURPOSES:
1971 SPRING ACTION CALENDAR

PEOPLES PEACE TREATY--The American and Vietnamese
people are not enemies. The war is carried out in the name
of the people of the United States but without our consent.
The conditions to end the war are clear and acceptable to the
majority of Americans but not acted upon by the government.
The Peoples Peace Treaty will help mobilize the majority
opinion for peace now, and provide a basis for building powerful, diverse mass action to force the government to end the
war.

March 8--INTERNATIONAL WOMENS DAY

April 1-4--TRIBUTE IN ACTION TO MARTIN LUTHER KING,
      JR.

Theme--"Freedom from Hunger, War and Oppression."

Nationwide Local Activities such as Hunger Marches to dra-
matize hunger for housing, hunger for jobs, and for peace.
Fasts: Teach-ins and other special programs in schools on
April 2. Tax Protest and Resistance Activities on a com-
munity level relating to reordering priorities: Rallies on
April 3. Religious Tributes to Martin Luther King on Sunday,
April 4. April to May people will be urged to live on the
welfare food budget (Money collected from Hunger Marches.
Fasts and Rallies will be divided among local and national
welfare, poverty action, and community groups, and the
Peoples Coalition for Peace and Justice)

May 2--MASSIVE ASSEMBLY IN WASHINGTON, D.C.--de-
manding:
1. Immediate withdrawal of all U.S. military air, land, and
sea forces from Vietnam, and that the U.S. set the date now
for completion of withdrawal.
2. $5500.00 Guaranteed Annual Income for family of four--
set the date.
3. Free all political prisoners--set the date.
The May 2 Massive Assembly begins a period of sustained

nonviolent struggle in Washington and nationwide.
May 3--Peoples Lobby at Congress, government agencies and
other appropriate locations focused on Demands for Social
Justice.

May 4--Peoples Lobby at Congress, government agencies and
other locations focused on Militarism.

The Peoples Lobby on May 3 and 4 will carry on urgent dialogue with government employees as well as officers of the
government departments and Congress to demand support for
the Peoples Peace Treaty and the three demands put forward
in the Massive Assembly on Sunday. Government workers
will be urged to stop business as usual on May 5.

May 5--Nationwide Moratorium on Business as usual
Washington, D.C.:
--Early morning: leafleting and nonviolent picketing at government buildings & other locations urging employees to stop
business as usual and to join us
--12 noon: assembly for March to the Capitol to begin sustained nonviolent action at the Capitol and other locations.
The Washington Scenario might serve as a model for activities in other cities beginning the first week in May.

May 16--ACTIONS IN SOLIDARITY WITH G.I.s

Note: The National Peace Action Coalition has called for a
massive legal assembly for April 24 in Washington and San
Francisco. The Peoples Coalition is holding discussions with
NPAC in the hope that a joint call for the massive assembly
on May 2 in Washington can be issued.

PEOPLES COALITION for Peace and Justice--1029 Vermont
Avenue, N.W. (Room 900) Washington, D.C. 20005
Phone (202) 737-8600

(Collected at Roosevelt University, Chicago, February 15,
1971.)

46. NATIONAL PEACE ACTION COALITION

8th Floor
1029 Vermont Avenue N. W.
Washington, D. C. 20006

April 29, 1971

Dear Friend:

We believe that April 24 will prove to be a turning point in the fight to end the Indochina war. It was the biggest demonstration in American history. In Washington, more than half a million people jammed the staging area, the march routes down Pennsylvania and Constitution Avenues and the huge rally site in front of the Capitol. Additional thousands simply couldn't get into the city. The Washington police report that charter buses were backed up on the highway 12 miles into Maryland.

The antiwar rally on the steps of the Capitol was an historic first and the message was broadcast across the nation and, indeed, around the globe. It came through loud and clear: OUT NOW!

In San Francisco, the crowd estimate ranged between 300,000 and 400,000, the largest ever in that city.

But while we're convinced that we struck a powerful blow for peace, we also understand that the fight is far from over, and we're determined not to rest until we achieve our declared goal, the withdrawal of all U.S. forces from Indochina.

Our next major action will be May 5, the Moratorium commemorating the Cambodian invasion and the killings at Jackson State College and Kent State University. The Student Mobilization Committee, along with the National Student Association and Association of Student Governments, are organizing a campus moratorium on business as usual. NPAC affiliates and other antiwar forces will be organizing the off-campus communities to join with the students in massive rallies

172

and other actions throughout the country to make May 5 one more powerful demonstration behind the demand, **OUT NOW!**

Then on May 15, we will be joining with GI and veteran groups in building GI Solidarity Day demonstrations at military bases across the country.

On the weekend of June 5-6 there will be workshops in New York, Detroit, and San Francisco for summer organizers who will then organize new peace action coalitions around the country.

Meanwhile, we will be mobilizing community sentiment to build pressure on Congress not to extend the draft which expires June 30.

All of these activities, and more, will lead toward our July 2-4 convention here in Washington. On the basis of the huge turnout April 24 and the broad new support that NPAC has consolidated, we are looking forward to the convention as the biggest, most representative yet held by the peace movement. There will be full discussion and debate and democratic decision making based on one person, one vote. Plans will be elaborated for a massive summer and fall program to end the war. ALL OF THIS MEANS THAT ONCE AGAIN WE MUST APPEAL TO YOU FOR FINANCIAL SUPPORT.

April 24 was an enormous undertaking and the breakthrough into the media came only after persistent, costly alternate forms of publicity--New York Times advertisements, broadside mailing, posters, bumper stickers, buttons, etc. We estimate that expenditures for April 24 exceeded $150,000. Unfortunately, our collection procedure did not run as smoothly as the rest of the demonstration, which puts us in a desperate financial situation. In order to ensure that our ongoing activities are not hampered by a burden of debts, we need $60,000 now.

We hope you will again be able to contribute generously. We do feel that our plans for the weeks and months ahead ensure that your contribution will be as sound an investment in the cause of peace as were those that made possible April 24.

Yours for Peace,

Ruth Gage-Colby   Jerry Gordon   Don Gurewitz   James Lafferty   John T. Williams

(NPAC Coordinators)

(Received from the National Peace Action Coalition on May 2, 1971.)

47. NATIONAL PEACE ACTION COALITION

2101 Euclid Avenue
Cleveland, Ohio 44115
Telephone (216) 621-6518

National Coordinators:

Ruth Gage-Colby
Women's International League for Peace and Freedom,
New York

Jerry Gordon
Cleveland Area Peace Action Council

Don Gurewitz
Student Mobilization Committee, New York

James Lafferty
Detroit Coalition to End the War Now

John T. Williams
V.P. Local 208, International Brotherhood of Teamsters,
Los Angeles

Organization affiliation for identification only.

November 27, 1970

TO: All Antiwar Activists
RE: National Convention of U.S.
Antiwar Movement, Chicago,
December 4-6.

Dear Friend,

The world is awaiting the response by the U.S. anti-war movement to Nixon's latest escalation of the fighting in Indochina. Laird's warning of total resumption of the bombing of North Vietnam, following the heavy bombing attacks of

175

November 20-21, coupled with the threat to mount new inva-
sions of North Vietnam following the raid of November 20,
should dispel any illusions that the war is winding down.

These blatant acts and expressions of military aggression by the Nixon Administration provide a compelling reason
for every antiwar activist to attend the National Convention
of the peace movement in Chicago on December 4-6. Obviously whatever action we are to take must be decided collectively and democratically. A convention opened to everyone in the antiwar movement is the ideal place to decide
where we go from here.

We strongly urge and warmly encourage you to attend
the convention. But in addition to attending, we hope you
will write out and circulate any proposal you may have for
future actions of the antiwar movement. It goes without saying that all who submit proposals will have the opportunity at
the convention to speak in their support and the decisions
will be made on the basis of majority vote.

Harold Gibbons, International Vice President of the
Teamsters Union; Pat Gorman, Secretary-Treasurer, Meatcutters Union; Carol Lipman, SMC West Coast leader; and
Attorney Stanley Tolliver, a leader in the Black liberation
and antiwar movements in Cleveland will keynote the convention.

Enclosed are materials relating to the convention.
Child care centers will be available so that parents may attend.

We look forward to seeing you in Chicago on December 4-6.

In peace,

Ruth Gage-Colby   Jerry Gordon   Don Gurewitz   Jim Lafferty

John T. Williams, NATIONAL COORDINATORS, NPAC

National Peace Action Coalition--Steering Committee 11/21/70

Vivian Abeles - Referendum '70, Boston
Katie Baird - Co-chairwoman, Cleveland Area Peace Action
      Council

Bill Banta - Co-chairman, October 31 Peace Action Committee, Chicago
Abe Bloom - Washington Area Peace Action Coalition, Washington, D.C.
Ernest Benjamin - Prof., Wayne State University, Detroit
Rick Brown - Strike Coordination Committee, Berkeley
Kay Camp - Pres. Women's International League for Peace and Freedom, Philadelphia
Orie Chambers - Chairman Black Caucus, Newark Teachers Union, Local 481
Bill Chaisson - New Jersey Libertarian Alliance
Chicago Medical Committee for Human Rights
Chicago Women's Liberation Union
Chicago Moratorium Committee, Los Angeles
Bill Cirone - Atlanta Peace Coalition
Vicki Cole - Augsburg College Republicans
Spec. 4 David Cortwright - Ft. Bliss GIs United
John Craig - Local P575 Amalgamated Meat Cutters & Butcher Workmen, Boston
Clara Demiha - Jeanette Rankin Rank and File, New York
Spec 4 Paul Dix - Ft. Hamilton GIs United
Marion Dockhorn - Philadelphia YMCA
Rev. Jonathan Ealy - United Pastors Association, Cleveland
Ozzie Edwards - Pres. National Federation of Social Service Employees
Robert Ferrera - Society for Individual Liberty, Philadelphia
Bob Ford - Seattle Mobe, Concerned Black Citizens of Tacoma
Ralph Fucetola - Radical Libertarian Alliance
Ruth Gage-Colby - Women's International League for Peace and Freedom, New York
Maurice Geary - American Federation of State, County and Municipal Employees, Local 50
Grady Glenn - Pres. Frame Unit Local 600, United Auto Workers, Dearborn
Jerry Gordon - Co-chairman, Cleveland Area Peace Action Council
Richard Gunn - Cleveland Lawyers Against the War
Don Gurewitz - Exec. Sec. Student Mobilization Committee, New York
Sandy Glassberg - Women's Liberation Center, Philadelphia
Fred Halstead - Socialist Workers Party
Ann S. Hampton - Program Director, Mid-City YWCA, Philadelphia
Monica Heilbrun - Military Wives for Peace
David Herreschoff - New University Conference, Detroit
Rachel Jacobs - Women's Liberation Union, Chicago

Ceil Keel - Atlanta Federation of Teachers
Stuart Kemp - Director National Council to Repeal the Draft,
     Washington
Cappy Kidd - Tampa Area Peace Action Coalition
Bruce Kimball - Columbus Peace Action Coalition
Ashley King - Neighbors for Peace, New York
Daren Kurth - Minnetonka Peace Action Coalition, Minn.
Abdeen Jabarah - Editor of Free Palestine
James Lafferty - Detroit Coalition to End the War Now
Shalom Lebowitz - Vets for Peace, Chicago
Norma Lengyel - Parents Plea for Peace, Modesto
Sidney Lens - Chicago trade unionist
Marilyn Levin - Coordinator, Greater Boston Peace Action
     Coalition
Carol Lipman - West Coast Coordinator, SMC
Jim Luggen - Peace, Power and People
Michael Lux - National Alliance of Postal and Federal Em-
     ployees
Herb Magidson - Individuals Against the Crime of Silence,
     Los Angeles
Sam Manuel - Black Student Union, Atlanta
Naomi Marcus - Womens International League for Peace and
     Freedom, Philadelphia
W. E. Mead - Pittsburgh Friends Meeting
Eileen Menotti - Women's Center, Los Angeles
Mark Michaels - Penn State Coalition for Peace
Joe Miles - Boston, formerly of GI's United, Ft. Bragg
Sandy Miller - Michigan Council to Repeal the Draft, Ann
     Arbor
Geoff Mirelowitz - High School Student Mobilization Commit-
     tee, Chicago
John E. Mitchell - Int'l. Rep., Amalgamated Meat Cutters &
     Butcher Workmen, Boston
Kate Moore - Chicago NAACP
National Medical Committee for Human Rights
Deborah Notkin - October 31 Peace Action Committee, Chi-
     cago
John T. Nowlan - Catholic Diocese, Detroit
Sam Pollock - Pres. District Union 427, Amalgamated Meat
     Cutters & Butcher Workmen
Joseph Paul - Cincinnati Peace Coalition
Jack Powers - Beacon Hill Support Group, Boston
Lou Renfrew - Chairman of the Ohio New Party
Marvin Rogoff - Washington D.C. Labor for Peace
Auda Romine - Sec.-Treas. Amalgamated Meat Cutters &
     Butcher Workmen, Local 500, C
Don Rucknagel - Chairman Ann Arbor Committee to End the
     War

David Ruhland - Ann Arbor Peace Action Coalition
Jean Savage - Philadelphia National Peace Action Day Committee
Betty Schneider - Detroit Area Laymen
Carl Schove - Houston Committee to End the War in Vietnam
Dan Seigel - Pres. Associated Students, Univ. of California at Berkeley
David Skuza - Park Action Committee, St. Louis Park
Floyd Smith - Pres. Local 500 Amalgamated Meat Cutters & Butcher Workmen, Cleveland
Ken Smith - Pacific Northwest New Mobe
Tom Snell - Augsburg SMC
Francis Somlyo - Cooks Union, Local 209, Washington, D.C.
Dr. Anthony Sterret - Coordinating Committee Health Professions for Peace, New York
Diana Sugg - Women's Liberation, University of Florida
Milton Tamber - AFSCME, Local 1640
Ethel Taylor - Women Strike for Peace, Philadelphia
Michael Tinkler - National Caucus of Labor Committees, Philadelphia
Stanley Tolliver - Attorney, Cleveland
UAW Local 1065
UAW Local 1083
Ruth Warrick - CBS Television Actress
Ernie Weiss - Asst. Education Director, District Local 37, AFSCME
Sue Welch - Macalester Coll. SMC
Ted Werntz - Computer People for Peace, New York
Jack White - "Great Speckled Bird"
Bob Wilkinson - GI Press Service
John T. Williams - VP Teamsters Local 208, Los Angeles
Mamie Williams - Principal, Miami High School
Reed Wolcott - West Side Peace Committee, New York
Ron Wolin - Coordinator, New York Peace Action Coalition
Sue Vass - University of Minnesota SMC
Roger Yockey - Retail Clerks Union #1001, Seattle

(Distributed by the National Peace Action Coalition, November 27, 1970. Collected in the Special Collections, Syracuse University, Syracuse, New York, December 29, 1973.)

48. NATIONAL COALITION AGAINST WAR,
RACISM AND REPRESSION

1029 Vermont Ave., NW Washington, D.C. 20005
(202) 737-8600

For most of you since June 28, this will be the first
information of substance that you have received about what
exactly has happened since the first Milwaukee conference in
June. Well, a lot has happened and there is still a lot to
do, and what we want to attempt to do in this newsletter or
this report is to bring you up-to-date and thus describe to
you our present status as a new and infant coalition.

When the 800 of you left Milwaukee on June 28, a
number of individuals remained, and without a formal mandate felt compelled to implement your firm decision on regional conferences, making it possible for local people in the
areas across the country to decide on priorities and the
steps of implementation of the projects that we discussed in
Milwaukee. A tentative network of about 16 to 18 people volunteered to return to their communities and work toward
those regional conferences. That network was to be co-ordinated by Rennie Davis in Washington. Due to conflicting and
time consuming responsibilities that Rennie already had,
William Douthard has volunteered to assist Rennie, and eventually wound up taking his place. With the assistance of
Dick Fenandez of Clergy and Laymen Concerned About Viet-
nam, Ron Young and Allen Brick of FOR, Trudi Young of
Women Strike for Peace, Susan Miller of the Episcopal Peace
Fellowship, Joe Miller of Sane in Philadelphia, Sid Lens,
Jack Spiegel, and Sylvia Kushner of the Chicago Peace Coun-
cil, and most notably, Norma Becker, Abe Weisberg, and
Thomas Hayes of the Vietnam Peace Parade Committee in
New York, funds were constantly provided to assist William
Douthard, Kathy Sophos and Mary Rouse to maintain an office
in Washington and to work full time on organizing regional
conferences around the country. By August 28 there had been
conferences held in Seattle, Pittsburgh, New Haven, Rochester, N.Y., Detroit, Philadelphia, New York City and the
Midwest area in Chicago. There were organizing attempts

under way for conferences in Baltimore, Washington, D.C.,
Los Angeles, San Francisco, Miami, New Orleans, Atlanta,
and Boston. On the whole, the conferences were well attended, often chaotic, usually confusing and with few exceptions, traditional forces of the local and national anti-war
movement, but there was a difference. That difference was
the issues being discussed, such as genocide, the $5,500 or
fight campaign of N.W.R.O., and local issues of significance
relative to each region. There were new kinds of people
too. There were Black people and Brown people who had not
been customarily found in the ranks in any significant number
of the anti-war movement.

This marked the second step of the Milwaukee conference in June and it was an important second step, for it was
the only way a beginning could be made to build firm leadership from the bottom or grass roots level up and to stimulate local and regional activity in a new way that sought to
educate, organize and then confront the interrelated issues of
war, racism, repression, sexism and all the other ills within this society. The third step was a meeting September 11
through 13th in Milwaukee of delegates from these regional
conferences and organizing committees, as well as from national organizations, who came together to formulate programs
and actions responsive to the decisions made and the feelings
of those regional conferences. That meeting of some 85 representatives adopted a proposal put forward by Stewart Meacham of the American Friends Service Committee that gave
us both a structure and a name----The National Coalition
Against War, Racism, and Repression.

The meeting at that time selected an interim committee, whose membership was decided by caucuses of various
interest groups. Those caucuses and their selections are
listed as follows:

Students - Terry Cook (Seattle)
Welfare Rights - Lucille Berrien (Milwaukee)
Religious - Stewart Meacham (Milwaukee)
           Dick Fernandez (New York)
Women - Beverly Sterner (New York)
Blacks - Muhammed Kenyatta (Philadelphia)
Radical Collectivists - Frank Joyce (Detroit)
November 15 Demonstration (Genocide) - Willie Jenkins (NY)
New York Region - Victoria Stevens (New York)
Southern Region - Marie Clark (Miami)
Midwest Region - Mike Crosby (Indianapolis)

California Region - Kent Weber (San Francisco)
Resistance Movement - Jerry Coffin (New York City)
Spring Action - Mike Lerner (Seattle)
Chicano Moratorium - Roberto Elias (Los Angeles)
Convenor - William Douthard (New York City)

      The purpose of this temporary committee was two-fold:
      (A) to identify and contact all groups, regions and organizations to be invited as members of the national council of the coalition. In so doing, this fact would follow the guide agreed upon in the proposal adopted from Stewart Meacham. (A copy of that outline with details of all groups is enclosed for your information and scrutiny.)

      (B) To meet together as a working body with the authority to make decisions for the Coalition until that national council was convened.

      In forming the interim committee, the meeting also formed a consultative committee whose purpose was to gather the feelings and opinions of the national organizations and groupings in respect to the proposed spring action program as adopted in this Milwaukee Conference. That consultative committee was to report its findings to the interim committee and from there to the entire Coalition. The committee consists of the following people:

Bill Briggs - NWRO-National Staff-Washington, DC
Trudi Young - National Director-Women Strike for Peace, New York
Michael Lerner - Seattle Liberation Front-(Originator of one of the Spring Plans)
Sylvia Kushner - Chicago Peace Council
Dick Fernandez - Director-Clergy and Laymen Concerned About Vietnam-New York City
Sid Peck - New Mobe-Cambridge, Mass.
Doug Dowd - New Mobe-Cornell University-Ithaca, N. Y.
Miss Bobbie McMahon - Chairman-Family Rights Council-Washington DC
Jerry Coffin - War Resisters League-New York City
William Douthard - Coalition Staff

      A synopsis of resolutions and programs adopted at Milwaukee is also enclosed.

      Since September 13, there have been two meetings of

the interim committee, one on September 17 in New York
City, and a second one October 5 in Washington DC. A third
meeting is scheduled for October 13 in New York with an ac-
companying press conference on October 14 that will announce
the coalition and its program for the months of October and
November.   The first order of business at the first interim
committee meeting was the Rev. Carl McIntyre rally in
Washington on October 3, with the announced speaking of Vice
President Ky of South Vietnam.   There was a plan of action
adopted for a counter-demonstration against the Ky rally on
the same day in Washington. On learning of Ky's cancella-
tion September 26, a press conference was called in Washington, in which we cancelled our plans for a counter-demonstration. (If you wish copies of that press release, please
call or write in to the office and we will send them to you.)

On October 5, the second meeting of the interim committee was held in Washington, and at this meeting three important decisions were made:

1.   A listing of groups and organizations was agreed
upon which would constitute the national council.   As stated
before, that listing is enclosed in this letter.

2.   It was decided that the coalition would play a major role in the genocide campaign by planning a one-week or
two-week non-violent civil disobedience demonstration period
at the United Nations on or about November 15, 1970.   A
task force was created and being co-ordinated by Willie Jenkins in New York City that would decide on a draft program
of action to be presented to the next interim committee on
October 13.   Once the draft outline has been accepted, a national call for the demonstration will be issued near the end
of October.

3.   The national office for the Coalition will remain
in Washington from now through June, and the national staff
will be created to be responsible for the following:
        (a) To assist local organizations and regions in
building the regional coalition and maintaining communication
between each region.
        (b) To implement whatever national programs or ac-
tion is decided upon by the council.
        (c) To issue a newsletter of the Coalition.   (mini-
mum of one per month)

Enclosed with this report is a calendar of actions as

planned by each of the regions within the Coalition. We ask
that everyone relate to these action plans as outlined for their
respective regions. You will note that on the enclosed coalition outline, there are still areas throughout the country
where, due to either lack of contacts or organizers, there
are no committees formed that relate to this National Coalition. We need your assistance in identifying groups or individuals in those areas so that we may contact them and inform them of the Coalition's formation, intent, and program.
If you have any knowledge pertaining to these areas, please
call or write us as soon as possible. If any of you desire
to form coalitions as listed in the outline, by all means do
so and let us know of your progress.

If any of you desire a copy of the press statement
that will be released on October 14, please call or write the
office.

In ending this report, we want to remind you that the
last three months has seen the beginning of this collective
effort to unify and assist the various struggles in our communities around the country. Please do not forget that the
specific nature of this Coalition is to aid that process where
local people can decide on the issues of importance in their
communities and move on those issues. This then becomes
your Coalition, and it is up to you to make the Coalition productive and meaningful for your area. One can't wait for
the Coalition to aid you for that would be like waiting for the
broom to sweep your house. If it's going to serve and aid
the development of the grass roots movement around this
country, then you must make it do that. It needs your participation in your community, city, and region. It needs
your participation on its national council.

GET IT TOGETHER--------DO IT!

In Peace and Freedom
William Douthard
Coordinator

PS The National Office wishes to thank the staff and volunteers of the Chicago Peace Council, specifically Allan Amato,
who through their daily handwork produced this report and
mailing.

PPS In our list of people who contributed of their time,
energies and resources to the organizing effort of this Coali-

tion, through fatigue and undersight we left off the following
people who also merit your thanks and "endearment":
Sidney & Louise Peck, Doug Dowd.

(Received from the National Coalition Against War, Racism
and Repression on October 10, 1970. The meetings referred
to in the document were convened during 1970.)

49. MIDWEST REGIONAL NEWSLETTER OF THE NATIONAL COALITION AGAINST WAR, RACISM AND REPRESSION

Why It Was Formed

There has been a growing realization for some time amongst people active in "the movement" that the individual issues on which we have all been fighting are in fact integrated, and that it would be helpful if some means could be found by which those of us who have been working to end the war, racism, repression, poverty, and sexism, could collaborate in a common effort.

To implement this idea, a conference of 750 people was called in Milwaukee in June. Present were representatives of the New Mobe, various anti-war coalitions, some of the leaders of the Southern Christian Leadership Conference, some of the leaders of the National Welfare Rights Organization, Chicano Moratorium groups, Women's Liberation, a number of collectives (the Seattle Liberation Front, and collectives from Indianapolis and Baltimore), and a number of trade unionists. The idea of a broad coalition was unanimously endorsed, and a staff formed to implement it. In order to build a firm leadership from the bottom up and to stimulate local and regional activity, the next step was to hold a dozen or more regional conferences--mostly in August. And the third step was a meeting Sept. 11-13 in Milwaukee of delegates from these regional conferences, as well as from national organizations, to formulate a program of action and select an interim committee. That meeting--of some 85 representatives --took the official name of NATIONAL COALITION AGAINST WAR, RACISM AND REPRESSION, and is now in business trying to stimulate and coordinate activity in a wide variety of fronts.

What has worried most of us in recent times is that we engage in a dramatic demonstration two or three times a year, but do little in-between; that each of our organizations is forced to act on its own, because there is little communication, contact, or coordination between us. The new COALI-

TION makes it possible to remedy these defects.

The Midwest Region, which covers an area from Indianapolis and St. Louis in the south to Minneapolis in the north, held its conference at Wheeling, Illinois, elected a 21-member steering committee, and a six-member interim committee to carry on the communication and coordination Headquarters will be at 343 S. Dearborn, Room 1416, Chicago, Illinois 60604, with Sylvia Kushner and Pat Richartz as staff. One other staff member--hopefully from Black or Chicano movements--will be added in the near future, to do travelling in our region.

The Program of Action This Fall

The COALITION has no desire to tell any group what it should or should not do, nor is it suggesting that any group give up any of the activities it is normally engaged in. It is hoped, however, that we can cooperate on a program of action for this fall that will take place in many cities simultaneously. That program includes the following.

1. A demonstration of support to the Black Panther Party members on trial in Milwaukee, September 26th-27th. You are asked to send by car, train, or busload, as many people as possible, to show our solidarity against repression. In the Chicago area, carloads will be leaving from the Chicago Peace Council, 343 S. Dearborn, and the Evanston Peace Center, 926 Chicago Ave., Evanston, at 1:30 on Saturday the 26th. If you want to go, call 922-6578 and make arrangements.

2. Local demonstrations in front of welfare offices on Friday, September 25th in behalf of the Welfare Rights Organization program of "FIFTY-FIVE HUNDRED OR FIGHT." You should immediately call the Welfare Rights group in your area to work out a common plan; and the WRO brothers and sisters are asked to communicate their plans to others. In Chicago, a demonstration is planned at 10 a.m. at 160 N. LaSalle. CWRO office number is 312 538-7080.

3. October 3rd. Washington demonstration against the visit of General Ky to the United States. Some arrangements are being made to go to Washington by

people at the Chicago _Seed_, 929-0133. If you cannot
go to Washington, plan a local demonstration in your
area, such as a vigil in front of a courthouse, post
office, etc. In Chicago, plans are being made for
guerrilla theatre and mass leafleting on State Street.
Call 922-6578 for more information.

4.   The regional conference at Wheeling decided to call
and promote TWO WEEKS OF CITY MOBILIZATION
prior to the elections November 3rd. It is hoped that
you will organize teams in those two weeks--at universities and in communities and elsewhere--to distribute
leaflets, knock on doors, and hold rap sessions around
the issues of war, racism and repression. Some
groups will want to coordinate this with their electoral work, and will strive to be legal and work "within
the system." Others will want to do it outside the
electoral process and may decide on nonviolent acts
of civil disobedience, such as holding a meeting in a
bank, in a department store, the Standard Oil offices,
draft boards, etc.

5.   On October 30th, a Friday, it is planned to hold demonstrations at the welfare offices, at induction centers,
and if possible, at factories, to dramatize the related
issues of war, the draft, poverty, unemployment.
Each city and town will have to work on its own details, but it is our hope that something takes place in
every community in this region where there are COA-
LITION affiliates or friends.

6.   On October 31st there will be mass vigils or marches
in each city and town, to dramatize our opposition to
the war, and related issues.

7.   During the week of November 15th there will be a
massive national action in New York, at the United Nations building, in opposition to American genocide at
home and abroad. You are asked to begin planning
now to send autos and busses to New York for that
event. Copies of the Genocide Petitions are available
at your regional office, to be circulated.

8.   Finally, a gigantic action is planned for early in May
1971, if the war is still on, which will include nonviolent civil disobedience and other nonviolent mass action. The details of this are being worked out, and

the plans will be relayed to you as soon as formu-
lated.

On Going Activities

One of the major dividends we hope will come out of
the NATIONAL COALITION AGAINST WAR, RACISM AND
REPRESSION is continued, ceaseless, steady, ongoing activity on the local level, and on a dozen fronts. We hope that
teams--or "collectives"--will form as widely as possible to
give such on-going actions full scope. The Midwest Regional committee can hardly enumerate all the activities possible, but here are a few suggestions:

1. Leafletting factories on a regular basis to rap with the
    workers about the issues we are interested in, espe-
    cially the war, as it causes inflation and unemploy-
    ment.
2. Soliciting speaking engagements to unions, churches,
    schools, women's organizations, etc.
3. Distribution of leaflets and guerrilla theatre in front
    of churches and other institutions.
4. Opening of coffee houses, especially near military in-
    stallations and at universities, where Movement people
    can congregate and plan action.
5. Draft counselling.
6. Leafletting military installations and USO offices.
7. Leafletting at unemployment offices and welfare of-
    fices.
8. House to house leafletting, especially in black and
    brown areas.
9. Formation of teams that will work together on a con-
    stant basis and will figure out their own specific ac-
    tivities. These collectives should focus on problems
    of their own communities.
10. Holding of vigils in the center of town on a regular
    basis, with signs and leaflets.
11. Formation of a media committee to solicit appear-
    ances on radio and television; as well as to secure
    newspaper coverage and, perhaps arrange debates.

There are many other ideas for action, but for the
moment, to build, we need to hear from you--what you're
trying and what works in your community, for joining the issues together. Send these reports to us, so we can publicize them through a printed newsletter.

How Else Can We All Help?

   If the NATIONAL COALITION and the Midwest Region
are to achieve their full potential, each of us must dedicate
ourselves to its work.   Specifically, we ask you:

   1.   To formally affiliate.   Just send in a letter stating your desire--and if possible some money to help the
work along.
   2.   To send us names and addresses of groups that
may be willing to join.
   3.   To send as large a contribution as possible--so
that we can hire additional staff and take care of the usual
expenses an organization like ours must contend with.

   If you want to discuss the COALITION program or any
activities further, don't hesitate to write:

       Midwest Region
       National Coalition Against War, Racism and
          Repression
       343 So. Dearborn - Room 1416
       Chicago, Illinois 60604

Or phone: Sylvia Kushner, 312-922-6578, or Pat Richartz
312 HA 7-3072.

THE FOLLOWING ARE SIX RESOLUTIONS STRONGLY SUP-
PORTED AT THE COALITION CONFERENCE IN MILWAU-
KEE SEPTEMBER 11-13, 1970:

1.   UAW STRIKE: Because the UAW strike is made necessary by the combination of war-induced inflation and reces-
sion, and the normal exploitative policies of the giant auto
corporations, we urge regional and national organizations to
work together in support of striking UAW workers.   Our support for the workers' needs, and for the efforts of the rank
and file movements to democratize the union to realize those
needs, does not imply uncritical support for the present union
leadership.
       Suggested techniques include: a) help in picketing; b)
distributing leaflets in public places calling for a boycott of
GM and Chrysler cars, and showing the relationship between
the strike and the pressing problems in our country;   c) hold-

ing meetings in support of the strike; d) bringing coffee and doughnuts to the strikers, raising support funds, helping in the publication of strike bulletins where useful; e) calling demonstrations for the strike and against the war, poverty, sexism and racism; f) bringing workers into contact with NWRO, anti-war activists, Panthers and leaders of the black struggle.

2. MOTION ON FALL ACTIONS: That we go on record as supporting the efforts already under way to make the period of October 15, 1970, to November 15, 1970, one of intensive mass actions on war, racism, welfare rights, and repression, with local committees deciding whether these be single or multiple actions. That this month of action wind up in a national action at the United Nations on the issue of genocide. That we give fullest support and help to rally large numbers to any demonstration called in defense of Bobby Seale. That we issue a call for international protest during this period in solidarity with these actions.

3. MOTION ON SPRING ACTION: We support in principle, a proposal for massive non-violent civil disobedience and other forms of nonviolent mass actions in Washington, D.C., and other cities, in early May, 1971.

That we commend the action to a variety of national organizations and groups and regional coalitions.

That the timing of the call for the action be the earliest result of extensive consultation with these other national and regional forces.

That a consultation committee be established for this purpose.

4. MOTION ON NATIONAL WELFARE RIGHTS ORGANIZA-TION: We urge this Strategy-Action COALITION to start taking positive steps in relationship to dealing with the NWRO. The attitude which has been projected, both at this conference and the first one, is one of verbal commitment only; we are asking for a more positive and relevant commitment. The following steps should be taken by this conference in order to move in a more positive manner:

a) This Coalition, in its long-range projections for actions and involvement, should maintain an involvement with NWRO actions on both a national and local level. NWRO has an action calendar and there is always some drive or problem which all of you attending this conference can relate to on the basis of ending the war being a major solution.

b)   Friends groups should be established by all Coalition groups.

c)   There should be an immediate policy of contacting the local NWRO chapter in the different regions, and the maximum input should be made.   This is to take place at the end of this conference.

5.   MOTION ON CHICANO MORATORIUM: That we have solidarity with the Sept. 16 Mexican Independence Day marches and rallies which will be sponsored by Chicanos across the country.

That groups and individuals help the bail fund for the August 29 Chicano Moratorium police riot.   Thousands of dollars are still needed.   Bail money can be sent to:

> Chicano Legal Defense Fund
> 920 S. Atlantic Blvd.
> Los Angeles, California   90022

The major actions on September 16 will be in Los Angeles, Cal., and in Denver, Colorado.

Prensa Libre, a Chicano newspaper in Chicago, has a film which shows the police riot on August 29 in East L.A.   Their address is 1831 S. Racine, at the Casa de Aztlan, in Chicago.

6.   MOTION ON STANDARD OIL BOYCOTT: Because Standard Oil is one of the largest war contractors (591,000,000 in military contracts in 1969), and because Standard Oil urged the U.S. government into Vietnam in the first place (Rockefeller Brothers Report, 1958), and because S.O. has lobbied for a great build-up of the U.S. military, a National Boycott of Standard Oil is being organized.

Other reasons for boycotting Standard Oil includes its unfair labor practices, its exploitation of the people and resources of Latin America, its support of the racist apartheid government of South Africa, its racial and sexual discrimination in hiring, its disregard for ecology (oil slicks, poison chemical fertilizers, etc.), its opposition to subsidies for good, cheap public transportation--and many others.

What is needed now is organizers on every level, everywhere.   This is an action project that local organizations can adopt.   We intend to distribute widely two educational pamphlets on Standard Oil.   Also, we will issue a Standard Oil DIScredit card.   Certain demands will be made of Standard Oil.   Everyone's help is needed.   Groups interested in working on this should contact the:

Standard Oil Boycott Committee
c/o Chicago Peace Council
343 South Dearborn, Room 1416
Chicago, Illinois 60604

We hope to hear from you soon; give us your reaction to the activities planned by the COALITION as presented in this newsletter.   Let us know what your group is doing, and how you can help to further actions planned by the COALI-TION.

Peace,
Freedom,

Midwest Regional Committee
9/22/70

(Received from the Midwest Regional Committee of the National Coalition Against War, Racism and Repression, September 25, 1970.)

50.   STRATEGY ACTION CONFERENCE

New Mobilization Committee to End the War in Vietnam
Washington Action Office: 1029 Vermont Avenue, N.W.,
Washington, D.C.   20005

August 24, 1970

Dear Friend,

On behalf of the Strategy Action Conference of the New
Mobilization Committee, I wish to thank you for your recent
contribution.   With your assistance we were able to launch
regional conferences around the issues of poverty, racism,
repression of all kinds, and the war.   People from the entire
spectrum of the Movement are getting together to plan re-
gionally targetted and coordinated actions as well as mass national actions focussed on these issues.   The need for "grass
roots" organizing is being emphasized.

Your continuing support is both needed and appreciated; if we're ever going to form a broad-based coalition to
combat the repressive forces evident in America today, now's
the time!

Power to the People!

(signed: Kathy Sophos)

Strategy Action
New Mobe

STRATEGY ACTION CONFERENCE

REGIONAL CONFERENCE ORGANIZERS COORDINATION
MEETING, CHICAGO, SUNDAY, JULY 20, 1970

MINUTES:

1.   Roll Call: People identified themselves and briefly told

194

what was going on in their regions.

A.   Chris Robson, San Francisco, Northern California SAC organizing committee.   Others from the West Coast committee could not attend because of lack of funds: Moeice Palladino, NWRO; Robert Grove NCSACOC; Robert Elias, Chicano Moratorium; Irving Sarnoff, Los Angeles Peace Action Council.   Robson reported that an office had been secured and people throughout the West were being contacted and that the following areas would probably have their own regional conferences, the only definite date given was for an expanded LA meeting within 3 weeks.   Seattle, Northern California, Southern California, Denver, Hawaii, and possibly Alaska if contacts can be made.   Robson also reported that the NCSACOC consisted of former New Mobe West people, Peace and Freedom Party, local National Welfare Rights Organizations, Northern California Chicano Moratorium, Student Strike Committees, Representative delegates to the Chicago Rank and File Labor Conference, and that other groupings were being contacted to form a broad based coordinating committee before any decisions were actually made regarding the mechanics of the conference.   The tentative date for the conference was projected for August 15-16.

B.   Rennie Davis reported on the developments in Seattle. Mike Lerner was expected, but the Seattle Liberation Front expected to have a regional conference within three weeks. Three activities were raised by the SLF.   A draft confrontation at Ft. Lewis; Support for a Washington action (SWP walked out of a broad based coordinating meeting); the possibility of setting up a closed circuit T.V. hookup of the Vietnamese in Paris, Eldridge Cleaver in Algiers, and various campuses across the country in the beginning of the Fall.

C.   John Froines discussed the division of the Northeastern into two regions, at this point only proposed, Boston, New Hampshire, Maine and Western Mass., Vermont, Connecticut.

D.   William Douthard gave a report from the Philadelphia region.   They have about thirty people and want to have their own regional conference.

E.   Judy Munaker, Rennie Davis, Frank Greer reported on the status of the Washington, D.C.-Baltimore regional conference.   Judy indicated that people in Baltimore were upset and curious as to why and how this meeting was called.

F.   Tom Houck gave his report from Atlanta that many groups
had come together and he was meeting again with them this
Tuesday to get their conference off the ground.   He said he
would give the SCLC report later in the meeting.   Bill
Briggs, NWRO would be working on the regional conferences
in the South and in Washington, D.C.

G.   Anne Perry, Jean Kenney and Frank Joyce reported on
the Detroit, Cleveland, Pittsburgh, and the rest of Ohio.
The areas might be subdivided, with Anne contacting people
in Pittsburgh, and the rest of Ohio.   The areas might be subdivided, with Anne contacting people in Pittsburgh.   Frank
reported that the Motor City Coalition was getting it together
in Detroit, also in Lansing.   (Pittsburgh contact: Marsha
Landy).

H.   New York State area was divided into three separate re-
gions: Newark and Northern New Jersey; New York City; and
Upstate New York.   Allison Raphael was contact person for
Newark, William Douthard was coordinating NYC, and Dave
Dowd up in the hills.   The City and the State have slated re-
gional conferences for the weekend of August 15-16.   NYC
had already adopted the five delegate idea for the National
Coordinating Committee to meet after the regional conference.

I.   William Douthard explained the reason for the meeting
and his role as ad-hoc coordinator.   After Milwaukee, Rennie
Davis had agreed to do the day to day work from Washington
to see that regional conferences did occur.   But he went out
of the country, and William took over that responsibility.
He felt there were a number of unanswered questions in people's minds and confusion, caused by the release of the Waskow proposal for example, about the real purpose of the regional conferences.   The problem of timetable, and follow-up
structure had to be discussed by those who were organizing
the regional conferences, along with other specific problems,
such as finance, etc.

J.   Sid Lens discussed a rationale for the regional conferences: a) to create the broadest possible coalition, b) true
grass roots organizing, c) to give a perspective for a national action for the fall.

K.   Dave Dowd responded that now was the time to get people together, that it would be improper for us in this meeting to put the cart before the horse.   We should be organizing from the bottom up around multi-issues.   Others joined

in to respond to Lens by stating that the whole idea of the
regional conferences was to get away from the top heavy
leadership of the movement as in the past.

(At this point in the meeting several errors were
found in the Milwaukee report, from individuals phone numbers to entire texts of workshop proposals; rather than enter
all these in the minutes, they will be added to a revised
Milwaukee Conference Report and mailed out.)

The Agenda was discussed and revised as follows:
- I. Report from SCLC by Tom Houck
- II. Regional Conferences: Timetable, finances, reports.
- III. National Coordinating Meeting: When and where and who.
- IV. Finances
- V. Mechanism for distribution of regional conference reports.
- VI. Structure
- VII. Money for this meeting's cost.
- VIII. Relating to the Cleveland Oct. 31 proposal.
- IX. Reaction to the Seattle plan for closed circuit TV hookup.

AGENDA

----I.   SCLC Report.

Tom Houck explained that there had been two meetings
to determine the SCLC position. The proposed fall action
will not conform to the SCLC program in the South this fall
and therefore nothing more than verbal or written endorsement can be expected from SCLC in the South. There is no
disagreement on tactics for the proposed Washington action,
but it should be encouraged for the Spring; then the SCLC
could place more emphasis and energy on it. They will send
delegates and support the regional conferences, but will not
be able to actively organize for them since their national
conference is on August 14. They did vote not to support the
October 31 marches and rallies.

----II.   REGIONAL CONFERENCE.

It was agreed to discuss the aspects of each RC by
region, moving from the West eastward.
A. West Coast. Chris Robson indicated a lot of confusion about the Waskow proposal and that many felt that it
would not be possible or desirable to relate to the Washington

fall action. Since there is no weather problem many people were proposing regional conferences later than August dates now projected elsewhere in the country. For example the LA Peace Action Council had proposed their conference for sometime in September to build for actions in November. In three weeks time, they will have an expanded meeting to deal with the conference and actions prior to September.

Northern California is attempting to gear itself for an August 15-16 Conference date. But this will not be finalized until a broad coordinating committee is formed. Denver needed promoting and this would be worked on by people with contacts there.

B. The Midwest conference would take place in Chicago on August 15. The Chicago Peace Council was working on its coordination. It was suggested that the area might be subdivided because of its size.

C. Ohio, Detroit, East Michigan and Pittsburgh would begin working on subdivision and get it on.

D. Virginia was moved into the Baltimore-D.C. region.

E. The South, 11 states, had a planning meeting that would be followed up in Atlanta this Tuesday.

F. NY and other regions seemed to have it pretty much together, but concern was evidenced about certain areas that were excluded from the centralized regions: the southwest, Idaho, Montana, Texas, Okla., Arkansas, and the Dakotas. A Traveling Cadre was supposed to go into areas where there are few contacts to see if regionals could be sparked in those areas (See attached list for people in that area).

----III. NATIONAL COORDINATING MEETING:

The members of delegates from the regionals and from national organizations were discussed at some length as were the site and date of the meeting. It was finally decided to propose the following to the regional conferences; That each region select a delegation with one vote to go to a national coordinating meeting on September 12 for the purpose of coordinating the decisions of the regional conferences into a national perspective. In addition to regional representation, national organizations would have representation. All of these structural considerations would be decided by the regional conferences. Sites proposed for the meeting were Louisville, Detroit or Chicago. The regional conferences should notify William Douthard after their RC's who their delegates will be.

----IV.   FINANCES:

   Most people felt they could raise the necessary funds
to hold the conferences but that some national fund raising
was necessary to cover the expenses of the coordinating office in Washington and the travel money for the organizing
Cadre.

ATTENDANCE LIST OF CHICAGO SAC - REGIONAL OR-
GANIZING COMMITTEE

                    July 20, 1970

ATLANTA	Tom Houck	SCLC
BALTIMORE	Judith Munaker	
BUFFALO	James Rivard	
CHICAGO	Jerry Hyman	Chicago Vietnam Morator-ium
	Pat Richartz	Clergy and Laymen Con-cerned, Chicago Viet-nam Moratorium
	Barbara Kessel	New University Conference
	Sylvia Kushner	Chicago Peace Council
	Diane Applebaum	Chicago Peace Council
	Sidney Lens	New Mobe
	Ken Love	Non-violent Training and Action Center
	Ginger Mack	Chicago Welfare Rights Organization
	Jack Speigel	Trade Union Committee for Peace
CLEVELAND	Sidney Peck	New Mobe
DETROIT	Frank Joyce	Motor City Coalition
ITHACA (NY)	Doug Dowd	New Mobe
MILWAUKEE	John Gilman	Milwaukee Coalition
NEW HAVEN	Michael Friedman	New Haven Liberation School
	John Froines	New Haven Liberation School
NEW YORK	William Douthard	5th Ave. Peace Parade Comm.
	Bob Greenblatt	New University Conference
SAN FRANCIS-CO	Chris Robson	Northern Calif. Strategy Action Conference Or-ganizing Committee
SPRINGFIELD	Carol Hinchen	Springfield Collective

WASHINGTON,   Rennie Davis   New Mobe
  DC
                   Frank Greer   D.C. Area Movement Comm.
YELLOW   Ann Perry   Ohio Peace Action Council
  SPRINGS

TRAVELING CADRE - SAC

7/20/70

1. Wm. Douthard, Coordi-   6. Rennie Davis
   nator   c/o New Mobe Office
   5th Ave. Peace Parade   1029 Vermont Ave. N.W.
   17 E. 17th Street   Washington, DC 20005
   New York, NY 10003   202 737-8600
   home - 212 857-1384   or
   work - 212 255-1075   1811 Wyoming Ave. N.W.
     or   Washington, DC
   c/o New Mobilization   home 202-265-4757
   1029 Vermont Ave., NW
   Washington, DC 20005   7. Judy Munacher
   202-737-8600   3011 Guilford Ave.
                                  Baltimore, Md. 21218
2. Chris Robson   301-235-0261
   1360 Howard St.
   San Francisco, Calif. 94103 8. John Froines
   home 415 771-1835   214 Winthrop Ave.
   work 415-626-1424   New Haven, Conn.
                                  203-777-3185
3. Bob Grove
   1360 Howard St.   9. Sidney Lens
   San Francisco, Calif. 94103   5436 So. Hyde Park Blvd.
   home 415 681-7583   Chicago, Ill. 60615
   work 415-626-1424   home 312 NO 7-5437
                                  work 312 FI 6-1857
4. Doug Dowd
   1004 E. Shore Drive   10. Ken Love
   Ithaca, NY, 14850   7313 Bennet St.
   home 607-272-6584   Chicago, Ill.
   work 607-256-4892   312-493-8382

5. Frank Greer   11. Diane Appelbaum (Oklahoma)
   c/o New Mobe Office   Chicago Peace Council
   1029 Vermont Ave. N.W.   343 So. Dearborn
   Washington, DC 20005   Chicago, Ill. 60604
   home 301 585-0662   home - 312 955-4972
   work 202 737-8600   work - 312 922-6578

12. Pat Richartz
    Chicago Vietnam Moratorium
    542 So. Dearborn
    Chicago, Ill.
    312 HA 7-3072

(Received from the New Mobilization Committee to End the
War in Vietnam, 1027 Vermont Avenue, N.W., Washington,
D.C., August 27, 1970.)

51. CALL TO STRATEGY ACTION CONFERENCE

Milwaukee, Wisconsin
June 27-28

Killings in Jackson, Mississippi... Augusta, Georgia...
Kent, Ohio... Expanding police attacks on the Black Panther
Party... Rising unemployment... Continuing inflation...
a dramatic escalation of the war throughout S.E. Asia...

America is in a crisis.

Squandering our limited resources on war has created a
torrent of dissent. The government has been forced into a
sharp choice. Either withdraw from S.E. Asia immediately
and redirect vast sums of money into reparations and economic assistance payments at home and abroad. Or clamp
down on unrest and gamble on a rapid and devastating military
assault in Indo-China.

At the present time, it seems all too clear which course
the government is pursuing. The probable consequences in
Indo-China are intensified bombing of North Vietnam, including Hanoi and Haiphong, and possible use of nuclear weapons.
The inevitable consequences at home will be a deepening economic crisis taking its heaviest toll on Blacks, the poor, and
through inflation on all working people. We will face an escalation of repression and further usurpation of legislative authority.

This sense of crisis has struck home across the country.
In hundreds of communities new coalitions have sprung into
action--developing tactics of massive, disciplined, non-violent
resistance, confronting the draft, forcing ROTC and military
contracts off campus, reaching out to middle America at the
factory gates and the front door.

Now we must learn from these actions and build a national response strong enough to STOP the war and repression.

Compelled by this sense of urgency and a desire for unity

among many groups, we are calling an <u>emergency</u> Strategy
Action Conference in Milwaukee on June 27-28.   We will
bring together community activists and regional/national organizers.   We will share experiences in small, informal
workshops.   We will explore the new potential for joint actions by Blacks, students, labor, women, clergy, Chicanos,
GIs, and anti-war forces.

We will be meeting in close liaison with the national conference of students from schools on strike.   We support the
student strike's three demands, that the US end repression of
dissent and release all political prisoners, such as Bobby
Seale and other Black Panthers; that the US cease expansion
of the Vietnam War and immediately withdraw all forces from
S.E. Asia; that universities end complicity in the war machine
by ending defense research, ROTC, counter-insurgency research and other such programs.

Delegations for this working conference will be chosen
jointly by community groups working on problems of racism,
welfare organizing, ending the war, GI rights, campus complicity, labor organizing, sexism, political action, etc.

Registration for the Strategy Action Conference starts
Friday, June 26, at 8:00 p.m. in room 114 of Engleman Hall,
University of Wisconsin at Milwaukee, Hartford and Maryland
Streets.   Registration will start again on Saturday morning at
9:00 a.m. in Milwaukee, contact the conference office, (414)
228-5121.

(Sponsors listed on other side)*
Strategy Action Conference office
Suite 900, 1029 Vermont Ave., N.W.
Washington, D.C. 20005
(202) 737-8600

Shirley Williamson   Michael Woods
4663 N. Morris   2817 Central
Milwaukee   Lafayette, Indiana
332 5345
                             MOE
Sandy Wiscarson
2639 N. Prospect   SANE
Milwaukee
223 4146

Brian Yaffe
217 2nd Ave.
NYC
212 CA 8 2576
Quaker Project

Becky & Betty Younger
7131 Edgerton
Pittsburgh, Penn.
243 3273
AWRG; Peace & Freedom

Ann Zwicker
1639 Alta Vista Ave.
Milwaukee
661 1693
C11

Mrs. L. Willingham
2047 E. 88th
Chicago

Welfare Rights

Stephen Witt
10 Livingston Pkway.
Snyder, NY
839 0032

Judith Wyer
4710 Warrington Ave.
Philadelphia
215 SA 4 5272
Plain Dealer

Trudi Young
126 Greenbush Rd.
Tappan, NY
914 359 2599
WSP; Mobe

Betsy Zelt
2239 Walnut St.
Waukegan, Ill.
244 1347

Melody Wilson
RR 1 Box 164
Mukwonego, Wisconsin
369 7612
WILPF

Marty Wolfson
1862 Hintwood Pl., N.W.
Washington, DC
462 5606

Jim Wysocki
202 W. Gilman St.
Madison, Wisconsin
256 0857
YSA; Socialist Workers

Ron Young
Box 271
Nyack, NY
914 358 4601
FOR

Irene Zvalgznitis
1004 A South 22
Milwaukee
344 7171
AWRO

*Partial list consisting of only sixteen of a large number of sponsors.

(Received from the Special Collections, University of Wisconsin at Madison, March 4, 1974. Collected by the library staff June 26, 1970.)

52. MAY DAY TACTICAL MANUAL

INTRODUCTION

This manual is a first for a national action. The Ann Arbor Student and Youth Conference on a People's Peace decided to organize Mayday on a regional decentralized basis. This means no "National Organizers." You do the organizing. This means no "movement generals" making tactical decisions you have to carry out. Your region makes the tactical decisions within the discipline of nonviolent civil disobedience laid down by the Ann Arbor Conference. That is why this manual was produced.

This manual is a supplement to the Mayday Orientation Sessions, which will be held April 3, 10, 17. If it is impossible for your region to send representatives to one of the sessions this manual will give you the basic information you need.

Coordination is being handled by the Tactics and Logistics section of the Mayday Collective, in D.C. The last page of this manual has a form you should send in as soon as you can answer the listed questions about your region. If you fail to mail or call in the answers to the questions there will be no D.C. logistical support for your region.

The words and target photographs in this manual were done by the Tactics and Logistics section of the Mayday Collective. The Mayday Collective is politically responsible to the Student and Youth Coordinating Committee which grew out of the Ann Arbor Conference. The Ann Arbor Conference is responsible for Mayday.

All graphics, layout, and production on this manual were done by brothers and sisters from WIN magazine, located at 339 Lafayette St., N.Y.C. 10012. We were lucky they thought enough of Mayday to do this manual. WIN is published every two weeks and relates to what's happening-- the anti-war movement, counter-culture, ecology, etc. -- from a nonviolent perspective. Subscribe if you can. It only costs $5.00 a year.

I. <u>ON NONVIOLENT CIVIL DISOBEDIENCE</u>

This is not a polemic. It is not designed to convince you to become a pacifist or argue against the theory of armed revolutionary struggle or people's war. It is an explanation of the tactic we will be using during the Mayday actions. The tactic is nonviolent civil disobedience. It was decided by the Ann Arbor Student and Youth Conference on a People's Peace which issued the call for the Mayday actions that this was the most valid tactic for this period.

In brief, the aim of the Mayday action is to raise the social cost of the war to a level unacceptable to America's rulers. To do this we seek to create the spectre of social chaos while maintaining the support or at least toleration of the broad masses of American people. It is felt that given the current political climate in this country, it is suicidal to isolate ourselves from the 73% of the American people who wish an immediate end to the war.

The strategy that was developed at the Ann Arbor Conference sought to build support among the American people through the mass distribution and ratification of the People's Peace Treaty. With that basic "base building" well under way we would engage then in disruptive actions in major government centers, primarily Washington, D.C. (creating the spectre of social chaos) that would be supported by the "base." The tactic of nonviolent civil disobedience was chosen because it could be used effectively to disrupt government functions and yet still be interpreted favorably to the broad non-demonstrating masses of Americans. Also by engaging in nonviolent disruptions we severely limit the containment and dispersal options of the government and lessen the likelihood of coming into violent conflict with the G.I.s who will be ordered to disperse us and who we wish to win to our side.

America is a violent country. We are raised on a diet of violence, and therefore we feel we understand it. Nonviolent civil disobedience on the other hand is widely misunderstood and the extent of most people's knowledge is inaccurate characterizations. We need to be clear that we are not talking about an exercise in martyrdom; we are not talking about negotiated arrests; we are talking about using a tactic to attain an objective. The tactic is nonviolent civil disobedience. The objective is to close down the Federal gov-

ernment sections of Washington, D.C., by blocking traffic
arteries during the early morning rush hours of May 3 and
4.

A working definition of nonviolent civil disobedience
in this context would be: A) the actions we engage in are
nonviolent which means we don't trash or street fight;   B)
we are "civil" which means we will try to express our solidarity and friendship with G. I.'s and attempt to see the rank
and file policeman as a member of the working class who's
simply on the wrong side; C) we will be disobedient which
means no matter what anyone says, no matter what laws we
break--we are going to reach our action target--the roads,
bridges, and traffic circles leading into the Federal areas of
Washington--and we will not leave our action targets until we
have succeeded in our target objective or until we are arrested.

In earlier days the small pacifist groups developed
out of necessity and preference a type of nonviolent civil disobedience that we could call the traditional school.   Crudely
put, this involved a very small group of people engaging in
a "moral witness" of action that involved them breaking a
specific law, almost always with advance notice to authorities.   Much of the early civil rights actions--such as lunch
counter sit-ins--followed this model.   Recently another form
of nonviolent civil disobedience has developed.   This con-
forms more with our new life style.   It is free, joyous, exciting, fun.   It's yippies throwing money on the floor of the
N. Y. Stock Exchange, draft card burnings in Central Park,
the invasion and takeover of the N. Y. Tass offices during the
invasion of Czechoslovakia and Sgt. Sunshine of the S. F. Police dept. lighting up a joint in front of the S. F. Police
Building.

At the same time this new mode of action was developing among the white youth movement, nonviolent civil disobedience was being used in new ways by third world groups.
Martin Luther King, Jr. pioneered the use of mass nonviolent civil disobedience in this country to challenge government racist policies.   The Birmingham movement is perhaps
the best example of these actions.   Cesar Chavez   and the
United Farmworkers Organizing Committee consistently broke
injunctions and picketing laws as they organized California
farm workers and used nonviolent civil disobedience including sit-ins and shop-ins to enforce the grape and now the
lettuce boycott.   We're talking of combining this experience

with our life culture to create Mayday in Washington.

   Flash on Gandhi. --An organic food vegetarian, a strong Indian culture freak who met the English Viceroy of India in a loincloth and organized civil disobedience campaigns which paralyzed entire sections of India--what comes to mind is thousands of us with bamboo flutes, tamborines, flowers and balloons moving out in the early light of morning to paralyze the traffic arteries of the American military repression government nerve center. Creativeness, joy, and life against bureaucracy and grim death. That's nonviolent civil disobedience; That's Mayday.

   Finally, if for philosophical, political, or emotional reasons any people feel they cannot adhere to the tactic adopted by the Ann Arbor Conference we strongly urge them to stay home or engage in actions they organize at other times or other places. We feel it is reprehensible and manipulative to expose people who respond to the Mayday call for nonviolent civil disobedience to be exposed to forms of actions for which they are not prepared. In addition we expect large numbers of agent provocateurs to be present during Mayday. We think it would be unfortunate for brothers and sisters who are unable to adopt the style, discipline and tactics decided on through a long collective process to be mislabeled and dealt with as agent provocateurs.

II. THE SPRING PERIOD

   The Mayday actions are to occur in the May 1-7 period. Mayday, however, should be seen in the context of an entire spring offensive that will begin the first week of April, reach a high point in May and continue on into the summer.

   The schedule for the Spring Offensive is:

APRIL 25: "Tribute in Action to Martin Luther King." These actions are organized by the Southern Christian Leadership Conference, the National Welfare Rights Organization and the People's Coalition for Peace and Justice. There is a special emphasis on New York with a march on Wall Street on Monday, April 5, led by the SCLC Mule Train.

APRIL 10: Women's March on the Pentagon.

APRIL 18-23: Operation Dewey Canyon III organized by the Vietnam Veterans Against the War will take place in Washington, D.C. Vietnam vets, their families and the families of POW's and GI's killed in Vietnam will engage in intensive lobbying, vigils and guerrilla theater depicting search and destroy missions, torture and other activities of US forces in Indochina.

APRIL 24: "Algonquin Peace City," the encampment area for Mayday, opens in Rock Creek Park in Washington, D.C.

APRIL 24: Mass, legal, peaceful anti-war demonstration in Washington, D.C. by National Peace Action Coalition and PCPJ.

APRIL 26-30: Peoples Lobby in Washington, D.C. organized by People's Coalition for Peace & Justice. Will include civil disobedience at selected government buildings and congressional offices.

MAY 1-7: Mayday International--Major demonstrations will take place in large cities around the world. These actions will express solidarity with our Mayday and will focus on U.S. foreign policy. In South Vietnam the people of the large cities will rise up in massive street demonstrations challenging the U.S. presence.

MAY 16: Armed Forces Day. Support for anti-war GI actions at bases across the country.

MAY 25-28: NATO International Conference on Cities in Indianapolis. Nixon and other heads of state will be greeted with massive demonstrations.

THE MAYDAY SCENARIO

Saturday, April 24: Algonquin Peace City Opens

The first national implementation of the peace treaty is planned in Rock Creek Park, an Indian woodlawn area of 1,754 acres about 4 miles long and one mile wide in Washington, D.C. Algonquin Indians were the first inhabitants in the ancient mountain range. In late April, we'll settle again, along the drier ridges with the pignut and mockernut, white ash, black cherry, the yellow poplar and beech, being careful and loving of nature. Regions and constituent groups

can set up living communities or villages in one of the 70
odd picnic groves where there are tables, benches, sanitary
facilities and usually a fireplace. People should bring their
own tents, blankets, flashlights, transistor radio, rice and
other foods, along with a cooking pot.

To cut down on confusion and ecological injury to our
peace city, cars should not be driven into Rock Creek Park.
Some people may want to park on the edge of Washington and
walk into the city. Others may want to drive into the downtown Washington area and take buses to their villages. Bus
transportation between Washington Monument Grounds and Algonquin Peace City will be provided at 11:00 A.M. and 6:00
P.M. every day by Mayday Motors. Detailed maps showing
the village of every region in Algonquin Peace City will be
available from information centers on the Monument Grounds.
Any large group wanting to be listed on the map should call
Mike Maslow (202) 347-7613.

It is in the interest of the government to provide us
this park, for training in nonviolence and to keep us out of
the streets at night. Should police clear the park at any
time during the two weeks, however, it will be necessary
that we know the various exits from our area of encampment.
There are 15 miles of trails through Algonquin Peace City.
Maps will be provided.

Algonquin Peace City is opening early in order to provide housing areas for the thousands of people staying after
the demonstrations of April 24. Many of these people, as
well as early Mayday arrivals will participate in the P.C.P.J.
People's Lobby. Others will act as construction battalions
to prepare the park for the massive May 1 influx of people.

Map number one in this manual shows you the layout
of Rock Creek Park. Two weeks prior to May 1st, maps
will be available from the Mayday Washington office giving
the location of regional campsites.

If bloodroot, fawnlily, toothwort and spring beauty
bloom doesn't turn you on, Mayday has secured housing for
twenty-two thousand people in churches, universities and private homes.

SATURDAY, MAY 1:

CELEBRATION OF THE PEOPLE'S PEACE

Most Mayday participants will arrive on May 1st. People will be coming in by chartered bus, car caravans, and long walks. The morning will be devoted to the May 1st arrivals setting up camp in their regional area villages and getting to know the land.

In the early afternoon the celebration will begin. The Mayday Collective is currently assembling a list of well-known rock groups that will play. The list of groups playing in the Peace Treaty Celebration Rock Show will be released as soon as possible.

The Celebration, with rock bands, and dancing, singing, and smoking in the fields will last late into the night. Bring along bamboo flutes, drums, guitars and tamborines, and the woods will be filled with people's music.

Sometime during the day of May 1st the SCLC Mule Train and hundreds of people who marched with them from Wall Street to Washington will arrive in Algonquin Peace City. They'll set up camp and join us in the Celebration of the People's Peace.

SUNDAY, MAY 2

We'll sleep late. In the late morning, the population will follow the SCLC mule train out of the park to the Sylvan Theatre near the Washington Monument grounds. We will march down Rock Creek Parkway.

At the Sylvan Theatre we'll join SCLC, National Welfare Rights Organization and the United Farmworkers Organizing Committee in a rally calling for an end to the war against American Poor People. This will be the last opportunity for Nixon to announce an end to the war before we fulfill our promise: If the government won't stop the war, we'll stop the government.

In the evening we march back to Algonquin Peace City for food, cultural activities and turning in early for a good sleep.

MONDAY & TUESDAY, MAY 3 and 4, at 6 A.M. :
NONVIOLENT CIVIL DISOBEDIENCE

The population of Algonquin Peace City will disperse
in regional groups to their target areas for Nonviolent Civil
Disobedience (see sections III, IV, VI, for details). PCPJ
joins with us along with religious forces, such as Clergy
and Laymen Concerned About Vietnam, SCLC, NWRO, and
pacifist organizations, such as the War Resisters League,
and the American Friends Service Committee.

WEDNESDAY, MAY 5-7

All across the country, on May 5, people respond to
the call for "No Business as Usual" in a massive people's
strike Against the War. At Algonquin Peace City the people
not arrested on Monday and Tuesday take camping gear and
food and move camp to the Capitol Building where we lay a
nonviolent siege demanding that congress ratify the Peoples
Peace Treaty (See Section VI for details).

We will be joined by masses of people from the
PCPJ, SCLC, NWRO, AFSC, WRL, CALCAV, Women's
Strike for Peace, and other groups. We'll stay at our siege
encampment until the treaty is ratified or all are arrested.

III.   ORGANIZATION FORM

The decision of the Ann Arbor Student & Youth Conference on a Peoples Peace was that the organization for
Mayday be decentralized with organizational forms being decided on a regional basis. Because of this the entire Tactics and Logistics section of the Mayday Collective in Washington is oriented toward providing information, support, and
coordination only. There are no movement "generals" sitting
in closed rooms making decisions binding on any participant.

All organizing and preparation for the action must be
done at the regional level. No "National Office Organizers"
will do it for you (or to you). What the Tactics and Logistics section has done is number the targets, prepare this
manual, prepare intensive orientation sessions for regional
representatives, and act as a coordination center for various
regions which have selected targets.

Once you have established a regional structure and

begun organizing for Mayday, contact the Tactics and Logistics Section of the Mayday Collective at (202) 347-7613 (ask for Jerry Coffin, Lynne Shatzkin, Nancy Fowler, or Rick Lubin).

Arrange to send two or three regional representatives to Washington on Saturday April 3, Saturday April 10 or Saturday April 17 to attend a Mayday orientation session. The subjects covered will include an overview of the Mayday actions, discussions of specific targets, Algonquin Peace City information, medical and legal information. In addition there will be tours of Washington and Rock Creek Park. Following the orientation sessions the regional representatives will be asked to select a target for their region and, on the basis of projected numbers of people from their region, select a campsite in Rock Creek Park.

Every phase of the Mayday actions is organized on a regional basis. Individuals coming into Washington will be asked to join with whatever apparatus represents their region in Washington. Prior to Mayday, maps and leaflets will be published listing the target areas and campsite locations of every region the Mayday Collective is in touch with.

This May we will see the culmination of an exciting and important experiment. Can national actions dependent on self motivated regional organization succeed? Our politics, our style and our instincts say it will work. Mayday will be the test.

Note: There are several constituency groups (Gays, Women, Third World) planning to function as distinct groups outside of the regional structure. These groups will function much the same as the regions with their own targets and campsite areas.

IV.   MAYDAY NONVIOLENT CIVIL DISOBEDIENCE:
      THE TACTICAL OVERVIEW

OUR APPROACH

Washington, D.C., is a colony. It is ruled by a committee of Congress made up of racist white southerners. The overwhelming number of people living in Washington are black. Virtually the only industry in Washington is the Federal Government, with the overwhelming majority of the em-

ployees being white, and, with a few exceptions, all upper
echelon employees being white. This means that most employees of the Federal government commute to work each day
from the suburbs of Virginia and Maryland.

Because of the racist nature of the Federal government, closing down the apparatus that controls the War
against Indochina and America's oppressed is a relatively
easy operation if it is coordinated.

Twenty-one targets have been selected for the Mayday
nonviolent civil disobedience. The targets (see Map no. 2)
are broken into two general categories: (1) traffic circles
and (2) bridges. These targets if blocked during the early
morning rush hour will seal off the Federal Triangle area of
Washington and the Pentagon. All of the targets selected
deal directly with the Federal Government and blocking these
targets will have a minimum impact on the surrounding black
community. These targets were specifically chosen to minimize disruption of the black community. No disruptive actions will take place North of Massachusetts Avenue NW or
East of 6th Street SE and NE, which are the boundaries of
the black community.

Actually sealing off a section of an American city
through nonviolent direct action has never been attempted before in an organized fashion. The experience of May, 1970,
however, shows that it can be done. During the Cambodian
crisis many cities had main thoroughfares blocked by nonviolent action, including sit-downs and street parties. In
several instances the thoroughfares were six and eight lane
expressways. It can be done!

From a propaganda point of view, and to minimize the
number of enemies we will produce, the style and method of
our actions are crucial. Our disruption of Washington must
be seen as an attack on the Federal Government, specifically
those sections dealing with the war against the people of Indochina and America. It must not be seen as an attack on the
employees of the Federal Government. We wish to win them
as allies and so we need to minimize their antagonism towards us.

To divert our attention from institutions to persons
employed in those institutions would be a serious political error.

Therefore, the days of May 3 and 4 are being projected as a government employees strike against the war. Our nonviolent civil disobedience actions are enforcing a two-day strike of government employees. If this is successful any employees caught in traffic jams will blame themselves for attempting to get to work and therefore, not us. In the happy event that the government orders all federal employees to be on the job, those caught in traffic jams will blame the government, and not us. One benefit of this will be an unconscious gratitude towards the anti-war movement for getting government employees a two-day holiday.

Our tactical approach to stopping the government is decentralization and concentration. By this we mean that the targets are decentralized and our demonstrators are concentrated. No target will have less than a thousand demonstrators and no major target (see map no. 2, targets bearing asterisks) will have less than three thousand demonstrators. Our targets are decentralized to a) insure the total halt of traffic and b) to increase the difficulty of Federal forces containing our demonstrations.

Government Response

On the basis of a careful reading of public and confidential government plans for containment of Mayday type actions and information secured from our sources inside the Federal bureaucracy and the military, the following is a general overview of the Federal Government's efforts to deal with Mayday. Specific late intelligence will be supplied by the Mayday Tactics and Logistics sections on May 1st.

General

The current plans call for a cooperative force of US Military (National Guard & Federal troops) and the DC police force. There will be no outside civilian police called in for Mayday. Agent provocateurs will say that Virginia and Maryland State Police have been called in to D.C. This is a lie designed to spread panic about the supposed brutality of Virginia and Maryland State Police.

Because of the limited number of D.C. police (5100 total, including clerks and 1000 headquarters personnel) the bulk of the defensive activities will be handled by the military.

The central tactic of the defensive forces will be psychological warfare.   There will be a maximum display of military hardware; agent provocateurs will seek to spread panic and exacerbate normal tensions in Algonquin Peace City (Rock Creek Park) in order to break our morale. There will be extensive use of helicopters to attempt to intimidate us and rumors will be spread that a helicopter with gas spraying devices (M 5 disperser) are about to attack Algonquin Peace City and/or target areas.

GI's, meanwhile, will be subjected to intensive "Psychological preparation" and indoctrination.   They will be told we are armed, we intend to verbally harass troops, we intend to throw shit and bags of urine at them, that we will throw bottles, rocks, and we will all be carrying clubs.

Prior to moving into defensive positions, GI's will be told that Mayday forces have beaten several GI's.   This is designed to create fear and resultant hostility among GI's and overcome the natural feelings of solidarity with us.

While temporary detention facilities are being prepared, the general defensive tactic will be dispersal and containment.   Through the use of troop movement (wedges, etc.) there will be an attempt to break our concentration into easily contained small units and gas may be used at low levels and selectively (large amounts of gas will block the roads more efficiently than we could).

The primary removal tactic will be short term detention.   This means people will be "arrested" and then released on the promise that they leave town.   Threats of severe punishment for those breaking the promise will be made.   The threats will be phony since they cannot be legally supported.   In a last resort people will be arrested, booked and jailed in temporary detention facilities.   Because of limited detention facilities an intense effort will be made by the Federal gov't to get everyone to bail out within twelve hours and leave town under "bail conditions," threatening severe punishment.   Once "bail conditions" are set, the severe punishment can be carried out.

Because of the volatile condition of the Washington Black community and the active participation of SCLC and NWRO forces, physical brutality against demonstrators will be avoided unless defensive forces feel themselves physically threatened.   Small scale selective brutality may be used

to panic and disperse demonstrators. Weapons of troops
will be plainly displayed as well as jeep mounted machine
guns (up to .30 calibre) and other armor, but because of the
experience with the Kent-Jackson reaction, ammunition will
not be issued. Rumors to the contrary will be encouraged
by agent provocateurs.

Command

        The main command for the Washington defense will be
located in the Pentagon in a special "Washington Situation
Room." There additional command centers are projected but
the number may be expanded. An effort will be made to
maintain "Unit Integrity" with certain military units being responsible for the defense of certain Mayday targets. These
units will be under a "decentralized command" with the highest ranking officer on the scene being responsible, within
defined limits, for the defense of the Mayday target using
his own discretion.

        Issuance of ammunition will be tightly controlled by
the command centers.

        · Overall command will rest with the military, though
our intelligence reports Chief Jerry Wilson and Mayor Walter
Washington will be given the "illusion of control."

Intelligence

        Many Mayday regions have already been infiltrated.
An intensive Army intelligence operation is underway. In
addition, there is close cooperation with the Justice Department and the FBI. The intelligence objectives are to identi-
fy leaders, numbers of participants, unstable elements, target areas, etc.

        Agent provocateurs are assigned to project the image
of Mayday as an undisciplined violent action. Mayday radio
communications will be monitored and in some instances
jammed with static or police information.

Logistics

        Helicopters will be used extensively. Chinook helicopters are projected for use in the event of Mayday "stall-ins" to airlift cars off roads. Helicopters and small spotter planes will be used to track our movement. Jeeps will be equipped with barbed wire fences mounted on the front and machine guns for psychological purposes. Tanks will be highly visible.

There will be extensive use of fencing and barricades including, but not limited to, chain link, concertina, and barbed wire.

Troops will be housed in government buildings and on selected billet sites in and around Washington. There will be hot food for troops in most cases.

Bridge Defense

Troops will be used in large concentrations to line roads and prevent entry to bridges by pedestrians where practicable. In most cases troops will be behind barricades. Efforts will be made to prevent communication between troops and demonstrators.

Traffic Circle Defense

Defense of circles will be left mostly to D.C. police though military reinforcements will be used. Attempts will be made to prevent concentrations of demonstrations with gas and arrests used as a last resort.

OUR RESPONSE

In essence, our response is to maintain communica-tions, prevent panic, and not allow ourselves to be chased out of town. We cannot prevent infiltration so efforts at keeping information "secret" will only serve to confuse par-ticipants. It is important that we consistently project that Mayday is a nonviolent action. Any fuzzing of that point will lend legitimacy to the rumors spread by provocateurs and cause people to stay away from Washington. The worst thing that can happen is a small, politically isolated action.

We need to work actively with GI's prior and during the action. At this time we can't expect a mutiny but we can expect the overwhelming majority of GI's to be sympathetic though some will be outright hostile, but we should recognize that these will be isolated.

For communications, we suggest regions secure bull horns and short range talkies. The walkie talkie operators need to be familiar with the equipment and establish codes to prevent interception and false information from being beamed in on their frequencies. The radios can be easily jammed or be made useless by false messages being beamed in, so you should establish an alternate system such as runners. The Mayday tactics and logistics section will maintain several coordination centers and is setting up several alternative means of communication. We will monitor all police and military frequencies to provide up to date information for all participants. The information will be sent out over AM radio frequencies from special mobile transmitters. These transmitters will broadcast May 3 and 4 over clear channels and cover all twenty-one target areas. Every participant should bring a transistor radio.

Our own logistic preparation should be oriented towards individual self contained units. People should bring wire cutters for fences, squeeze bottles of water for gas, bamboo flutes, tamborines for people's music, balloons and flowers for joy, dope and food to share with the GI's and fellow demonstrators. And a transistor radio so we are all informed of what is happening.

V. TACTICAL APPROACHES TO TARGET AREAS

The following are a few of the nonviolent civil disobedience tactics being planned by various regions.

WAVES. The regional groups will be broken into units of 10-25 people. Monday morning the units will move in waves, one unit in each wave, onto the road. They will sit down in a circle, and pass the pipe and play music until arrested. The next wave will then move to the road. This will last until noon when the remaining people will return to Algonquin Peace City. The same thing will happen Tuesday. Any people remaining will move on Wednesday to the Capitol and stay until everyone is arrested. This tactic is particularly useful at traffic circles where there are many roads leading into the circle.

STREET PARTY. The regional group will move in mass to
their circle target playing music and dancing, getting as
close as they can to the target. They will disperse if
gassed or charged with batons but always regroup. They
stay put if threatened with arrest.

TROOP TEACH-IN. The region will encircle troops guarding a circle or line up several deep along troop lines protecting bridges. They will establish a one to one relationship to GI's and demonstrate solidarity. Food and dope will
be passed. If a large group of GI's come over to our side
the breech will be filled with demonstrators moving through
and sitting in on the target road. The Mayday legal facilities will have special sections to serve troops who join us
and a special GI counseling center will be located in Algonquin Peace City. These regions are bringing wire cutters
to get through fences to the GI's. Wedges and other forma-
tions sent to break up the concentration of demonstrators
will be absorbed amoeba-like and given intensive arguments
about why they should join us.

SIT-IN. The region will march up a street towards a circle
or bridge and when confronted by police or troops will sit
down. They will maintain their ground until arrested.

VI.   TACTICAL DESCRIPTIONS

Lay of the Land

        The District of Columbia is most likely one of the
easiest cities to understand and travel within, for it was one
of the few which was laid out by a city planner.

        The district is sectioned off into four areas, desig-
nated North West, North East, South West, and South East.
Base lines for these sections are North, East, and South
Capitol Streets and an imaginary line extending West from
the Capitol Building.

        Numbered streets run north to south; the lettered
streets travel east to west. House and building numbers for
each section start at each base line. For example, the 900
block on "C" Street, NW, is between 9th and 10th Streets,
NW. The 300 block on 7th Street, SW is between "C" and
"D" Streets, SW.

As one travels North, and the single lettered paths
and trails in D.C. end, a new sequence appears, of one-syl-
lable words, starting with "A" and continuing in alphabetical
order. Once this order is finished, two-syllable words,
starting again with "A" begin. For instance, in one part of
NW Washington, Benton, Calvert, Davis, Edmunds, Fulton,
Garfield, etc. appear, following "W" Street.

Pennsylvania Avenue is numbered the same as lettered trails. Connecticut Avenue is the same as a numbered
path. Most other diagonal paths and trails have no standard
pattern.

The plans of D.C. were made, based upon the lessons
and experiences of the French Revolution of 1789. The ar-
chitect for the city, an aristocratic Frenchman, designed the
District so that it could be easily defended against a general
insurrection of the populace.

All the main avenues were purposely built wide, with
all the original streets being fed into a series of circles.
The Paris experience showed that the avenues needed to be
wide so trees felled from both sides would not meet and
block the street.

For the defenders of the city, this enabled cavalry
charges, one of the fiercest tactics of the period, to be used
to clear the avenues of insurrectionists and maintain communications. The circles joining every street were designed
for the purpose of mounting cannon.

With cannon in the circles, every street of the Capital could be swept with grape and chain shot, in the event of
street demonstrations or insurrections.

Washington was the most militarily secure capital of
the Nineteenth Century. That security, however, is now its
insecurity, as the following tactical descriptions will reveal.

1. Site One

Site one, Rosslyn Plaza, is on the Virginia side of
the Francis Scott Key Bridge, which connects George Washington Parkway, Lee Highway, Route 66 and Fort Myer Drive.
It is probably one of the most heavily traveled single areas
in the entire Metropolitan area.

Site one affords excellent, low, flat, open areas which are adjacent to nearly all the aforementioned major highways from Northern Virginia.

North of Rosslyn Plaza is the Marriot Hotel, where it was found, the "High Command" of the Pentagon regularly dine. As one leaves Key Bridge, traveling West, the Marriot Hotel is clearly visible on the right and it provides an excellent staging area and superb parking facilities.

Traffic, during rush hour, is normally stalled and it is believed that it would present extreme problems for the defense forces of the Federal Government to prevent any disruption from occurring. Massive defense of Rosslyn Plaza would normally disrupt traffic, one-third of which travels to the Pentagon, and the defense forces would thus be doing our job.

Also, use of gas in Rosslyn Plaza may be impossible since it is directly adjacent to the business section of Arlington and the "prestigious" Marriot Hotel. Their reluctance of using gas, however, is naturally not certain; we are merely speculating on probability.

2.   Site Two

Site two, the D.C. side of Key Bridge, is restrictive in area and severely limited in mobility. "M" Street can be easily secured by defense forces.

Thirty-fourth and thirty-fifth streets are extremely steep, and can be easily blocked by police without affecting the flow of traffic at all.

The traffic both to and from Key Bridge is intense; congested traffic is normally a problem during rush hour. Whitehurst Highway, which travels under Key Bridge, is a major thorofare and can be relatively easily disrupted from a flat, open area which is directly adjacent to Key Bridge, "A" Street and Whitehurst. One word of caution: this open area is extremely small, perhaps supporting only several hundred people.

3.   Site Three

This area is a comparatively isolated region, leading to the Theodore Roosevelt Bridge from the Virginia side.

There is a very great expanse of open grassy plains which
lies next to the George Washington Parkway, Arlington Blvd.,
which leads, directly to the Pentagon, and Route 66, which
directs traffic onto the TR Bridge.

This area, normally, carries relatively little traffic.
However, if Rosslyn Plaza is disrupted, there is the possibility that traffic could be diverted to TR Bridge via Route
66.

4. Site Four

The D.C. entrance to the TR Bridge has one open
land area which can accommodate large numbers of people.
This area is the grounds for the Kennedy Performing Arts
Center, presently under construction.

The Kennedy Arts Center lies adjacent to Rock Creek
Parkway, a major interchange.

5. Site Five

The Virginia side of the Arlington Bridge contains
acres upon acres of open space leading to the bridge. In the
event that Fort Myer Drive is disrupted at Rosslyn Plaza
(see Site one), Memorial Drive may be used as an auxiliary
road to Fort Myer by Federal authorities.

Also, in the event all points South are effectively disrupted, Arlington Ridge Road, which changes into Route 110,
may be utilized as one of the prime access roads, from
Northern Virginia to the Pentagon.

6. Site Six

There is much land which can sever the Arlington
Bridge entrance from the Lincoln Memorial grounds and the
entrance to Rock Creek Parkway, and Ohio Drive South.
There are very large grassy areas west of Lincoln Memorial
facing the Potomac adjacent to Ohio Drive.

7. Site Seven

Washington Blvd., containing the only direct access
roads to the Pentagon from northern points, contains large
expanses of flat open areas.

Specifically, the first access route fed from Arlington Blvd. leads to the Pentagon North Parking Area, where tens of thousands of cars arrive daily. The terrain is flat and open and is bounded from the north by the Boundary Channel.

The second access route, Highway 110, leads from the area near Rosslyn Plaza directly to the Pentagon grounds itself. It travels under Washington Blvd. and splits off into a small operational access road which leads onto the Pentagon grounds itself.

There exist, in and around the Pentagon grounds, very large flat open spaces, particularly the area just north of the Pentagon.

Resistance from authorities is expected to be very rough, although it will be difficult to execute without a general disruption of traffic, which achieves our potential goal.

8. Site Eight

The loop just west of the Pentagon serves the Naval Annex, the US Marine Corps, and the Pentagon personnel via Washington Blvd., north to south, from the Arlington Bridge, Columbia Pike, and Shirley Highway, East and West.

Just south of the loop, massive road construction is underway. There are acres upon acres of flat open space at the loop on Washington Blvd. and the access ramp from Shirley Highway "West" are vulnerable to disruption particularly.

The Loop, specifically, is the main feedin to the Pentagon South Parking Area, and disruption of this general area could have demonstrable effects.

9. Site Nine

Shirley Highway, just south of the Pentagon South Parking Area boasts large flat open areas of land. Bordering the Pentagon Parking Area are large bushes which tend to obscure visibility of the Pentagon Parking Area considerably.

Shirley Highway is probably the key road to the Pentagon, the US Naval Annex and Henderson Hall, headquarters

for the US Marines, the latter two both off Washington Blvd.
west of the Pentagon South Parking Area.

Expect, however, to find tight restriction on mobility,
as Federal, local and military authorities will attempt to
keep these areas, particularly Shirley Highway, open.

10/11. Sites Ten and Eleven

The Rochambeau Bridge and George Mason Bridge are
possibly the two most heavily travelled bridges leading to and
from Washington, D.C. The Rochambeau Bridge directs
traffic into D.C. and the Mason Bridge directs traffic into
Virginia. Both bridges, for simplicity, are known as the
14th Street Bridge complex.

In addition, the 14th Street Bridge is added greater
importance because over 70% of the traffic flows to and
from the Pentagon.

The two main arteries are the George Washington
Parkway and Shirley Highway. There is a large open area
of several acres between both the Rochambeau and Nixon
Bridges, which also shares its borders with the George
Washington Parkway and the Potomac River.

Just north of the 14th Street Bridge is the Marriot
Hotel which offers a large parking lot. East of the Marriot
Hotel and south of Shirley Highway, an additional several
acres of open flat land exists.

There appears little likelihood that gas would be utilized here, because of the proximity to the Pentagon and the
Marriot Hotel.

12. Site Twelve

The D.C. side of the 14th Street Bridge is one of the
more heavily travelled thoroughfares in D.C. Approximately
70% of the traffic here will be Pentagon personnel.

The Jefferson Memorial grounds provide low level
open spaces for massive gatherings. The area, however,
will provide many logistical problems as the dispersal and
containment tactic the federal authorities can employ can be
ideally implemented at the Jefferson Memorial grounds.

The importance of this juncture is the fact that an enormous rate of traffic flow will be travelling to the Federal Triangle, where most of the government operates.

Specifically, the most vulnerable area is the exit of the 14th Street Bridge leading to the Case Memorial Bridge and 14th Street. There is one intersection which joins both immediately following the exit of the Bridge.

13. Site Thirteen

Washington Circle itself is massive and can accommodate large numbers of people. However, other than the Circle, there is little room for gathering. Adjacent to the circle is the George Washington University Hospital, with its emergency entrance facing Washington Circle.

There are several prestigious luxury apartments north of the circle which occupy most of the immediate land. K Street, in addition to intersecting with the circle, travels under the circle which might provide other complications.

It is, however, a major site, intersecting Pennsylvania, six blocks from the White House, with main artery, New Hampshire Avenue.

14. Site Fourteen

Dupont Circle, a crucial intersection where much traffic flows from the downtown "Federal Triangle" to the affluent, predominantly white NW section and Maryland suburbs.

The circle itself is open and provides easy accessibility to any of the particular arteries joined at Dupont.

Some of the more notable landmarks at Dupont are the Iraq Embassy, Riggs National Bank, the Washington Club and a Peoples Drug Store.

Some caution must be exercised at Dupont for Connecticut Avenue travels under the circle, from north to south.

15. Site Fifteen

Scott Circle, three blocks from Dupont Circle, sports much open land not only on the Circle green itself, but also in front of the Gramercy Hotel, which is south of the Circle

on Rhode Island Avenue.   Also, there is a small lot adjacent
to Scott Circle where the abandoned Philippines Embassy
stands.

The main arteries, Massachusetts, Rhode Island Avenues, and 16th Street are often heavily travelled.

There is also much open space in front of the Australian Embassy and the infamous National Rifle Association,
which are at opposite ends of Scott Circle on 16th Street.

16.   Site Sixteen

Thomas Circle is a key junction for Massachusetts
and Vermont Avenues.   Massachusetts Avenue runs beneath
Thomas Circle, yet there is a large open area, capable of
sustaining several hundred people, directly south and adjacent to the Western end of the Massachusetts underpass.

Thomas Circle green is long and thin, divided into
three separate areas by the circle access roads.

The Sonesta Hotel provides some area for mobility,
which lies directly north of Thomas Circle.

Between 14th Street and Massachusetts Avenues, just
east of the Circle green is a large parking lot which is un-
restricted.

17.   Site Seventeen

Mt. Vernon Square, joining Massachusetts and New
York Avenues with K Street, provides a large area for ma-
nueverability in the green itself, where the D.C. Public Library is located.   Directly west of the Library there is much
land, which is increased by a church on K and Massachusetts Avenues, overlooking the Library.

18.   Site Eighteen

The Commodore intersection, near Union Station has
a large open area directly across from the US Post Office
and National Guard Headquarters.

The two main arteries at Commodore, Massachusetts
Avenue and North Capitol Street, lie adjacent in this open
area, where perhaps 1/2 acre of land is available.   The
area is also several blocks from the Senate Office Bldg.

19. Site Nineteen

Stanton Park, a lower-middle class residential area,
two blocks east of the Senate Office Bldg, is a small open
area, measuring approximately 75 yards in length and 20
yards in width.

With the exception of Massachusetts and Maryland
Avenues, which intersect at Stanton Park, there is little of
importance.   A gas station, a small church and a laundro-
mat fill its borders.

20. Site Twenty

Seward Square, two blocks away from the 5th pre-
cinct of the D.C. Police Department, and three blocks away
from the House of Representatives Office Building, has a
small area of open land, where North Carolina and Pennsylvania Avenues intersect.

It is one of the major crossroads into the Federal
Triangle from points east and southeast of D.C.

One disadvantage is that Seward is divided into four
sections, thus forcing any large group to be vulnerable to
the dispersal and containment strategy of the defense forces.

21. Site Twenty-one

Folger Park, although seemingly insignificant, does
serve a vital purpose.   Should the Seward Square disruption
succeed, all eastbound traffic would be detoured to Folger.
A tie-up at Folger would prevent much traffic arriving from
eastern points to the Federal Triangle from reaching their
destination.

Folger is a small park in a semi-residential, semi-
commercial area.   It is relatively isolated and is two blocks
south of the House Office Buildings.

CAPITOL BUILDING

On May 5, Algonquin Peace City will shift its camping grounds from Rock Creek Park to the U.S. Capitol Building.

There, it is expected that we will lay a nonviolent

siege of the Congress, forcing it to remain in session until
it ratifies the People's Peace Treaty or until we are all arrested.

At the present time, it seems very unlikely that the
defensive forces of the Federal Government can do anything
substantial in deterring us. The Capitol Building is endowed
with massive areas of low, flat open space which logistically
is difficult to defend.

If the Federal defense forces attempt to lay a 360 degree ring around the Capitol Building, we can merely ring
them. If however, such a dubious plan is implemented by
the Federal Government, they will have accomplished our
task.

Come prepared to stay, bringing tents, blankets, etc.
so that we can exist together and be as self-sufficient as
possible.

VII.   ARREST AND JAIL

It is said that the level of civilization of a society is
measured by the quality of its prisons. It is certainly true
in America that you cannot appreciate what repression and
oppression are about until you have done a bit of time in jail.

The mere threat of jail has traditionally been an effective weapon against movements for social change. So long
as our actions are limited to easily controlled "legal dissent" they are easily dealt with. Mayday is nonviolent civil
disobedience. We expect most of the participants to be arrested and all participants to be prepared for possible arrest.
It greatly enhances our tactical position if the jails and detention facilities are filled with demonstrators. The spectre
of thousands of people jailed in the government's unsuccessful attempt to control Mayday will graphically demonstrate the
political isolation of the warmaking government. The stopping of Washington will slow our power. Tens of thousands
of us risking jail--going to jail--will make the choices painfully clear to America's rulers. End the War or face social
chaos. On the other hand if we allow brief detention and/or
the threat of arrest to chase us out of town Mayday may be
contained.

Given our numbers, arrest, booking, detention, and

court procedures will be run on an assembly line basis. Upon arrest demonstrators will be photographed with their "arresting officers." When arrests occur in areas defended by the military, U.S. Marshals will be the "arresting officers." The photographs will be for identification purposes in the event of court action. After arrests people will be put in buses and transported to a booking area, usually adjacent to the detention area. Prior to busing men and women will be segregated. All arrest and booking procedure will be observed by the Mayday legal cadres. There will be, with rare exception, the same misdemeanor charge laid against all people arrested. Any people booked with a trumped-up charge (such as someone beaten by police and then charged with assaulting an officer) will immediately have his or her case assigned to a Mayday lawyer.

Detention facilities will be of a barracks variety. Upwards of 250 people will be housed in the same dormitory. This presents the opportunity for high energy non stop raps, political education, singing, etc. At this point it is important that group solidarity be developed and maintained. The food and facilities will be shitty. Extreme pressure will be placed on individuals to bail out immediately. Recognizance bail (meaning free) will be offered to those who will leave immediately. If solidarity is maintained and only those who absolutely must bail out leave everyone will be released together when Mayday is over. In jail, organization and solidarity can defeat efforts to divide and control us.

Experienced cadre will be present in all detention facilities to interpret the actions of the special courts that will be convened to deal with us. All Mayday lawyers will have special identification cards. Be wary of lawyers not holding these cards since they will not be aware of the politics and purposes of Mayday.

Finally, rumors of extreme fines and jail terms will be rampant. Ignore them. The maximum fine levied in Washington in mass arrest situations has been $25. In most cases the fine and bail has been $10. If we maintain our solidarity we should all be released with no charges.

Note: As with everything in this manual this section will be updated and copies available in Algonquin Peace City on May 1.

Conclusion

You've read the Manual. Now a list of things that need to be done.

1. If you don't have a regional organization, organize one. When it's done, let us know. Call 202-347-7613.
2. Send regional representatives to an orientation session. Call 202-347-7613 to set it up.
3. Fill out the following form and get it into the Mayday Collective, Tactics and Logistics Section.

Logistics Preparation Form

1. Area your region covers_____

2. Name of region_____

3. How many from your region will be in D.C. Mayday (best estimate)_____

4. What is your target_____

5. Who's your regional contact person?

Name_____

Address_____

Phone_____

Mayday Collective
Tactics and Logistics
1029 Vermont Ave., N.W. Rm. 906
Washington, D.C.

or call: 202 347-7613 (Coffin, Lubin, Fowler, or Shatzkin)

(Received from the Mayday Collective on March 22, 1971.)

53. PEOPLES COALITION FOR PEACE & JUSTICE

1029 vermont avenue n. w.
washington d. c.   20005
room 900, 202-737-8600

COORDINATING COMMITTEE (in formation)

Mia Adjala
Althea Alexander
Irving Beinin
Allan Brick
Bill Briggs
Kay Camp
Sally Chancey
Mary Clark
Theirrie Cook
Dave Cortright
Jay Craven
Carlos Dabezies
Rennie Davis
Stu Davis
Dave Dellinger
William Douthard
Jim Duffy
Don Duncan
Dick Fernandez
Alan Fisher
Carleton Goodlett
Gil Green
Terrance Hallinan
Dave Hauseman
Dave Ifshin
Willie Jenkins

Louis Kampf
Sylvia Kushner
Sid Lens
Marcia Landy
Brad Lyttle
Josh Markel
Paul Mayer
Dave McRenolds
Stewart Meacham
Chris Meyer
Susan Miller
Dr. Luther Mitchell
Rosalio Munoz
Sidney Peck
Claudette Piper
Pat Richartz
Irving Sarnoff
Rev. Ken Sherman
Jack Spiegel
Bill Tate
Leonard Tinker
Jarvis Tyner
Deborah Wallace
Cora Weiss
Ron Young
Trudi Young

May 14, 1971

Dear Sisters and Brothers,

The People's Coalition faces a severe financial crisis.

232

The spring campaign has been expensive. Bills total more than $10,000. Sound systems cost more than $16,000. Renting tents cost $2700. We owe the Vietnam Peace Parade Committee more than $8000.

Until now, much of our money has been raised in the worst possible way--through bank loans. One person alone has signed bank notes for more than $25,000. A people's movement shouldn't rely on banks or a few wealthy contributors; it should have a broad financial base.

Although we have debts on one hand, we have enthusiastic people on the other. The nation's largest nonviolent civil disobedience resistance has left people everywhere asking us what next they can do to oppose war, poverty, and repression.

A people's movement needs people's money. Please send all you can.

Yours in peace
and unity,

Dave Dellinger

Sidney Peck
Bradford Lyttle

(Received from the Peoples Coalition for Peace and Justice on May 15, 1971.)

54. PEOPLES PEACE

This conference was called for and organized by the
U.S. National Student Association, Midwest Peace Treaty
Coordinating Committee and a group of students of the University of Michigan at Ann Arbor. The Conference was
called because the three sponsoring groups felt it important
that American students and young people who are against the
war and committed to the People's Peace Treaty meet to discuss the current situation in Indochina, particularly South
Vietnam; the People's Peace Treaty and how to organize
around it; and enforcement of the People's Peace Treaty.

Responsibility for the conference rests with the Conference Organizing Committee which is made up of four people from each of the sponsoring groups. This Committee
has made decisions leading up to the Conference and shared
responsibilities for work on the Conference with other groups
and individuals who support the conference call. During the
Conference the Committee will carry out its responsibilities
through a Conference Steering Committee. This Committee
is made up of three people from each of the sponsoring
groups and will be expanded during the Conference to include
an elected representative from each of the Saturday afternoon
workshops (see "proposed agenda").

All the people working on the conference are trying to
structure it so that it is flexible and loose, yet enables serious discussion to take place. We want to provide an atmosphere which is creative, which recognizes our common
culture, and which is not paralyzed by either inefficiency or
authoritarianism.

It's damn near certain that during the Conference a
number of participants will get pissed off, offended, feel
pushed around or be ignored. It's always happened at conferences and probably always will. If at any time you are
dissatisfied or angry, critical or have a suggestion to make,
go to the Message/info room on the third floor of the Union.
In that room there will be a member of the Conference
Steering Committee who will attempt to respond to whatever
problems arise.

234

The rest of this special supplement provides information of the conference including facilities, services, housing, and general information. The people working on the conference have done their best to make this a worthwhile and productive weekend. In the final analysis, however, whatever this conference is or can be, whatever it does or does not do to end the war against the people of Indochina, is dependent on you.

> Jerry Coffin, Conference Coordinator
> Allyne Rosenthal, for the Organizing Committee
> Marnie Heyn and Brian Spears, for the
> Conference Facilities Group

PROPOSED TREATY OF PEACE BETWEEN THE PEOPLE OF THE UNITED STATES AND THE PEOPLE OF SOUTH VIETNAM AND NORTH VIETNAM

1. The Americans agree to immediate and total withdrawal from Vietnam and publicly to set the date by which all American forces will be removed.

   The Vietnamese pledge that as soon as the U.S. Government publicly sets a date for total withdrawal:

2. They will enter discussions to secure the release of all American prisoners, including pilots captured while bombing North Vietnam.

3. There will be an immediate cease-fire between U.S. forces and those led by the provisional revolutionary government of South Vietnam.

4. They will enter discussions of the procedures to guarantee the safety of all withdrawing troops.

5. The Americans pledge to end the imposition of Thieu-Ky-Khien on the people of South Vietnam in order to insure their right to self-determination and so that all political prisoners can be released.

6. The Vietnamese pledge to form a provisional coalition government to organize democratic elections. All parties agree to respect the results of elections in which all South Vietnamese can participate freely without the presence of any foreign troops.

7. The South Vietnamese pledge to enter discussion of pro-
    cedures to guarantee the safety and political freedom of
    those South Vietnamese who have collaborated with the
    U.S. or with the U.S.-supported regime.

8. The Americans and Vietnamese agree to respect the in-
    dependence, peace and neutrality of Laos and Cambodia
    in accord with the 1954 and 1962 Geneva Conventions and
    not to interfere in the internal affairs of these two coun-
    tries.

9. Upon these points of agreement, we pledge to end the
    war and resolve all other questions in the spirit of self-
    determination and mutual respect for the independence and
    political freedom of the people of Vietnam and the United
    States.

        By ratifying the agreement, we pledge to take what-
ever actions are appropriate to implement the terms of this
joint treaty and to insure its acceptance by the government
of the United States.

CHALLENGE: THE PEOPLE'S PEACE TREATY IS A RE-
TREAT FROM THE "IMMEDIATE WITHDRAWAL" POSITION
TO ONE OF "NEGOTIATIONS."

RESPONSE: Actually, the People's Peace Treaty is an advance based on the immediate withdrawal position. Implicit
in the treaty is that discussions between the American and
Vietnamese peoples have already taken place and the only
thing left is to enforce the treaty on the American government. Further, the People's Peace Treaty gives guts to demands for immediate and total withdrawal because it shows
folks an eminently reasonable way the total withdrawal can
take place. The treaty even says "the Americans agree to
immediate and total withdrawal from Vietnam..." Finally,
it does something that hasn't been done before and demands
that Americans "... publicly set the date by which all U.S.
military forces will be removed." This fact turns the whole
Nixon strategy for defusing domestic anti-war sentiment back
on him by saying, in effect, "okay, smart guy, if you're
really withdrawing troops why don't you publicly set the date
when they'll all be out."

CHALLENGE: WHAT THIS TREATY REALLY DOES IS EN-
DORSE THE PROGRAM OF ONE GROUP OF VIETNAMESE

AND IS NOTHING MORE OR LESS THAN AMERICANS PRAC-
TICING REVERSE IMPERIALISM BY SUPPORTING A DIF-
FERENT VIETNAMESE FACTION THAN NIXON IS SUPPORT-
ING.

RESPONSE: The key thing to remember, however, is that
the People's Peace Treaty originated as a Vietnamese proposal.   It was written by North Vietnamese and PRG and non-
PRG South Vietnamese.   It was, in fact, non-PRG South Vietnamese who took the lead.   The points in the treaty have
the endorsement and support of literally every organized
group of Vietnamese not in the hire of the U.S.   It is falling into Nixon's propaganda trick to pretend the Vietnamese
don't have a program for ending the war.   While Nixon's
agents talk of "old wine in new bottles," the People's Peace
Treaty proves to Nixon's own constituency that indeed there
is a very reasonable Vietnamese proposal for ending the war.

CHALLENGE: THE PEOPLE'S PEACE TREATY IS NOTH-
ING BUT ANOTHER PETITION.

RESPONSE: The power of the People's Peace Treaty is that
it can be enforced on the U.S. government.   What this means
is that after individuals or groups ratify the treaty they will
take concrete action to force the U.S. government to comply
with the provisions of the treaty.   With millions of people
ratifying the treaty, the last shreds of legitimacy will be removed from the war against Indochina.   The U.S. government will have to withdraw, or force an unprecedented crisis
of confidence and all that follows.   Finally, a petition is a
request and the People's Peace Treaty is a declaration.   We
aren't asking for peace, we are declaring a peace we intend
to enforce, and a peace we intend to implement by finding
ways to directly aid the Vietnamese people.

CHALLENGE: WE'VE NEVER BEEN AT WAR WITH THE
VIETNAMESE SO THERE'S NO NEED TO MAKE A TREATY.

RESPONSE: Sure, people in the movement don't consider
themselves at war with the Vietnamese but the treaty is designed to reach out to millions of Americans who think they
are at war with the Vietnamese because our government says
we are.   The People's Peace Treaty is a convincer and not
designed for the already convinced.

CHALLENGE: THE PEOPLE'S PEACE TREATY IS READY
MADE TO BE CO-OPTED BY THE LIBERAL ESTABLISH-
MENT.

RESPONSE: How can a declaration of peace that is based on self-determination for the Vietnamese and total withdrawal of American forces be coopted? If what's meant by co-options is that the liberal establishment will ratify the Treaty, then right on! It won't be the Treaty that is co-opted but the liberal establishment.

CHALLENGE: RATIFYING THE PEOPLE'S PEACE TREATY IS A VIOLATION OF THE LOGAN ACT AND AVERAGE AMERICANS ARE NOT GOING TO VIOLATE THE LAW.

RESPONSE: The Logan Act is the first law ever passed in this country against an individual. A Quaker named Logan went to France in 1789 to negotiate a treaty between the French and the American people, in order to end the undeclared warfare between the respective governments. Needless to say, the property owning class in the U.S., then attempting to reassert their control over a people who thought they'd made a revolution, weren't too happy with Friend Logan and thus the Logan Act. The law has never been used to prosecute anyone, not even Logan.

So long as the sanctity of the President's warmaking power is respected by the people, even when it is only protected by the most tangential of laws--like the Logan Act-- we will continue to see Indochinese people slaughtered. No one will be prosecuted by the obscure Logan Act though ratifying the treaty will be technically civil disobedience. It probably boils down to a difference of opinion about whether or not this technical civil disobedience will deter people from signing the treaty. Many people think mass concern about the war is real enough so that millions of Americans will follow Friend Logan's honorable example.

CHALLENGE: THE PEOPLE'S PEACE TREATY IS SIMPLY A COVER FOR SOME KIND OF HIDDEN AGENDA BY AN ELITIST GROUP, AND IF IT ISN'T THAT THEN IT'S ANOTHER LIBERAL SCHEME, AND IF IT ISN'T THAT IT'S UNDEMOCRATIC BECAUSE THE MILLION PEOPLE IN THE MOVEMENT DIDN'T VOTE TO DO IT, AND IF IT ISN'T THAT THEN THE YIPPIES LIKE IT SO IT'S CRAZY, AND IF IT ISN'T THAT THEN IT'S RACIST BECAUSE IT DOESN'T CALL FOR BLACK LIBERATION AND BLACKS DON'T CARE ABOUT THE WAR, AND IF IT ISN'T THAT IT'S SEXIST BECAUSE AMERICAN WOMEN DON'T CARE ABOUT VIETNAMESE WOMEN AND ... AND ...

RESPONSE: And some people who are sincerely against the
war are, unfortunately, living in a society which makes
them feel that their ideas are illegitimate and which immobi-
lizes them.   The People's Peace Treaty is an idea, the form
of which has yet to be determined.   We must work to insure
that the form which the idea takes is none of those ugly
things.

SAIGON: RISING UP

A Suppressed Story: The Anti-American
Establishment in S. Vietnam

-by Cynthia Fredrick

        In a country at war, "national security" gets top pri-
ority.   This may take the form of curfews, rationing, or
universal conscription.   In South Vietnam, it simply means
hiding the truth.

        Generally speaking, the Saigon authorities have been
fairly successful in their campaign against free speech.   Although Vietnamese papers like to publish fact (and therefore
must be heavily censored), the U.S. press corps in South
Vietnam nearly always plays the government's tune.   Most
American journalists are so wrapped up in their spectacular
body counts and casualty reports that they find little time to
delve into the political intricacies of a "people's war."   The
few exceptions to this rule--Americans who learn the language, establish contacts with Vietnamese outside the (tiny)
ruling circles, and attempt to follow the political struggle in
the south--obviously cannot be tolerated.   Either their press
credentials will suddenly be revoked without explanation or
especially of late, they are simply expelled.

        This November 1, I returned to Saigon for a brief
visit--briefer than planned, incidentally, as I too was promptly expelled six days after entering the country.   Before arriving in Vietnam, I had heard very optimistic reports about
important political changes in the South.   But I was hardly
prepared for what has taken place since I was in Saigon in
1966-67.   Public opinion about the war has undergone a radical transformation.   While little publicized in the U.S., the
events of the past nine months reflect a new and vigorous
opposition to Thieu-Ky-Khiem.   Particularly significant, this

opposition is no longer centered primarily in the country, but
has surfaced in urban areas also. Students, workers, veterans, politicos, women's organizations, and religious leaders (including Roman Catholics, formerly one of the most
anti-Communist, pro-war groups), have all taken a public
stand in favor of hoabihn--peace.

Moreover, for the first time, they have linked this
peace with the withdrawal of "foreign" (i.e., American)
troops from the South and with it the ouster of the puppet
trio in Saigon.

Much has happened to bring about such overt manifes-
tation of war-weariness and revulsion. First, it is no longer possible for anyone to avoid the physical and moral damage of the war. Few families remain unscathed. Over a
quarter of the South Vietnamese population is confined to
refugee camps. An estimated 50,000 persons sleep on the
streets of Saigon every night. International public reaction
to the My Lai massacre also encouraged more outspoken
criticism of the U.S. presence in South Vietnam, for although the Vietnamese know that My Lai's happen every week,
their protests had remained unheeded abroad.

Vietnamization is a second factor contributing to a
stiffening of Vietnamese public opinion. With the withdrawal
of American troops the Saigon government is forced to rely
on increased repression in order to compensate for its rapidly dwindling support. As many as 200,000 political prisoners are now being held under intolerable conditions in "in-
terrogation centers" and jails. Such repressive measures
have in turn alienated even larger segments of the urban
population. Thirdly, the economic situation continues to de-
teriorate, and despite the recent devaluation, inflation is still
rising. An ARVN soldier earns about 3,500 piastres a
month; one egg costs 32 piastres in the Saigon market.
Hence many women--perhaps 400,000--have been forced to
work as bar girls or prostitutes to help their families survive.

Since early 1970, a new trend has developed, initially
centered on rather specific, often personal grievances, it has
evolved into a concerted effort for peace that has so far
proved impossible to suppress. A few of the more dramatic
events reflecting this trend have been picked by the Western
press. Generally speaking, however, fragmented reports
about the growing urban unrest have conveyed virtually none

of the urgency and significance of the actual situation. Once again, the American public has been kept in the dark of a news black-out, and information which would have exposed the political bankruptcy of U.S. policy in Vietnam has remained unpublished.

Events were set in motion by the students. Last February, they renewed their demands for the "autonomy of the university"--i.e. that the Thieu police stop meddling with student activities in university buildings. Soon thereafter, the two top ranking Roman Catholic bishops in the South publicly issued a 7-point program for peace. Addressed to the Vietnamese delegations in Paris, their statement was the first openly political stand by the official Vietnamese Catholic hierarchy on the secular issues of war and peace. In March, Congressman Tran Ngoc Chau was illegally sentenced to ten years of hard labor for having "unauthorized" connections with a Communist agent (his brother). Shortly thereafter, Thieu carried out a "pre-emptive strike" against the student leaders, arresting and seriously torturing several of them. The student body responded by launching a new wave of protests demanding the immediate release of their comrades. In a letter to Thieu and his advisors, they declared that "if only you care to get out of your ivory tower where you live in high luxury, you will see the discontent and anguish of our compatriots and hear their afflicted laments."

A university boycott was organized, and demonstrators poured into the streets. Hard on their heels followed a new group: a pathetic mass of war invalids, who protested bitterly about the government's refusal to help them find housing and jobs. While they roamed the city looking for empty plots of land for squatting purposes, the students continued making news. In the national Assembly building, they tried to stage a hunger strike and played cat and mouse with Thieu's police.

The invasion of Cambodia sparked a new series of protests. The struggle again escalated; student demands grew from what had been some rather timid legal-constitutional points to a condemnation of the Lon Nol regime and its brutal massacres of Vietnamese in Cambodia. The Cambodian Embassy in Saigon (empty for the past two years) was "liberated" by the students, and militant peace banners appeared with increasing frequency during the mass protest marches. The disabled vets not only joined in these public denunciations, but brought pressure on the Congress to

clean up corruption in the government. Some independent-
minded Senators did act on this issue with considerable success and wide press coverage.

On July 11, the students issued a statement demanding: 1. Immediate withdrawal of foreign troops from South
Vietnam and immediate end of support to the Thieu-Ky-
Khien regime; and 2. that the question of peace should be
left to the Vietnamese to decide on the sole basis of self-
determination.

These long-withheld demands for peace were not a
student monopoly. During the summer months, new anti-
war organizations were formed to provide focus and direction for mounting public outrage in all segments of South Vietnamese society. With familiar irony, their membership
grew and solidified thanks to the government itself. For at
the end of August, Thieu's police renewed their obtuse attacks against the student leaders, thereby, provoking a new
public denunciation of police brutality and repression. When
the detained students initiated a hunger strike "to the death,"
students throughout the country demonstrated their solidarity
by fasting with them. Yet, despite these actions, and despite the fact that a high Saigon court early in September had
actually refused to try the students because evidences of
guilt are not clear enough, still the government held and tortured the students for over a month, finally releasing them
on October 5.

At the same time, in Saigon, the anti-war groups
moved to enlarge their base of support. On October 11,
four of these organizations (the Committee of Women's Action for the Right of Life, the National Movement for Self-
Determination, the High School Teachers Union, and the Student Committee for Human Rights) convened to discuss the
possibility of forming a mass-based peace front. Over one
thousand delegates including students, workers, women, intellectuals, politicians, and religious leaders were present
at this session.

Three weeks later, on November 7, the principal
spokesman of these groups met again at a pagoda near Saigon to pledge their official support for the new movement--
the Popular Front for the Defense of Peace. Not just any
peace, and above all, not a Nixonian "peace," but "independent peace and national self-determination." In fact, the
new front position as expressed in their official 10-point

program is even stronger than that of the NLF. For rather
than demand a "negotiated" withdrawal of American troops,
they have called for 1) the departure of all U.S. and Allied
troops as a necessary prerequisite to ending the war, and
2) the establishment of a "truly representative government
so that the South Vietnamese people can establish an end to
the war as soon as possible which corresponds to the wishes
of the whole people."

Not surprisingly, one of the main themes of this long
and emotional meeting was the deep hatred felt by the Vietnamese toward the U.S. government. Listening to their ve-
hement denunciation of American war crimes, I found it difficult to believe that the wounds inflicted on Vietnam by our
country will ever heal. But these speakers also stressed
the need to distinguish the real feeling of the American public from that of its leaders, and their desire to encourage
cooperation and understanding between our two peoples.

On the basis of the political prestige of several of the
founders of the new movement, as well as the representa-
tiveness of its membership, attuned observers in Saigon consider its establishment to be the potentially most important
political development since the Tet offensive. The urban
activists realize the enormous risks they run in challenging
those in Saigon whose power and influence depend on prolonging the fighting. Nonetheless, the Saigon peace advocates
insist that regardless of any short-term success by the government in repressing their organizations, new people will
come to the foreground to continue the struggle to end the
war. Ultimately, they assured me, an independent peace
must come.

Now, more than ever, the resolution of the war depends on our demands to know the truth about what is really
happening in Vietnam. For the surfacing of the new struggle
in Saigon is the strongest clue so far as to what is wrong
in Indochina--its support of an illegitimate regime, its use
of high technological terrorists as a means of breaking Vietnamese resistance and morale, and its grand scale use of
the making "Asians fight Asians"--the so-called Nixon Doc-
trine. The Saigon peace movement needs our support. Letters, telegrams, and demonstrations for solidarity will provide crucial encouragement to our Vietnamese brothers and
sisters--and at the same time, bring to the American public
attention the fact that Vietnamese opposition to the war has
reached a new and significant stage. For twenty-five years,

they have been bearing the weight of the war. It is time we
shared this burden.

When thinking about the forms of activities in which
people can become involved in making a people's peace, there
are many programs for "positive" implementation of their
peace treaty. Positive forms of activity around the peace
treaty can be thought of as normalizing relations with the Vietnamese people. Thus, people-to-people programs can be
set up. Peoples who are at peace with one another often exchange information on common problems, often try to find
ways to build cultural understanding, and in general look for
programs to work for the benefit of both peoples.

One such program for "positive" implementation of a
treaty between peoples at peace is the one which follows. It
has been taken up by Science for the People, an organization
of American scientists. For better information on this program, please write: Levin/Lewinton, Science for the People, Department of Biology, University of Chicago, Chicago
60637.

The science for Vietnam program is being developed
to promote direct scientific cooperation with the Vietnamese
people to demonstrate that we--American scientists, re-
searchers, teachers, students of science, and workers in scientific industry--are not at war with Vietnam. We conduct
this program in order to make it possible for us to place our
skills at the service of the people. The program includes:

1. Research on problems facing Vietnam today, including
the medical treatment of pellet bomb victims, the rehabilitation of defoliated and bombed land, and some problems of agriculture.

2. General scientific support--the preparation of literature
packets (books and reprints) on topics of use to Vietnamese
universities, reviews of subjects for Vietnamese journals, collections of agricultural seed, information on some computer
science problems, and materials needed for developing science education.

3. Direct pairing of groups of American scientists from particular departments or institutions with Vietnamese groups including universities, research institutes, computer centers,
scientific societies, and the society for the popularization of
science and technology.

4. <u>Promoting the publication of</u> Vietnamese works in our
journals, the inclusion of Vietnamese scientists on editorial
boards and governing bodies of professional societies, the
nomination of Vietnamese scholars for honorary degrees,
etc.

5. <u>Some of us will apply through</u> our universities for research grants from the Provisional Revolutionary Government
and the state committee on science of Vietnam, and will devote much of our research effort to Vietnam. (Since much
of the work is library research, you don't have to be a scientist to help. Anyone who is literate and can use a library
is welcome.)

It is of course expected that science establishment institutions will disapprove of these activities, and that we will
necessarily be challenging the hierarchy of science, its structure, and its links to the centers of power in America. So
far, only a minimum of organization is required. Most
work can be done by groups within institutions. However,
communication is useful, especially for those who want to
make contact with Vietnam. Since the strongest local group
is in the biology department of the University of Chicago,
members of that chapter of Science for the People will act
as temporary coordinators.

News Service International DISPATCH maintains correspondents throughout Southeast Asia. Most of their correspondents speak native languages and have spent considerable periods of time independently traveling and living in the
countryside. As a result they tend to be more attuned to
what is really happening amongst the majority of the people.

Dispatch exposed the My Lai massacre. The character of their reporting is further attested by the recent ex-
pulsion of Michael Morrow from Vietnam for attending the
founding meeting of the Popular Front for the Defense of
Peace, and the revocation of Don Luce's press credentials.
(Luce exposed the Con Son Island prison camp tiger cages.)

This news service publishes a six-page-four-article
newsletter every week. It can be had by organizations or
individuals for the meager price of only $10.00 per year--
at 19¢ a week, hardly enough to cover postage and printing.
For subscriptions write to DISPATCH News Service International, 1826 R Street, N.W. Washington, D.C., 20009, or
come to the Committee of Concerned Asian Scholars' litera-

ture table in the Union during the People's Peace Treaty Conference.

Transportation Center - Third Floor Union
Information Center - Third Floor Union
Health Care - Third Floor Union
Women's Center - International Center (adjacent to West
    Quad and Union)
Child Care Center - International Center
Legal Aid Office - 050 Office in Union (665-6146)
Transportation Center - Third Floor Union
Message and Information Center - Third Floor Union
Health Care - Third Floor Union
Women's Center - International Center (adjacent to West
    Quad and Union)
Child Care Center - International Center
Legal Aid Office - 050 Office in Union (665-6146)
Conference Office - UAC Offices - Second Floor Union
                    763-1107
                    761-4648
                    763-2130
Meals - Basement of Union
Registration - Main Lounge - First Floor Union
Union Ballroom - Second Floor Union

Those of us in Ann Arbor who have worked to organize the conference have worked hard to try to provide all the services which you need. If there is a need which is unmet, and one which you feel we can provide, please let us know. Someone will be staffing a "messages and complaints" room as much of the time of the Conference as possible; please register any requests or complaints at that office.

AGENDA FOR STUDENT YOUTH CONFERENCE
ON THE PEOPLE'S PEACE

FRIDAY, 5 FEBRUARY

Registration
Films and literature
Women's Caucus
Organic Food Feast
    PLENARY: Speeches (10 minutes each)
               1.   General Introduction
                    Allyne Rosenthal

    2. Nixon strategy -
        Dr. Eqbal Ahmad
    3. S. Vietnam situation -
        Trudy Young
    4. N. Vietnam situation -
        Cynthia Fredrick
    5. GI situation -
        Winter Soldier GI
    6. NSA presentation and introduction
        NSA delegate

Agenda ratification
Correctives

SATURDAY, 6 FEBRUARY

Large workshops: NSA summation and in-depth study of
    Peace Treaty
Lunch
Constituency workshops (labor, students, GI's, women, people of color, press)
    1. Organizing skills
    2. Treaty enforcement
Cultural events

SUNDAY, 7 FEBRUARY

PLENARY: Nature of agenda to be determined by committee comprised of 3 members of NSA, Midwest Peace Treaty Coordination Committee, and 1 representative of each workshop.
Lunch
Regional meetings

Transportation Service

In the event that someone needs transportation in order to return to his/her home city, a transportation service room is being provided. We ask that anyone who has space in their car or bus notify us by filling out the transportation service card at registration or by coming to the room. Anyone needing rides should contact us at the room, which is located in the Services Area in the Michigan Union.

Women's Center

The Women's Center is located in the International Center, south of the Michigan Union. It is being staffed by

women of Ann Arbor.   A feminist literature collection is
available for reading.

Legal Aid Service

Legal Aid Services will be located at 340 Office of
Student Organizations, in the Michigan Union.   The office
will be staffed by members of Lawyers Guild.   The phone
number of the office is 665-6146.   A lawyer will be on call
at all times during the Conference.

Child Care Center

The Child Care Center is located in the International
Center, which is adjacent to the West Quad and the Michigan
Union.   It is being staffed by members of an Ann Arbor
men's collective, and members of an Ann Arbor junior high
people's organization.   Children's toys have been donated by
the Ann Arbor Child Care Center.

Health Care Facilities

Health Care Facilities will be located in the services
area of the Michigan Union.   Members of the Ann Arbor
Free Clinic and Drug Help service will be helping to staff
the room.   If you need help, and our room is not open,
please call Ozone house - 769-6540; Drug help--761-HELP;
or Free Clinic--761-8952

                          AN NAM

                                        Munchen
                                        27 May 1965

Dear Friends,

I have just passed ten days in Vietnam.   This country
of the coup d'état showed enough enthusiasm to warrant my
giving fifteen lectures during my short stay.

Only Saigon, Cholon and a few other cities are under
the government of the American-Vietnamese--a total population of three million.   The rest of the population--thirty
million--is Viet Cong or its sympathizers.   Thirty million
as opposed to three million--ten to one!

For 80 years, the French tried to "establish" peace
in Vietnam, and failed. In the end, they gave up. And now
Amerika...

Says a Vietnamese university professor:

"Every day millions of Amerikan dollars fall from the
skies. The Americans are rich! What a shame that these
millions are in the form of bombs and bullets, which kill an
average of fifty women and children a day--peaceful people
working barefoot in the fields. What a pity for the Americans! Spending so much money, and yet being considered
the most evil murderers! Believing that peace can be established by force. What low judgment!"

The Vietnamese people are the most docile and peaceful, the most gentle, submissive, and tender people I know
of in this world. The Vietnamese woman is so lovely and
girlish, so blushful, smiling and smart. She is a worker
without match in the world, and strong, very strong, the
mother of 7 or 8 on the average. Eating and drinking lightly, the Vietnamese woman weighs an average of 85 pounds.

No one shouts, Vietnamese women and men speak very
soft and low. In fact, they don't speak; they whisper. Even
when wearing shoes, they make no noise as they walk.

On 28 April 1965, five Japanese--four engineers (Mr.
Suzuki, 58; his assistant, Professor Sakaida, 55; and two
young experts) and an interpreter--were captured by the Viet
Cong while surveying the ground around Saigon. After four
weeks of captivity, they were released. Newsmen rushed to
their hotel, and the next day all the Saigon newspapers, as
well as French, English, and American, reported the:

Cruelty and brutality of the Viet Cong. The Japanese prisoners were outrageously abused, for four
weeks in the jungle, their only food was rice with
a little salt and two or three leaves of manioc.
Nothing else! They tried to starve them with an
incomplete food, poor in minerals, vitamins, and
protein!

Early the next day, I went with my wife to interview
the freed men. They were having breakfast, in the French
manner, for the first time in a month, and seemed happy.
"Could you tell us a little about your jungle experience, Mr.
Suzuki, Mr. Sakaida?"

First of all, we deeply regret that the papers have
reported 'facts' which are unknown to us. How
strange, really strange. Could it be they are controlled by invisible forces? Abused!? Not on your
life! We had an unforgettable time in the jungle.
We have learned much.

We were fed rice, with a soup of manioc leaves--
every day, and three times a day, it is true.
But this was not exceptional; everyone was eating
this way--soldiers and officers alike--except that
they ate only twice every day.

Each soldier carries a week's supply of rice in a
long sack slung over his shoulder. From time to
time, young mountain girls appear, pixie-like,
bringing the paddy rice (still covered with rice
straw) to replenish the supply. The soldier himself,
with a small mallet, husks his daily ration of rice.

It is truly amazing that we never got sick from this
freshly husked cereal. No malaria! And we were
hiking 20 to 30 miles a day through thick pathless
jungle.

It is very natural that these Japanese never fell ill.
They were fed macrobiotic diet number 7, with which I have
seen so many thousands of "incurable" patients cure themselves.

Why Do We Eat Rice?

As stated earlier in this article, the nutritional value
of whole brown rice is far greater than that of milled white
rice. We eat brown rice as our principal food in order to
maintain our health.

We eat it in preference to animal food because we
wish to establish peace within ourselves. Brown rice has a
balance of certain elements (particularly sodium and potassium) which are in a ratio very similar to that of our blood
cells. By eating primarily grains, which are very close to
this balance (about 5 potassium to 1 sodium) our health and
mental clarity improve, and our judgment becomes higher.

How did the Viet Cong learn to apply macrobiotic diet
no. 7 so well?

The fundamental basis of daily life in the teaching of Lao-Tzu, where Yin and Yang are explored and explained in depth, teaches how to win without fighting, convince without talking, and achieve without stress. With the magic spectacles of Yin and Yang, one can change hardship into ease, sickness to health, pain to pleasure.

Chinese philosophy, and especially Taoism (Lao-Tzu's philosophy) has very strongly influenced Vietnam, which was for many years under Chinese dominion, and many of whose people are, therefore, of Chinese ancestry. In 1434, Vietnam began using Chinese curricula in their schools (Chinese history, literature, Taoism, Confucianism, the philosophy of Mencius, etc.)

In the East, Vietnam is also known as AN-NAM: PEACE (AN) and SOUTH COUNTRY (NAM)--the country of peace in the south. Annam is the country where people lived and still live in complete harmony with the philosophy of absolute freedom, happiness and justice of Lao-Tzu.

At the far end of the Asiatic continent, in perfect peace and freedom for thousands of years, poor and humble, barefoot and lightly clothed, the people of Vietnam are satisfied with whatever Nature gives them. Living in the most primitive huts, built in a few hours from coconut leaves, they thrive on the bare necessities--air, water, a handful of brown rice, a little tea, salt, and a few vegetables--macrobiotic diet no. 7 which cures, before we contract it, any disease, physical or mental.

Two years ago, Zen macrobiotics was translated from the Japanese and published in Vietnamese. The first and second editions are already out of print, and have won over about 10,000 practicing macrobiotics. In fact, after witnessing several "miraculous" healings, one entire village of 500 went completely macrobiotic.

Vietnam is the country where vivere parvo (living the life of joyous and unfettered simplicity) has been practiced for years. It is truly the country of origin of macrobiotics.

The Amerikan killing machines can never destroy the Viet Cong completely. In fact they kill an average of seventy Viet Cong women and children only, each day.

War: Amerika against Viet Cong ... the civilized

way against the primitive ... the eating of poisoned food
plus the taking of poison-like medicine as opposed to the
Macrobiotic no. 7 diet!

Civilization versus primitive people in the jungle ...
useless fighting. In one hundred years, Americans may
with great difficulty overcome the Viet Cong. Long before
then, however, (in the next ten or twenty years), the Americans will retire completely just as the French did before
them.

Yours sincerely,

George Ohsawa

CHI HOA PRISON, South Vietnam (LNS).--The "tiger cages"
on Con Son Island, South Vietnam made headlines last July
when a fact-finding tour of Amerikan congressmen stumbled
upon these cells where Vietnamese political prisoners are
held. Con Son, described as a "re-education center" before
the scandal broke, was exposed in the press as a complex
of inhuman torture chambers.

Official U.S. opinion reflected in the straight press
was one of polite horror. The U.S. had "nothing directly"
to do with the conditions, of course, but we were chastised
for not bringing our standards of humaneness to bear on
South Vietnamese prison officials. Reform was promised.
Pressure would be put on.

A document smuggled out of Chi Hoa Prison by wom-
en who had been imprisoned in Con Son recently found its
way to Don Luce. Luce was in Vietnam with International
Voluntary Services for 12 years, until he resigned to protest
the war. He was recently fired from his post as an AP
reporter. Still in Vietnam on a grant from the World Council of Churches, Luce translated the letter and sent it to
this country.

The women who wrote the letter were political prisoners. They had been taken to Con Son as punishment for a
hunger strike in another jail protesting the murder of a fellow inmate.

All of the prisoners on Con Son Island are being

confined, tortured, and murdered, for protesting the American presence in their country, for demanding peace, or for not "actively denouncing the Communists."

The women were transferred to Con Son after they went on strike demanding that conditions of prisons be improved, that prisoners not be beaten and tortured, and that women unsentenced or with expired sentences, as well as the sick and crippled, be released.

In the middle of the night, a loudspeaker told them to "Pack your luggage and get ready to move on to another place. You will find better conditions and comforts at the new place." They were reassured that "Military police will help the women with packing, and will not beat the women."

As soon as the loudspeaker went off, a shower of lime dust and tear gas fell on the women, and they were beaten and dragged from their cells by armed police, under the direction of the wardens and in the presence of officials from the Ministry of Interior, Police Headquarters, and National Directorate of the jail.

Dragging us down the steps, they threw us one on top of the other and stepped on our bodies. Lime was thrown on two of the babies who were about two months old. We thought they could not survive. At the prison gate they threw us into the trucks like animals. Our bodies burned--our bleeding wounds were mixed with lime dust. Our clothes were torn, some of us were naked. Some big trustees got into the truck, shackled us, and threw more lime on us. While waiting at the airport, shackled, the trustees and military field police continued to beat us and threw more bags of lime. Then they threw us onto the U.S. military planes. The Americans who were watching laughed.

The tiger cages were built with U.S. dollars and so is the detention equipment. The U.S. has an advisory body to handle such matters on the island. The 450,000 dollars they spend each year for the prisons in South Vietnam are not meant to improve them, but to build more. Four prisons are needed to "detain" the population who oppose the present Saigon regime and its complicity with the U.S. All "trouble-makers" are herded into concentrated zones, otherwise known as detention camps, "rehabilitation" or "re-education centers"-- or "tiger cages."

A tiger cage is five feet wide, ten feet long and eight feet high. The walls are made of stones a foot thick. Above us were the iron bars. In each cell there is a cement bench, less than 3 feet wide, 6 feet long and 2 feet off the ground.

The cells were narrow and hot. Five of us were in one cell so that we had to divide the space: two people lay on the cement bench and three persons lay below, squeezed together like canned fish, the limited space occupied by the iron bars used to shackle us. One of us had to lie sideways, close to the latrine bucket, with her legs bent day and night. Over our heads a barrel of lime dust. The trustee prisoners were allowed to place canvas beds over the iron bars where they could sleep and watch us day and night.

Across from the tiger cages are the outdoor toilets which continuously send out bad smells. Each gust of wind brings the dust from the toilets and covers our head, eyes, and nose as well as our food and water. At night we could not sleep because of the cold, the mosquitos, our dirty clothes, thirst, and because of the trustees sleeping above our heads.

We were never given enough food and drink. If we asked for more they sometimes answered by mixing our rice with petroleum or mixing our dried rotten fish with soap, or giving us uncooked rice. Often they did not allow us to wash our bowls, so we had to eat out of dirty bowls which the flies, dogs and poultry stepped on, and the mice ran over. Rice was usually mixed with the dust from the outdoor toilets.

Each day, they allowed us to empty our latrine bucket once. The narrow hot cells always smelled of excrement and urine. Each day when they opened the cell door, flies came into the cell in swarms. At night the bugs crept all over the walls and mosquitos flew around sucking the prisoners' blood until morning. There were thousands of mosquitos and bugs, their bellies swelling with the blood they sucked until they could not fly or creep anymore. Ants and worms also bit us, our bodies itched and we were festering from scratching.

Each week we were allowed to wash ourselves three times. Each time they gave us five minutes, time enough to quickly undress and pour one or two cans of water over our bodies. Sometimes before we could put our clothes on, the trustees would push the door open and come in with their whips, looking at us naked, swearing and kicking over the bucket and the remaining water, not allowing us to wash our clothes.

The conditions at Con Son caused many of us to suffer intestinal diseases, stomach disorders, diarrhea, cholera, malaria, TB, typhoid, as well as open wounds and vomiting. When any of us fell seriously ill and when we called for emergency treatment, not only did the trustees do nothing but they also threatened to throw more lime on us and swore:

"This is a cattle cage."

"These are brick and lime kilns."

"If you do not obey and if you keep demanding things, we'll give you more lime dust."

"Death is common in Con Son. If you die, we'll send you to the cemetery of Hang Duong."

One of the women had cholera and called for the nurses. However, no nurse was sent down. She was accused of being a "peace disturber" and her arms and legs were shackled to an iron bar. She lay there in the midst of her feces.

In the eight months the women were at Con Son, they were "repressed" twice with lime dust. (Lime was used in Nazi Germany to cover and slowly dissolve the bodies of Jews who were thrown alive into trench graves.) On the fourth day of Tet (the lunar New Year), a sacred day in Vietnamese tradition, the women were beaten in the dispensary and in their cells. When they protested, they were immediately showered with lime dust. The second time, the women began protesting when they heard men in nearby tiger cages screaming.

We heard orders given to "throw lime on them until they die." So the trustees rushed toward us, throwing bags and buckets of lime upon us, which had been set on the iron bars above. Buckets of water flowed. We were choked and burned by the lime mixed with water. Many fainted, others vomited blood. One woman was seriously injured when a block of hard lime fell on her head. At the same time, they went into the dispensary and threw lime onto the patients four

times until all of them collapsed.   They stuck the rest of the
lime into the noses, mouths, and eyes of the patients so that
some were blinded, others vomited and coughed up blood.
After this, our bodies were all covered with lime.   Yet they
did not allow us to wash ourselves or clean the walls.   So
for two months, we kept lying in the lime.   We did not have
a bit of water to cool ourselves.   We had to wash our
clothes with urine, consequently we itched and were covered
with wounds.

One hundred and eight women were finally taken to
Chi Hoa, another jail on the mainland.   Here, they made demands that contacts between prisoners and their relatives be
allowed and that prison conditions be improved.   Shortly after, the trustees came into their new cells and beat them
with clubs, table legs, iron rods and iron wheels.

These are only partial facts about the cruelty of Con
Son and our present prison.   We know that:

*The denial of freedom of thought is against interna-
tional law.

*The detention of prisoners who have never been sen-
tenced or with expired sentences, or of crippled and chroni-
cally ill prisoners is an illegal act.

*The act of leaving the prisoners in thirst and hunger,
not giving them adequate medicine, killing them slowly, is an
inhumane act.

*The disrespect of the prisoners: human rights,
treating the prisoners as if they were animals, are violations
of human rights.

We, the women prisoners, denounce the repression,
the beatings, the killing, and the violation of the prisoners'
dignity.

We strongly protest against the ministry of the interior, police headquarters and the directorate of corrections
which have given orders to the managers of the prisons to
terrorize, repress, beat, and shackle the prisoners and send
them to Con Son prison.

We ask the Committee for Prisoners' Relations, Wom-
en's Committee for Human Rights, Saigon Student Union and

all other organizations to denounce the cruel acts and crimes of these people in front of the people in our country and throughout the world.

We put all our faith in you and impatiently wait for your intervention.

--Chi Hoa, 20 Sept 1970

Trinh Cong Son is a South Vietnamese guitarist and composer whose popularity seems to be above that of any military or political leader, but whose songs are not known in the west. They have a western beat and admittedly have been strongly influenced by Bob Dylan and Joan Baez.

In 1969 the Saigon government banned his songs, but the ban was eased as the army political warfare people three times asked him to confer with them. The communists claim his support, but he maintains his independence. 'I am against the war in general,' he says. 'I don't want to do what some people do: to draw a clear difference between just and unjust wars.' Khanh Ly is a 23-year-old performer who for several years has sung only Trinh Cong Son's songs. When he sings the following song at the Queen Bee in downtown Saigon, no one claps; it is not a song to applaud.

--Igal rodokenko

LOVESONG OF A MADWOMAN

I have a lover who died in the Ashau battle.
I have a love who died, lying clumsily in a valley,
Who died beneath a bridge, feeling bitter, with no shirt on.
I have a lover who died in Bagia.
I have a lover who just died last night, a sudden death.
With nothing to say, nurturing no hatred,
Lying dead as in a dream.

(Received from Jerry Coffin, Coordinator of the National Youth Convention, Ann Arbor, Michigan, on March 7, 1971. The convention transpired February 5-7, 1971.)

55. PEOPLE'S PEACE TREATY

To End the War in Indochina
156 Fifth Avenue, New York, N.Y. 10011
(212) 924-2469

"People want peace so much that one of these days governments had better get out of their way and let them have it." --President Dwight D. Eisenhower, August 31, 1959, in a televised conversation with Prime Minister Macmillan.

The government is not making peace. President Nixon, like his predecessors, speaks the words of peace and expands the war. Cambodia, Laos. And now the threatened invasion of North Viet Nam and confrontation with China.

Every segment of the population has expressed opposition to the war. Students have protested for years, some at the cost of their lives. Marches have been held. Members of Congress have been lobbied. Active duty GI's and Viet Nam veterans protest war in growing numbers. And a recent Gallup Poll says 73% of the American people want the U.S. out of Viet Nam by the end of 1971.

We have waited long enough.

The people will make the peace. With the PEOPLE'S PEACE TREATY.

What is the PEOPLE'S PEACE TREATY?

It is a document which sets forth the realistic conditions under which the war could end honorably for the people of the United States and Viet Nam. If President Nixon accepted the terms of this treaty, the killing and destruction in Indochina could stop immediately.

Where does the PEOPLE'S PEACE TREATY come from?

The idea was developed among Americans active in the

anti-war and student movements in the spring of 1970. The
U.S. National Student Association, acting on a mandate from
its 23rd National Student Congress, organized delegations to
Saigon and Hanoi where discussions were held with their Vi-
etnamese counterparts in December, 1971. The text of the
PEOPLE'S PEACE TREATY is a result of those discussions.

Who supports the PEOPLE'S PEACE TREATY?

The treaty has the support of numerous individuals
and organizations in the United States, in South Viet Nam
(both the N.L.F. and U.S.-held sectors), and in North Viet
Nam (see partial list on reverse side). In the United States
these include such national organizations as the American
Friends Service Committee, Clergy and Laymen Concerned
About Viet Nam, Fellowship of Reconciliation, National Student Association, National Welfare Rights Organization, Southern Christian Leadership Conference, Women's International
League for Peace and Freedom, Women Strike for Peace,
and the People's Coalition for Peace and Justice. Successful
referenda have already been held on campuses from Florida
to Oregon and others are underway on campuses and cities
across the nation.

A JOINT TREATY OF PEACE
BETWEEN THE PEOPLE
OF THE UNITED STATES, SO. VIET NAM & NO. VIET NAM

Introduction

Be it known that the American and Vietnamese people
are not enemies. The war is carried out in the name of the
people of the United States, but without our consent. It de-
stroys the land and the people of Viet Nam. It drains America of her resources, her youth and her honor.

We hereby agree to end the war on the following terms,
so that both peoples can live under the joy of independence
and can devote themselves to building a society based on human equality and respect for the earth. In rejecting the war
we also reject all forms of racism and discrimination against
people based on color, class, sex, national origin and ethnic
grouping which form a basis of the war policies, present and
past, of the United States.

PRINCIPLES OF THE JOINT TREATY OF PEACE

AMERICANS agree to immediate and total withdrawal from Viet Nam, and publicly to set the date by which all U.S. military forces will be removed.

> Vietnamese agree to participate in an immediate cease-fire with U.S. forces, and will enter discussions on the procedure to guarantee the safety of all withdrawing troops, and to secure release of all military prisoners.

AMERICANS pledge to stop imposing Thieu, Ky and Khiem on the people of Viet Nam in order to ensure their right to self-determination, and to ensure that all political prisoners are released.

> Vietnamese pledge to form a provisional coalition government to organize democratic elections, in which all South Vietnamese can participate freely without the presence of any foreign troops, and to enter discussions of procedures to guarantee the safety and political freedom of persons who cooperated with either side in the war.

AMERICANS and VIETNAMESE agree to respect the independence, peace and neutrality of Laos and Cambodia.

> Upon these points of agreement, we pledge to end the war in Viet Nam. We will resolve all other questions in mutual respect for the rights of self-determination of the people of Viet Nam and of the United States.

As Americans ratifying this agreement, we pledge to take whatever actions are appropriate to implement the terms of this joint treaty of peace, and to ensure its acceptance by the government of the United States.

. . . .

I'd like to contribute $_____   I endorse the Principles of the
                                      Joint Treaty
I'd like to distribute the treaty.   Signed _____
Send me_____copies
                                  Name _____
Occupation_____   (please print)

                                  Address_____
Send to: People's Peace Treaty   City _____
156 Fifth Avenue,
New York, N.Y. 10010   State _____Zip _____
(212) 924-2469

Make checks payable to
People's Peace Treaty.

Organization Preamble: Each organization ratifying the treaty
is encouraged to write and attach a preamble appropriate to
its members, setting forth its reasons for ratification and
its methods of implementation.

Endorsers of People's Peace Treaty
(partial listing)*

Ralph Abernathy, President,
    Southern Christian Leadership Conference
Congresswoman Bella Abzug, New York
Barbara Ackerman, Cambridge City Councilwoman
Barbara Avedon, San Francisco
Congressman Herman Badillo, New York
Richard Barnet, Co-director, Institute for Policy Studies
Rev. Daniel Berrigan, S.J.
Rev. Philip Berrigan, S.S.J.
Joseph Betheil, Albert Einstein School of Medicine
Julian Bond, State Representative, Georgia
Rev. Malcolm Boyd
Allan Brick, Fellowship of Reconciliation
Rabbi Balfour Brickner, Union of American Hebrew Congre-
    gations
Wagner H. Bridger, Albert Einstein School of Medicine
Allan Brotsky, Attorney
Robert MacAfee Brown, Stanford University
Roscoe Lee Browne, actor
Timothy Butz, Vietnam Vieterans Against the War
Godfrey Cambridge, actor
Kay Camp, Women's International League for Peace and
    Freedom

Noam Chomsky, MIT
Kenneth Cockerel, Attorney
Rev. William Sloane Coffin, Jr., Yale
Judy Collins, singer
Congressman John Conyers, Jr., Michigan
Rt. Rev. Daniel Corrigan, Dean, Colgate Theological
    Seminary
Bishop William Crittenden, Erie, Pa.
Bishop C. Edward Crowther, Santa Barbara
Rt. Rev. William Davidson, Episcopal Bishop of Western
    Kansas
Leon J. Davis, President, National Union of Hospital and
    Nursing Home Employees, ARWDSU, AFL-CIO
Rennie Davis, May Day Collective
Rt. Rev. Robert L. DeWitt, Bishop of Pennsylvania
Dave Dellinger, People's Coalition for Peace and Justice
Congressman Ron Dellums, California
Joseph Duffey, National Chairman, Americans for Demo-
    cratic Action
Jane Dudley, mother of P.O.W.
Congressman Don Edwards, California
Joseph & Helen Eisner, New York
Ronnie Eldridge, New York
Sister Joques Egan, Religious Order of the Sacred Heart
    of Mary
Daniel Ellsberg, Center for International Studies, MIT
Richard Falk, Princeton
Jules Feiffer, artist
Abe Feinglass, Amalgamated Meat Cutters and Butcher
    Workmen of North America
Rev. Richard Fernandez, Clergy & Laymen Concerned About
    Vietnam
Thomas Flavell, Manager, Local 169, Amalgamated Clothing
    Workers of America
Jane Fonda, actress
Henry Foner, President, Fur, Leather & Machine Workers
    Unions Joint Board
Moe Foner, Executive Secretary, Local 1199, Drug and
    Hospital Workers Union
Betty Friedan, author
Charles P. Garry, attorney
Ben Gazzara, actor
Alan Geyer, editor, Christian Century
Senator Charles E. Goodell, New York
Dr. Carleton Goodlett, San Francisco
Mitchell Goodman, author
Patrick Gorman, Secretary-Treasurer, Amalgamated Meat

Cutters and Butcher Workmen of North America, AFL-CIO
Cleve Gray, artist
Francine Plessix Gray, author
Dick Gregory, actor
Father James Groppi, Milwaukee
Thomas J. Gumbleton, Roman Catholic Auxiliary Bishop, Archdiocese of Detroit
Julie Harris, actress
Mrs. Philip Hart, Washington
Dave Hawk, Vietnam Moratorium Committee
Tom Hayden, Berkeley
Karl Hess, Institute for Policy Studies
Abbie Hoffman, WPAX, New York
Al Hubbard, Vietnam Veterans Against the War
Ericka Huggins, Black Panther Party
Rock Hudson, actor
David Hunter, Deputy General Secretary, National Council of Churches
Rev. Jesse Jackson, Operation Breadbasket
Rafer Jackson, athlete
Jennifer Jones, actress
Bernard Kelly, Roman Catholic Auxiliary Bishop, Providence, R.I.
Kenneth Keniston, Yale
Arthur Kinoy, attorney, Rutgers University
Mrs. Martin Luther King, Jr.
Jerome Kretchmer, administrator, Environmental Protection Agency, New York City
William Kunstler, Center for Constitutional Rights, New York
Rabbi Arthur Lelyveld, Cleveland
Denise Levertov, poet
Robert Z. Lewis, Staff Council, United Electrical Workers
Rober Jay Lifton, Yale
Roz Lichter, Assistant Commissioner, Economic Development Administration, NYC
David Livingston, President, District 65, New York
Salvatore E. Luria, Institute Professor, MIT, Nobel Laureate
Sister Elizabeth McAlister, Religious Order of the Sacred Heart of Mary
Senator Eugene J. McCarthy
Rev. Richard McSorley, Georgetown University
Francis J. McTerman, attorney
Stewart Meacham, American Friends Service Committee
Charles E. Merrill, headmaster, Commonwealth School
William & Ruth Meyers, New York

Kate Millett, author
Jonathan Mirsky, Dartmouth
Congressman Parren Mitchell, Maryland
Ashley Montagu, anthropologist
Rt. Rev. Paul J. Moore, Jr., Episcopal Bishop Coadjutor
    of New York
Stewart Mott, New York
Bess Myerson Grant, Commissioner of Consumer Affairs,
    NYC
Ngo Vinh Long, Vietnamese Students for Peace, Harvard
Grace Paley, author
Linus Pauling, Stanford University
Sidney Peck, People's Coalition for Peace and Justice
Ben Peckin, Business Executives Move for Peace, Chicago
Marcus Raskin, Co-director, Institute for Policy Studies
Rev. Peter Riga, St. Mary's College
Catherine G. Rorback, Attorney
Janice Rule, actress
Robert Ryan, actor
Congressman William F. Ryan, New York
Irwin Salk, Salk, Ward & Salk, Chicago
Roberta Salper, Visiting Distinguished Professor of Women's
    Studies, San Diego State College
John P. Scanlon, Assistant Administrator, Economic Devel-
    opment Administration, NYC
Berta Scharrer, Albert Einstein School of Medicine
Franz Schurmann, University of California, Berkeley
Bobby Seale, Chairman, Black Panther Party
Erich Segal, Yale
Sam Seifter, Albert Einstein School of Medicine
Sol Silverman, President, Local 130, Bedding, Curtain &
    Drapery Workers Union
Marge Sklencar, Vietnam Moratorium Committee
Burt Schneider, Los Angeles
Benjamin Spock, New York
Gloria Steinem, author
I. F. Stone, journalist
Paul M. Sweezy, editor, Monthy Review
Amy Swerdlow, editor, Women Strike for Peace Memo
Joseph Tarantola, President, Local 1, International Jewelry
    Workers Union
Studs Terkel, author
Sister Margaret Traxler, chairman, National Coalition of
    American Nuns
Dalton Trumbo, author
Jackie Vaughn, III, State Representative, Michigan
George Wald, Nobel Laureate, Harvard

Mr. & Mrs. James Warner, parents of P.O.W.
Arthur Waskow, Jews for Urban Justice
Salome Waelsch, Albert Einstein School of Medicine
Cora Weiss, Women Strike for Peace
George Wiley, executive director, National Welfare Rights
    Organization
Melvin Wulf, American Civil Liberties Union
Ron Young, Youth Work director, Fellowship of Reconcilia-
    tion
Trudi Young, National Coordinator, Women Strike for Peace

    American Friends Service Committee Peace Education
    Clergy and Laymen Concerned About Vietnam
    National Lawyers Guild
    New University Conference
    People's Coalition for Peace and Justice
    Women's International League for Peace and Freedom
    Women Strike for Peace

The People Will Make the Peace

SOME WAYS TO BEGIN:

We have the power to bring the war to an end now if we
act in a united way and exert maximum pressure.   The
People's Peace Treaty provides the means for such unity in
action.   Special efforts must be made to invoke new groups
in the process of ratifying the treaty.   And this must be followed up by plans to implement it.

Ratifying the Peace Treaty

Referenda and canvassing campaigns are now underway
in several cities and dozens of campuses.   These efforts
must spread into every community, school and membership
organization.   Every American should have the opportunity
to consider and endorse the Principles of the PEOPLE'S
PEACE TREATY.

City Councils, state legislatures, unions, student and
faculty senates and other bodies can be approached by organizational endorsement of the Treaty.   Such efforts will be
successful in many cases and can provide a creative focus
for further educational and organizing work.

Community leaders and personalities should be approached for their public support. These can be dramatized at mass meetings and press conferences to give added visibility to our campaign.

All endorsements should be sent to the PEOPLE'S PEACE TREATY, 156 Fifth Avenue, New York, N.Y. 10010 and a copy retained for local use. We will make periodic reports to the American people on the progress of the ratification campaign.

Making the Peace

The Treaty will be as real as we make it. The list of endorsers can form a basis for implementation committees within every sector of the population and every institution in American life. The forms of implementation will reflect the commitment, imagination and diversity of the American people who want peace.

Making peace means continuing many of the things we have done before but with renewed energy and focus. It means extricating ourselves from the war and ending the complicity of those institutions within our reach. These activities should range from draft and tax resistance to boycotts, strikes and other campaigns against draft boards, war corporations and research centers in our communities.

Making peace means joining together in new ways with the movements in the forefront of the struggle to end the war and the people who pay the highest price for its continuation: GI's and Veterans, welfare recipients and millions of other Americans fighting for a liveable minimum income, workers and consumers caught in the inflation unemployment squeeze brought on by the war, farm workers whose union struggle is being sabotaged by the Pentagon, and those subject to political repression for speaking out and acting against the oppression they see in America.

Many of these groups have come together to work with a United Spring Action Calendar for local and national demonstrations.

Business as usual must stop while the war goes on. We must determine and effect our honorable peace, based on the truth that we know and the life that we want.

Literature of the Resistance   267

Regional Contacts:

People's Coalition for Peace   Chicago Peace Council
   and Justice   343 South Dearborn
1029 Vermont Ave., NW   Chicago, Ill. 60604
Washington, D.C. 20005   (312) 922-6578
(202) 737-8600
                                      Los Angeles Peace Action Coun-
National Student Association   cil
2115 S. Stree, NW   55 Northwestern Ave.
Washington, DC   20008   Los Angeles, Calif. 90026
(202) 387-5100   (213) 462-8188

People's Peace Treaty (De-   People's Coalition for Peace and
   troit Area)   Justice
13100 Woodward   400 Missouri St.
Highland Park, Mich. 48203   San Francisco, Calif. 94107
(303) 869-6775   (415) 648-2125

. . . .

Information for Peace Treaty NEWSLETTER:

Name_____   Projects for implementation:
                                     Describe briefly:_____
Address_____Phone____
                                     _____
City_____State____Zip____
                                     _____
Local Peace Treaty Office:
                                     _____
_____
                                     _____
_____Phone_____   Planned activities_____

Interested in organizing? Yes   _____

_____   No _____   _____

Where? Church_____

School_____Club _____   Ideas, suggestions_____

Community___ Union___   _____

Other_____   _____

If organization, give name and   _____

address:_____

_____

(Received from the Special Collections Division, Indiana University, Bloomington, Indiana, January 17, 1974.   Collected on campus by the library staff on April 28, 1971.)

56. STOP NIXON
Stand Up and Be Counted--April 24

DEMONSTRATION

Your Golden Opportunity
GIGANTIC DEMONSTRATION IN SAN FRANCISCO FOR PEACE
Sponsored By All the Peace Groups in the United States

THIS IS LABOR'S GOLDEN OPPORTUNITY--AND YOUR OP-
PORTUNITY--TO JOIN WITH MANY THOUSANDS IN A MAS-
SIVE RALLY TO TELL NIXON WHAT WE THINK OF HIS
PHONEY PROGRAMS INCLUDING:

1. Attack on Building Trade; wages (Suspension of Davis-
   Bacon Act)
2. Unemployment.
3. High Taxes going for war.
4. Failure to come up with any program for the benefit
   of the American people.

WHAT YOU CAN DO--

(a) See that your union participates with banners.
(b) Urge your union officials to organize the members,
    make this the greatest demonstration the west has
    ever seen.
(c) Wave the union banner, carry the union sign!

APR. 24   Northern California Committee for
                           Trade Union Action and Democracy
(labor donated)   P.O. Box 8173
                           Emeryville, CA 94608

(Collected from the National Peace Action Coalition headquarters, San Francisco, April 14, 1971.)

269

57. UNITED WOMEN'S CONTINGENT FOR APRIL 24

1029 Vermont Ave., Washington, D.C. 20005

FOR IMMEDIATE RELEASE:

The United Women's Contingent for April 24 announces the opening of the Women's Center at George Washington University (800 21st St SW) Rms 402-406. The center is open to all women from 10 a.m. to 10 p.m., & offers many activities through the week preceding April 24. The press is invited to come to the center to interview women on Thursday and Friday (April 22 & 23) and is especially invited to the first major activity on Wed. April 21--Women Speak Out Against the War 12:00 noon McPherson Square (15th & K NW) speakers will include Barbette Blackington--International Director Women's Studies American University--Tina Hobson-- Member of Federally Employed Women: Marcia Sweeten- ham--Coordinator of the United Women's Contingent: Jeanne Walton--Washington Teachers Union & any sister who wishes to speak about the war, and its effects on women.

CALENDAR FOR THE CENTER:

April 20 - The Center will be a distribution site for leafletting & poster and banner making for the April 24th Contingent.

April 21 - 12:00 Noon - Women speak out against the war - McPherson Square, 7:30 pm - Workshop on Women's Right to Abortion led by the Metropolitan Abortion Alliance

April 22 - 12: Noon - Women speak out against the war - McPherson Square, Afternoon - Marshal training for women - Theatre workshop
8 pm - Films on Women & the War

Women's groups and organizations are invited to bring their literature and participate in all activities at the Center.

270

April 24 - MARCH WITH THE WOMEN'S CONTINGENT
      ASSEMBLE: 10:00 Ellipse Marshals will indicate
             location of Women's Contingent)

MARCH 12:00 Noon
RALLY 2:00 Women speakers include:
BETTY FRIEDAN - WRITER
BELLA ABZUG - CONGRESSWOMAN, NY
RUTH GAGE-COLBY - COORDINATOR OF NPAC
CORETTA SCOTT KING
DEBBY BUSTIN - STUDENT MOBILIZATION COMM.
TINA MANDEL - GAY LIBERATION
SANDRA MONDYKOWSKI - YOUNG WOMEN COMMIT-
TED TO ACTION (YWCA)

INITIAL LIST OF ENDORSERS
OF THE UNITED WOMEN'S CONTINGENT FOR APRIL 24TH

Sidney Abbott	Gay Liberation Front, Women's Caucus, NYC
Terry Anderson	San Diego Women's Center
Bobbie Arrington	Kalamazoo Women's Liberation
Rene Backkan	The Guardian
Katherine Baird	Cleveland Area Peace Action Council
Bobbie Jean Bishop	San Diego Women's Center
Barbette Blackington	Director, International Institute of Women's Studies, Washington, DC
Annie Blanton	Tallahassee Women's Liberation
Carol Bloom	Richmond College Women's Liberation
Louise Bruyn	Boston
Myena Burkholder	Women in City Government, NYC
Deborah Bustin	Natl. Student Mobilization Committee
Anne Childs	Virginia Commonwealth University
Cindy Cissler	New Yorkers for Abortion Law Repeal
Sue Cleary	Virginia Commonwealth University
Nancy Clinch	President, Greater Washington, NOW
Claire Cohen	Chwm, Women Against the War, Florida State U
Ruth Gage-Colby	Natl. Coordinator, NPAC
Polly Connelly	Chicago Women's Liberation Union
Leslie Corin	Women's Abortion Project, NYC
Flora Crater	President, Northern Virginia, NOW
Cara Crosby	Temple U, Women's Liberation
Dr. Mary Daly	Boston, NOW
Dr. Adelaide M. Delluva	Univ. of Pennsylvania
Clara de Miha	Jeannette Rankin Rank & File, NYC

Meril Dobrin	Douglass College
Sarah Dolly	Manhattan Church Women United
Betsy Downing	Virginia Commonwealth Univ.
Anne Draper	Reg. Dir., Union Label Dept., Amalgamated Clothing Workers of America
Dorothy Eldridge	President, New Jersey, SANE
Kay Estes	San Diego Women's Center
Elizabeth Fisher	Aphra, Editor
Cheryl Fricke	Virginia Commonwealth Univ.
Karen Gentemann	Univ. of Pittsburgh
Eileen S. Gersh	Univ. of Pennsylvania
Ruth Greenhouse	Welfare Rights Mothers, NYC
Helen Gurewitz	Washington Area Peace Action Coalition
Rennie Hanover	Attorney, Chicago
Helen Fugh Hayes	Coord., Chinese Culture & Education Center, Federal City College
Isabel Hendricks	Vice-Chwm, New Democratic Coalition, Cleveland
Chris Hildebrand	Coordinator, New England Women's Coalition
Tina H. Hobson	Federally Employed Women, Washington, D.C.
Hofstra College Women's Liberation	
Lucile Iverson	New York Radical Feminists
Danessa Johnson	Temple University
Elisie C. Karo	Pres., Washington Church Women United
Jeanne Lafferty	Boston Female Liberation
Fortune La Marca	Florida State Univ.
Myrna Lamb	Playwright, NYC
Jeanne Lawrence	Chicago Teacher's Union, House of Representatives, member, Teachers' Mobilization Comm.
Lillian Levine	Exec. Sec'y, Cleveland SANE
Barbara Lipman	Case-Western Reserve U Women's Liberation
Caryl Loeb	Democratic Party Precinct Committeewoman, Cleveland
Barbara Love	Gay Liberation Front, Women's Caucus, NYC
Carolyn Love	San Diego Women's Center
Marilyn Lurkin	Adelphi U School of Social Work
Ginger Mack	Chwm, Chicago Welfare Rights Organization
Mae Massie	Civil Rights Director, IUE, New Jersey

Susan Miller   Episcopal Peace Fellowship
Kate Millett   Writer, NYC
Sandra N. Mondykowski Young Women Committed to Action,
                           Boston, YWCA, New England
                           Women's Coation
Sue Moore   National Assoc. of Social Workers,
                           Chicago
Arlene Newman   Women's Liberation, Hofstra U
Anne Nunez   San Diego Women's Center
Sheila Ostrow   Temple U Women's Liberation
Dorothy J. Perkins   WILPF, Temple U
Karen Pewitt   Florida State U Women's Liberation
Queens College Wom-
    en's Liberation
Nagda Ramirez   Latin American Student Union, Chicago
Adele Rickett   Univ. of Pennsylvania
Valerie Robinson   Abortion Project Coalition, Cleveland
Pauline Rosen   Women's Strike for Peace, NYC
Ann Rosenberg   Press Co-or., Computer People for
                           Peace
Dr. Judy Rosenthal   Univ. of Pittsburgh
Muriel Rukheyser   Poet, NYC
Lula A. Safford   Women's Peace & Unity Club, Chicago
Ann Sanchez   New York Women's Center
San Diego Women
    United Against the War
Robbie Scheer   SMC, Case-Western Reserve U
Evonne Schulze   San Diego Women's Center
Kathie Scott   San Diego Women's Center
Jane Shetler   National Student Committee, Natl. Stu-
                           dent YMCA
Marge Sloan   Women Mobilized for Change, Chicago
Rose M. Somerville   San Diego State College, Faculty
Susan Sowers   Virginia Commonwealth U
Gloria Steinem   Writer, NYC
Marijean Suelzle   Berkeley, NOW
Mary Windell   Reporter, Cleveland Press
Hanna Takashige   Boston
Dr. Beatrice Tucker   Chicago Maternity Center
Barbara Kaston   San Diego Women's Center
Ilene Katz   El Cerrito, California
Florynce Kennedy   Lawyer, NYC
Rusty Krausz   Rutgers University
Jeanne Walton   DC Committee to Free Angela Davis
Isabel Wasserman   Another Mother for Peace, San Diego
Murill White   Graphics Designer, Chicago
Linda Wieser   Univ. of Pennsylvania

Nancy Williamson   Boston Female Liberation
Arlen Wilson   The Spark, Evanston, Illinois
Women's Studies Program,
    San Diego State College
Sharon Zundel   Young Women Committed to Action,
                              Cleveland
Columbia University Women's
    Liberation
Betty Friedan   Writer
Long Island Women's
    Liberation Front

Additional Endorsers

Bay Area Council on Jail
    Reform
Anita Bennett   Female Liberation, Berkeley
Bertha Dertz   Coordinator, NPAC, San Francisco
Antonia Dolar   Program Director, YWCA, San Fran-
                              cisco
Louise Garry   Women's International League for
                              Peace and Freedom
Susan Griffin   Poet, Berkeley
Ilone Hancock   Berkeley City Council
Charity Hirsch   President, Women for Peace, Berkeley
Peggy Holmes   Berkeley High School
Carol Hughes   Lawyer, San Francisco
Ella Hill Hutch   International Longshoreman Workers
                              Union
Carolyn Jasin   Sisters in Solidarity, Denver, Colo.
Gladys Jenkins   Berkeley
Joan Jordan   ICW, Women's Party
Zide Kirtley   President, San Francisco NOW
Andrea Land   Candidate for Berkeley City Council
Pat McCormick   Calif. State College, Hayward
Ruth McElhinney   Berkeley NOW
Patricia McGinnis   Association to Repeal Abortion Laws
Ruth Rosen   UC Berkeley, T. A. in Women's History
Nina Ryan   Board of Directors, Community Chil-
                              drens Nursery
Sharon Simms   Association to Repeal Abortion Laws
Sue Schulman   Female Liberation, Berkeley
Sylvia Siegel   Exec. Dir., Calif. Consumer Assoc.
Carol Ruth Silver   Candidate for Berkeley City Auditor
Leslie Sirag   Candidate for Berkeley School Board
Fay Stender   Lawyer, Los Siete

Louise Stoll	Berkeley School Board
Judy Tyfers	ICW, Women's Party, Writer
Beverly Von Dohre	Gay Women's Liberation, Berkeley
Evelyn Williams	Glide Memorial Church, San Francisco
Becky Williamson	Gay Liberation Front, San Jose
Ruth Young	Redevelopment Agency, San Francisco

East Bay Women for Peace
Jo Kuney, Mari Waters, Pat Helloran, Kathy Kornblith, Jean Crossman - Connections

Joan Hybald, Claire Miller, Judy Knoop, Cathy Caed - Women's Liberation, S. F.

(Received April 15, 1971.)

58. SAVE THE PEOPLE

Join Our Struggles with the Struggle of the Vietnamese

U.S. GET OUT OF VIETNAM NOW

The following is a summary calendar of the actions planned for Oct. 8-11 by the Revolutionary Youth Movement.

WEDNESDAY: street corner rallies throughout the city, participation in various serve the people programs such as the Young Lords day care center and the Black Panther Party's various Breakfast for Children programs. We want to emphasize that the struggles of suppressed and exploited people in this country are the same--must be linked--with the struggles of the Vietnamese people.

THURSDAY: a high school and college boycott linking the fight against the jail-like repression of the schools with the fascist repression against leaders of the people's movements in this country. There will be a rally at 12 noon at the Federal Building around the trial of the "Conspiracy 8."

AFTERNOON: at 3 p.m. there will be a rally at International Harvester Tractor Works Plant (near 26th and California). The plant is being closed down and the land is to be used to build an addition to Cook County Jail. About half the workers at Harvester are black. The UAW, the union there, recently organized the Harvester plant in Libertyville (a lilly white town) and agreed secretly with Harvester before they were even authorized to negotiate for the workers that those who will lose their jobs at Harvester will not be allowed to transfer their seniority rights to the Libertyville plant. Why? to keep it all white. In addition, Harvester has just bought some land in South Vietnam for future "development." So the joining of the issues is clear here.

FRIDAY: a rally will be held at Cook County Hospital at 2:30 in the afternoon. The purpose of the rally is Free and Adequate Medical Care for all. The conditions of

workers in the hospitals throughout the city who are mostly
women and predominantly black and brown, the enforced
sterilization of women at Cook County, the total failure of
health services in this city to meet the needs of poor people
in this city--all these issues will be raised. Support for
the Black Panther Party's Peoples Free Medical Center as
an alternative to medicine for profit.

SATURDAY: there will be the main march to demand
that the U.S. GET OUT OF VIETNAM NOW. Hooked with
the rally will be a rally in memory of Albizo Campos, the
great leader of the Puerto Rican liberation struggle, in order
to raise the demand of Free Puerto Rico, and support for
the Young Lords Organization's Peoples Day Care Center.
The rally will begin at noon in the People's Park.

SUPPORT FROM OTHER ORGANIZATIONS. National-
ly the Young Lords Organization, the Black Panther Party,
and the New Universities Conference have officially endorsed
the action. Locally and around the country a host of organi-
zations--many women's groups, varied anti-war organizations,
and so on. Medical assistance is being provided by the SHO
(Student Health Organization) and the Medical Committee for
Human Rights.

WE NEED YOUR HELP. This will be a highly disciplined series of actions. In order to give the thousands of
people from outside the city directions about housing, where
to go and when, to provide education programs, to have a
relatively safe place for them we need places to serve as
MOVEMENT CENTERS. Preferably they should be open 24
hours, so that people coming into town anytime can be taken
care of and so that emergencies can be met promptly. There
will be two captains of security in charge of each movement
center. They will be in charge of security and discipline
there and liaison with officials of the building.

HOUSING. We need individuals, churches, and organizations to make a concerted effort to find housing for the
folks from out of town. It is essential, if we are to prevent a bloodbath, that people have a place (which means a
floor, not a bed) to go to sleep. Especially helpful would be
larger facilities to accommodate bigger groups.

WE NEED assistance in raising bail funds, your help
in distributing leaflets and information, volunteers to do
calling, run mimeo machines, etc. We need your participation in the activities Oct. 8-11.

The Notes: This action is an attempt to reach ordinary
working people, to take the issues of the war in Vietnam,
white supremacy in this country, and the liberation struggle
of black and brown people here, to the mass of the people in
this city and in the country. We are trying to show that the
just demands of the people in this country and our fights
here are the same as the struggle of the people of Vietnam.
The only road to victory is to unite with the Vietnamese.

POWER TO THE PEOPLE   U.S. OUT OF VIETNAM NOW

For further information contact: Revolutionary Youth Movement 348-2246

(Collected October 7, 1969 at the University of Chicago.
Distributed on the same day by the Revolutionary Youth
Movement.)

59.   THE ANTI-WAR MOVEMENT

The Demand for Immediate Withdrawal

The demand for immediate and complete withdrawal is the only demand which is consistent with the right of the Vietnamese to self-determination.   It makes a clear demand on the capitalist U.S. government, placing responsibility for the war squarely on the imperialists.   Expressed in the slogan, "Bring All the GIs Home Now!," it is a demand which can reach out to the broad masses of the American people and unite them in common action against their government.

Non-Exclusion

The principle which allows the participation of any person, party or organization which is opposed to the war has been essential to the strength and success of the antiwar movement.   The role of the revolutionary socialist vanguard, whose participation depends on this principle, has been indispensable in keeping the movement on a course of independent growth.

Democratic Decision-Making

The democratic making of decisions at periodic open mass meetings and conferences has also been a necessary element in maintaining the strength, independence and growth of the antiwar movement.   Only frequent and open discussions where the deciding vote is cast by the rank and file antiwar activists can ensure the firm adherence of the movement to the other central principles.

Antiwar Coalitions 1965-1969

The history of the antiwar movement has been a history of continued struggle over the four basic principles of mass action, immediate withdrawal, non-exclusion and democratic decision-making.   Each of the national antiwar coalitions which developed prior to 1970 was able to thrive so long as it adhered to these principles and organized mass actions.   Each

279

coalition declined and fell apart as it strayed from the four basic principles.

The first viable national antiwar coalition, known as the National Mobilization Committee, organized national demonstrations in April and October, 1967. Under the pressure of the 1968 elections, it abandoned mass action and disintegrated. Antiwar actions were continued by the Student Mobilization Committee during the period between the collapse of the National Mobilization Committee and the formation of the New Mobilization Committee. The New Mobilization Committee was formed in July, 1969, and organized the November 15 March on Washington. After November 15 the New Mobe retreated from mass action and degenerated.

Neither of these coalitions was a stable, long-term formation because of the centrifugal political forces which operated on its constituent elements; while the New Mobe contained forces which were not in the National Mobe, both of these coalitions rested in large part on three main elements: the Trotskyists, the Communist Party and the radical pacifists. The demise of each coalition came about when the CP and pacifists fled mass action.

The Antiwar Movement in 1970:
The Growth of NPAC

The past year has been marked by shake-ups and realignments in the organized antiwar movement.

The Vietnam Moratorium Committee, formed in late spring of 1969, was organized by forces tied to a section of the Democratic Party. The VMC oriented toward capitalist politicians from the outset, and with the approach of the 1970 elections and the capitulation of the Congressional "doves" to Nixon, this orientation destroyed the VMC. The VMC made no real effort to organize the protests it had called for on April 15, 1970, and it decided to disband on the eve of the invasion of Cambodia. Consequently, the VMC played no role in the May events.

The leadership of the New Mobilization Committee, dominated by the CP, pacifists and a handful of ultraleftists, changed its orientation after November 15, 1969, away from mass action toward support for capitalist "peace" candidates, combining this with an attempt to substitute small-scale acts of civil disobedience and adventurism for mass demonstrations.

Like the VMC, the New Mobe called for protests on April 15,
1970, but refused to build them as mass actions.

The sole activity of the New Mobe in May was to call
for the May 9 demonstration in Washington, D.C. Because
of the intervention of other forces and the massive numbers
who came to the capital, May 9 was a successful mass action. But the New Mobe leadership, which had attempted to
organize May 9 as a confrontationist trap for those who attended, viewed it as a disappointment; New Mobe leaders published vicious red-baiting attacks on the SMC, YSA and Socialist Workers Party for the role of these organizations in
marshalling the action and preventing the kind of bloody police attack the New Mobe considered a "militant" confrontation.

The antiwar activity led by the SMC during the New
Mobe's decomposition and the widespread mobilizations of
May set the stage for reorganizing a national antiwar coalition. In June, 1970, at the national antiwar conference held
in Cleveland, the October 31 demonstrations were called and
the National Peace Action Coalition was formed. NPAC set
itself the task of involving new forces that had been jolted into readiness for antiwar action by the May protests.

NPAC was organized on the basis of agreement to
build the October 31 actions and adherence to the four basic
principles of non-exclusion, democratic decision-making, mass
action and immediate withdrawal.

The success of the October 31 demonstrations, which
brought out tens of thousands of people in more than 40 cities
proved the viability of NPAC and the correctness of its perspective. While the turnout was modest compared to some
previous mobilizations, it is by far the largest which has
ever taken place in a pre-election period.

Moreover, the process of building the actions and involving a broader base of forces in NPAC was carried out in
the face of active hostility and red-baiting by the CP and other remnants of the New Mobe, as well as red-baiting and vi-
olence-baiting by the government and sections of the trade union bureaucracy. The CP and a handful of ultraleftists from
the old New Mobe created a new multi-issue reformist organization, the National Coalition Against War, Racism and Repression. This formation has been unable to mount any successful activities in the fall. As a result, some of the former

elements of the New Mobe who had not associated with NPAC previously, can now be won to its perspective for antiwar action in the spring.

The YSA supports NPAC, but unlike the previous coalitions, NPAC does not have the support of the pacifists and the Communist Party. NPAC is based on local antiwar groups and forces with a mass base like the SMC, trade unions, Third World organizations and others. NPAC has been particularly successful in involving support from the trade union movement, laying the groundwork for participation by social forces whose power will be decisive in forcing Washington to withdraw its troops.

Some of the forces around the old New Mobe have joined NPAC in the past several months, and more should be encouraged and expected to do so. However, the predominant base for NPAC's leadership is firmly rooted in the more substantial organizations which have come into the antiwar movement during the past year.

The prospects for a successful mass action in the spring depend largely on the movement's ability to tap the energy and power of students, who have furnished the bulk of the participants in the mass actions and who have been the main base for the militant, independent left wing of the antiwar movement.

The Student Mobilization Committee

Since its inception in December, 1966, the SMC has been the major vehicle for organizing the students in antiwar action. The SMC is by far the largest student antiwar organization with many thousands of members and chapters at hundreds of colleges and high schools all over the country.

The SMC was originally organized as a coalition resting on the same three elements as the old national adult coalitions. But when the pressure of the 1968 elections drove the CP and the radical pacifists away from mass action into campaigning for capitalist "doves," the YSA was able to lead a victorious fight against these forces in the SMC from the perspective of continued mass action. The pacifists and the CP then walked out of the SMC.

In 1968 and early 1969 the SMC continued to organize mass actions and succeeded in prodding others to support them while the National Mobilization committee fell to pieces. The SMC was instrumental in helping to form the New Mobilization Committee and winning the call for a mass action in Washington on November 15 as the focus for that coalition. The SMC again played the role of continuing the mass action perspective after November 15 when the New Mobe went the way of its predecessor.

Since the fall of 1969, major changes have occurred in the student movement. SDS declined dramatically after its 1969 summer convention, at which it split apart into three small groups. The only organization which continues to use the name of SDS is a narrow group dominated by the Progressive Labor Party. The other splinters barely exist, and no new organization has arisen which acts as the kind of all-inclusive radical youth organization SDS used to try to be. During the same period, the SMC made major advances, particularly in the course of building the October 15 Moratorium, the November 15 March on Washington, and the May 1970 student upsurge.

(Distributed at Antioch College, Ohio, November 30, 1970. Collected August 22, 1971 from the Antioch College Chapter of the Students for a Democratic Society.)

60. A HISTORY OF THE NATIONAL PEACE
     ACTION COALITION

The National Peace Action Coalition (NPAC) was founded at a "National Emergency Conference Against the Cambodia-
Laos-Vietnam War" held June 19-21, 1970, in Cleveland,
Ohio. The conference was attended by 1500 antiwar activists
of which 869 were students and 296 were workers. The students came from 240 colleges and 73 high schools. Thirty-
four trade union organizations were represented. Delegates
came from 30 states.

The conference was held in the aftermath of the Cambodian invasion and the mass upsurge which followed it. The
initial Call was signed by Noam Chomsky, Professor of
Linguistics, Massachusetts Institute of Technology; Jerry Gordon, Co-Chairman, Cleveland Area Peace Action Council
(CAPAC); James T. Lafferty, Co-Chairman, Detroit Coalition to End the War Now; Leo Fenster, Secretary, Cleveland
District Auto Council, United Auto Workers, AFL-CIO; New
York Moratorium Committee; Sam Pollock, President, District Union 427, Amalgamated Meatcutters and Butcherworkmen of North America, AFL-CIO; Auda Romine, Secretary-
Treasurer, Local 500, Amalgamated Meatcutters and Butcherworkmen of North America, AFL-CIO; Stanley E. Tolliver,
Cleveland civil rights attorney, attorney for Ahmed Evans and
legal advisor, Operation Black Unity; Carol Lipman, National
Executive Secretary, Student Mobilization Committee to End
the War in Vietnam.

The Call to the conference announced its purpose:

> The purpose of the emergency conference is simple
> and to the point: to plan anti-war demonstrations
> and other anti-war activities of the most massive
> kind centering on the crucial issue of withdrawal
> from the war and conducted in a peaceful and order-
> ly fashion. This is the way to involve immense
> masses of ordinary people, trade unionists, G.I.'s
> and their families, students, moderates, liberals
> and radicals, young and old, and all those who op-
> pose the war regardless of their differences on var-
> ious other matters.

284

Reflecting the emphasis that those organizing the conference were already playing on involving trade unionists in the antiwar movement, the initial announcement of the gathering was made at a press conference held on May 25, 1970, in the office of Gus Scholle, president of the Michigan AFL-CIO (See the Detroit Free Press, May 26, 1970). Scholle called for a coalition of labor and students in the antiwar effort.

The conference was convened at Cuyahoga Community College. It heard keynote speeches on Friday night from Rosalio Munoz, the National Chairman of the Chicano Moratorium; John T. Williams, Teamsters organizer from Los Angeles; Carol Lipman, National Executive Secretary of the Student Mobilization Committee; and Paul Silver, a UAW International Representative from Wayne County, Michigan. Greetings were received from two Ft. Bliss GI's; Father Eugene Boyle, Sacred Heart Church in San Francisco; Canadian Moratorium Committee; Edgar Collins, President of Local 2195, American Federation of Government Employees; Democratic Republic of Vietnam; Murray Finley, Manager, Midwest Regional Joint Board, Amalgamated Clothing Workers of America; John Gergen, Greater Cleveland Council of Churches of Christ; Tom Hill, State Representative, Ohio; Jose Irrizary, Movement for Puerto Rican Independence; Valentino Munoz, N. California Moratorium; National Liberation Front; Provisional Revolutionary Government of South Vietnam; Gus Scholle, President of Michigan AFL-CIO; Cleveland Mayor Carl Stokes; Jackie Vaughn III, State Representative, Michigan.

The sessions concluded Sunday with the adoption of an action resolution calling for a summer of intensive organizing and educational work; local antiwar demonstrations on August 6-9, to commemorate the 25th Anniversary of the atom bombings of Hiroshima and Nagasaki; support for the August 29 Chicano Moratorium antiwar demonstrations by Mexican-Americans in Los Angeles; and a day of nationally coordinated massive antiwar demonstrations on Saturday, October 31 centered around the political demand for immediate U.S. withdrawal from Indochina. The National Peace Action Coalition was established to implement this program. A steering committee of some 25 persons was elected with the committee given the power to add to its numbers. In addition the following five national coordinators were elected:

Ruth Gage-Colby - journalist; delegate from the Women's International League for Peace and Freedom to the United Nations.

Jerry Gordon - Cleveland attorney; co-chairman of
the Cleveland Area Peace Action Council; member
of the Executive board of the American Civil Liberties Union of Greater Cleveland.

Don Gurewitz - Field Secretary of the Student Mobilization Committee to End the War in Vietnam
(SMC).

James Lafferty - Detroit attorney; co-chairman of
the Detroit Coalition to End the War Now.

John T. Williams - Teamsters Union organizer,
Los Angeles.

The national office was established at 2102 Euclid Avenue,
Cleveland, Ohio. Telephone: 216-621-6516.

What distinguished the NPAC conference above all else
was the fact that for the first time in the history of the anti-
war movement a significant number of trade unionists attended a peace gathering. (See the Cleveland Plain Dealer, June
22, 1970). NPAC's central thrust was and is to unite workers, students, GI's, women, Third World people and all others who oppose the war in a broadly based movement focused
on the demand for immediate withdrawal and conducting its
activities in legal, peaceful and orderly ways. Other basic
positions approved by NPAC and incorporated in the resolution adopted at the Cleveland conference called for: internal
democracy; non-exclusion ("all who oppose the war are welcome in the coalition irrespective of their views on other
questions and regardless of other affiliations"); and non-par-
tisanship.

In the months following the June conference, NPAC
carried out the program that had been adopted. The culmination came on October 31, 1970, when nearly 100,000 people
demonstrated against the war under the NPAC banner in some
30 cities. The rallies were especially significant for two
reasons:

1. Following President Nixon's speech of October 7,
   1970, leading Senate doves called for a moratorium
   on antiwar dissent. A resolution was unanimously
   passed in the Senate hailing the Nixon message.
   The National Peace Action Coalition denounced the
   speech, characterized it as demagogy, and warned

that Nixon was planning to escalate the war as part of his basic strategy of winning it. NPAC said there would be no moratorium on dissent against the war as long as the war continued. The only organized antiwar voice in the nation of substance during the election campaign was NPAC's. The October 31 demonstration provided the forums.

2. Although the October 31 demonstrations were much smaller on a national scale than October 15, 1969, they were still the largest antiwar demonstrations held in the country during an election year. The largest gathering was in Austin, Texas where close to 15,000 people turned out. A tremendous amount of organizing went into building the October demonstrations and NPAC emerged from them substantially strengthened.

The NPAC coalition is composed of a wide diversity of groups: local labor unions; state federations; women's liberation groups; Student Mobilization Committee; Third World committees; community peace organizations, etc. But the basic component of the national coalition is the local coalition (such as the "New York Peace Action Coalition"). The local coalition exists on a city or regional scale and seeks to bring together all groups and individuals in the area who support the demand for immediate withdrawal. When NPAC was first formed, there were 3 such local groups affiliated with it; by the time of its second convention there were 35; presently there are some 50 and new peace coalitions and new ones are being formed all over the country.

On December 4-6, 1970, NPAC held its second convention at the Packinghouse Labor Center in Chicago. The 1500 delegates heard speeches from Hilton Hanna, Executive Secretary to Patrick Gorman, Int'l. Secretary-Treasurer of the Amalgamated Meatcutters and Butcherworkmen; Stanley Tolliver, Cleveland Civil Rights attorney; Carol Lipman, West Coast Coordinator of the Student Mobilization Committee; A. A. "Sammy" Rayner, Chicago Alderman; Leon Page, Cairo (Ill.) Black United Front; and representatives of the Japan Congress Against A & H Bombs. Greetings were received from Noam Chomsky; the Australian Vietnam Moratorium Committee; U.E. Local 767; the Chicago Women's Liberation Union; Cesar Chavez; and the Provisional Revolutionary Government.

The Chicago Convention reaffirmed the basic NPAC principles developed in June. The NPAC structure was maintained with a steering committee of over 100 elected and the same five coordinators retained. The action proposal adopted featured plans for local meetings April 3-4, 1971, commemorating the assassination of Dr. Martin Luther King, "a major leader of the U.S. antiwar movement and of the struggle for human dignity; and a march on Washington, DC and San Francisco April 24 in support of the demand "Immediate Withdrawal of all U.S. forces from Southeast Asia" and "End the Draft Now." A subsequent meeting of the NPAC steering committee endorsed plans for nationwide demonstrations on campuses and in local communities on May 5, 1971, to mark the anniversary of the Cambodian invasion and the murder of students at Kent State (May 4) and Jackson State (May 6). The steering committee also voted support for the demonstrations planned by GI and veteran groups at army bases across the country on May 16. Civilians will travel to the bases during "Armed Services Day" (renamed by the antiwar movement as "Solidarity Day") to express their support for antiwar GI's.

On or about February 1, 1971, NPAC opened additional offices on the 8th floor of 1029 Vermont Avenue NE, Washington DC, as the center for the Washington action. Phone number is 202-638-6601. Shortly thereafer an NPAC office to coordinate the San Francisco demonstration was opened at 50 Oak St., San Francisco. Phone number is 415-864-5835. The Washington office has a full time staff of 12 and the staff is constantly being augmented.

Responding to Nixon's escalation of the war in Laos, NPAC secured broad endorsements for a 3/4 page ad which appeared in the February 14 and February 17, 1971, New York Times. Eight members of Congress, labor leaders, actors and actresses, writers and journalists, female liberation leaders and other prominent persons signed the ad calling for financial support for NPAC's spring offensive against the war. The ad also appeared in the February 21 Washington Post.

NPAC is now deeply involved in building its spring program, particularly the April 24th march on Washington and San Francisco. The coalition continues to grow rapidly and solidly. In cooperation with the Peoples' Coalition for Peace and Justice, NPAC expects the April 24 antiwar demonstrations to be the largest ever organized by the peace movement.

Upon conclusion of the spring events, NPAC will convene another national convention at which time a new action program against the war will be adopted.   The convention will be held July 2-4, 1971, probably in Cleveland.

(Distributed at Ohio State University, Columbus, Ohio on March 28, 1971.   Collected by the compiler on the same day.)

61. PEACE ACTION COALITION--INTRODUCTION

Peace Action Coalition
2102 Euclid Ave.
Cleve., Ohio 44115
tel: (216) 621-6516

Dear Friend,

The establishment of the Peace Action Coalition (PAC) as a national anti-war coalition opens the way for rapidly building the alliance of labor, students, and other sectors of the anti-war movement. As the Cambodian debacle further unfolds and as the frenzy of the Nixon administration further develops, the need for unity of all anti-war forces, particularly workers and students, becomes all the more imperative.

We hope you share our enthusiasm in the new beginnings forged by the Cleveland conference. The unprecedented participation of people from the labor movement coupled with the resolution and organizational structure produced by the conference give hope that in the months ahead fresh powerful new forces will add their substantial weight to the anti-war movement. PAC has a key role to play in assuring that the opportunities for building the anti-war movement spawned by the Cambodian invasion, and reflected in the Cleveland conference, are fully realized.

Our immediate problem is money. We still have some commitments to meet from the conference itself and, of course, we need funds for immediate national mailings, as well as to staff and operate the national office. Since significant anti-war activity is planned for the summer and since new crises could erupt in Indochina at any time, there can be no delay in meeting financial obligations.

We are appealing to you now to be as generous as you can. Developing the labor-student alliance--something we have dreamed of for years--requires work, consciousness, energy and money. Please help!

Jerry Gordon   Ruth Gage-Colby   John T. Williams

(Cleveland Area   (Women's Internation-   (V. P. Teamsters
Peace Action   al League for Peace   Local #208, L. A.)
Council)   and Freedom)

   Don Gurewitz   James Lafferty

   (Student Mobilization   (Detroit Coalition to
   Committee)   End the War Now)

(The above are national coordinators of the Peace Action
Coalition)

Sam Pollack

(Pres., Dist. 427,
Amalg. Meatcutters)

(Collected in the Special Collections, Ohio State University library, Columbus, on May 17, 1971.   Mimeo.)

62. PEACE ACTION COALITION

2102 Euclid Avenue
Cleveland, Ohio 44115
(216) 621-6516

NATL. EMERGENCY CONFERENCE SPONSORS (partial listing)

(Organizations listed for identification purposes only)

Atlanta Mobilization Committee
BAPAC
Berkeley Strike Coord. Comm.
Chicago Strike Council
CAPAC
Det. Coalition to End the War Now
Houston Comm. to End the War in Vietnam
New Jersey New Mobe
N. Y. Moratorium Committee
Pacific NW New Mobe
Student Mobilization Committee

Bella Abzug, N.D.C., New York
Katherine Camp, Natl. Chmn., WILPF
Betty Friedan, Natl. Org. of Women
Noam Chomsky
Ruth Gage-Colby, WILPF
Dick Gregory
Don Gurewitz, SMC
Fred Halstead
Phil Hirschkop, Atty., Virginia
Prof. S. E. Luria, MIT
Jeannette Rankin, Ga.

Fr. Eugene Boyle, S.F.
Clergy & Laymen Concerned About Vietnam, Detroit
Rev. Earl Cunningham, Clevel.
Fr. Don Nolan, Detroit

Atlanta Amer. Fed. of Teachers
Ozzie Edwards, Pres., Natl. Fed. of Social Service Employees

Leo Fenster, Dist. Counc., UAW, Cleveland
Grady Glenn, Pres. Frame Unit, Loc. 600, UAW, Dearborn
Sam Pollock, Pres., Dist. 427, Amal. Meatcutters, Cleve.
Gus Scholle, Pres., Mich. AFL-CIO
Tom Burner, Pres., Metro, AFL-CIO, Detroit
Washington, D.C. Labor for Peace

Chicago Women's Liberation Union
Independent Campus Women, S. F. State College
Amer. Servicemen's Union, Selfridge, AFB, Mich.
GIs United, Wright-Patterson AFB, Ohio
Vets for Peace, Chicago
Vets for Peace, Cleveland
Vets for Peace, Madison
Vets for Peace, Mass.
Vietnam Vets for Peace, Cleveland.

Roberto Elias, Chicano Moratorium
Corky Gonzalez, La Raza Unida Party, Colorado
Jose Irrizary, MPI
Mary Kochiyama, Asian Americans for Action, NYC
Manuel Lopez, La Raza Unida Party
Manhattan Comm. Coll. 3rd World Coalition, NYC
Movimiento Pro Independencia, NYC
Rosalio Muñoz, Chicano Moratorium
SCLC, Cleveland

INTRODUCTION

The National Emergency Conference Against the Cambodia-Laos-Vietnam War, held in Cleveland June 19-21, was
probably the most significant meeting in the history of the
antiwar movement. The fact that more than 1/4 of the over
200 sponsors were trade union officials represents a major
breakthrough into the ranks of labor.

The conference opened Friday evening with speeches
by Rosalio Muñoz, the National Chairman of the Chicano
Moratorium, John T. Williams, the Vice-President of Teamsters Local 208 in Los Angeles, Carol Lipman, the National
Executive Secretary of the Student Mobilization Committee,
and Paul Silver, the UAW International Representative from
Wayne County, Michigan. Greetings were received from
Cleveland Mayor Carl B. Stokes, Gus Scholle, the President
of Michigan AFL-CIO, the Democratic Republic of Vietnam,
the Provisional Revolutionary Government of South Vietnam, and
others.

Nearly everyone from the Conference, along with over 1000 people from Cleveland, demonstrated against the war in front of the Cleveland-Sheraton Hotel where Vice-President Agnew was speaking Saturday evening.

Sunday afternoon, the Conference voted overwhelmingly to endorse the Action Proposal, submitted by Jerry Gordon, the Chairman of the Cleveland Area Peace Action Council, and Jim Lafferty, the Co-Chairman of the Detroit Coalition to End the War Now, which is included in this brochure. The Conference also voted to establish the Peace Action Coalition (PAC) to carry out the decisions of the Conference.

Of the 1447 people who registered for the Conference, 869 were students and 296 were workers. The students came from 240 colleges and 73 high schools, with Wayne State University in Detroit sending the largest contingent of 54 students. People attended from 30 states and 4 foreign countries, the largest contingents coming from Ohio, New York, and Massachusetts.

Ages of the participants ranged from 10 to 71, with the bulk in the 16-23 year-old category. Individuals from over 100 organizations participated in the Conference.

It was obvious that, through trade union participation, that the antiwar movement has begun a new stage in its development and growth. It is now up to everyone sincerely interested in ending the war to take advantage of these opportunities.

Build the August 6-9 demonstrations. Prepare and plan mass demonstrations for October 31. Build a movement of the American people that can really end the war by Bringing ALL the Troops Home Now!

Note: An "Action Proposal" adopted by the National Peace Action Coalition has been edited out here. That same "Action Proposal" appears in the document numbered 71, p. 329-35.

LABOR AND THE WAR

Workshop Proposal

The labor workshop supports the proposal for action submitted by Jerry Gordon and Jim Lafferty.

We pledge that when we return to our areas we will devote our energies and urge others to work on the activities and build the mass actions outlined in this proposal.

We urge everyone in the antiwar movement to take advantage of the opportunities which today exist for the antiwar movement to deepen and broaden the involvement of working people, especially the organized sector, in the antiwar movement.

We think it is especially important to realize the opportunity for obtaining official trade union endorsement for antiwar actions, thus opening the door for participation in the antiwar movement by those who have the power to force the government to bring the troops home and end the war, that is, the working men and women of the United States.

We urge that this conference issue an invitation to all unions to send official representatives to local antiwar organizing committees, and participate in the work of organizing mass antiwar demonstrations in this country until all the troops are brought home.

Chairing: John T. Williams,
        Teamsters Local 208

        Auda Romine,
        Meatcutters

ORGANIZATION OF P.A.C.

1. This Conference shall constitute itself as a national antiwar coalition to be known as the Peace Action Coalition (PAC).

2. National headquarters to be located, at least on a temporary basis, at the Peace Center, 2102 Euclid Ave., Cleve., O. 44115. 216-621-6516.

3. The Steering Committee of PAC shall be the members of the presiding committee elected at the Conference with the understanding that the steering committee will be enlarged to include representatives of antiwar groups from all over the country. The steering committee shall be authorized to add to its numbers.

4.   The National Coordinators of PAC are:
       Ruth Gage-Colby, WILPF
       Jerry Gordon, CAPAC
       Don Gurewitz, SMC
       Jim Lafferty, Detroit Coalition
       John T. Williams, Teamsters Loc. 208
(organizations listed for identification purposes only)

5.   PAC shall strive in every way to unify all groups, individuals and forces that oppose the war in Indochina and support the demand for immediate withdrawal.

(Distributed by Peace Action Coalition July 18, 1970.   Collected in the Special Collections Suzzallo Library, University of Washington, Seattle, June 22, 1973.)

63. CALL TO ACTION
   OCTOBER 31

Nixon's invasion of Cambodia triggered an unprecedented wave of opposition to the war in Southeast Asia. Many people who had previously tolerated Nixon's token troop withdrawal policy were drawn into action for the first time as they saw that the real intention of the administration was to continue the war and even to escalate it.

The sentiment for "bringing all the troops home now" has never been more widespread than today. The demonstrations in May, following the Cambodian invasion, proved one thing: the American people have the power to curb the administration's aggressive militarism. Nixon was forced to withdraw U.S. troops from Cambodia because millions of Americans took to the streets in opposition to Nixon's invasion of that nation. Only the continued building of the antiwar movement can prevent new escalations. The possibility now exists to involve massive numbers of unionists and black and brown people along with students, women, professionals and others in the most massive movement ever to bring the war to an end: to get out of Indochina now.

It is essential at this time that nationwide activities which can involve broad new layers of society be held. Therefore, we the undersigned call for massive, peaceful demonstrations throughout the country, in every major metropolitan area, on October 31 to demand the immediate withdrawal of all U.S. forces from Southeast Asia.

The working people of this country have paid a high price for the war in Southeast Asia. The spiralling inflation brought on by the war has made it impossible for working people to maintain their standard of living. Our sons, nephews, and friends have been called on to fight, and many to die, in a war which is clearly not in their interests. The war has eaten up the money that is so desperately needed for domestic programs such as housing, education, health care, air pollution and the rehabilitation of our cities.

297

Organized labor has the power to end the war, it is time that power was exercised. A great step forward was taken on May 21, when tens of thousands of workers joined with students in New York City in a massive anti-war protest. This forward motion must continue. Therefore, we the undersigned, endorse the call for mass anti-war protests on October 31 and call upon all unions, union organizations and working people to join with us.

Third World people pay the heaviest price for the war in Vietnam. We fight, and die, in numbers disproportionate to our percentage of the population. The cities in which we are so often concentrated suffer most acutely from budget cuts instituted to help pay for the war. Rising unemployment, hailed by the Nixon administration as a necessary cost of the war, means rising unemployment for us. All these sacrifices to pay for a war which is not in our interest. We, the undersigned, endorse the call for the October 31 mass anti-war actions and urge all our brothers and sisters to join with us.

Please clip and mail to: National Peace Action Coalition. 2102 Euclid Ave., Cleveland, Ohio 44115

_____ I (my union, organization) endorses the call for October 31.

_____ List me as a labor endorser. _____ List me as a Third World endorser.

_____ Enclosed is my donation of $____ to help cover costs of publicizing October 31.

Name:_____Union/Organization:_____

Address:_____City, State & Zip_____

Labor Donated:_____

(Distributed by the National Peace Action Coalition, June 5, 1970. Collected in the Special Collections, Suzzallo Library, University of Washington, Seattle, June 22, 1973.)

64. STRATEGY FOR PEACE

Ending the war in Southeast Asia should be one of the primary goals of progressive forces in the United States today. To end this seemingly endless war, an approach must be developed that can bring together all the divergent forces and interests of the American people and together demand that the ruling class of this country end the killing. The strategy of forming united fronts with existing groups around their particular interests turns out to be the best approach to moving masses of people. As you know, people move on their understanding of what their interests are. A few examples of this will serve to clarify the point.

How was it that students came to the peace movement? If we look back to the early sixties on the college campuses, we find that there were very few who spoke or acted against the war and that those who were courageous enough to raise his or her voice in protest of the war were risking at best severe criticism and at worst a severe beating. As the war continued and expanded and fewer and fewer students were coming back to school in the fall, students started speaking out. Moreover, the first form student anti-war sentiment took, the burning of draft cards, illustrates their particular interest in the war.

How was it that labor joined the anti-war struggle? Just a few months ago labor in general was termed "hawkish." But as the unemployed rolls increased, as the burden became heavier, as prices skyrocketed, and as benefits decreased, labor started coming to realize that "peace was their struggle also."

What this tells us in terms of our strategy is that we must move to show all that peace is their struggle on the basis of their interests. We cannot wait until the broad masses come to this realization by themselves. We must step boldly out and provide the framework for this level of consciousness. Our sons, brothers, friends, etc., and the Vietnamese people cannot wait.

COME TO THE APRIL 24 MASS PEACE RALLY

NAME_____

ADDRESS_____

Clip and send to: YWLL, c/o 110 34th St. #304, S.E. D.C.

YOUNG WORKERS LIBERATION LEAGUE

(Distributed by the Young Workers Liberation League during April, 1971. Collected from the Young Socialist Alliance, City College of New York, April 20, 1971.)

65. CALL FOR AN EMERGENCY NATIONAL CONFERENCE AGAINST THE CAMBODIA-LAOS-VIETNAM WAR

President Nixon has expanded the war in Southeast Asia against the will of the majority of the American people. His latest reckless move in Cambodia dooms thousands of additional GIs, Cambodians and Vietnamese to death and threatens a confrontation with China. The frenzy and recklessness which now characterize the U.S. foreign policy do not preclude the end result of nuclear holocaust.

Nixon has acted against the clearly expressed desires of the American people who want to get out of the war. His order to invade Cambodia was issued without the consent of Congress. It is now perfectly clear that Nixon's real policy is not to withdraw from Southeast Asia but to "win" the illegal, immoral Indochina war.

In this historic crisis for humanity it is imperative that the American anti-war movement be a beacon light for the tens of millions of Americans who will join the struggle to end the war if given leadership. The movement must provide a focus and a form for the expression of the broadest opposition to Nixon's course and for the immediate withdrawal of all U.S. forces from Southeast Asia. That is the only way to spare the lives involved: to save humanity from the horrors to which Nixon is leading it; to protect the living standards of American workers which are being destroyed by war-inspired inflation; and to achieve a reordering of national priorities away from a war economy. It is imperative-- and at this time it is possible--that the movement expand to embrace the millions of Americans who have not previously protested. It is imperative and it is also possible that significant elements of such powerful social forces as organized labor be involved and integrated in the anti-war struggle. This is the time for those opponents of the war who understand the importance of immense masses in action, for those who understand the importance of giving form to the majority sentiment against the war, to unify for that task and launch a program of action on which such broad forces can agree.

301

For these reasons the undersigned issue this call for
a NATIONAL EMERGENCY CONFERENCE AGAINST THE
CAMBODIA-LAOS-VIETNAM WAR to be held in Cleveland
June 19-20, 1970. The Cleveland Area Peace Action Council, which hosted the conferences which gave birth to the
largest anti-war demonstrations in American history--includ-
ing April 15, 1967 and Nov. 13-15, 1969--has agreed to host
this conference.

June 20 is the date when Vice President Agnew is
speaking in Cleveland at a $250-a-plate Republican fund-rais-
ing dinner. CAPAC is organizing a massive, peaceful demonstration to confront Agnew on this occasion. The conference itself will be an effective answer to Agnew and all participants in the conference will be urged to join the demonstration.

The purpose of the emergency conference is simple
and to the point: to plan anti-war demonstrations and other
anti-war activities of the most massive kind centering on the
crucial issue of withdrawal from the war and conducted in a
peaceful and orderly fashion. This is the way to involve immense masses of ordinary people, trade unionists, GIs and
their families, students, moderates, liberals and radicals,
young and old, and all those who oppose the war regardless
of their differences on various other matters.

This conference is not intended to solve or even necessarily to discuss all the problems of our crisis-ridden society. It is not a conference to hammer out the strategy or
tactics of social revolution or to found a new political party
or movement. It is not a conference in competition with any
tendency or movement for social change. IT IS A CONFER-
ENCE TO ORGANIZE MASSIVE OPPOSITION TO THE WAR.
All those who want to see such opposition organized are welcome to participate regardless of their political ideas or affiliation.

Preliminary list of sponsors, individuals and organizations:

Noam Chomsky, Professor of Linguistics, Massachusetts In-
    stitute of Technology*
Cleveland Area Peace Action Council (CAPAC), Jerry Gor-
    don, Chairman
Detroit Coalition to End the War Now, James T. Lafferty,
    Co-Chairman
Leo Fenster, Secretary, Cleveland District Auto Council,

United Auto Workers, AFL-CIO*
New York Moratorium Committee
Sam Pollock, President, District Union 427, Amalgamated
    Meatcutters and Butcherworkmen of North America,
    AFL-CIO*
Auda Romine, Secretary-Treasurer, Local 500, Amalgamated
    Meatcutters and Butcherworkmen of North America,
    AFL-CIO*
Stanley E. Tolliver, Cleveland civil rights attorney and at-
    torney for Ahmed Evans; legal adviser, Operation Black
    Unity
Student Mobilization Committee to End the War in Vietnam,
    Carol Lipman, National Executive Secretary

*Organizations listed for identification purposes only.

Please fill out and mail to the Cleveland Area Peace Action
Council, 2102 Euclid Avenue, Cleveland, Ohio 44115.

(1) (Our organization) agrees to be a co-sponsor of the
"Emergency National Conference Against the Cambodia-Laos-
Vietnam War."

(Please Print)

NAME:_____

ADDRESS:_____

PHONE NO.:_____

Date of Mailing:_____

Note: Please attach list of other co-sponsors secured from
       your area with their names signed by them, their ad-
       dresses and phone numbers.

(Distributed by the Cleveland Area Peace Action Council during June, 1970. Collected July 11, 1970 from the "People
File," Cleveland State University Library, Cleveland, Ohio.)

66. CLEVELAND AREA PEACE ACTION COUNCIL

2102 Euclid Ave.
Cleveland Ohio 44115
216-621-6516

June 10, 1970

TO: All anti-war groups and supporters

Dear Brothers and Sisters:

As preparations for the Cleveland anti-war conference move forward, the crucial importance of the conference becomes increasingly clear. For the first time in the several years' effort to end U.S. military intervention in Southeast Asia, a significant number of trade unionists have endorsed an anti-war conference and have expressed a desire to meet with students and others to plan united actions against the war.

Because the conference has this great potential, it is truly unfortunate that some leaders of the New Mobilization Committee to End the War in Vietnam (New Mobe) have elected to oppose it. Some of these people are even making phone calls and sending letters all over the country to discourage people from attending the conference.

What explains the hostility of these New Mobe Leaders? It is not because they were excluded from participating in the conference. Quite the contrary! There was a sustained five month effort to get New Mobe to convene a national conference at which workers, students, the black movement, GIs, religious groups, the traditional peace forces and others could join together and map anti-war plans. New Mobe leaders consistently rejected all proposals for such a conference. Even after Nixon's invasion of Cambodia, an emergency meeting of the New Mobe coordinating committee said "no" to the idea of a national conference.

In the face of this, the Cleveland Area Peace Action Council (CAPAC) unanimously voted on May 5, 1970, to join with the other anti-war coalitions, in particular the Detroit Coali-

304

tion to End the War Now (which has the support of many trade unionists in Detroit), to initiate plans for an emergency national anti-war conference. We told the New Mobe leaders we would make no public announcement of the conference until after their steering committee meeting of May 23-24. Our hope was that they would join us as sponsors and that this would be a united effort. Again they voted "no." On May 25, therefore, a press conference was convened in Detroit and Gus Scholle, president of the Michigan AFL-CIO, and others announced plans for the Cleveland conference. In the succeeding days further efforts were expended to involve New Mobe in sponsoring the conference but with no success whatever.

Why did New Mobe leaders refuse to call a national conference? Why did they refuse to join in sponsoring the Cleveland conference? Why are some of them now wasting time, energy and money in opposing our conference when all of their time, energy and money ought to be spent in organizing opposition to the continued U.S. military intervention in Indochina?

The answer to these questions lies in the political position of some of the New Mobe leaders. They believe that a nuclear confrontation may well be imminent and that the anti-war movement must act decisively NOW. They seek to substitute civil disobedience and "direct action" for mass, peaceful demonstrations. Yet they lack confidence in their ability to persuade a majority of those attending an open national conference that civil disobedience and "direct action" are the proper tactics for the anti-war movement today. These New Mobe leaders fear hearing from trade unionists because they know that trade unionists with rare exceptions oppose confrontation tactics and civil disobedience.

Typical of the thinking of these New Mobe leaders were the plans they made for the Washington May 9 demonstration. Over 100,000 people went to Washington on a few days notice to register their profound opposition to the Cambodian invasion. The demonstration dramatized for millions of Americans the depth and breadth of opposition to the invasion in a way few other anti-war demonstrations ever have. The anti-war movement gained wide public support as a result of this demonstration in no small part because it was conducted in a peaceful and orderly fashion. But credit for this goes to the good sense of the thousands of demonstrators and to the skill of the marshals--over 4,000 students--who

frustrated the high risk confrontation plans of the New Mobe
coordinating committee. Heading up the marshals together
with Fred Halstead was Brad Lyttle, who has himself advo-
cated and practiced civil disobedience for years. Yet Lyttle
opposed the plans of action advanced by New Mobe leaders
and he explained why in a memorandum:

> We calculated that it would take more than an hour
> to move 100,000 people out of the H Street area.
> A gas attack or a police charge with clubbing in a
> situation like that could result in hundreds of peo-
> ple being trampled to death. Victims would be
> those who had come just to attend a peaceful rally
> as well as people who were prepared for the dan-
> gers of a sit-down. The idea that the enormous
> crowd should surround the White House posed many
> of the same problems.

Dave Dellinger, a key spokesman for the New Mobe,
wrote an article in the June 4, 1970 Village Voice which reveals how some of the New Mobe leadership views the historic May 9 demonstration and the dangerous possibilities described by Lyttle above. Dellinger begins his article by explaining what he considers the need for "open, disciplined,
carefully focused non-violent resistance" and he cautions
against mass marches and demonstrations that "fail to prepare people for more militant forms of resistance." He
then explains that "non-violent direct action" was "the de
facto tactic called for by the New Mobe when it invited people to protest in Washington on May 9 not only without government permits but in an area near the White House which,
as the Mobe clearly pointed out, had been declared 'off limits' to protesters." "Because the Mobe clearly called for
massive protest without permits in a banned area," he says,
"thousands of persons came conscious of the fact that they
might be arrested, gassed, or otherwise assaulted." He then
laments "the mistake ... of asking for the Ellipse" and explains that "if there was a 'failure of nerve' and a 'betrayal'
that weekend, it occurred when this decision [to ask for the
Ellipse] was made."

Similar thinking was revealed in a paper written by
Arthur Waskow, another of the top spokesmen for the New
Mobilization Committee, in a paper he wrote shortly after the
Washington event. Waskow characteristically wrote:

If even just 15,000 (let alone 75,000) had nonvio-

lently sat down in the D.C. streets as they were
prepared to do, and waited (in shifts, etc.) until
the Monday 50-governors' meeting or until mass
arrested or until gassed, I think there would have
been numerous massive imitations of that action all
over the country by Tuesday or Wednesday. New
York City and San Francisco would have been shut
down, the national crisis would have been intensified, and the war might well have been ended within six weeks.

Is the cause of the anti-war movement aided by such
confrontation schemes? Do we win workers by such tactics?
These are questions that ought to be discussed out in the
open and there is no better place than in a national anti-war
conference. The New Mobe leaders could attend the Cleveland conference and could present their views on questions of
confrontations and civil disobedience.

But they have apparently concluded that such views
have little chance of winning acceptance and therefore they
will not attend the conference. That is their right. But the
tragedy is that they are not content to simply boycott the
Cleveland conference. They are attacking it at every turn.
What a shame! For years people in the anti-war movement
have dreamed of the day when workers would join the fight
for peace. Now it's beginning to happen! Is there any wonder that we are excited and enthused at the prospects of
building a much broader anti-war coalition with labor playing
a leading role? And is it right for some New Mobe leaders
to denounce our conference when such prospects exist?

The Cleveland conference is open to everyone wishing
to attend. And every person attending will have vote as well
as voice. This will be a democratic conference and future
programs for the anti-war movement will be determined on
the basis of free and healthy discussion. Who can legitimate-
ly complain about a conference organized in such a manner?

To the leaders of New Mobe we urge: Join with us in
building a united anti-war movement. But if you cannot join
us, at least let us have our conference without interference
or invective. And in this moment of great crisis, but also
of great opportunity for the anti-war movement, isn't it fair
to ask you whether the cause of peace is aided when you attack groups and individuals in the anti-war movement who
only want to get everybody together--including yourselves!--

to decide the future of the anti-war movement?

> For peace,
>
> Jerry Gordon,
> Chairman of the Cleveland Area
>   Peace Action Council

(Distributed by the Cleveland Area Peace Action Council
June 10, 1970. Collected July 11, 1970 from the "People
File," Cleveland State University Library, Cleveland, Ohio.)

67. WASHINGTON AREA PEACE ACTION COALITION

1346 CONNECTICUT AVE., N.W.   SUITE 1122 WASHING-
TON, D.C.   20016
(202) 293-3855

June 14, 1971

Dear Friend:

The spring of 1971 brought with it the largest antiwar demonstration in history on April 24 and the most sustained period of antiwar activity to date, from the dramatic presence of the Veterans to the Maydays to the lobbying groups still converging on Washington. The antiwar movement has turned a corner; millions of people are ready to work in a sustained, united, organized way to deliver the knockout blow against the war.

It is clear that massive, effective demonstrations do not happen overnight. The call for April 24 came at the December, 1970 convention of the National Peace Action Coalition. Work was begun immediately to build that historic day. In the same way, activists must begin NOW to build the fall offensive. To this end, NPAC is calling a National Antiwar Convention in New York City, July 2-4.

We strongly urge and cordially invite you to attend. All who register have voice and vote. A thorough exchange of views on what people think is the most effective way to end the war. Only an open, democratic convention can guarantee this and also guarantee that what comes out of it will represent the majority view. The exchange and debate is an enlightening experience which can only be fully comprehended by being there.

The Washington Area Peace Action Coalition is mobilizing people for the convention: we want to have the broadest spectrum possible of antiwar activism in our area represented. It is of first importance that YOU be there. But if this is impossible, please contribute something to help those

309

attend who want to but cannot afford it.   Also urge any group
that you work with to send representatives.

A new optimism and vigor and power exist in the anti-
war movement.   We can end the war.

Yours for Out Now,
(signed)
Marilyn Lerch, WAPAC Staff

Partial list of local endorsers: organizations listed for
identification purposes only.   Black Moratorium Committee,
D.C. Statehood Party, Student Mobilization Committee, Wash-
ington Teachers Union, Federal Employees for Peace, D.C.
Employees for Peace, Washington Peace Center, Vets for
Peace, Concerned Officers Movement, Maryland Council to
Repeal the Draft, Metropolitan Chapt. of the National Assoc.
of Social Workers; Marion Barry, Exec. Dir. of Pride, Inc.;
Rev. Dave Eaton, All Souls Unitarian Church; William Sim-
ons, Pres., Wash. Teachers Union; Charles Cheng, Exec.
Assistant to the President, WTU; Jeanne Walton, Free Angela
Davis Committee; Pat Strandt, Wash.-Balt. Newspaper Guild,
Local 35; Endraft; D.C. Labor for Peace; Florian Bartosic,
Counsel, International Brotherhood of Teamsters; WILPF,
D.C. Chapter; Frank Somlyo, Cooks Union, Local 209.

(Distributed at the University of Delaware, Newark, Delaware, during June, 1971.   Collected from the files of the
University of Delaware News, June 22, 1973.)

68. NATIONAL PEACE ACTION COALITION

2102 Euclid Avenue
Cleveland, Ohio 44115
Telephone (216) 621-6518

AN OPEN LETTER TO ALL COLLEGE STUDENTS
From: the National Peace Action Coalition (NPAC)

On June 19-21, students from 240 universities joined
with 296 workers from 33 labor unions, representatives from
Third World organizations, women's leaders, high school students, and others at the "Emergency National Conference
Against the Cambodia, Laos, Vietnam War" held in Cleveland. The purpose of the conference, attended by nearly
1500 people, was to plan massive demonstrations in the fall
to support the demand for immediate withdrawal of all U.S.
troops from Southeast Asia.

The conference decided to call for mass antiwar demonstrations on October 31, National Peace Action Day, in
every major regional center. The conference also established the National Peace Action Coalition (NPAC) to unite
all antiwar forces in the struggle to end U.S. intervention in
Indochina.

As the school year begins, the entire world is watching to see whether American college students will pick up
where they left off last May when millions demonstrated
against Nixon's Cambodian invasion and the killing of young
people at Kent State, Jackson State and Augusta. A tre-
mendous--if only partial--victory was won when Nixon was
forced to pull the troops out of Cambodia by June 30. Yet
the vile war goes on, the slaughter continues, the bombs
wreak systematic destruction, and young Americans, Vietnamese, Cambodians, and Laotians continue to die. It is
clear that intensified efforts are needed if this unjust, anti-
human, colonial war is to be finally ended.

We feel confident that the students will resume their
offensive against the war. As the fall term begins, as the
mass meetings begin to take shape on campuses around the

311

country, we would urge you to place building mass demonstrations on October 31 National Peace Action Day high on your list of antiwar priorities in conjunction with other antiwar groups in your area.

The U.S. antiwar movement needs organization and unity to achieve its aim. The circulation of this letter on campuses throughout the nation is part of an unprecedented effort to bring all antiwar forces together under one roof. The effort has been greatly bolstered by the affiliation to the National Peace Action Coalition of a significant number of trade unionists who are anxious to join with students in the fight to end the war.

Please be sure that your campus representative is present at the NPAC steering committee meeting in Chicago on October 11.

For Peace in Southeast Asia,

(signed)

Ruth Gage-Colby   Jerry Gordon   Don Gurewitz   James Lafferty   John T. Williams, Coordinators, National Peace Action Coalition

(For identification purposes: Ruth Gage-Colby is a national leader of the Women's International League for Peace and Freedom; Jerry Gordon is co-chairman of the Cleveland Area Peace Action Council; Don Gurewitz is the National Executive Secretary of the Student Mobilization Committee; James Lafferty is co-chairman of the Detroit Coalition to End the War Now; and John T. Williams is Vice President of the Teamsters Local 208 in Los Angeles.)

(Distributed by the National Peace Action Coalition, September 14, 1970. Collected in the Special Collections, Suzzallo Library, University of Washington, Seattle, June 22, 1973.)

69.   NATIONAL PEACE ACTION COALITION

815 17th Street NW Washington DC
628-5876
628-6834

February 1, 1971

Dear Friend:

"There will be no U.S. ground personnel in Cambodia except for the regular staff of our embassy
in Phnom Penh"...the President

CBS filmed American servicemen on the ground in
Cambodia.

"We will conduct...air interdiction missions against
the enemy efforts to move supplies and personnel
through Cambodia..."
the President

"... we are using air power, including close-in
support from helicopter gunships, anywhere local
American commanders see a need to help the Cambodians with their own defense."
(Washington Post editorial, January 27, 1971)

The American people are once again faced with a
wider, deadlier war.   Despite his promises of "withdrawal"
Nixon has escalated the war in Indochina in clear violation
of the sentiments of the people of this country and the world.
A situation exists where only a broad and massive mobilization of the American people can keep Nixon from further desperate escalations.

With the widespread rebellion of GIs in South Vietnam,
with more and more American workers rejecting the idea
that they should sacrifice their real wages for military and
industrial interests in Southeast Asia, the opportunity exists
to bring these constituencies into the antiwar movement in

greater numbers than ever before. Moratoria on the scale
of October 15 and November 15, 1969 are possible.

The NPAC calendar 'of antiwar actions this spring
must be translated into days of vital, unprecedented, massive,
nonviolent opposition to the war. To do this, we must reach
people and that takes money. Without our permission 125
million dollars a day is spent to maim and kill. NPAC's entire budget for the spring actions is a tiny fraction of that:
$100,000. We need money to purchase one-minute spots,
300,000 buttons and literally tons of literature.

By the time this appeal goes out, the intervention in
Cambodia and Laos may have reached disastrous new proportions. We can't afford not to make the most generous contribution possible.

Please contribute what you can.

Thank you.

Yours for Peace,

Clive Barnes
Journalist
New York City

Patrick E. Gorman
Secretary-Treasurer
Amalgamated Meatcutters &
Butcherworkmen of N.A.
AFL-CIO

Dick Gregory
Chicago

Julius Hobson
Civil Rights Activist
Washington, D.C.

Murray Kempton
Journalist
New York City

Kate Millett
Author
New York City

Ashley Montagu
Anthropologist
Princeton

2nd Lt. Rob Olson
Concerned Officers Movement
Washington, D.C.

Stanley Sheinbaum
Author
Santa Barbara, Calif.

Rev. Fred Shuttlesworth
National Secretary, SCLC
President, SCEF

LOCAL COALITIONS
AFFILIATED OR ASSOCIATED WITH NPAC

In addition to scores of peace, community and religious organizations that have been co-ordinating their activity with
the National Peace Action Coalition, there are now established coalitions of local organizations in the following areas:

CALIFORNIA
    Los Angeles Out Now Committee
    Bay Area Peace Action Coalition (San Francisco)
    San Diego Peace Action Coalition

COLORADO
    Rocky Mountain Peace Action
    Coalition (Denver)

CONNECTICUT
    New Haven Peace Action Coalition

FLORIDA
    Florida Peace Action Coalition (Tampa)
    Orlando Peace Center
    South Florida Peace Action Coalition (Miami)

GEORGIA
    Atlanta Mobilization Committee

ILLINOIS
    Chicago Peace Action Committee

IOWA
    Cedar Falls Peace Action Coalition
    Des Moines Area Moratorium

KANSAS
    Lawrence Peace Action Coalition

LOUISIANA
    New Orleans Peace Action Coalition

MASSACHUSETTS
    Greater Boston Peace Action Coalition
    Connecticut Valley Peace Action Coalition (Northampton)

MICHIGAN
    Ann Arbor Peace Action Coalition
    Detroit Coalition to End the War Now

MINNESOTA
    Minnesota Peace Action Coalition (Minneapolis)

MISSOURI
    St. Louis Peace Action Coalition

NEW YORK
    Capitol Area Peace Action Coalition (Albany)
    New York Peace Action Coalition (NYC)

OHIO
    Cleveland Area PAC
    Cincinnati Peace Council
    Columbus PAC
    Trumbull County PAC

OREGON
    Portland Peace Action Coalition

PENNSYLVANIA
    Philadelphia National Peace Action
    Day Coalition

RHODE ISLAND
    R.I. PAC (Providence)

TEXAS
    Texas Oct. 31 Coalition (Austin)
    Houston Comm. to End the War Now

UTAH
    Wasatch Area PAC (Ogden)

WASHINGTON
    Seattle PAC

WASHINGTON, D.C.
    Washington Area PAC

WISCONSIN
    Madison Area PAC

(Distributed by the National Peace Action Coalition February
1, 1971.   Received from NPAC by mail on February 3,
1971.)

70. NATIONAL PEACE ACTION COALITION

1029 Vermont Avenue, N.W.
8th Floor
Washington, D.C. 20005
628-5388, 5483

PARTICIPANTS IN THE NATIONAL PEACE ACTION COALITION NEWS CONFERENCE

February 3, 1971

Jerry Gordon--Cleveland Attorney and an NPAC Coordinator
Congressman Ronald Dellums, California
Kate Millett, author
Charles Cassell, member District of Columbia School Board
Stuart Kemp, National Director, National Council to Repeal the Draft
Robert Glenn, Business Agent, Hod Carriers and Laborers Union
2nd Lt. Rob Olson, Andrews AFB, Concerned Officers Movement
P.O. 2 Hal Rankin, Ft. Meade
Deborah Bustin, Student Mobilization Committee to End the War in Vietnam

Statement by Jerry Gordon, one of five national coordinators of the National Peace Action Coalition (NPAC)

President Nixon is again systematically expanding, intensifying and escalating the Indochina War. The air strikes over North Vietnam, the land raid into its territory, the saturation, 24-hour-a-day inhumanly destructive bombing of Cambodia; and now the U.S. sponsored invasion of Laos should dispel any remaining illusions concerning President Nixon's intentions in Indochina.

Nixon is not winding down the war. He is mounting a desperate, all-out effort to win it. The latest escalations result from the complete failure of Nixon's "Vietnamization"

318

program.   No matter how hard he tries to shore up puppet
military dictatorships in South Vietnam, Cambodia, and
Laos, he cannot save them from their own people.   The genocidal bombing attacks being unleashed against the Indochinese people may kill large numbers of them and destroy
much of their countries.   But Thieu, Ky, Lon Nol and Sou-
vanna Phouma still face collapse.

It is clear now that President Nixon and the American people are travelling in opposite directions.   The people
want out of Indochina; Nixon is getting us further in.   The
people want their sons brought home alive; Nixon assures the
death of many by forcing them to stay.   The people want an
end to the draft; Nixon, reneging on his pre-election promise, demands its continuation.   The people want full employ-
ment in a peace-time economy; Nixon provides mass, mounting unemployment in a war-time economy.   The people want
a curb on war-inflated prices; Nixon has ordered a wider war
which inevitably means higher prices.   The people want to be
told the truth; Nixon tells them nothing but lies.   His attempt
to conceal his violation of the Cooper-Church Amendment by
sending U.S. troops into Cambodia dressed in civilian clothes
is especially pernicious.

The administration is also trying to deceive the public about the new aggression in Laos.   The Pentagon is in-
sulting the intelligence of the American people by asserting
that the present news blackout is for reasons of military security.   The Laotian people don't have to read the American
press to know their country is being invaded.   The purpose
of the blanket censorship is to keep the American people
from knowing the truth about the crime that is being committed in their names and without their consent.

Richard Nixon exhibits an absolute contempt for the
American people's desire for peace.   And for that reason he
is well on his way to becoming the most detested and de-
spised president in American history.   Just as Lyndon Johnson was retired from politics because he insisted on continuing the Vietnam war, so a similar fate inevitably awaits
Richard Nixon.

We call today upon all sections of the U.S. Antiwar
Movement to organize large demonstrations wherever Nixon
appears.   Nixon may have selected Agnew as his vice-president as insurance against being impeached, but the U.S.
Antiwar Movement will see to it that both Nixon and Agnew
are a one-term team.

The current escalation of the war will not go unchallenged. The U.S. Antiwar Movement is launching its own massive offensive; an offensive for peace.

The GI's in Vietnam are refusing to fight in the dirty war any longer. And major antiwar actions have been called by the National Peace Action Coalition on the following dates:

April 2-4: local meetings and demonstrations to mark the assassination of Martin Luther King, an ardent opponent of the Vietnam war and fighter for human dignity.

April 24: a mass peoples' march on Washington, with a simultaneous demonstration in San Francisco, in support of the demand for immediate withdrawal of all U.S. military forces from Indochina and abolition of the draft. We plan to hold our rally on the steps of the Capitol as the police did last October 13. We have retained counsel and applications are being made for the necessary permits.

May 5: demonstrations on campuses and communities across the country to note the anniversary of the Cambodian invasion and the massacre of students at Kent State and Jackson State.

May 16: demonstrations at U.S. military bases to show solidarity with antiwar GI's.

And now, in response to the current ominous new escalation, we are inviting antiwar activists from all over the country to attend an emergency meeting of the National Peace Action Coalition steering committee scheduled for next Saturday, February 13 at the Laborers Hall, 525 N. Jersey Ave. N.W. The meeting will begin at noon and will discuss plans for a united, massive response to the latest expansion of the war. The power of our protest lies in the number of people who participate. While Agnew will predictably raise the specter of violence, our demonstrations are planned to be completely peaceful and orderly--we leave all the violence to Nixon. Our objective is to involve far greater numbers of GI's, trade unionists, women, Black and Third World people, students and others in the fight to end the war. Given the level of antiwar sentiment today and Nixon's reckless and bloody policies of escalation, there is every reason to expect a vast turnout on April 24. The large and representative list of endorsers already obtained is encouraging, and indicates that large masses of Americans will move this spring to curb the warmaniacs.

Statement to the NPAC News Conference from
Congressman Ronald Dellums, California

Today's number one priority for Congress--as indeed
for the entire American people--is to end the illegal, immoral and insane war in Southeast Asia as soon as possible.

I believe the majority of Americans support quick
termination of America's tragic adventurism in Indochina.
The majority of American citizens realize that there is a
vast gulf between the Nixon Administration's objectives of
winding down U.S. operations in Southeast Asia and restor-
ing a just and equitable peace for the Vietnamese, for the
Laotians, for the Cambodians, and for the Siamese.

As long as the Nixon Administration clings to its ab-
surd rhetoric of "Vietnamization," "Cambodiazation," "Lao-
tization,"--or whatever term they apply on a particular day
--I believe it is incumbent upon American citizens to undertake peaceful, responsible dissent to these policies.

I endorse the objectives outlined by the National Peace
Action Coalition and it is my sincere hope that NPAC activities this Spring will have a positive effect in achieving a
rapid withdrawal of American forces from Southeast Asia.

Statement to NPAC News Conference from Charles I. Cassell

The United States of America, supposedly a nation of
the people, by the people and for the people, has reached
the edge of an extremely dangerous precipice. Nearly a
year ago, an insane, power-mad administration, through deception and surreptitious intrigue, plunged this nation further
into unconscionable pillage and plunder of yet another small
Asian country, Cambodia.

Nationwide reaction to that disgraceful aggression
thousands of miles from our shores forced the administration
to assume a posture of withdrawal.

The new invasion of Laos by U.S.-supported South
Vietnamese forces and the strange self-conscious secrecy
surrounding U.S. involvement in this 1971 version of Ugly
America should make it clear to all decent Americans that

we have no alternative but to sue for peace immediately and
to accept no further claims that peace is just around the
corner.

Statement for NPAC News Conference from Stuart Kemp,
National Council to Repeal the Draft

    The National Council to Repeal the Draft is an inde-
pendent organization with a single purpose: complete and immediate repeal of the Military Selective Service Act of 1967.
It has no other political ties or positions nor official ties
with other groups.

    The American people are sick and tired of the draft.
They are sick of a system which forces young men to fight
old men's wars. They reject a system which forces men to
die in a war they do not support. They will not tolerate a
system which by arbitrary caprice drags some men to involuntary servitude while others go free.

    There is no way to make the draft fair. Reforms
such as ending student deferments are an attempt to trim
spoiled meat. It can never be fair to use compulsion to exploit any minority.

    The open-ended power to draft, essential to those who
would wage war by administrative decree, allows the President to prosecute and prolong wars in spite of the will of the
people. Despite his talk of the volunteer army Nixon is asking for a two-year extension of the Selective Service Act and
wants to keep the power to activate the stand-by draft at any
time.

    It is the duty of the Congress to hold full and open
hearings at which all views are fairly represented. Yesterday the Senate Armed Services Committee heard Melvin
Laird, Roger Kelley and Curtis Tarr. Tomorrow several
senators will testify. The Committee has not extended a
single invitation to testify to groups or individuals outside the
government.

    It is past time for the government to listen to the
people. On April 24 thousands of men and women will march
in Washington to demand, peaceably and openly an end to the
draft as well as an end to the war. There is no justifiable
reason to extend the draft when it expires in June.

Statement to the NPAC News Conference
from the Concerned Officers Movement

The Concerned Officers Movement is a group of active-duty officers in the Armed Forces who want to publicly express their opposition to the war in Indochina. We believe that we have the constitutional right to make our convictions known. The Armed Forces Officer, a Department of Defense manual, insists that a good officer "... says and believes what he thinks to be true even though it would be the path of least resistance to deceive himself and others."

Many officers disagree with the Government's policy in Vietnam, but remain quiet to avoid controversy, flipping into apathy and counting the days until their obligated service is completed. We believe that officers should not be passive and unquestioning, because of threats of harassment or "legal" punishment. We have sought guidance from the military on how we can responsibly express our dissent, and have encountered only vague threats and unofficial disapproval. Many of us have been separated from active duty, despite our objections, shortly after we announced our association with Concerned Officers Movement. Many others have experienced punitive transfers or threats of court martial. We believe that the military must recognize the right of all active-duty servicemen to freely express dissent from public policy.

Because of our obligations as citizens and military officers and our knowledge and convictions about the Indochina War, we believe that it is both right and necessary that we voice our convictions. The war is a ruinous failure! Its devastating effects on both our society and on the people of Indochina cannot be justified by any strategic goal. The war will not stop until Americans who are deeply committed to duty, honor and loyalty freely voice their total opposition to the Indochina War.

The Concerned Officers Movement endorses the demonstration to be held on April 24. An active-duty officer will be speaking at the rally. COM urges our fellow servicemen and servicewomen to join us there. All Americans must voice their opposition now. Bring all the troops home now!

Statement from P. O. 2 Hal Rankin, Ft. Meade,
to the NPAC News Conference

I've been asked to speak today from the viewpoint of
a man in the military. This is probably my final opportunity to express myself on that basis as I am being dis-
charged from the Navy as a C.O. The military man has
traditionally been expected to conduct himself according to
the credo: "ours is not to reason why." And there are
still a great many leaders in the military who rather naively
expect their men to continue to be blindly subservient. However, the day of the Automaton Soldier is happily behind us.
Sailors, soldiers, marines and airmen everywhere are beginning to realize that a muzzle is not part of their uniform.
They're beginning to realize that each time they are asked
to kill (or to die) they have not really the right but an obligation to make a personal moral evaluation of the situation.

The importance of this personal moral decision by
each military man is rather pointedly demonstrated in the
present situation in SE Asia.

For some time now the American people have been
attempting to make it clear (through their representatives
in Congress, through mass demonstration, through referenda) that we want an end to the war NOW, not next month,
nor next year.

But as long as young American men allow themselves
to be used as pawns, the military-industrial establishment
will be able to continue to circumvent the will of the people.
As long as young American men allow themselves to be
drafted and shipped off to Vietnam and Cambodia without a
word of protest, the devastation of SE Asia will continue.

Approximately four years ago the American people
were promised an end to the draft. The American people
were promised an end to the war. We are now being asked
to accept an extension of the draft. We are now being asked
to countenance the continuation of the war.

Thomas Fuller, a 17th Century English scholar, once
noted that "a man apt to promise is a man apt to forget."
On April 24 here in Washington and in San Francisco, the
American people are going to produce a massive reminder
and with massive GI participation we can make it a most effective reminder.

Statement to NPAC News Conference from The Student Mobilization Committee to End the War in Vietnam

The Student Mobilization Committee to End the War in Vietnam calls for convocations and teach-ins on campuses to expose the major escalation of the war. Students in this country are not going to accept press blackouts and lies concerning the ongoing escalation of the war in Southeast Asia. Massive convocations of students on campuses across the country will examine the treachery of the Nixon administration and discuss further antiwar action. To focus this student investigation of the Nixon Administration's criminal maneuvers, there will be an emergency national student antiwar conference at Catholic University in Washington, D.C. on Feb. 19-21.

This conference, called by the country's largest student antiwar group, will bring together youth from every section of the country: college and high school students, women, GIs, and Third World youth. These constituencies will rededicate themselves to build unceasing pressure against any U.S. presence in Southeast Asia. The lessons of May have shown the youth antiwar movement the role it can play in galvanizing antiwar sentiments in the community. We pledge to reach out again to the American people in a united action which can make the demand for immediate and unconditional withdrawal one which can no longer be ignored.

On April 24 hundreds of thousands of students will join with antiwar forces from every city in the country in massive demonstrations in Washington and San Francisco.

Statement to the NPAC News Conference from The Washington Area Peace Action Coalition

The Washington Area PAC is the local Washington organization affiliated with the NPAC which is dedicated to ending the war in all of Indochina. We are developing support here in Washington on the main actions being planned for this spring. The first will be on April 2, 3, 4 and is being planned with key people and organizations in the Black community in Washington. It will commemorate the date of the assassination of Martin Luther King Jr. as a great civil rights leader and a great leader in the peace movement.

There will be a meeting this afternoon between NPAC and local community leaders to plan the memorial actions.

On April 24 there will be a mass peaceful protest demonstration here in D.C. We have been successful in obtaining endorsement of this action from key people and organizations in this community: (Organizational affiliation for identification)

> Florian Bartosic, Counsel for the Teamsters
> Concerned Officers Movement
> Ozzie Edwards, Pres., Nat'l. Fed. of Social Service
>   Employees
> Rev. Joe Gipson, Nash Methodist Church
> Julius Hobson
> Etta Horn, Citywide Welfare Alliance
> Rev. Robert Hovda, Liturgical Conference
> E. James Lieberman, M.D., Howard University
> SANE, D.C.
> Frank Somlyo, Cooks Local 209
> Vietnam Veterans Against the War
> Womens International League for Peace and Freedom,
>   D.C.

One of the important concerns of the people and organizations operating in the Washington, D.C. area is that the demonstration on April 24 incorporate in its demands "an end to the colonial status of Washington, D.C." Not only will we be calling for self-determination of the Vietnamese people, but also for the people of the District of Columbia.

Statement to NPAC News Conference by
Representative Shirley Chisholm, NYC

I have always been one of this country's staunchest advocates of the antiwar movement. I vowed in my maiden speech before the House of Representatives that I would vote against every piece of legislation to provide funds for the military, and this is still my position.

Not only is our war involvement morally wrong, but our priorities are wrong also. There are too many mouths to feed here, too many people to house, too many children to be clothed, too many elderly being neglected--too much poverty--too much despair--too much hopelessness in this nation of plenty for us to be involved in immoral wars elsewhere.

The National Peace Action Coalition has my best wishes in its endeavors to attain peace in this country, as does every individual who is totally committed to bring about world peace.

(Distributed by the National Peace Action Coalition on February 3, 1971.   Collected in the Social Protest Archives, Bancroft Library, University of California at Berkeley, July 14, 1971.)

71. NATIONAL PEACE ACTION COALITION

2102 Euclid Avenue, Cleveland, O. 44115
216-621-2561
_____

Washington Area Peace Action Coalition
P.O. box 1314 Wheaton, Maryland 20902
(202) 628-6834   (202) 628-5876

On December 4-6, 1970, at the Packinghouse Labor
Center in Chicago, over 1500 people, representing 29 states,
34 labor unions, 150 colleges, 40 high schools and hundreds
of community peace groups met in a National Convention of
the U.S. Antiwar Movement. Speakers at the convention included Hilton Hanna, Executive Secretary to Patrick Gorman,
Int'l. Secretary-Treasurer of the Amalgamated Meatcutters
and Butcherworkmen; Stanley Tolliver, Cleveland Civil Rights
Attorney; Carol Lipman, West Coast Coordinator of the Student Mobilization Committee; A. A. "Sammy" Rayner, Chicago Alderman; Leon Page, Cairo (Ill.) Black United Front;
and representatives of the Japan Congress Against A & H
Bombs. In addition, greetings were received from Noam
Chomsky, the Australian Vietnam Moratorium Committee,
U. E. Local 767, the Chicago Women's Liberation Union,
Cesar Chavez, and the Provisional Revolutionary Government.

MARCH ON

WASHINGTON DC

SAN FRANCISCO

BRING ALL THE TROOPS HOME NOW!
END THE DRAFT NOW!

APRIL 24, 1971

The week of April 19-24 to be designated National
Peace Action Week to culminate in massive, peaceful and orderly national demonstrations in Washington, DC and San Francisco on Saturday, April 24.
   --from the Action Proposal endorsed by the National Convention of the U.S. Antiwar Movement.

ACTION PROPOSAL ADOPTED BY THE CONVENTION

For Immediate Withdrawal

The U.S. bombing of North Vietnam and the invasion of its territory provide fresh proof that the Nixon administration's real policy in Indochina is to win a military victory. It is perfectly clear now that Nixon's pre-election "peace plan" was a fraud and a hoax designed to fool the people into believing that he is serious about ending the war.

While he unceasingly attempts to persuade the American people that all the troops will be brought home soon and that a generation of peace lies ahead, events--aided by an active and effective antiwar movement--will expose his demagogy. When the people see that his words of peace are accompanied by the deeds of war, any illusions about Nixon will be dispelled. This process will be hastened if Nixon orders a full scale escalation of the war as he now threatens to do. The use of nuclear weapons is not precluded.

As the war drags on, the war weariness of the American people deepens. And as the economic vice of high prices and high unemployment squeezes the people beyond endurance, their toleration of further continuation of the war will end. The prospect rapidly grows that support for the demand for immediate withdrawal will assume tidal wave proportions.

Even if Nixon is permitted to stretch out the period for his declared policy of troop withdrawals, a crisis of major proportions looms ahead. If, to preserve the South Vietnam military dictatorship, he puts a stop to withdrawals, he will expose his true intentions and evoke an astronomical growth of "out now" sentiment. If on the other hand he continues periodic withdrawals, the peoples of South Vietnam, Cambodia, and Laos will quickly put an end to the domestic tyrannies maintained by the Nixon administration. Whatever the future holds, the demand of the United States antiwar movement must remain at all times crystal clear: immediate, unconditional and total withdrawal of all U.S. military forces from Southeast Asia.

End the Draft!

The Selective Service Act expires on June 30, 1971. The President has already repudiated his pre-election promise to end the draft. He now seeks its extension for another two years.

Senator Stennis, Chairman of the Senate Armed Services Committee, said, "As long as we are in that war, there will have to be a renewal of the Selective Service Act and it will have to be used." His words are confirmed by the fact that 90% of the combat troops in Vietnam are draftees. The Administration has concluded that the draft is to this war what the heart is to the human body, that is, unless troops are forcibly pumped into Indochina, U.S. military intervention there will fail. Not enough young Americans are going to jeopardize their lives voluntarily to support a war which they wholeheartedly oppose.

The antiwar movement must campaign to end the draft as a key part of its fight to end the war. Opposition to the draft runs deep among many sections of the population. The young generation can be united to oppose its extension and to put an end to the involuntary servitude which the draft imposes upon their lives. Opposition to the draft can help build an antiwar movement of unprecedented scope, one that has the potential of drawing in working class and Third World youth who are the particular victims of the draft.

No More Vietnams!

The danger of new U.S. military intervention in the affairs of other countries is ever present whenever Nixon deems the "national interest" of the United States to be threatened. The U.S. antiwar movement must be ready to respond on a mass scale to any move by Nixon to send American troops into other countries. Our demand must be: "No More Vietnams."

We Are the Majority!

The results of the November 3 referenda particularly in heavily working class Detroit where nearly 2 out of 3 voters cast their ballots for immediate withdrawal, indicate

that the antiwar movement now speaks for a majority of the
American people. As the ranks of labor have increasingly
turned against the war, one union after another has come out
for immediate withdrawal. These include: United Auto
Workers (UAW); Amalgamated Meatcutters and Butcher Workmen; Teamsters; American Federation of State, County and
Municipal Employees (AFSCAME); Amalgamated Clothing
Workers; American Newspaper Guild; National Alliance of
Postal and Federal Employees; Retail Store Employees Union
and numerous others. Masses of workers know that their
living standards are being destroyed by the war, and that to
curb inflation, the war must be ended.

Third World people are also a vital force in the majority movement to end the war. Chicanos have marched by
the tens of thousands in antiwar demonstrations. The Black
community solidly opposes the war and increasingly participates in antiwar actions. The same is true of Puerto Ricans
and other Third World people.

The polls confirm that the overwhelming majority of
women oppose the war and on a percentage basis higher than
men. Women possess an untold power and can be a determin-
ing force in ending the killing.

GIs in unprecedented numbers are thoroughly disil-
lusioned with the war. They are a key part of the antiwar
movement and possess a unique power to stop the war.

Students remain the most vital, energetic and dynamic
sector of the antiwar movement. That is why they have been
targeted for heavy repression. The antiwar movement as
part of its fight to end the war must defend the students and
roll back the repressive attacks against them.

Sentiments of workers, Third World people, women,
GIs and students are overwhelmingly antiwar. The job of the
U.S. antiwar movement is clear: to unite this majority sent-
iment against the war and organize it into mass action.

Proposal for Action

I. A variety of activities, including rallies, meetings, picket lines, vigils, teach-ins, press conferences, referenda,
etc. to be organized on a local basis to build opposition to
Nixon's escalation and continuation of the war.

II.   April 3-4, 1971 to be a commemoration of the assassination of Dr. Martin Luther King, a major leader of the U.S.
antiwar movement and of the struggle for human dignity.   Appropriate activities to be organized locally.

III.   The week of April 19-24 to be designated NATIONAL
PEACE ACTION WEEK to culminate in massive, peaceful and
orderly national demonstrations in Washington, D.C. and San
Francisco on Saturday, April 24.
        Local and regional activities to be organized during
the first days of the week as determined by area Peace Action Coalitions.
        The central demand of antiwar activities to be organ-
ized during the week to be "Immediate Withdrawal of All U.S.
Forces from Southeast Asia."   The demand to "End the Draft
Now" to have special prominence.

IV.   As part of an intensive nationwide effort to galvanize
maximum numbers of people into action against the war and
the draft during National Peace Action Week, efforts be made
to bring together women, Trade Unionists, Third World
people, GIs and Veterans, and students according to their
constituencies for the purpose of building support for the April 24 demonstrations.   In addition, state and regional conferences to be convened by area Peace Action Coalitions for
the purpose of uniting all antiwar forces in support of the actions planned for the spring.

V.   In the event of a new military intervention into the affairs of other countries, the antiwar movement to organize
an appropriate response.

Organization

1.   The National Peace Action Coalition (NPAC) to continue
as a national antiwar coalition which strives in every way to
unify all individuals, groups, and organizations that support
the demand for immediate withdrawal of all U.S. military
forces from Indochina.

2.   NPAC to maintain a national headquarters to coordinate
its activities.

3.   NPAC's present steering committee to continue with the
understanding that it be constantly enlarged to include representatives of antiwar groups from all over the country.   The

steering committee is authorized to add to its numbers.

4. The national coordinators of NPAC to be Ruth Gage-Colby, Womens International League for Peace and Freedom; Jerry Gordon, Cleveland Area Peace Action Council; Don Gurewitz, Student Mobilization Committee; Jim Lafferty, Detroit Coalition to End the War Now; John T. Williams, Teamsters Local 208.

5. NPAC shall function on the basis of the following principles:

I.   Immediate Withdrawal

The National Peace Action Coalition demands the immediate and unconditional withdrawal of all U.S. forces from and the dismantling of all U.S. bases in Indochina. The right of the Indochinese people to self-determination must be supported as a matter of principle. The U.S. had no right to be in Vietnam in the first place and it has no right to be there now.

Many Americans who oppose the war are attracted to the idea of withdrawal at some fixed date in the future. We will engage these people in friendly dialogue and strive to win them to the immediate withdrawal position. Any prolongation of the war means more deaths of American GIs, Vietnamese, Cambodians and Laotians. It also means the continued massive destruction of Indochina. Continuation of the war also contains the risks of further escalation and even of nuclear warfare.

II.   Non-Exclusion

The desire for peace cuts across political, racial, religious, and national lines. A basic principle of the National Peace Action Coalition is non-exclusion by which is meant all who oppose the war are welcome in the coalition irrespective of their views on other questions and regardless of other affiliations.

III.   Tactics

The National Peace Action Coalition employs a variety of tactics to win adherents to its program of immediate withdrawal. But whatever tactic is used, NPAC functions in a peaceful, orderly and disciplined fashion. Confrontational

adventures hurt the antiwar movement by alienating otherwise sympathetic sections of the population, particularly labor and Black and Brown people.

Violence in our society springs from the administration's policies of war abroad and repression at home. Nixon and his military-industrial supporters seek always to conceal this fact and to ascribe violence to those who seek to
end violence. The antiwar movement must counter violence-
baiting directed against it. But mere announcements stating
our peaceful intentions are not sufficient. All demonstrations need careful preparation--including the training and
presence of marshals to insure that these events occur as
planned. Then it can be made clear that the responsibility
for any violence or disorder rests with the warmakers.

IV. Mass Demonstrations

Mass demonstrations remain the National Peace Coalition's most effective method of communicating its message
to, and involving the largest numbers of people. By the
sheer weight of numbers that can be mobilized at a given
time and place, the antiwar movement gains credibility and
visibility. It provides a way for new people drawn into the
movement to register their opposition to the war.

Demonstrations by themselves do not end the war.
Nor do other methods of protest suggested by those who dis-
parage demonstrations. The war will end when its catas-
trophic consequences become unbearable to those waging it
and those burdened by it; and when workers, women, GIs,
Third World people, and students act decisively to end the
killings. The job of the antiwar movement is to educate,
organize, and mobilize tens of millions of people to hasten
the day when those that have the power to change the governmental policy use that power to end the war.

V. Political Action

The National Peace Action Coalition is non-partisan
and seeks to unite people of all political persuasions and affiliations in support of the demand for immediate withdrawal.
NPAC does not endorse candidates for political office. However, individuals and groups within NPAC are free to endorse and work for political candidates of their choice, and
to inform NPAC groups of such activities. Such a formula
permits the unity of the movement in mass actions and

simultaneously allows those within it to follow their own political bent. Referenda calling for immediate withdrawal provide the antiwar movement with an opportunity to work in a united and energetic fashion in the electoral arena to register the depth and breadth of antiwar sentiment. All NPAC affiliates are urged to explore the possibilities of putting such referenda on the ballot.

VI. Democracy

The National Peace Action Coalition and its affiliates on a local and national level must be completely democratic. The decision-making process can never be the exclusive province of a select few. Periodic conferences and conventions, open to the entire movement, are indispensable to democracy within the movement.

National Peace Action Coalition
2102 Euclid Avenue, Cleveland, Ohio 44115
Washington Area Peace Action Coalition
  P.O. Box 1314 Wheaton Maryland 20902

____Please add my name to your mailing list

____I want to help organize for spring activities in my area

____I/My organization endorses the call for spring actions

____Enclosed is my donation of $____

Name_____

Address_____

City _____State_____Zip_____

Phone _____

Organization/Union/School_____

FUNDS URGENTLY NEEDED FOR BUILDING THE SPRING ANTIWAR ACTIVITIES.
PLEASE SEND A CONTRIBUTION TO THE ABOVE ADDRESS.

California

Out Now Committee
717 South Parkview
Los Angeles, Calif.
213-389-1351

San Francisco P.A.C.
50 Oak Street
San Francisco, Calif.
415-864-5835

San Diego P.A.C.
P.O. Box 5762
San Diego, Calif. 92105
Jeff Powers -714-282-5628
San Diego SMC 286-6568

Colorado

Rocky Mountain P.A.C.
P.O. Box 86
Denver, Colorado
303-333-7936

Connecticut

Connecticut P.A.C.
53 Wall Street
New Haven, Conn. 06510
203-777-4265
203-562-1669

Florida

Orlando Peace Center
316 East Marks Street
Orlando, Florida
305-424-6232

South Florida P.A.C.
Peace Center
3356 Virginia St.
Miami, Florida
305-443-9836
305-444-7278

Tampa Area P.A.C.
7717 Huntley Av.
Tampa, Florida 33604
813-635-9176

Tallahassee P.A.C.
United Ministries Center
Corner of Park & Copeland
Tallahassee, Fla.   32304
904-222-6320

Palm Beach P.A.C.
P.O. Box 3233
West Palm Beach, Fla.   33402

South Florida P.A.C.
P.O. Box 6803
Hollywood, Florida

Georgia

Atlanta Mobilization
18 Yonge Street
Atlanta, Georgia   30312
404-525-9810

Illinois

Chicago P.A.C.
407 S. Dearborn #935
Chicago, Illinois   60605
312-922-1068

Springfield P.A.C.
c/o O. R. Sutherland
842 South 5th Street
Springfield, Illinois   62703

Iowa

Cedar Falls P.A.C.
2119 Coll. #7
Cedar Falls, Iowa 50613
319-268-1374
515-576-4372

Kansas

Lawrence P.A.C.
c/o SMC
1005 Kentucky
Lawrence, Kansas   66044
913-842-8957
913-843-1606

Louisiana

New Orleans P.A.C.
8017 Palm Street
New Orleans, Louisiana
504-865-7711

Massachusetts

Greater Boston P.A.C.
7 Brookline Street
Cambridge, Mass. 02139
617-491-3917

Michigan

Ann Arbor P.A.C.
1532 Student Act. Bldg.
University of Michigan
Ann Arbor, Mich. 48104
313-769-8249

N.P.A.C.
6535 Third Avenue
Detroit, Michigan 48202
313-874-4410

Grand Rapids P.A.C.
Wilbur Walkoe
4505 Lake Michigan Dr.
Allendale, Michigan

Minnesota

N.P.A.C.
1813 University Ave. S.E.
Minneapolis, Minnesota
612-376-7386

Missouri

St. Louis P.A.C.
2910 Lawton
St. Louis, Missouri 63103
314-755-3172

New York

New York PAC
137 W. 14th St. - 3rd Floor
New York, N.Y. 10011
212-924-0894

Capitol Area P.A.C.
727 Madison Avenue
Albany, N.Y. 12208
518-463-8297

Mohawk Valley P.A.C.
Box 568
Utica, N.Y. 13503
315-797-5580

Niagara P.A.C.
c/o WATTS
423 Elmwood Ave.
Niagara Falls, N.Y. 14301

New Jersey

Peter Schucter
c/o New Jersey SANE
201-744-3263

Ohio

Cleveland P.A.C.
2102 Euclid Ave.
Cleveland, Ohio 44115
216-621-6518

Cincinnati P.A.C.
c/o Julie Haley
4 E. Interwood Place
Cincinnati, Ohio
513-751-0284

Trumbull County P.A.C.
c/o Joe Paul
1717 Gypsy Rd.
Niles, Ohio 44460
216-652-5736

Oregon

Portland P.A.C.
c/o Jean Belord
10127 S.E. Cambridge
Milwaukee, Oregon
503-654-9847
503-236-7285

Pennsylvania

N.P.A.D.C.
928 Chestnut Street
Philadelphia, Pa.   19107
215-923-0797

Rhode Island

R.I. P.A.C.
Box 351
Annex Station
Providence, R.I.
401-863-3340

Texas

Austin P.A.C.
2330 Guadalupe
Austin, Texas   78705
512-478-0609

Houston P.A.C.
c/o Ann Springer
4014 Woodleigh
Houston, Texas   77023
713-741-2577

Fort Worth - Dallas P.A.C.
c/o Robert Mansel
2302 Mitchell
Arlington, Texas   76010
817-261-9944

Dallas - 214-521-6650
Fort Worth - 817-534-2470

Utah

Wasatch Valley P.A.C.
963 E. 900 N.
Logan, Utah   84321

Washington

Seattle P.A.C.
P.O. Box 487
Seattle, Washington
206-522-2222

Washington, D.C.

W.A.P.A.C.
1029 Vermont Ave. N.W., 4th
   floor
Washington, D.C.
202-628-5375

Tennessee (addition)

Nashville P.A.C.
c/o SMC
Box 61, Station B.
Vanderbilt University
Nashville, Tenn. 37203
615-292-8827

(Distributed by the National Peace Action Coalition during
April, 1971. Collected in the Social Protest Archives, Bancroft Library, University of California at Berkeley, July 14,
1971.)

72. SPEAK OUT AGAINST THE WAR

April 1st

Hunter Auditorium

at: HUNTER COLLEGE

68th St. & LEXINGTON AVE.

7 P. M.

CHARLES GOODELL: former U.S. Senator from New York

BELLA ABZUG: congresswoman, 19th district

HERMAN BADILLO: New York congressman

LT. FONT: West Point Graduate Concerned Officers Movement

ALLARD LOWENSTEIN: former U.S. congressman 5th dist.

ED GRAY: Asst. Regional Director U.A.W. (Region 9)

MYRNA LAMB: Playwright

DAVID HALBERSTAM: Pulitzer Prize Winning Journalist

DON GUREWITZ: National Field Secretary, Student Mobilization Committee

SISTER ELIZABETH McALLISTER, Harrisburg 6 Defendant

Sponsored by: NYU Law Students Against the War,
N.Y. Peace Action
Coalition & Student Mobilization Committee

April 24th---March in Washington!!!

Every day it becomes increasingly clear that Nixon is trying to win a military victory in Indochina. The overwhelming majority of Americans oppose Nixonization of the war and the April 1st Speak Out will begin to mobilize public opinion against the government's war policies.

339

Clip and Mail to: April First Speak Out, 249 Sullivan St.,
New York, N.Y.   10003

Phone: 598-2342 or 675-8465

____I want more information on Spring anti-war activity

____I want to volunteer to help

____I want further information on transportation to Washing-
  ton on April 24   Buses $10   Trains $15

Enclosed is $____ to help defray costs of advertising

Name_____Address_____

City_____ State _____

School/Organization_____

Phone_____ Zip Code_____

(Distributed March 29 and 30, 1971 at Hunter College, New
York City.   Collected in the Special Collections, New York
University, April 21, 1971.)

73. STOP THE ESCALATION--STOP THE WAR NOW!

The world now faces a deadly new peril as the Nixon administration presses ahead with its drive for military victory in all of Southeast Asia. This means a heavy new toll in blood and even greater risk of ultimate nuclear combat.

Only a broad and massive mobilization of the American people can keep President Nixon from further desperate escalations.

With the widespread rebellion of GIs in South Vietnam, with more and more American workers rejecting the idea that they should sacrifice their real wages for military and industrial interests in Southeast Asia, the opportunity exists to bring these constituencies into the antiwar movement in greater number than ever before. Massive mobilization on the scale of October 15 and November 15, 1969 are possible.

The National Peace Action Coalition (NPAC) calendar of antiwar actions this spring must be translated into days of vital, unprecedented, massive, non-violent opposition to the war. To do this we must reach people and that takes money. Without our permission, 15 billion dollars a year is spent to maim and kill. NPAC's entire budget for the spring actions is a tiny fraction of that: $100,000. We need money to purchase one-minute TV spots, 300,000 buttons and literally tons of literature.

By the time you read this, the intervention in Cambodia and Laos may have reached disastrous proportions. We can't afford not to make the most generous contribution possible. Please contribute what you can.

ROBERT ABRAMS
Borough President

JAMES ARONSON
Author and Editor

ROBERT ALAN AURTHUR
Author and Film Director

FLORIAN BARTOSIC
Counsel, International Brotherhood of Teamsters

HON. HERMAN BADILLO
Member of Congress
31st District, N.Y.

341

ERIC BENTLEY
Writer

HERMIT BLOOMGARDEN
Producer

HON. SHIRLEY CHISHOLM
Member of Congress
13th District, N.Y.

HON. JOHN CONYERS
Member of Congress
1st District, Michigan

EDWARD CROSS
Sec'y-Treas., Local 147
Tunnelworkers Union

LEON DAVIS
Pres., Local 1199
Drug & Hospital Union,
RWDSU/AFL-CIO

HON. RONALD V. DELLUMS
Member of Congress
7th District, California

HON. JOHN G. DOW
Member of Congress
27th District, N.Y.

HON. DON EDWARDS
Member of Congress
California

JULES FEIFFER
Cartoonist and Writer

HENRY FONER
Pres., Joint Board for
   Leather & Machine
   Workers Union

BETTY FRIEDAN
Writer, Women's Liberation

STEPHEN H. FRITCHMAN
Unitarian Minister
Los Angeles, Calif.

RUTH GAGE-COLBY
U.N. Representative of Wom-
   en's Intl. Leage for Peace &
   Freedom, Co-Coordinator of
   NPAC

MARTIN GERBER
Director, Dist. 9
United Automobile Workers

JACK GILFORD
Actor

MADELINE LEE GILFORD
Producer

JERRY GORDON
Attorney
Co-Coordinator NPAC

PATRICK GORMAN
Secretary-Treasurer
Amalgamated Meatcutters &
   Butcher Workmen of N.A.

DICK GREGORY
Chicago

CAROL GREITZER
Councilwoman
New York City Council

DON GUREWITZ
Student Mobilization Committee
   to End the War in Vietnam
   Co-Coordinator of NPAC

VINCENT HALLINAN
Attorney-San Francisco

PETE HAMILL
Columnist

E. Y. HARBURG
Author and Lyricist

SHELDON HARNICK
Lyricist

MICHAEL HARRIS
Pres., Howard University
Student Association

JOSEPH HELLER
Author

JULIUS W. HOBSON
Teacher, The American U.
Washington, D.C.

MURRAY KEMPTON
Journalist

STANLEY KUNITZ
Poet

JAMES T. LAFFERTY
Attorney
Co-Coordinator of NPAC

CORLISS LAMONT
Author & Educator

HELEN LAMB LAMONT
New York City

BURTON LANE
Composer

RING LARDNER, JR.
Writer

DAVID LIVINGSTON
Pres., District 64, Nat'l.
   Council, Distributive
   Workers of America

SHIRLEY MACLAINE
Actress

KATE MILLETT
Author

ASHLEY MONTAGU
Anthropologist
Princeton Univ.

RT. REV. J. BROOKE MOSLEY
Pres., Union Theological Seminary

PAUL O'DWYER

2ND LT. BOB OLSON
Concerned Officers

LINUS PAULING

CHANNING E. PHILLIPS
Democratic Nat'l. Committeeman
   for Washington, D.C.

VICTOR RABINOWITZ
Attorney

TONY RANDALL
Actor

HON. CHARLES RANGEL
Member of Congress,
18th District, N.Y.

HON. BENJAMIN ROSENTHAL
Member of Congress
6th District, N.Y.

REV. FRED L. SHUTTLEWORTH
Nat'l. Secretary, S.C.L.C.

JOAN L. SIMON
Writer

GLORIA STEINEM
Writer

LOUIS UNTERMEYER
Poet and Critic

JOHN T. WILLIAMS
Teamsters Trade Union
Co-Coordinator of NPAC

CALENDAR OF SPRING ANTIWAR EVENTS

> All activities of the National
> Peace Action Coalition are planned
> as legal, peaceful and orderly manifestations
> of opposition to the war.

APRIL 2-4

---Local demonstrations to mark the assassination of Martin Luther King, Jr., who among his many contributions to the cause of social justice, opposed the Vietnam War.

APRIL 24

---Mass march on Washington, D.C. and San Francisco in support of the demand for immediate withdrawal of all U.S. forces from Southeast Asia and the abolition of the draft.

MAY 5

---Antiwar demonstrations on campuses and in communities around the country to commemorate the massacre of students at Kent State and Jackson State and the nationwide outcry against the invasion of Cambodia.

MAY 16

---(ARMED FORCES DAY)---Civilians will make this Solidarity Day with antiwar GIs by joining them in peace activities at military bases.

MAIL TO: PEACE ACTION COALITION, 1029 Vermont Ave., N.W., Dept. A., Washington, D.C.

Here is my contribution of $_____

____I endorse the spring antiwar program. Put me on the mailing list in my area.

____My organization_____endorses the spring antiwar program.

___Send me April 24 transportation information to Washington or San Francisco from my area.

Make checks payable to National Peace Action Coalition.

_____
Name   Address

_____
City or State   Zip   Organization or School

Sponsored by NATIONAL PEACE ACTION COALITION, 1029 Vermont Avenue, N.W., Washington, D.C.

MARCH ON WASHINGTON AND SAN FRANCISCO APRIL 24 TO END THE WAR NOW!!!

(Distributed March 15, 1971 at San Francisco State College. Collected in the Social Protest Archives, Bancroft Library, University of California at Berkeley, July 14, 1971.)

74. NATIONAL ANTIWAR CONVENTION

July 2-4   1971

HUNTER COLLEGE   N. Y. C.

695 Park Avenue (68th Street)

Registration begins 6:00 PM Friday

called by

NATIONAL PEACE ACTION COALITION

Congressman Richard Ichord, chairman of the House Internal Security Committee, claims that the antiwar movement is a Communist conspiracy. He thinks the massive demonstrations on April 24 were planned by "subversives. "

He's right about one part.

The April 24 demonstrations in Washington and San Francisco were planned. They were planned at an open, democratically organized convention in Chicago in December of 1974. April 24 was decided on in free discussion and open debate and democratic vote.

The convention which organized the historic April 24 demonstrations was called by the National Peace Action Coalition. This year NPAC is doing it again. A National Antiwar Convention sponsored by NPAC will be held in New York City on July 2-4, 1971. It will take place at Hunter College beginning with keynote speakers at 7:30 Friday evening, July 2. On Saturday and Sunday there will be plenary sessions and workshops to plan the Fall Offensive. On Monday, July 5 (a holiday), the National Steering Committee of the SMC will meet to decide whether to endorse the decisions of the antiwar convention. As the organized student arm of the antiwar movement we must not wait to plan our role in the fall antiwar offensive. All who register will have a voice in the Steering Committee.

We in the Student Mobilization Committee think this

346

convention can consolidate the gains made in the Spring Offensive of 1971. A call for mass, legal and peaceful demonstrations for immediate withdrawal of all U.S. forces from Southeast Asia can further cement the links made between students, labor, GIs and veterans, gays, Black and Brown people, women, professionals and others.

Students have been a driving force in uniting the American people against the war, and our presence at the National Antiwar Convention will help insure its success.

We have brought the country together in a way the Nixons and Ichords can't stand. Because we are the majority and we discuss things out in an open, democratic way-- because we speak and act for the American people, who want "OUT NOW!"

Return to

STUDENT MOBILIZATION COMMITTEE
133 Fifth Avenue, 6th Fl.
New York, N.Y. 10003

Please register me for the National Antiwar Convention. Enclosed is____ $6(adults)____ $3(college) ____ $2(junior high or high school)
Note: Low cost housing and hotel reservations will be available. Childcare facilities will be provided.

I cannot attend. Enclosed is $____donation. (Make checks payable to the Student Mobilization Committee. FUNDS URGENTLY NEEDED.)

I want to join the SMC. Enclosed is $1.00 for membership.

Please send me more information about the SMC and the National Antiwar Convention.

NAME_____

ADDRESS_____PHONE_____

CITY _____STATE_____ZIP_____

SCHOOL/ORG_____

(Distributed during June, 1971 at Southern Illinois University at Edwardsville.   Received from the SIU Director of Special Collections on September 4, 1971.)

75. PEOPLES COALITION FOR PEACE & JUSTICE

MOVIN' TOGETHER

july 15, 1971

1029 vermont ave. nw, washington dc 20005

202-737-8600

FAP, Anti-War Action Scenario Mapped Out by People
At National Peace and Justice Conference Last Month to discuss the program of the People's Coalition. On Saturday evening, before the plenary began, Mrs. Sallye Davis, mother of
Angela Davis, not only brought us up to date on Angela's case
but stirred the Conference delegates toward continued resistance to Government acts of repression. In the evening
plenary much of the discussion centered on a proposal initiated by several labor leaders to achieve a unified calendar
for Fall actions. Over the preceding month, these labor
leaders, had met representatives of the Peoples Coalition and
the National Peace Action Coalition. They had developed a
memorandum proposing local actions around the Hiroshima-
Nagasaki Commemoration (Aug. 6-9), a National Moratorium
on business as usual on Oct. 13, and a series of regional
massive anti-war demonstrations.

The National Conference for Peace and Justice drew
over 1200 representatives of more than 150 movement groups
--clergy, blacks, whites, Chicanos, Indians, labor, rank and
file, men, women, children--to Milwaukee over the weekend
of June 25-27. For two and one-half days the delegates eval-
uated the Spring offensive and laid plans for local and national actions this Summer and Fall aimed at stopping the war in
Vietnam and poverty and repression here at home.

The tone for the weekend deliberations was set by a
number of brief presentations at a Friday evening open plen-
ary-rally. Among those who spoke were Father James Groppi, Mrs. Virginia Collins, mother of jailed black-draft resister, Walter Collins, David Livingston, President of Dist.
65, Abe Feinglass, V. President of Meat Cutters Union, Al

349

Hubbard, Executive Director of VVAW, Lucille Berrien,
Nat'l Representative of NWRO, and David Ifshin, President of
NSA. All of the speakers stressed the importance of maxi-
mizing unity in the anti-war movement, while at the same
time strengthening the ties between the anti-war movement
for social justice. They also stressed the need to intensify
militant tactics of non-violent civil disobedience designed to
move the government to respond to the will of the American
people.

(Received July 18, 1971 from the Seton Hall University chapter of the Peoples Coalition for Peace and Justice, South
Orange, New Jersey.)

76. PEOPLE'S COALITION FOR PEACE
AND JUSTICE

June 25, 1971

1029 Vermont Ave., N.W., Room 900
Washington, D.C. 20005
Phone: (202) 737-8600

Milwaukee Conference
Information, phone
344-8282, 8283
Carole Cullum
Jack Stetbens
Sally Chencey

BACKGROUND INFORMATION

The People's Coalition for Peace and Justice contains
a wide range of over 100 organizations active in the struggle
for peace and justice in America. Among the groups affiliated or associated with the People's Coalition are poor people's groups, such as the Southern Christian Leadership Conference and the National Welfare Rights Organization: religious groups such as the American Friends Service Committee, the Catholic Peace Fellowship, the Episcopal Peace
Fellowship, Clergy and Laymen Concerned, the Interfaith
Conference for Peace; traditional peace groups such as the
War Resisters League, the Fellowship of Reconciliation;
women's peace organizations such as the Women's International League for Peace and Freedom, and Women Strike for
Peace, resistance groups such as War Tax Resistance and
Resist; local peace organizations such as the Los Angeles
Peace Council, the Vietnam Peace Parade Committee of New
York, the Chicago Peace Council, Buffalo Peace Council;
and Coalition regional groups such as the Milwaukee, Boston
and Cleveland Coalitions for Peace and Justice. Among the
other groups associated with the Coalition are the New University Conference, the Committee of Returned Volunteers,
the National Student Association, Vietnam Veterans Against
the War, Trade Unionists for Peace, Jews for Urban Justice,

the People's Peace Treaty and the Ann Arbor Youth Conference.

The People's Coalition for Peace and Justice sponsored the highly successful spring offensive, including the April 24 mass march, the week-long People's Lobby and the May Day actions, all in Washington, D.C. The Coalition was founded at a Chicago conference of over 500 representatives, held January 8-10, 1971. It is a linear descendant of the New Mobilization Committee to End the War, which was formed in July 1969 and which sponsored the November 15, 1969 rally against the war in Washington, and the May 9, 1970 demonstration in response to the invasion of Cambodia and the murder of students at Kent and Jackson State Universities. The New Mobe was a descendant of the National Mobilization Committee, which sponsored anti-war demonstrations on April 15, 1967 in New York and San Francisco, October 21, 1967 in Washington; and at the Chicago Democratic Convention in August 1968.

The Coalition believes in using broadly based, mass non-violent direct action to combat racism, poverty, repression and the war. The Coordinators who are responsible for the day-to-day operations of the Coalition include:

Sidney M. Peck, 44, Professor of Sociology now on sabbatical from Case Western Reserve University, Cleveland, Ohio. Peck was Chairman of the National Mobilization Committee and Co-Chairman of the New Mobilization Committee and was a principal organizer of their demonstrations. In October 1970, Peck went to Hanoi and brought back 571 letters from American POW's. Peck received his PhD from the Univ. of Wisconsin and is the author of Rank and File, a study of American labor. He is married to Louise Peck, a psychiatric social worker, and they have two children - Sylvia, 18, and Danny, 16. Peck is Convener of the People's Coalition.

Rennie Davis, 30, a graduate of Oberlin College, received his MA from the Univ. of Illinois and did graduate work at the Univ. of Michigan and the Univ. of Chicago in political science. He was a founder of Students for a Democratic Society, was the National Director of Community Organizing Projects for SDS in 1964, and worked on the JOIN Community Union project, organizing poor Appalachian whites in Chicago from 1965 to 1967. Davis made a fact-finding trip to Hanoi in 1967 and returned to Hanoi in August 1969

to negotiate the release of three American POW's. He was
Project Director for the National Mobilization Committee,
helped organize the 1968 Chicago Convention demonstrations,
and was a National Coordinator for the New Mobe from 1969-
70. Davis was a defendant in the Chicago 8 trial.

   William J. Douthard, 28, studied at Dillard University, New Orleans, and the New School for Social Research
and City College in New York. From 1955 to 1960, he was
a Youth Coordinator for the Alabama Christian Movement for
Human Rights in Birmingham. From 1960 to 1964, he
worked as a field worker and field secretary for the National Congress of Racial Equality and was a field representative
for the Southern Christian Leadership Conference. In 1964,
Douthard became Education Coordinator for James Farmer
for Congress Campaign. From 1969 to 1970, he worked as
a community organizer, Area Director and Deputy Director
of Training for the Addiction Service Agency of New York
City. Douthard was a participant in the Stockholm Conference on Indochina in November 1970.

   Bradford Lyttle, 43, has a B.A. in Philosophy from
Earlham College, Richmond, Indiana, and an M.A. in English Lit. from the Univ. of Chicago. He has been active in
the peace movement from 1960 to the present as a member
and Executive Committeeman for Nonviolent Action and the
War Resisters League. At present, he is Coordinator of
War Tax Resistance. He was Co-Coordinator of Logistics
for the November 13-15, 1969 and May 9, 1970 mobilizations in Washington. He is author of You Come With Naked
Hands, the story of the San Francisco to Moscow Walk for
Peace, and National Defense thru Nonviolent Resistance, as
well as articles in WIN and Liberation magazines. In 1965,
he was a member of a delegation of pacifists who went to
Saigon to stage a protest against the war.

   Ron Young, 28, is the National Student Secretary of
the Fellowship of Reconciliation, Nyack, N. Y. Young worked
as a Student Minister in an all-black membership church in
Memphis, Tenn., and worked closely with SCLC in Selma,
Alabama during the struggles there. He is a graduate of
Wesleyan Univ., Middletown, Conn. Young is a Co-Founder
of the Resistance, a draft resistance group, and on April 15,
1967, he burned his draft card in Central Park, N.Y.
Young was Coordinator of the November 15, 1969 Mobilization in Washington, and worked on the May 9, 1969 demonstration against the invasion of Cambodia. In July 1970,

Young went to Saigon as part of a delegation for peace, and was beaten when he demonstrated against the war. He traveled to Hanoi Christmas 1970 as part of a delegation to negotiate the release of American POW's and to negotiate the People's Peace Treaty. He is married to Trudi, a leader of Women Strike for Peace.

(Collected by the library staff at the University of Virginia, Charlottesville, Virginia, on June 27, 1971. Received from the library May 15, 1973.)

77. FACT SHEET ON THE NATIONAL PEACE ACTION COALITION (NPAC)

WHAT IS NPAC?

An umbrella coalition of more than 400 peace groups, NPAC was founded with the purpose of mobilizing millions of Americans against the war in Southeast Asia. Its program calls for building periodic mass demonstrations for immediate, total withdrawal of all U.S. troops, planes and material from Indochina.

WHAT KIND OF DEMONSTRATIONS?

Peaceful, legal demonstrations such as the Marches on Washington and San Francisco on April 24 are the type of demonstrations NPAC sponsors.

HOW DOES NPAC DETERMINE ITS PROGRAM?

Through periodic national conventions where everyone who opposes the war is invited with everyone attending having voice and vote.

WHO ELECTS NPAC's OFFICERS?

The five coordinators of NPAC are elected at the national conventions. The steering committee which meets between conventions is also elected by the convention. The committee can vote to add additional steering committee members during convention intervals.

WHO ARE NPAC's PRESENT NATIONAL COORDINATORS?

Ruth Gage-Colby: journalist, delegate from the Womens' International League for Peace and Freedom in the United Nations.
Jerry Gordon: staff coordinator in the NPAC national office.
Don Gurewitz: field secretary of the Student Mobilization Committee to End the War in Southeast Asia.
James Lafferty: Detroit attorney; co-chairman of the Detroit

355

Coalition to End the War Now.
John T. Williams: Teamsters Union organizer, Los Angeles.

WHO BELONGS TO NPAC?

All those who believe in the need for mass antiwar actions
of a legal, peaceful, non-confrontational nature are welcome
in NPAC. NPAC holds to the principle of non-exclusion.
Thus individuals of any political affiliation can belong to
NPAC. When the House Internal Security Committee charged
in May that there were socialists and communists in NPAC,
Jerry Gordon, national coordinator, answered HISC sharply.
"That's true and so what?" he said. But he said that HISC's
allegations that NPAC is dominated by such groups "is ab-
surd." NPAC is open to all groups and individuals opposed
to the war and vigorously repudiates the attempt to red-bait
the antiwar movement. When HISC subpoenaed NPAC's bank
records last month, NPAC secured an injunction, stopping
HISC from taking more records.

(Received from the University of Wisconsin at Milwaukee Special Collections on January 17, 1974. This fact sheet was
collected at the National Peace and Justice Conference June
25-27, 1971.)

78. THE FIGHT FOR FREEDOM IS HERE--
Bring the brothers home Now!

    The struggle of Black and Brown Americans is not in
the rice paddies of Indochina but in every city and town all
over this racist country. The racial oppression that we're
quite familiar with at home is even more rampant in the
Army against our brothers. The fact is that 25,000 brothers
have been killed; that is, 55% of all American casualties are
Black and Brown and we constitute only 16% of the whole
population of this country! Education, housing, medical care,
welfare, transportation are all deteriorating--millions of our
people literally go to bed hungry every night--and the government has the nerve to draft us to help oppress our brothers
and sisters. The U.S. spends $125 million a day on the
racist war to destroy the SE Asian people. That's our
money!--and we don't want it used to destroy our sisters
and brothers in SE Asia. Just imagine what we could do
with $125 million a day for the benefit of our own people!

* * *

    With the expansion of the war into Laos and Cambodia
it is urgent that Black and Brown Americans build the most
massive movement this country has ever known. This is the
best way to let our sisters and brothers in Indochina know
that we support their struggle for self-determination. Let's
get ourselves together--brothers and sisters--and build the
mass actions on April 2-3-4 and also for April 24!

All Out April 2-4!

March on Washington & San Francisco April 24!!

Third World Task Force Against the War in Southeast Asia--
            National Peace Action Coalition

Mail to: THIRD WORLD TASK FORCE, Chicago Peace Ac-
            tion Committee
          407 S. Dearborn, Rm. 760, Chicago Ill 60605
          Tel. 427-7055

357

____Enclosed is a donation of $____. FUNDS URGENTLY
    NEEDED!

____I want to organize Third World participation in the spring
    antiwar activities.

____My organization endorses the spring antiwar activities.

____Add my name to the mailing list.

____Enclosed is $____, send me:____Apr. 24 Third World
    buttons (30¢ ea) ____Apr. 2-4 posters (Martin L.
    King Memorial) (50¢ ea) ____Apr. 24 buttons (30¢
    ea) ____Apr. 24 GI posters (50¢)

Name_____Address_____

Phone_____Zip_____School/Organization_____

(Received from the Third World Task Force on April 22,
1971.)

79. HOMOSEXUALS MARCH FOR PEACE

GAY TASK FORCE

On April 24, 1971, we witnessed what may have been the largest march for peace yet. An estimated 500,000 people (official police figures put the estimate much lower, as usual) marched to show their opposition to the war in Southeast Asia. My lover Marc Rubin and I left New York for Washington to take our part in the Gay Contingent.

Somehow, we decided, the march had been more of a "people's march" than those on previous occasions. More blacks, more working people, more of our elders and conservatively dressed folks were in evidence. And of course, there were more gays than ever before.

We had spent the day looking for the Gay Contingent, but the contingent itself was only the tip of an iceberg. I saw two middle-aged males, conservatively dressed, sitting on the lawn near us outside the Capitol grounds. They were not "movement types"--but there they were, unself-consciously holding hands, being themselves, and doing their thing. And how beautiful they were.

---Pete Fisher

We've all tried to conform to societal pressures, and where has it got us? No money for schools, which could do more than imprison our children (and lesbians are mothers too!)--no money to feed the hungry (and lesbians know poverty too!)--A war that burns babies, defoliates rice fields and turns our young men into criminals--and lesbians are angry too!

The gay community is now insistently entering the mainstream of American life and participating with our fellow American citizens in all aspects of that life. That's why I'm here today. That's why there are lots of gay people here today.

---Frank Kemeny

"On the weekend of July 2-4, at Hunter College in
New York City, there will be a National Antiwar Conference,
called by the National Peace Action Coalition to plan the next
series of massive antiwar actions for the summer and fall.
During the conference, constituency workshops will be held,
including a national Gay Liberation and the War workshop.
The same government that is responsible for the oppression
of Gays is carrying out a racist, sexist war of aggression
in Southeast Asia.   We as Gay people have an interest in ending the war NOW!   All Gays opposed to the war--women or
men, young or old, Black, Chicano, or white--are urged to
participate in the National Antiwar Conference." --Excerpt
from a Gay Task Force statement endorsed by: Jim Owles,
President, Gay Activists Alliance; Franklin E. Kemeny,
President, Mattachine Society, Washington; Rev. Troy Perry,
Metropolitan Community Church, Los Angeles; Morris Knight,
Christopher Street West, Los Angeles; Jack Baker, President
of Minnesota Student Association, University of Minnesota;
Don Teal, author of The Gay Militants; and others.

GAY TASK FORCE   133 5th Avenue   260-0210

(Distributed by the Gay Task Force in New York City on
April 24, 1971.   Collected in the Columbia University Special
Collections August 19, 1973.)

80. STUDENT MOBILIZATION COMMITTEE

1029 Vermont Avenue N.W.
Washington, D.C., 20005
(202) 628-5893

April 21, 1971   FOR IMMEDIATE RELEASE

WASHINGTON--The Student Mobilization Committee (SMC), the nation's largest anti-war student organization will hold a national press conference Thursday, April 22 at the SMC MOVEMENT CENTER located at 3rd and A Streets, Southeast, to discuss plans and objectives of Saturday's demonstrations in Washington.

Jay Ressler of SMC said today that student government leaders, campus press editors, and student political leaders at the national level will be present to offer a counter statement to a Washington Post news story on Monday April 19 which characterized the student movement on campuses as filled with "apathy, skepticism, cynicism, and caution." Ressler said in a press briefing:

> The students of this nation are going to take their case to the people, the Congress, and the White House on Saturday to present the expression of the national will to end the war now, today, not at some future politically expedient date. Our answer to random speculations that the movement is dead among the nation's youth will be an influx of hundreds of thousands of dedicated peace workers in the nation's capital Saturday, representing all segments of American society.

Included in the press conferences to begin at 11:00 a.m. will be:

Debby Bustin	Student Mobilization Committee
Frank Boehm	Young Socialist Alliance
Frank Grear	National Student Association
Duane Draper	Association of Student Governments
Barry Holtzclaw	United States Student Press Assoc.

361

Matty Berkelhammer Young Workers Liberation League

STUDENT MOBILIZATION COMMITTEE PRESS
SERVICE   call: (202) 628-5893

(Distributed by the Student Mobilization Committee on April
21, 1971.   Collected from SMC, Kent State University, on
May 28, 1971.)

81. THIRD WORLD MOVING AGAINST THE WAR

March 29, 1971

For immediate release

For further information
contact: Herman Fagg
Charles Stephenson
Lynne Watson

Washington--Third World peoples across the United States are organizing anti-Indochina War actions in memory of Dr. Martin Luther King Jr., an early and forceful critic of America's murderous involvement in Asia.

The <u>Washington, D.C.</u> Third World Task Force Against the War in Southeast Asia reports that it will proceed with its Spring schedule despite the refusal of D.C. Police to grant a parade permit for the April 3 march. The Washington Task Force schedule is as follows: April 2--Teach-in at Howard University's Crampton Auditorium, from noon to 5 p.m. The speakers will be Joe Miles, GIs United Against the War; Etta Horn, City-wide Welfare Alliance; Charles Cheng, Assistant to the President of Washington Teachers Union; John Gibson, Washington Urban League; Marion Barry, PRIDE, Inc.; R. H. Booker, Urban Law Institute; Imma Jean Williams, Church of What's Happening Now; Leon Page, Cairo, Ill. Black United Front. April 3--mass march and rally. Third World people will assemble at 10 a.m. at Malcolm X Park (16th and Euclid Sts.), and march down 15th St. to U St., down 14th St. to Lafayette Park. The rally will begin at noon. Speakers for April 3 will be Julius Hobson, D.C. Statehood Party; Joe Miles, GIs United Against the War; Jeanne Walton, D. C. Angela Davis Defense Committee; Leon Page, Black United Front, Cairo, Ill.; Michael Harris, President, Howard University Students Association; Ozzie Edwards, President, National Federation of Social Service Employees; Herman Fagg, Third World Task Force. April 4--Martin Luther King Memorial at Our Lady of Perpetual Help Church, 1600 Morris Road, S.E., co-sponsored with the D.C. Angela Davis Defense Committee. The speakers will be Rev. Joe Gibson; Jeanne Walton; Edell Lydia; Charles Stephenson, Third World Task Force.

In Detroit the Black Moratorium Committee Against the War held a successful teach-in March 24th on "Black America and the War in Southeast Asia." This Committee plans a mass march and rally on April 3, with support from ex-GIs, United Black Trade Unionists, Inc.; Black student unions.

In Chicago the Black and Brown Task Force is working with the Martin Luther King Jr. Commemorative Committee to build a mass march down State Street to the Chicago Coliseum. More than 10,000 marchers are expected to participate and hear speakers Rev. Jesse Jackson, SCLC; and Eqbal Ahmad, Harrisburg Six.

The Cleveland Area Peace Action Coalition reports that the NAACP, SCLC and the Urban League will sponsor a Martin Luther King Memorial action. The speakers will include John Williams, NPAC coordinator; Hattie McCutcheon of the Philadelphia Student Mobilization Committee; Rev. E. R. T. Osburn, SCLC director in Cleveland.

In New York there will be a high school student strike on April 2 at Manhattan Community College.

Among the endorsers of the Third World actions are: Froben Lozada, chairman of the Chicano Studies Department, Merritt College; Kate Moore, national staff of NAACP in Chicago; Warren Buxton, President of the Student Senate, Jackson State College; Dick Gregory; Jaime de la Iola, President of the University of Houston; Rep. John Conyers (D-Michigan); Rep. Parren Mitchell (D-Maryland); Rep. Ronald Dellums (D-California) and the Mexican-American Youth Organization--plus others.

(Distributed by the Third World Task Force Against the War in Southeast Asia on March 29, 1971. Collected at Howard University, Washington, D.C., November 4, 1972.)

82. CONDAO PRISON*

To:

Our Fellow Countrymen, Distinguished and Notable Guests, Fellow University and High School Students who have already been in prison and who have not yet been in prison, including also the fathers, the mothers, the older brothers, the younger brothers and sisters, and the young friends of all the prisoners in all the prison wards of South Viet Nam.

Distinguished guests; Deputies from the Joint Committees of Interior and Justice of the House of Representatives; dear friends; student representatives from the Saigon Student Union, from the Joint Council of the Faculties of Hue University, and from Can Tho University; Chairman of the Committee to Oppose Repression of University and High School Students; Chairman of the General Confederation of High School Students of Saigon; and close relatives of the prisoners on Con Son Island.

If we had to report to you everything about Con Son Prison, a prison which was established in 1939 and which has experienced many cruel regimes--colonialist, fascist, French, Japanese, and the one existing today--, it would be impossible to do so.

To report about their existence, we are not yet able to act as the official representatives of the more than 10,000 prisoners on Con Son Island. So we only intend, for the present, to simply report to you about a small portion of the situation of the prisoners on Con Dao, based on facts from our own experience, since we were the principal victims of a system they call "RE-EDUCATION," a system we lived under, endured, and suffered under for the year and more just

---

*Report of five students who have been returned from Con Dao Prison. They were released from Con Son Island on May 25, 1970.

365

past.   We are prepared to testify in more detail before any
agency related to the government about the incidents, the affairs, the facts which we report here.

We appeal to the enlightenment and the frankness of
our guests and honored deputies, those remaining people in
this regime that we can still believe in.   Guests, deputies,
distinguished persons and our brothers who have been in prison, as well as those who have not yet been in prison, we
hope that with the help of your spirit, we can eradicate completely all of the evils of the prison system, and re-establish justice and reason for all those people who have lost
their freedom.

We also call on all the communications media, both in
and outside the country, particularly the Saigon press, to
print this report, which reflects accurately and fully the prison system of Con Dao, though this is only a very small part
of the infinitely tragic situation that has existed there for
many years.

After being beaten and held in the Central Police
Headquarters for more than two months; and having appeared
before the so-called "Field" court; and having received a
sentence of imprisonment from two to three years based on
a prepared statement, forcibly signed after many beatings,
the members of the Field Court could find no way to clarify
what they called our "crime" except by calling it a "disturbance of national security" as the government had already decided in advance.   The frankness of our self-defense before
the members of the Court was met with threats from the
Military Police who also escorted us wherever we went, revealing their violent intentions in the face of and with the
consent of the men on the bench (that is, the Field Court),
who chose to ignore what was happening.   The right of self-
defense of a person convicted on no grounds, as we had all
been, was rudely denied.   The arguments of the Government
Commissioner now only revolved clumsily around the words,
"stubbornness, stubbornness..." and we were sentenced for
"two years imprisonment," "three years imprisonment."
Today we have returned for all to see.   What do those sitting on the bench think of the sentences which they have
passed in the name of justice?   What does the government
think of the years we were ill-treated in their prisons, of the
months we were tortured to confess in the police stations?
I am sure you know whose responsibility it is.

After being held for many months "imprisonment" in Chi Hoa prison, it was decided by the Prison Master there to transfer us to "hard labor." His intention to transfer us resulted in deportation to Con Son Island. Of course we could never accept this sentence, especially as he had decided by himself to change the sentence from "imprisonment" to "hard labor." Without warning, the Chi Hoa Prison Master sent us off to the island in an enclosed truck aboard a Navy boat #403; our legs shackled from the time we left the vessel and arrived on the Island, where we were welcomed by more than 300 Prison Orderlies (these are the prison's beating-specialists). We were forced to keep our heads bent down toward the ground and were hurried off to the prison ward amid sounds of rude cursing and swearing, amid the whipping rods of the people welcoming us. "This is Con Son, boy, do you hear!" "The Last Place They Will See." One old man, over sixty years old, from Bien Hoa, could not keep up as we went along because he was so old and weak. The orderlies beat and kicked him, rapped him on the head with a cane. "Be smart and you'll live." "Slowness Means Being Whipped, do you hear, boy?" The old man was beaten numberless times and suffered more than anyone during the welcoming that day. After one day in the prison ward they sent us to the Tiger Cage where our legs were shackled together from that day on, until we left the Island.

There is a room, or more correctly a small cage about 3 meters (10 feet) long and 1-1/2 meters (5 feet) wide, in an area separated from the other cages by many walls and totally isolated from all life outside. They threw five people into this narrow cage. On the average, each person had only about two hand-breadths of space in which to lie and live. The legs were shackled and held high day and night--even while eating, sleeping, washing--fastened to a metal rod about 4 or 5 meters (14 to 17 feet) long. They forced us to lie in silence; we couldn't sit or stir in this hot, narrow, dark cage. The cages are separated by stone walls more than a meter thick. A small door is kept tightly shut all day, except for a few minutes when it is opened and reclosed during meals. Above it are metal bars running horizontally lengthwise, with a small space or passageway left for the orderlies who make regular checks. We had to lie there all day. Sitting or standing (during the first months) was not allowed. We only had to murmur one or two words ever so softly under our breath and we had to pay for it with the cruel lashings of the orderlies, as ordered by the Administration of the prison. Even when the latrine barrel was open

and leaking all over so the floor had a pasty covering, we
still had to lie quietly and endure it. The tile roof had
leaked for years and never been repaired, and during the
rains the water poured down into the cage, not to mention the
sand pebbles and blinding dust that came in on windy days.
The ground where we lay was uneven, rough, bumpy with
sand, pebbles and dirt since it was many years since the last
time it had been cleaned. We were kept here continuously
for the first four months. They now throw girls and women
prisoners into these places.

The second place was the Cow Cage. This is a prison, located near a cattle feeding shed from the days of the
French, which was built by the government in 1970. It was
no different from the Tiger Cage except that it was bigger
and hotter, seventeen people being all thrown together into one
of these cages. We were put in chains, and existed as before. Let me describe here what sort of food the government reserved for us.

The food regimen was officially determined for the
more than 8000 prisoners in the various locations, wards,
and underground cells, according to the various categories
of prisoners that the government has set up here: military
prisoners, political prisoners, general security prisoners,
female prisoners (including children) and more than 2,300
prisoners whose cases were being re-examined.

We want to affirm clearly, at the beginning, that all
year round our fellow prisoners are continuously and regularly given just two main things to eat, namely, fish sauce
and a dried fish, along with rice. This was all decided by
the Administration, the quantity always being limited and
regularly insufficient, not to mention the quality of the food
we had to eat.

Besides the matter of allotting an insufficient amount
of rice, there were many other ways of keeping us hungry,
such as making us eat very fast (so it was impossible to eat
much or enough to make us full). Specifically, in the Tiger
Cage we were given three minutes to eat. A second way
was to cook the rice and gruel so it was pasty and liquid,
which rapidly filled your stomach so you could eat no more,
but then even more rapidly left you hungry again, only an
hour or two after eating. A third method the government
used to limit the prisoners' rice consumption was simply
that most of the rice was mixed with sand and pebbles.

Until the prisoners stand up to demand a re-organization of these conditions, they will continue to have little to eat and must accept a state of endless and constant hunger.

Finally, as you know, rice and gruel can't be eaten alone, but must have some flavoring to help get the rice past the throat, but here there was nothing but one kind of dried rotten fish that the prisoners all call dried Quinine because it is so bitter. People in the South of Viet Nam often buy this to use as compost for plants. Even among the most miserable Vietnamese or the people of the most remote minority groups, I have yet to see anyone use it for either human or animal food. There is no word that can adequately describe the quality of this dried Quinine. This dried substance was brought to the island in great quantities whenever it was selling cheap. They stored it for long periods, from three to six months, which made it even more bitter and decayed. If there was a little oil they half-fried it, if not they boiled it by pouring on a scalding liquid to make something called "stew;" if there was not enough they poured in more water. At times they roasted it until it was burned black like a piece of coal. For this reason, only prisoners know how to find the saltiness in the bitterness of this dry rot; choked with tears, they swallow the rice grains, washing them down with resentment.

Aside from this dried Quinine, there was also a "fermented sauce stirred into plain water." So much water was added to the sauce that you could only see a bit of shrimp residue barely coloring the bottom. We still remember, many times when this food was brought into the cage, it made us nauseous enough to vomit. So our deepest wish now is to eat rice with some grains of salt or sprinkled with a little salty water. That is enough to make it seem delicious. They only gave us salt a few times when they were in a good mood. But if they happened to be in a bad mood when you asked, you were liable to be beaten, as was one of our friends here who was called up to the Specialist Section and beaten and required to testify this past May 16th.

All year, month after month spent in the cage, not once did we ever see a bit of green vegetable or anything that could have been called fresh. Only a few times during New Years (the day when love appears among people). During the New Years holidays we only received a special piece of fried pork fat as big as the end of your finger. We understood that this little piece of fat was no bigger now be-

cause it had "evaporated" en route, through the intermediary
hands of the orderlies, the organizers, the overseers of the
prison.   For lack of fresh food over a long period of time,
most teeth became rotten and loose, even the biggest and
hardest teeth.   The only way to solve this condition was to
find some leaves to eat, even if they were those distributed
later to use to go to the bathroom, but which we had temporarily and painfully to call the "vegetables" of the Administration.   Or we could look for insects, crickets, flees, fly-
ing white ants, beetles, and even lizards, unfortunate enough
to fly past the prison door or unintentionally chased and falling off the top of the wall.   We ate them alive, biting off
and sharing pieces, saving some for the weakest among us
who had never once in all these years been given a vitamin
pill or eaten a bite of vegetable leaf that could serve as vitamins.

        In order to get some vitamins or something fresh,
sometimes after being called before the Specialist Section for
a beating, though totally exhausted we tried to pick some
blade of dry grass growing near the road and stick them
secretly under our arm to bring back to the sick prisoners.
That was the only "fresh" thing that we were ever able to
get for food throughout that whole year, month after month of
dried rotten fish and watery sauce.

        We ate and drank only twice a day, first around 8
a.m. which we called lunch, and then again around 2 in the
afternoon which we called dinner.   The time between the afternoon and next morning's meal was 18 hours, out of the
24.   They only gave us water to drink twice a day along with
our meals; each time we received a small sweetened con-
densed milk can about 1/3 full of water.   Since it was so hot
and humid all year round in the crowded and dark cell, we
mutually quenched our thirst with our collected urine.   In the
first terribly hot months our throats were so parched we
couldn't swallow any rice, the esophagus and tongue got numb
from thirst and there was only one other kind of water to be
had, the water that remained from the latrine barrel after it
had been roughly rinsed out.   And so we had to use this un-
sanitary germ-ridden water because of the cruelty of the
chief of the specialists and the tight squeeze of the prison orderlies, and we were prepared not to tolerate or submit ourselves to them though we had to accept germs, though we
had to accept sacrifice....

        Due to these conditions of eating and drinking, most

of us were sick, in addition to the symptoms we had after
the savage beatings of the prison system. Some had stomach trouble from eating too fast and from eating the mixture
of sand and pebbles, or suffered from chronic dysentery
from having to drink cold water as we did in the Cow Cage.
When we were sick like this, or physically exhausted, or
when we could not eat at all, the problem of reporting this
and getting permission to eat rice soup was very difficult indeed.   Each sick person could only have a small bowl of rice
soup and he had to talk endlessly before he even got that.
If he reported he was sick and still got no soup, he got so
hungry he had to stave off the hunger by eating a few spoon-
fuls of the gruel of one of the other prisoners beside him,
knowing that if the orderlies caught him he would be beaten
with a rod until he would have to give up eating for many
days ... as happened to one of our friends here who was
beaten by an orderly who used his elbows and knees to pound
him, ... and as happened to someone on a day in September
1969, because he had eaten one spoon of rice that a fellow
prisoner had saved for him when he was sick.   Though he
called out, "I am sick.   Why do you keep beating me so?"
the orderly did not cease striking him except to answer shortly, "You're sick.   Then let me beat you to death."

     To sum up the issue of food and drink, we constantly
were in a state of insufficiency, misery, and--compared with
an animal who has someone to feed him--we were much
worse off, even if you don't consider the savage beatings we
received as compared with the lot of a family pet.   But still
we continued to endure this for more than thirteen months,
because we dared oppose the injustice and bestiality of the
individuals who belong to the cruel government of Con Son Island.

     These living conditions were all created by the Island
Master and his committees, and the causes of these conditions originated in a policy called the "Five year plan for
economic self-sufficiency" which Mr. Le Canh Ve drew up in
1964.   In direct requests, the Island Master began going
around the usual contractor because he found that otherwise
he could not divide things up and get as much as he wanted.
On the economic self-sufficiency theory it was easy to deceive and flatter the government on the mainland.   He
achieved the goals of his policy by exploiting the prisoners,
limiting their food and drink, letting his men distribute the
food supply, over which he held a complete monopoly, as
they wished; he could also arrange for supply any way he

wished, he could grant anything he pleased. And at the end
of each contract bid term, he didn't have to laboriously run
up and down conniving with the contractor like the other
Province Chiefs did before him.... In this way Mr. Le
Canh Ve was filled to overflowing on the starving, suffering,
needy bellies of more than 8000 prisoners.

Many times when the prisoners stood up and demanded
an improvement in their living under the dynasty of Mr. Ve,
it seemed that a fierce accusation of the policy of economic
self-sufficiency he had created--which meant a direct colli-
sion with his interests--was always answered by the Island
Master with beatings, by the group of specialist orderlies
and security orderlies that he had set up and supported.
Many unscrupulously corrupt Province Chiefs in South Viet
Nam who exploit the very bones and marrow of their own
countrymen, have been protested by the people in favorable
situations, and have still managed to succeed without suffering revenge. In this case, uncovering the unscrupulous corruption of the Province Chief of Con Son was not so easy because the struggle of the prisoners could be labeled a "revolt," a "Communist rebel struggle," or "prisoners daring
to resist," by the Province Chief and his friends. Thus
their suspicious activities continue over many years con-
cealed from the eyes of the Saigon government and from public opinion despite the hatred and anger at injustices to the
prisoners and all the people.

All this time the ration allotted to the prisoners was
never made clear to the public. The Con Son government
has put the blame on the Ministry of the Interior. Since the
Re-Education Center has not granted them enough, the prisoners must accept their lot. Thus every struggle to demand
an improvement in the life of the prisoners has no base to
stand on and is always accused of "violating internal regulations" and is thus punished. Ultimately only two solutions
were left to the Con Dao prisoners, namely to either:

-Surrender and submit themselves to the cruelty, and
live forever a miserable existence, slowly dying in need and
oppression until the very end; or

-Continue the struggle by voluntarily sacrificing so
that one's fellow prisoners could live more easily than before, even though it was necessary to sacrifice one's body,
go on hunger strike to the death, slit one's stomach, or dis-
embowel oneself, in order to force the Island Master and

his cohorts to find solutions to the minimum and simple aspirations of the prisoners (as happened on May 14, 1970, in the 4th ward, where an unsuccessful request was made to meet with the head of the Specialist Section in order to demand a solution to the food problem of the prisoners).

Besides the "Food" problem, we also had to cope with a modern method of "Washing" that comes out of the Con Son Prison Master's many years of experience in overseeing the prison, as well as the extraordinary code of "Dressing" practiced in the prison in the Tiger Cages. We called it "bathing in shackles" and "dressing stark naked, at least nearly so."

The day they first pushed us into the Tiger Cages, our clothes, money, and medicines and all the other things an individual finds essential were taken, put all together and simply appropriated immediately by the orderlies, following the orders of the Administration. They purposely created a situation where everyone's personal possessions were all mixed up, and then used the pretext of having made a mistake in order to rudely steal from us. They deliberately recorded incorrectly the amounts of money they kept from us since a criminal in the "discipline cells" has no right to possess money. So each prisoner had to bear a loss of anywhere from 100$ VN to 1500$ VN piasters, which was a lot of money for us. Besides, the grand total of all this stolen money was not so small considering that there were over 1000 prisoners that they called "isolated" prisoners. As a classical example, in my case I lost all my clothes and possessions, including all the letters that my family sent. How can one tolerate a situation of injustice and robbery right in the place that the government calls a "re-education center," a "reformatory." If we complained, the overseer whom we called Mr. Chin Rong issued the order for a merciless beating as revenge for our complaint, which he called "daring to protest" (in the case of university student Nguyen van Chin). Sometimes the complaints were ignored and left unsolved as in the case of Mr. Nguyen Tuam Kiet and Mr. Tran van Long, not to mention all the other prisoners who have had similar experiences.

We still continued to struggle and complain about their oppressive, barbarian and inhumane actions until the morning we were returned to mainland. Only then did we get their answer: "You already have your freedom; what are all those little things you lost worth compared to that." How ironic and bitter is the price of freedom for a prisoner.

We could only keep one outfit. In this single outfit
we had to pass all the terribly hot days and months, as well
as the months of winter on Con Dao when the cold penetrated
us to the very bone. There were no blankets, no sleeping
mats; we lay flat on the earth floor, our skin covered with
ulcers from the gravel we lay on for long days and months.
As for washing, during the first months (April, May, June,
July) we were only allowed to wash once a week, and then
our feet were kept chained to this short metal bar. We sat
together and the orderly poured a tub of water over the five
of us. Naturally the water never got our whole body wet.
Moreover, during the past thirteen months, washing our
mouths or brushing our teeth was unheard of. Brushing the
teeth and washing the mouth was something the authorities,
the "discipline" keepers, absolutely forbade us. We couldn't
even go to the bathroom; for toilet paper we had to use a
small scrap of cloth ripped from a shirt or pants pocket,
which we carefully washed out with urine so it could be used
again and again.

Living under these conditions of eating, dressing, and
shelter, the prisoners had to endure confusion and serious
disease. Food was inadequate, beatings were regular, feet
were shackled day and night. Most of our fellow prisoners
in the cages were paralyzed, on the average two out of the
five persons were paralyzed, not to mention the number suffering from chronic dysentery (resulting from the drinking
water); tuberculosis due to long-term physical exhaustion;
stomach disorders from the beatings by the orderlies, from
eating sand and pebbles, from eating too fast; gangrenous
feet from a lack of vitamins; and endless other diseases and
medical problems such as mumps, swellings, etc. Medicine
was dispensed as the person in charge of medical problems
was inspired to do so. Here, every time we wanted to ask
for medicine we had to wait until we were in agony and then
generally only received a few aspirin tablets. Any medicine
more valuable than this was all hoarded by the orderlies and
their accomplices in the administration and was taken away
and sold. The situation now is even more tragic than when
we were in the Cow Cage around February, March, April,
May of 1970. Weakness, pain, or the effects of beatings
over many days and death during the subsequent period was
nothing unusual.

No matter what medical problem the prisoner has:
T.B., diphtheria, etc.., he is still thrown in with all the
others who are not sick, all still eat out of the same bowl,

sleep together, shackled to the same rope. We know of no
other place on earth where human lives are so cheap as in
Con Dao, to the degree that the government and the orderlies
there dared to state openly to us that "If you die it only costs
us a piece of paper." A sheet of paper which they call the
announcement to the Re-education Center of the Ministry of
the Interior. This evidence can serve to help you all see
clearly what our conditions of life and death were like.

Medical problems on Con Dao were entrusted to a
lieutenant in the medical corps. We had heard his name, but
never once did any of us see his face, even though we were
taking our very last breath. Seeing this doctor in charge was
a remote dream for us political prisoners because, in the
name of this ideal or that ideal, he avoided having to directly treat these people he called V.C..... especially the sick
who were in agony and really needed him. Thus medical
work was entrusted to people under him. Some were truly
capable but lacked the needed medicines and supplies; others
had just studied their profession for two or three months and
only understood the names of drugs. There was one male
nurse one time who was very capable and wanted to cure us
of our diarrhea and asked the administration for more drugs.
He was suspected of being an accomplice of the V.C. and
could have been thrown into the cells too, for doing something
like that. Though we were dying, the medicine our families
sent us never reached our hands, for the simple reason that
we were being disciplined and could not receive pills. Many
people have died in spite of the piles of medicine their families sent them, which was kept stored in the warehouse of
the specialists.

Deputies, student representatives and relatives of the
prisoners at Con Son:-

Through our report of the Con Son government's treatment as concerns our food, our diseases, the squeezing of
our means, and their robberies, the shameful acts of the
Province Chief and his fellows, we hope to have given you
some small view of the prisoners' life at Con Dao.

The corruption of the Con Son government has not been
reported despite the bitter resentment of the prisoners who
have lost their freedom and who have been in agony. These
facts are not as barbarous and violent as the beatings, repressions, mental and physical terrorisms they carry out on
us. To perform these cruel spectacles, special committees

have been set up. The security committee, responsible to
the Province Chief, has at its head a proctor with three
"grades" named "Mr. Chin Khuong." His assistant "Mr.
Chin Rong" has direct command over a thousand orderlies who
specialize in beatings. The office of beating is near Camp 2
area with its stores of lime powder, canes, chains, shackles
and other equipment for torture. Whenever the prisoner is
tortured and beaten, he must sign under the following statement: "Not being beaten at all," and similar statements
such as "The dried fish are deliciously fried and we prisoners ask for more," in case of food problems.

In order to explain the silent and subtle killing "machine" and the violent barbarian beating "machine" that the
Island Master set up, we will successively report the following situations.

Being political prisoners, we sympathize with and feel
pity for the fate of our fellow-prisoners who work as "orderlies," order and security specialists, which we recognize are
part of the terrible policy of "division for government" by
the Con Son government to crush the prisoners. A most
painful case, publicized by the press, was the death of seven
prisoners on May 31, 1970. Most of them were political
prisoners. The rest are seriously injured and in agony. At
Con Dao there are a number of prisoners convicted of robbery, murder, and rape who are sentenced from five to
twenty years of hard labor, and to death punishment. These
include military culprits who could have been re-trained by
the government in order to participate equally in the life of
the Vietnamese community. However the Con Son government encouraged their cruelty and barbarism by giving them
the title of "Order Guard" of the prison. They use materialistic means and allow a certain indulgence to attract and increase the cruelties of the "Order and Security" prisoners,
while they could have ended these acts.

Some of the prisoners who were attracted by these
materialistic means once again sold their souls to take the
responsibility of "keeping order." They are used as reform
cadres because they directly beat and control the lives of
prisoners in the various prison wards and cells. Their inhumane acts of beating, of killing and disposing of us increase the "prestige" of the administrators, and thus the confidence and favors on the part of the authorities. They have
much hope of having their sentences reduced if the Administrative Committee reports that "they are behaving well."

Thus the orderlies' killing actions are easy activities, even pastime hobbies.

The Con Son government's toleration of these barbarous acts of the orderlies encourages their bestial desires most clearly, through acceptance of their lusty activities: namely, visiting the prostitute houses, getting injections of marijuana and opium, and gambling. This type of life has been and is still going on publicly at Con Son. Smuggled opium is bought through the intermediary of the proctors. Gambling is tolerated by the higher authorities. Prostitution is provided by a series of girls. The orderlies fight in these activities, sometimes even killing each other. With the support of the Con Son authorities and with their assigned positions, they publicly grab our money. Some of them possess as great a sum as 4 or 500,000 piasters from these "activities" (as is the case of the orderly Tam Kinh) or they are released after having been able to kill too many political prisoners (as is the case of Muoi Mau).

The Island Master and the heads of the committees protect these acts that they themselves have planned, and destroy the evidences of robbery and acts of cheating the prisoners of their food ration in order to raise poultry for their own benefit.

At the island, a prisoner who wants to buy something must get it through the order-committee, i.e., through a "filter" who fixes the price of the item. The prisoner has only a choice either to buy it or not, either to need it from the prison or not. Money coming from the prisoners of the tiger-cages may reach a million piasters, and this is freely divided among the chiefs. Prisoners who want to get the money they had or the money sent to them by their families run into many difficulties, some of them have had to fight and sacrifice their lives in order to get it.

With the support of the government, the orderlies have a new profession: that of killing people without being accused, that of torturing--which was reserved only for the secret police, that of reformative cadres of the prison and the administration. A more tragic profession is that of the health assistant here. Such is the case of Mr. Phan Van Mong, who, after having beaten us to death, is now assigned the job of health assistant in order to try medicines on us and use us as experimental animals, shooting needles into our bodies in place of the previous clubbings on our heads.

Of course, we never forget the devoted help of the doctors,
health assistants who are here as political prisoners and who,
despite suffering and continuous threats by the authorities,
still manage to give cures to many of us. We also do not
forget some of the orderlies who still treat us with some
sympathy. We can never forget their grace. Some of them
were barbarously beaten by the Administration when they
tried to help us.

Once again, we are thankful to their sympathies and
help for us. On the other side we are forced to accept the
daily cruelty and the insults. Some of them use the most
vulgar words and in our struggles for improvement of conditions some of them have become torture-specialists by applying lime powder on our bodies so that some of the prisoners are choked and vomit blood. The orderlies are equipped
with masks and gloves while beating us. In one of the most
typical and recent cases in December, some women political
prisoners were covered with lime powder and two of them
were beaten to death. Each four orderlies are in charge of
torturing and beating one of us as in the case of February
28, 1970, at _____ Camp, where the repression was carried out under the direction of the proctors Tha, Chin Khuong,
Chin Rong and a high ranking officer named Duc. On May 5,
as we asked to see the head of the committee for improvement of conditions, we had to decide on the last means of
struggle--that we were ready to accept death through a nonviolent protest: an unlimited hunger strike. The strike
lasted over a week. Still we could not see Mr. Chin Khuong.
He remained indifferent to our minimum and just demands.
One fellow prisoner, Mr. Ho Van Chin, 23 years old, of
Dien Ban district, Quang Nam province, sacrificed himself in
this struggle. His corpse was robbed and his death was giv-
en a falsified reason, "dead because of illness," with the
complicity of the health service and the police department of
the Island. Under the direction of the Island Master Le Canh
Ve, we are constantly under threats of being beaten or killed.
Just an act of unbuttoning your shirt because of the heat, or
a noise caused by your leg as you involuntarily move it under the chains, or your not bending the head as you pass the
office, and you are punished with a series of beatings and insults for the reason of not observing the rules of the center.

Here, the orderlies have the opportunity to use the
modern methods of hooligans which are called "rubbing the
heel," "crushing the pepper," or "used bolts": they use
their feet or long heavy sticks which are used to bar the

doors (called Rod Bars) or iron bolts to hit on our heads and necks, especially on the weak parts of the body. Besides this, they continually keep us under shackles. In the past year, we were free from the shackles only for eight days, four days at New Years, three days at Wandering Souls holiday, and one day before we returned home. This "grace" to the prisoner is very valuable, as we were at ease, being able to move our legs when we slept after days and months of being paralyzed. We always remember these feelings and are grateful for those who have created these holidays, to save the conscience of these people here who have lost most of their human qualities.

> --shackles of the period of the French colonists which are round and smooth under the surface.

> --shackles of this present period which are made of F.8 iron, provided by U.S. Aid for the construction of houses.

These iron bars are shaped to the form of shackles. They are full of sharp, pointed thorns which cause violent pain reaching to your heart and brain when you have your leg under it. Later, these sharp teeth cut the legs and make painful wounds around them: each time he moves to one side or the other, is a misery for the prisoner. Such is the shrewdness and cruelty of this present regime and of F.8 iron aide.

As for the prisoners with hard labor sentences, whenever they struggle to ask for more rice and salt, they are punished by the "disciplinarians" who shut them up in cave-cells.

The shape of the caves is a half-circle. It is very narrow, without enough light and air for ten people jailed together. The prisoners collapse in extreme insufficiency and because of continuous tortures to death. The call, "Mr. Orderly, we have a dead man in our cell," or, "Mr. Orderly, someone is in agony," is very common to us. Each time we hear the call, our heart is broken and we think of our own fate.

To protest against this situation, the prisoner accepts sacrificing himself so that his friends may "live" in a better condition, or else he surrenders to the cruelty of the men, thus letting his friends live in a worse condition. We

choose the former, because we cannot let the proctors and
the island master exploit human strength through hard labor,
causing death to prisoners when they slip from the top of a
high hill or are smashed by a fallen tree. The master
robbed part of the wood that the prisoners chopped, and what
remained was divided among the other proctors (as in the
case of the Proctor Danh Sinh and his fellows). They used
about ten prisoners in their families as slaves, three to cul-
tivate land for the family's food, one to take care of their
children, two to cook, two to wash clothes, one to be mes-
senger. In case the prisoner has some education, he is
used as preceptor without wages to the administrators' children against his will. Selling their education in order not to
be whipped! Selling their education in order not to be
shackled! Such is the fate of the intellectual in prison who
is forced to accept the regime, to overlook it even though it
is cruel. Does one accept staying in prison in order to
learn more slavery or to learn to fight against injustice in
the tiger-cages. Most of us students in the whole country
take the second choice.

If in Saigon there are continuous campaigns to promote lowly romantic love, and family ties, to get rid of
struggles against injustice, this type of reformative education is strictly not applied to us in prison. The love of
brothers, sons, fathers in danger, in prisons ... is repressed by "discipline." One is not allowed to write letters
to his family, to meet his relatives. They publicly call
these love sentiments "lowly," so that the prisoner gives in to
his desire to see his relatives. The authorities have created
scenes of unhappy mothers and wives weeping day and night
for their sons, husbands and fathers. The authorities rudely accuse the prisoners of "having no sentimentality," i.e.,
having no lowly love as they expected, only because these
prisoners who dare struggle against cruelty have a higher
love and a higher and more determined love for their country.

However, faced with the infinite unhappiness of mothers and wives, can the authorities always remain silent?
For, no matter how violent they are, they cannot in the name
of cruelty destroy family relations and human love. We have
experienced the deprivation of love and we have escaped this.
But what is the fate of thousands of our fellow prisoners who
still remain there?

Here, we have to raise a question. How can the

authorities at Con Son plan and carry out these barbarous acts without being discovered? How can the Province Chief succeed in taking bribes, squeezing out the prisoners, if the "special committees," "the organization of the order committee," "the division of benefits among the Province Chief and the proctors" are being openly reported?

The Province Chief classifies the jails into different categories:

-jails for prisoners with and without sentence,
-jails for prisoners with hard labor sentences and isolated prisoners,
-jails for prisoners with a light sentence and political prisoners,
-but most typical are the jails for the "undisciplined" and the "disciplined."

The system of re-training the prisoners through series of barbarous whippings, through forcing their labor by the Chief of Con Son Island, has transformed these prisoners without freedom into complete physical and mental slaves. The degree of slavery depends on the degree of "correction" given by the Con Son Administration. At the very beginning when we first came to the prison, we were warned by Mr. Ve's words: "Obey us, bend to force and misery. Otherwise we'll treat your stubbornness by breaking your bones."

We had to obey, and follow the orders, sell our labor. If we protest, if we dare stand up against violence, whether we are numerous or not, no matter what means we use, we will be beaten to death. They try to correct us through violence, threats, cheating us of our food. Correction here means violence and robbery by the Con Son authorities. Yet, they are not yet satisfied. They deceive the outsiders who come and visit us through false "democracy at the island." How can there be democracy here? Only prisons. Therefore the master of the people is the King of the Island, Le Canh Ve. In order to see how powerful he is, how much authority he has over the slave prisoners, he had the idea of setting up a letter box to receive the people's opinions. For more than four years, he has only received several letters from the box. As a result, the authors of the letters were summoned to a special committee to get answers, in the form of terrible whippings. "Who tells you to denounce us?" "Who gives you the right to give opinions?" "Remember, boy, this is a prison." From then on, the letter box collects rust as time passes, still it remains on the wall. We wonder if any of the congressmen's groups who come to visit the island noticed the rust on the lock of the box, though the words "People's Opinion" still remain, together with Mr. Le Canh Ve.

When there are teams who come to visit, or investigate order, the special committee takes care of giving us some "wipe." We get a chance to wash ourselves lest we stink. They have us cut our hair and whiskers so that we look less wild and they do not forget to warn us carefully, "Don't you breathe a word to the team, beware of death, we will not forgive you. Hear it?" We note that when some of the members of the team have the generous idea of asking about the conditions in the tiger-cages, in cell no. 2, in the cow-cage, they are given such answers as, "that was in the French period; it no longer exists today." Stacks of firewood were piled in front of the doors of the cells to hide the cells, cow-cages, and the tiger cages. "It no longer exists," says Le Canh Ve.

Sirs, countrymen, friends, student representatives of the Saigon Student Union, the Joint Councils of the Faculties of Van Hanh University, Can Tho, and Hue Universities, the Committee to Oppose Repression of the Students of Van Hanh, Saigon, Hue and Can Tho Universities and of the Saigon High Schools, and relatives of the prisoners all over South Viet Nam.

We hope to have reported to you only a very small part of the violence and cruelty of the prison system. What does the Government think? Sirs, what must we do to re-establish equality and justice to the people deprived of freedom, those who can never speak out for their human rights, those who silently and continuously struggle against the injustices of a sinful and vulgar society?

Saigon, June 19, 1970

TRAN VAN LONG   CAO NGUYEN LOI
NGUYEN THANH TONG   NGUYEN TUAM KIET
NGUYEN MINH TRI

(Received from the Fellowship of Reconciliation on July 4, 1970.)

83. THIS MONK'S LIFE YOU CAN'T SAVE

He died last year, fasting for freedom.
You might help save 300 others.

On March 1, 300 Buddhist monks in a Saigon prison
began a fast which they declared would end only with their
release. The only nourishment they are accepting is water.
Because of their already weakened condition, spokesmen for
the Unified Buddhist Church of Vietnam fear that some may
already have died.

The "crime" for which these monks are imprisoned
is the advocacy of peace. They have spoken and worked for
a political compromise--a "third way" which would allow for
survival and coexistence within a reconciled society. Their
church is engaged in projects of reconstruction, the relief
of refugees, the war injured and orphans--work the imprisoned monks wish to rejoin.

On March 5 a delegation of Vietnamese Senators went
to the prison (Chi Hoa) but were not allowed to meet with
the monks. On March 12 the Associated Press reported that
142 more monks were arrested near Saigon. On that same
day a large delegation of Buddhist leaders went to the prison
but they were also turned away. Films and tapes of the
event made by CBS and NBC news teams were confiscated by
the police. All subsequent efforts to renew contact with the
monks have failed.

We protest the continued imprisonment of these
peaceful men, as well as of the tens of thousands of other
would-be peacemakers whose situation in U.S.-financed prisons is similarly desperate and unjust.

We plead for an immediate and massive public re-
sponse in the form of protest to every appropriate official.
Telephone or telegraph your Senators and Representatives.
Telegraph or write to Mr. Le Cong Chat, the Minister of the
Interior, Republic of Vietnam, Saigon; Ambassador Tran Kim

Phuong, Embassy of the Republic of Vietnam, Washington; and Ambassador Graham Martin, U.S. Embassy, Saigon.

Join us in Washington April 12 for a day of support to the prisoners in Vietnam.

Respond now, this minute, while at least some of the 300 remain alive.

Signers of the above statement include: Bishop James Armstrong, Bishop of the Dakotas, United Methodist Church; Anne Bennett, Churchwoman, Berkeley, Calif.; Dr. John C. Bennett, President Emeritus, Union Theological Seminary; Peggy Billings, Women's Division, Section of Christian Social Relations; Rabbi Balfour Brickner, Director of Interfaith Activities, Union of American Hebrew Congregations; Dr. W. Sterling Cary, President, National Council of Churches; Dorothy Day, Publisher, The Catholic Worker; Bishop Carroll Dozier, Roman Catholic Diocese of Memphis; The Right Rev. Paul Moore, Episcopal Bishop of New York; Dr. Robert V. Moss, President, United Church of Christ; William P. Thompson, Stated Clerk, United Presbyterian Church; Fr. Thomas Stransky, President, the Paulist Fathers and Dr. John Howard Yoder, President, Goshan Biblical Seminary. Associations are listed for identification purposes only.

The Fellowship of Reconciliation, Box 271, Nyack, N.Y. 10960

____Include my name as a signer of this statement. Keep me in touch with other things that can be done to help imprisoned dissenters in Vietnam.

____I want to help finance this project. Enclosed is my contribution for $____ (Tax deductible.)

____Please send information about the FOR and the April 12 day of prisoner support in Washington, D.C.

name_____

address _____

_____zip_____

Reading the text above will tell you why we thought it urgent to send this to you right away.   We and the Chi Hoa monks need your help.

TELEPHONE OR TELEGRAPH your Senators and Representatives.   Don't let them off the hook.   Our taxes pay Thieu's bills.

POST THIS in your church, synagogue, school or club, if possible.

PUBLISH as an ad in your local newspaper.

CONTRIBUTE to the Chi Hoa Fasters' Fund to extend efforts for their freedom.   Make checks payable to F.O.R. --tax deductible.

(Collected in the Special Collections, Harvard University, June 17, 1974.   Mimeo.   The events referred to occurred in 1970.)

84. FACT SHEET ON VIETNAM

1945-1954   French Renege on Agreements--Indochinese War
            Begins

   1945 Japanese surrender. Ho Chi Minh declares inde-
         pendent Democratic Republic of Vietnam.
   1946 French forces return, recognize authority of Ho
         regime over North, promise plebiscite in South.
         Later French establish separate puppet govern-
         ment in South and issue ultimatum to Ho to dis-
         band all Vietminh military forces in North. Ho's
         refusal results in open warfare.
   1949 French attempt to rally popular support, establish
         autonomous State of Vietnam based in Saigon un-
         der Emperor Bao Dai.
   1950 US and allies recognize Bao Dai government and
         US begins economic and military aid. Russia and
         China recognize Ho regime.
   1954 Dien Bien Phu symbolizes final defeat of French.

1954-1956   Geneva Accords Promise Elections--Diem and US
            Renege

   1954 Geneva Agreement provides for two temporary
         military regroupment zones, French in South and
         Vietminh in North. Reunification promised after
         nation-wide elections scheduled for July 1956.
         Political reprisals and foreign military bases or
         troops prohibited; US refuses to sign but agrees
         to honor agreement.
   1954 SEATO established. S. Vietnam designated as a
         "protected state."
   1955 Diem (Prime Minister under Bao Dai) refuses
         Hanoi proposal to consult on promised elections
         and proclaims self President of independent Re-
         public of Vietnam.

1956-1963   Diem Regime Alienates Vietnamese--US Involve-
            ment Increases

1956 Diem ordinance allows arrest of anyone consid-
     ered dangerous to public order.   Elected village
     councils replaced by government appointees.   Last
     French troops withdraw; US military advisory
     group remains to train and equip S. Vietnamese
     army.
1958 Clandestine radio (Voice of S. Vietnam Libera-
     tion Front) begins operation in South.   Denounced
     by Hanoi as provocative.
1960 Anti-communist leaders in South condemn Diem
     undemocratic policies.   Hanoi sanctions formation
     of United Front and overthrow of Diem regime.
     National Liberation Front of South Vietnam (NLF)
     formally established.
1961 Visits of Vice-President Johnson and other offi-
     cials to S. Vietnam result in increase in US ad-
     visors to 18,000.
1962 NLF calls for implementation of Geneva accords,
     withdrawal of US military personnel, and coali-
     tion government in South with neutral foreign pol-
     icy.
1963 Buddhist uprising against Diem.   Kennedy calls
     for popular reforms in S. Vietnam and suspends
     US aid.   Diem regime overthrown.

1963-1965 Neutralization Proposals Rejected--US Begins
         Widescale Bombing

1963/64 NLF proposes negotiated ceasefire and general
     elections.   U Thant supports.   Johnson labels
     neutralization "a Communist takeover."   Anti-
     neutralist elements overthrow Saigon government,
     reject NLF proposals for negotiations.   U Thant
     suggests reconvening Geneva Conference.   John-
     son rejects this as a conference to "ratify terror."
     US military mission increased to 21,000.
1964 (August) Gulf of Tonkin Incident.   Johnson orders
     retaliation before Navy has determined that attack
     on US destroyers did in fact occur.   Congression-
     al resolution authorizes "all necessary measures."
1965 (January-February) Continued instability of Saigon
     government results in armed forces control of re-
     gime under Thieu and Ky.   US begins widespread
     bombing of North and NLF areas in South.   US
     marines land in South.   U Thant again appeals for
     reconvening Geneva conference.

1965-1966 Hanoi Peace Plan Rejected--US Institutes
           Bombing Pause

   1965 (April-May) Hanoi four point proposal: withdraw-
         al US military; cessation hostilities against North;
         honor Geneva accords; Vietnamese to solve own
         problems. US orders bombing halt conditional on
         reduction in hostilities by other side. Bombing
         resumed 5 days.
   1965 (July-December) Johnson offers "unconditional dis-
         cussions" with "any government" and announces
         US troop increases to 125,000. Saigon refuses
         to negotiate with NLF. Repeated peace feelers
         from Hanoi bring US request for "clarification"
         while US carries out first air strike on Hanoi-
         Haiphong complex.
   1965/66 (December-January) Second US bombing halt.
         N. Vietnamese forces cease most aggressive ac-
         tions in South. US launches major offensive. Ad-
         ministration ignores Senate appeal for continua-
         tion of bombing pause. Hanoi calls for implemen-
         tation of Geneva accords.

1966-1968 Elections Held in South--Tet Offensive Shakes
           US Confidence

   1966 (March-September) Buddhist demonstrations in Hue
         put down with American military support and Sai-
         gon promise of national election. Only candidates
         acceptable to government allowed to participate in
         Constitutional Assembly elections; Buddhist boy-
         cott.
   1966 (October) At Manila conference, US agrees to with-
         draw troops 6 months after Hanoi and NLF with-
         draw to north of 17th parallel. US troop strength
         reaches 385,000 (8 times the number of N. Viet-
         namese troops).
   1967 (February) Johnson refuses to stop bombing until
         North stops all infiltration into South. Bombing
         resumed before reply received.
   1967 (September) Vietnamese presidential elections re-
         sult in Thieu-Ky victory with 35% plurality. All
         known advocates of peaceful settlement or negotia-
         tions with NLF are banned.
   1967/68 "Free fire" zones established, resulting in
         estimated 4 million refugees (25% of population).
   1968 (January-February) Tet offensive. Vietcong and

N. Vietnamese troops attack 36 of S. Vietnam's
44 provincial capitals, holding major portions of
Saigon and Hue. In heavy fighting over Hue,
civilian casualties estimated at 3600.

1968-1969 Johnson Announces Bombing Halt--Peace
Conference Bogs Down

1968 (April-June) Peace moves in US escalate following
Tet Offensive. Johnson announces bombing halt
north of 20th parallel as first step to "de-esca-
late the conflict" and "move immediately to peace
through negotiations." Total halt to follow signs
of restraint from other side. Hanoi agrees to
meet US representatives in Paris; talks begin in
May. Subsequent decline in N. Vietnamese offensive operations.

1968 (October) Johnson announces total bombing halt on
election eve. NLF and Saigon governments to join
peace talks.

1969 (January) Four-party talks begin in Paris.

1969 (April-May) Peace talks stalemate over issues of
troop withdrawals and interim government.
Hanoi/NLF demand US commitment to total withdrawal of US forces and call for provisional coalition government representing all who favor peace,
independence and neutrality.

1969 (May) Nixon announces start of gradual troop withdrawals (US troop strength in Vietnam 540,000).

1969 (November-December) US and world opinion
shocked by news of US troops killing Vietnamese
civilians at Mylai.

1969-1970 Stalemate in Paris and Vietnam--Escalation in
Laos and Cambodia

1969 (December-March) Senate Foreign Relations Committee increasingly critical of US involvement in
SE Asia. Senate-House Conference Committee
proposes legislation barring use of US combat
troops in Laos.

1969 (December) US chief delegate to Paris talks
(Lodge) resigns; neither he nor deputy replaced.
No progress in negotiations. Thieu government
closes two Saigon newspapers, seizes 15 student
leaders, purges and imprisons 3 critics in House
of Representatives. Vice-President Agnew, on

Asian tour, deems it inappropriate for US to
press Thieu to broaden his popular support.

1970 (January-February) Administration states that infiltration from N. Vietnam decreases.   US carries out retaliatory bombings on North for attacks
on US reconnaisance planes.

1970 (January-March) Increased fighting in Laos, with
US bombing wide areas in support of Laotian government troops.   Numerous civilian casualties and
large numbers of refugees.   Deep US involvement
in training, arming, financing and directing clandestine army of Meo tribesmen (non-Lao hill
peoples) revealed.   Laotian government requests
reconvening of Geneva Conference; Pathet Lao
(Pro-communist forces) seek to open direct negotiations with Laotian government and demand end
to US bombing.

1970 (March-April) Coup in Cambodia deposes neutralist leader Prince Sihanouk, calls for military actions against Vietcong and N. Vietnamese bases in
Cambodian border areas.   S. Vietnamese forces
begin attacks on suspected Vietcong base camps in
Cambodia with US helicopter support.   Many members of Cambodia's Vietnamese minority killed as
consequence of anti-Vietnamese campaign undertaken by new military regime in Phnom Penh.
Vietcong offensive moves westward close to capital; Cambodia appeals for foreign arms aid.

1970 (April 20) Nixon pledges to withdraw an additional
150,000 troops from Vietnam during 1970 because
progress in "Vietnamization" exceeding expecta-
tions.

1970 (April 30) Nixon Administration announces that US
and S. Vietnamese forces have launched first of
6 major attacks into Cambodia to root out Vietcong and N. Vietnamese bases in order to make
"Vietnamization" policy successful and insure continuing withdrawal of US troops.

Compiled by:
Committee of Concerned Asian Scholars
Cornell University

(Received August 17, 1970.)

85. PLEASE, MR. PRESIDENT

Must More Americans Die for Thieu and Ky?

Mr. President --

We approve in principle your desire, expressed in your Vietnam address of October 7, for "a political solution that reflects the will of the South Vietnamese people."

But we urge you to see that this can never come about as long as South Vietnam is controlled by the thinly legitimized dictatorship of General Thieu and Marshal Ky.

The negotiators on the other side of the table at the Paris peace talks must realize this only too well.

They have seen the jails and tiger cages of South Vietnam filled to overflowing with political prisoners arrested without cause and imprisoned without trial. Estimates of the number of these political prisoners have ranged as high as 200,000.

And they have seen how the South Vietnamese military junta manipulated the election and operation of a Constituent Assembly giving the President dictatorial powers.

And how General Thieu then manipulated the election machinery again to bestow upon himself the title of President.

How could such a government conduct a truly free election, no matter how many thousands of international observers were sent in to supervise it?

How could international observers, most of whom would be completely ignorant of Vietnamese language and customs, be able to observe and prevent gross election fraud?

And what would prevent Thieu's secret police from seizing and jailing any Vietcong election inspector who protested irregularities?

Is it not understandable why the other side in the Paris peace negotiations has steadfastly insisted on the need for a new provisional coalition government to be formed before any truly free national elections can be held?

Can we really blame them, Mr. President? Would not their giving up this requirement really amount to unconditional surrender on their part?

The chief negotiator for the National Liberation Front has said they will enter into discussions with anyone in the present government except Thieu, Ky, and one other.

Why must we cling to these unpopular military dictators who fought with the French colonial troops against their own people, Mr. President?

Why must we, in effect, send more American boys to fight and die for Thieu and Ky?

How can we console ourselves that "only" 4,000 American men died in Vietnam this year ... when we consider the possibility that a coalition government formed during your first year in office might have negotiated a peace which would have saved them all?

Mr. President, when the Tonkin Gulf resolution was rescinded by the Senate, and you were asked by reporters your legal justification for continuing to fight an undeclared war in Vietnam, your answer was--

"The President of the United States has the constitutional right--not only the right but the responsibility--to use his powers to protect American forces when they are engaged in military action."

What will you do, then, if the North Vietnamese launch a major offensive next summer, after you have reduced American forces to the promised level of 250,000 troops? Will you then feel you have the right and responsibility to send in more American troops to protect the troops still there?

Would there not be far greater protection of American troops in Vietnam if you accepted the offer of the National Liberation Front not to fire on our troops if we agree to withdraw them all by June 30 next year?

You have said, Mr. President, that you are against the United States "imposing" a coalition government in South Vietnam.

But isn't it really a question of permitting rather than imposing a coalition government?

"Without American support," Ky's foreign minister told an American study group in 1965, "this government would not last five days."

Has the situation really changed so much since then? And would we really be imposing a coalition if we simply withdrew our strong official support of Thieu and Ky?

Might there not even be a neutral provisional government formed which would be neither pro-Thieu nor pro-Communist? A South Vietnam National Assembly deputy, Ngo Cong Duc, made such a proposal recently and said that it was backed by the "silent majority" of the Vietnamese people who are "struggling for peace, independence, and national reconciliation."

Isn't such a proposal at least worth considering, Mr. President, if it might mean saving the lives of another several thousand G. I. 's between now and next summer?

Please, Mr. President, consider again if there is not a better way out of Vietnam than the course we appear to be locked into.

Must we allow the military dictators of South Vietnam to dictate our own national fate and the fate of our G. I. 's there as well as that of the war-weary South Vietnamese?

This appeal is sponsored by the undersigned organizations.

We will support the Administration in any genuine move toward a realistic peace settlement. But past experience has taught us that we must continue to work and speak out independently until peace is achieved.

To readers who agree with us--we urge you not to slacken in your own dedication to peace, but to continue to support peace organizations at a time when your support may prove more important than ever.

And please send whatever you can in the way of a contribution to help us carry on our work.   All proceeds will be divided equally among the sponsoring groups.

SANE
318 Massachusetts Avenue N.E.
Washington, D.C. 20002
Dr. EDWARD U. CONDON,
PROFESSOR SEYMOUR MELMAN, Co-Chairman

FUND FOR NEW PRIORITIES IN AMERICA
415 Lexington Avenue
New York, N.Y.   10017
WILLIAM MEYERS, President

LAWYERS COMMITTEE ON AMERICAN POLICY TOWARD
     VIETNAM
38 Park Row
New York, N.Y.   10038
WILLIAM STANDARD, Chairman

VIETNAM VETERANS AGAINST THE WAR
156 Fifth Avenue
New York, N.Y. 10010
AL HUBBARD, National Executive Secretary

THE FELLOWSHIP OF RECONCILIATION
Box 271, Nyack, N.Y.   10960
ALFRED HASSLER, Executive Secretary
ALLAN BRICK, Associate Executive

AMERICANS FOR PEACE
South Point Plaza
Lansing, Michigan   48910
ARNOLD SERWER, Chairman

To: SANFORD GOTTLIEB, Treasurer
        Joint Peace Ad Committee
        3308 South Cedar
        Lansing, Michigan 48910

I support your statement on Vietnam.

____ I am sending a copy of this flyer to my Congressman.

____ Enclosed is my contribution of $____ to help pay for
     the work of the sponsoring organizations.

____ Please send ____ hundred copies of this flyer, for
     which I am enclosing $10 per 100.

Name _____

Address _____

City _____ State _____ Zip_____

MAKE CHECKS PAYABLE TO "JOINT PEACE AD COMMIT-
TEE"

(Received from the Fellowship of Reconciliation, October 27,
1970.)

86. STAY IN THE STREETS...

See the Struggle Through to the Finish...

The Student Mobilization Committee is the national organization of high school and college students united in uncompromising struggle against the war in Vietnam.

Our goal is the immediate, total, unconditional withdrawal of all U.S. troops from Vietnam. Our strategy is to
mobilize millions of Americans in independent ACTION in the
streets for this end. This is our power.

The SMC is the nation's largest student antiwar group.
We've been in business since 1967 and have helped to build
antiwar actions ever since. We helped spearhead the Fall
Antiwar Offensive this year. And we'll be in business to-
morrow--until this war is over and every last GI is brought
home.

The SMC is part of the international movement of
young people who are fighting U.S. aggression in Vietnam.
We stand in solidarity with European students as they demand
an end to the NATO Treaty and with the Japanese students
working to halt renewal of the U.S.-Japan Security Treaty
and U.S. occupation of Okinawa.

The SMC is a democratic and non-exclusive organization. Our action program is made at twice-yearly national
antiwar conferences open to all antiwar activists.

Our program is clear and straightforward. Bring
ALL the GI's Home Now! Abolish the Draft! End Campus
Complicity with the Vietnam War! Self-Determination for
Vietnam and Black America! Free Speech for GI's and High
School Students! Free All Political Prisoners; No Political
Persecution!

WE DEMAND: WAR MACHINE OFF CAMPUS. As students
we are pledged to organizing on every high school and college campus to stop the use of educational institutions as

396

arms of the military machine.   U.S. students are against the
war and will not tolerate the complicity of their schools with
it.   We organize mass struggles against ROTC, military recruitment, warfare research, etc.

WE DEMAND: FREE SPEECH FOR GI'S.   SMC wholly supports and helps to expand the growing GI opposition to the
war.   We defend the constitutional rights of GI's as citizens
in uniform to speak out and demonstrate against the war.
Our twice-monthly publication, THE GI PRESS SERVICE, provides coverage of the GI antiwar movement on bases around
the country and overseas.

WE DEMAND: FREE SPEECH FOR HIGH SCHOOL STU-
DENTS.   This generation of high school students has been
the backbone of the student antiwar movement.   High School
SMCers work for an end to the repressive atmosphere in the
high schools and fight for the right to organize in school
against the war and exercise their freedom of speech, assembly, petition and organization.   FULL CITIZENSHIP FOR
HIGH SCHOOL STUDENTS!

WE DEMAND: FREE ALL POLITICAL PRISONERS; NO PO-
LITICAL PERSECUTION.   The antiwar struggle has taught
us that full rights to organize and act upon our political convictions must be protected at all times if we are to continue
to grow as a powerful movement.   We support this right for
all people and consider an attack on one as an attack on all,
rallying to the defense of all sections of the antiwar movement whose rights are trampled upon.

WE DEMAND: SELF-DETERMINATION FOR VIETNAM &
BLACK AMERICA.   We recognize the right of the Vietnamese
to determine their own future in their own way.   Only the
total removal of all U.S. interference from that country will
guarantee this elementary democratic right.   We see a direct link between the racist war in Vietnam and racism at
home and recognize this same democratic right for Black
America.

This fall's actions begin a new stage in the building of a
massive, militant movement that will end the war in Vietnam.
There is much to be done.   Join us to do the job.

Clip & mail to
    STUDENT MOBILIZATION COMMITTEE TO END THE
        WAR IN VIETNAM
    NAT'L OFFICE: 1029 Vermont Ave., NW No. 907,
    Washington, D.C. 20005
    phone (202) 737-0072

    N.Y. OFFICE: 857 Broadway, No. 307
    New York, N.Y. 10003
    phone (212) 675-8465

Name_____phone _____

Address_____City, State, Zip_____

School or Organization_____

____ I would like to be an SMC organizer at my school.

____ Please keep me informed of SMC conferences and ac-
     tivities.

____ I am not a student, but here is my contribution $____
     to help. Enclosed is $_____.

BRING ALL THE GI's HOME NOW!!!!!!

(Collected from the Student Mobilization Committee to End
the War in Vietnam, Berkeley, California, November 12,
1969.)

87. AN OPEN LETTER TO THE MOVEMENT:
    WHAT NEXT?

from the National SMC Staff

        There are all sorts of opportunities for expanding the
antiwar movement among high school and college students in
the next few weeks and months ahead. The success of the
April 5-6 demonstrations can only serve to inspire further actions this spring. This was just the beginning.

        If we are really activists determined to change things
and serious about our opposition to the war and complicity
with that war on the high school and college campuses, let's
act this spring! Following are suggestions for local actions
on high school rights to oppose the war, campus and high
school complicity with the war, Vietnam commencements, and
free speech for antiwar GIs.

High School Rights to Oppose the War

        Participation of high school students was phenomenal
in most of the seven areas on April 5-6. Much like the
movement developing within the military, it is now a new
movement that serves to inspire others to action.

        The Establishment and many high school administra-
tors try to create the image that high school and junior high
school students don't have political rights to oppose the war.
"They don't know better yet," some say. But who has a better right to oppose the war than those whose diploma this
spring means nothing but a ticket to Saigon University?

        High school students have the right to oppose the war
and to actively organize their opposition. High school students have the right to wear buttons and armbands in school;
pass out leaflets in and around the schools; use bulletin
boards to announce their activities; utilize school facilities
such as rooms and auditoriums for antiwar meetings; invite
antiwar speakers, such as antiwar GIs, to speak at school,

399

in classes and at graduation. We are projecting a campaign
to implement these rights and to back them up if the school
administration decides to try to take them away.

Major civil liberties organizations are willing to help
in this fight. Important high school rights cases involving
SMCers are now being fought in Chicago and Cleveland. The
Cleveland case, concerning a student who wore an April 5
button in his high school and was suspended, will almost certainly reach the Supreme Court. Important precedents like
the Tinker case have already been established.

Campus and High School Complicity with the War

When the Harvard U. students sat in against ROTC
among other issues, they revealed the administration's connections with the CIA and war policies of the U.S. government. The government has no right to use the educational
system as a tool and an arm of U.S. foreign policy in Vietnam or anywhere else. Digging deep enough will show that
the MSU scandal of 1964 is nothing but a mirror of how every
university in the country is used by the government--it may
be just a bit more subtle on the surface.

A few years ago large movements sprang up on the
college campuses opposing the universities turning over names
of graduating students to the draft boards. In many cases,
students were victorious in forcing a stop to this. The same
is done in the high schools. We can carry out the same
kind of campaign--and we can win victories. We want to see
many Harvards and many Stanfords this spring!

High School and College Graduations--Vietnam Commence-
ments

There is little doubt that something is going to happen
during both high school and college graduations. A nationally coordinated campaign will make a large impact far beyond
any scattered disturbances. There is no reason why the
graduation ceremonies shouldn't be run by the students themselves expressing their political convictions, not the administration's. Actions will vary from school to school depending
upon the strength of the movement. Some suggestions that
have already been raised are:

--Demand the right to run the graduation ceremony as an arena for expressing opposition to the effects of the war on your future and the future of American society.

--Petition for antiwar speakers at the ceremony, possibly an antiwar GI or a Vietnam veteran.

--Hold a counter-commencement involving underclassmen.

--Wear armbands and buttons. SMC may come out with a national armband and button.

--Find out who the valedictorian is--maybe he or she is against the war.

--Have draft counselors available for graduating seniors.

--Present petitions against the war at graduation.

--Organize parental support.

--Picket the commencement.

--Send a telegram of support to the Presidio 27 and the Ft. Jackson 8 and a telegram of protest to the Army.

--Unfurl antiwar banners at the ceremony.

--Tie in the black struggle for self-determination with the war, making that a significant part of counter-commencement actions.

--Find out who the special invited speakers are. Many local and national government figures will probably be speaking.

--Expose the complicity with the war on the campus from which antiwarriors are graduating.

Free Speech for GI's--Free the Ft. Jackson 8,
Free the Presidio 27!

         The fact that GIs are now openly expressing their anti-war sentiment has inspired the whole movement. The Establishment press hasn't gotten as excited over anything like this since the antiwar movement began in 1965. Neither has the brass. GIs have the constitutional right to oppose the

war as do high school students.   The brass attempts to create the image that GIs don't have political rights either.

At Ft. Jackson the military is threatening to court-
martial eight antiwar GIs for exercising their legal right to
protest the war.   The greater the support for the right of
GIs to oppose the war from the civilian movement, the easier
the victory in this important case.   If you are not yet an endorser of the GI Civil Liberties Defense Committee, please
fill out the endorser card below and send it in.   If you know
of a prominent individual who might endorse this case, help
out by asking him.   Funds are urgently needed. Make out
checks to the GI Civil Liberties Defense Committee.   Also
send in all clippings that appear in your local press about the
case.

Regional and Local SMC Meetings

We urge all SMCs and antiwar groups to hold regional or local meetings to discuss perspectives for the rest of
the school year.   If there is no SMC in your area, form one.
Contact the national SMC office and we'll get someone to help
you or send you more information.

That's about it for now.   The Spring Offensive is underway!

(Mimeographed leaflet collected from the Student Mobilization
Committee in Berkeley, California on April 22, 1969.)

88. SPRING OFFENSIVE BEGINS

Spring Action Reports

NEW YORK   APRIL 5

Over 100,000 people demonstrated including 200-300 active-duty GIs from 25 bases in the New York region. This was the largest demonstration against the war in New York since the April 27, 1968 mass march and rally. The demonstration was sponsored by the Fifth Avenue Vietnam Peace Parade Committee and endorsed by a large number of school, community and professional groups. By far the largest contingent was the high school students, while youth as a whole comprised about 80% of the demonstration.

SEATTLE   APRIL 5-6

About 300 people and 20 GIs attended the first day of Antiwar Basic Training Days on April 5-6. The demonstration was organized by the GI-Civilian Alliance for Peace. The Army placed Ft. Lewis on alert and gave GIs extra duty to keep them away from the activities. Speakers included Terrence Hallinan, defense lawyer for 14 of the Presidio 27; Aaron Dixon of the Seattle Black Panther Party; Sidney Mills, an Indian rights fighter; Stephanie Coontz, GI-CAP, among others.

ATLANTA   APRIL 6

Atlanta had its biggest antiwar demonstration ever on April 6 as 4,000 people from all over the south marched with over 50 active-duty GIs. The march was organized by the Southwide Mobilization Against the Vietnam War and for Self-Determination.

CHICAGO   APRIL 5

Over 30,000 people marched behind a 30-man contingent. Most of the demonstrators were young, with a large

403

segment being high school students. The demonstration was
sponsored by the Chicago Peace Council. This was the
largest demonstration against the Vietnam War ever held in
Chicago.

AUSTIN   APRIL 12

Austin's largest demonstration yet against the Vietnam
War took place with about 1,200 people demonstrating outside
the State Capitol. The march was sponsored by the Texas
Coalition Against the War. About 100 active-duty GIs from
Ft. Hood and Bergstrom Air Force Base joined the march.

A new GI antiwar newspaper called "GI Organizer" is
being published by GIs at Ft. Hood. Its first issue was devoted to organizing GI participation in the demonstration.

Speakers at the demonstration included Larry Caro-
line, SDS faculty advisor; Charles Cairns, faculty sponsor
for the University Committee to End the War in Vietnam; and
Pfc. Walter Kos of Ft. Hood. Several GIs spoke at the open
mike reserved for them

LOS ANGELES   APRIL 6

About 6,500 people demonstrated with about 50 GIs.
The demonstration was organized by the Los Angeles Peace
Action Council, GIs and Vietnam Veterans Against the War,
and the L.A. Student Mobilization Committee.   GIs have begun publishing an antiwar paper called "About Face" to organize antiwar sentiment within the military in this area.

SAN FRANCISCO   APRIL 6

Over 50,000 people marched to the Presidio gates led
by a contingent of 500 GIs. This demonstration had the twin
themes of "Bring the Troops Home Now!" and "Free the
Presidio 27!" This was the largest demonstration in San
Francisco since the April 15, 1967 march.

FREE THE FT. JACKSON 8 ACTIONS

Very soon the Army will decide if it will proceed in
the court martials of 8 Fort Jackson GIs whose only "crime"
is being against the Vietnam War and saying so. SMC urges
all local antiwar committees to plan meetings, rallies or
demonstrations for the defense of the Ft. Jackson 8. These

should take place on the opening day of the court martials.
SMC will notify groups of the exact date when it is announced and will send out up to date information on the case
then.   Groups planning actions should send in information of
plans to SMC.

CLEVELAND   MAY 21

The Cleveland Peace Action Council has called for a
mass march in Cleveland on May 21.   The march will assemble at the Lagoon in front of the Art Museum at noon
with the march going down Euclid Avenue for a rally downtown.

The theme of the march will be "Mourn those who
have died, bring the live ones home now!"   The march will
also feature two important defense cases going on now.   The
first is the Ft. Jackson 8 and the second is the defense of
Sid Peck.   Peck was attacked by police in Chicago during the
police riot during the Democratic Party national convention.
He was charged with assaulting a cop's club with his head.

NAG ANTIWAR ACTIONS

The National Action Group (NAG) sponsored demonstrations of "resistance and renewal" in 40 cities throughout the
country during the Passover-Easter weekend.   These actions
ranged from vigils to sit-ins at draft boards.   The actions
were carried out on the local level by chapters of the American Friends Service Committee, Womens International
League for Peace and Freedom, and the Resistance, among
others.

NAG does not have full-time staff or office at present
but was only an ad hoc group for the April actions.   It is
considering calling further actions.

(Mimeographed leaflet collected at Stanford University, Palo
Alto, Calif., June 17, 1969.   All events referred to occurred in 1969.)

89. THE CASE OF GIs UNITED
     AGAINST THE WAR IN VIETNAM

FT. JACKSON, S. C.

On the evening of March 20, 1969, at Fort Jackson,
South Carolina, a group of over 100 enlisted men gathered
together after dinner to discuss the war in Vietnam. The
meeting was called by members of GIs United Against the
War in Vietnam, a group of antiwar GIs who have been actively arguing against the war at Ft. Jackson. GIs United is
predominantly black and Puerto Rican in composition, but it
includes many white soldiers as well.

The March 20 meeting was one of a series of meetings held by GIs United, dating back to February, 1969.
These meetings have been held with the knowledge, and
therefore implicit approval, of the Army officials at Fort
Jackson. Officers were present at the March 20 meeting,
and, aside from criticizing the dress and haircuts of the anti-
war GIs, they did not interfere with the meeting.

But the following day Army officials arrested four of
the members of GIs United, and charged them with breach of
the peace, disrespect to an officer, disobeying an order,
holding an illegal demonstration, and breaking restriction.
Later, five additional GIs were placed under barracks arrest.
All of the charges refer to the evening of March 20. The
Army now claims that the peaceful meeting was in reality a
"demonstration" (which would make it a violation of Army
regulations), and that the soldiers refused to disperse after
they were ordered to do so. No orders to disperse were
given at any time during the meeting. Moreover, there was
no "breach of the peace" because the meeting was perfectly
orderly, and broke up of its own accord after about an hour.

A Political Frame-Up

Why is the Army trying so hard to imprison these
antiwar GIs? The answer lies in the fact that GIs United

has been vigorously fighting for the constitutional rights of
GIs as citizens to discuss the war in Vietnam.   As a result,
much national publicity has been focussed on Ft. Jackson.
The Army, in its own clumsy, authoritarian manner, has responded to this situation by trying to railroad these GIs into
the stockade.

GIs United began last February to circulate a petition
addressed to Gen. James Hollingsworth, the Commanding General at Fort Jackson, asking him to make facilities available
for an open meeting on the base at which the GIs could "hold
a peaceful, legal meeting open to any enlisted man or officer at Fort Jackson.   We desire only to exercise the rights
guaranteed to us as citizens and soldiers by the First Amendment to the U.S. Constitution."   Several hundred signatures
were obtained on this petition.   But when the GIs tried to
present it, Army officials refused to accept it because, said
the official spokesman, it represented "collective bargain-
ing."

In response to this blatant denial of their rights, ten
members of GIs United, through their attorneys Leonard Bou-
din of New York, David Rein of Washington, Howard Moore
of Atlanta, and Thomas Broadwater of Columbia, S.C., filed
suit in the U.S. District Court for the District of South Carolina.   The suit asks for a declaratory judgment by the court
that the plaintiffs and all other GIs at Fort Jackson have the
right to hold meetings on or off post to discuss matters of
concern to them, including the war in Vietnam, and that they
have the right to circulate petitions for redress of grievances.
The suit further asks for a court order directing the Commanding General to grant facilities for a meeting at which
GIs could discuss public issues.   It also requests the court
to enjoin the Army from harassing and attempting to intimidate the GIs who are trying to exercise their First Amendment rights.   This suit, if victorious, will have Army-wide
effect.

Of the ten plaintiffs who instituted the suit, five are
among those facing court martial; one other was given a punitive transfer to Fort Bragg; and one is being threatened with
a less than honorable discharge.

In short, the Army is responding to the fight by GIs
for their constitutional rights with a crude frame-up in an attempt to silence all antiwar or civil libertarian voices of dissent within its ranks.   That is why the GIs are now facing
court martials.

The McCarthyite procedures which the Army is following were made even clearer when it was disclosed that one
of the GIs originally arrested was, in fact, operating "in the
interest of the command." In other words, as a spy and
agent-provocateur within the ranks of GIs United. The fact
that this agent, who went by the name of John Hoffman, was
present at meetings where defense strategy was discussed by
the GIs with their attorneys, severely compromises the
Army's case. Charges against this man were, of course,
dropped. The "Fort Jackson Nine" became the "Fort Jackson Eight."

A Question of Fundamental Rights

The basic issues involved in the case of the Fort
Jackson GIs are simple, but they are fundamental questions
of civil liberties that affect all Americans.

Both the lawsuit against the Army and the frame-up
directed against the men deal directly with the same issues:
are soldiers, who are citizens in uniform, protected by the
U.S. Constitution, and in particular the First Amendment to
the Constitution? Do GIs have the same right to discuss and
take positions on the war in Vietnam and other issues of public concern as do citizens fortunate enough not to have been
drafted?

Can the Army really expect that, with the entire country divided about the correctness of America's policy in Vietnam, with millions of Americans demonstrating against the
war, with Senators and Congressmen daily expressing opinions pro and con, the very men who are asked to fight that
war will not have an opinion on the question? And don't they
have the right to express that opinion even though they are
members of the armed forces?

Writing in the April 20, 1969, issue of The New York
Times, Ben A. Franklin clearly exposes the Army's frame-
up attempt: "A classic case approaches a climax this week
at Fort Jackson, S.C. By harassing, restricting and arresting on dubious charges, the leaders of an interracial militant
enlisted group there called GIs United Against the War in Vietnam, Fort Jackson's brass has produced a cause celebre
out of all proportion to the known facts. It has also brought
about two court actions, directed by capable and contentious
civilian legal counsel, which may give a merely fractious
episode lasting effect.

"The Fort Jackson lawsuits, if they are upheld, will give the courts a clear opening to declare that American enlisted men do, indeed, have the same right to oppose by all lawful, orderly means the course chosen by their Government and military leaders...."

The Fort Jackson GIs need all the help they can get, from all those who believe that soldiers, as citizens, have the same rights as civilians to discuss the war in Vietnam.

Support for the GIs, both in their lawsuit against the Army and in their court martials, is being handled by the GI Civil Liberties Defense Committee. The GI CLDC was established in the fall of 1968 to help defend GIs whose constitutional rights are infringed upon by the Armed Forces. The GI CLDC has organized the support for the Fort Jackson case from the beginning. It has obtained the legal counsel mentioned above for the suit against the Army; and the same team of lawyers has agreed to handle the defense of the GIs who have been framed up. In addition to arranging legal counsel, the GI CLDC has undertaken an aggressive and successful campaign to get the word out about the situation at Fort Jackson. As a result of its efforts, national attention has been directed to the constitutional fight of GIs United at Fort Jackson.

The GI Civil Liberties Defense Committee urges all Americans to come to the support of these GIs in their fight for their civil liberties.

What You Can Do

. Send a donation to the GI Civil Liberties Defense Committee to help cover the extremely high expenses involved in this case. Send to: GI CLDC, Box 355, Old Chelsea Station, New York, N.Y. 10011.

. Send letters of protest to Gen. James Hollingsworth, Commanding General, Fort Jackson, S.C., and to Stanley Resor, Secretary of the Army, Washington, D.C. Copies of all messages should be sent to the GI CLDC. Urge prominent people in your area to send similar messages. Get messages of support from lawyers, professors, trade unionists, black and Puerto Rican leaders, etc.

. Become a sponsor of the GI CLDC, and urge others to do so also. (Use coupon on this brochure.)

. Organize meetings and conduct demonstrations in support
of the Ft. Jackson GIs. Speakers on the case can be obtained by writing to the GI CLDC.

. Express support to the GIs at Fort Jackson directly. Mail
can be sent to the GIs in care of the GI CLDC office in New
York, and it will be forwarded.

STATEMENT OF AIMS OF THE GI
CIVIL LIBERTIES DEFENSE COMMITTEE

The purpose of the GI Civil Liberties Defense Committee is to defend the rights of American citizens in uniform to
freedom of speech, freedom of the press, freedom of assembly and associations, and the right to petition the government for a redress of grievances. It supports the right of
GIs to use these and all other constitutionally guaranteed liberties to express their opinions on public affairs and political issues, including the war in Vietnam.

It extends this support by obtaining legal counsel for
GIs whose rights are violated and by publicizing their cases.

Toward this end it raises funds and solicits the endorsement and support of all those who uphold the constitutional rights of American servicemen.

------------------ Clip and Send to----------------------

GI Civil Liberties Defense Committee
Box 355, Old Chelsea Station
New York, N.Y.   10011

____   I support the constitutional rights of American GIs.
       Please add my name as a sponsor of the GI Civil Lib-
       erties Defense Committee. I understand that sponsor-
       ship does not necessarily denote agreement with the po-
       litical views of any of the defendants.

____   Please send me _____ copies of this brochure at
       $2/100.

____   Enclosed is $____ to help cover expenses of the GI
       CLDC.

Literature of the Resistance   411

Name_____

Address _____

City _____State_____Zip_____

Telephone _____

(Received from the GI Civil Liberties Defense Committee on
May 1, 1969.)

90. TO THE NATIONAL LIBERATION FRONT
OF SOUTH VIETNAM

August 29, 1970

(Huey P. Newton)

In the spirit of international revolutionary solidarity
the Black Panther Party hereby offers to the National Liberation Front and Provisional Revolutionary Government of South
Vietnam an undetermined number of troops to assist you in
your fight against American imperialism. It is appropriate
for the Black Panther Party to take this action at this time in
recognition of the fact that your struggle is also our struggle,
for we recognize that our common enemy is the American imperialist who is the leader of international bourgeois domination. There is not one fascist or reactionary government in
the world today that could stand without the support of United
States imperialism. Therefore our problem is international,
and we offer these troops in recognition of the necessity for
international alliances to deal with this problem.

Such alliances will advance the struggle toward the final act of dealing with American imperialism. The Black
Panther Party views the United States as the "city" of the
world while we view the nations of Africa, Asia and Latin
America as the "countryside" of the world. The developing
countries are like the Sierra Maestra in Cuba and the United
States is like Havana. We note that in Cuba the people's
army set up bases in the Sierra Maestra and choked off Havana because it was dependent upon the raw materials of the
countryside. After they won all the battles in this countryside the last and final act was for the people to march upon
Havana.

The Black Panther Party believes that the revolutionary process will operate in a similar fashion on an international level. A small ruling circle of seventy-six major companies controls the American economy. This elite not only
exploits and oppresses Black people within the United States;
they are exploiting and oppressing everyone in the world

412

because of the overdeveloped nature of capitalism. Having
expanded industry within the United States until it can grow
no more, and depleting the raw materials of this nation, they
have run amuck abroad in their attempts to extend their economic domination. To end this oppression we must liberate
the developing nations--the countryside of the world--and then
our final act will be the strike against the "city." As one
nation is liberated elsewhere it gives us a better chance to be
free here.

The Black Panther Party recognizes that we have certain national problems confined to the continental United States,
but we are also aware that while our oppressor has domestic
problems these do not stop him from oppressing people all
over the world. Therefore we will keep fighting and resisting
within the "city" so as to cause as much turmoil as possible
and aid our brothers by dividing the troops of the ruling
circle.

The Black Panther Party offers these troops because
we are the vanguard party of revolutionary internationalists
who give up all claim to nationalism. We take this position
because the United States has acted in a very chauvinistic
manner and lost its claim to nationalism. The United States
is an empire which has raped the world to build its wealth
here. Therefore the United States is not a nation. It is a
government of international capitalists and inasmuch as they
have exploited the world to accumulate wealth this country be-
longs to the world. The Black Panther Party contends that
the United States lost its right to claim nationhood when it
used its nationalism as a chauvinistic base to become an empire.

On the other hand, the developing countries have every
right to claim nationhood, because they have not exploited anyone. The nationalism of which they speak is simply their
rightful claim to autonomy, self-determination and a liberated
base from which to fight the international bourgeoisie.

The Black Panther Party supports the claim to nationhood of the developing countries and we embrace their struggle
from our position as revolutionary internationalists. We cannot be nationalists when our country is not a nation but an empire. We contend that it is time to open the gates of this
country and share the technological knowledge and wealth with
the peoples of the world.

History has bestowed upon the Black Panther Party the obligation to take these steps and thereby advance Marxism-Leninism to an even higher level along the path to a socialist state, and then a non-state. This obligation springs both from the dialectical forces in operation at this time and our history as an oppressed Black colony. The fact that our ancestors were kidnapped and forced to come to the United States has destroyed our feeling of nationhood. Because our long cultural heritage was broken we have come to rely less on our history for guidance, and seek our guidance from the future. Everything we do is based upon functionalism and pragmatism, and because we look to the future for salvation we are in a position to become the most progressive and dynamic people on the earth, constantly in motion and progressing, rather than becoming stagnated by the bonds of the past.

Taking these things under consideration, it is no accident that the vanguard party--without chauvinism or a sense of nationhood--should be the Black Panther Party. Our struggle for liberation is based upon justice and equality for all men. Thus we are interested in the people of any territory where the crack of the oppressor's whip may be heard. We have the historical obligation to take the concept of internationalism to its final conclusion--the destruction of statehood itself. This will lead us into the era where the withering away of the state will occur and men will extend their hand in friendship throughout the world.

This is the world view of the Black Panther Party and in the spirit of revolutionary internationalism, solidarity and friendship we offer these troops to the National Liberation Front and Provisional Revolutionary Government of South Vietnam, and to the people of the world.

(Collected from the Third World Liberation Front, University of California at Berkeley, October 2, 1970. Mimeo.)

91. LETTER FROM NGUYEN THI DINH

October 31, 1970

To: Mr. Huey P. Newton
Minister of Defense
Black Panther Party

Dear Comrade:

We are deeply moved by your letter informing us that the Black Panther Party is intending to send to the National Liberation Front and the Provisional Revolutionary Government of the Republic of South Vietnam an undetermined number of troops, assisting us in our struggle against the U.S. imperialist aggressors.

This news was communicated to all the cadres and fighters of the PLAF in South Vietnam; and all of us are delighted to get more comrades-in-arms, so brave as you, on the very soil of the United States.

On behalf of the cadres and fighters of the SVN PLAF I would welcome your noble deed and convey to you our sincere thanks for your warm support to our struggle against U.S. aggression for national salvation. We consider it as a great contribution from your side, an important event of the peace and democratic movement in the United States giving us active support, a friendly gesture voicing your determination to fight side-by-side with the South Vietnamese people for the victory of the common cause of revolution.

In the spirit of international solidarity, you have put forward your responsibility towards history, towards the necessity of uniting actions, sharing joys and sorrows, participating in the struggle against U.S. imperialism.

You have highly appreciated the close relation between our both uncompromising struggles against U.S. imperialism, our common enemy. It is well known that the U.S. government is the most warlike, not only oppresses and exploits the

American people, especially the Black and the coloured ones, but also oppresses and exploits various peoples the world over by all means, irrespective of morality and justice. They have the hunger of dollars and profits which they deprived by the most barbarous ways, including genocide, as they have acted for years in South Vietnam.

In the past years, your just struggle in the U.S. has stimulated us to strengthen unity, and rush forward toward bigger successes.

The U.S. imperialists, although driven by the South Vietnamese and Indochinese people in a defeated position, still have not given up their evil design, still seek to gain the military victories and to negotiate on the position of strength. On the SVN battle-fields, they are actively realizing their policy of "Vietnamization" of the war with a view to maintaining the neocolonialism in South Vietnam and prolonging the partition of our country.

The very nature of the policy of "Vietnamization" is prolonging indefinitely the aggressive war at a degree ever so cruel and barbarous. While Nixon puts forward his "initiative for peace," in SVN the aggressive war got harder and harder; after the "urgent pacification" came the "Eagle campaign"; after that, by the "special pacification" in the countrysides and the "for the people" campaign in the towns, Nixon and the Thieu Ky Khiem clique have perpetrated innumerable barbarous crimes towards the people of all strata in SVN.

The 5-point proposal of Mr. Nixon, put forth on October 7th exposes more clearly his stubborn, perfidious and deceitful nature to U.S. and world opinion. It is clear that Nixon is unwilling to accept a peaceful settlement on the Vietnam problem, but tries to stick to South Vietnam as a neo-colony and U.S. military base, as well as to legalize the U.S. aggression in Indochina as a whole.

The U.S. government must seriously respond to the September 17th statement of the RSVN PRG, for it is the just basis, the reasonable and logical solution of the SVN problem. These are also the urgent aspirations of the whole Vietnamese people, of the progressive Americans and of those the world over who cherish peace, freedom and justice.

Dear Comrades, our struggle yet faces a lot of hardships, but we are determined to overcome all difficulties,

unite with all progressive forces, to heighten our revolutionary vigilance, to persist in our struggle, resolutely to fight
and win. We are sure to win complete victory.

So are our thinkings: At present, the struggles, right
in the United States or on the SVN battle-fields, are both
making positive contributions for national liberation and safe-
guarding the world peace. Therefore, your persistent and
ever-developing struggle is the most active support to our resistance against U.S. aggression for national salvation.

With profound gratitude, we take notice of your enthusiastic proposal; when necessary, we shall call for your volunteers to assist us.

We are firmly confident that your just cause will enjoy sympathy, warm and strong support of the people at home
and abroad, and will win complete victory; and our ever closer coordinated struggle will surely stop the bloody hands of
the U.S. imperialists and surely contribute to winning independence, freedom, democracy and genuine peace.

Best greetings for "unity, militancy, and victory" from
the SVN people's liberation fighters.

NGUYEN THI DINH,
Deputy Commander
Of the SVN People's
Liberation Armed Forces.
Republic of South Vietnam

(Collected from Black Panther Party Hdqtrs., Oakland, November 15, 1970.)

92. TO MY BLACK BROTHERS IN VIET NAM

(Eldridge Cleaver)

I'm writing this on January 4, 1970. We are starting out a new year. On August 31, I'll be 35 years old. I'm married, and I have one child with another one on the way. I am in love with my wife and I would like to enjoy a happy life raising a family. But I am not free to live the type of life that I would like. Pigs--the racist fascist rulers of the United States--won't let me.

And I would like to ask you Brothers: are you living the life that you want to live? Are these same pigs cramping your style? I don't believe that you actually prefer to be way over there, fighting against our Vietnamese Brothers and Sisters who are fighting for their freedom. Because your own people, whom you left behind in Babylon, are also fighting for their freedom against the very same pigs who have you over there doing their dirty work for them. And your people need you--and your military skills--to help us take our freedom and stop these racist pigs from committing genocide upon us, as they have been doing for the past 400 years.

I am the Minister of Information of the Black Panther Party, and I am speaking to you now for the Party, but I want to put a personal note into this because I know that you niggers have your minds all messed up about Black organizations, or you wouldn't be the flunkies for the White organization--the U.S.A.--for whom you have picked up the gun. The Black Panther Party has picked up the gun too, but not to fight against the heroic Vietnamese people, but rather to wage a war of liberation against the very same pigs whom you are helping to run their vicious game on the entire world, including upon your own people. Dig it. I wonder, can you dig it? Can you dig niggers, brothers and sisters off the block, who have said later for the pigs and have picked up guns in Babylon, to bring to fulfillment the dreams of freedom that have kept our people alive for 400 years, under the racist yoke of the White man. From the sad days of slavery in the cotton

418

fields of the South, to the present bleeding years of the Dem-
ocrats, Republicans, Uncle Toms, Lyndon B. Johnson, and
now, the foulist racist pig ever to become president of the
United States, Richard Meally Moth Mouth Nixon--your Commander in Chief and the Number One Enemy of our people.

The struggle of our people for freedom has pro-
gressed to the form where all of us must take a stand either
for or against the freedom of our people.   You are either
with your people or against them.   You are either part of the
solution or part of the problem.   We either help our people
or, by refusing to help them, make it easier for the enemy
to destroy us.   There are no two ways about it.

While you are over there in Vietnam, the pigs are
murdering our people, oppressing them, and the jails and
prisons of America are filling up with political prisoners.
These political prisoners are your own Black Brothers and
Sisters.   We have a desperate, life and death struggle on our
hands, and if we as a people are going to survive, then we must
save ourselves.   We need your help, desperately, before it
is too late.

This is the moment in history that our people have
been working, praying, fighting, and dying for.   Now, while
the whole world is rising up with arms against our oppressors, we must make a decisive move for our freedom.   If
we miss this chance, this golden opportunity, who knows when
we will get another chance?   We cannot afford to gamble with
this chance by putting things off.   Now is the moment for decision.   This very moment, right where you are.   You do
not have to wait until later, until after you are back home
and out of the army.   You can make your move now, while
you are still inside the army, because the army is one of the
key weapons which the pigs have up their sleeves to use
against us when the time comes.   And make no mistake about
it, that time is coming and it is almost here.

The pigs are using G.I.'s from Vietnam on the police
forces and National Guard units inside Babylon.   Many of our
Black Brothers go to Vietnam and learn how to kill human
beings, then when they are released from the army they return home and end up on the police force.   On the police
forces, they carry out the same dirty work against us, in the
name of "Law and Order" that they carried out against the
Vietnamese people.

In 1968-69, the pigs murdered 28 members of the
Black Panther Party and nobody even knows how many other
of our Black Brothers and Sisters were shot down by the
pigs.   But it is a long list.   Scores of our Party members
are being held as political prisoners because they took a
stand for the freedom and liberation of our people.   Huey P.
Newton, Minister of Defense of the Black Panther Party, our
leader, is in prison in California.   Our Chairman, Bobby
Seale, is in jail and the pigs are trying to put him in the
electric chair, in Connecticut, on trumped up charges.   Pigs
in Chicago murdered Fred Hampton while he was asleep in
his bed.   Shot him in his head with a shotgun, with 00 Buck-
shot.   The pigs have been making mass arrests of our Party
members, with 21 arrested in New York, 14 in New Haven,
18 in Los Angeles, and 16 in Chicago.

We appeal to you Brothers to come to the aid of your
people.   Either quit the army, now, or start destroying it
from the inside.   Anything else is a compromise and a form
of treason against your own people.   Stop killing the Vietnamese people.   You need to start killing the racist pigs who
are over there with you giving you orders.   Kill General Abrams and his staff, all his officers.   Sabotage supplies and
equipment, or turn them over to the Vietnamese people.
Talk to the other Brothers and wake them up.   You should
start now weeding out the traitors against you.   It is better
to do it now than to allow them to return home to help the
pigs wipe us out.   Especially the Uncle Tom officers should
be dealt with now, because the pigs will use them as effective tools against our people.   When you can no longer take
care of business inside the army, then turn yourself over to
the Vietnamese people and tell them you want to join the
Black Panther Party to fight for the freedom and liberation
of your own people.   If you do cross over, you don't have to
worry about the Vietnamese people abusing you.   They will be
glad to see you drop out of the army because what they want
most in life is to stop the fighting in their land.   You have
a duty to humanity as well as to your own people not to be
used as murderous tools by racist pigs to oppress the people.

Think about it, Brother, and act on it, because you
don't have much time.   Organize all the Brothers around you
and move.   Force the pigs to understand that you will no
longer be their slave and hired killer.   Let the pigs know
that, instead, you want the persecution of your Black Brothers
and sisters to stop and that you intend to help stop it.   Demand that Huey P. Newton and Bobby Seale be set free.

Especially, help us force the pigs not to murder Bobby Seale in the electric chair.

We have dedicated our lives, our blood, to the freedom and liberation of our people, and nothing, no force, can stop us from achieving our goal. If it is necessary to destroy the United States of America, then let us destroy it with a smile on our faces. A smile for the freedom and liberation of our people. The Black Panther Party calls for freedom and liberation in our life time, because we want to leave behind us a decent world for our children to grow up in. Let's turn 1970 into a year in which people make a heroic drive for freedom and liberation.

ALL POWER TO THE PEOPLE!

SEIZE THE TIME!

> Eldridge Cleaver
> Minister of Information
> BLACK PANTHER PARTY

(Mimeographed statement collected from the Black Panther Party Headquarters, Oakland, California, on March 11, 1970.)

93. MUTINY DOES NOT HAPPEN LIGHTLY

by Marjorie Heins

It is strange that there is
(a) lack of books on mutinies
of the past.
They have had no small effect
on events, shaking empires
and social systems,
ending wars and leading
to considerable reforms.
It seems probable that one
reason for history's reticence
is the difficulty in passing
judgment on those who took part
in these events.
Mutinies--revolts by men
under discipline of life and death--
do not happen lightly,
and in most cases
when the reasons for the mutiny
are sought,
they appear clearly to be...
conditions of life that few of us
could find tolerable.
The puzzle becomes
not why did the mutiny occur,
but why did men,
for years or generations,
endure the torments
against which, in the end,
they revolted?

-- "Mutiny," by T. H. Wintringham

San Francisco's Presidio stockade was jammed to emergency density for weeks before the October 14 sit-in the Army has called mutiny. Unstable prisoners were driven to the edge of madness; and suicide gestures were so frequent

that they ceased to be an event. Cockroaches floated in the
orange juice; excrement floated on the floor.

Stockade prisoners have documented the gruesome details. A soldier sits dumbly on his bunk, wiping imaginary
cobwebs from his face. Another feels something warm and
sticky on his neck: it is the blood from a friend's vein,
spurting thirty feet in the air. Another jumps on a mess
hall table and kicks a fellow prisoner in the jaw. Still another, who enlisted as an alternative to being committed to
Modesto State Hospital, is so shaky that "if you come up behind him and talk in a normal voice, he will jump through
the ceiling" (Guard Roger Broomfield).

For a while after the sit-in, defendant Steve Rowland
kept a chronology of the madness:

> 5 Dec. Hoflin hit Woodring today, which was a
> climax to growing tensions ... in box.
>
> 9 Dec. Hoflin--in box--apologized to Woodring--
> has asked to see the shrink but they won't let him.
> Today severely cut both wrists and stabbed inner
> thighs with a pencil.
>
> 9 Dec. Heaston (in box) cut neck again--about
> thirty stitches.
>
> 10 Dec. Harrington is in box blowing it--hiding
> under bunk, banging head a full run against door
> and yelling things like "Mother, I didn't do it."
>
> 15 Dec. A guy [Hayden] in cell 2 stuck an inked
> safety pin in right eye just now. He's married
> with four daughters and here on AWOL. He told
> the sarge this afternoon he was going to do it.
> Taken to LGH [Letterman General Hospital] and re-
> turned to box.

Captain Robert Lamont, the slight, high-strung stockade commander, and his brutal sidekick Sergeant Thomas
Woodring are two remarkable characters. Woodring is an
archetypal sadist:

> Then he [Woodring] grabbed my wrist with one hand
> and while with the other he took hold of my fingers.
> Then slowly and methodically he twisted my fingers

until one of them was broken. He twisted for at
least a full minute while raving at me. In the
meantime I was crying and screaming for help and
asking him to stop.--(defendant Roy Pulley)

Then, there was the death of Richard Bunch. A thin
young kid, veteran of many bad drug trips, Bunch was obviously one of the sickest prisoners in the stockade. He told
his mother he was a warlock; he believed he could walk
through walls, and sometimes tried. "He would wake up
screaming, and he'd ask questions of himself and answer them
like he was another person" (Pulley).

When Bunch asked his shotgun guard if he would fire
in the event of an escape attempt, the guard told him he'd
have to try it and see. Now, it is a moot point whether
Bunch's death was suicide or murder. One thing it wasn't
was justifiable homicide, as the Army claimed. The prisoners were outraged at the death. They found Bunch's suicide
notes and "carried them around as if they were sacred"
(Steve Rowland).

Bunch died on Friday, October 11. During the weekend, the already neurotic atmosphere in the stockade grew
more tense. Outside, the prisoners knew, a GI march for
peace was going on. Inside, the chaplain held a memorial
service for Bunch while "the officers were sitting around
laughing" (defendant Buddy Shaw).

The mutiny of October 14 has become a near-legend.
The prisoners wanted their grievances heard by the public,
and by Provost Marshal Ford, who would hopefully be more
responsive than Lamont. At first, a majority of the prisoners planned to participate. By Monday, most thought better
of it, including the blacks, who reasoned they'd be punished
more harshly than the whites.

But twenty-seven followed through. They left their
7:30 formation, sat down on the stockade lawn, sang freedom
songs, flashed the V, read their grievances, and later were
quietly carried back inside. When the trials finally ended,
twenty-two of the twenty-seven were convicted of mutiny.
Two of Attorney Terence Hallinan's clients were convicted on
lesser charges; and three of the prisoners escaped.

Certainly, there was ample reason for the demonstration, whether you think the twenty-seven rationally planned an

act that would bring attention to their miserable condition;
or whether you take Hallinan's line of defense, that the men
acted out of irresistible impulse, were temporarily insane
by legal standards.

But military prisons have existed for a long time.
They have never been known for their ideal sanitary conditions or the sweet dispositions of their guards.   Other
forces were at play in the Presidio mutiny.   To find out
what these forces were, we have to ask: who are the Presidio 27?   And what was the nature of their act?

"Are you old enough to remember Ferdinand the Bull?"

Ricky Lee Dodd was noted for his numerous suicide
attempts: slashing his wrists, then trying to hang himself
with the bandages; drinking lye.   Once, Ricky was pronounced
Dead on Arrival at Letterman General Hospital.   But he re-
vived, so they sent him back to the stockade, where he was
put in the box.

Ricky Dodd is the oldest child and only son of a lower
middle class family in Hayward, California, a dreary Oakland suburb.   Tim Harris, Ricky's best friend for many
years, remembers Mrs. Dodd as a religious fanatic, who
covers her walls with the kind of Jesus pictures that seem to
move when you walk.   "She makes much of telling you that
Ricky was raised in a Christian home," says Howard Dinike,
Dodd's attorney.   Mrs. Dodd made an appearance during
Ricky's trial: she was conspicuous at that time for her outspoken opinion that the Army should keep Ricky in order to
straighten him out.

Mr. Dodd, now separated from his wife, is a baker
by trade--"a regular guy," says Dinike, "a fairly strong individual."   Tim Harris says that Ricky and his father were
always fighting.   Soon after high school, Ricky left home,
or was kicked out--probably mutual agreement--and came to
live with Tim's family.   Tim's stepfather, Ernest Bicknell,
always had room for several boys to live.

Bicknell's big farmhouse stands anomalously behind
rows of motel-like cardboard dwellings in residential Hayward.   He showed me where Ricky slept: a large closet
with a slanting ceiling and just enough room for a cot.
"Ricky always came back here on his AWOL's," Bicknell said.

Ricky blossomed into a flower child. He was gentle and peaceable, willing to help around the house or garden, but just not willing to be told what to do. He wore his blond hair shoulder-length and began to turn on with the dedication of a young man who has found his first true calling. Tim and Ricky did some hitchhiking up and down the coast, living briefly in communes. Ricky still saw his parents: on one occasion, Tim relates, Mrs. Dodd burned Ricky's hippie clothes while he was home taking a shower; and on another, Ricky returned to Bicknell's with blood on his T shirt, explaining he's had a fight with his father. Mr. Dodd would come to the farmhouse looking for his son, but Mrs. Bicknell would chase him away.

"When I met him," Tim said, "he didn't have any political ideas." There were frequent discussions of conscientious objection in Bicknell's household, but Ricky resisted forming any plans. He preferred living from day to day: as Tim said, "He just wanted to be left alone ... get loaded, party ... go traveling, meeting people." Or, as Bicknell put it, "Are you old enough to remember Ferdinand the Bull? He was trained to be a killer, but he just wanted to sit under a tree and smell flowers."

Bicknell assumed Ricky would resist induction. He was shocked when one day Dodd set out for the Induction Center and didn't return. Ricky had indeed wanted to refuse, and Tim was supposed to meet him at the center that morning, for moral support. The night before, Ricky went home. "His parents really pounded him out," Tim said. "He was weak." When Tim arrived at the Induction Center, Ricky was already gone.

From Fort Bliss, Texas, Ricky wrote to Tim and his girlfriend:

> I am an American fighting man. I serve in the "farces" which guard my country and our way of life. I am prepared to give my life in their defense. I will trust in my God and in the USA. What can I say except bullshit to what they feed us all day and part of the night?
>
> ... Did you go to the Dylan concert?...
>
> (Very serious) I have thought it over and made a decision. War may go on but it will go on without

me. No farmer will see his fields ploughed by my
bullets, no child will be burned by bombs I release,
and no man will die at my hands.

... P.S. Do your own thing wherever you have to
do it and whenever you want. Turn on every
straight person you can reach, if not to drugs, then
to beauty, love, honesty, fun.

A few years of hippiedom had not prepared Ricky for
Army life. It took about eight men to hold him while a dry
shave GI haircut was administered. During bayonet practice,
he would yell LOVE LOVE LOVE instead of KILL KILL
KILL, an antic which did not endear him to the noncoms.
Many stockades and AWOLs later, Ricky retained his cheer-
ful defiance. "Upon arrival at the Presidio stockade from
the comparative utopia of the Fort Lewis stockade, Ricky
found himself back in the box because he said okedoke to an
officer instead of yes sir" (Phil Farnum, a clergyman and
frequent stockade visitor).

Phil Farnum knew Dodd as a bright, straightforward
kid with ambitions to go to college and study anthropology.
Bicknell found Ricky articulate but unmotivated. Tim Harris,
who knew him best, said he was loving and happy-go-lucky.
His parents, who knew him worst, thought he was a weak-
kneed, lazy kid. Captain Lamont considered Ricky a mutiny
leader, and one of the worst of the prisoners. Ricky himself, when asked at his trial if he had won any honors in
school, said, "Well, I was elected class clown."

"He thought that's what his Dad wanted."

Buddy Shaw, like Ricky Dodd, is from Hayward. As
a child, he was sickly and nervous, had asthma, nephritis,
dropsy, ulcers, and finally had to leave school. He studied
at home for a while, then got a job at Highland Hospital,
where he talked vaguely of becoming a doctor. But he soon
got bored and discouraged. At the age of seventeen, Buddy
got a doctor's release for the ulcers, didn't tell the Army
about the other ailments, and enlisted. "He was so proud
of that uniform," says his mother, adding that Buddy was
searching desperately for something to do. Why did he enlist? "He thought that's what his dad wanted." Mr. Shaw
has emphysema, fibrosis of the lungs, and a heart condition.
The constant care he requires makes him feel guilty and
burdensome.

Mrs. Shaw is a thin handsome woman with lines of work and worry in her face. From six in the morning often till ten at night, she runs the Green Shutter Coffee Shop in downtown Hayward. Her older son Bob, who just finished a two and a half year stay in Vacaville Prison, helps her. Bob is a big muscular guy with tattoos (including "Born to Raise Hell") all over his mammoth biceps. He is the physical opposite of brother Buddy, who is small and thin and blinks compulsively.

Buddy has a proud history of AWOLs; and was in the Presidio stockade on and off since February, 1968. Mrs. Shaw, describing him as slightly spoiled, thinks stricter discipline in the Army would have kept him in line. The Army is training boys, just as parents do, she reasons. If they're not strict, the boys will never learn.

Bob Shaw, the handsome, meaty ex-con, has another point of view. "These twenty-seven are probably twenty-seven of the most courageous soldiers there ever have been in the service," he says. Men in prison, whether civilian or military, have "rebelled against authority." This rebellion is an all-important act. But he "finally found something in life he could go along with ... this may be the only thing he accomplishes in life, but some people don't even do that."

*   *   *

Keith Mather is one of the three who escaped. Weighing grim solidarity against uneasy freedom, Keith chose freedom. Said Mrs. Mather, "He couldn't stand the harassment, the ridicule ... the pressures got so great."

Keith's mother says she always "taught him to be against wars." But his father "had that old traditional feeling." There followed verbal battles, but in the end, Keith didn't resist induction; he even tried to enlist in the Air Force first. "He felt that's what his dad expected him to do." And unlike Ricky Dodd, Keith hadn't the benefit of informal draft counseling. He assumed induction was inevitable; conscientious objection was confined to the college set.

The Mathers live in a comfortable San Bruno house; there are four younger children. Mrs. Mather sat behind a coffee table covered with Life, TV Guide, and Woman's Day. Eisenhower had just died, and the popular magazines were full of America's vulgar ritual of mourning. "Eisenhower

caused the death of thousands of our boys," Mrs. Mather
said.   She went on to describe her visit to Oak Knoll Naval
Hospital, where, in every bed, "one or two or three limbs
were gone." Mrs. Mather, always anti-war but never vocal
about it before, is becoming active in the local peace movement.   "When it comes to raising your sons for cannon fod-
der," she says, "I'm not patriotic in the least....there is no
just war; it's just the rich men planning all the wars."

Mather was a sociable, fun-loving kid, "always rebel-
lious of authority." He too had his trip around the country
during those uncertain years between high school and induction.   He never let the Army discipline get to him too much;
he went AWOL and surrendered when he felt ready.   In the
stockade, he maintained his defiance.   "I really thought they
would whip his spirit," Mrs. Mather said.   But Keith at
first refused to wear a uniform, later fasted (as did Dodd and
several of the others), and spent a good deal of time in the
box.   He didn't mind it so much as "somebody standing over
him rapping out orders."   And before he left for points north,
Keith told his mother: Though he'd hated every minute of
his time in the stockade, he wouldn't trade it--the experiences
he had--an awakening--to know what freedom really means.

*   *   *

Like several of the twenty-seven, Steve Rowland
comes from a military family, and he spent his childhood
shuttling from one Air Force base to another.   "I didn't particularly like the military," he said.   "Just watching my
father, he was always worrying about what his superior officers would do."   Steve dropped out temporarily after two
years of pre-med at the University of Missouri, and decided
to get the Army over with.   He'd always been told that "if
you're going to live in this country, you've got to pay the
rent," and like most of the twenty-seven, he never really
thought about resisting.

Steve signed up as a medic and was eventually sent to
Fort Lewis, Washington.   There, he married his college girl-
friend, Sue.   Sue says Steve had changed in the Army: like
most soldiers, he was smoking grass, and like many, he was
becoming anti-military and anti-war.   He soon applied for non-
combatant C.O. status; the Army replied with orders to Vietnam.

Steve and Sue went to San Francisco on leave.   There

they decided he would go AWOL for ninety days, after which
time his name would be dropped from the Vietnam roster.
Then he would turn himself in and serve six months for
AWOL, instead of five years for refusing orders. While he
was serving he would file a new C.O. application, this time
requesting discharge.

Everything seemed well-planned. Sue and Steve had
ninety days to kill: they spent the first part in Berkeley, observing with some midwestern amazement the freaky Telegraph Avenue scene. Steve's father, an Air Force lieutenant
colonel, still afraid what his superior officers might do, gave
the Army Steve's address, and with MP's nearly pounding at
their door, the Rowlands fled to Mendocino for a month of
berry-picking. Steve's father, divorced from his mother,
has since disowned him.

Sue and Steve returned to San Francisco in time for
the October 12 peace march. Steve turned himself in, and,
now unwilling to do any work for the Army, lasted about an
hour in the Special Processing Detachment before being sent
to the stockade. There, he found a "nonviolent lynch mob"
atmosphere following Bunch's death. Steve was immediately
caught up in the madness and tension. He joined the sit-in,
during which he got up to ask for Colonel Ford. "I stood up
because it was kind of obvious that I wasn't a ringleader.
I'd just gotten there." Unfortunately, the Army thinks otherwise. They consider Steve a troublemaker planted by Hallinan in the stockade.

After the sit-in, the mutiny charges came down. Os-
cipinski and Reidel, two of the sickest of the twenty-seven,
got sixteen and fourteen years; and these sentences weren't
reduced (to two years each) till months later. In the meantime, the glory began wearing off; Mather and Pawlowski escaped, and Steve was considering it. When Linden Blake,
the third escapee, left, encouraging Steve to come along, Rowland wavered but finally remained. The same impulse that
drew Steve into the mutiny compelled him then to stay.

Rowland is a nervous but very articulate guy. Sue,
unlike the wives and girlfriends of most of the twenty-seven,
wears her blonde hair straight and long, not teased. At the
Fort Ord trial, she became friendly with Gloria Stevens,
whose husband Rick was also a defendant. Gloria has two
young children and is living with her parents. Sue was trying to convince her to move to Leavenworth and maybe rent
a house together there.

*   *   *

Rick Stevens comes from Fremont, another Oakland suburb, where his father is pastor of Stonybrook Full Gospel Church. Rick quit school after eighth grade and joined the Army because "I knew I was going to have to go in sooner or later so I figured I might as well get it over with." His father had been in the service. Rick had a year and a half of good time before he began going AWOL first to get married, then to see his baby born, then to help his wife financially. "They was living with her parents and they didn't have no money coming in, sir."

Rick has a strangely religious face: penetrating eyes and a soft-spoken manner. Hallinan asked him if during the sit-in he intended to override military authority and Rick said no. On cross-examination, the bullish prosecutor, John Novinger, asked, "How would you define 'override'?"

"Blowing up things, sir," said Rick.

*   *   *

Richard Gentile, a big strong boy with thin, set lips and vacant eyes, has the unmistakable look of a soldier who's been in combat. He returned from Vietnam strongly opposed to the war, and joined the GI march against Presidio orders. Charged with AWOL he arrived in the stockade about the same time as Rowland. Since then, Gentile's emotional disintegration has been swift: he attempted suicide and later suffered a total breakdown. "I couldn't take no more of the stockade, sir," he testified, displaying the forty-four stitches it took to put his arm back together. One day during the Fort Ord trial, Gentile bolted suddenly from the courtroom, yelling that he couldn't stand it. Hallinan said he'd been in the box the night before, as punishment for flashing a V sign. A few weeks later, one of the prosecutors made a threatening gesture at one of the defense attorneys. Gentile stood up angrily and said, "Ain't nobody going to hit my lawyers!"

Gentile's father is a career noncommissioned officer. His mother attended the Fort Ord trial faithfully, and has become sympathetic to the peace movement. At the time of the sit-in, Richard had only fifty days left in the Army.

*   *   *

Alan Rupert, on the other hand, has in two years

since induction accumulated fewer than two months good time.
Intimidated by induction officers into taking the oath (he
wanted to refuse), Alan went AWOL thirteen days after entering the Army and then again a few hours after being apprehended. According to Phil Farnum, "Alan felt his AWOL pattern was a relatively rational way to try to get out ... and
was about to make it when he decided to join the sit-in. Now
he feels he is doing something worthwhile."

     Alan's mother has been married and divorced twelve
times, and Alan was a ward of the state at fifteen. Sue Rowland describes how his friends arranged for a girl to come
visit him at the stockade, posing as his fiancee. Now they
are engaged.

                    *   *   *

     The average age of the twenty-seven on October 14 was
nineteen. Rowland is the only one who's been to college; a
few have not gone beyond ninth grade. Among them can be
found almost any common physical or mental ailment. Of
Hallinan's fourteen clients, thirteen were recommended for
medical discharge. They have accumulated thirty-one attempted suicides of record. Mostly, they come from lower
middle class or working class homes, often broken homes.
In a handful of cases, their families are sympathetic; in many,
they are hostile. Most often they are utterly bewildered by
their sons' acts.

     These twenty-seven are not the demonstrators at the
Oakland Induction Center two years ago. They are the boys
on the inductee buses the demonstrators were trying to stop.

     But the basic fact about them was obvious as they sat
in the Fort Ord courtroom. They are boys. Their faces
are very young. Some still have pimples on their necks or
cheeks. During a brief recess, Buddy Shaw ran over to his
mother and kissed her. "That's my baby," she told him.
Roy Pulley tugged at Sue Rowland's hair on his way into court,
and gave her a playful grin. During the breaks, they talked
with their parents or girlfriends or wives, holding hands,
hugging, or just staring, in the warmth of human feeling.
As Mrs. Mather observed in describing visiting day at the
stockade: "There was a feeling among all of them--together-
ness, even though they were in the stockade--just to touch
each others' hands."

Rowland said that at the sit-in, "everyone was really excited, really almost happy." For the twenty-seven, no matter what is said about their sanity, the mutiny is an act of communion. As Buddy Shaw wrote to his mother: "Forgive me for the hurt I've caused you, but not for what I've done.... Don't just pray for me, pray for all twenty-seven. We're doing it, and we're not backing down."

(Pamphlet published in offset print and distributed by the American Deserters Committee. Collected from the San Francisco office of ADC, June 20, 1969.)

94. CADAVER 1467

Today at the Gateway
to the Pacific
Travis AFB California
we loaded a cattle
truck full with
bodies fresh off
the plane from Con Thien.

Vacuum sealed in
smooth extrusions as
shiny and neat
as your latest poptop
beer can:

Container, Cadaver
Aluminum, PROS 1467, Reusable

Nomenclature of Contents
The human remains of
Transportation #757XOD3967
Cpl E4

(or some kind
of sergeant once
that weighed 143 lbs. net.)

Tarp over to protect
motorists from the glare
on the highway
to Oakland the truck
pulled out and we watched
silent
        wiping wet palms
on our green thighs.

Tom V. Schmidt

(Poem by dissident Vietnam veteran Tom V. Schmidt. Collected
July 17, 1969 at the University of California at Berkeley.
Mimeographed.)

95. SHAFT THE DRAFT

The <u>Los Angeles Free Press</u> carried a column
entitled "Shaft the Draft" during the Vietnam War.
It answered potential draftees' questions as to how
they mght resist the draft. The January 30, 1970
"Shaft the Draft" column appears below:

Shaft the Draft

The Seven Mighty Anvils

Q: I just got my shooting papers from my Riverside board.
I'm a graduate student. I thought Slimy Dick had decreed
grads were in a DMZ till June.

A: He didn't exactly decree it--that is, he didn't issue an
executive order. However, when a San Diego board tried to
rip off a grad, he wrote to State Director of SS Carlos P.
Ogden, 814 I St., Sacramento. Ogden honored his Commander-in-Chief's unofficial directive and cancelled the induction. As far as I know, Riverside is the only board in the
country arrogant enough to nix Nixon. Write the State Director (registered mail, return receipt requested)--and the
National Director, Slimy Dick himself, your congressman,
local newspaper, college paper, Mort Sahl, Joe Pyne. Raise
hell.

Q: My Riverside board shanghaied me although I'm in school.
I had the school notify them I'm enrolled full-time as an un-
dergrad so I could get a 1-SC, as I thought regulations said.
The board says they won't give me one until I ask for it in
writing. I refuse because I think they're bullshitting me.
Right?

A: Right. Write to the State Director. And the National
Director. And Slimy Dick. Demand an investigation from
your Congressman.

Q: I'm a medical student. For Christmas, my Riverside

435

board sent me a 1-A because I'm not making "normal progress." I can stall on appeals and CO for a year or so but
not long enough to finish school. Any advice?

A: Graduate students in medical and allied subjects are not
required to make "normal progress." Remind your Riverside ripoffs of that--and the State Director, National Director, Slimy Dick, etc.

What can we do about these Riverside people who have
such callous disdain for the lives behind the numbers they
shuffle around? Steal Union Oil credit cards, buy gas and
siphon it into their swimming pools? Hold SNCC integration
parties in their parlors? Give them money and drive them
crazy with confusion?

It's hard to take any action because under the regs,
SS--which stands as much for Secret Service as Selective
Service--is required to make public only names of draft board
members. In urban areas, keeping addresses secret also
conceals identity.

As a public service, Shaft the Draft is publishing the
names of Riverside board members. Although many members of Secret Service shun telephone directory listings, some
may still be found there. The rest usually occupy ample
space in the property-holder tax register in the Hall of Records. We even offer a bonus clue--one of them is a college
administrator.

We have two motives for listing the names:

1) Registrants can call them up and invite them to
dinner, where they can exercise moral suasion to convince
them to desist in their illicit activities.

2) Citizens with identical names--victims every bit,
as much as registrants of Secret Service anonymity tactics--
will receive phone calls meant for their namesakes and thus
obtain legal grounds for invasion-of-privacy and harassment
suits against Secret Service.

These are the members of Riverside Local Board 137,
"who have voluntarily donated their time and services without
pay:"

Fred Lewis
William Sullivan
James Linehan
Dr. Jack Hargan
George Shibata

Mr. Linehan, according to one of the abused registrants we counseled, actually advised him of correct procedures to follow after being illegally classified. In fact, most
of the dirty work--indeed, most of the work--done by boards
is the not the skullduggery of the members but of the "executive
secretary," or chief clerk, of the board. We don't have the
Riverside clerk's name, but you can take her a bouquet any
time during work hours. And when you do--tell her The
Seven Mighty Anvils sent you. Tune in next week.

(Send draft problems to The Seven Mighty Anvils,
LAFP, 7813 Beverly Blvd., LA 90036. Include stamped return envelope; questions too specific to interest a general
readership will be answered privately.

We urge no one to act on the basis of information that
appears here. The answer to every question in addition to
the words we write, is to See a counselor.)

96. HOW TO START A GI UNDERGROUND PAPER

Casual observers viewing the growth of the Armed Forces underground newspaper network since its birth a short sixteen months ago might very easily gain the misconception that such papers are printed at little or no risk to the persons involved. We wish it were so, but to date scores of GIs have been court-martialed, jailed, spirited off to Vietnam, or kicked out of the service altogether for working on them. Their crimes were often nothing more than a lack of experience or too much trust in the military establishment. We know better now; we've learned pretty much what works and what doesn't. In this leaflet we've compiled a brief guide for the potential GI underground newspaperman. It doesn't contain all the answers but should keep you out of jail long enough to learn the rest.

For starters you'll need to locate other GIs to work with you. So begin watching for guys who've had some college experience, draftees, or just anyone who seems to be the working type. Strike up conversations with them, sound them out, steer the topics to war protests, racial problems, or GI rights. If they sound pretty squared away then get them alone sometime and hit them with the paper idea; have a copy of one of the other papers with you and show them what you have in mind. If you've judged them reasonably well and sound like you know what you're doing, you shouldn't have any problems.

With several GIs together you can then start to produce the actual newspaper. Unless you're rich or something, this requires first locating free or very inexpensive office space, typewriters, a printing press of some sort and other essential items. Difficult? Not at all; many civilian organizations are more than willing to help. Check first at the student activities building of your nearest university; both there and off campus look for groups involved in the peace movement, draft counseling, civil rights, civil liberties, coffee houses, or minority group problems. Don't avoid the "radical" organizations in your search, as generally the more antimilitary the group is, the more they'll do to help you. Also,

438

don't be discouraged if you can't find anything near your
base; it's not at all unusual to have to do your actual printing many miles from where you're stationed.   In any case,
just sound them out like you do GIs and you'll soon find what
you're looking for.

Another essential is an off-base post office box.
They're generally very inexpensive, easy to obtain, and most
important of all, they're fairly safe from military snoopers.
Having the box allows you to communicate with many organizations that you couldn't through your military address.   Also, it will allow you to offer mail subscriptions to your paper which by far is the most painless means of distribution.

Along that line, whenever you mail anything (your paper included) to servicemen, use plain envelopes, first class
postage, and make CERTAIN that nothing showing on the outside of the envelope gives the material away as being political in nature.   Seriously, don't even put your full return address on the envelope if it sounds political or "subversive":
peace signs, obscene words, anti-war slogans--for heaven's
sake give us a break!   Most of us receive our mail via lifers
and that sort of thing just gets us into trouble.

The actual printing of your paper (How to run a mim-
eograph machine in three easy lessons, etc.) is something
you're going to have to learn for yourselves.   However,
again there are several things to keep in mind.   Keep your
articles truthful.   Keep your language reasonably clean.
DON'T print your staff members' names on the paper.   Borrow articles, ideas, and cartoons freely from the other GI
underground papers but credit them to the originating paper.

Distribution is the part that really gets sticky.   No
other single area has caused more grief than this one.   On-
base distribution in particular is the rough one:

1)   To legally distribute printed materials on a military base you must first obtain a written permit from the
commanding officer.

2)   No such permit has been granted in recent history
without court action; so be prepared with attorneys before
you make application.

3)   Your application should be in the form of a letter
to the commanding officer and should include ONLY a copy

of what you intend to distribute, and the dates, times and places you intend to distribute it. The letter should be signed by a civilian (preferably an attorney) and should NOT contain the names of any GIs. If the C.O. asks for additional information (your staff members' names, your financial supporters' names, etc.), DON'T give it to him! At that point he's only trying to stall or trick you. He has NO right to any information other than what you first gave him; if he says that isn't enough, go to court.

4) Even if you obtain a permit, DO NOT let GIs attempt to hand out the papers openly. Use only civilian volunteers. GIs doing it WILL be black-listed whether they have a permit or not and probably will end up in jail on some petty charge. Use only civilians, make sure that they hand out only what, where, and when the permit specifies and you'll do OK. Do anything else and somebody's going to jail.

5) As an alternative to that route, the most commonly used method of on-base distribution is to simply forget the permit and hand out your papers secretly. As this method is clearly illegal, no one suggests that you use it--however, I will admit that my old paper distributed over twenty thousand copies altogether this way and never had any problems. We smuggled them on base in small bundles and left them lying about when no one was watching: in the theater, on benches, in rest rooms, along the road, any place. By taking our time and being careful, none of us ever got caught. If your staff is composed entirely of GIs (as ours was) or you can't obtain a permit, do what you will.

Off-base distribution is much easier and may be accomplished by either civilians or out-of-uniform GIs. Suggested places to distribute are coffee houses, transportation centers (bus stations, etc.), entertainment centers, or any place else frequented by servicemen. But, again, the safest method of distribution is the secret, flop a copy down when no one's looking method.

Most of the rest of your operations you can play pretty much by ear or learn from the other GI papers. However, let me stress:

1) Never, never, never make public the names of your GI staff members.

2) Never "borrow" any government property for use in your paper.

3) Never print classified material.

4) If any of your staff use grass or drugs, tell them to keep their stuff away from your paper operations.

5) Keep well informed on Canadian immigration procedures.

6) Don't keep large quantities of material in your locker on base.

7) Don't be afraid to ask the other GI papers if you have a problem.

The GI newspaper underground is as young as it is exciting and productive. To date it has been expanding at a fantastic rate--if this is to continue we need new workers, more money, new papers. We need anything anyone cares to contribute. The personal risks involved in participating and not taming this military-industrial, war-producing racist animal known as the U.S. Armed Forces are even higher. We need your help. With the use of a little care and a lot of common sense yours' can be a valuable contribution in this struggle. So do it! All we have to lose is war...

---A Marine Lance-Corporal

This is a complete list of G.I. newspapers:

About Face
(Pendleton)
PO Box 54099
Terminal Annex
L.A., Calif. 90054

Aboveground
(Carson)
PO Box 2255
Colorado Springs
Colorado 80901

ACT Newsletter
c/o Rita Act
12 Passage du Chantier
Paris 12, France

The Ally
PO Box 9276
Berkeley, Cal. 94709

As You Were
(Ft. Ord)
PO Box 1062
Monterey, Cal. 93940

The AWOL Press
(Riley)
PO Box 425
Manhattan, Kan.   66502

Baumholder Gig-Sheet
(Germany) same address
as ACT Newsletter

The Bond
156 5th Ave., Rm. 633
New York, N.Y. 10010

Bragg Briefs
(Bragg)
Box 437
Spring Lake, N.C. 28309

Broken Arrow
(Selfridge)
Box 9571
North End Station
Detroit, Mich. 48202

The Chessman
(Beaufort MCAS)
Box 187
Frogmore, S.C. 29920

Counterpoint
(Lewis & McChord)
515 20th E.
Seattle, Wash.   98102

Duck Power
751 Turquoise St.
San Diego, Cal. 92109

Dull Brass
(Sheridan)
9 S. Clinton, Rm. 225
Chicago, Ill. 60606

Eyes Left!
(Travis)
Box 31387
San Francisco, Cal. 94131

Fatigue Press
(Hood)
101 Ave. D
Killeen, Texas 76541

Fed Up!
(Ft. Lewis)
PO Box 244
Tacoma, Wash.   98409

Final Flight
(Hamilton)
Box 31387
S.F., Calif. 94131

Flag-in-Action
(Campbell)
New Providence, Tenn. 37040

A Four-year Bummer
(Chanute)
PO Box 2325
Station A
Champaign, Ill. 61820

Forward March
(N. Severn)
310 6th St.
Annapolis, Md.   21401

Fun, Travel & Adventure
(Knox)
Box 336
Louisville, Ky.   40201

The GI Organizer
(Hood)
Box 704
Killeen, Texas 76541

GI Voice
Box 825
New York, N.Y.   10009

Gig-Line
(Bliss)
G.A. Carter, Box 2143
El Paso, Tex. 79951

Huachuca Hard Times
mailing address unknown

Last Harass
(Gordon)
Box 2994
Hill Station
Augusta, Ga. 30904

Left Face
(McClellan)
Box 1595
Anniston, Ala. 36201

Marine Blues
(MC reserves)
Box 31387
S.F., Cal. 94131

The Oak
(Oakland Nav. Hosp.)
Box 31387
S.F., Cal. 94131

OM (D.C. area)
c/o Link
1029 Vt. Ave., NW
rm 200
Wash., D.C. 20005

Open Sights
(D.C. area)
Box 6585 T St. Station
Wash., D.C. 20009

RAP! (Ft. Benning)
PO Box 894
Columbus, Ga. 31902

Rough Draft
Box 1205
Norfolk, Va. 23501

The Second Front
M. Billaudot,
33 Rue Vauttier,
92-Boulogne, France

Shakedown
(Dix)
Box 68
Wrightstown, N.J. 08562

Short Times
(Jackson)
Box 543
Columbia, S.C. 29202

Spartacus
(Ft. Lee)
Box 4027
Petersburg, Va. 23903

SPD News
(Ft. Dix)
same address as:
The Bond

Task Force
(Bay Area)
Box 31268
S.F., Cal. 94131

Top Secret
(Devens & Boston)
595 Mass. Ave., Rm. 205
Cambridge, Mass. 02139

The Ultimate Weapon
(Dix)
Box 8633
Philadelphia, Pa. 19101

Up Front
Box 60329
Terminal Annex
L.A., Cal. 90060

Vets Stars & Stripes
Box 4598
Chicago, Ill. 60680

Vietnam GI
Box 9273
Chicago, Ill. 60690

WE GOT THE brASS   Your Military Left
same address as   (Sam Houston)
The Second Front   Box 561
                                San Antonio, Tex. 78206

Where It's At
1 Berlin 12
Postfach 65, Germany

(Collected December 29, 1969 at the University of Texas at
El Paso.)

97. THE NEXT TASK

American society is entering one of the most decisive decades in history.

The 1960s--the decade of dawning popular consciousness--will achieve its symbolic zenith Nov. 15 when millions of people in Washington, San Francisco and in their home towns demand that the American ruling class withdraw an imperialist army from an oppressed nation struggling for liberation.

Most of those millions would not use these words to describe their actions Nov. 15--but it is an objective fact. And if their political consciousness is such that a clear understanding of the meaning of Vietnam is lacking, it must not be overlooked that these people have come a long way in a few years.

At the beginning of this decade, at mid-decade and often just a year or two ago perhaps a majority of the people who will participate in what may be the most politically important popular demonstration in this nation's history could not even perceive the sickness rampant in American society, much less prescribe a remedy.

Only the most benighted among the American people have been immune to the changes which have taken place in the collective consciousness during this last decade brought about by the vanguard actions of the blacks, the youth, the poor and the antiwar movement at home and the beginning of the collapse of the U.S. empire due to the struggle of national liberation forces abroad.

Once stimulated, this consciousness has often proliferated to an understanding of the corrupt quality of American culture, the emptiness of conventional mores, the hypocrisy of the ruling authorities, the absence of ideological difference between the two bourgeois political parties and of the real poverty of America's vaunted affluence.

445

Some, unable to cope with the realization that the American Dream is a nightmare, have retreated further into tradition, into belief and into political reaction. Many, the millions who will demonstrate Nov. 15 and the millions more who share their understanding but not yet their commitment, have moved forward, attempting to act in concert with their new consciousness, seeking ever more complex answers to questions they previously never thought to ask. The majority--the "silent majority" President Nixon presumes support the policies of the American ruling class--have also been affected by the changes in our society in the last decade but not enough as yet to determine a course for themselves.

The American people are awakening, stimulated by the revolt of the most oppressed sections of the population and the developing contradictions in the capitalist system. In just 10 years the black masses have transformed themselves from a totally subjugated people into a conscious force for rebellion against the institutionalized racism of American society. Other national minorities--Mexican-Americans and Puerto Ricans in particular--are likewise beginning to rebel against the racism and poverty that is their assigned position in the hierarchy of U.S. class relations. Hundreds of thousands of liberal Americans have been radicalized through participation in the anti-Vietnam war movement. Young people by the millions no longer believe in the shibboleths about the greatness of America and are turning away from their patriotic elders in disgust. Thousands of women--potentially millions--are beginning a political struggle against male supremacy and economic discrimination. Sections of the American working class, without which all talk of revolution is meaningless, are starting to take steps toward breaking the chains of capitalist and conservative union domination.

Revolutionary forces in all these groups must unite to the greatest degree possible and focus their attention during the tumultuous decade to come--a decade which for our purposes begins the morning of Nov. 16--on elevating the consciousness of the mass of Americans. The changes of the 1960s have prepared the people for a radical critique of racism, economic exploitation, imperialism, male supremacy, the domination of American education by corporate-military interests and other aspects of the American Way of Life. The people of the U.S. do not have to be told that their society is corrupt and crumbling. They have to be told how and why and the means by which they can construct a better life for themselves and their neighbors.

The "silent majority," the masses of Americans being challenged to embrace or deny the American nightmare,
must be brought to our side. This cannot be done willing it
so. The Nixon administration is frantically attempting to
propel the "silent majority" to the right, playing upon themes
of white superiority, insecurity, conformity, and fear. This
is but one aspect of the ruling class drive to gain the support of the American people, of course. Simultaneously, the
capitalist system is trying to rationalize its own contradictions in order to placate an increasingly restive population
and also is seeking to discredit and smash the most politically advanced sectors.

Radical America has learned a great deal during the
decade of dawning consciousness--and it has made many mistakes.

The knowledge gained from our success and failure
must be reevaluated and composed into an effective instrument in the primary struggle of the 1970s--the struggle to
change the consciousness of the American masses and to convert ignorance and apathy into understanding and action. The
remnants of the American Dream must be destroyed and an
alternative must be constructed to take its place--an alternative society and way of life for which people are willing to
live, fight and die.

Merely to proclaim that our goal is a communist society or that we are Marxist-Leninists is not enough. We
must develop a deeper analysis of the existing capitalist society, of its institutionalized white supremacy and male supremacy, and win the American people to the struggle against
it. We must develop a vision of an authentic communist society based on the conditions of 1970s America and convince
people we are correct. The most penetrating critique and
the most marvelous model of a new society are as nothing
if the people do not embrace them as their own.

This is perhaps the greatest failure of the radical left
of the 1960s--not only was our critique inadequate, not only
was our model ill-formed but the understanding that we must
convince the people, the masses of people, was lacking.

Frustrated by the enormity of the task and by the inability to coordinate analysis, model and mass organizing,
the radical left over the years has been largely ineffective.
But in the process of internal trial and error the radical

left approaches the 1970s with a qualitatively higher political consciousness than ever before.

Objectively, America offers opportunities as never before for radicals and revolutionaries. From President Nixon on up to the tiniest backwater community, the American people realize the country is in the process of falling apart. Although it is possible the ruling class will ultimately resort to overt fascism to protect its interests, the situation now, at least, is extremely fertile for radical organizing. Were we to fulfill our organizing task of reaching the masses, this would at the same time be an instrument for use against fascism.

What is lacking is ideological coherence--the analysis and the glimmer of a model--a strategy, viable tactics and organizational forms. The radical left has come so far in the last decade that achieving these objectives is not impossible. If we are to take advantage of the opportunities of the 1970s--the opportunity to elevate the consciousness of the American people and channel that consciousness in a socialist direction--we must resolve these subjective problems.

As the radical left and the left-liberals on Nov. 15 and in building a mass and effective antiwar movement, these problems and objectives must be kept uppermost in mind.

(Mimeographed flier collected from Young Socialist Alliance, San Francisco State College, October 22, 1969. The November 15 demonstrations referred to in the flier occurred in 1969.)

98. CAMPUS ROTC AND THE VIETNAM WAR

When reading through the reams of material published
by the Harvard students during the course of their struggle
against ROTC, some interesting sidelights come out that have
been little publicized outside of the Boston-Cambridge complex.   These will be of great interest to the movement as a
whole.   The struggle at Harvard which has broadened far beyond the struggle against ROTC, encompassing black student
demands, opposition to university expansion into the black
and white working class communities, is very important.
Without trying to present an analysis of the struggle, it is
important to realize that because of the widespread opposition to the war, the presence of ROTC on campuses has become an explosive issue, and Harvard is just one dramatic
example.

The student population in its majority is opposed to
the Vietnam War.   Therefore, it should be able to wage mass
struggles and win important demands concerning university
complicity with the war and war-related industries, or at
least through such struggles raise the consciousness of the
student body as a whole.

Debates have arisen over how and why ROTC should
be dealt with.   But sentiment against the war is so overwhelming that ROTC can be abolished from many academic
institutions.

Why have university administrations so firmly resisted getting rid of ROTC?   Many people underestimate the
importance of ROTC for the Army, the Government, and the
Vietnam War.   One interesting sidelight in the Harvard fight
is an Army ROTC memorandum to the Harvard University
Committee on Educational Policy (CEP).   It appeared last
fall in the OLD MOLE, an independent Boston underground
paper.   Excerpts are as follows:

"... the armed forces cannot function ... without an
officer corps comprised largely of college graduates...   Who
is prepared to trust their sons--let alone a nation's destiny--
to the leadership of high school boys and college drop-outs?

449

"Equally disturbing must be the knowledge that there
are brilliant young Harvard men with God-given leadership
abilities who seem content to waste two years of their life
by allowing themselves to be drafted as a private.

"There is no acceptable program in existence at this
time to substitute for ROTC as a broad-based source of college educated citizen-soldier leaders for our armed forces.
About 45% of all Army officers currently on active duty are
ROTC graduates; 65% of our 1st Lieutenants come from the
ROTC program and 85% of our 2nd Lieutenants. The Army
needs 18,000 new 2nd Lieutenants each year to meet normal
attrition ...

"ROTC is under attack at Harvard now because a
small group of student extremists--a tiny minority of the student body--have played upon the inherent antiwar sentiment
shared by a majority of peace loving, traditionally isolation-
ist Americans..."

So we find out from the horse's mouth that (1) the
Dept. of the Army cannot function without an officer corps
comprised largely of college graduates; (2) they don't trust
the poor and "uneducated" to run their Army; (3) they admit
that a majority of U.S. citizens oppose the Vietnam War.

Therefore: (1) We don't care if the Army is unable
to function while carrying out the Vietnam War which, as the
Army admits, is not supported by the majority of Americans.
(2) ROTC doesn't belong in any educational institutions in
this country. Our fight should be for abolishment.

And it is more than a question of just ROTC. The
government utilizes the high schools and campuses as arms
of its reactionary policies in Vietnam and other countries (as
well as in this country), through ROTC and other channels.
During the Harvard events certain facts to back this up were
revealed about the university being used as a tool of the government and its war policies. Direct links with the CIA
were exposed.

There seems to be two main reasons why the administration finds it hard to submit to student demands: (1) The
Army needs ROTC. (2) The struggle against ROTC serves
to reveal the nature of the university--that of being a serv-
ant and labor pool for the CIA, corporations such as DOW,
and the military. But it becomes all the harder to maintain

this role when the majority of the student body actively oppose it.   The antiwar movement can win significant victories
over ROTC and university complicity with the war through an
expanded campaign against them this spring.

John Baker
Harvard Students for Abolition of ROTC

(Mimeographed flier collected at Harvard University, February 24, 1969.)

99. IMPERIALISM--HOW IT WORKS

Imperialism is a word that most people in the Anti-Vietnam war movement have avoided. Some worry it might alienate middle class supporters. Others fear recognition of America's worldwide economic empire would force them into a longer and more intense struggle than simply forcing the U.S. out of Vietnam. Still others believe that the Vietnam war is an accident and the word imperialism just doesn't apply to the United States.

Little can be done for those who would rather ignore America's role in the world, but a leaflet such as this might help those who don't understand America's economic relations with the world.

America's prosperity is to a great degree the result of its worldwide economic dominance. What foreign traveler in London, Mexico City, Tokyo, Caracas, or Leopoldville can ignore the American-owned factories and stores, the U.S. banks, the Coca-Cola signs and the American goods that fill up the stores. Venturing away from the city, U.S.-owned plants, mines, smelters, and plantations can be found everywhere. In fact, many giant U.S. corporations sell more and earn more profits abroad than they do at home.

America exports about $30 billion worth of goods--primarily manufactured products--and imports $30 billion--primarily raw materials--making it by far the dominant force in international trade. In addition, the U.S. corporations have invested more than $60 billion in mines, smelters, oil wells and manufacturing plants abroad.

Giant corporations dominate U.S. foreign investment as well as export and import trade. They reap the benefits of America's worldwide role. For instance, it is estimated the top 60 U.S. corporations account for over two-thirds of all foreign investments and the top 200 U.S. corporations account for all of it.

The American economy is dependent on foreign invest-

ment, exports and imports for its health and prosperity because the giant corporations are dependent on these foreign
markets. In their search for stable and cheap raw materials, U.S. corporations have been the primary force and the
beneficiary in American expansion overseas. Their quest for
growth and profit has led them deep into the affairs and politics of Europe, Latin America, Africa and Asia.

Few people realize how important foreign markets, investments and sources of raw materials are to American
corporations and thus to the American economy. Liberal
economists dismiss any mention of U.S. "dependence" by raising one statistic--U.S. exports are less than 4% of the gross
national product. This is true but highly misleading fact.

The key industrial sector of the American economy
depends heavily on foreign markets. By comparing exports
to GNP, the liberal economists compare apples with eggs.
The GNP includes in its accounting advertising expenditures,
federal, state, and local expenditures and all banking and financial transactions. If we compare exports to a more useful figure--the domestic production of goods--we find that in
1964, 8.6% of American goods (not 4%) had to find foreign
outlets for sales.

The 8.6% figure is for all industry and agriculture.
Specific industries, particularly those of high technology, are
more dependent on foreign markets. For example, in the agricultural sector over 20% of the products of American farms
cannot find markets in the U.S. and must be sold overseas.
Other examples from the year 1968 are 19.1% of all coal
production, 14.8% of all engines and turbines, 26.9% of all
construction and mining machinery and 14.0% of all metal
working machinery was exported.

The great trend in recent years has been for U.S.
corporations to set up or buy manufacturing plants abroad,
not just increase exports. The amount of sales by U.S. corporations abroad is enormous. In 1964 for instance, while
the U.S. exported only $24 billion in goods, investments
abroad either from direct ownership of factories or through
equities produced approximately $143 billion worth of goods
sold overseas. (These figures, as others above, are from
The Age of Imperialism by Harry Magdoff, Monthly Review
Press, 1969.)

In other words American corporations were dependent

on foreign markets to buy approximately $186 billion worth
of their production in just one year. Magdoff estimates that
this foreign market is approximately 40% of the domestic
market. Thus U. S. corporations depend on overseas markets for their sales perhaps ten times more than the 4% figure liberal economists throw at us all the time.

In fact, a growing percentage of American corporations were forced to earn either half their profits or sales
from foreign operations. In 1961, for example, Yale &
Towne earned 80% of its profits from abroad and the Aluminum Corp. of America got 65% of its income from abroad.
The following corporations were just some of those that received over 50% of their business abroad: Eastman Kodak,
Pfizer, H. J. Heinz, Singer, National Cash Register, Wool-
worths, Colgate Palmolive, International Harvester and Cat-
erpillar Tractor. The list grows every year.

This business pays off. In 1964, over 22% of U. S.
manufacturing profits came from their foreign operations.
U. S. investments overseas have been so profitable (to the
corporation) that investments abroad as a percentage of total
U. S. investments each year have risen rapidly. In 1957,
investments abroad were 8% of the total. By just 1965, investments abroad had grown to 17.3% of the total.

How Raw Materials Are Supplied

Furthermore, the U. S. is also dependent on foreign
sources of supply for most of the raw material its economy
needs. Steel can't be made without manganese. The only
countries with sufficient deposits beside China and the U. S.
S. R. are India, Gabon and South Africa. The same situation prevails with most of the other critical raw materials.

The mineral yearbook for 1963 computed how much of
each mineral needed by U. S. industry had to be imported.
At the top of the list was the important metal chromium, of
which 100% had to be imported, 98% of cobalt, 94% of manganese, 86% of nickel, 85% of bauxite and 78% of tin had to
be imported. among other minerals.

Another study surveyed the entire raw material situation, revealing that in 39 commodities critical to the American economy more than 80% had to be imported, In only
23 commodities of the 97 commodities surveyed could the
U. S. be called self-sufficient.

Corporate investment and foreign policy must of course be closely linked to assure politically secure and cheap sources of these raw materials. Besides manganese, the only place the U.S. can get chromium from is either South Africa or Rhodesia. New Caledonia has most of the "free world's" nickel deposits. Indonesia and Thailand have two-thirds of the world's tin reserves. Chile, Zambia, the Congo and Peru have two-thirds of the foreign copper reserves.

The importance of these imports to the American economy cannot simply be calculated by the cost of the imports themselves. What must be calculated is the value of the industry which depends on them. The steel and iron industry --$22.3 billion in sales--must have manganese and other critical imports or the furnaces will have to be shut down. Cheap sources of bauxite are a must for the $3.9 billion a year aluminum industry.

In many ways America's worldwide diplomatic and military expansion is a result of the worldwide expansion of American corporations. Their constant search for markets, investments and raw materials moves the U.S. deeper and deeper into the political life of every nation in the world.

(Mimeographed leaflet collected from the Radical Student Union on May 24, 1969 at the University of California at Los Angeles.)

100. BUILDING AN ANTI-IMPERIALIST MOVEMENT

The coalition of radical groups leading last week's demonstrations against Massachusetts Institute of Technology's counterinsurgency program is an example of a means toward building an anti-imperialist movement. Directed against the use of this "distinguished institution" as a site for weapons research and development projects, the action was one model for raising the antiwar struggle to a higher level.

The demonstrations sought to demystify the university's liberal veneer by revealing that it serves corporate military interests, even if it does hire left-liberal and radical scholars to legitimize claims to status as a leading center of pure and humane research. Tactics employed by the demonstrators were militant, but militancy does not by itself, of course, constitute radical activity. More significant was the target of the demonstration and the character of the demands.

Similar efforts are underway to expose the role of "institutes of international affairs" and other corporate-oriented agencies at the University of Wisconsin and Columbia. In Minneapolis, the "Honeywell Project" is attempting to show how the Honeywell Corp., a great "civic-minded corporation," is benefiting from and fostering the war.

These attempts to link the university with the war and giant corporations are more valuable for raising political consciousness than abstract marches "against death." Death certainly is not the enemy. The enemy, among others, is the giant corporations and professional servants in the universities and research institutes. In this constellation of power, the government acts as the intermediary and financial base for research and development too costly for the companies. The government is less the originator of policy in this sphere than its handmaiden. A major center of economic and military decision-making resides in the private corporations and the corporate university.

The most practical places for developing new methods

456

of destruction are the privately-endowed prestige schools, only indirectly subject to public scrutiny. It is to these schools that the most talented scientists and engineers are attracted. The enormous volume of research and development has also made necessary the extension of government-sponsored research for war purposes into the state universities and colleges.

The transformation of these "academic" institutions into knowledge factories for the production of new techniques in weapons manufacture and military strategies constitutes a major target for radicals seeking to expose the real role of public higher education in our society and the penetration of corporate interests into this sector of American society.

The MIT demonstrations illustrated a fundamental class approach to the antiwar struggle, adding a new dimension to the movement by exposing the unambiguous relationship of the university to capitalist society. The radical coalition at MIT declared its anti-imperialist aims and succeeded in attracting widespread attention, pinpointing the real character of the war rather than engaging merely in rhetorical admonitions to oppose imperialism.

Making Connections

Artificial attempts to build "worker-student alliances" and "labor committees" which try to establish contacts with workers engaged in traditional trade union struggles seem pale in contrast. The MIT demonstrators understood the complexity of the class struggle, its manifestations within the university and its broad social implications. Other attempts to make the connections between students and working class have an air of Victorian romanticism which would make Marx shudder.

The time has come for a link-up of those radicals on campuses and in local communities who recognize that the fight against the Vietnam war through purely political pressure can neither result in victory for the antiwar forces nor raise the critical issues which lie behind the reasons for the war itself.

The basic strategy for an anti-imperialist movement is to connect the Vietnam war to the realities of corporate capitalist control over all major social institutions, to show

how the repression of opposing political movements and individuals is linked to the authoritarian character of the capitalist system in its last stages and to point out that the end of the Vietnam war will not halt the drive of U.S. corporations to repress national liberation movements all over the world.

Embryonic Stage

Such a movement exists only in embryonic form. It manifests itself in student and faculty demonstrations on isolated campuses against corporation recruiters, against counterinsurgency research departments and in spasmodic efforts to expose the hypocrisy of various corporations which profit from the war. These activities are not characteristic of the antiwar movement as a whole. With the exception of GI organizers, striking at the heart of imperialist ability to conduct wars, most radicals have tailed the left-liberals in the antiwar movement in concentrating efforts in the political arena.

Much of the antiwar movement acts as if the state is still the major perpetrator of foreign policy. It has failed to perform the necessary analysis to determine the seat of power--clearly within the key financial and industrial corporations.

Exposing Complicity

The task for radicals is to expose corporate complicity and domination over U.S. foreign policy, corporate responsibility for the intensification of repression against the black liberation and radical movements and increasing corporate control over major educational institutions. This task will not be performed by liberals who insist the antiwar movement remain a pressure group which implicitly accepts the tenets of pluralistic politics according to which the splits in the capitalist class permit effective mass action against the war. Such splits do exist, but are not deep enough to turn the powerful forces of Eastern capital from the escalation of foreign investments, counter-revolution abroad and a continuing commitment to armed conflict.

Radicals will march with the liberals Nov. 15, despite liberal pressure to prevent independent actions such as the demonstration at the Justice Department in behalf of The

Conspiracy. But it is important that we do not repeat the mistakes of the past.

The inability of the left-liberal coalition to articulate the central issues of the war makes necessary the formation of anti-imperialist, anti-fascist groups which can begin the task of radical education and action on the local level. These groups need national coordination because the system itself is both national and international. For example, if a decision were made to boycott Honeywell or GE products, a national network would make the campaign more effective. Further, our presence as a force within the movement as a whole would be greatly boosted by such coordinates.

Armed with a class analysis, such a movement could begin the arduous task of organizing beyond the largely middle-class constituency of the antiwar movement. The facile belief that the workers are on the side of the imperialists reflects a failure of the antiwar movement to connect corporate control over foreign affairs to questions such as taxes, social services, labor struggles and racism.

(Distributed at Ohio State University, Columbus, November 14, 1969. Collected in the Special Collections at Ohio State on February 24, 1973. Mimeographed flier.)

101. SECOND COMING

There are four fronts to the Vietnamese war. The first front is on the battlefield of Southern Vietnam and the bombed areas of the North. The second front is the struggle of the antiwar movement in America and the effect it can have on the war against the Vietnamese. The third front is the negotiations between the U.S., Saigon, the PRG, and the DRV in Paris. (Those who criticize the Vietnamese policy of negotiation in Paris fail to distinguish between negotiation as a tactic and as a grand strategy.) And the fourth front is among the nations of the world, about two dozen of which have recognized the PRG as the legitimate government of Vietnam.

The Vietnamese liberation fighters have called on their American friends to build a second front here in the U.S. They do not expect us to end the war or to take power in Washington. What they ask is that we initiate mass, broad-based actions against the war which will have the effect of weakening the ability of the Nixon regime to wage all-out war against them.

Building Our Movement

Our problem, especially in terms of mass actions, is how to support this need of the Vietnamese and at the same time to build our own movement which will not be the politics of the least common denominator. There has been the feeling that every time we engage in mass actions our radical politics must be submerged in order to keep liberals and reform movement types from leaving the many tenuous antiwar coalitions. What "Second Coming" hopes to do this week is to approach this problem on three levels--organization-structure, politics and tactics and to suggest some ways out of this dilemma.

In terms of organization, despite some good elements, the New Mobilization Committee is not a suitable group to be entrusted with taking a radical initiative against the war. It

has too many built-in limitations that keep it from being an
active day-to-day radical organizing force. Its main strength
to date has been its ability to call mass actions on an annual or semiannual basis. The New Mobe has the weakness of
putting forward what are often good political slogans that are
divorced from the practice of its following. This results
from the separation between Mobe organizers and the people
who answer its call to action. On the question of militant
tactics, the coalition nature of the Mobe makes it virtually
impossible to push beyond passive-type actions without antag-
onizing the different factions. This, however, does not mean
radicals should ignore the Mobe. A radical caucus within
the New Mobe is important to keep the coalition from sway-
ing too far to the right under Moratorium and other conservative influences. Perhaps the best groups to compose this
caucus are some women's liberation organizations, SDS
(RYM-2), one or two black organizations and some representation from the radical news media. On most questions this
would be a minority caucus but its importance would be in
continually putting forward a radical position in antiwar activity.

On a more permanent basis, radical organizers should
begin to build committees of solidarity with the people of Vietnam in local areas around the country. These committees
could relate to real community bases and deal as well with
domestic problems that are an outgrowth of the war such as
high prices and inflation. Already existing radical community groups could simply form a Vietnam solidarity committee within the structure of that organization. Then these committees could have a loose link-up on a regional basis and for
occasional local actions. The result would be to attract new
people to antiwar activity who have some sense of the war
and how the quality of American life feeds directly into it.
Also on the organizational level it is unrealistic to expect
many third world groups to enter into New Mobe-type coalitions. The frame of reference of both the New Mobe and
most of the antiwar movement is very "white" and often
comes across not too different from the white-dominated institutions the third world groups are fighting. However these
reasons should not be a strategy for non-action. Third world
solidarity committees should be set up all around the country
such as the one in New York or the Black Antidraft Union in
Chicago headed by Bob Lucas and the numerous third world
groups in the Bay Area. Three universal demands might be:
(1) support of the Vietnamese people's revolution, as a colored people fighting international white power, (2) immediate

U. S. troop and economic withdrawal and (3) condemnation of
the same power structure that oppresses black people and
makes war on our Vietnamese brothers. In terms of mass
actions these groups would be able to have separate actions
against the war or joint demonstrations with white groups as
the occasion demands.

On the political front the most basic demand is that of
immediate military and economic withdrawal. There are
those who will want to press for support of the NLF or the
PRG. Instead of dogmatic approval of the NLF-PRG it is
more important for us to tell people why given the reality of
Vietnam the demands of the NLF and PRG represent the only hope for peace, independence and unity in Vietnam. Besides, to anyone who knows the political-military situation in
Vietnam, to declare for immediate withdrawal is to support
the NLF without actually saying it. What is important politically is to make demands that continually show that Vietnam
is no mistake and is only a place where U. S. policies of
neocolonialism have met with active resistance. If Vietnam
is understood to be a product of the normal workings of U. S.
power, then the need for revolution in the U. S. becomes obvious.

Militant Tactics

As for tactics, militant tactics for the sake of militant tactics lead nowhere. Any tactic which obscures or con-
fuses political demands or alienates potential support is incorrect. If the political situation calls for militant tactics
to press home a point, obviously militant tactics should be
used. Militancy should be used for the sake of political education. After all, armies are to carry out the political
tasks of a revolution.

Finally, some suggestions for actions that a radical
antiwar movement can initiate and carry out: (1) strikes,
work slow-downs and walk-outs in industries and plants which
support the war effort; (2) radical "truth squads" to travel
around the country and to harass administration spokesmen
with the truth about Vietnam; (3) women's action in the spring
of 1970 as a women's strike against the war which could involve secretaries, working women, and others who want to
show that women will no longer support the war; (4) conferences around U. S. imperialism in Asia; (5) third world convention possibly in Chicago around Easter of prominent

third world personalities and organizations who are opposed to the war.

These ideas are not so much a specific program for action as ideas suggested to revitalize the radical antiwar movement.

(Collected at Stanford University, Stanford, Calif., November 15, 1969.   Mimeographed leaflet.)

102. THE WAR GAME

Defense of Profit

From all the newspaper accounts of Congressional agitation, one might get the impression that the Military-Industrial Complex suffered a major setback this year. But a quick look at the $20 billion 1970 defense budget indicates no substantial cuts have been made in controversial weapons systems.

On Sept. 9, the Senate defeated a measure proposed by Sen. William Proxmire (D-Wis.) to cut $533 million from the budget for 23 additional C-5A supertransport planes. Proxmire wanted to limit procurement of the C-5A to the 58 already on order from Lockheed Aircraft, the prime contractor. Cost overruns on the jet, which is designed to ferry U.S. troops to troublespots abroad during future Dominican-type interventions, have already reached $2 billion.

Also on Sept. 9, the Senate Armed Services Committee voted to retain a $55.4-million budget item for continued development of the MBT-70 heavy tank, which is being designed jointly with West Germany. Critics of the MBT-70 (Main Battle Tank for the 1970s) have complained of excessive development costs and question the very need for such a weapon at this time.

On Sept. 16, the Senate voted $100 million for full-scale engineering development of the Advanced Manned Strategic Bomber (AMSA), the proposed replacement for the obsolete B-52 intercontinental bomber. Military strategists in and out of the Pentagon have ridiculed plans for the AMSA on the grounds that intercontinental ballistic missiles (ICBMs) and submarine-launched Poseidon missiles are much more reliable weapons for deterrence than ordinary aircraft. But the aerospace industry has too much at stake to let go of AMSA without a struggle (planned procurement costs are estimated at $24 billion). So industry lobbyists and Air Force spokesmen teamed up to persuade hesitant Senators to vote for the measure.

464

SPIW It Out

Even while the Pentagon is going ahead with plans to arm all U.S. troops with the M-16 high-velocity rifle, work is continuing on a new infantry weapon, the Special Purpose Individual Weapon (SPIW). Instead of firing ordinary bullets, SPIW will fire a burst of "flechettes"--razor-sharp splinters of metal which will literally tear its victim to shreds.

The SPIW weapon is the first product of an Army program to apply the methodology of systems analysis to what is called the "man-weapon-ammunition system." Flechette ammunition is attractive to the military because of its high "lethality."

The SPIW is known officially as the XM19 Rifle, 5.6 mm., Primer Activated, Flechette Firing. The AAI Corporation, a major producer of weapons for both the military and the police, will produce the first prototype SPIW in 1970.

MIT announced it would attempt to shift the emphasis of its two large defense laboratories to domestic work. The two facilities--Lincoln Laboratory and the Instrumentation Lab--have become the target of a growing radical movement at MIT, which seeks to end all war research at the Institute .... The University of Kansas will profit from recent personnel changes at the U.S. Army's chemical warfare laboratories at the Edgewood, Md. Arsenal. Dr. Charles Reynolds, Edgewood's top scientist and Technical Director, will leave his Army post to become a professor of chemistry at Kansas.... Many universities have acquired, or are planning to acquire, Triga Mark II nuclear reactors for research on atomic energy. For a list of the universities, and a description of the reactor and possible dangers, write for "Atoms on the Campus" from the Committee on Radiological Hazards (Box 148, 150 Christopher, New York, N.Y. 10014).

(Collected at the SDS literature table at the University of Kansas student union, Lawrence, Kansas, June 21, 1969.)

103. U.S. INVOLVEMENT IN VIETNAM
IS NOT AN ACCIDENT

The most glibly diffused myth about U.S. involvement
in Vietnam is that it was an unfortunate accident, something
Washington unwittingly drifted into. "Too bad, it was wrong
but we're stuck with it..." the apologists say and go on to
suggest that the Vietnamese sacrifice half their country so the
U.S. can save face and withdraw with "honor."

In fact, American involvement in Vietnam was the result of policies as deliberately planned and calculated as any
other post-war U.S. policies in Europe, Asia and elsewhere.

That it was done behind the back of Congress and the
public does not alter the fact. It was a very precisely graft-
ed piece of the mosaic of the famous "roll-back" policy--a
policy which was transformed into "containment" when socialist and national independence movements refused to be rolled
back. Eventually if "honor" is to be saved it will have to
transform further into "disengagement."

Anyone believing the "accident" myth would do well to
read the chapter on Vietnam in James Gavin's "Crisis Now."
He reveals that having failed to keep the French in the fight
against the Vietminh despite a last minute U.S. offer of A-
bombs to the French government--the Pentagon, CIA and former Secretary of State John Foster Dulles agreed immediately after the 1954 Geneva Agreements that the U.S. had to
"assume the full burden of combat against Communism in the
area." And "... In this atmosphere the Joint Chiefs (of
staff) began with the highest priority to study a proposal to
send combat troops into the Red River delta of North Vietnam...."

Gavin Plots Occupation

Gavin, as chief of plans of the Army staff, was sent
to Vietnam to work out what size force would be necessary
to occupy the Red River delta area including Haiphong and

Hanoi.   He came up with the figure of "eight combat divisions, supported by 35 engineer battalions and all the artillery and logistical support such mammoth undertakings require...." In parenthesis Gavin noted with quiet pride as proof of his good judgment: "At the time of my trip to Vietnam in November, 1967 there were eight and two-thirds U.S. divisions in Vietnam...."

In the latter part of 1954, a decision was made by Pentagon chiefs to commit unprovoked aggression against North Vietnam. This was approved, according to Gavin, by Admiral Radford, chairman of the Joint Chiefs of Staff, by the Chief of Staff of the Air Force and the Chief of Naval Operations.   Only the Army Chief of Staff, General Ridgway, opposed it.   He did so on Gavin's advice because the prospect of getting involved in another land war in Asia with a good chance (as Ridgway was painfully aware from his Korean war experience) that China would intervene, was too awful to contemplate.   Ridgway in a rare burst of indiscipline, went over the head of his immediate boss direct to President Eisenhower and persuaded the latter to veto the scheme. (Eisenhower as an Army general was more prone to listen to advice from the Army than from the Air Force and Navy.) The invasion was to have taken place well before July, 1956, when all Vietnam elections were to be held in accord with the 1954 Geneva Agreements.   The plan was dropped.

"However," continues Gavin, "there was a compromise.   We would not attack North Vietnam, but we would support a South Vietnamese government that we hoped would provide a stable, independent government...."   This was the U.S.-imposed dictatorship of Ngo Dinh Diem, whose overthrow and assassination of Diem--with CIA connivance--is now ironically celebrated every Nov. 1 as an official national holiday in Saigon.

The invasion plan itself was only a substitute for Dulles' failure to organize a Korean-type internationalization of the Indochina war to avert a French defeat--inevitable despite the fact that the U.S. was footing 80% of the war costs by 1954.   Those of us who attended the Geneva Conference know that Dulles spent all his time during the early stages in bullying representatives of nations who joined in the Korean intervention (who were in Geneva for the abortive first part of the conference on Korea) to commit troops for a new war of intervention in Indochina.   But only South Korea and Australia agreed on specific troop commitments and the plan failed.

The real substitute for the invasion of the Red River
delta was to build up a U.S.-trained and equipped army in the
South capable of carrying out its own invasion of the North.
"March to the North" was a national slogan of the Diem regime.   Graduates from the U.S.-run military academy were
issued "March to the North" shoulder patches and had to take
an oath to this effect at graduation ceremonies.

According to the Geneva Agreements, Vietminh forces
South of the 17th parallel were to be regrouped in the North;
French forces North of the 17th parallel were to be regrouped in the South prior to their total evacuation.   This
was part of the package deal, the other part being nationwide
elections by July, 1956, with consultations to arrange the
modalities of the elections by July, 1955.   The reward, in
other words, that the Vietminh was to have for permitting the
French to withdraw from their encircled positions in the Red
River delta and evacuate their own liberated bases in the
South was the total departure of the French and nationwide
elections to reunify the country under a single government by
July, 1956.   In agreeing to such a bargain, the leadership of
the Vietnamese revolution consciously made a sacrifice to the
line of "peaceful coexistence" unanimously supported by the
socialist camp at that time.

The regroupment was to take place within a period of
300 days, the final enclave for the evacuation of French
forces from the North being centered on Haiphong.   During
that period, the CIA took over from the French the most ruth-
less and efficient of their puppet agents, whisked them off to
special CIA training centers for crash courses in American-
type espionage, subversion and sabotage methods and infil-
trated them back into the North via the Haiphong enclave.
By the beginning of 1955, these agents were feeding back data
on potential landing beaches, targets for bombers and naval
guns, etc.   They were the sort of advance guard for the intended invasion which never came off.

It is an axiom that you do not start a war unless you
have a solid rear.   It was certain that those Vietnamese in
the South who had taken part in, or supported in some way
or other, the resistance war against the French would resist
a U.S.-backed attempt to invade the North.   The Diemist regime, with the help of police specialists supplied by Michigan
State University, opened up a vast campaign aimed at elimi-
nating those who had been active in the anti-French resistance.   Once French and puppet forces had been safely with-

drawn from the North and Vietminh armed forces from the
liberated areas of the South, the first phase of "Denounce
Communists" was launched, essentially to draw up lists of
former resistance workers.   All Vietnamese citizens were
given "A," "B" or "C" security ratings.

No Elections

        July, 1955 passed and there were no consultations for
elections; July, 1956 passed and there were no elections, because Ngo Dinh Diem with official U.S. blessing had denounced the Geneva Agreements and declared the Saigon regime would no longer be bound by them.

        Successive waves of repression were launched, culmi-
nating in Law 10/59 (passed in May, 1959) under which only
one of two sentences, death or life imprisonment, was levied
on anyone "committing or intending to commit" crimes against
state security.   Death sentences were executed on the spot by
mobile guillotines which were trundled through the country ac-
companying the special military tribunals.   This was the final phase aimed at liquidating all those listed or arrested
during the previous phases.

        During 1959, in various parts of the country, widely
separated in place and time, people started to resist: pre-
ferring "to die on our feet and not on our knees," as one resistance leader put it.   By 1960, resistance had become fairly widespread and with the formation of the National Liberation Front in December, 1960, it was put on an organized
basis, especially with the NLF's appeal for a nationwide uprising.   By the end of 1961, most of the countryside was in
the hands of the NLF.   It was then that the U.S., faced with
the total collapse of the puppet regime, decided to intervene
with "special war"; that is, with dollars, arms, air support,
strategic and tactical command by "advisors"--everything except U.S. combat troops.   During 1962-63, the U.S.-Saigon
forces were able to win back many areas because of the overwhelming force at their disposal, the massive use of helicopters, amphibian tanks and other new elements in guerrilla
warfare.   But towards the end of 1963, the NLF troops had
also grown up and dealt devastating blows one after another
to the Diemist forces.   When it was clear to Washington that
the U.S. could not "win with Diem," he was murdered and
a succession of new "strong men" played a game of musical
chairs in Saigon, exile being the least of the penalties for failure.

Binh Gia Is Turning Point

    Throughout 1964, the NLF continued to whittle away
the forces of "special war" built up under Gen. Maxwell Taylor's command until at the turn of the year 1964-65, at the
battle of Binh Gia, the NLF won a Dien Bien Phu-type victory wiping out in a few days--in classical day-time battles--
nearly one-third of Saigon's strategic reserve of elite troops.
This started another series of coups and counter-coups in
Saigon, because the complete disintegration of the puppet
army was only a matter of months away.

    That was the fateful moment when anyone with an
ounce of intelligence in the White House would have said:
"Enough.   Stop pouring good money after bad...."   Instead,
the decision was made to start bombing the North "to inject
morale into the Saigon regime," to commit U.S. combat
troops and to escalate "special war" to "limited war."   What
Eisenhower hesitated to do in 1955 Johnson rushed in to do
in 1965.

    In 1965 and 1966, with the overwhelming weight of
manpower and equipment, the U.S. expeditionary force was
able, at considerable cost, to occupy some strategic positions in what had been NLF held territory.   But not too
many.   The NLF still held the strategic initiative because it
held the greater part of the countryside and had the total
support of the people.   If it was true that General Westmoreland could strike more or less where and when he wanted
during those first two years, it was also true that within
each operation it was the NLF forces that decided when and
where to give battle.

    By late 1967, the NLF regular forces, most of which
had been withdrawn to base areas for regrouping, retraining
and re-equipping, began to make themselves felt.   Just when
Westmoreland was boasting that there were only small (maximum, battalion-sized) guerrilla groups left, he was hit in
October, 1967 with a division-sized unit.   While he was explaining that this was a last desperate fling, he was hit by
another division-sized unit.   The U.S. forces have never re-
covered from this.   Westmoreland started panic measures,
splitting up divisions, rushing component parts to widely differing parts of the country.   He was caught in a classical
Vo Nguyen Giap strategy, torn between dispersing his troops
to maintain occupation and concentrating them for offensive

operations. Forced to disperse, Westmoreland opened the
way for the NLF's mighty Tet offensive in late January,
1968. That sealed the fate of "limited war" because Westmoreland from then on and General Abrams after him was
forced on to the strategic and tactical defensive. Two months
after the Tet offensive, Johnson played for time by agreeing
to the talks which eventually started in Paris in May, 1968,
the major result of which was the ending of the abortive
(from a military viewpoint) bombings of the North and the
start of quadripartite talks in Paris at which the NLF was
seated as an equal partner.

"Limited war" having failed, President Nixon now
thinks he can do better than his predecessors at the White
House by moving into a "war of attrition" in which U.S.
troops will retire indefinitely into a sort of "Maginot line" of
concrete and barbed wire bunkers in a series of enclaves,
sallying forth from time to time to rescue puppet troops when
they are too hard-pressed. With a couple of hundred thousand troops in the enclaves, another 20,000 or so as military "advisors" in a back-to-Diemism style "special war,"
Nixon has been persuaded by his Pentagon advisers, he can
eventually emerge victorious in a test of "staying power"
with the Vietnamese people. In this he is doomed to defeat.

The Paris talks have not made one iota of progress
from the time Henry Cabot Lodge took over as Chief of the
U.S. delegation, if only because he is one of the main archi-
tects of the New Nixon concept. The only purpose of the
Paris talks from the Nixon-Lodge viewpoint is that they serve
to hoodwink U.S. public opinion, with judicious phony leaks
from time to time of "progress," "private contacts," and the
like. These were smoked into the open for what they were
recently when the DRV and a PRG delegation in Paris actually proposed private contacts between the U.S. and PRG delegations. Lodge rejected the idea.

The end result of this long history of very deliberate
but badly calculated U.S. aggression in Vietnam is that militarily, politically and diplomatically the mighty U.S. is on
the defensive in South Vietnam and Paris; at home and abroad
U.S. prestige has never been at a lower ebb.

Years ago, North Vietnamese Premier Pham Van Dong
said, "If the U.S. intervenes on a small scale in Vietnam,
she will be faced with a small defeat; if in a big way, with
a big defeat." The longer the war lasts, the more clearly

this prophecy is proved to be true.

(Collected from the Radical Student Union at the University
of California at Berkeley on December 11, 1969.   Mimeographed leaflet.)

104. DRAFT COUNSELING ADS

The Selective Service System became such a serious concern in young men's lives during the Vietnam War that many sought draft counseling. To
find help, they often read the ads in the underground press. The following is the draft counseling advertisement section of the December 19, 1969
issue of the Los Angeles Free Press, p. 28:

DRAFT

Los Angeles Resistance is now located at the Haymarket, a
new coffee house and community center in the Silverlake
area (507 N. Hoover St.). The office and Haymarket is (sic)
open almost all day and night. Call us for other times
draft counselors will be here or if you have any questions.
Resistance office: 666-2066 Haymarket: 386-9645

DRAFT COUNSELING

Orange County Peace Center 204 1/2 W. 3rd St., Santa Ana.
Mon., Wed., Thurs., 8-10 PM, or call (714) 836-8669 or
(714) 838-1137.

Complete draft counseling now in downtown L.A. Right be-
hind the induction center. Open every day from 6:30-4:30.
Attorney available Wednesday Nite at 8. For information
Call RI 7-5461. LA DRAFT HELP 1018 So. Hill St.

DRAFT COUNSELING
FULLERTON

2500 E. Nutwood, Suite 22M (second floor, College Park -
across street from Cal. State Fullerton) Call 774-9429.

SAN DIEGO DRAFT COLLEGE

is a volunteer service organization dedicated to helping young
men cope with the Selective Service System. We have experienced, lawyer-trained counselors to help you understand
the draft law and your rights and privileges under that law.

FREE INFORMATION
FREE COUNSELING

San Diego Draft College

714-276-8866

RESISTANCE
DRAFT COUNSELING

PASADENA
Peace House
724 N. Marengo St.
449-8228

WEST L.A.   WHITTIER
11317 Santa Monica Blvd.   7201 S. Bright St.
478-2374   698-8717

FEEL THE DRAFT?

Venice Draft Information Service, 73 Market St., Rm. 2,
Venice, Mon., Tues., Wed., Thurs. 7:30 to 10 pm, Sat
1-5 pm. Call 399-5812. We need draft counselors and other
volunteer help. Attorneys Mon & Wed.

Group and individual counseling every Tuesday, 7:30 pm,
Hollywood-Los Feliz Jewish Community Center, Sunset-
Bates (1 blk. E. of Sunset-Fountain-Hoover in Silverlake).
Call Jerry Habush, 663-2255, for further info. and EMER-
GENCY referrals.

FREE CLINIC

offers draft counseling Mon thru Thurs from 7 to 9:30 pm.,
115 N. Fairfax, L.A.   938-9141

FREE DRAFT COUNSELING

Spons. by Student Association Cal. State, Dominguez Hills,
809 E. Victoria Avenue.   Every Wed., 12-3 pm.
Ph. 532-4300, ext. 239.

SO. BAY PEACE

Draft Counseling and Resistance aftrn and evng appt. available.   Call 372-0038 after 5:30 pm.

DRAFT COUNSELING

643-8749 VENTURA 525-8043.   Free draft counseling provided every Thurs. nite at 4949 Foothill, Ventura, first
driveway west of Arroyo Verde Park at 7:30 to 10:30. Unitarian Church.   Experienced draft counselors and free information there.

DRAFT COUNSELING
LONG BEACH

1st and 3rd Sundays at 7:30 PM, 5450 Atherton Street.

105. REPORT ON WASHINGTON, D.C. MORATORIUM

The Washington, D.C. Moratorium was a combination of soulful beauty and unexcusable disgrace.

The march down Pennsylvania Avenue was colossal--about half a million mostly young people moving through a very cold day with a lot of color and spontaneous music, sometimes militant, occasionally Beatles--all in defiance of Spiro Agnew's great conspiracy to make them stay home and listen to patriotic radio programs.

I got really pissed at the National Mobe's marshals, who outpigged the police in their efforts to keep the march orderly and traffic within white lines.

The job of marshal is one infiltrating pigs take to most easily. It is the part of our movement which most resembles the society we are trying to change.

"It's larger than Woodstock," was Tim Leary's comment when he looked out at the fantastic crowd that was bunched together in gigantic warmth.

There were large contingents of the AmeriCong carrying NLF and Yippie flags. Lots of little American flags were being waved by the moderates, but they seemed colorless in comparison.

The stage raps were, as usual, boring. An audience overwhelmingly young listening to old men talking about reforming a society that no longer exists. A mixture of Senators, labor leaders, businessmen and movement bureaucrats talked about changing American priorities when even young liberals figure a revolution is necessary.

Of the speakers, only Dave Dellinger was right on time with a heavy rap about how the entire system was fucked up. He woke up the crowd electricity which was deadened by the programmed pettiness of the rally.

476

Dave and Jerry Rubin, Abbie Hoffman and John Froines, all comrade Conspirators, by his side while he spoke. The Mobe agreed to let these wildmen on the stage but refused to allow them even a groan into the microphone. Jerry received an ovation when he doffed his wig to the crowd.

The ecstatic moment of the day was born of Pete Seeger's voice. This great friend of my late progressive childhood is still as dangerous to the rat-infested establishment as he and Woody and Leadbelly always were.

"All we are saying is give peace a chance," Pete sang, and sing-along Mitch Miller waved his arms and got almost everybody to join in. If beauty is the name of our revolutionary desire, it was there at the foot of the Washington Monument and we were for a few minutes in its possession.

At around four o'clock a march on the Justice Department erratically began. It was called by the Youth International Party to protest the judicial lynching that Nixon and Agnew are trying to execute in the Chicago Conspiracy trial.

The march was scheduled for five o'clock, but the militants left early. Originally the Mobe opposed this march because they were afraid of violence and more than one "issue," but when they saw the march would happen anyway they allowed Dellinger to announce it from the stage.

All day the pigs wore a smiling mask. They were very polite and let the Mobe marshals do the police work for them. But this march was a very different matter. It was called by the crazies and only had semi-support from the respectable left. The pigs decided to kick ass.

About eight thousand sisters and brothers surrounded the Justice Department, a few rocks were thrown and the NLF flag was run up. I saw the Washington Police Chief order the demonstration to disperse and then an instant later throw a tear gas grenade into a center of humanity.

The tear and pepper gassing that followed was as vicious as People's Park. These pigs were venting the hatred that was building in them, but under the sunlight of CBS cameras was not permitted daytime circulation.

About 60 people were busted and some were badly burned by the gas. One friend's eyes were blistered closed when a teargas canister smashed her head.

The Mobe marshals did their sellout best to protect the building from justice by urging the brothers and sisters not to fight back.

There has been an informal conspiracy on the part of the media, leading liberal politicians, pigs, the Moratorium and the National Mobe to pretend this brutality never happened. The Moratorium wants to keep its skirts clean of unpleasantness. Pigs always like to shove their shit under the rug, and the liberal media supports a respectable movement and doesn't want the silent majority to think too much about NLF flags and broken federal windows.

Attorney General Mitchell, who was in the Justice Department building and was gassed, has complained about the violence. In his patriotic tight ass he thinks anyone who raises a commie flag over the Justice Department deserves to stand in the gas chamber.

When I returned to Chicago for the trial and another day of undercover police bullshit-artists on the witness stand, a Federal Marshal gleefully asked me how I liked the gas in Washington.

It was strong stuff which would not easily leave our clothing. In a moment the happy sadist began to inhale my fumes and his suffering face was the proper answer to the question.

The official left has sold us out again in their passionate crawl for respectability. But we have been complaining about these paper people for a long time. We must begin to put our fury into practice. A revolutionary organization must be built that can call half a million sisters and brothers to Washington without needing a Senator to pronounce the feast kosher. If we can do this it might be possible not only to end the war but to crash in the White House.

Stew Albert

(Mimeographed flier available from Radical Student Union, University of Illinois at Chicago Circle following the November 15, 1969 Washington, D.C. Moratorium. Collected in the Chicago Circle Special Collections October 11, 1974.)

106. SERVING ONE'S COUNTRY IN THE ARMY

The Case of E4 William T. Gaugush

Approximately two months ago, the UCLA Student Peace Union began a correspondence with William T. Gaugush, an E4 who is serving in the Military Police and stationed at Camp Pendleton. His letters present a clear and sincere picture of the struggle that any man of honor must undergo in attempting to keep his head and "serve his country" at the same time. For the benefit of those who've had the good fortune not to personally experience the armed forces, here is an all-too-typical case history.

"I am presently a member of the armed forces of the United States," Bill Gaugush's first letter began.

"I am of German nationality and have not as yet applied for American citizenship; nor do I intend to."

"I am seriously contemplating requesting release from the service on the grounds that I am an alien. I am aware that by (doing this) I will be compelled to leave the country and relinquish the possibility of acquiring American citizenship in the future. I have considered this stipulation with utmost care and sincerity. However, I feel that truth, justice and freedom are more important than possessing a piece of paper declaring me a citizen of the United States of America."

Bill Gaugush had volunteered for the Marines in July 1968 and had no trouble at all until November 1969 when First Lieutenant Theodore Lee Carlson became the executive officer of his company.

After Lt. Carlson had been with MP headquarters a few weeks many of the enlisted men he commanded began to question the Lieutenant's qualities of leadership, according to Gaugush.

Gaugush specified the following in a letter to his Representative, Morris King Udall, of Arizona:

"As Lt. Carlson became more familiar with the company and its personnel, his attitude became increasingly harsh, biased, detrimental and derogatory towards individuals' emotional attributes and physical well being.... I personally know two individuals he has threatened to throw out the window while holding office hours on them; of one individual whom he has managed to throw out the door; of another (whom Carlson threatened) to "kick his ass"; and numerous other minor incidents ... Lt. Carlson has been known to require personnel to salute him while that particular individual has had his hands full or was on a working detail. The military does not require one to salute while on a working detail if it is reasonably obvious that he cannot salute without first emptying his hands.

"I have personally seen (Carlson) evaluate and judge an individual solely on his education.... Perhaps we should all obtain a business degree (such as) he possesses and seems mighty hung up on...."

On January 6, Bill Gaugush sat down and wrote a poem expressing his feelings about Lt. Carlson. It reads in part as follows:

"... we are humans and can only survive if our insatiable human rights are thoroughly and concretely preserved and advanced toward good will.... This is why we must and will judge you....

"A man? Most assuredly you are not.

"For what is a man, but one who is instilled with justice, truth, righteousness, and the ability to reason and understand his fellow man...."

Gaugush showed the poem to a friend in his company. The friend felt that the poem expressed his sentiments also, and the two decided to use the poem as a petition of sorts, with the stipulation that the poem would not be presented to Lt. Carlson unless at least 25 EM signed.

Gaugush stated that he went around the company and asked each man privately to state his opinion of Carlson. Only in the cases when the GI definitely had negative feelings about the Lieutenant did Gaugush offer the petition.

Twenty-four signatures had been collected by January

10 when Captain Byron L. Watson, Commanding Officer of the MP Company, and Staff Sergeant Thomas Milsapp cornered Gaugush in his barracks, informed him that he had a piece of paper with signatures concerning Lt. Carlson in his wall locker, and demanded that Gaugush hand it over. Gaugush complied.

Twenty-one of the 24 signers received two weeks restriction and/or loss of seven days pay. One individual had punishment suspended and another requested a court martial. Gaugush was forwarded to Batallion officer within hours with the recommendation that his rank be reduced to E-3, and he receive the maximum fine.

"(On February 9) I went to the MPCo Officer to talk to Capt. Watson...." Gaugush wrote: "As I started to leave, 1st Lt. Carlson came in the door and asked me what I was doing in his office. I explained, or tried to explain, that I came in to see the Captain and my friend (who works there).

"He told me to get out of the office. Well, I was leaving anyway. As I was walking toward the door he called me a 'turd' and began walking toward me in a threatening manner. I politely told him that I was not a 'turd.' At that point he grabbed me by the throat and commenced choking me while at the same time pushing me backwards out of the door."

In his letter to Representative Morris Udall, Gaugush commented the following:

"I am writing you only because I feel that I and 23 others are being unjustly punished.... It is my opinion that the officers within the command are trying to silence the incident and the individuals involved by use of fear and threats of severe repercussions so that Lt. Carlson's record might be kept 'clean.'

"Yes, so help me God I signed my enlistment contract because I believe I would attain the ability, the adroitness to understand, to comprehend, to perceive, and to experience a man's life.

"I did not sign to give up freedom of speech, liberty, and equality."

   Bill Gaugush is still awaiting a date to be set for his
court martial. He has a civilian lawyer from the offices of
Melvin Belli, and also a military lawyer whom he reports is
very interested and willing to help. One of the other signers
of the petition just received 30 days correctional custody,
which is being repealed.

(Collected from the UCLA Student Peace Union, March 27,
1970.   Mimeographed.)

107. DRAFT EXEMPTION THROUGH ORDINATION

Purchasing an ordination certificate from a transitory and ersatz religious group was one of the desperate ways to beat the draft. This technique was highly suspect and the editor knows of no exemption resulting. Below are ads from the Missionaries of the New Truth, the Church of the Universal Brotherhood, and the Padua Order offering ordination and possible draft exemption, for a price. The ads appeared in the February 13, 1970 issue of the Los Angeles Free Press:

A.   WE WANT YOU TO JOIN OUR FAITH AS AN

ORDAINED MINISTER

with a rank of

DOCTOR OF DIVINITY

AS REPORTED IN LIFE MAGAZINE

We are a fast growing faith, actively seeking new members who believe as we do that all men should seek the truth in their own way, by any means they deem right. As a minister of the faith you can:

1.   Set up your own church and apply for exemption from property and other taxes.
2.   Perform marriages and exercise all other ecclesiastic powers.
3.   Seek draft exemptions as one of our working missionaries. We can tell you how.
4.   Get sizeable cash grants for doing missionary work for us.
5.   Some transportation companies, hotels, theaters, etc., give ministers reduced rates.

GET THE WHOLE PACKAGE FOR $10.00

Your ordination is completely legal and valid anywhere in this country. Your money back without question if this packet isn't everything you expect it to be. Print your name the way you wish it to appear on your DOCTOR OF DIVINITY and ORDINATION CERTIFICATE.

SEND $10.00 TO: MISSIONARIES OF THE NEW TRUTH
                   P.O. Box 1393, Dept. A2,
                   Evanston, Illinois 60204

B.   YOU CAN BE DOCTOR AND REVEREND

The Number-One Titles In The World and Get

   * CAREER ENRICHMENT

   * PRESTIGE IN SOCIAL LIFE AND COUNSELING

   * FULL MINISTERIAL PRIVILEGES OF MARRYING,
     COUNSELING, VISITING THE IMPRISONED AND
     SICK.

   * POSSIBLE DRAFT EXEMPTION

You will receive in one package, your honorary degree as a D.D., legal in all states and territories, your certificate of ordination, your I.D. card, and complete information on getting maximum benefits from your new status, including how to start your own Church, plus a good Karma Surprise. Your money refunded if not delighted.

      Please type or print your own name exactly as you wish it to appear on your degree and your minister's certificate.

Send $12.50 to:
CHURCH OF UNIVERSAL BROTHERHOOD
6311 Yucca St., Dept. F.P., Hollywood, California
Please allow 3-4 weeks for delivery

FOR FREE INFORMATION SEND STAMPED, SELF-ADDRESSED ENVELOPE.

C.   BECOME AN ORDAINED MINISTER

      with a title of Dr. and Rev. in the Padua Order.

1. You receive lessons on how to marry, baptize, and per-
    form other sacraments.
2. Bible lessons with a diploma upon completion.
3. Receive immediately a Dr. of Divinity Degree.
4. Credentials, and Ministers Certificate.
5. Information on how to open your church, and receive
    certain funds.   How to get funds for non-profit projects
    and other information.

Your credentials are legal in any state.   Remember--to be
ordained without proper schooling is against church law.
You must know how to perform certain sacraments in case
of emergencies such as death, birth, etc.

Send $20.00 to:

ST. ANTHONY
BOX 36471
L.A., Calif. 90036
Information $1.00 applies to all

108. PLEDGE TO RESIST THE DRAFT

This is a Pledge, not a Petition--
Understand that Before You Sign.

My signature on this pledge means four things.

A. I feel that the present draft system in America is in violation of my constitutional rights and/or simply immoral.

B. I am nevertheless presently cooperating with the system and am liable to be inducted into the armed forces or some type of alternate service.

C. I pledge that, when a hundred thousand draftable men have signed pledges like this, I will return my draft card to my local or national resistance headquarters where it will be forwarded with the other returned cards to the proper authorities. I pledge that after that time I will cease to cooperate with any type of draft system in any way.

D. I recognize that I am in no way immune from Federal prosecution either for resisting the draft or conspiring to resist the draft.

Name..

Address at present ·······································

Permanent address.......................................

Please return to: 128 Chancellor St., Charlottesville, Va.
                   22903

(Collected at the University of Colorado at Boulder, July 17, 1968.)

109. UPTIGHT WITH THE MILITARY OR DRAFT?
    CALL THE RESISTANCE

PASADENA

The Peace House
724 N. Marengo Street
Phone 449-8228
Come over and rap anytime.

WHITTIER RESISTANCE

7201 S. Bright Street
Phone 698-9304
4:00 p.m.-9:00 p.m., Mon.-Fri.
Noon thru 6:00 Saturday

W.L.A. - PAPA BACH BOOKSTORE

11317 Santa Monica Boulevard
Phone 478-2374
Mon., Wed., Thurs. --7:30-10 p.m.

(Collected at the University of California at Los Angeles,
January 2, 1970. Mimeographed.)

110. THE ARMY IS REVOLTING

Andy Stapp

Thirty-eight soldiers are being held for court martial by the Army brass in the aftermath of the June 5 rebellion in the Fort Dix Stockade. With many of the men facing virtual life imprisonment, the importance of the case takes on Presidio-like proportions.

Ten of the thirty-eight have been singled out for especially severe charges. Terry Klug has been framed up with the heaviest indictments: Riot (ten years), inciting to Riot (six years), Conspiracy to Riot (ten years), Willful Damage of Government Property (six months) and Aggravated Arson (twenty years). Under Willful Damage of Government Property the charge reads that "Terry G. Klug did on or about 5 June 1969 destroy a footlocker of the value of $13.36." On the charge of Aggravated Arson the indictment reads that "on or about 5 June 1969 Terry G. Klug did set fire to Cell Block 67 of the value of $12,169."

Others selected for the heaviest charges are Bill Brakefield (Riot, Conspiracy to Riot, Inciting to Riot, and Aggravated Arson).

Thomas Catlow (Riot, Inciting to Riot, Conspiracy to Riot).

Donald Hill (Riot, and Inciting to Riot).

George Irrizzari (Riot and Inciting to Riot).

Jeffery Russell, whose wife is about to have a baby (Riot, Inciting to Riot, and Conspiracy to Riot).

Dennis Kirby (Riot and Inciting to Riot).

William Miller (Riot and Inciting to Riot).

Tom Tuck (Riot and Willful Damage of Government

488

Property). Tuck, who is Black and an organizer for the
American Servicemen's Union, received the full brunt of the
Brass' rage after the revolt. He was kept totally without
food for three days in an unsuccessful attempt to make him
"confess." During these three days he was often taken from
his segregation cell and paraded in leg irons in front of the
other prisoners as an "example." Of course, it is because
Tuck is an example to the other men that the Brass fear
him so much.

Politics of the Uprising

The May 20 issue of The Bond, the ASU (American
Servicemen's Union) newspaper, had been clandestinely circulated in the Dix Stockade shortly before the rebellion. Almost two hundred prisoners had a chance to read in it this
statement from Tuck. "I call upon all Afro-American servicemen to give support to oppressed people in the effort to
destroy U.S. Imperialism and to refuse by any means necessary to serve in these racist wars. The only way we can
really win is through total mass revolution."

Like Tuck, Brakefield and Klug are also ASU organizers. Both men were immediately hustled off after the uprising to maximum security cells under a Code 14 (very
sensitive person). Klug has already begun to serve a three
year sentence for desertion. He was convicted last April of
splitting from the 525 Military Intelligence Packet A in June,
1967, five days before it shipped to Vietnam. Klug spent a
year and a half in Europe doing anti-war work with GIs on
the bases. As he stated at the time, "My reasons for going
AWOL and remaining AWOL are not pacifistic. The U.S. is
fighting an illegal war. It is fighting a war of capital interest. It is killing and maiming the brave people of Vietnam
for the interest of Big Businessmen. The Vietnamese people
have been fighting against aggression in their country for
many hundreds of years. They will not lose this war!"

Gestapo Tactics

On July 9th Brakefield had his Article 32 hearing,
which is similar to a grand jury hearing. In a highly irregu-
lar maneuver the Ft. Dix Brass insisted that the Article 32
take place inside the stockade instead of at the Courts and
Boards Bldg. Brakefield was represented by Roland Watts

of the Workers Defense League at the request of the ASU.
At one point in this star chamber proceeding (no civilians
besides Watts were permitted to be present), the brass got
tripped up on its own Gestapo tactics. A GI prisoner on the
stand as a government witness against Brakefield was asked
by the prosecutor to acknowledge a statement he had signed
that said Brakefield had conspired to riot. "Is this really
my statement," the GI asked ingeniously, "when you consider
that the interrogators for the Criminal Investigation told me
that if I didn't sign it I would probably be in prison for quite
a few more years and if I did sign it I might be allowed to
have more food and a few movies and even get out soon?"
The Army prosecutor became flustered and quickly called the
next witness.

In a letter to the National Office of The American
Servicemen's Union, Colonel James C. Shoultz, the Pentagon's Acting Provost Marshal General, wrote that "Weekly in-
spection indicates that conditions at the Fort Dix Stockade
are far from intolerable." Brass-brained Shoultz apparently
never asked to see those inmates in the Wolson Army Hospital psyche ward who completely flipped out while being tortured in the straps in the Dix Stockade. When Major Casey
orders his flunkies to give a man a few hours in the straps
the prisoner's wrists are strapped to his ankles and he is
repeatedly dropped on his face until Casey has decided that
he has been properly punished for whatever infraction of the
stockade rules the man committed. Shoultz' letter continues.
"There was a show of force by military policemen, but there
was no physical contact between military policemen and prisoners. Nine prisoners were treated for minor cuts and
bruises sustained during the mass evacuation from the barracks. They were treated at the post hospital...." Shoultz
claims that there was no physical contact between guards and
prisoners during the riot, but that nine prisoners had to be
treated at the post hospital! It is obvious that the Brass is
prepared to pile lie upon lie to obscure what really happened
on the night of June 5th at the Ft. Dix Stockade.

But there are other voices telling the story of an uprising of men who were oppressed so hard they could not
stand voices from inside the stockade itself.

In a letter smuggled out three weeks after the rebellion, Terry Klug, facing 46 years in prison writes, "I think
one of the biggest factors in this case and a thing which will
decide whether we win or not is outside support. We need

a great amount of publicity and support or we're as good as
lost.   What I am working up to say is that we are going to
have to depend on your help.   We're going to have to put our
faith in the Union and the Union in turn will have to trust us.
It will have to know that under no circumstances will we
back down, make any agreements, or accept any bargains or
deals.   It's all I live for Andy; to fight.   That's my every
hope, my every desire, my every dream.   For me the revolution is all powerful, all great, all pure, all sacred. Hasta
la victoria siempre!"

(From the GI underground newspaper, The Bond, July, 1968
issue.)

111. LETTER FROM FORT DIX

Friends:

   To introduce myself, I shall only say that I am one of the prisoners that is being charged with involvement in events taking place in the Ft. Dix stockade on the 5th of June, 1969. I am referring, of course, to the riot that took place in cell blocks 66, 67, and 84. The military is trying its utmost to keep this happening out of the press and away from the eyes of the people by saying that what happened was only a "minor disturbance" and that they now have everything under control. The facts that I wish to present are that it was not a minor disturbance and the Machine does not now nor will it ever have us under their control. The riot itself proved that the conditions in the stockade were humanly unbearable. Riots do not happen because they are fun to be in; they happen because people, real people and sensitive people, react to inhuman and insensitive treatment. Therefore, I hold it to be the lawmakers themselves who are responsible for instigating this riot! If the Machine wishes to press charges, let them charge those who are truly guilty; the stockade officials themselves! In other words the Machine should clean its own house because it's filthy!

   I will not at this time attempt to fill in the blanks by elaborating on the riot itself--it could prove detrimental to our case. I wish only to use this opportunity to expose the Military for the illegalities that they have used against us since the riot, and ask for your support on this.

   So far as I know 8 prisoners are going to be tried by general court martial for their participation (?). Six of us will be facing general court martial for AGGRAVATED ARSON, DESTRUCTION OF GOVERNMENT PROPERTY, PARTICIPATING IN A RIOT and CONSPIRACY TO RIOT! These prisoners are Thomas Catlow, William Miller, Allen Farrell, Jeff Russell, Bill Brakefield and Terry Klug. They are facing 40 years and six months as a maximum penalty for the charges against them. (The other two will not be facing the conspiracy charge.) About 22 others will be court martialed

492

by special court--maximum penalty is 6 months confinement.

Those of us facing "trial" by general court are all in
maximum security cells now.   We are strong and our morale
is at its highest.   We CAN and WILL win!--with your help!
We need you, all of you, to stand up on the outside with those
of us standing tall on the inside.   We need the publicity and
strength you can give us.   We want to expose all of this!

After the first day of Investigation about 12 or 13 of
us were thrown into maximum security cells.   The first night
we were denied mattresses, blankets, sheets or pillows.   For
two days we were placed on DS (disciplinary restriction) and
were not allowed out to exercise, shave or shower, to smoke,
to read and our visitors were turned away at the gates that
Sunday.   Also we were not allowed to attend religious services.   But the main fault lies in the fact that for the first
two days we were openly refused the right to notify our lawyers, congressmen, senators or even President or loved ones.
After two days the Machine realized that we had a beautiful
case against them and quickly gave us privileged correspondence to our lawyers, etc., opening them up, reading them
and then returning them to us saying that they were not addressed properly or some such nonsense.   Those letters they
read were pertinent to our cases! Also they would hold up our
personal mail for periods often exceeding one week and then
return them to us with some off-the-wall excuse. They did this
because they wanted to keep the news off the streets--they
wanted to deny the public the truth!

Now, as I said, we are to be court-martialed.   Eight
of us are risking the possibility of spending the rest of our
lives in a military prison, while the Machine grows constantly
stronger and goes on to commit more and more illegalities
against the people.   We have put our foot down and raised our
hands in a clenched fist.   Will you stand with us against this?
Can we expect your help in writing letters of support to Senators, congressmen, the President and the Department of the
Army?   Will you spread the word for us so that the masses
will come to learn of these things?

The military is trying to rush this through and send
us off to Leavenworth as quickly as possible--there is not
much time left for us to act.   PLEASE DO YOUR THING
NOW!

In solidarity,

Terry G. Klug
RA16884493
Ft. Dix, N.J.

(Collected from the Young Socialist Alliance, Stanford University, August 11, 1969. Mimeographed.)

112. ESCAPING TO CANADA

Canada, the new Promised Land: for the growing legions of America's dispossessed young men of conscience this high sounding epigraph has the ring of truth about it. How long now has the procession been struggling northward. It seems a decade since their exodus began. In fact perhaps it's only been half that much time, and yet it could have easily been a score of years. The clear-eyed escapees are everywhere, scattered across vast Canada as if by a whirlwind. They come from all walks of life, all stations and situations. Some of the wealthy and influential upper class, some from the pain faced poor and a few long suffering swarthy ones are interwoven into the whole of the flesh fabric comprised mainly of omnipresent, common-and-durable-as-cotton middle class.

The reaction here in Canada seems generally to be favorable regarding her "draft-dodging" U.S. immigrants, as is evidenced in most Canadian mass media and, more important yet, official government policy. First and foremost is that little piece of paper: The Canadian Extradition Treaty. It's the golden key that opens the door to the "New Promised Land," and makes it the attractive citadel of safety and sanctuary that it is for war exiles. In this document there are listed 22 various crimes. Only if an American immigrant was accused or convicted of one or more of these offenses can he be forced to return to his country. Some of the crimes that warrant extradition from Canada in accord with the treaty between the two countries are murder, piracy, arson, robbery, forgery, voluntary manslaughter, counterfeiting, embezzlement, fraud, perjury and rape. The treaty does not recognize refusal of induction or desertion from the U.S. military establishment as criminal. So that there could be no mistaking the government's position on this vital issue, the following statement was issued in the summer of 1967 (a time when American Immigration was heavy) by none other than John Munro, secretary to the Minister of Immigration at that time.

"... compulsory military service in his own country

495

has no bearing upon his admissibility to Canada either as an immigrant or as a visitor; nor is he subject to removal from Canada because of unfulfilled military obligations in his country of citizenship."

What more could a prospective immigrant ask for than official approval and a generally favorable press? There is more, and true to form one only need ask, knock or inquire to receive information, job prospects, shelter, special assistance, et al. Across the nation, from Nova Scotia to British Columbia, groups of sympathetic citizens have rallied to meet the pressing needs of young anti-war refugees. In Ontario alone there are ten anti-conscription groups or contacts available. Below are the names, addresses, and phone numbers of the Ontario draft aid people.

> ---AID (Assistance with immigration and the Draft) 237-
>   3149/Box 2362, Ottawa 4.
> ---Southern Ontario Committee on War Immigrants, Box
>   155, Hamilton 15.
> ---Lakehead Committee to Aid American War Objectors,
>   344-8559/98 Peter St., Port Arthur.
> ---Miss C. Cartwright, 89 Clarence St., Kingston.
> ---Guelph Anti-Draft Programme, 35 Fairview Blvd.,
>   Guelph.
> ---Walter Klaasen, 745-4116/109 William St. W., Water-
>   loo.
> ---Information 68-69, 254-5520/Box 1233, Windsor.
> ---Glen Tenpenny, 432-4718/230 Platt's Lane, London.
> ---Union of American Exiles, 929-9433/44 St. George St.,
>   Toronto.
> ---Toronto Anti-Draft Programme, 481-0241/Box 41, Sta.
>   K, Toronto, 12.

The last of the groups listed, the Toronto Anti-Draft Programme, is the longest and best equipped in Canada. During the early fall of last year they were handling as many as 50 visitors per day. Besides furnishing information to persons about immigration, they also provide special services to U.S. immigrants who have recently arrived. Medical aid, shelter and job counseling are among the services offered. Free of any charge, of course. When one takes into consideration that the money-addicts of the American Empire, Unlimited, have usually-mild-mannered Canada by the economical balls, it becomes clear that her stand, and the stand of her many citizens in aiding and comforting those who refuse to act as "Cops of the World" for the Empire, is indeed a gutsy and honorable one.   Other faults aside, Canada is on terra firma when she stares down the bullying barrel of Yankee imperialism and shouts into it in such a fashion that the echo is heard 'round the world: No! No! No!!!!!!

Red Rover
Toronto

(Collected February 8, 1970.   Mimeographed.)

113. A SOCIALIST ANALYSIS OF THE NOVEMBER 15, 1969 MASS ANTI-WAR DEMONSTRATION

A million and a half? A million? Half a million?

Only one man in America probably has accurate estimates of the number of people who demonstrated in Washington and San Francisco Nov. 15 for immediate withdrawal of U.S. troops from Vietnam and he's not talking--presumably because he does not intend to be affected by the activities of such "noisy minorities."

The exact number (probably a million on both coasts) doesn't really matter. It is obvious the majority has spoken, louder and clearer than ever before. For every person who traveled many miles under difficult circumstances, experienced the cold winds of Washington and the rain of San Francisco, marched and then listened for hours to speeches condemning the war and to antiwar music, finally returning home again, exhausted, there were dozens, scores, who for one reason or another were unable to attend the massive demonstrations. Millions lived too far away to travel to the demonstration cities and many could not afford to travel. Many were too old or too young. Many were afraid of violence or reprisal. Many just let others do their protesting for them. Many differed with the "immediate withdrawal" demand but agreed on the basic idea of bringing U.S. troops home.

It was no "noisy minority," Vice President Spiro Agnew notwithstanding. And no President can remain unaffected, regardless of Richard Nixon's pretensions.

Nixon Exerts Pressure

Unaffected? In the week preceding the demonstrations the Nixon administration exerted more pressure than any administration in recent history to coerce the American people in an effort to diminish the size of the Nov. 15 protests. Beginning with Agnew's calculated remarks to smear the demonstrations; Nixon's Vietnam speech Nov. 3, intended to create a pro-war backlash which never materialized; Justice Department intransigence about granting permits in Washington, consciously seeking to raise the possibility of bloodshed in the capital; FBI harassment of bus companies; the sensationalization of the New York bombing cases; the Vice President's threats against the news media, which did to an extent reduce news coverage; Nixon's surprise visit to Congress -- all were aimed at minimizing the Nov. 15 turnout. And all failed.

Recognizing, from a radical point of view, that there were serious problems with each demonstration and that important political questions have been raised by the conduct of the New Mobilization Committee, the entire left must extend a comradely "well done" to the organizers of the Nov. 15 actions. Only the most sectarian forces will weigh these problems and questions against the fact of a million people demonstrating for immediate withdrawal from Vietnam and see the demonstrations as set-backs in comparison.

For the left, Nov. 15 was critically important in two big respects. First, for the impact the action will have on the American people and U.S. domestic politics and for the solidarity that was evidenced for the struggle of the Vietnamese people against U.S. imperialism. The contradictions in U.S. society can only have been increased by the protests. Second, for having provided a vehicle for tens and hundreds of thousands of people to make a transition to an immediate withdrawal position and for vastly increasing the identifiable reservoir of people who have made that political transition and who are now open to the possibility of radical persuasion and organization.

All of this does not mean, of course, that the problems and questions posed for the left by the Nov. 15 actions should be minimized or disregarded. They are extremely relevant for the future development of the movement. In the months to come before the next important mass demonstrations, the left must exert its full strength in the struggle to radicalize the politics of the antiwar movement.

Rightward Direction

The major political question raised by the Nov. 15 action is the rightward direction of the leadership of the antiwar coalition. The liberal Vietnam Moratorium Committee,

despite having hardly organized at all for the Nov. 15 demonstrations, gained a significant influence within the Mobilization Committee coalition in the days leading up to mid-
November. This was more covert than overt. The existence of the Moratorium Committee and the millions of people
who attended the Moratorium demonstration in October gave
considerable leverage to liberal elements within the Mobilization coalition and to the more conservative left wing elements
which traditionally seek the opportunity to minimize radical
politics to attract greater numbers. The end result of this
as far as today's antiwar movement is concerned could be a
truly massive liberal movement which would ultimately be
brought to exert a "progressive" influence safely within the
confines of the capitalist two-party system.

This ideology was expressed in many ways in Washington Nov. 15. The appearance by two liberal U.S. Senators and a liberal businessman on the speaker's platform
was, to say the least, unfortunate. These men have nothing
in common with what must become the ultimate goal of the
antiwar movement--the removal of U.S. troops and counter-
insurgency forces not only from Vietnam but from Thailand,
Laos, and all over the globe. Let them attend antiwar rallies, let them even support antiwar rallies, but to deliver
political statements as part of the apparent leadership of
these rallies and thus influence political direction of the
movement can only lead to the defeat of the movement. The
800,000 people who traveled to the capital did not do so because they wanted to hear Goodell and McGovern deliver
pompous sermons on their views of the Vietnam war. They
came to Washington because they wanted to end a war, not
to be patronized by liberal politicians on the make for votes.

A major error in Washington was the lack of attention
given the black liberation movement and the battle against
white supremacy. With very few and brief exceptions, the
black struggle was hardly mentioned. Among the speakers,
Phil Hutchings was the only one who could be said to represent the revolutionary forces within the black liberation
struggle. While this situation did not obtain in San Francisco it was glaringly apparent in Washington. The antiwar
movement must become aware that unless it is able to articulate the demands of the national minorities in the U.S. and
the oppressed peoples of the world it will never be able to
develop into an anti-imperialist movement, much less ever
attract substantial support from black and brown people in
the U.S.

Where People Were At

Of course the Washington rally gave the liberals a respectful hearing and of course everyone participated in a genuinely moving mass chorus of the prayerful lines, "Give peace a chance" and of course people responded to the chants of "peace now"--this was a reflection of where a lot of people were at. As well as mobilizing numbers for a peacefest, however, the task of the Nov. 15 action was to create an environment for moving these people one step closer to where they must be if we are to end the Vietnam aggression and prevent future imperialist wars. Fortunately, Dave Dellinger and a very few other speakers articulated a clear antiimperialist politics, but this was not at all the general tone.

A major omission in Washington on Nov. 15 was the absence of relevant literature distributed by the Mobe. The committee's special four-page Nov. 15 newspaper contained a map and schedules--no politics. Although the Mobe issued some press statement demanding immediate withdrawal of troops, this demand and the eight other secondary demands were submerged during the march and rally. Just two days before the rally Stewart Meacham and Cora Weiss, two cochairmen of the Mobe, sent a letter to President Nixon in behalf of the committee requesting a meeting with the President to discuss their "demands for the announcement and initiation of swiftly phased withdrawal" from Vietnam. Nixon declined the request, although he might have been intrigued by the apparent change in the leadership line from immediate withdrawal to "swiftly phased withdrawal."

The several thousand Mobilization committee marshals who lined the parade route and kept order at the rally were occasionally overzealous in their duty. In future mass demonstrations movement marshals should be confined to directing traffic and giving assistance, not to acting as surrogate cops.

The Source of Violence Forgotten

The extraordinary precautions against violence and illegality taken by the Mobilization Committee must be criticized--but in a particular way. No responsible radical sought violence at the Washington protest and illegal actions, on this particular day, only tended to detract from the broader

demonstration (though on a comparative scale of values we
fail to understand how illegal actions and confrontations staged
by a relative handful of demonstrators could equal in terms
of political error the inclusion of brothers Goodell and Mc-
Govern on the platform).   The point is that by incessantly
projecting the Washington gathering to the public and press as
"nonviolent and legal," the Mobilization Committee ultimately
came to project its politics, rather than its tactics, as those
of nonviolence and legality.   What was lost in the rhetoric
was a perspective on the real source of "violence and illegality"--an imperialist ruling class.   This renewed stress on
nonviolence--as a philosophy--is part of the coalition's rightward drift.

Those who purposefully sought a violent confrontation
with police in Washington and those who seem to measure
their revolutionary fervor by the diameter of the holes they
can produce in a plate glass window must also be criticized.
They ended up providing a very uptight news media with an
opportunity to prove to Spiro Agnew that it is as patriotic as
ever.   No one was organized to our side.   As soon as night
fell they were spoiling for the chance to play with their gas
bombs and try out their new anti-riot techniques.   Unfortunately,
the zeal of a few militants to experience a confrontation dove-
tailed too well with the desire of the police to do the same--
and what could have been a militant and consciousness-lifting
demonstration at the Justice Department to protest the Conspiracy trial merely ended up in a lot of people getting
gassed and tremendous confusion.   The press took note.

The Future

The question, of course, is what now?   These are
just some of the lessons the movement should learn from Nov.
15 and some of the points which must be interjected in future
debates about mass actions.

What is the movement going to do with the million
people who showed up Nov. 15?   How is Nixon going to respond?   What is the role of the radical left?

The situation appears this way: Ever greater numbers of people are coming over to the immediate withdrawal
side.   The Mobilization Committee, which reflects the total-
ity of its constituent organizations, is displaying a tendency
to drift to the right.   The radical left is in confusion.   The

Nixon administration is toying with the dual tactic of co-optation and outright repression.   The movement could grow or
be co-opted or split into impotence.

We believe the antiwar movement will continue to
grow.   But an intelligent left--one capable of dealing both
with the mindless tactical militancy of the ultraleft and the
liberal accommodations of the conservative left--is essential
to this process.

One of the most important benefits of Nov. 15 was
that a great many people have moved further to the left.   A
considerable number of these people probably took their first
step against the Vietnam war during the Oct. 15 Moratorium.
We must insure that their next step is left, as well.   People
are becoming politicized much faster these days as the contradiction over the war continues to sharpen.

It is necessary for the left at this point to play a
conscious anti-imperialist role in the antiwar movement, inside the coalition and outside, to halt the rightward drift and
fight against co-optation and splits caused by Nixon administration repression.   It must recognize the opportunities for
radicalizing those newly involved in the antiwar movement by
mounting campaigns--such as one to free The Conspiracy or
to support and build the GI movement or to demonstrate
against corporations which profit from war--which transcend
elementary "peace now" demands and begin to dig into the
oppressive inner heart of the capitalist system.

(Collected from Young Socialist Alliance, UCLA, December
14, 1969.   Mimeographed.)

114. SPEECH BY RENNIE DAVIS AT NOVEMBER 15, 1969 SAN FRANCISCO PEACE RALLY

<u>Editor's Note:</u>

The following is the text of a speech delivered by Rennie Davis, a New Mobilization Committee leader and member of The Conspiracy, tried in Chicago as an aftermath of the disruption of the 1968 Democratic National Convention. At the time of the speech, Davis had recently returned home from a visit to North Vietnam where he had participated in discussions with the Provisional Revolutionary Government (PRG).

Speech

I want Spiro Agnew to know that I bring this assembly a message of greetings and solidarity to the American people from the "Vietcong" (NLF).

I want Agnew to know that this generation is establishing its own diplomatic relations, because we are not at war with the people of Vietnam or Korea or China or Cuba. Our war is with the Pentagon, Wall Street and Spiro T. Agnew.

I have another message from one of the most exciting and courageous young men I know, Bobby G. Seale.

After Bobby had been chained and gagged for trying to simply defend himself and his Constitutional rights, after he had been beaten literally in the chest and the testicles in the courtroom, after the spectacle of a black man chained and gagged in an American court became too much for their public relations and they had to sever him from the case and sentence him to four years for the crime of defending his Constitutional rights. Bobby Seale said what I think should be said here today. Bobby said to us, "They can hang me upside down for the rest of my life, they can railroad us to prison for 10 years, they can strap me in the

504

electric chair, but this damn Conspiracy is so beautiful that
as fucked-up as we defendants are, this Conspiracy is going
to tear this capitalism down and set us free!"

Bobby Seale showed the nation that this trial is no
joke, that judge Hoffman is no joke and that what is at stake
here is far more than eight individuals who have been singled
out for trying to do at the Democratic convention what we are
doing here today.   What is at stake here is a strategy, a
strategy that was hatched the first six months of the Nixon
administration, a strategy that is being carried out by a Justice Department that has been taken over by a band of reactionary, defeated politicians, who call us ideological criminals and say we should be rounded up and put in detention
camps.

When the jury goes out in Chicago, Nixon will be undertaking a vicious plan to win in Vietnam coupled with a
new fascism at home--and I think that if we leave here with
anything, it must be with an understanding of this two-part
Nixon scheme and how we are going to smash it.

Nixon plans not "Vietnamization."   Nixon plans to win
in Vietnam.   First by escalating the air war, by using weapons that were in the experimental stage in 1967, like magnesium, incendiary weapons, thermite, napalm, cluster bomb
units--using them on a mass scale in 1970.   Second by withdrawing enough troops to deflate antiwar sentiments at home,
while fortifying the East Coast and the major cities like Hue
and Saigon and from this position of fortification carry out
the raging air war against the countryside that most students
of Vietnam now understand is controlled some 80% by the
National Liberation Front.

Finally, Nixon's plan calls for turning up all the
burners of domestic repression.   Crucial to the Nixon scheme,
in my judgment, is time.   Nixon knows that this plan will
succeed or fail depending on his ability to turn back the opposition around the world in the next 12 months.

But what Nixon does not know is that his time has
run out--the Vietnamese are going to defeat his plan in Vietnam just as we are going to defeat it here in the United
States.

Nixon does not know what I am about to say, and listen to this: The debate that is going on in the Central Com-

mittee of the National Liberation Front today over how to
achieve self-determination in Vietnam is a debate between a
strategy that uses the diplomatic front in Paris coupled with
a military strategy that accents American casualties in South
Vietnam versus—I repeat versus—a strategy of the general
uprising, a strategy that will give the American imperialists
their Dien Bien Phu. Anyone who does not understand that
the "Vietcong" are not out of breath is out of touch with the
reality of Vietnam today and is making the same mistake as
the French made in the 1950s.

Pham Van Dong, the premier of North Vietnam, told
me that August of 1970 will see the fiercest fighting of the
war and I tell you after having traveled from Hanoi to the
DMZ that Vietnam is a nation that is mobilizing. Every
young person, old person, man, woman in Vietnam is mobilizing today around the last public appeal of President Ho Chi
Minh for total victory.... This decade will not end in the
defeat of Vietnam as Nixon believes, but rather Vietnam is
going to give this country the most profound political lesson
of the 20th century: that against the B-52s, the F-105s,
against the thermite and the magnesium, against the most advanced military force in world history, against all of this
and more, ordinary people can win.

And if the people of Vietnam are about to give the
U.S. imperialists their first military defeat in history, can
we do less than compel the Nixon outlaws to stop this war
and give the American people their greatest victory in decades?

I think now that we must, as has been said again and
again from this stage, talk about the next steps. It is obvious that these monthly demonstrations that have brought millions of people into the street must continue. But I think
now that it has to be said that they must continue with a new
militancy. A militancy that brings the mutiny that was
started by Company A in Vietnam into every factory and every schoolhouse and every Army base in this land. I think
the next concerted campaign has got to begin to support
American GIs who are organizing against this war. Because
when GIs and freaks, short hairs and long hairs, unite
against imperialism, Richard Nixon better turn himself into
an astronaut if he wants to find a safe place to travel.

(Received from the New Mobilization Committee, Nov. 27,
1969. Mimeographed.)

115. BUILDING THE WHITE MOTHER COUNTRY
ANTI-IMPERIALIST MOVEMENT

National actions against the war have played a tremendous part in building the revolutionary movement in this
country and in aiding the struggles of oppressed peoples
throughout the world. They have helped concentrate our numbers and strength and thus allowed us a level of militancy
impossible in local areas. They have enabled us to smash
through the liberal web of words, polite protest and impotence that passed for dissent in this country in the fifties and
well into the sixties. They have focussed the attention of the
world on the resistance in the United States, thus giving freedom fighters in other lands encouragement and a sense of
world-wide solidarity. (Remember how we were all jolted
by the Vietnamese take-over of the American Embassy in
Saigon; by the TV pictures of scores of thousands of Ger-
mans converging on Berlin, marching rows upon rows, chant-
ing Ho, Ho, Ho Chi Minh, and then taking on the German
pigs; by the Watts, Newark and Detroit uprisings--the pictures of battlefields right here in the Motherland; by the
French uprisings last May; and by the Columbia uprising
last year.) From the Pentagon and Oakland Induction Center
demonstrations in the fall, 1967, to the battle of Chicago
last summer, we had that kind of electric effect in Vietnam,
Latin America, Cuba, and western Europe. A few pictures
demonstrated, as no number of articles, reports, or
speeches could have, that a movement was growing in the
United States and that it was becoming increasingly serious
and increasingly identified with the struggles of oppressed
peoples in other lands.

Here in the United States those demonstrations set the
terms for the struggle and gave the movement a push forward in gutsiness and in the targets it chose to attack. Remember the Pentagon, and the nearly simultaneous west
coast Oakland Induction Center demonstrations in October '67.

Two and a half years before, in the spring, 1965, a
young student-based, mainly-from-elite-schools organization,
the Students for a Democratic Society, sponsored a march

507

on Washington against the war. The White House sent out
coffee. The mood of the march was anger at the war, but
was contained, channeled and polite. It rested upon the assumption that the government "should" not commit aggression and atrocities rather than upon the assumption that this
government must use its armed might against the people of
the world. The vast majority of people want US occupying
troops out of their countries. Teach-ins, petitions, and
scattered draft refusals characterized the anti-war movement
up until 1967. And, there were the annual or semi-annual
Easter and fall marches. We called for negotiations and believed if only our leaders would hear us and our reasoned
arguments, peace and justice could be achieved for South
Vietnam.

Slowly the lessons of Johnson's campaign lies not to
escalate the war, the Invasion of the Dominican Republic;
the bombing of North Vietnam; the massive escalation of the
war against South Vietnam; the secret wars in Laos and
Thailand, convinced us that we must move past liberal protest in our conceptions and our actions, and confused the
liberal professors who had worked so hard to reason with
the US government. In the spring, 1967 large peace marches
were held in New York--beginning in Central Park and ending at the UN--and in San Francisco--winding through Hippie-
land and ending up in Kezar Stadium. A few nuts announced
that they intended to burn their draft cards before or during
the march in New York. The big guns had a shit fit. Phone
calls, panicked mid-night visits, and other means were used
to try to prevent these "illegal" acts from marring the giant
march. Well, in Central Park the cards were burned in the
midst of a Be-In before the march, the idea caught on, and
by the next day they were all heroes in the peace establishment. We made a cautious step toward symbolic attacks on
the government and slowly made our break with it in our
minds. Thousands marched through the streets of New York
and for the first time, as the peace marchers were attacked
by the lumpen right and pig provocateurs, black kids--who
were also something new on a peace march--waded in and
smashed the mother-fuckers. Martin Luther King, who had
finally come out against the war a few days earlier, spoke,
and so did Stokely who said in response to the moderate cry
for "Negotiations"--there were none in those days before the
Tet Offensive--"when you are being raped you don't call for
negotiations but for immediate withdrawal."

Stokeley's remarks and King's very brief appearance

underscored the tension between those who wanted to fight against the government.

After the march in San Francisco, ministers, professors, and trade union leaders addressed the scores of young people. There were two demonstrations -- one for the demonstrators and one for the outside world. The platform contingent provided the image for the outside world. While there were ministers on the stage, there were few if any church people in the crowd; trade union leaders but few trade unionists; professors but few academics. For young people on the marches in New York and San Francisco, the energy and exhilaration of being part of a strong and vital mass was a powerful experience which helped us to overcome our feelings of isolation and impotence.

Arguments couldn't show why this was wrong but history did. For the fall action, Bay Area activist Jerry Rubin flew in to join the Mobilization Committee as Project Director--up until then the staff had been dominated by the rather more restrained SCLC members (Martin Luther King's outfit)--and join the old time march leader Dave Dellinger. In Berkeley massive events had long provided the focus for political activity: the Free Speech Movement in 1964 and the Vietnam Day Committee stand-off against the Oakland pigs are just examples--and the infusion of militant west coast extravaganza mixed with peace movement organization led to the Pentagon.

The slogans, targets, and militancy were almost totally new. We moved from individual acts of moral protest -- the spring before, draft card burning had been considered the very limit of the movement--to massive attacks on the centers of the military power in this country. The Pentagon and the vast Oakland Induction Center were real; in Oakland, the slogan changed from "Hell No! - We Won't Go" to "HELL NO, NOBODY GOES." We had begun to realize that to stop the war we had to stop the United States government. In Oakland the movement controlled the streets for a few exhilarating days.

Thousands saw in the demonstration the growth of a movement they wanted to join. The demonstration enabled us to overcome our limited means for propaganda and our restricted access to new audiences. It reached out to millions where our organizing in the past could only reach thousands. We used the media and the potential of technology for our

ends. We had, in fact, overcome localism, provincialism,
and the tendency for "sewer socialism" (the term for those
in the era of Socialist organizing before the First World War
who wanted to concentrate on local issues, prove that socialists could deliver street lights faster than the bosses could,
and to build socialism in one city).

   The demonstrations had a double effect: 1) they created a culture of resistance in which GI's revolted, white
working class gangs turned political, and hippies, sensing the
end of the love trip, acted as shock troops in street actions;
and 2) they projected a seriousness and strength of the movement which made many on campuses see that there was more
to this thing than just a few white college missionaries in
their neighborhood. The irony, of course, is that local projects have come and gone, but now youth across the country
are organizing themselves in response to what's happening
and a part of what is happening is that a fighting movement
has come to dominate the news in a dramatic way.

   The Pentagon and Oakland also began to lay the basis
for a new way of looking at organizing. We had often talked
of the "decisions that affect our lives," and somehow had all
too often become bogged down in bread and butter issues.
Now our action began to change some people's minds in the
direction that the real issues that affected the people were
not the most narrow and seemingly immediate ones but were
in fact the large social, political, and moral ones--issues of
militarism, racism, hunger, and imperialism. In the days
of a growing war demanding more and more young men; of a
gold crisis threatening to bring down the American Empire;
of assassinations of liberal leaders; of increasing police control of our communities, the problems of stop lights in the
community and questions of in loco parentis on campus did
not grip people in the manner organizers had assumed they
would. Ideologically, we began to grasp the idea that the
system as a whole was the enemy; tactically, we began to try
to attack the system as a whole organism. We gradually
abandoned the notion that if we fought and fought for reforms,
we might succeed in reforming the system away or that consciousness would somehow arise out of enough local fights so
eventually the local rent strike group would spring into action
as a guerrilla force.

   Nevertheless, the old way of viewing organizing held
on. SDS failed to endorse the Pentagon action until the very
last moment when the government failed to give the Mobiliza-

tion Committee permits and then it endorsed the action in a
hedged manner. Nine months later, at almost the last minute, SDS endorsed the Chicago action in a limited fashion after much debate.

Last, but not least, militant actions affected the liberals. 1967-68 was their year to end their war. After the
Pentagon action, Allard Lowenstein scurried around the country a little faster looking for a legitimate liberal to de-fuse
the growing movement. The Pentagon action convinced Eugene McCarthy that he must enter the race for the Democratic Party nomination for president in order to move the
protest from the streets back to electoral politics. On one
hand, 1967-68 witnessed the "clean for Gene" kids all over
New Hampshire and Wisconsin; Senator Fulbright's hearings
on TV attacking Johnson's war and vainly trying to stem the
war tide; and finally on April Fool's eve, LBJ dropped out
and halted the regular bombing of North Vietnam.

On the other hand, after the Pentagon, came the Hilton Foreign Policy Association demonstration in New York,
the Dow demonstrations on campuses throughout the country,
and finally Columbia. Columbia transferred to a single
campus the ideas of the Pentagon: Bring the War Home and
hit where it hurts. We had moved from individual attacks
on the centers of power, attacks on the home ground of the
war machine. Columbia drew in those whom we hadn't seen
since the Pentagon. The action and the realness of the attempt to close down the universities convinced many to join
us.

The year which began in Washington ended in and
around the Hilton Hotel in Chicago. McCarthy entered the
city the hero of thousands of youth and left a forgotten dream.
McCarthy entered the race to take us out of the streets and
back into electoral politics; McCarthy pushed his own kids into the streets and to dramatically illustrate to the country
the bankruptcy of the "legitimate" way of affecting government decisions, Daley had McCarthy campaign workers beaten
in their hotel room.

The Pentagon to Chicago: a year of ascending militancy and power for the movement in the United States.
Those two events mark the conception and birth of a white
mother country anti-imperialist movement. A movement conceived in battle and willing to die in battle. In the next year,
the example and the experience of those events spread across

the country.   Revolts in colleges, neighborhoods, and high schools spread throughout the land.   Radio reports gave battle reports like baseball scores: hundreds of thousands of black and brown high school students in the streets; San Francisco State College draws on community support; riots in Berkeley, Madison, and Ann Arbor ... on it went.

This fall, on hundreds of campuses throughout the country many times more students will show up in the first weeks of school, looking for a more real way of fighting than the local organizations know how to use.   Chicago 1969 is the focus.   In thousands of high schools and street scenes throughout the country that movement organizers have never reached, stone revolutionaries are itching to get into the fray, yet searching for a way.   Chicago is the way.   Come with your friends, run with your friends, learn with your friends.

People in small-town Ohio, in West Virginia, in industrial towns and rural towns throughout America have come to hate those who have taken their sons and sent them back in flag-draped wooden boxes, as the promises of the Kennedy brothers turn sour in their hungry children's bellies --they have come to hate imperialism and to say: Avenge our sons; Vengeance to the Mass Murderers. Enough Already.

The focus for the hate and anger of those skrewed over, the center for those relatively isolated from the movement will be a massive street demonstration in Chicago on October 11th.   It will coincide with the "conspiracy" trial and show support by continuing the fight around the issues that caused the indictments.

The war continues.   Occupation troops remain in the Third World, black and brown communities and our schools. Only our united actions can pull out all of the occupation troops and free all political prisoners.

Chicago sets the terms for the action in the coming year.   History waits in Chicago.   If you missed Harper's Ferry, the Alamo, the Seattle General Strike, or Dien Bien Phu, don't let it pass you by again.   Scores of thousands of Americans have said, "Enough!" and have started to move forward!   Join Us.

(Collected from UC Students Against the War, University of Chicago, July 22, 1969.   Mimeographed.)

116. SAFE RETURN
AMNESTY COMMITTEE

A Message from Daniel Ellsberg:

The recent disclosure of portions of the White House transcripts reveal what many of us have known for some time; that Richard Nixon went to extraordinary lengths to shield himself and his associates from prosecution for their offenses against our Constitution. Yet, for tens of thousands of young men who resisted the Indochina war, he hasn't shown one ounce of compassion nor understanding. Last year, he said: "those who deserted must pay their price ... a criminal penalty for disobeying the law."

I know from my own experience and that of others, that the decision to resist further participation in the Indochina war often followed a long and painful period of deliberation on the obligation of an American citizen to refuse collaboration in a war conceived and carried out in violation of both U.S. and International law. The decision to resist has been a costly one for thousands of young Americans. They've been jailed in federal prisons, forced to live underground or in exile and denied jobs and veterans' benefits. Today, there are literally hundreds of thousands of draft resisters, military deserters and Vietnam era vets with "bad" discharges, whose futures depend significantly on our ability to win a just amnesty.

While our country grapples with the legacy of Watergate lawlessness and the complicity of our highest leaders, few acts would do more to right past wrongs than the declaration of a universal, unconditional amnesty for all war resisters. Such an amnesty, of course, will not be easily obtained. President Nixon and his allies have millions of our tax dollars at their disposal to combat the movement for amnesty. SAFE RETURN, the organization in the forefront of the drive for universal amnesty, has only your support on which to rely in this difficult fight. It's essential that they intensify efforts in the coming months.

SAFE RETURN needs your support now. It's crucial that you contribute as generously as you can; the futures of nearly one million young men depend on it. Please return the enclosed envelope with your contribution to SAFE RETURN today.

Yours truly,

Daniel Ellsberg

A Word About Safe Return

We're a national committee with the objective of winning a universal, no-strings amnesty for all categories of war resisters. We've developed several different strategies for advancing this campaign.

SAFE RETURN recently launched Campaign '74, a national program to insure that the question of amnesty is a central issue in every Congressional race this year. Local committees will poll all candidates--regardless of party affiliation--as to their position on amnesty. In many districts, discussion and debate with the candidate will be an important part of the polling process. SAFE RETURN will supply educational materials on amnesty to be used locally. Where candidates are reluctant to declare their position on amnesty, we will publicize this fact. When a candidate declares his or her support for universal amnesty, the local Campaign '74 committee will attempt to publicize that position as broadly as possible. This should generate pressure on the competing candidates to speak out and to further educate the electorate on the issue.

On the legislative front, we've organized two Ad Hoc Congressional Hearings for Unconditional Amnesty in the last year. A panel of lawmakers, chaired by Congresswoman Bella Abzug, heard testimony from family members of resisters. The families spoke to the human cost of resistance, and their sons and brothers' need for a just amnesty. At the second session, co-chaired by Congressman John Conyers, Vietnam veterans who had received "bad discharges" as a result of their opposition to the war and racist conditions in the military were heard. SAFE RETURN representatives testified at the Katenmeier Committee's hearings in March, 1974. We also provide a regular distribution of amnesty materials to all members of Congress and assist family members to lobby with their individual Congressmen.

SAFE RETURN has sponsored the public surrender of five Vietnam veterans who have refused further military service out of opposition to the Vietnam war. All had lived for several years either underground or in exile. Most recently, Lewis Simon and Edward McNally returned to military control after their dramatic appearance at a SAFE RETURN homecoming reception. We waged a vigorous defense campaign for them based on their duty to refuse to execute criminal military policies in Indochina, and we will continue to advise resisters who decide to return to military control.

We also provide speakers for public events and debates; publish materials relevant to amnesty; and act as a clearinghouse for people seeking suggestions and ideas on implementing local amnesty work.

FORA, Families of Resisters for Amnesty, has been organized with the aid of SAFE RETURN. Several thousand families are already conducting petitioning and letter writing campaigns, distributing resister bracelets, and in some communities, working on local electoral referendums on amnesty.

(Received by the compiler June 22, 1974.)

117. APPLICATION FOR MEMBERSHIP:
     AMNESTY INTERNATIONAL OF THE U.S.A.

Please enroll me in Amnesty International.   My membership
dues/contribution, in the amount I have indicated below, is
enclosed.

Contributions to A.I.U.S.A. are tax deductible.
I would like to contribute (check one):

____$1,000   ____$500   ____$100   ____$50

____$25   ____$15   Other _____

              Gary L Heath
              806 W Locust
              Bloomington Il   61701

Please enclose this form with your contribution.

_____

KEEP THIS STUB FOR YOUR RECORDS

AMNESTY INTERNATIONAL
of the U.S.A.

200 West 72nd Street
New York, New York 10023

Contributions to A.I.U.S.A. are tax deductible.

Date _____

Amount _____

Check No. _____

_____

AMNESTY INTERNATIONAL
of the U.S.A.

200 West 72nd Street
New York, New York 10023

West Coast Office
1590 Union Street
San Francisco, California 94123

West Coast Coordinator:
Ginetta Sagan

EXECUTIVE DIRECTOR
Dr. Amelia Augustus

HONORARY CHAIRMEN
Victor Reuther
Judge Francis Rivers
Michael Straight

BOARD OF DIRECTORS
Chairman:
Prof. Ivan Morris

Vice-Chairman:
Arthur Michaelson

Treasurer:
Arnold Price

General-Secretary:
Prof. Arthur Danto

Roger Baldwin
Mark K. Benenson
Nelson Bengston
Theodore Bikel
Prof. Zbigniew Brzezninski
Ramsey Clark
Maurice Goldbloom
Frances Grant
Dr. Hanna Grunwald
Prof. James Harrison
Sheldon Lipson
Prof. Stanley Plastrik
Millard Pryor
Ginetta Sagan
Norman Schorr
Robert Schwarz
Rose Styron
Melvin Wolf

NATIONAL ADVISORY COUNCIL
Philip W. Amram
Joan Baez
Prof. Daniel Bell
Charles Benenson
William Buckley
David Carliner
Rep. Don Edwards
Prof. Richard A. Falk
Jules Feiffer
Stephen Goldman
Prof. Gidon Gottlieb
Sanford Gottlieb
Rep. Michael J. Harrington
Nat Hentoff
Dr. Prynce Hopkins
George M. Houser
Sen. Jacob Javits
Max M. Kampelman
Sally Hellyer Lilienthal
Edward Mosk
James Nabritt III
Guy Nunn
Dr. Jan Papanek
Nathan Perlmutter
Richard D. Perry
Rex Stout
William S. Thompson
Marietta Tree
A. Buel Trowbridge
William L. White
June A. Willenz

INTERNATIONAL ASSOCIATES
Daniello Dolci
Prof. Eric Fromm
Sir Brian Horrocks

INT'L ASSOCIATES (cont.)
Jean-Flavien Lalive
Salvador de Madariaga
Yehudi Menuhin
Gunnar Myrdal
Dr. Martin Nemoller
Alan Paton
Sean MacBride
Giorgio La Pira
Archbishop Arthur Ramsey
Prof. Julius Stone

(Received by the compiler June 19, 1974.)

118. AMNESTY INTERNATIONAL OF THE U.S.A.

200 West 72nd St.   West Coast Office
New York, New York 10023   1590 Union Street
                              San Francisco, California 94123

Dear Friend:

First I would like you to know that your brother died
as well as could be expected.

I don't think they wanted him to die just yet, but they
were frustrated by his refusal to recant. One of the guards
told me that the commandant lost his temper and that when
your brother went into convulsions the commandant laughed
and said it was an excellent dance.

Your brother asked me to tell you that he hoped you
would understand that he had not broken as yet--but that if
he did you would know that it was because of what they were
doing to him. So please if you hear of a "confession"--even
if they have it taped--don't pay any attention. They can get
you to say anything.

Your brother believed that freedom of conscience is
the fundamental freedom. I am truly sorry that he is dead
but feel sure you are proud of your brother. He was a good
man.

                    *   *   *

Dear Friend:

It is up to you whether or not you wish to actually acknowledge kinship with the "brother" described above.

The deceased was a "prisoner of conscience" who disagreed with the methods of a regime and had the audacity to
say so. Prison, torture and death resulted. He did not
commit or advocate a violent act. But his life was forfeited
because he refused to deny his conscience.

519

The question is whether the decedent was "your brother." It would seem that the family of man owes much to gentle heroes. But it is one thing to acknowledge such kinship in history and altogether another to step forward and say, "I am his brother" today.

If you do recognize such a kinship, then you should know that tens of thousands of men and women are suffering imprisonment, torture and death as you read this. Their "crime"? They do not agree with a regime.

You should also know that no matter where these people are imprisoned--even in the deepest pit of the most remote chamber of horrors--there is a way you can help them regain their freedom.

And by you--I mean you.

Amnesty International was formed by a group of lawyers in London in 1961. It espouses no political philosophy and supports no particular government.

Amnesty International keeps out of politics for obvious reasons. Because we are without bias we can help the prisoners of conscience. In fact we investigate each case meticulously before we decide whether or not we can aid a person, because we must retain our credibility for fairness and impartiality before the world.

We are a relatively small organization--and probably always will be until enough people care about prisoners of conscience.

We were started by lawyers--but we have been sustained by all kinds of people from literally all over the world: housewives, students, ministers, businessmen, laborers, men and women of the cloth, journalists, bankers, farmers and teachers. We have members from some sixty countries and incredibly in our twelve years of existence we have actually succeeded in getting over 10,000 prisoners of conscience released!

I will tell you how we do it in a moment--it is quite interesting I think--but first, if I may, I would like to offer you a personal interpretation of the cold hard fact that we have opened the doors for over 10,000 men and women whose only "crime" was their refusal to turn their backs on their consciences.

In 1945 I was arrested along with a young physician by the Nazis. We disagreed with the regime so we were tortured. My companion died under the torture but I escaped.

I escaped from a place where the walls were splattered with human flesh and blood. Where the torturers amused themselves by seeing who could elicit the loudest screams. Can you imagine my joy at being free from such a place? It was like escaping from hell.

The only reason I have mentioned my story is to try to put some real meaning into the statement, "We have freed over 10,000 men and women." I know what I am talking about. And right now there are thousands of men and women still locked up, still being tortured and still dying because they have not knuckled under. Here is how Amnesty International is helping them:

> Amnesty International's mission is to seek out and secure freedom (or improved conditions of imprisonment) for the world's 'prisoners of conscience'-- individuals imprisoned for their political beliefs, religion, race or ethnic background who have not used or advocated violence.

Amnesty International has been granted consultative status with the United Nations, the Council of Europe, UNESCO, the Organization of American States, the Interamerican Commission of Human Rights and the Organization of African Unity. This status gives us the right to petition these organizations and to have our observers attend conferences and debates. It means, too, that we have direct access for making our views known. Amnesty International representatives on official missions are generally accorded treatment comparable to that accorded UN officials.

Amnesty International's reputation for reliability is such that the United Nations Organization and individual nations turn to us for authoritative information on mass arrests, trials and imprisonment in situations such as the crisis in Chile. We have devised ways for our network of informants to penetrate even the most closely knit veils of secrecy.

Almost all member states of the UN have agreed to observe and abide by the principles set forth in the Universal

Declaration of Human Rights. And yet, hundreds of thousands of prisoners of conscience are interned today by these same countries. Indeed, virtually every country which signed the Universal Declaration of Human Rights is--or has been--guilty of profound violations of human rights.

Many of the prisoners were never tried or were tried under laws and by means of legal processes that mock justice and mock even the most rudimentary concepts of human rights. Many have never been told why they are in prison. Many are forbidden any contact with the outside. Many have no idea of when, if ever, they will be released, because they have indeterminate sentences or never actually were sentenced at all.

The conditions under which many are held range from abominable to ghastly. Many prisoners of conscience are underfed, undernourished and diseased. Many live in constant fear that they will be executed; many others live in constant fear that they won't be, that they will survive to be tortured again.

It is remarkable, I suppose, that an organization armed with nothing more than moral authority and the consciences and energies of its members actually has been effective in the age-old struggle against tyranny and oppression. But Amnesty International does get results. Not always, but a good portion of the time.

From correspondents and observers throughout the world, we learn of prisoners of conscience. Depending on the government involved and the circumstances of the prisoner's case, members may write to the prisoner, to his family or friends, to the officials in charge at his prison, to the news media in his or other countries, even to the head of state or other government leaders. Meanwhile, the International Secretariat protests through diplomatic channels, including the appropriate international bodies. "Embarrassment" works wonders, especially on torturers who pretend they are something else.

Amnesty International consists entirely of concerned private citizens who have come to realize that by changing one life for the better, they change the world. Many of our active members become emotionally tied to the prisoners. We know them by name, know their families, occasionally even know the names of their torturers.   To be part of this "resistance movement" is often to rejoice, unfortunately more often to weep, but always to know in your heart that you are part of the most unrelenting force ever to set itself against the bastions of tyranny and inhumanity.

I hope you will help us liberate a "brother" or "sister" from a torturer's cell by giving as much as you can. If you can afford $15, make a sacrifice and give $25.   If you can afford $50, give $100.

Please remember, many good people are counting on you.   You are their hope.   Imagine what it would be like-- to have done nothing wrong and yet to be imprisoned, tortured, near death.   Imagine what it would be like for you, then decide how much you can help.   Thank you.

Sincerely,

Ginetta Sagan

P.S.   All contributions are tax deductible.   Please be as generous as you can.

(Received by the compiler July 17, 1974.)

VII. SELECT BIBLIOGRAPHY ON VIETNAM

A vast body of literature developed as the Vietnam War expanded and lengthened. This bibliography is a selective one focusing on works that illuminate the context and substance of The Resistance to the United States' misadventure in Vietnam. It is intended
to guide the reader to works that will enable him to interpret the
documents compiled in this volume. The entries have been grouped
under six categories: A. Articles and Chapters; B. Books; C.
Government, University, Foundation and Citizen Group Reports; D.
Dissertations and Theses; E. Microfilm; and F. Film.

A. ARTICLES AND CHAPTERS

1. Apple, R. W. "Vietnam: The Signs of a Stalemate," New
   York Times, August 7, 1967.

2. Beech, Keyes. "How Uncle Sam Fumbled in Laos," Saturday
   Evening Post, April 22, 1961.

3. Bigart, Homer. "Saigon Is Losing Propaganda War," New
   York Times, January 18, 1962.

4. _____. "U.S. Prods Saigon on Resettlement," New York
   Times, May 9, 1962.

5. Bombwall, K. R. "Presidential Leadership in the Republic of
   Viet-Nam," International Studies (New Delhi), October, 1961.

6. Bowles, Chester. Excerpts from testimony to the Joint Economic Committee of Congress, January, 1971. Boston Sunday
   Globe, February 14, 1971.

7. Branfman, Fred. "Presidential War in Laos, 1964-1970" in
   Laos: War and Revolution, edited by N. Adams and A. Mc-
   Coy. New York: Harper and Row, 1970.

8. Carver, George A. "The Faceless Viet-Cong," Foreign Affairs, April, 1966.

9. _____. "The Real Revolution in South Vietnam," Foreign

Affairs, XLIII (April, 1965), 387-408.

10. Chomsky, Noam. "Mayday: The Case for Civil Disobedience,"
New York Review of Books, June 17, 1971.

11. Clark, Blair. "Westmoreland Appraised: Questions and Answers," Harper's, November, 1970.

12. "Commitment in Saigon" (Editorial), The New Republic, May
22, 1961.

13. Davies, James C. "The Circumstances and Causes of Revolution," The Journal of Conflict Resolution, XI (June, 1967),
247-257.

14. _____. "Toward a Theory of Revolution," American Socio-
logical Review, XXVII (February, 1962), 5-19.

15. Devillers, Philippe. "The Struggle for the Unification of Vietnam," China Quarterly, IX (January-March, 1962), 15.

16. Dommen, Arthur J. "Laos: The Troubled 'Neutral,'" Asian
Survey, VII (January, 1967).

17. Donovan, Robert J. "Dilemma Over Indo-China" in his Eisenhower: The Inside Story. New York: Harper and Brothers,
1956, 259-268.

18. Dorsey, John T., Jr. "Bureaucracy and Political Development
in Vietnam" in Bureaucracy and Political Development, edited
by Joseph LaPalombara. Princeton, N.J.: Princeton University Press, 1963.

19. Dudman, Richard. "Asia's Frontiers of Freedom. U.S. Policy: Pluses, Minuses and Questions," St. Louis Post-Dis-
patch, February 3, 4, 5, 1963.

20. _____. "Political Reaction a Problem in the Use of 'Dirty'
Tactics to Fight Viet Cong Guerrillas," St. Louis Post-Dis-
patch, February 6, 1963.

21. Duncanson, Dennis J. "How and Why--The Viet Cong Holds
Out," Encounter, December, 1966, 77-84.

22. Duong Son Quan. "Land Reform?," Thoi Bao Ga, October 10,
1970.

23. Duong Van Minh. "Vietnam: A Question of Confidence," Foreign Affairs, XLVII (October, 1968), 84-91.

24. Durdin, Peggy. "The Grim Lesson of Laos," The New York
Times Magazine, May 21, 1961.

25. Ellsberg, Daniel. "Laos: What Nixon Is Up To," New York Review of Books, March 11, 1971.

26. Fall, Bernard B. "The International Relations of Laos," Pacific Affairs, XXX (March, 1957).

27. _____. "The Laos Tangle," International Journal, XVI (Spring, 1961).

28. _____. "Master of the Red Job," The Saturday Evening Post, November 24, 1962.

29. _____. "North Viet-Nam's Constitution and Government," Pacific Affairs, September, 1960, 282-290.

30. _____. "The Pathet Lao: A 'Liberation' Party" in Robert A. Scalapino, ed., The Communist Revolution in Asia: Tactics, Goals, and Achievements. Englewood Cliffs, N.J.: Prentice-Hall, 1965.

31. _____. "The Political-Religious Sects of Viet-Nam," Pacific Affairs, XXVIII (September, 1955), 235-253.

32. _____. "La politique americaine au Viet-Nam," Politique Etrangère, July, 1955, 299-322.

33. _____. "Reappraisal in Laos," Current History, XLII (January, 1962).

34. _____. "South Viet-Nam's Internal Problems," Pacific Affairs, September, 1958.

35. _____. "A Talk With Ho Chi Minh," The New Republic, October 12, 1963.

36. _____. "Tribulations of a Party Line: The French Communists and Indochina," Foreign Affairs, April, 1955, 499-510.

37. _____. "Viet-Cong--The Unseen Enemy in Viet-Nam" in The Viet-Nam Reader, edited by Marcus G. Raskin and Bernard B. Fall. New York: Random House, Vintage Books, 1965.

38. _____. "Viet-Nam's Twelve Elections," The New Republic, May 14, 1966.

39. _____. "What deGaulle Actually Said About Vietnam," The Reporter, October 24, 1963.

40. _____. "Will South Viet-Nam Be Next?," The Nation, May 31, 1958.

41. _____. "The Year of the Hawks," New York Times Maga-
     zine, December 12, 1965.

42. Finney, John W. "Soviet Operational Role Is Seen in North
     Viet-Nam's Air Defense," New York Times, October 4, 1966.

43. Fishel, Wesley R. "Vietnam's Democratic One-Man Rule,"
     New Leader, November 2, 1959, 10-13.

44. FitzGerald, Frances. "The Tragedy of Saigon," Atlantic
     Monthly, December, 1966, 59-67.

45. Frederick, Cynthia. "Cambodia: Operation Total Victory No.
     43," Bulletin of Concerned Asian Scholars, II (April-July,
     1970), 3-19.

46. _____. "The Vietnamization of Saigon Politics," Bulletin of
     Concerned Asian Scholars, III (Winter-Spring, 1971), 5-14.

47. Grant, J. A. C. "The Viet-Nam Constitution of 1956," Amer-
     ican Political Science Review, June, 1958.

48. Grose, Peter. "Soviet Announces New Pact for Aid to Hanoi's
     Regime," New York Times, October 4, 1966.

49. Halberstam, David. "Coup in Saigon: A Detailed Account,"
     The New York Times, November 6, 1963.

50. _____. "Return to Vietnam," Harper's, December, 1967,
     47-58.

51. _____. "Voices of the Vietcong," Harper's, January, 1968,
     45-52.

52. Hammer, Ellen J. "Progress Report on Southern Viet-Nam,"
     Pacific Affairs, September, 1957, 283-294.

53. Henderson, William. "South Viet-Nam Finds Itself," Foreign
     Affairs, January, 1957.

54. Ho Chi Minh. "Problèmes de l'Asie," Temps Nouveaux (Mos-
     cow), XLVII (November 22, 1961), 4-6.

55. Humphrey, Hubert H. "Viet-Nam: The Case for the Admin-
     istration," Diplomat, August, 1966.

56. Hunebelle, Danielle. "North Vietnam: Communism's Most
     Disquieting Experiment," Réalités (English ed.), May, 1963.

57. Huntington, Samuel. "The Bases of Accommodation," Foreign
     Affairs, XLVI (July, 1968), 642-656.

58. "The Impossible Choices in Viet-Nam," The Washington Post,

May 22, 1966.

59. Jumper, Roy. "Mandarin Bureaucracy and Politics in South Vietnam," Pacific Affairs, XXX (March, 1957), 47-58.

60. Kissinger, Henry. "Viet Nam Negotiations," Foreign Affairs, XLVII (January, 1969), 211-234.

61. Komer, Robert W. "The Other War in Vietnam--A Progress Report," Department of State Bulletin, X (October, 1966), 549-600.

62. Ladejinsky, Wolf I. "Agrarian Reform in the Republic of Vietnam" in Problems of Freedom: South Vietnam Since Independence, edited by Wesley R. Fishel. New York: Free Press of Glencoe, 1962, 153-175.

63. Lansdale, Major-General Edward G. "Two Steps to Get Us Out of Vietnam," Look, IV (March, 1969), 64-67.

64. _____. "Vietnam: Do We Understand Revolution?," Foreign Affairs, XLIII (October, 1964), 75-86.

65. Le Duan. "Under the Glorious Party Banner, for Independence, Freedom and Socialism, Let Us Advance and Achieve New Victories," Vietnam Documents and Research Notes, U.S. Mission, Saigon, LXXVII (April, 1970).

66. Lifton, Robert Jay. "The Circles of Deception--Notes on Vietnam," Trans-Action, March 1968, 10-19.

67. McAlister, John T., Jr. "America in Vietnam," Portion of unpublished MSS, Princeton University, 1969.

68. _____. "The Possibilities for Diplomacy in Southeast Asia," World Politics, XIX, No. 2 (January, 1967), 258-305.

69. Martin, Everett G. "Viet-Nam: Correcting the Crucial Error," Newsweek, September 12, 1966.

70. Mende, Tibor. "Les deux Vietnam," Esprit, June, 1957, 945-946.

71. "The Michigan Winter Soldier Investigation," Excerpts from the Congressional Record, 6-7 April, 1971, Harvard Crimson, XIV (May, 1971).

72. Millet, Stanley. "Terror in Vietnam: An American's Ordeal at the Hands of Our 'Friends,'" Harper's Magazine, September, 1962.

73. Mitchell, Edward J. "Inequality and Insurgency: A Statistical Study of South Vietnam," World Politics, XX (April,

1968), 421-438.

74. Mus, Paul. "Cultural Backgrounds of Present Problems,"
    Asia, IV (Winter, 1966), 10-21.

75. _____. "Les Religions de l'Indochine" in Indochine, edited
    by Sylvain Lévi, 2 vols. Paris: Société d'Editions Geo-
    graphiques Maritimes et Coloniales, 1931.

76. _____. "The Role of the Village in Vietnamese Politics,"
    Pacific Affairs, XXIII (September, 1949), 265-272.

77. _____. "The Unaccountable Mr. Ho," New Journal, XII
    (May, 1968), 9.

78. _____. "Viet Nam: A Nation Off Balance," Yale Review,
    XLI (Summer, 1952), 524-538.

79. Nguyen Ngoc Bich. "The Poetry of Vietnam," Asia, Spring,
    1969.

80. Nguyen Tuyet Mai. "Electioneering: Vietnamese Style,"
    Asian Survey, November, 1962.

81. Nguyen Van Phong. "La Diffusion du confucianisme au Viet-
    nam," France-Asie, XXI (Winter, 1966-1967), 179-196.

82. O'Daniel, Lieutenant General John W. "A Finger in the Dike
    Is Not Enough," TVN Magazine, April 29, 1962.

83. "Our Options in Viet-Nam," The Reporter, March 12, 1964.

84. Pfaff, William. "Rhetorical Escalation," Commonweal, March
    17, 1967, 673-674.

85. _____. "Rivals for the Vietcong?," Commonweal, March
    3, 1967, 615-617.

86. _____. "What Else Can We Do?," Commonweal, March 10,
    1967, 641-642.

87. Phan Boi Chau. "Memoires," Edited by Georges Boudarel,
    France-Asie, XXII (Autumn, 1968), 263-471.

88. Pool, Ithiel de Sola. "Political Alternatives to the Viet Cong,"
    Asian Survey, VII (August, 1967), 555-566.

89. Poore, Simon. "General McGarr's Jungle Tigers of Viet-Nam,"
    Saga, October, 1961.

90. Race, Jeffrey. "How They Won," Asian Survey, X (August,
    1970), 628-650.

91. Rigg, Robert B. "Catalog of Viet Cong Violence," Military Review, December, 1962.

92. Rose, Jerry A. "I'm Hit! I'm Hit! I'm Hit!," The Saturday Evening Post, March 23, 1963.

93. Rossi, Mario. "U Thant and Vietnam: The Untold Story," The New York Review of Books, November 17, 1966.

94. Rowen, Hobart. "Saigon Turns a Profit, U.S. Loses More Gold," The Washington Post, August 17, 1966.

95. Sacks, I. Milton. "Marxism in Viet-Nam" in Marxism in Southeast Asia, edited by Frank N. Trager. Stanford, Calif.: Stanford University Press, 1960, 102-170.

96. _____. "Restructuring Government in South Vietnam," Asian Survey, VII (August, 1967), 515-526.

97. Schell, Jonathan and Orville. Letter to the New York Times, November 26, 1969.

98. Scigliano, Robert G. "Political Parties in South Vietnam Under the Republic," Pacific Affairs, XXXIII (December, 1960), 327-346.

99. Shaplen, Robert. "The Enigma of Ho Chi Minh," The Reporter, XII (January 27, 1955), 11-19.

100. _____. "Letter from Indochina," New Yorker, May 9, 1970, 130-148.

101. _____. "Letter from Saigon," New Yorker, February 18, 1967, 150-166; June 17, 1967, 37-92; October 7, 1967, 149-175; January 20, 1968, 35-82; March 2, 1968, 44-81; March 23, 1968, 114-125; June 29, 1968, 37-61; September 21, 1969, 100-150; January 31, 1970, 40-55.

102. _____. "Letter from South Vietnam," New Yorker, June 17, 1967, 37-91.

102a. _____. "A Reporter at Large," New Yorker, November 16, 1968, 193-206; July, 1969, 36-57.

103. _____. "A Reporter in Viet-Nam: The Delta, the Plateau, and the Mountains," New Yorker, August 11, 1962.

104. Simmonds, E. H. S. "Breakdown in Laos," World Today, XX (July, 1964).

104a. _____. "A Cycle of Political Events in Laos," World Today, XVII (February, 1961).

105. _____. "Laos and the War in Vietnam," World Today,
     XXII (May, 1966).

105a._____. "Laos: A Renewal of Crisis," Asian Survey, IV
     (January, 1964).

106. Smith, Roger M. "Laos in Perspective," Asian Survey, III
     (January, 1963).

107. Stavins, Ralph. "Kennedy's Private War," New York Review
     of Books, July 22, 1971.

108. Stone, I. F. "A Reply to the White Paper" in The Viet-Nam
     Reader, edited by Marcus G. Raskin and Bernard B. Fall.
     New York: Random House, Vintage Books, 1965.

109. Taillefer, Jean. "Les Elections au Sud-Viêtnam," France-
     Asie, XXI (Spring-Summer, 1967), 447-458.

110. Taylor, Milton C. "South Viet-Nam: Lavish Aid, Limited
     Progress," Pacific Affairs, XXXIV (Fall, 1961), 242-256.

111. Thomson, James C., Jr. "How Could Vietnam Happen: An
     Autopsy," Atlantic Monthly, April, 1968, 47-53.

112. Tongas, Gérard. "Indoctrination Replaces Education" in P. J.
     Honey, ed., North Vietnam Today: Profile of a Communist
     Satellite, New York: Praeger, 1962, 93-103.

113. Trumbull, Robert. "Laos-Based Reds Use Tribes in South
     Viet-Nam as Guerrillas," New York Times, June 5, 1961.

114. Unna, Warren. "One Year Later, Money and Men Bring Light
     to Viet-Nam," The Washington Post, December 17, 1962.

115. Valéry, Paul. Extract from History and Politics No. 10. New
     York Times, March 25, 1971.

116. "The War in Viet Nam," The Economist, May 19, 1962.

117. "The War in Viet-Nam: We Are Not Told the Truth," The
     New Republic, March 12, 1962.

118. Whiteside, Thomas. "Defoliation," New Yorker, February 7,
     1970, 32-38.

119. Woodside, Alec. "Some Southern Vietnamese Writers Look at
     the War," Bulletin of Concerned Asian Scholars, II (October,
     1969), 53-58.

120. Wurfel, David. "The Saigon Political Elite: Focus on Four
     Cabinets," Asian Survey, VII (August, 1967), 527-539.

B. BOOKS

1. Adlai Stevenson Institute of International Affairs. No More
    Vietnams? The War and the Future of American Foreign
    Policy. New York: Harper and Row, 1968.

2. Adler, Bill (ed.). Letters from Vietnam. New York: Dutton,
    1967.

3. Alsheimer, Georg W. Vietnamesische Lehrjahre: Sechs Jahre
    als Deutscher Arzt in Vietnam. Frankfurt am Main: Suhr-
    kamp, 1968.

4. American Friends Service Committee. Peace in Vietnam: A
    New Approach in Southeast Asia. New York: Hill and Wang,
    1967.

5. Aptheker, Herbert. Mission to Hanoi. New York: Internation-
    al Publishers, 1966.

6. Arlen, Michael. The Living-Room War. New York: Viking,
    1969.

7. Armbruster, Frank E. et al. Can We Win in Vietnam? Hud-
    son Institute Series on National Security and International Or-
    der. New York: Praeger, 1968.

8. Arora, Gloria. Vietnam under the Shadows: A Chronological
    and Factual Book that Records the Tragedy of Vietnam.
    Bombay: Jarco Publishing House, 1965.

9. Ausenev, M. M. Democratic Republic of Vietnam: Economy
    and Foreign Trade. New York: Crowell Collier and Macmil-
    lan, 1960.

10. Bain, Chester Arthur. Vietnam: The Roots of Conflict.
    Englewood Cliffs, N.J.: Prentice-Hall, 1967.

11. Baruch, Jacques. Bibliographies des traductions françaises
    des littératures du Viet-Nam et du Cambodge. Bruxelles:
    Editions Thanh-Long, 1968.

12. Bator, Victor. Vietnam, A Diplomatic Tragedy: The Origins
    of the United States Involvement. Dobbs Ferry, New York:
    Oceana Publications, 1965.

13. Baxter, Gordon. Vietnam: Search and Destroy. Cleveland:
    World, 1967.

14. Beechy, Atlee and Winifred. Vietnam: Who Cares? Scotts-
    dale, Pa.: Herald Press, 1968.

15. Bernard, Martin (comp.). Vietnam and Trade Unionists. London: Vietnam Solidarity Campaign, 1967.

16. Berrigan, Daniel. Night Flight to Hanoi: War Diary with Eleven Poems. New York: Macmillan, 1968.

17. Bisignano, Flavio. Vietnam.... Why? An American Citizen Looks at the War. Torrance, Calif.: Frank Publications, 1968.

18. Blanchet, Marie Therese. La naissance de l'Etat associé du Viet-Nam. Paris: M. T. Genin, 1954.

19. Bloomfield, Lincoln Palmer. The U.N. and Vietnam. New York: Carnegie Endowment for International Peace, 1968.

20. Bly, Robert (ed.). A Poetry Reading against the Vietnam War. Madison, Minn.: Sixties Press, 1966.

21. Boba, Antonio. Saigon Diary. New York: Vintage Press, 1970.

22. Bodard, Lucien. La Guerre d'Indochine. Paris: Gallimard, 1963.

23. _____. The Quicksand War: Prelude to Vietnam. Translated by Patrick O'Brian. Boston: Atlantic-Little, Brown & Co., 1967.

24. Boettiger, John R. (comp.). Vietnam and American Foreign Policy. Boston: Heath, 1968.

25. Bøgholm, Karl. Vietnam Kalder. København: Nyt Nordisk Forlag, 1967.

26. Bommarito, John E. The Truth about Viet Nam. St. Louis: Alert Publications, 1966.

27. Bonnet, Gabriel. La Guerre Revolutionnaire du Vietnam: Histoire, Techniques et Enseignements de la Guerre Americano-Vietnamienne. Paris: Payot, 1969.

28. Bouscaren, Anthony T. The Last of the Mandarins: Diem of Vietnam. Pittsburgh: Duquesne University Press, 1965.

29. Bozek, David A. Artillery Medic in Vietnam. New York: Vantage Press, 1971.

30. Brandon, Henry. Anatomy of Error: The Inside Story of the Asian War on the Potomac, 1954-1969. Boston: Gambit, 1969.

31. Brass, Alister. Bleeding Earth: A Doctor Looks at Vietnam.

Melbourne: Heinemann, 1968.

32. Brelis, Dean. The Face of South Vietnam. Boston: Hough-
    ton Mifflin, 1968.

33. Brinch, Esther. Vietnam. København: Vietnam-Komiteen,
    1966.

34. Briscoe, Edward. Diary of a Shorttimer in Vietnam. New
    York: Vantage Press, 1970.

35. Bromley, Dorothy. Washington and Vietnam: An Examination
    of the Moral and Political Issues. Dobbs Ferry, N. Y. :
    Oceana Publications, 1966.

36. Broughton, Jack. Third Ridge. Philadelphia: Lippincott,
    1969.

37. Brown, Robert McAfee, Abraham J. Heschel, and Michael
    Novak. Vietnam: Crisis of Conscience. New York: Asso-
    ciation Press, 1967.

38. Brown, Sam and Len Ackland (eds.). Why Are We Still in
    Vietnam. New York: Random House, 1970.

39. Browne, Malcolm W. The New Face of War. Indianapolis:
    Bobbs-Merrill Co., 1965.

40. Buell, Harold G. Viet Nam: Land of Many Dragons. New
    York: Dodd, Mead, & Co., 1968.

41. Burchett, Wilfred G. The Furtive War: The United States in
    Vietnam and Laos. New York: International Publishers,
    1963.

42. _____. My Visit to the Liberated Zones of South Vietnam.
    Hanoi: Foreign Languages Publishing House, 1966.

43. _____. North of the Seventeenth Parallel. Delhi: People's
    House, 1956.

44. _____. Pourquoi le Vietcong Gagne. Paris: Maspero,
    1968.

45. _____. Vietnam: Inside Story of the Guerrilla War. New
    York: International Publishers, 1965.

46. _____. Vietnam North. New York: International Publish-
    ers, 1966.

47. _____. Vietnam Will Win! New York: Monthly Review
    Press, 1968.

48. Burling, Robbins. Hill Farms and Paddy Fields. Englewood
    Cliffs, N. J. : Prentice-Hall, 1965.

49. Bushner, Rolland H. (ed.). American Dilemma in Viet-Nam.
    New York: Council on Foreign Relations, 1965.

50. Buttinger, Joseph. The Smaller Dragon: A Political History
    of Vietnam. New York: Praeger, 1958.

51. _____. Vietnam: A Dragon Embattled. 2 vols. New
    York: Praeger, 1967.

52. Cadière, Léopold. Croyances et Pratiques Religieuses des
    Viêtnamiens. 3 vols. Saigon: Ecole Francaise d'Extrême
    Orient, 1955, 1957, 1958.

53. Cairns, James. The Eagle and the Lotus: Western Interven-
    tion in Vietnam. Melbourne: Lansdowne Press, 1969.

54. Calley, William and John Sack. Lt. Calley: An American
    Tragedy with a Complete Account of My Lai Four and Exclu-
    sive Coverage of the Trial. New York: Viking Press, 1971.

55. Cameron, Allan W. (comp.). Viet Nam Crisis: A Documen-
    tary History. Ithaca, N. Y. : Cornell University Press, 1971.

56. Cameron, James. Here Is Your Enemy: Complete Report
    from North Vietnam. New York: Holt, Rinehart and Win-
    ston, 1966.

57. Cannon, Terry. Vietnam: A Thousand Years of Struggle.
    San Francisco: Peoples Press, 1969.

58. Chaliand, Gerard. Peasants of North Vietnam. Translated by
    Peter Wiles. New York: Penguin Books, 1970.

59. Chaumont, Charles. Analyse Critique de L'intervention Ameri-
    caine au Vietnam. Bruxelles: Commission permanente d'en-
    quete pour le Vietnam, 1968.

60. Chen, King C. Vietnam and China, 1938-1954. Princeton,
    N. J. : Princeton University Press, 1969.

61. Chesneaux, Jean. Le Vietnam. Paris: Maspero, 1968.

62. Child, Frank C. Essays on Economic Growth, Capital Forma-
    tion, and Public Policy in Viet-Nam. Saigon: Michigan
    State University Viet-Nam Advisory Group, 1961.

63. _____. Toward a Policy for Economic Growth in Vietnam.
    Saigon: Michigan State University, Vietnam Advisory Group,
    1962.

64. Chomsky, Noam. American Power and the New Mandarins. New York: Random House, Vintage Books, 1967.

65. _____. At War with Asia. New York: Pantheon, 1970.

66. Chung, Ly Q. (ed.). Between Two Fires: The Unheard Voices of Vietnam. New York: Praeger, 1970.

67. Civic Education Service. Two Viet Nams in War and Peace. Washington, D.C.: Civic Education Service, 1967.

68. Clark, Alan. The Lion Heart: A Tale of the War in Vietnam. New York: Morrow, 1967.

69. Clubb, Oliver E., Jr. The United States and the Sino-Soviet Bloc in Southeast Asia. Washington, D.C.: The Brookings Institution, 1963.

70. Clutterbuck, Richard L. The Long, Long War: Counterinsurgency in Malaya and Vietnam. New York: Praeger, 1960.

71. Coe, Charles. Young Man in Vietnam. New York: Four Winds Press, 1968.

72. Committee for Economic Development. The National Economy and the Vietnam War. New York: CED, 1968.

73. Committee of Concerned Asian Scholars. Indochina Story: A Critical Appraisal of American Involvement in Southeast Asia. New York: Pantheon Books, 1971.

74. Cooke, David. Vietnam: The Country, The People. New York: Norton, 1965.

75. Cooper, Chester L. Lost Crusade: America in Vietnam. New York: Dodd, Mead & Co., 1970.

76. Corson, William R. The Betrayal. New York: Norton, 1968.

77. Critchfield, Richard. The Long Charade: Political Subversion in the Vietnam War. New York: Harcourt, Brace and World, 1968.

78. Cronkite, Walter. Vietnam Perspective: CBS News Special Report. New York: Pocket Books, 1965.

79. Crozier, Brian. Southeast Asia in Turmoil. London: Penguin Books, 1965.

80. Dang, Nghiem. Viet-Nam: Politics and Public Administration. Honolulu, Hawaii: Eastwest Center Press, 1966.

81.   Dareff, Hal. The Story of Vietnam: A Background Book for
      Young People. New York: Parents' Magazine Press, 1966.

82.   Deane, Hugh. The War in Vietnam. New York: Monthly Re-
      view Press, 1963.

83.   Dedra, Don. Anybody Here from Arizona? A Look at the Vi-
      etnam War. Phoenix: The Arizona Republic, 1966.

84.   Devillers, Philippe. End of a War: Indochina, 1954. New
      York: Praeger, 1969.

85.   _____. Histoire du Viêt-nam de 1940 à 1952. Paris: Edi-
      tions du Seuil, 1952.

86.   Dommen, Arthur J. Conflict in Laos: The Politics of Neutral-
      ization. New York: Praeger, 1964.

87.   Donlon, Roger H. C. Outpost of Freedom. New York: Mc-
      Graw-Hill, 1965.

88.   Donoghue, John D. My Thuan: The Study of a Delta Village
      in South Vietnam. Saigon: Michigan State University Advis-
      ory Group, 1961.

89.   Dooley, Thomas A. Deliver Us from Evil: The Story of Viet
      Nam's Flight to Freedom. New York: New American Li-
      brary, 1956.

90.   Dorsey, John T. Report and Recommendations on the Reor-
      ganization of the Presidency of Vietnam. Michigan State Uni-
      versity: Vietnam Advisory Team, Saigon, 1955.

91.   Do-Van-Minh. Viet Nam: Where East and West Meet. New
      York: Paragon Book Reprint Corporation, 1968.

92.   Doyon, Jacques. Les Viet Cong. Paris: Denoel, 1968.

93.   Drachman, Edward R. United States Policy toward Vietnam.
      Rutherford, N.J.: Fairleigh Dickinson University Press,
      1970.

94.   Draper, Theodore. Abuse of Power. New York: Viking
      Press, 1967.

95.   Drendel, Lou. Air War in Viet Nam. New York: Arco
      Publishing Company, 1968.

96.   Drinan, Robert F. Vietnam and Armageddon: Peace, War,
      and the Christian Conscience. New York: Sheed and Ward,
      1970.

97.   Dudman, Richard. Forty Days with the Enemy. New York:

Liveright, 1971.

98. Duffett, John (ed.). Against the Crime of Silence: Proceedings of the Russell International War Crimes Tribunal, 1967. New York: Simon and Schuster, Clarion Books, 1970.

99. Duncan, David Douglas. I Protest! New York: New American Library, 1968.

100. Duncan, Donald. The New Legions. New York: Random House, 1967.

101. Duncanson, Dennis J. Government and Revolution in Vietnam. London: Oxford University Press, 1968.

102. Dunn, Mary Lois. The Man in the Box: A Story from Vietnam. New York: McGraw-Hill, 1968.

103. Dunn, William. American Policy and Vietnamese Nationalism, 1950-1954. Chicago: University of Chicago Press, 1960.

104. Duong-Chau. The Seventeenth Parallel. Translated by Vietnam Translation Service. Saigon: Cong Dan, 1958.

105. Durdin, Tillman. Southeast Asia. New York: Atheneum, 1966.

106. Dykes, Hugh and Reginald Watts. Vietnam: Threat and Involvement. London: Bow Publications, 1966.

107. Economic Impact of the Vietnam War. New York: Renaissance Editions, 1967.

108. Eden, Sir Anthony. Toward Peace in Indochina. Boston: Houghton Mifflin, 1966.

109. Effros, William G. (ed.). Quotations Vietnam: Nineteen Fifty to Nineteen Seventy. New York: Random House, 1970.

110. Eide, Asbjørn. Intra-statlige Konflikter og Intervensjon Utenfra: Folkerett og Politikk i Var Tid. En Analyse med Vietnam som Utgangspunkt. Oslo: Universitetsforlaget, 1968.

111. Einbinder, Harvey. Mah Name Is Lyndon. New York: Lady Bird Press, 1968.

112. Ennis, Thomas. Vietnam: Land without Laughter. Morgantown, West Virginia: Cooperative Extension Service, West Virginia University, 1966.

113. Falk, Richard A., Gabriel Kolko, and Robert Lifton (eds.). Crimes of War: After Songmy. New York: Random House,

Vintage Books, 1971.

114. Falk, Richard A. The Six Legal Dimensions of the Vietnam
     War. Princeton, N.J.: Center of International Studies,
     Princeton University, 1968.

115. _____. A Vietnam Settlement: The View from Hanoi.
     Princeton, N.J.: Center of International Studies, Princeton
     University, 1968.

116. _____. (ed.). Vietnam War and International Law, Vol. 1,
     Princeton, N.J.: Princeton University Press, 1967.

117. Fall, Bernard B. Hell in a Very Small Place: The Siege of
     Dien Bien Phu. Philadelphia: Lippincott, 1967

118. _____. Last Reflections on a War. Garden City, N.Y.:
     Doubleday, 1967.

119. _____. Street without Joy: Insurgency in Indochina, 1946-
     1963. 3rd edition. Harrisburg, Pa.: Stackpole, 1963.

120. _____. The Two Vietnams: A Political and Military Analy-
     sis. New York: Praeger, 1963.

121. _____. Le Viêt-Minh: La République démocratique du
     Viêt-Nam, 1945-1960. Paris: Colin, 1960.

122. _____. The Viet-Minh Regime: Government and Adminis-
     tration in the Democratic Republic of Vietnam. Revised edi-
     tion. New York: Institute of Pacific Relations, 1956.

123. _____. Viet-Nam, dernieres Reflexions sur une Guerre.
     Translated by Daniel Martin. Paris: Laffont, 1968.

124. _____ and Marcus G. Raskin (eds.). Vietnam Reader.
     New York: Random House, 1965.

125. _____. Viet-Nam Witness, 1953-1966. New York: Praeger,
     1966.

126. Faltis, Joseph. Quickie Lessons in Vietnamese, Using the Ab-
     sorbomatic Method. Palo Alto, Calif.: Winston, 1967.

127. Fanon, Frantz. Black Skin, White Masks. Translated by
     Charles Lam Markmann. New York: Grove Press, 1967.

128. _____. The Wretched of the Earth. Translated by Con-
     stance Farrington. New York: Grove Press, 1965.

129. Farmer, James. Counterinsurgency Principles and Practices
     in Viet-Nam. Santa Monica, Calif.: Rand Corporation, 1964.

130. Favre, Claude. Les Os du Tigre. Paris: Editions France-Empire, 1965.

131. Feinberg, Abraham L. Rabbi Feinberg's Hanoi Diary. Don Mills, Ontario, Canada: Longmans, 1968.

132. Fernandez, Benedict J. In Opposition: Images of American Dissent in the Sixties. New York: Da Capo Press, 1968.

133. Fifth Avenue Vietnam Peace Parade Committee. In the Teeth of War: Photographic Documentary of the March 26th, 1966, New York City Demonstration against the War in Vietnam. New York: OAK Publications, 1966.

134. Finan, John. Guns and Blood for Butter. New York: Vantage Press, 1969.

135. Findlay, P. T. Protest Politics and Psychological Warfare: The Communist Role in the Anti-Vietnam War and Anti-Conscription Movement in Australia. Melbourne: Hawthorn Press, 1968.

136. Fishel, Wesley R. (ed.). Problems of Freedom: South Vietnam Since Independence. New York: Free Press of Glencoe, 1962.

137. _____ and T. A. Bisson. The United States and Viet Nam: Two Views. New York: Public Affairs Committee, 1966.

138. _____. Vietnam: The Anatomy of a Conflict. Itasca, Ill.: F. E. Peacock, 1968.

139. FitzGerald, Frances. Fire in the Lake: The Vietnamese and the Americans in Vietnam. Boston: Little, Brown and Co., 1972.

140. Ford, Daniel. Incident at Muc Wa. Garden City, N. Y.: Doubleday, 1967.

141. Ford, Herbert. No Guns on Their Shoulders. Nashville: Southern Publishing Association, 1968.

142. Foreign Policy Association. Vietnam: Issues for Decision. New York: Foreign Policy Association, 1968.

143. Fourniau, Charles. Le Vietnam de la Guerre à la Victoire. Paris: Editions du Pavillon, 1969.

144. French, Walter. Pattern for Victory. New York: Exposition Press, 1970.

145. Friedman, Edward and Mark Selden (eds.). America's Asia: Dissenting Essays on Asian-American Relations. New York:

Random House, 1971.

146. Friends, Society of. American Friends Service Committee
     (AFSC). Peace in Vietnam: A New Approach in Southeast
     Asia. New York: Hill and Wang, 1967.

147. Friends, Society of (London). Vietnam: Facts and Figures.
     London: Friends Peace and International Relations Commit-
     tee, 1967.

148. Fulbright, J. William. Vietnam Hearings. New York: Ran-
     dom House, 1966.

149. Galbraith, John Kenneth. How to Get out of Vietnam: A
     Workable Solution to the Worst Problem of our Time. New
     York: American Library, 1967.

150. Gellhorn, Martha. A New Kind of War. Manchester: Guard-
     ian and Evening News, 1966.

151. Georg, Anders. Opgør i Vietnam. København: Berlingske
     Forlag, 1966.

152. Gerassi, John. North Vietnam: A Documentary. London:
     Allen and Unwin, 1968.

153. Gershen, Martin. Destroy or Die: The True Story of Mylai.
     New Rochelle, N.Y.: Arlington House, 1971.

154. Gettleman, Marvin E. Vietnam. New York: New American
     Library, 1970.

155. _____ (ed.). Viet Nam: History, Documents, and Opinions
     on a Major World Crisis. Greenwich, Conn., Fawcett, 1965.

156. Gheddo, Piero. The Cross and the Bo-Tree: Catholics and
     Buddhists in Vietnam. Translated by Charles Quinn. New
     York: Sheed and Ward, 1970.

157. Giap, Vo Nguyen. Banner of People's War: The Party's Mili-
     tary Line. New York: Praeger, 1970.

158. _____. Big Victory, Great Task: North Vietnam's Minis-
     ter of Defense Assesses the Course of the War. New York:
     Praeger, 1968.

159. _____. Military Art of People's War: Selected Writings.
     Edited by Russell Stetler. New York: Monthly Review
     Press, 1970.

160. _____. People's War, People's Army: The Viet Cong Insurrection Manual for Underdeveloped Countries. New York:
Praeger, 1962.

161. Gigon, Fernand. Les Americains face au Vietcong. Paris:
Flammarion, 1965.

162. Giuglaris, Marcel. Vietnam: Le Jour de L'Escalade. Paris:
Gallimard, 1966.

163. Glorvigen, Bjørn. Ved Fronten i Vietnam. Oslo: Elingaard,
1967.

164. Glyn, Alan. Witness to Viet Nam: The Containment of Communism in South East Asia. London: Johnson, 1968.

165. Goodwin, Richard N. Triumph or Tragedy: Reflections on
Vietnam. New York: Random House, 1966.

166. Gore, Albert. Eye of the Storm: A People's Politics for the
Seventies. New York: Herder and Herder, 1970.

167. Gosselin, Charles. L'Empire d'Annam. Paris: Perrin,
1904.

168. Grant, Jonathan S. (comp.). Cambodia: The Widening War in
Indochina. New York: Washington Square Press, 1971.

169. Grauwin, Paul. Doctor at Dienbienphu. New York: John Day
Co., 1955.

170. Greene, Felix. Vietnam! Vietnam! Palo Alto, Calif.: Fulton Publishing Co., 1966.

171. Greene, Graham. The Quiet American. New York: Viking,
1956.

172. Griffiths, Philip. Vietnam Inc. New York: Macmillan, 1971.

173. Groslier, Bernard P. Indochina. Cleveland: World Publishing Co., 1966.

174. Gruening, Ernest. Vietnam Folly. Palo Alto, Calif.: National Press Books, 1968.

175. Guevara, Ernesto. Guerrilla Warfare. New York: Monthly
Review Press, 1961.

176. _____. On Vietnam and World Revolution. New York:
Pathfinder Press, 1971.

177. _____. Open New Fronts to Aid Vietnam! London: The
     Week, 1967.

178. Guillain, Robert. Vietnam: The Dirty War. London: Hous-
     mans, 1966.

179. Gurtov, Melvin. The First Vietnam Crisis: Chinese Commu-
     nist Strategy and United States Involvement, 1953-1954. New
     York: Columbia University Press, 1967.

180. Halberstam, David. The Best and the Brightest. New York:
     Random House, 1972.

181. _____. Ho. New York: Random House, 1971.

182. _____. The Making of a Quagmire. New York: Random
     House, 1965.

183. _____. One Very Hot Day. Boston: Houghton Mifflin,
     1968.

184. Halstead, Fred. GIs Speak Out against the War: The Case of
     the Ft. Jackson 8. New York: Pathfinder Press, 1970.

185. Hamilton, Michael P. (ed.). The Vietnam War: Christian
     Perspectives. Grand Rapids, Mich.: Eerdmans, 1967.

186. Hammer, Ellen J. The Emergence of Vietnam. New York:
     International Secretariat, Institute of Pacific Relations, 1947.

187. _____. The Struggle for Indochina. Stanford, Calif.: Stan-
     ford University Press, 1954.

188. _____. Vietnam Yesterday and Today. New York: Holt,
     1966.

189. Hammer, Richard. The Court-Martial of Lieutenant Calley.
     New York: Coward-McCann, 1971.

190. _____. One Morning in the War: The Tragedy at Son My.
     New York: Coward-McCann, 1970.

191. Handache, Gilbert. L'Oeil de Cao Dai. Paris: Julliard, 1968.

192. Hanh, Thich N. Cry of Vietnam. Santa Barbara, Calif.:
     Unicorn Press, 1968.

193. _____. Vietnam: Lotus in a Sea of Fire. New York:
     Hill and Wang, 1967.

194. Harrigan, Anthony. A Guide to the War in Viet Nam. Boulder,
     Colo.: Panther Publications, 1966.

195. Hartke, Vance. The American Crisis in Vietnam. Indianap-
     olis: Bobbs-Merrill, 1968.

196. Harvey, Frank. Air War--Vietnam. New York: Bantam
     Books, 1967.

197. Haskins, James. War and the Protest: Vietnam. Garden
     City, N.Y.: Doubleday, 1971.

198. Hassler, R. Alfred. Saigon, U.S.A. New York: R. W. Bar-
     on, 1970.

199. Haviland, H. Field, Jr. et al. Vietnam after the War: Peace
     Keeping and Rehabilitation. Washington, D.C.: Brookings
     Institution, 1968.

200. Hawley, Earle (ed.). The Face of War: Vietnam, The Full
     Photographic Report! North Hollywood, Calif.: Milton Lur-
     os, 17600 Gledhill North, 1965.

201. Hay, Stephen N. and Margaret Case. Southeast Asian History:
     A Bibliographic Guide. New York: Praeger, 1962.

202. Heaton, Leonard D. Military Surgical Practices of the United
     States Army in Viet Nam. Chicago: Year Book Medical
     Publishers, 1966.

203. Hendry, James. The Study of a Vietnamese Rural Community.
     Saigon: Michigan State University, Viet-Nam Advisory
     Group, 1959.

204. _____. The Small World of Khanh Hau. Chicago: Aldine,
     1964.

205. Herbert, Jean. An Introduction to Asia. New York: Oxford
     University Press, 1965.

206. Herman, Edward S. America's Vietnam Policy: The Strategy
     of Deception. Washington, D.C.: Public Affairs Press,
     1966.

207. _____. Atrocities in Vietnam: Myths and Realities. Phil-
     adelphia: United Church, 1970.

208. Hersh, Seymour M. My Lai 4: A Report on the Massacre
     and Its Aftermath. New York: Random House, 1970.

209. Heymard, Jean. Verité sur l'Indochine. Paris: Nouvelles
     Editions Debresse, 1962.

210. Hickey, Gerald C. Village in Vietnam. New Haven, Conn.:
     Yale University Press, 1964.

211. Higgins, Marguerite. Our Vietnam Nightmare. New York:
     Harper and Row, 1965.

212. Hilsman, Roger, et al. Vietnam: Which Way to Peace?
     Chicago: University of Chicago, Center for Policy Study,
     1960.

213. Hirsch, Phil (ed.). Vietnam Combat. New York: Pyramid,
     1967.

214. Hoang Van Chi. From Colonialism to Communism: A Case
     History of North Vietnam. New York: Praeger, 1964.

215. _____. (ed. and trans.). The New Class in North Vietnam.
     Saigon: Long Dan, 1958.

216. Hoang Van Thai. Some Aspects of Guerrilla Warfare in Viet-
     nam. Hanoi: Foreign Languages Publishing House, 1965.

217. Ho Chi Minh. Ho Chi Minh on Revolution: Selected Writings,
     1920-1966. Edited by Bernard B. Fall. New York: Prae-
     ger, 1967.

218. _____. Oeuvres Choisies. Paris: Maspero, 1967.

219. _____. Prison Diary. Translated by Aileen Palmer.
     Hanoi: Foreign Languages Publishing House, 1962.

220. Holzer, Werner. Vietnam: oder, die Freiheit zu sterben.
     Munchen: Piper, 1968.

221. Honey, P. J. Communism in North Vietnam: Its Role in the
     Sino-Soviet Dispute. Cambridge, Mass.: M.I.T. Press,
     1963.

222. _____. Genesis of a Tragedy: The Historical Background
     to the Vietnam War. London: Benn, 1968.

223. _____ (ed.). North Vietnam Today: Profile of a Commu-
     nist Satellite. New York: Praeger, 1962.

224. Hoopes, Townsend. Limits of Intervention. New York: David
     McKay, 1970.

225. Huard, Pierre and Maurice Durand. Connaissance du Viêt-
     nam. Hanoi: Ecole Française d'Extrême Orient, 1954.

226. Huber, Bert. Vietnam. Berlin: Verlag der Nation, 1968.

227. Huberman, Leo, et al. Vietnam: The Endless War. New
     York: Monthly Review Press, 1971.

228. Hughes, Larry. You Can See a Lot Standing under a Flare

in the Republic of Vietnam: My Year at War. New York:
Morrow, 1970.

229. Hull, Roger H. Law and Vietnam. Dobbs Ferry, N.Y.:
Oceana Publications, 1968.

230. Hutchens, James M. Beyond Combat. Chicago: Moody
Press, 1969.

231. Huyen, N. Khac. Vision Accomplished? The Enigma of Ho
Chi Minh. New York: Collier Books, 1971.

232. Hymoff, Edward. The First Air Cavalry Division, Vietnam.
Philadelphia: M. W. Lads, 1967.

233. _____. The First Marine Division, Vietnam. Philadelphia: M. W. Lads, 1967.

234. Isard, Walter (ed.). Vietnam: Some Basic Issues and Alternatives. Cambridge, Mass.: Schenkman, 1969.

235. Johnson, Raymond W. Postmark: Mekong Delta. Westwood,
N.J.: Revell, 1968.

236. Jones, Rennie C. Vietnam: Historical Background, The 1954
Geneva Conference, The International Commission for Control. Melbourne: State Library of Victoria, 1966.

237. _____. Vietnam: A Select Reading List. Melbourne:
State Library of Victoria, 1966.

238. July, Mark. The Vietnam Photo Book. New York: Gross-
man, 1971.

239. Just, Ward S. To What End: Report from Vietnam. Boston:
Houghton Mifflin, 1968.

240. Kahin, George (ed.). Governments and Politics of Southeast
Asia. Ithaca, N.Y.: Cornell University Press, 1964.

241. _____, and John W. Lewis. The United States in Vietnam.
New York: Dial Press, 1967.

242. Kalb, Marvin L. Roots of Involvement: The U.S. in Asia,
1784-1971. New York: Norton, 1971.

243. Kang, Pilwon. The Road to Victory in Vietnam. New York:
Exposition Press, 1970.

244. Karlsson, Per Olof. Kriget i Vietnam. Stockholm: Raben
and Sjogren, 1966.

245. Karnow, Stanley. Southeast Asia. New York: Time, Inc., 1962.

246. Kastenmeier, Robert W. Viet-Nam Hearings: Voices from the Grassroots. Waterloo, Wisc.: Art Craft Press, 1965.

247. Keesing's Publications Ltd. South Vietnam: A Political History, 1954-1970. New York: Scribner, 1970.

248. Kelly, George A. Lost Soldiers. Cambridge, Mass.: M.I.T. Press, 1965.

249. The Kennedys and Vietnam. Interim History Series: The Bridge Between Today's News and Tomorrow's History. New York: Facts on File, Inc., 1971.

250. Kirk, Donald. Wider War: The Struggle for Cambodia, Thailand and Laos. New York: Praeger, 1971.

251. Klemm, Edwin O. You, Viet-Nam and Red China. Saginaw, Mich.: Multicopy Printing Services, 1968.

252. Knobl, Kuno. Victor Charlie: The Face of War in Viet-Nam. Translated by Abe Farbstein. New York: Praeger, 1967.

253. Knoll, Erwin and Judith McFadden (eds.). War Crimes and the American Conscience. New York: Holt, Rinehart and Winston, 1970.

254. Kolko, Gabriel (ed.). Three Documents of the National Liberation Front. Boston: Beacon Press, 1971.

255. Kolpacoff, Victor. The Prisoners of Quai Dong. New York: New American Library, 1967.

256. Kraslow, David. The Diplomacy of Chaos. London: Macdonald and Co., 1968.

257. _____. The Secret Search for Peace in Vietnam. New York: Random House, 1968.

258. Krueger, Carl. Wings of the Tiger. New York: Fell, 1966.

259. Labin, Suzanne. Sellout in Vietnam? Arlington, Va.: Crestwood Books, 1966.

260. _____. Vietnam: An Eye-Witness Account. Arlington, Va.: Crestwood Books, 1964.

261. Lacouture, Jean. Ho Chi Minh: A Political Biography. Translated by Peter Wiles. New York: Random House, 1968.

262. _____ and Philippe Devillers. La Fin d'une guerre: Indochine 1954. Paris: Editions du Seuil, 1960.

263. _____. Vietnam: Between Two Truces. Translated by

Konrad Kellen and Joel Carmichael. New York: Random House, Vintage Books, 1966.

264. Lamb, Alastair. Mandarin Road to Old Hue: Narrative of Anglo-Vietnamese Diplomacy from the Seventeenth Century to the Eve of the French Conquest. Hamden, Conn.: Shoe String Press, 1970.

265. Lamb, Helen. The Tragedy of Vietnam: Where Do We Go from Here? New York: Basic Pamphlets, 1964.

266. Lancaster, Donald. The Emancipation of French Indochina. New York: Oxford University Press, 1961.

267. Lane, Thomas A. America on Trial: The War for Vietnam. New Rochelle, N.Y.: Arlington House, 1971.

268. Lang, Daniel. Casualties of War. New York: McGraw Hill, 1969.

269. Langer, Paul F. and Joseph Zasloff. North Vietnam and the Pathet Lao: Partners in the Struggle for Laos. Cambridge, Mass.: Harvard University Press, 1970.

270. Larson, Donald. Vietnam and Beyond. Durham, N.C.: Rule of Law Research Center, Duke University, 1965.

271. Lartéguy, Jean. Yellow Fever. Translated by Xan Fielding. New York: Dutton, 1965.

272. Le Chau. La Révolution paysanne du Sud Viet-Nam. Paris: Maspero, 1966.

273. _____. Le Viet Nam socialiste: une economie de transition. Paris: Maspero, 1966.

274. Lederer, William J. Our Own Worst Enemy. New York: Norton, 1968.

275. Le Thanh Khoi. Le Viêt-nam, histoire et civilisation. Paris: Editions de Minuit, 1955.

276. Le Van Dinh. Le Culte ancêtres en droit annamite. Paris: Editions Domat-Montchrestien, 1934.

277. Lee Van Chat. Guerre non declaree au Sud Viet Nam. Hanoi: Editions en langues etrangeres, 1962.

278. Leifer, Michael. Cambodia: The Search for Security. New York: Praeger, 1967.

279. Lidman, Sara. Samtal i Hanoi. Stockholm: Bonnier, 1966.

280. Lindholm, Richard (ed.). Viet-Nam: The First Five Years, an International Symposium. East Lansing: Michigan State University Press, 1959.

281. Liska, George. War and Order: Reflections on Vietnam and History. Baltimore: Johns Hopkins Press, 1968.

282. Liss, Howard. The Mighty Mekong. New York: Hawthorn, 1967.

283. Little, David. American Foreign Policy and Moral Rhetoric: The Example of Vietnam. New York: Council on Religion and International Affairs, 1969.

284. Lovy, Andrew. Vietnam Diary: October Nineteen Sixty-Seven to July Nineteen Sixty-Eight. New York: Exposition Press, 1970.

285. Lowenfels, Walter (ed.). Where Is Vietnam: American Poets Respond. New York: Doubleday, 1967.

286. Lucas, Jim. Dateline: Viet Nam. New York: Award House, 1966.

287. Luce, Don and John Sommer. Viet Nam: The Unheard Voices. Ithaca, N.Y.: Cornell University Press, 1969.

288. Luu Quy Ky. Escalation War and Songs about Peace. Hanoi: Foreign Languages Publishing House, 1965.

289. _____. The Vietnamese Problem. Hanoi: Foreign Languages Publishing House, 1967.

290. Ly Qui Chung (ed.). Between Two Fires: The Unheard Voices of Vietnam. New York: Praeger, 1970.

291. Lynd, Alice. We Won't Go: Personal Accounts of War Objectors. Boston: Beacon Press, 1968.

292. Lynd, Staughton. The Other Side. New York: New American Library, 1966.

293. Maiwald, Helga. Vietnam: Information über ein aktuelles Weltproblem. Berlin: Dietz, 1966.

294. Maneli, Mieczyslaw. War of the Vanquished: A Polish Diplomat in Vietnam. New York: Harper and Row, 1971.

295. Mangiolardo, Michael. My Days in Vietnam. New York: Vantage, 1969.

296. Manning, Robert and Michael Janeway. Who We Are: An Atlantic Chronicle of the United States and Vietnam, 1966-1969.

Boston: Little, Brown and Co. , 1969.

297. Mannoni, Otare. Prospero and Caliban: The Psychology of
      Colonization. Translated by Pamela Powesland. New York:
      Praeger, 1964.

298. Maretzki, Hans. Was suchen die USA in Vietnam? Berlin:
      Staatsverlag der Deutschen Demokratischen Republik, 1967.

299. Marks, Richard E. The Letters of Pfc. Richard E. Marks.
      Philadelphia: Lippincott, 1967.

300. Marr, David G. Vietnamese Anticolonialism, 1885-1925.
      Berkeley: University of California Press, 1971.

301. Marshall, Samuel. Ambush: The Battle of Dau Tieng. New
      York: Cowles Book Co. , 1969.

302. _____. Battles in the Monsoon: Campaigning in the Cen-
      tral Highlands, Vietnam, Summer 1966. New York: Morrow,
      1967.

303. _____. Bird: The Christmastide Battle. New York:
      Cowles, 1965.

304. _____. Fields of Bamboo: Dongtre, Trung Luong and Hoa
      Hoi, Three Battles Just Beyond the South China Sea. New
      York: Dial Press, 1971.

305. _____. West to Cambodia. New York: Cowles, 1968.

306. McAleavy, Henry. Black Flags in Vietnam: The Story of a
      Chinese Intervention. New York: Macmillan, 1968.

307. McAlister, John T. Vietnam: The Origins of Revolution.
      New York: Knopf, 1969.

308. _____ and Paul Mus. The Vietnamese and Their Revolu-
      tion. New York: Harper and Row, 1970.

309. McCarthy, Joseph E. Illusion of Power: American Policy
      Toward Viet-Nam. New York: Carlton Press, 1967.

310. McCarthy, Mary. Hanoi. New York: Harcourt, Brace and
      World, 1968.

311. McGarvey, Patrick J. (comp.). Visions of Victory: Selected
      Vietnamese Communist Military Writings, 1964-1968. Stan-
      ford, Calif.: Hoover Institution on War, Revolution and
      Peace, Stanford University, 1969.

312. McGrady Mike. A Dove in Vietnam. New York: Funk and
      Wagnalls, 1968.

313. Mecklin, John. <u>Mission in Torment: An Intimate Account of the U.S. Role in Vietnam.</u> Garden City, N.Y.: Doubleday, 1965.

314. Meeker, Oden. <u>The Little World of Laos.</u> New York: Scribner, 1959.

315. Melin, Karin. <u>Vietnamkonflikten i Svensk Opinion, 1954-1968.</u> Stockholm: Raber. and Sjogren, 1969.

316. Melman, Seymour. <u>In the Name of America: The Conduct of the War in Vietnam by the Armed Forces of the United States as Shown by Published Reports, Compared with the Laws of War Binding on the United States Government and on its Citizens.</u> New York: Clergy and Laymen Concerned About Vietnam, 1968.

317. Mensel, Paul. <u>Moral Argument and the War in Vietnam.</u> Nashville, Tenn.: Aurora Publications, 1971.

318. Mertel, Kenneth D. <u>Year of the Horse--Vietnam, First Air Cavalry in the Highlands.</u> New York: Exposition Press, 1968.

319. Meyerson, Harvey. <u>Vinh Long.</u> Boston: Houghton Mifflin, 1970.

320. Mohn, Albert. <u>Vietnam.</u> Oslo: Gyldendal, 1965.

321. Moinet, Bernard. <u>Opium Rouge.</u> Paris: Editions France-Empire, 1965.

322. Monroe, Malcolm. <u>The Means Is the End in Vietnam.</u> White Plains, N.Y.: Murlagan Press, 1968.

323. Montagu, Ivor. <u>Vietnam: Stop America's Criminal War.</u> London: Communist Party of Great Britain, 1967.

324. Montgomery, John. <u>The Politics of Foreign Aid: American Experience in Southeast Asia.</u> New York: Praeger, 1962.

325. Moore, Barrington, Jr. <u>The Social Origin of Dictatorship and Democracy: Lord and Peasant in the Making of the Modern World.</u> Boston: Beacon Press, 1966.

326. Moore, Gene D. <u>The Killing at Ngo Tho.</u> New York: Norton, 1967.

327. Moore, Robert. <u>The Green Berets.</u> New York: Crown Publishers, 1965.

328. Morgenthau, Hans. <u>Vietnam and the United States.</u> Washington, D.C.: Public Affairs Press, 1965.

329. Mulligan, Hugh A. No Place to Die: The Agony of Viet Nam. New York: Morrow, 1967.

330. Mulling, Jay. Terror in Vietnam. Princeton, N.J.: D. Van Nostrand, 1966.

331. Munson, Glenn (ed.). Letters from Viet Nam. New York: Parallax Publishing Co., 1966.

332. Mus, Paul. Viêt-Nam: Sociologie d'une guerre. Paris: Editions du Seuil, 1952.

333. _____. Le Viet-Nam chez Lui. Paris: Paul Hartman, 1946.

334. Myrdal, Gunnar. USA och Vietnamkriget. Stockholm: Vietnam-press, 1967.

335. Navarre, Henri. Agonie de l'Indochine, 1953-54. Paris: Plon, 1958.

336. Newman, Bernard. Background to Viet Nam. New York: New American Library, 1971.

337. _____. Let's Visit Vietnam. London: Burke, 1967.

338. _____. Report on Indo-China. New York: Praeger, 1954.

339. Nghiem Dang. Viet-Nam: Politics and Public Administration. Honolulu: East-West Center Press, 1966.

340. Nguyen Anh Tuane, Mme. Les Forces politiques au Sud Viet-Nam depuis les Accords de Geneve 1954. Louvain: Offset Frankie, 1967.

341. Nguyen Cao Dam. Vietnam, Our Beloved Land. Rutland, Vt.: C. E. Tuttle, 1968.

342. Nguyen Cong Vien. Seeking the Truth: The Inside Story of Viet Nam after the French Defeat. New York: Vantage, 1966.

343. Nguyen Du. Kim Van Kieu. Translated by Xuan Phuc and Xuan Viet. Paris: Gallimard, 1961.

344. Nguyen Kien. L'Escalade de la guerre au Vietnam, vers un conflit nucleaire mondial? Paris: Editions Cujas, 1965.

345. _____. Le Sud-Vietnam depuis Dien-Bien-Phu. Paris: Maspero, 1963.

346. Nguyen Trung Viet. Mon Pays, Le Vietnam. Montréal: Editions Parti Pris, 1967.

347. Nhat-Hanh, Thich. Vietnam: Lotus in a Sea of Fire. New
     York: Hill and Wang, 1967.

348. Norden, Eric. America's Barbarities in Vietnam. New Delhi:
     Mainstream Weekly, 1966.

349. Nørland, Ib. Mode med Vietnam. København: Tiden, 1966.

350. Oberdorfer, Don. Tet! New York: Doubleday, 1971.

351. O'Connor, John. A Chaplain Looks at Vietnam. Cleveland:
     World Publishing Co., 1968.

352. O'Daniel, John W. The Nation that Refused to Starve: The
     Challenge of the New Vietnam. New York: Coward-McCann,
     1962.

353. O'Neill, Robert. The Strategy of General Giap Since 1964.
     Canberra: Australian National University Press, 1969.

354. Osborne, Leone. Than Hoa of Viet-Nam. New York: Mc-
     Graw-Hill, 1966.

355. Osborne, Milton E. Strategic Hamlets in South Viet-Nam.
     Ithaca, N.Y.: Cornell University Press, 1965.

356. Paine, Lauran. Viet-nam. New York: Roy Publishers, 1965.

357. Pfeffer, Richard M. (ed.). No More Vietnams?: The War
     and the Future of American Foreign Policy. New York:
     Harper and Row, 1968.

358. Phan Thi Dac. Situation de la personne au Viet-Nam. Paris:
     Centre national de la recherche scientifique, 1966.

359. Pic, Roger. Au Coeur du Vietnam. Paris: Maspero, 1968.

360. Pickerell, James H. Vietnam in the Mud. Indianapolis:
     Bobbs-Merrill, 1966.

361. Pike, Douglas. Viet Cong: The Organization and Techniques
     of the National Liberation Front of South Vietnam. Cam-
     bridge, Mass.: M.I.T. Press, 1966.

362. _____. War, Peace, and the Viet Cong. Cambridge,
     Mass.: M.I.T. Press, 1969.

363. Possony, Stefan. Aggression and Self-defense: The Legality
     of U.S. Action in South Vietnam. Philadelphia: University
     of Pennsylvania, Foreign Policy Research Institute, 1966.

364. _____ and J. E. Pournelle. Congress Debates Vietnam.
     New York: Dunellen, 1971.

365. Pratt, Lawrence. North Vietnam and Sino-Soviet Tension. Toronto: Baxter, 1967.

366. Presbyterian Church in the U.S.A. (General Assembly). Vietnam: The Christian, the Gospel, the Church. Philadelphia: Presbyterian Church in the U.S.A., 1967.

367. Pruden, Wesley, Jr. Vietnam: The War. Princeton, N.J.: National Observer, 1965.

368. Quang Loi. South of the Seventeenth Parallel. Hanoi: Foreign Languages Publishing House, 1959.

369. Quigley, Thomas E. (ed.). American Catholics and the Vietnam War. Grand Rapids, Mich.: Eerdmans, 1968.

370. Race, Jeffrey. War Comes to Long An. Berkeley: University of California Press, 1971.

371. Raffaelli, Jean. Hanoi: Capital de la Survie. Paris: Grasset, 1967.

372. Ramparts Editors et al. (eds.). Two, Three--Many Vietnams: The Wars in Southeast Asia and the Conflicts at Home. San Francisco: Canfield Press, 1971.

373. Raskin, Marcus G. and Bernard B. Fall (eds.). The Viet-Nam Reader: Articles and Documents on American Foreign Policy and the Viet-Nam Crisis. Revised edition. New York: Random House, Vintage Books, 1965.

374. Ray, Michele. Des deux rives de l'enfer. Paris: Laffont, 1967.

375. Reed, David E. Up Front in Vietnam. New York: Funk and Wagnalls, 1967.

376. Reich, Ebbe (comp.). Til Vietnam. København: Dat Internationale Krigsforbrydelses Tribunals Københavnskontor og Vietnamindsamlingen, 1967.

377. Reicher, Reuben. Une Paix immediate au Viet-Nam, est-elle possible? Paris: S.G.R.A.D.I., 1966.

378. The Reporter. Vietnam: Why? A Collection of Reports and Comments from The Reporter. New York: Reporter Magazine Co., 1966.

379. Riboud, Marc and Philippe Devillers. Face of North Vietnam. New York: Holt, Rinehart and Winston, 1970.

380. Richard, Pierre. Cinq ans prisonnier des Viets. Paris: Editions de la Serpe, 1964.

381. Riffaud, Madeleine. Au Nord Viet-nam (Ecrit sous les bombes). Paris: Julliard, 1967.

382. _____. Dans les maquis "vietcong." Paris: Julliard, 1965.

383. Rigg, Robert B. How to Stay Alive in Vietnam: Combat Survival in the War of Many Fronts. Harrisburg, Pa.: Stackpole Books, 1966.

384. Roberts, John. Vietnam. London: Association for World Government, 1968.

385. Rohrer, Daniel M. By Weight of Arms: America's Overseas Military Policy. Skokie, Ill.: National Textbook Co., 1969.

386. Rosenberg, Milton J. Vietnam and the Silent Majority: The Dove's Guide. New York: Harper and Row, 1970.

387. Rostow, W. W. The Stages of Economic Growth: A Non-Communist Manifesto. Cambridge: Cambridge University Press, 1960.

388. Rovere, Richard. Waist Deep in the Big Muddy: Personal Reflections on 1968. Boston: Little, Brown, and Co., 1968.

389. Rowe, James N. Five Years to Freedom. Boston: Little, Brown, & Co., 1971.

390. Rowe, John. Count Your Dead. Sydney: Angus and Robertson, 1968.

391. Roy, Juoes. The Battle of Dienbienphu. New York: Harper and Row, 1965.

392. Rupen, Robert A. and Robert Farrell (eds.). Vietnam and the Sino-Soviet Dispute. New York: Praeger, 1967.

393. Russ, Martin. Happy Hunting Ground. New York: Atheneum, 1968.

394. Russell, Bertrand. Appeal to the American Conscience. London: Bertrand Russell Peace Foundation, 1966.

395. _____. War Crimes in Vietnam. New York: Monthly Review Press, 1967.

396. Sager, Peter. Report from Vietnam. Translated from the German by Ian Tickle. Bern: Swiss Eastern Institute, 1968.

397. Sainteny, Jean. Histoire d'une paix manquée, Indochine, 1945-1947. Paris: Fayard, 1967.

398. Sakka, Michel. Vietnam, la guerre chimique et biologique, un peuple sert de champ d'experience. Paris: Editions sociales, 1967.

399. Salisbury, Charlotte Y. Asian Diary. New York: Scribners, 1967.

400. Salisbury, Harrison. Behind the Lines: Hanoi, December 23, 1966-January 7, 1967. New York: Harper and Row, 1967.

401. Sanders, Jacquin. The Draft and the Vietnam War. New York: Walker, 1966.

402. Sandvig, Anders. Fred i Vietnam. Oslo: Normannaforlaget, 1968.

403. Sansom, Robert L. The Economics of Insurgency in the Mekong Delta of Vietnam. Cambridge, Mass.: M.I.T. Press, 1970.

404. Sartre, Jean Paul. On Genocide. Boston: Beacon Press, 1968.

405. Scharnberg, Carl. Vietnam--blot en begyndelse? Du skall ikke adlyde ordrer! Århus, Denmark: Aros, 1967.

406. Scheer, Robert. How the United States Got Involved in Vietnam. Santa Barbara, Calif.: Center for the Study of Democratic Institutions, 1965.

407. Schell, Jonathan. The Military Half. New York: Random House, Vintage Books, 1968.

408. _____. The Village of Ben Suc. New York: Random House, Vintage Books, 1967.

409. Schlesinger, Arthur M., Jr. The Bitter Heritage: Vietnam and American Democracy. Boston: Houghton Mifflin, 1967.

410. Schoenbrun, David. Vietnam: How We Got In, How to Get Out. New York: Atheneum, 1968.

411. Schoenman, Ralph. A Glimpse of American Crimes in Vietnam. London: Bertrand Russell Peace Foundation, 1967.

412. Schoofs, Rudolf. Israel, Vietnam: The Horrors of War. New York: George Wittenborn, 1968.

413. Schultz, Gene. Third Face of War. Austin, Tex.: Jenkins Publishing Co., 1969.

414. Schurmann, Franz, Peter Dale Scott, and Reginald Zelnik. The Politics of Escalation in Vietnam. Boston: Beacon Press, 1966.

415. Schweitzer, Carl Christoph. Die U.S.A. und der Vietnam-
     Konflikt, 1964-1967. Koln: Westdeutscher Verlag, 1969.

416. Scigliano, Robert G. South Vietnam: Nation under Stress.
     Boston: Houghton Mifflin, 1964.

417. Shah, Ikbal Ali. Viet Nam. London: Octagon Press, 1960.

418. Shaplen, Robert. The Lost Revolution: The U.S. in Vietnam,
     1946-1966. Revised edition. New York: Harper and Row,
     Harper Colophon Books, 1966.

419. _____. Road from War: Vietnam 1965-1970. New York:
     Harper and Row, 1970.

420. Shchedrov, I. Fighting Vietnam. Moscow: Novosti Press
     Agency Publishing House, 1965.

421. Sheehan, Neil et al. The Pentagon Papers: The Secret His-
     tory of the Vietnam War ... as Published by the New York
     Times. New York: Bantam Books, 1971.

422. Sheehan, Susan. Die nicht gefragt werden Menschen in Viet-
     nam. München: Claudius-Verlag, 1968.

423. _____. Ten Vietnamese. New York: Knopf, 1967.

424. Sheldon, Walter J. Tigers in the Rice: A Short History of
     Vietnam. New York: Macmillan, 1969.

425. Sivaram, M. The Vietnam War: Why? Rutland, Vt.: Tuttle,
     1966.

426. Slingsby, H. G. Rape of Vietnam. Wellington, New Zealand:
     Modern Books Press, 1966.

427. Smith, George E. P.O.W.: Two Years with the Viet Cong.
     Berkeley, Calif.: Ramparts, 1971.

428. Smith, Ralph. Viet-Nam and the West. Ithaca, N.Y.: Cor-
     nell University Press, 1971.

429. Solomon, Richard H. Mao's Revolution and the Chinese Politi-
     cal Culture. Berkeley, Calif.: University of California
     Press, 1971.

430. Sontag, Susan. Trip to Hanoi. New York: Straus and Giroux,
     1968.

431. Spock, Benjamin. Dr. Spock on Vietnam. New York: Dell,
     1968.

432. Standard, William L. Aggression: Our Asian Disaster. New

York: Random House, 1971.

433. Starobin, Joseph R. Eyewitness in Indochina. New York: Greenwood Press, 1968.

434. _____. Viet-Nam Fights for Freedom: The Record of a Visit to the Liberated Areas of Viet-Nam in March, 1953. London: Lawrence and Wishart, 1953.

435. Stavens, Ralph (ed.). Warmakers: The Men Who Made the Vietnam War and How They Did It. New York: Outerbridge and Dienstfrey, 1971.

436. Steinberg, David (ed.). In Search of Southeast Asia: A Modern History. New York: Praeger, 1971.

437. Stern, Kurt. Bevor der Morgen graut: Vietnam zwischen Krieg und Sieg. Berlin: Verlag Neues Leben, 1969.

438. Stewart, George. What's So Funny about Vietnam? Tampa, Fla.: Tampa Art and Publishing Co., 1968.

439. Stone, Gerald L. War without Honour. Brisbane: Jacaranda Press, 1966.

440. Strong, Anna Louise. Cash and Violence in Laos and Viet Nam. New York: Mainstream Publishers, 1962.

441. Suarez, Luis. Guerra en la paz: Vietnam, Camboya y Laos. Mexico: Editorial Nuestro Tiempo, 1969.

442. Sully, Francois (ed.). We the Vietnamese: Voices from Vietnam. New York: Praeger, 1971.

443. Sweezy, Paul (comp.). Vietnam: The Endless War. New York: Monthly Review Press, 1971.

444. Syme, Anthony. Vietnam: The Cruel War. London: Horwitz, 1966.

445. Takman, John. Krigsforbrytelser i Vietnam. Stockholm: Vietnampress, 1967.

446. _____. Vietnam: Ockupanterna och Folket. Malmö, Sweden: Cavefors, 1965.

447. Tanham, George K. Communist Revolutionary Warfare: From the Vietminh to the Viet Cong. Revision of initial 1961 edition. New York: Praeger, 1967.

448. _____. War without Guns. New York: Praeger, 1966.

449. Taylor, Telford. Nuremberg and Vietnam: An American

Tragedy. New York: Bantam Books, 1971.

450. Thich Nhat Hanh. Vietnam: Lotus in a Sea of Fire. New York: Hill and Wang, 1967.

451. Thompson, Sir Robert. Defeating Communist Insurgency. New York: Praeger, 1966.

452. _____. No Exit from Vietnam. New York: McKay, 1969.

453. Thompson, Virginia. French Indo-China. New York: Octagon, 1968.

454. Thorin, Duane. The Need for Civil Authority over the Military. Bryn Mawr, Pa.: Intercollegiate Studies Institute, 1968.

455. Thuong Vinh Thanh (ed. and trans.). La Constitution religieuse du Caodaisme. Paris: Editions Derby, 1953.

456. Tong, Andre. Dix mille annees pour le Vietnam! le dossier. Paris: La Table Ronde, 1967.

457. Tongas, Gerard. J'ai vecu dans l'enfer communiste au Nord Viet-Nam. Paris: Nouvelles Editions Debresse, 1960.

458. Tournaire, Helene. Livre jaune du Viet-Nam. Paris: Librairie Academique Perrin, 1966.

459. Toye, Hugh. Laos: Buffer State or Battleground. London: Oxford University Press, 1968.

460. Trager, Frank N. Why Vietnam? New York: Praeger, 1966.

461. _____, et al. Marxism in Southeast Asia: A Study of Four Countries. Stanford, Calif.: Stanford University Press, 1960.

462. Tran Minh Tiet. Problemes de Défense du Sud-Est Asiatique. Paris: Nouvelles Editions Latines, 1967.

463. _____. Le Viet-Nam dans le contexte mondial. Paris: Nouvelles Editions Latines, 1967.

464. Tran Van Dinh. No Passengers on the River. New York: Vantage Press, 1965.

465. Tran Van Tung. Le Vietnam face au communisme et à la feodalité. Viry-Chatillon, France: Editions du Parc, 1962.

466. _____. Viet-nam. New York: Praeger, 1958.

467. Tregaskis, Richard W. Vietnam Diary. New York: Popular Library, 1963.

468. Truong Buu Lam. <u>Patterns of Vietnamese Response to Foreign Intervention, 1858-1900.</u> New Haven: Yale University Press, 1967.

469. Truong Chinh, pseud. (Dang Xuan Khu). <u>President Ho Chi Minh: Beloved Leader of the Vietnamese People.</u> Hanoi: Foreign Language Publishing House, 1966.

470. _____. <u>Primer for Revolt: The Communist Takeover in Viet-Nam.</u> New York: Praeger, 1963.

471. Truong Son. <u>A Bitter Dry Season for the Americans.</u> Hanoi: Foreign Languages Publishing House, 1966.

472. _____. <u>The Winter 1966-Spring 1967 Victory and Five Lessons Concerning the Conduct of Military Strategy.</u> Hanoi: Foreign Languages Publishing House, 1967.

473. Tucker, Robert W. <u>Nation or Empire? The Debate over American Foreign Policy.</u> Baltimore: Johns Hopkins Press, 1968.

474. Tung, Tran Van. <u>Vietnam.</u> London: Thames and Hudson, 1958.

475. Van Dyke, Jon M. <u>North Vietnam's Strategy for Survival.</u> Palo Alto, Calif.: Pacific Books, 1971.

476. Van Tien Dung. <u>After Political Failure, the U.S. Imperialists Are Facing Military Defeat in South Vietnam.</u> Hanoi: Foreign Languages Publishing House, 1966.

477. _____. <u>South Vietnam: U.S. Defeat Inevitable.</u> Hanoi: Foreign Languages Publishing House, 1967.

478. Van Vinh, Nguyen. <u>Disengagement and Disenchantment.</u> New York: Carlton Press, 1970.

479. Vance, Samuel. <u>The Courageous and the Proud.</u> New York: Norton, 1970.

480. Vernon, Hilda. <u>Vietnam: The War and Its Background.</u> London: British Vietnam Committee, 1965.

481. <u>Vietnam, l'heure decisive, l'offensive du Tet (fevrier 1968).</u> Paris: Laffont, 1968.

482. Vinde, Victor. <u>Vietnam--den beskidte krig.</u> Stockholm: Raben and Sjøgren, 1966.

483. Wagenaar, Dan. <u>Letters from Nam.</u> New York: Carlton Press, 1971.

484. Walt, Lewis W. Strange War, Strange Strategy: A General's Report on Vietnam. New York: Funk and Wagnals, 1970.

485. Warbey, William. Vietnam: The Truth. London: Merlin Press, 1965.

486. Warner, Dennis. The Last Confucian. Harmondsworth, England: Penguin Books, 1963.

487. Waterhouse, Charles H. Vietnam Sketchbook: Drawings from Delta to DMZ. Rutland, Vt.: C. E. Tuttle Co., 1968.

488. _____. Vietnam War Sketches, from the Air, Land, and Sea. Rutland, Vt.: C. E. Tuttle Co., 1970.

489. Waters, Mary A. G.I.s and the Fight Against War. New York: Pathfinder Press, 1971.

490. Watt, Sir Alan Stewart. Vietnam, An Australian Analysis. Melbourne: Australian Institute of International Affairs, 1968.

491. Weatherly, Marjorie. Pig Follows Dog. Hanoi: Foreign Languages Publishing House, 1960.

492. Weinstein, Franklin B. Vietnam's Unheld Elections: The Failure to Carry out the 1956 Reunification Elections and the Effect on Hanoi's Present Outlook. Ithaca, N.Y.: Southeast Asia Program, Department of Asian Studies, Cornell University, 1966.

493. Weiss, Peter. Notes on the Cultural Life of the Democratic Republic of Vietnam. New York: Dell, 1970.

494. West, Francis J., Jr. Small Unit in Action in Vietnam: Summer 1966. New York: Arno Press, 1968.

495. West, Fred. Getting to Know the Two Vietnams. New York: Coward-McCann, 1963.

496. West, Richard. Sketches from Vietnam. London: Cape, 1968.

497. Westmoreland, William C. Report on the War in Vietnam. Washington, D.C.: Government Printing Office, 1969.

498. White, Ralph K. Nobody Wanted War: Misperception in Vietnam and Other Wars. Garden City, N.Y.: Doubleday, 1968.

499. Whiteside, Thomas. Defoliation. New York: Ballantine Books, 1970.

500. Whitmore, Terry. Memphis, Nam, Sweden: The Autobiography of a Black American Exile. New York: Doubleday, 1971.

501. Williams, Marion. My Tour in Vietnam: A Burlesque Shocker. New York: Vantage Press, 1970.

502. Williams, Roger Neville. The New Exiles: American War Resisters in Canada. New York: Liveright, 1971.

503. Woito, Robert S. (ed.). Vietnam Peace Proposals. Berkeley, Calif.: World Without War Council Publication, 1967.

504. Wolf, Eric R. Peasant Wars in the Twentieth Century. New York: Harper and Row, 1969.

505. Woodside, Alec. Vietnam and the Chinese Model. Cambridge, Mass.: Harvard University Press, 1971.

506. Woolf, Cecil and John Bagguley (eds.). Authors Take Sides on Vietnam: Two Questions on the War Answered by the Authors of Several Nations. New York: Simon and Schuster, 1967.

507. Zagoria, Donald S. Vietnam Triangle: Moscow, Peking, Hanoi. New York: Pegasus, 1967.

508. Zinn, Howard. Vietnam: The Logic of Withdrawal. Boston: Beacon Press, 1967.

C. GOVERNMENT, UNIVERSITY, FOUNDATION AND CITIZEN GROUP REPORTS

1. American Civil Liberties Union, Southern California Branch. Day of Protest, Night of Violence, The Century City Peace March: A Report. Los Angeles: Sawyer Press, 1967.

2. Ball, George W. The Issue in Viet-Nam. Department of State. Washington: U.S. Government Printing Office, 1966.

3. _____. Viet-Nam, Free-World Challenge in Southeast Asia. Department of State. Washington: U.S. Government Printing Office, 1962.

4. Bundy, William P. South Viet-Nam: Reality and Myth. Department of State. Washington: U.S. Government Printing Office, 1965.

5. Clark, Joseph S. China and the Vietnam War--Will History Repeat? Report to the Committee on Foreign Relations, United States Senate. Washington: U.S. Government Printing Office, 1968.

6. _____. Stalemate in Vietnam. Report to the Committee on Foreign Relations, United States Senate. Washington: U.S. Government Printing Office, 1968.

7.   Conley, Michael Charles.   The Communist Insurgent Infrastruc-
     ture in South Vietnam: A Study of Organization and Strategy.
     Pamphlet No. 550-106.   Washington, D.C.:   Center for Re-
     search in Social Systems, American University, 1967.

8.   Davison, W. P.   "Some Observation on Viet Cong Operations
     in the Villages."   RAND Corporation Collection RM-5267/2-
     ISA/ARPA.   Santa Monica, Calif.:   RAND Corporation, July,
     1967.

9.   Ellsberg, Daniel.   "The Day Loc Tien Was Pacified."   RAND
     Corporation Collection P-3793.   Santa Monica, Calif.:   RAND
     Corporation, February, 1968.

10.   _____.   "Escalating in a Quagmire."   Paper read at annual
     meeting of the American Political Science Association, Sep-
     tember 8-12, 1970.

11.   Great Britain.   Central Office of Information, Reference Divi-
     sion.   Vietnam: Background to an International Problem.
     London: Her Majesty's Stationery Office, 1970.

12.   _____.   Foreign Office.   Recent Exchanges Concerning At-
     tempts to Promote a Negotiated Settlement of the Conflict in
     Viet-Nam.   London: H.M.S.O., 1965.

13.   _____.   Foreign Office.   Vietnam and the Geneva Agree-
     ments: Documents Concerning the Discussions between Rep-
     resentatives of Her Majesty's Government and the Government
     of the Union of Soviet Socialist Republics Held in London in
     April and May, 1956.   London: H.M.S.O., 1956.

14.   Hickey, Gerald C.   "Accommodation and Coalition in South
     Vietnam."   RAND Corporation Collection P-4213.   Santa
     Monica, Calif.:   RAND Corporation, January, 1970.

15.   _____.   "Accommodation in South Vietnam: The Key to
     Sociopolitical Solidarity."   RAND Corporation Collection P-
     3707.   Santa Monica, Calif.:   RAND Corporation, October,
     1967.

16.   Ho Chi Minh.   Against U.S. Aggression for National Salvation.
     Hanoi: Foreign Languages Publishing House, 1967.

17.   _____.   President Ho Chi Minh Answers President L. B.
     Johnson.   Hanoi: Foreign Languages Publishing House, 1967.

18.   Hosmer, Stephen T.   "Viet Cong Repression and Its Implica-
     tions for the Future."   Report prepared for Advanced Re-
     search Projects Association.   RAND Corporation Collection
     R-475/1 ARPA.   Santa Monica, Calif.:   RAND Corporation,
     May, 1970.

19. International Commission for Supervision and Control in Viet-
    nam. Interim Report, August 11, 1954-February 10, 1955.
    London: Her Majesty's Stationery Office, 1955.

20. _____. Special Report to the Co-chairmen of the Geneva
    Conference on Indo-China, Saigon, February 13, 1965. Lon-
    don: H.M.S.O., 1965.

21. _____. Special Report to the Co-chairmen of the Geneva
    Conference on Indo-China, Saigon, February 27, 1965. Lon-
    don: H.M.S.O., 1965.

22. International War Crimes Tribunal, Stockholm and Copenhagen,
    1967. Against the Crime of Silence: Proceedings of the Rus-
    sel International War Crimes Tribunal, Stockholm, Copen-
    hagen. New York: Bertrand Russell Peace Foundation, 1968.

23. International War Crimes Tribunal, Stockholm and Roskilde,
    Denmark, 1967. Le Jugement final. Paris: Gallimard,
    1968.

24. "Interviews Concerning the National Liberation Front of South
    Vietnam." RAND Corporation Documents from Series FD and
    G. Santa Monica, Calif.: RAND Corporation.

25. Johnson, Lyndon Baines. The Nation's Commitment in Viet-
    nam. Statement of the President of the United States, July
    28, 1965. Washington: U.S. Government Printing Office,
    1965.

26. _____. U.S. Halts Bombing of North Viet-Nam. Depart-
    ment of State. Washington: U.S. Government Printing Of-
    fice, 1968.

27. _____. Viet-Nam: The Struggle to Be Free. Washington:
    U.S. Government Printing Office, 1966.

28. _____. Viet-Nam: The Third Face of the War. Washing-
    ton: U.S. Government Printing Office, 1965.

29. _____. We Will Stand in Viet-Nam. Washington: U.S.
    Government Printing Office, 1965.

30. Johnson, Ural Alexis. Viet-Nam Today. Washington: U.S.
    Government Printing Office, 1966.

31. Joint Development Group. The Postwar Development of the Re-
    public of Vietnam: Policies and Programs. New York:
    Praeger, 1970.

32. _____. Postwar Development of Viet Nam: A Summary
    Report. Saigon: Vietnam Council on Foreign Relations,
    1969.

33. Kennedy, Edward M. Refugee Problems in South Viet-Nam
     and Laos. Washington: U.S. Government Printing Office,
     1965.

34. Lawyers Committee on American Policy Towards Vietnam
     (Consultative Council). Vietnam and International Law: An
     Analysis of the Legality of the U.S. Military Involvement.
     Flanders, N.J.: O'Hare, 1967.

35. Leites, Nathan. "The Viet Cong Style of Politics." RAND
     Corporation Collection RM-5487. Santa Monica, Calif.:
     RAND Corporation, May, 1969.

36. Lowenstein, James G. and Richard M. Moose. Vietnam: De-
     cember, 1969. A staff report compiled for the Committee
     on Foreign Relations, United States Senate. Washington:
     U.S. Government Printing Office, 1970.

37. Mansfield, Michael. Vietnam and the Paris Negotiations. Re-
     port of Senator Mansfield to the Committee on Foreign Rela-
     tions, U.S. Senate. Washington: U.S. Government Printing
     Office, 1968.

38. McNamara, Robert S. United States Policy in Vietnam. De-
     partment of State. Washington: U.S. Government Printing
     Office, 1964.

39. Meeker, Leonard C. The Legality of U.S. Participation in the
     Defense of Viet Nam. Department of State. Washington:
     U.S. Government Printing Office, 1966.

40. Merton Council for Peace in Vietnam. The Truth about Viet-
     nam. London: Merton Council for Peace in Vietnam, 1967.

41. Michigan State University, East Lansing. What to Read on
     Vietnam: A Selected, Annotated Bibliography. New York:
     Institute of Pacific Relations, 1959.

42. Mus, Paul. "The Buddhist Background to the Crises in Viet-
     namese Politics." Mimeographed. New Haven, Conn.:
     Southeast Asia Studies Program, Yale University.

43. NLF of South Vietnam: The Only Genuine and Legal Repre-
     sentative of the South Vietnamese People. Saigon: Liberation
     Editions, 1965.

44. Nguyen Van Vinh, Lieutenant General. The Vietnamese People
     on the Road to Victory. Hanoi: Foreign Languages Publish-
     ing House, 1966.

45. Nixon, Richard M. Cambodia Concluded: Now It's Time to
     Negotiate. President Nixon's report to the nation, June 30,
     1970. Washington: U.S. Government Printing Office, 1970.

46. _____. Cambodia in Perspective, Vietnamization Assured.
     President Nixon's report of June 3, 1970. Washington: U.S.
     Government Printing Office, 1970.

47. _____. The Pursuit of Peace. President Nixon's address
     of November 3, 1969. Washington: U.S. Government Print-
     ing Office, 1969.

48. Oka, Takashi. "Buddhism as a Political Force. No. 5: Da-
     nang and Afterwards." Paper for Institute of Current World
     Affairs, May 29, 1967.

49. Opinion Research Corporation. The People of South Vietnam:
     How They Feel about the War, A CBS News Public Opinion
     Survey. Princeton, N.J.: Opinion Research Corporation,
     1967.

50. Osborne, Milton E. Strategic Hamlets in South Vietnam. Data
     paper No. 55. Ithaca, N.Y.: Southeast Asia Program, De-
     partment of Asian Studies, Cornell University, 1965.

51. Pfaff, William. "A Vietnam Journal." Discussion paper.
     Hudson Institute, New York, HI-807-DP, February 23, 1967.

52. Pike, Douglas. "The Viet Cong Strategy of Terror." Mono-
     graph. U.S. Mission, Saigon, February, 1970.

53. Pond, Elizabeth. "The Chau Trial II: Denouement," April-
     July, 1970. "The Chau Trial III: Aftermath," October, 1970.
     New York: Alicia Patterson Fund, 1970.

54. Porter, D. Gareth. "The Myth of the Bloodbath: North Viet-
     nam's Land Reform Reconsidered." International Relations of
     East Asia Project, Cornell University, New York, 1972.

55. Principales victoires des F.A.L. du Sud Vietnam pendant la
     saison seche (de novembre 1965 à mars 1966). Saigon: Edi-
     tions Liberation, 1966.

56. Rogers, William. Viet-Nam in Perspective: An Address.
     Department of State. Washington: U.S. Government Printing
     Office, 1969.

57. Rusk, Dean. The Heart of the Problem: Secretary Rusk and
     General Taylor Review Viet-Nam Policy in Senate Hearings.
     Department of State. Washington: U.S. Government Printing
     Office, 1966.

58. _____. Viet-Nam: Four Steps to Peace. Department of
     State. Washington: U.S. Government Printing Office, 1965.

59. Shore, Moyers S. The Battle for Khe Sanh. Historical
     Branch, G-3 Division, Headquarters, U.S. Marine Corps.

Washington: U.S. Government Printing Office, 1969.

60. Solomon, Richard H. "The Chinese Revolution and the Politics of Dependency." Mimeographed. Center for Chinese Studies, University of Michigan, Ann Arbor, Michigan, August, 1966.

61. _____. "Communications Patterns and the Chinese Revolution." Paper prepared for Annual Meeting of the American Political Science Association, September 5-9, 1967, Chicago.

62. Symposium on the Viet-Nam War, East Carolina University, 1968. Essays on the Vietnam War. Greenville, N.C.: East Carolina University Publications, 1970.

63. Ten Years of Fighting and Building of the Vietnamese People's Army. Hanoi: Foreign Languages Publishing House, 1955.

64. Terrorist Raids and Fascist Laws in South Viet Nam: Documents. Hanoi: Foreign Languages Publishing House, 1959.

65. Truong Buu Lam. Patterns of Vietnamese Response to Foreign Intervention, 1858-1900. Monograph Series No. 11. New Haven, Conn.: Southeast Asia Studies, Yale University, 1967.

66. United Nations Association of Great Britain and Northern Ireland. Vietnam: A Plea for Self-Determination. London: United Nations Association, 1966.

67. U.S. Congress, House of Representatives, Special Subcommittee on National Defense Posture. Review of the Vietnam Conflict and Its Impact on U.S. Military Commitments Abroad: Report. Report authorized by House Resolution 124. Ninetieth Congress, Second Session. Washington: U.S. Government Printing Office, 1968.

68. U.S. Congress, House of Representatives. American Prisoners of War in Vietnam Hearings. Ninety-first Congress, First Session, November 13 and 14, 1969. Washington: U.S. Government Printing Office, 1969.

69. U.S. Congress, Joint Economic Committee. Economic Effect of Vietnam Spending. Hearings, Ninetieth Congress, First Session. Washington: U.S. Government Printing Office, 1967.

70. U.S. Congress, Senate. Air War against North Vietnam. Hearings, Ninetieth Congress, First Session. Washington: U.S. Government Printing Office, 1967.

71. _____. Moral and Military Aspects of the War in Southeast Asia. Hearings, Ninety-first Congress, Second Session, May 7 and 12, 1970. Washington: U.S. Government Printing

Office, 1970.

72. _____. Report on Indochina: Report of Mike Mansfield on
a Study Mission to Vietnam, Cambodia and Laos. Washington: U.S. Government Printing Office, 1954.

73. _____. Situation in Vietnam. Hearings before the Subcommittee on State Department Organization and Public Affairs
of the Committee on Foreign Relations, United States Senate,
Eighty-Sixth Congress, First Session. Washington: U.S.
Government Printing Office, 1959-1960.

74. _____. Southeast Asia Resolution. Joint Hearings before
the Committee on Foreign Relations and the Committee on
Armed Services, August 6, 1964. United States Senate,
Eighty-eighth Congress, Second Session. Washington: U.S.
Government Printing Office, 1966.

75. _____. Submission of the Vietnam Conflict to the United
Nations. Hearings, Ninetieth Congress, First Session, on
Resolutions 44 and 180, October 26, 27, and November 2,
1967. Washington: U.S. Government Printing Office, 1967.

76. _____. Vietnam Policy Proposals. Hearings, Ninety-first
Congress, Second Session. Washington: U.S. Government
Printing Office, 1970.

77. _____. Senate Committee on Foreign Relations. The Vietnam Hearings. Introduction by J. William Fulbright. New
York: Random House, 1966.

78. U.S. Department of Defense. Aggression from the North: The
Record of North Viet-Nam's Campaign to Conquer South Viet-
Nam. Washington: U.S. Government Printing Office, 1965.

79. _____. Viet-Nam: The Struggle for Freedom. Washington:
U.S. Government Printing Office, 1964.

80. U.S. Department of State, Office of the Deputy Ambassador,
Saigon. "Ky's Candidacy and U.S. Stakes in the Coming
Elections." Memorandum for the Record, by Daniel Ells-
berg, May 4, 1967.

81. U.S. Treaties (Kennedy Administration). Treaty Between the
United States of America and Viet-Nam. Signed at Saigon,
April 3, 1961. Washington: U.S. Government Printing Of-
fice, 1962.

82. Vermeersch, Jeannette. Pais immediate au Viet-Nam, dis-
cours prononce à l'Assemblée nationale le 27 janvier 1950.
Paris: Parti communiste francais, 1951.

83. Vietnam (South). Clearing the Undergrowth: What Are the

Facts about Defoliation in South Vietnam? Saigon: Ministry of Information, 1964.

84. Vietnam (North). Documents relatifs à l'execution des Accords de Genève concernant le Viet-Nam. Hanoi: Ministry of Foreign Affairs, 1956.

85. Vietnam (South). The Measure of Aggression: A Documentation of the Communist Effort to Subvert Vietnam. Saigon, 1966.

86. _____. Ngo Dinh Diem of Viet-Nam. Saigon: Press Office, Presidency of the Republic of Viet-Nam, 1957.

87. _____. La politique agressive des Viet Minh communistes et la guerre subversive communiste au Sud Vietnam: periode de mai 1961 à juin 1962. Saigon, 1962.

88. _____. Seven Years of the Ngo Diem Administration, 1954-1961. Saigon, 1961.

89. _____. Un danger pour la paix mondiale: l'agression communiste au Sud Viet-Nam, periode de juin 1966 à juillet 1963. Saigon, 1963.

90. _____. Les violations des accords de Geneve par les communistes Viet-Minh. Saigon, 1959.

91. Weiss, Peter and Gunilla Weiss. "Limited Bombing" in Vietnam: Report on the Attacks against the Democratic Republic of Vietnam by the U.S. Air Force and the Seventh Fleet, after the Declaration of "Limited Bombing" by President Lyndon B. Johnson on March 31, 1968. London: Bertrand Russell Peace Foundation, 1969.

92. Why Vietnam. Washington: U.S. Government Printing Office, 1965.

93. Woodside, Alec. "Some Features of the Vietnamese Bureaucracy under the Early Nguyen Dynasty." Papers on China, Vol. 19. Cambridge, Mass.: East Asian Research Center, Harvard University, December, 1965.

94. Zablocki, Clement J. Report on Vietnam. Committee on Foreign Affairs, House of Representatives. Washington: U.S. Government Printing Office, 1966.

95. Zasloff, J. J. "Origins of the Insurgency in South Vietnam, 1954-1960: The Role of the Southern Vietminh Cadres." RAND Corporation Collection RM-5163/2-ISA/ARPA. Santa Monica, Calif.: RAND Corporation, May, 1968.

96. _____. "Political Motivation of the Viet Cong and the Viet-

minh Regroupees." RAND Corporation Collection RM-4703/
2-ISA/ARPA. Santa Monica, Calif.: RAND Corporation,
May, 1968.

D. DISSERTATIONS AND THESES

1. Henry, John Bronaugh, II. "March 1968: Continuity or
   Change?" B.A. thesis, Department of Government, Harvard
   University, April, 1971.

2. Hickey, Gerald C. "Social Systems of Northern Viet Nam."
   Unpublished Ph.D. dissertation, Department of Anthropology,
   University of Chicago, 1958.

3. Hoskins, Marilyn W. "Life in a Vietnamese Urban Quarter."
   Unpublished M.A. thesis, Southern Illinois University at Car-
   bondale, 1965.

4. King Chen. "China and the Democratic Republic of Viet Nam,
   1945-1954." Unpublished Ph.D. dissertation, Pennsylvania
   State University, September, 1962.

5. McCall, Davy Henderson. "The Effects of Independence on the
   Economy of Viet Nam." Unpublished Ph.D. dissertation, Department of Economics, Harvard University, 1961.

6. Nguyen Thai. "The Government of Men in the Republic of Vietnam." Thesis. Michigan State University, East Lansing,
   Michigan, 1962.

7. Popkin, Samuel L. "The Myth of the Village: Revolution and
   Reaction in Vietnam." Ph.D. dissertation, Department of
   Political Science, Massachusetts Institute of Technology, Feb-
   ruary, 1969.

E. MICROFILM

1. Bain, Chester. "The History of Viet-Nam from the French
   Penetration to 1939." Ann Arbor: University Microfilms,
   1957.

2. Fall, Bernard B. "Political Development of Vietnam." Ann
   Arbor: University Microfilms, 1955.

3. Kyriak, Theodore E. "North Vietnam, 1957-1961: A Bibliography and Guide to Contents of a Collection of United States
   Joint Publications Research Service Translations on Microfilm." Annapolis: Research and Microfilm Publications,
   1962.

F.   FILM

1.   "The Year of the Pig."   Documentary film.   Directed by Emile
     de Antonio, 1969.

INDEX

573